Praise for the Book

"This text invites students to develop an in-depth understanding of core concepts in research methods; it clearly guides them through real-life examples and offers tools needed for the development of strong analytical skills highly valued in the labor market."

—Maria Aysa-Lastra, Winthrop University

"This is an incredibly useful textbook, showing students how to interpret others' quantitative research, think about quantitative research of their own, and communicate the findings of that research. I learned several great tips myself on writing effectively about quantitative research findings!"

—Susan A. Dumais, Lehman College, CUNY

"*Making Sense of Numbers* is an excellent companion for those learning to navigate the world of quantitative research."

—Marc Isaacson, Augsburg University

Making Sense of Numbers

To the next generation of number aficionados.

Making Sense of Numbers

Quantitative Reasoning for Social Research

Jane E. Miller

Rutgers University

Los Angeles | London | New Delhi
Singapore | Washington DC | Melbourne

FOR INFORMATION:

SAGE Publications, Inc.
2455 Teller Road
Thousand Oaks, California 91320
E-mail: order@sagepub.com

SAGE Publications Ltd.
1 Oliver's Yard
55 City Road
London EC1Y 1SP
United Kingdom

SAGE Publications India Pvt. Ltd.
B 1/I 1 Mohan Cooperative Industrial Area
Mathura Road, New Delhi 110 044
India

SAGE Publications Asia-Pacific Pte. Ltd.
18 Cross Street #10-10/11/12
China Square Central
Singapore 048423

Acquisitions Editor: Helen Salmon
Product Associate: Ivey Mellem
Production Editors: Natasha Tiwari and
                     Gagan Mahindra
Copy Editors: Linda Gray and Will DeRooy
Typesetter: C&M Digitals (P) Ltd.
Indexer: Integra
Cover Designer: Candice Harman
Marketing Manager: Victoria Velasquez

Printed in Canada

Library of Congress Cataloging-in-Publication Data

Names: Miller, Jane E. (Jane Elizabeth), 1959- author.

Title: Making sense of numbers : quantitative reasoning for social research / Jane E. Miller.

Description: Thousand Oaks, California : SAGE Publishing, [2022] | Includes bibliographical references and index. |

Identifiers: LCCN 2021011968 | ISBN 9781544355597 (paperback) | ISBN 9781544355603 (epub) | ISBN 9781544355610 (epub) | ISBN 9781544355627 (pdf)

Subjects: LCSH: Social sciences—Research—Methodology. | Quantitative research. | Reasoning.

Classification: LCC H62 .M44225 2022 | DDC 300.72/1—dc23
LC record available at https://lccn.loc.gov/2021011968

This book is printed on acid-free paper.

21 22 23 24 25 10 9 8 7 6 5 4 3 2 1

Brief Contents

Detailed Contents

List of Figures

(Continued)

(Continued)

(Continued)

(Continued)

List of Tables

(Continued)

(Continued)

Preface

Numbers provide important information for addressing many different topics and tasks. Even if you aren't thinking of research as a major focus of your career—what I refer to as "Research with a Capital R"—you will need to conduct research in various ways as you go about your daily life, act as an informed citizen, and perform the functions of your profession. To make sense of all the numbers you run across, you need to know how to use research methods and quantitative reasoning skills to find, analyze, interpret, and communicate numeric information.

Too often, however, research methods and math are taught as a bunch of definitions and formulas to be memorized rather than as a set of principles for critical thinking that will prepare you to handle those tasks. Unless you are a mathematician who analyzes numbers in the abstract, most of the time the numbers you work with are not "just numbers"; they are essential pieces of information to help you understand a topic or answer a real-world question. In other words, most people use numbers by applying them to a particular topic and context, defined, measured, and analyzed in specific ways. This book is designed to help you master a set of concepts and skills that prepare you to make sense of numbers, providing you with a comprehensive and cohesive approach to quantitative reasoning for social research and beyond.

Teaching and Learning Goals

The first major goal of this book is to teach you how to avoid common errors of reasoning, calculation, or interpretation by introducing a systematic approach to working with numbers, teaching you a set of questions that will help you figure out what a particular number means. A second goal is to convince you why it is important to apply a healthy dose of skepticism to the numbers you encounter, so you can understand how those numbers can (and cannot) be interpreted in their real-world context. A third goal is to teach you the basic skills necessary to be both a consumer and a producer of quantitative research—able to read about, collect, calculate, and communicate numeric information.

For those of you who believe that you "can't do math," I hope this book helps you realize that not only can you learn to make sense of numbers but also learn to appreciate and even enjoy that process. For those of you who are already friendly with numbers, I hope this book helps you take your comfort and capacity for quantitative reasoning to the next level.

How This Book Is Organized

This book is organized into six major parts. Part I lays the groundwork for the rest of the book, with an introductory chapter about common uses of numbers and challenges in learning how to interpret them (Chapter 1) and a chapter that defines some basic research methods terminology and quantitative reasoning principles (Chapter 2). Part II covers the importance of topic (Chapter 3), measurement (Chapter 4), and context (Chapter 5) in making sense of numbers. Part III explains and illustrates the structure, purpose, interpretation, and design of tables (Chapter 6) and charts and other visualizations (Chapter 7) to prepare you to both read and design those types of exhibits for presenting data.

Part IV covers how to evaluate what numbers mean and whether their values are reasonable based on how they were measured and calculated: Chapter 8 explains how to choose the right-size contrast and comparison groups or values for conducting comparisons—a key facet of quantitative research. Chapter 9 describes common numeric measures and mathematical computations, with a focus on how the formula for each type of calculation affects the level and range of values it can produce. Chapter 10 covers how to describe the distributions of single variables and associations between two or three variables. For each of those topics, I discuss how to understand the meaning of numbers you read about, including how to tell whether the authors interpreted their numeric results correctly.

Part V considers factors that affect the quality of numeric estimates—the reasons for that healthy skepticism I mentioned earlier. Chapter 11 covers how study design and data collection can introduce bias—an important thing for you to think about when interpreting the numbers you encounter. Chapter 12 explains how you can assess whether a relationship can be interpreted as cause-and-effect—a key element in determining whether research results can be used to identify possible solutions to real-world problems. Chapter 13 introduces the idea of statistical uncertainty, how it is calculated, and why it is important for you to consider as you interpret results based on samples rather than populations—a very common situation in social science research.

Finally, Part VI pulls together ideas from all the earlier chapters, explaining how you can use them together to make sense of numbers. Chapter 14 discusses how to use prose along with tables and charts to present numeric information effectively and shows how to apply general expository writing techniques together with guidelines specifically related to writing about numbers. It also explains how results of calculations can be reported so that the wording matches the math and is easy to understand—another useful skill whether you are reading or writing about research. Chapter 14 also includes a short section on the structure and contents for presenting quantitative research to different audiences. Chapter 15 helps you understand the big picture of whether a numeric result is (or isn't) "important," tying together several criteria covered in earlier chapters. It closes by discussing how you can apply the principles and skills from throughout the book to each of the four main quantitative research tasks: reading about, collecting, calculating, and communicating numeric information.

The book also includes three appendixes. Appendix A explains why and how to create new variables—a skill that is often needed to prepare data for analysis.

Appendix B covers the derivation and use of sampling weights, tying those concepts to ideas introduced in Chapter 11, and providing background for how sampling weights are used in results shown in Chapters 10, 13, and 14. Appendix C provides brief supplementary information about inferential statistics, helping students who have had prior coursework in statistical methods link that material to concepts introduced in Chapter 13.

Features of the Book

In addition to boxes that make it easy to find **definitions** of terms and concepts, each chapter includes **principles boxes** that summarize important research methods or quantitative reasoning approaches to making sense of numbers. Another key feature is **annotated examples** of text, figures, tables, and other materials. For instance, one example might be a chart that presents numbers to address a question of interest; in the associated **annotation** (indented below the **example**) new terms and concepts are underlined to show how they apply to that example. The annotated examples are designed to make abstract ideas concrete, building from simple illustrations of definitions to more advanced skills such as applying several related concepts and skills together.

The examples in the book are a mixture of the kinds of "research" you do as part of your everyday life and topics and tasks like those you will be asked to do for school and in your career. The topics range widely, from some that might be very familiar to others that you are learning about in school or might encounter in the future. The idea is to practice initially with less challenging examples and then move to new or more complex ones so that you learn to make sense of unfamiliar numbers—something you can expect to have to do often in the future.

At the end of each chapter is a list of the terms and concepts that were introduced in that chapter along with highlights about the research methods and quantitative reasoning approaches covered there. I also provide a set of exercises and discussion questions to help you practice applying the new ideas from the chapter to various topics and tasks. Also at the end of each chapter is a short list of references that provide more depth and detail about the concepts and skills covered in that chapter.

Notes for Instructors

Material in this book spans several overlapping domains, including quantitative reasoning, social science research methods, basic statistics, data analysis, and communicating quantitative information. To do justice to the entire book requires a full academic year (two-semester or three-trimester) course that provides enough time for students to not only read about, but also discuss and practice, the many concepts and skills covered in the full set of 15 chapters.

Adapting This Book for Different Types of Courses

For instructors teaching one-semester courses, I have recommended different subsets of the chapters, each built around one or two of those domains. All these recommended subsets include Parts I and II (Chapters 1 through 5), which lay the foundation on which other chapters are built.

For **quantitative reasoning courses** that focus on preparing students to become educated consumers of numeric information, assign Chapters 1 through 9 and perhaps Chapter 15.

For **research methods courses**, assign Chapters 1 through 5 and Chapters 11, 12, and 15. For survey (overview) courses on social science research methods, ethics, and qualitative methods are usually considered key curricular elements, so several weeks of such courses would typically be devoted to those topics, assigning additional resources for students to read. Although qualitative methods are mentioned briefly in Chapter 2 of this book, they are not covered in sufficient depth to provide an adequate overview of those methods. See Mack et al. (2005) or other resources on the SAGE Research Methods site for materials on qualitative research. For content on the ethics of social science research, consider having students complete an online Human Subjects Certification course, such as the Basic Course on Social/Behavioral/Epidemiologic Research provided by the Collaborative Institutional Training Initiative (CITI, 2020) through contracts with colleges and universities.

Statistics or **data analysis courses** can complement a standard statistics textbook with the material in Chapters 1 through 5 plus Chapters 8, 9, 10, and 13 and Appendix C. Ideally, students in such courses would be provided with an electronic data set so they can conduct data preparation and analysis using the associated end-of-chapter exercises; see below.

For **quantitative communication courses**, assign Chapters 1 through 7, and 14.

Instructional Features

In addition to the standard PowerPoint slide sets, test bank, and other resources found at **edge.sagepub.com/millernumbers1e**, I include several instructional features both within the book and as supplemental resources for instructors.

Annotated Examples

During my decades teaching research methods, research writing, and quantitative reasoning, I have learned the importance of making abstract ideas concrete, helping students move from general definitions of terms and concepts to being able to use those ideas in applied work. To address that need, I developed a teaching device called **annotated examples**: text, figures, tables, and other materials, accompanied by explanations of how newly introduced terms, concepts, and approaches are used in that example. For instance, one example might be a table to organize numeric data; in the associated annotation, new terms and concepts are bolded to identify how they apply to that specific table. Another example might be a text description of a study design, with the associated annotation showing how new concepts are used in that description. This approach is used throughout the book and can also be used independently by instructors who develop and annotate additional examples that fit their course, audience, and newer topics and data.

Engagement Activities

At the end of each chapter is a set of exercises designed to help students engage with the concepts and skills from that chapter by applying them to real-world quantitative reasoning and research tasks. Some of these exercises are short and self-contained enough to be done as part of a live class session; longer, more complex or detailed exercises can be given as homework assignments. I have field-tested many of these exercises in my own undergraduate teaching.

The exercises are organized into five major types of activities:

- Quantitative reasoning and research in everyday life
- Identifying ideas and interpreting information from research publications
- Planning research, including study design and question writing
- Analyzing data using comparisons or calculations
- Communicating research in tables, charts, or prose

These exercises are divided into those intended for students to conduct individually and those intended for group discussion or planning activities that involve peer review of calculations or writing and editing–revising exercises. They, too, can be used as templates for instructor-designed activities using different research articles, websites, data sets, or topics.

Whereas the assessment materials are designed to test students' ability to recall and understand new concepts—the most basic levels of *Bloom's Taxonomy of Educational Objectives* (Anderson & Krathwohl, 2001)—the end-of-chapter exercises are designed to help students progress to the more advanced levels: applying, analyzing, evaluating, and creating material using those concepts and skills.

Reference

Anderson, L. W., & Krathwohl, D. (Eds.) (with Airasian, P. W., et al.). (2001). *A taxonomy for learning, teaching, and assessing: A revision of Bloom's Taxonomy of Educational Objectives*. Longman.

Acknowledgments

Many people contributed formally and informally to this book. Most notably, the thousands of students whom I have taught in undergraduate research methods courses and the Project L/EARN undergraduate research training program served as guinea pigs, testing the examples and strategies I developed for teaching the quantitative reasoning, research methods, and communication skills covered in this book. I also appreciate what I learned from field-testing ideas with participants at various "Writing About Numbers" workshops I taught based on my earlier books, and from students in courses on data visualization and communicating quantitative research. I would also like to thank the members of StatLit.org and the Statistical Literacy section of the American Statistical Association for encouragement and feedback about my early work related to quantitative reasoning.

I'd like to give special recognition to Dawne Mouzon and Diane (Deedee) Davis, with whom I worked for many years on the instructional staff of Project L/EARN at Rutgers University. I learned a lot from them about conducting and teaching quantitative research. Many other colleagues from Rutgers and beyond provided invaluable feedback, suggesting topics to cover, examples to use, pitfalls they encountered with their students or in their own research, and a plethora of other helpful perspectives on the challenges of teaching and learning how to make sense of numbers. They include Francis Barchi, Debbie Borie-Holtz, Sharon Bzostek, Jocelyn Crowley, Andrea Hetling, Allan Horwitz, Rebecca Horwitz-Willis, Ian Miller, Clara Moore, Hal Salzman, Mi Shih, Tamara Swedberg, Jermaine Toney, Jon Unger, and Marc Weiner. I could not have completed this book without the assistance of Genesis Arteta, who provided essential support on a variety of administrative tasks.

I'd like to thank the following reviewers for providing feedback during the development of this book:

Maria Aysa-Lastra, Winthrop University

Shannon Bert, University of Oklahoma

Derrick M. Bryan, Morehouse College

Patricia Campion, Saint Leo University

Susan A. Dumais, Lehman College, CUNY

Eric Gaze, Bowdoin College

Nathan Grawe, Carleton College

William J. Haller, Clemson University

Marc Isaacson, Augsburg University

Finally, I'd like to thank several generations of my family for the inspiration and pleasure they have provided for working and playing with numbers. My parents were role models of ways to use numbers scientifically (my father) and visually (my mother). My children carry the thread forward, using numbers in myriad ways both for fun and for work. And my grandchildren exemplify the possibility and promise of approaching numbers with curiosity, confidence, and joy.

About the Author

Jane E. Miller is a professor at the Edward J. Bloustein School of Planning and Public Policy at Rutgers University, where she is lead instructor for the undergraduate research methods course and instructor for the undergraduate honors research program. She also teaches graduate courses on data visualization and quantitative research and communication. She was previously faculty director of Project L/EARN—an intensive social science research training program for undergraduates from historically underrepresented groups.

Dr. Miller has written two other books: *The Chicago Guide to Writing About Numbers* and *The Chicago Guide to Writing About Multivariate Analysis* (University of Chicago Press)—both in their second editions and also available in Chinese translation (Xinhua Publishing). She has also authored a series of articles in teaching and research journals on how to communicate about quantitative research. Dr. Miller's research interests include relationships between poverty, child health, health insurance, and access to health care. She earned her bachelor's degree in economics from Williams College and her MA and PhD in demography from the University of Pennsylvania.

Introduction

Introduction to Making Sense of Numbers

Learning Objectives

After reading this chapter, you will be able to do the following:

1. Recognize the scope of topics and applications for which numbers are used.

2. Identify common tasks for using numbers to answer real-world questions.

3. Define plausibility and how it relates to making sense of numbers.

4. Anticipate some challenges of learning to make sense of numbers.

5. List ways people typically learn about the applied use of numbers.

The Many Uses of Numbers

Numbers are used as evidence about a huge variety of topics in today's complex global society. For instance, being able to interpret numeric information helps you understand issues such as whether a proposed increase to the minimum wage will mean fewer entry-level jobs in your area or whether e-cigarettes are less risky for your health than conventional cigarettes. Knowing how to work with numbers gives you the tools to make important decisions like how to save toward buying a car or other major purchase. Being able to recognize how data were collected and analyzed can help you distinguish between "fake news" and reliable information from the media and other sources. Understanding what numbers mean for a social issue can motivate you to take action, such as advocating for change after reading about inequitable treatment of certain groups in society.

It takes only a quick scan of today's media to see just how many aspects of life require you to understand and apply numeric information. For instance, a major newspaper might feature cover stories on national election results, cancer rates, Chinese population trends, elementary school education, and crime, each of which present and discuss several numeric facts. Other sections of that day's paper might include articles on the stock market, a few scientific topics, the economy, wages, housing, the environment, several sports, the weather, and many other topics that involve various numeric facts and patterns. That is a lot of different topics (and numbers) to become familiar with!

> Numbers provide important information for addressing many different issues and tasks in school, everyday life, and in the workplace.

A key objective of this book is to teach you how to avoid making common errors of logic, calculation, and interpretation by introducing a systematic approach and a healthy dose of skepticism to understanding and applying the numbers you encounter.

Common Tasks Involving Numbers

As you go through your everyday life at school, in your job, or doing volunteer work, you will need to use numbers in several different ways. You might use numeric facts to make decisions. Suppose you see an ad for a new cell phone plan that looks really cheap. To make an informed choice about whether it is worth changing from your current plan with a different provider, you will need to do some research to find and compare several pieces of numeric data for the two plans, including the type of phone or device, whether the pricing is based on usage (e.g., gigs/month) or a flat rate per month, whether you are locked in for a long term (like two years), and the cost of early termination penalties.

Another common task is doing simple comparisons using numeric facts from books, reports, or websites. Perhaps your first job after college is at an environmental monitoring company and your supervisor has asked you to find some statistics about water quality in a nearby lake and to present those numbers at a staff meeting. To do that job well, you need to know what information to look for, how to find comparison values to help interpret the measures of water quality such as levels of pH or bacteria in the water, and be able to communicate the results clearly to the people who will attend the meeting.

A third common task is analyzing a set of data that someone else has collected. Suppose your economics professor assigns you to use data from a government survey to test whether differences in unemployment rates show real differences between occupations or whether those variations could be explained by random variation. To ace that assignment, you need to do some research on how the data were collected and how unemployment was measured, be able to identify and conduct the relevant types of statistical tests, and know how to write up the results in ways that answer the professor's question.

A fourth type of research task is collecting quantitative data. Imagine that you have a summer internship at a marketing firm where you are asked to design and carry out a survey of 400 consumers to learn about their preferences among three different brands of potato chips. To convince that company to hire you for a permanent job, you need to know how to design the study and write the questions to collect data in a form that can be used to answer the questions your supervisor has posed.

A fifth common task is communicating numeric results. Suppose you are working for an organization that lobbies for better housing for low-income families. To enlist new volunteers and persuade potential funders to donate to that cause, your supervisor asks you to design some snappy charts and social media messages to get the word out about the issues and what people can do to help. To be effective at your job, you need to know how to identify and communicate a few key numbers using charts and prose that will quickly and clearly convey the seriousness of the issues to your intended audiences.

To become adept at identifying, assessing, calculating, interpreting, and presenting numbers, you must master a set of concepts and skills that prepare you to think critically about numbers. You need to know how the topic, context (setting), and ways things were measured attach meaning to numbers so you can interpret and use that information. You need to be able to identify which calculations and contrasts are best suited for answering the questions of concern to you. You need to know how to assess the quality of numeric estimates and understand enough about statistical tests that you can grasp the meaning of those numbers without guidance from experts. Finally, you need to be able to write or speak about numeric information in ways that allow your audience to make sense of the numbers and understand how they help answer the question at hand.

> Common quantitative research tasks include interpreting numbers that you read about, analyzing data that others have collected, collecting data, and communicating numeric results to others.

Plausibility of Numeric Values

Making sense of numbers involves figuring out what values are **plausible** (realistic) for the topic, setting, and way of measuring whatever is being quantified, be it price, population growth, temperature, or other characteristic. A value that is well-suited for some topics or settings might be totally absurd—**implausible**—for others. In other words, not all numeric values fit all topics, contexts, and ways of measuring things.

> A **plausible** numeric value is one that is possible and realistic for the particular topic, context, and way of measuring.

Although numeric information is widely used, many newspaper articles, blogs, websites, and even scientific papers sometimes present numeric facts without enough information to help readers understand what those numbers mean. They report what I call "naked numbers"—facts reported without context or interpretation. For instance, is a price advertised by a local vendor cheap or expensive? Do trend data suggest rapid or slow population growth? Is today's temperature typical for the season and location or one that suggests climate change?

Challenges in Making Sense of Numbers

For some topics, you know from experience which numeric values make sense. For instance, you probably have a good idea how much a concert ticket costs and what temperatures to expect in your hometown in winter. However, you might have heard your grandparents lament how much cheaper it was to go to a concert "back in the day," and if you've gone on a trip to another part of the country over winter break, maybe you didn't know what clothes to pack for the weather there. In other words, which numeric values make sense and how you interpret them often depend on time and place as well as topic.

When you run into a new topic, the fact that you don't know how it was measured, what typical levels are, and how much those values vary make it really hard to understand what a particular numeric value means. For instance, suppose your friend goes to the doctor and learns that he has diabetes. For the first time, he has to interpret and make decisions based on information about his A1C level so he can learn to manage his condition. Most newly diagnosed diabetics will have no idea what A1C measures, what constitutes a "good" or "bad" level of A1C, or how much of a change (or in what direction) would represent a meaningful improvement. Without understanding those things, how can your friend know whether his efforts to control his diabetes are working?

Making it even more challenging to interpret numeric information is the fact that a particular number can have very different meanings depending on whether it is a single data point (such as the price of a certain style of jeans at your favorite store), a summary statistic for a set of data points (such as the average price of jeans at several different stores), a mathematical contrast (such as how the price of jeans has changed over time), or the result of an inferential statistical test (such as whether there is a statistically significant difference in the price of jeans from bricks-and-mortar stores versus online stores).

A value or difference between values that is "big" for one topic, context (place, time, and group), and type of units might be "small" for another topic, context, or units.

- A value of 10,000 is possible if counting the number of people in a town but impossible as the height of a person in inches.

- A final score of 105 to 98 makes sense for basketball but is way too high for ice hockey. On the other hand, a score of 3 to 0 would be a pretty typical score for a hockey game, but outrageously low for any but a preschool basketball game. And it is a rout when an international football (soccer) team wins by 3 points, but a close game when a U.S. football team wins by the same margin.

The type of measure, calculation, or contrast also determines which numeric values do (and do not) make sense.

- Certain numeric measures can only take on positive values or can only be counted in whole numbers. For example, the number of students in your class cannot be negative or include fractions of people.

- On the other hand, the change in number of students between the beginning and end of the school year could be negative if some people dropped out or moved away, and average class size at your school could include decimal places (e.g., 24.7 students per class).

> Not all numeric values fit all topics, contexts, or ways of measuring and analyzing data, so it is important to learn how to determine which values make sense for whatever, whenever, and whomever you are studying and in whatever way you are measuring the concepts.

Making sense of numbers also involves knowing whether higher values represent an improvement or deterioration in whatever you are measuring.

- For some things, a higher score is better. For example, a higher credit rating will help you qualify for credit cards, more favorable interest rates on loans, and other financial advantages.

- For other topics, a lower score is what you're aiming for. For instance, you want to minimize points added to your driver's license because more points mean higher car insurance premiums and greater chances of your driving privileges being revoked.

For many topics and research questions, there are numeric cutoffs and benchmarks that help us interpret what a particular numeric value means for that topic and units. Numeric goals, thresholds, and standards can also help convey whether a particular numeric value is high or low, favorable or unfavorable. You will learn more about cutoffs, thresholds, and target values in Chapter 8.

Example: The value 32 °F is the freezing point of water.

> *Although that **threshold** is highly relevant for topics related to physical properties of water, there probably aren't many other **topics** for which the value "32" is relevant for defining a concept or differentiating between meaningfully different categories. Besides, 32 °C (Celsius) = 89 °F (Fahrenheit), and the freezing point of water is 0 °C, so clearly knowing the **units** matters as well.*

Example: The World Bank set a goal for the year 2030 of reducing child mortality rates to less than 25 deaths per 1,000 children under age 5 years. Figure 1.1 shows how each of the world's developing regions 2017 child mortality rates compared to that target.

> *By viewing which regions' child mortality rates remain <u>above</u> the **target** and by how much, policymakers can identify which regions need the most resources to meet that **goal**.*

Figure 1.1   Observed Mortality Compared to a Sustainable Development Goal

Of the developing regions, as of 2017 only Latin America and East Asia had under-5 mortality below the **2030 target**
Sub-Saharan Africa's rate was 3 times the target value

2030 Sustainable Development Goal
< 25 deaths per 1,000

Sub-Saharan Africa	South Asia	World	Arab World	Latin America & Caribbean	East Asia & Pacific
76	45	39	37	18	16

Under-5 mortality = # deaths before age 5 years per 1,000 live births

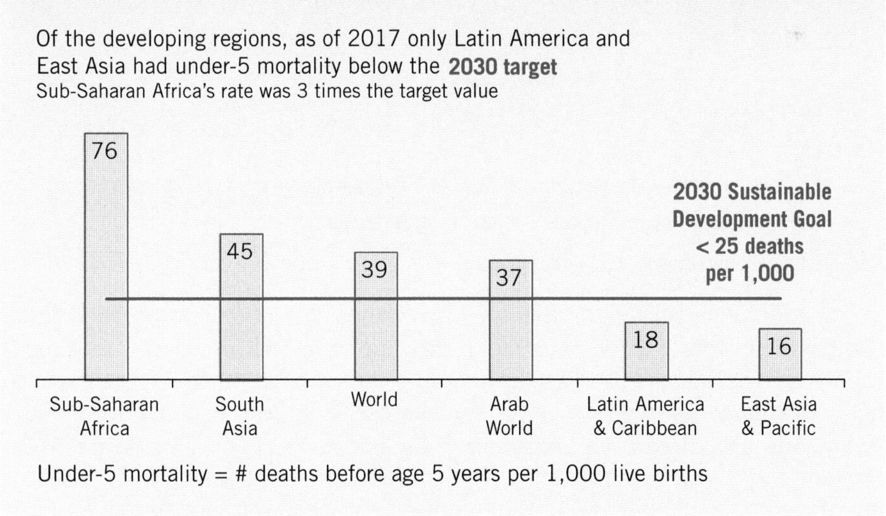

Source: Data from World Bank (2018). © World Bank. License: CC BY 3.0 IGO.

A Cautionary Tale

The following true story underscores how crucial it is to learn how to interpret the numeric values that relate to a particular topic, units, and setting before you work with those numbers. A young researcher was analyzing infant birth weight using survey data from a developing country from the year 2002, which she had downloaded from a website but hadn't learned much about before she started analyzing it. In the sample of cases she was studying, birth weight values ranged up to 9,999 with an average of about 8,000. Had she taken the time to look up the expected range of values for that concept (birth weight) and units (grams), she would have immediately seen a red flag because 9,999 grams is roughly 22 lbs.—a typical weight for a 1-year-old child (Figure 1.2a), not a newborn baby (Figure 1.2b)!

Figures 1.2a and 1.2b   The Importance of Checking Whether Numbers Make Sense for the Topic and Units

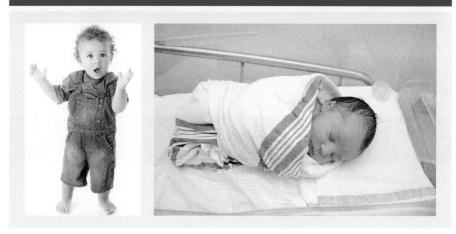

Notes:

a. A 1-year-old, average weight approx. 22 lbs. (9,999 grams)

b. A newborn, average weight approx. 7.5 lbs. (3,409 grams)

Source: iStock.com/JBryson, iStock.com/USGirl.

In addition, it turned out that the birth weight question was <u>not</u> asked about children who were 5 to 17 years old at the time of the survey, so kids those ages were given the value "9999" as shorthand to indicate that birth weight information was missing for them. Once the student researcher learned what those 9999s meant, she had to redo all the analyses for her final paper at the last minute, excluding the cases with missing values so that the remaining numbers could be interpreted as actual birth weight in grams. This book will help you avoid those kinds of mistakes and all that stress by teaching you the right questions to ask about the numbers for your topic and data <u>before</u> you use them!

How We Learn to Make Sense of Numbers

We learn how to make sense of numbers in several ways, including formal instruction, on-the-job training, and experiential learning. Some topics are taught in school. For instance, you learned the basics of how to tell time in preschool and how to recognize common monetary denominations and make change in elementary school. Within your major area of study in college, you take courses that familiarize you with the key numeric concepts and measures in that field. For example, if you are majoring in economics, you will learn how to calculate and interpret things such as interest rates, measures of labor force participation, and inflation. If your roommate is a premed student, she will instead learn about numeric concepts in biology, chemistry, and physics.

We learn about some other numeric topics through on-the-job training. For instance, someone with a new job in retail will learn about sales commissions and how they affect their earnings, whereas a trainee in the mental health services field will be taught how to interpret data from questionnaires used to screen for depression or anxiety.

Obviously, you can't be formally taught about the numbers used in every topic; there are just too many subjects for which numbers are used, as you can see from the examples used so far in this book. Besides, people's interests and jobs change, and new topics and measures emerge all the time. For instance, in 2005, personal "data usage" was a completely irrelevant concept, but by 2015 that term was widely understood by just about everyone over the age of 12! Also, standards and thresholds used to interpret numbers for various topics are updated every now and then. For example, recommendations about healthy blood pressure ranges were revised in 2017 by medical experts based on the latest research.

In other situations, we learn about numeric topics through educational pamphlets or websites, sometimes with guidance from an expert, other times on our own. Social services offices have brochures to familiarize clients with eligibility criteria for programs such as the Supplemental Nutrition Assistance Program (SNAP) or childcare tax credit. Banks and nongovernmental organizations (NGOs) disseminate information about microloans to potential borrowers in a variety of formats. WebMD and other health-related websites have fact sheets that people can download to learn about the numeric measures related to a particular disease and the chances of recovery for each of several treatment options.

You might have learned about other numeric measures experientially, often as hobbies you share with friends or family members or perhaps through intensive individual "study." A budding baseball fan gradually learns the various statistics that pertain to that sport from reading the sports section and listening to commentators: what each statistic measures, whether higher numbers are good (batting average) or bad (earned run average—ERA), what range of values is possible for each measure, and what level typically earns a player a Cy Young award or Golden Glove award versus what value will get them sent down to the minor leagues. An aspiring cookie baker will quickly learn that although sugar is often measured in cups, salt should be measured in teaspoons.

However, your interests are likely to change over time and might be different from those of your family members or friends. That means that you can't always rely on a relative or friend to teach you how to interpret statistics about an unfamiliar sport such as bocce or cricket, or count on knowing someone who can explain how to measure the ingredients used to brew beer. These issues mean that it is vital that you master a set of research concepts and critical-thinking skills so you will be prepared to teach yourself how to understand and interpret numbers for many different topics and applications.

> With numbers and quantitative analysis used for so many different issues, it is impossible to be formally taught how to use and interpret numbers for every issue. As a consequence, it is important to master the research and quantitative reasoning skills needed to make sense of numbers for new topics you encounter.

Hopefully, this introduction has convinced you that in your daily life, in school, and at work, you will encounter many different topics for which numbers are essential, some of which will be unfamiliar to you. Obviously, you want to avoid a haphazard approach to learning about the relevant numbers for each topic, which could be very confusing, waste a lot of time, and allow for many mistakes. To help you be more efficient and effective at teaching yourself about numbers for topics that are new to you, in this book I define and illustrate a series of research methods and quantitative reasoning principles. I also show how concepts and skills from other disciplines—including fields from which the topic is drawn, basic statistics, and expository writing—will help you learn to make sense of numbers.

TERMS AND CONCEPTS

Benchmark 7
   Threshold 7
   Target 7
Context 4
   Setting 4

Implausible (impossible, unrealistic) value 4
Plausible (possible, reasonable, believable) numeric value 4

Quantitative reasoning 10
   Critical thinking 10
Topic 7
Units 7

HIGHLIGHTS

- Being able to **make sense of numbers** is a critical skill set for addressing many different issues and tasks in school, daily life, and in the workplace.

- **Quantitative research tasks** include **interpreting numbers** that you read about, **analyzing data** that others have collected, **collecting data**, and **communicating** numeric results to various audiences.

- Not all numeric values fit all **topics**, **contexts**, or **ways of measuring** and analyzing data, so it is important to learn ways to distinguish between values that are **plausible** (make sense) and those that are not.

- Although some numeric tasks are taught as part of **formal education** or **training**, others require that you be prepared to teach yourself how to use and interpret numbers to suit new topics and tasks.

- Making sense of numbers involves concepts and skills from **many different fields**.

EXERCISES

Individual Exercises

Quantitative Reasoning in Everyday Life

1. Describe courses, paid or volunteer positions, or other situations where you've been asked to do the following tasks: (a) use numbers from published or online sources, such as choosing which of several brands to buy; (b) analyze a set of data, such as calculating a rate, average, or change over time; (c) collect numeric data, such as conducting a survey; and (d) presenting numeric information using words, a chart, or other diagram.

   [Example answer to (d): As a volunteer for my local congresswoman, I was asked to create a chart comparing the costs of solar, wind, and coal power sources.]

2. For each of the tasks you listed in answer to the previous question, describe which aspects of conducting those tasks you found challenging.

3. Describe an example of when you've been asked to learn about numbers in each of the following ways, including information on the topic, measure, method of learning, and source of information: (a) been formally taught about numeric measures for a specific topic—for example, in a course at school; (b) been taught about numeric measures for a task outside of school—for example, by a supervisor at a job or volunteer position; (c) learned about numeric measures for an unfamiliar topic by reading a website or brochure; and (d) learned from a friend or taught yourself about numeric measures for a new interest or hobby.

   [Example answer to (d): I learned how to complete a baseball box score (including runs, hits, errors, strikeouts, bases on ball) by attending games with my uncle.]

4. For each of your answers to the previous question, list aspects of making sense of the numbers that you found challenging.

5. Think of a situation in which you were given numeric information about a topic, setting, or type of measure that was unfamiliar to you. Identify the resources you used or could have used (e.g., people, websites, reference materials) to figure out what values were plausible for those numbers.

6. Think of a situation in which you misunderstood the meaning of a numeric measure or its value. Describe how you (or someone else) caught your error and what you did to learn the correct understanding of that number.

Group Exercises

Quantitative in Everyday Life

7. Make a list of the tasks your group members identified for Exercise 1 above. Then compare the aspects of making sense of numbers in those tasks that you found challenging (from Exercise 2).

8. Repeat the instructions to the previous question but for your answers to Exercise 3.

9. Repeat the instructions to Exercise 7 but for your answers to Exercise 5.

10. Identify a numeric measure of some aspect of COVID-19. Discuss the types of resources you used (or could have used) to learn how to interpret the meaning of those numbers.

CHAPTER 2

Foundational Concepts for Quantitative Research

Learning Objectives

After reading this chapter, you will be able to do the following:

1. Define basic terms for quantitative research.

2. Describe the research circle.

3. Identify the four major goals of social research.

4. Write a checklist of the W's.

5. Understand the reasons for both reporting and interpreting numbers.

6. State the importance of specifying the direction and magnitude of a pattern.

In this chapter, I lay the groundwork for the rest of the book by defining and illustrating some basic research methods terminology. I then describe the research circle and the strategies it encompasses and identify the four major goals of research. Finally, I introduce some basic principles for working with numeric information.

Terminology for Quantitative Research

To begin learning how to make sense of numbers, you need to become familiar with the terminology that researchers use when discussing quantitative data and research methods. The term **data** refers to information that has been collected on characteristics such as age, educational attainment, and place of residence of individual people or information on type of cuisine, price range, and customer satisfaction ratings for individual restaurants.

Utts (1999) makes a useful distinction between **data** and **numbers**, stating that "data are numbers to which meaning has been attached" (p. 15). **Data** is the plural form of the singular **datum**, which is why we write "data <u>are</u>" rather than "data <u>is</u>."

Example: "2" is a number, but 2 people in a family or $2 for a cup of coffee are data.

> *The numeral "2" in the first phrase is a **number** (<u>not</u> data) because it <u>isn't</u> associated with a topic or units. When used to describe family size, it has a **topic** (family size) and **units** (number of people), so that same numeral is now **data**. "2" is also **data** when it pertains to price of coffee (**topic**) and $ per cup (**units**).*

Raw data refers to category labels (such as type of religion or name of country) or numeric information that has been collected but not yet processed or manipulated in any way (Utts & Heckard, 2014, p. 15). To turn raw data into useful evidence, those data have to be organized, summarized, and compared with other values to help interpret what they mean for the question at hand. We'll see some introductory examples in the section on Reporting and Interpreting Numbers.

An **observational unit** is an individual **entity** (such as a person, institution, or geographic area) about whom data are collected. However, for studies that collect information on the same cases across time (longitudinal studies; Chapter 12), each data collection time point is called an **observation**. In those situations, each observational unit is referred to as a **respondent** (for studies of people), **case**, or **study subject**. (Note that this usage of "study subject" refers to study participants, <u>not</u> to the topic of the study.)

Example: Consider two different studies: A survey of college students and a study of family leave policies at different corporations.

> *In the survey of college students, the type of **entity** is a student, and each student is an **observational unit** (or **study subject**). In the family leave study, the type of **entity** is a corporation, and each corporation is a **case**.*

Example: For a longitudinal study of how tree growth is affected by climate change, scientists measure the diameter of each tree in their study plot every year for 20 years.

> *Each individual tree is a **case** and each annual measurement of tree diameter is an **observation**.*

Data are information that has been collected about characteristics of **entities**. An **observational unit** (sometimes called a **case, respondent,** or **study subject**) is an individual **entity** about which data are collected, such as people, neighborhoods, or schools. These are also known as **units of analysis** or **levels of aggregation**. In studies that follow cases across time, there are multiple **observations** for each case.

A **variable** is a characteristic that can vary from one case to another. Each case has a **value** for each variable, capturing the nature or extent of that characteristic for that case. In contrast to a variable, a **constant** is a characteristic that has the same value for all cases being studied, often due to restrictions on which cases are included in the data set.

Example: In 2020, Canada was a democracy, whereas North Korea was a communist country.

> Type of political system is a **variable**, but date is a **constant**. The type of **entity** is a nation.

Example: Heights of each child in a kindergarten class are measured. Maria is 115 centimeters (cm.) tall.

> For each of her classmates, the **variable** height will take on the **value** that captures their height—e.g., 112, or 115, or 119 cm. Every student in Maria's class is a human being, so in that context, "species" is a **constant**.

However, which characteristics are constants and which are variables depends on the topic and context.

Example: A study of the Metropolitan zoo collects data on all the different animals, including information on their ages.

> In this study, "species" is a **variable** because some of the zoo residents are lions, some are eagles, some are rattlesnakes, and so on. Age is also a **variable**, with some young and some older animals. However, all of the zoo residents are animals, so in that study, type of biological **entity** is a **constant**.

Example: In Maria's kindergarten class, every student is 5 years old at the beginning of the school year.

> For that topic, setting, and time point, age is a **constant**. However, if the study also included other grades within her elementary school or followed the kids in her class for several years, age would be a **variable**.

A **data set** is an organized collection of information on a consistent set of variables for each of the cases in a study. **Missing values** occur when a respondent did not provide information on a particular variable. In longitudinal studies, there may be some variation in the amount of information collected for different participants, based on how often each of them participated.

Example: A social survey asks each of 1,000 respondents the same set of questions about their demographic traits, volunteer activities, and attitudes about current policy issues. Some of the study participants did not answer the question about a proposed health care policy.

> A **data set** for that survey would contain answers to each of those questions for each **respondent**. In other words, that survey does not have

one set of questions for some respondents and a completely different set of questions for others. Participants who didn't answer the policy question would have a **missing value** for that **variable**.

Example: An online shopping website collects data on each customer's shipping address, searches, and purchases.

*Location, search topics, items purchased, and dates of purchase are some of the **variables** on which data were collected from every customer (**case**) who shopped on that site. The **data set** will include more information on each of those topics for people who visited the site several times than for those who visited the site only once.*

A **variable** is a characteristic or attribute that can vary (differ) from one case to another. Each case takes on a **value** for a variable, measuring the type or degree of that characteristic for that case. A **constant** is a measure that has the same value for every case in the context under study. A **data set** or **database** is a compilation of information on the same set of variables for each of the cases under study. Cases that do not provide information on a particular variable have a **missing value** for that variable.

Figure 2.1 is a schematic diagram of a hypothetical school health data set, with one row for each student in the school and one column for each attribute about which data were collected. For each of the 432 cases (students in the school), the data set includes information on each of the variables (attributes). The ". . ." in the row between ID 105 and ID 432 shows that there were additional students in the data set, even though they are not included in the diagram.

Figure 2.1   Hypothetical Data Set of School Health Records

ID	School code	Date of medical record	Age (years)	Gender	Height (cm.)	Weight (kg.)	Date of most recent vaccination	Transfer status	Code of prev. school
101	1227	9/15/18	5	M	117	20	9/15/18	No	NA
102	1227	9/2/18	8	M	129	26	7/10/17	No	NA
103	1227	8/27/18	6	F	119	19	3/22/17	Yes	3418
104	1227	8/28/18	10	M	140	33	11/2/17	No	NA
105	1227	9/7/18	8	F	123	25	4/30/18	No	NA
. . . .		. . .							
432	1227	9/15/18	7	F	118	23	12/5/16	Yes	5009

Example: Student 101 is a 5-year-old male who was 117 centimeters tall and weighed 20 kilograms when he visited his doctor September 15, 2018. His most recent vaccination took place on that same date.

*That sentence reports the **case's** values for the **variables** age, gender, height, weight, and dates of medical record and vaccination. Those same **variables** take on different **values** for other **cases** (students) in the **data set.***

Example: The ages of the students in School 1227 range from 5 to 10 years; two of the cases shown are both 8 years old.

*In large data sets, many cases can share the same **value** of a **variable**— in this example, age. School code is a **constant** for every student in the data set because they all attend the same school. If the study included more than one school, then school code would be a **variable** because different students would come from different schools.*

If certain questions pertain to only some of the cases in a data set, those questions will be not be asked about those for whom they do not apply. We'll learn more about missing values and "not applicable" responses in Chapter 4.

Example: Students 103 and 432 both transferred in from other schools midyear, whereas the other students attended School 1227 from the beginning of the academic year.

*As shown in the two right-hand columns of Figure 2.1, for the students who transferred to School 1227, the **value** of the transfer status **variable** is "yes," and the "previous school" variable has a code for another specific school. For the students who attended School 1227 from the beginning of the year, the value of the transfer status variable is "no," and the "previous school" variable is coded "NA" for **not applicable**. By indicating the cases to which a particular question does not apply, the **data set** can have a consistent list of variables for every case, with their respective values filled in.*

The Research Circle

A wide variety of types of methods can be used to conduct research: **Quantitative methods** use numbers as evidence, collecting information from sources such as surveys, censuses, surveillance data, and "big data" (Chapter 11). By definition, quantitative methods can only be used to study phenomena that can be quantified in some way, whether by counting things or measuring their dimensions or characteristics. **Qualitative methods** are used to study phenomena that cannot easily be quantified, working with data collected using focus groups, participation/observation, or in-depth interviews or sources such as audio, video, or text documents. **Mixed-methods** research uses a combination of quantitative and qualitative approaches within a research study or set of related studies to take advantage of their particular strengths.

With its objective of teaching how to make sense of numbers, this book focuses on quantitative research methods. To learn more about qualitative research methods, see Chambliss and Schutt (2018) or Mack et al. (2005).

> **Quantitative research methods** are used to study phenomena that can be counted or measured numerically. **Qualitative research methods** are used to study phenomena that cannot easily be quantified. **Mixed-methods research** uses a combination of quantitative and qualitative approaches.

There are two major types of research strategies: **Inductive** and **deductive**. **Descriptive research** is an intermediary step that involves making empirical generalizations based on the data, where **empirical** refers to <u>observed</u> data rather than to ideas based solely on theory or logic. The overall research process combines descriptive, inductive, and deductive research to create the **research circle** shown in Figure 2.2. As the circle implies, the research process does not have any built-in starting or ending point: A researcher can start at any point on the circle moving from theory to data (deductive—the arrow that starts at the top of Figure 2.2) or from data to theory (inductive—starting at the bottom of the circle), depending on the objective of their study.

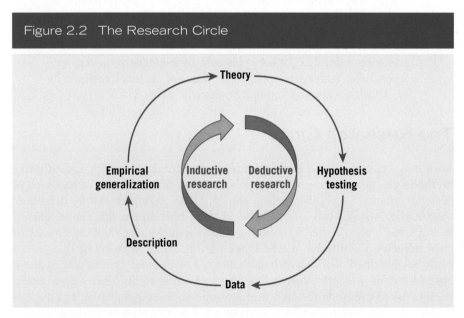

Figure 2.2   The Research Circle

Source: Chambliss & Schutt (2016). Reprinted with permission.

Inductive Research

Inductive research starts with data and uses it to generate a theory about observed patterns. Put differently, a theory is "induced" (proposed) to account for patterns in the data. In everyday conversation, the word **theory** is used to simply refer to an idea, whether or not it has a factual basis. In research terminology, however, it has a much more formal and specific meaning: a hypothetical explanation of some aspect of the world that has been developed from observing data and describing patterns.

> Example: A study of drunk driving started with descriptive data showing that the rate of alcohol-related traffic accidents in the boroughs of New York City decreased by 24% to 35% after introduction of ride-hailing apps such as Uber, but only in the four boroughs where such apps were rapidly adopted (Peck, 2017). The author then developed a theory based on that pattern, surmising that availability of ride-sharing made it easier for people to avoid driving drunk.
>
> > *This research was **inductive** because it started with data on alcohol-related traffic accidents and **described** that the accident rate dropped after introduction of ride-hailing apps. That generalization **induced** the **theory** about a possible mechanism linking increased availability of ride-sharing services to observed (**empirical**) reductions in traffic accident rates.*

Inductive research is often conducted using qualitative or descriptive quantitative methods.

Deductive Research

Deductive research develops a hypothesis from theory and tests that hypothesis using data. In other words, a specific expectation about a relationship between two variables is **deduced** based on (reasoned from) a theory. A **hypothesis** is an educated guess or supposition about a relationship between two or more variables, specifying how the researcher anticipates the value of one variable will differ or change as some other variable differs or changes. A hypothesis should be developed based on a combination of theory and empirical evidence from descriptive studies or from previous research on the topic under study. Deductive research is often conducted using quantitative research methods.

> Example: A study of alcohol-related car crashes might start with a theory about the influence of ride-hailing apps and from it develop a hypothesis that greater availability of ride sharing is responsible for the observed decline in alcohol-related crashes.
>
> > *This research is **deductive** because it starts with theory and develops a **hypothesis**.*

The **research circle** shows how descriptive, inductive, and deductive research relate to data, theory, and hypotheses. **Empirical** means verifiable by observation or experience rather than based on theory or logic alone. **Inductive research** starts with data and develops a theory about why the observed patterns occur. A scientific **theory** is a hypothetical explanation of a relationship between concepts. **Deductive research** starts with a theory and develops a hypothesis, which is then tested using data. A **hypothesis** is a tentative statement predicting how variables are associated with one another.

In a hypothesis about a cause-and-effect relationship, the variable we think is the cause is referred to as the **independent variable**. We hypothesize that it predicts or explains variation in the dependent variable. The variable thought to be the effect (or **outcome**) is referred to as the **dependent variable**—so called because we hypothesize that it <u>depends</u> on, or <u>changes in response to</u>, variation in the independent variable. You will learn more about cause-and-effect relationships in Chapter 12 and how to test hypotheses in Chapter 13.

An **independent variable** is the characteristic that is thought to be the "cause" in a cause-and effect relationship. Synonyms for independent variable include **risk factor**, **predictor**, or **explanatory variable**. A **dependent variable** is the characteristic that is thought to be the "effect" in a cause-and effect relationship. Other commonly used terms for dependent variable are **outcome** or **response variable**.

<u>Example</u>: Keith et al. (2017) hypothesized that people with darker skin color would experience more frequent or severe racial discrimination.

> *Their hypothesis implies that extent of racial discrimination <u>depends on</u> skin color, so skin color is the **independent variable** and racial discrimination is the **dependent variable**.*

A hypothesis can be worded in an "if–then" format, implying that <u>if</u> the independent variable changes (or varies) in a certain way, <u>then</u> the dependent variable is expected to change (or vary) in a specified direction.

<u>Example</u>: <u>If</u> ride-sharing becomes more widely available, <u>then</u> alcohol-related traffic accidents will decrease.

> *Availability of ride-sharing services is the **independent variable**, while traffic accident rate is the **dependent variable**. In other words, the*

hypothesis conjectures that traffic accident rates (the "effect") are influenced by availability of ride-share services (the "cause"). The Peck (2017) study did <u>not</u> have data on individuals' actual usage of ride-sharing, so a **deductive** *study would need to collect such data to test this* **hypothesis**.

The decision of whether to use a descriptive, inductive, or deductive strategy for a particular study should be based on what is already understood about the topic and what additional questions have been raised by prior research or new circumstances. The overall body of research on a particular topic typically involves all three types of strategies to provide a more complete understanding of that topic. Some researchers specialize in either inductive or deductive research, complementing studies of the same topic that other researchers have conducted using a different research strategy. Other researchers conduct both inductive and deductive research over the course of their career, designing each study to fill in gaps in what they had learned from their own prior work and that of others studying that topic.

Goals of Quantitative Research

A research project can have any of several **goals**: descriptive, exploratory, explanatory, and evaluation. Any of these goals can be pursued using either quantitative or qualitative approaches, however, given the focus of this book, the examples below describe hypothetical quantitative studies.

Descriptive Research

Descriptive research is exactly what it sounds like: It seeks simply to describe a pattern or relationship <u>without</u> aiming to explain the reasons for or implications of that pattern; those are covered by one or more of the other research goals. Descriptive research starts by defining what is meant by each concept (aspect of the question) and determining how that attribute will be measured.

Example: A consulting company wants to ensure that their clients are satisfied with the services provided through their online portal. First, they decide to define "satisfaction" as encompassing ease of finding information, coverage of topics clients want to learn about, and accessibility and quality of their web customer support. They develop a survey to measure those dimensions and then analyze the data to identify which aspects of their portal need the most improvement.

This **descriptive study** *uses data collected via the survey to describe what percentage of clients have low satisfaction based on the way they <u>defined</u> and <u>measured</u> that concept.*

Descriptive research is often conducted when getting to know a new topic or to see how some phenomenon occurs in different locations, times, or groups. Other times, descriptive research is conducted to find out what can be learned about a topic using a different definition or measure of a concept. The observed patterns may then be used to generate theories about the relationship between the variables or to develop hypotheses to be studied with one of the other types of research. You will learn more about how to define concepts in Chapter 3 and how to specify approaches to measuring those concepts in Chapter 4.

Exploratory Research

Exploratory research seeks to understand how a phenomenon works, such as what problems people face in a certain social setting, how they cope, and how they think about their experiences. Findings of exploratory research can be used to identify concepts about which to collect data for future descriptive studies or to develop theories about relationships between the attributes of that setting.

> Example: A study of immigration collects data on where respondents came from, their reasons for leaving their home country, barriers they encountered along the way, and strategies they adopted to overcome those barriers.
>
> > This hypothetical **exploratory study** was designed to provide insight into what motivates people to emigrate, and to describe the <u>problems and solutions</u> they developed during their immigration experiences.

Explanatory Research

Explanatory research seeks to identify causes and effects of social, biological, or other phenomena and to predict how an outcome differs or changes in response to variation or change in some other characteristic. Explanatory research often involves formulating and testing a hypothesis about the relationship of interest. Results of explanatory research might then be used to design an intervention that could be tested with an evaluative study or inform a study to explore reasons for the observed patterns.

> Example: To test the theory that social comparison can be used as a "nudge" to reduce household energy consumption, researchers sent one of three messages to each of several thousand households as part of their monthly electric bill—either (1) comparing that household's energy consumption with their neighbors', (2) including a link to a website about the health consequences of pollution associated with energy consumption; or (3) pointing out the extra financial

cost to the household of higher electricity usage (Allcott & Rogers, 2014). They found that the households that received the "keeping up with the Joneses" message substantially reduced their electricity consumption, whereas those sent either of the other two approaches hardly changed their consumption at all (Figure 2.3; Benartzi et al., 2017).

> This **explanatory** study aimed to understand whether a social-comparative message (value of the **independent variable**) predicted greater change in household energy reduction (the **dependent variable**) than messages that did not involve social comparison.

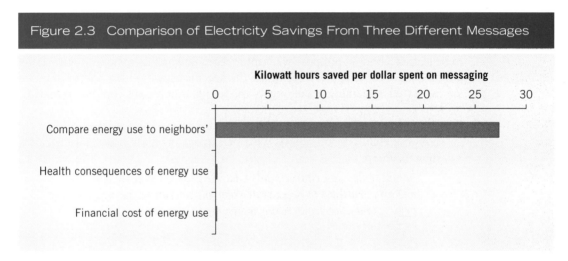

Figure 2.3 Comparison of Electricity Savings From Three Different Messages

Source: Benartzi et al. (2017) with data from Allcott & Rogers (2014). Reprinted with permission.

Evaluation Research

Evaluation research seeks to determine the effects of programs, policies, or other efforts to impact social, health or other outcomes, whether by government agencies, private nonprofits, or for-profit businesses.

> Example: Concerned with rising obesity rates, a city imposes a tax on soda and other sweetened beverages. They compare obesity rates among their residents for the 3 years before and the 3 years after the tax was introduced.

> This study sought to **evaluate** whether <u>changing</u> the **independent variable** (presence of the soda tax) was associated with a change in the **dependent variable** (obesity rate).

> **Descriptive research** aims to define the concepts to be studied, and to characterize patterns in those phenomena. **Exploratory research** seeks to learn how a phenomenon works, such as how people get along in a particular social setting, what issues concern them, and what meanings they attach to their behaviors. **Explanatory research** strives to identify causes and effects of social or other phenomena and to predict how an outcome (dependent variable) varies or changes according to variation in some other characteristic (an independent variable). **Evaluation research** aims to assess the impact of programs, policies, or other interventions.

The topic of a study doesn't necessarily determine which type of research is appropriate. In fact, often, all four types of research will be conducted on a particular topic depending on what is already known about that topic and what remains to be learned about it. Suppose we want to learn how family socioeconomic status affects child well-being. Depending on the specific aspect of that relationship we are interested in learning about, any of the four research goals could be pursued.

Example: A study compares asthma rates for poor, near-poor, and nonpoor children, and reports what percentage of children are in each income group.

*Results of this **descriptive study** could be used to identify groups at high risk of asthma or to generate theories about the relationship between poverty and child health that could be used to develop hypotheses for an explanatory study.*

Example: A survey asks parents in low-income families what worries them about their children's health and safety and how they cope with low income while trying to provide for their children.

*This **exploratory study** is aimed at identifying possible reasons for patterns observed in prior descriptive studies of the relationship between poverty and child well-being. By learning the different ways parents in low-income families provide for their children, specific strategies could be identified to investigate in future studies using descriptive, explanatory, or evaluative approaches.*

Example: A study uses data on family income, what women ate while pregnant, and how much their babies weighed at birth to test whether inadequate intake of certain nutrients is the reason that low birth weight is more common among children from poor than nonpoor families.

*This **explanatory study** is aimed at figuring out what mechanisms explain the findings of a descriptive study showing that the percentage of babies that were low birth weight declined with increasing family income.*

Results of such a study could be used to design interventions to reduce low birth weight among children from low-income families.

Example: A study evaluates whether a pilot program to improve nutritional intake among children born into low-income families improves their health outcomes.

*This **evaluation** project tests whether an intervention to change the hypothesized cause (nutritional intake) results in better health outcomes for children in low-income families.*

Note that each of the four of the hypothetical studies is intended to learn more about the same topic—poverty and child well-being—but each type of research has a different goal in terms of what aspect of that topic is to be studied and why.

Several basic principles are central to making sense of numbers, affecting virtually every other quantitative reasoning skill you will learn in this book. They include using the W's as a checklist, reporting and interpreting numbers, and specifying the direction and magnitude of a pattern.

The W's

Information on **the W's** (who, what, when, where, and how) of a study is crucial for making sense of numbers. The W's are so essential that all of Part II of this book is devoted to explaining how those attributes affect many aspects of quantitative studies. Chapter 3 discusses the importance of the scope and definition of the topic: **what** is under study. Chapter 4 discusses the implications of **how** that concept was measured, and Chapter 5 covers the relevance of **when, where**, and to **whom** (or **which** cases) the data pertain. Later chapters cover other aspects of **how** the data were collected, analyzed, interpreted, and communicated as well as **how many** cases were studied.

> The W's consist of **what, when, where**, and to **whom/which** cases the data pertain; **how** data were defined, measured, collected, and analyzed, and **how many** (cases) are granted honorary W status because they, too, are vital to making sense of numbers.

For now, the key point is to pay attention to those W's for any numbers you work with, making note of them as you read about data that others have collected or analyzed, and writing about them as you present information about your own data collection or analysis.

> The W's affect many aspects of how data are collected, analyzed, and interpreted and should be reported along with the associated numeric information.

Report and Interpret Numbers

In most quantitative research, numbers should be both reported <u>and</u> interpreted to help the audience understand the meaning of those numbers. **Reporting** numbers means including them in a sentence, table, or chart so readers can evaluate or analyze those values further. **Interpreting** numbers involves explaining what they mean in terms of the questions the author seeks to address, such as by comparing them to other numbers or explaining whether they are consistent with a hypothesis about the pattern under study. I introduce and define those concepts briefly here; we will return to many facets of reporting and interpreting numbers throughout the rest of this book.

Reporting the numbers is an important first step in communicating numeric information. By presenting (**reporting**) numbers in the text, table, or chart, researchers provide their audience with the raw data with which to perform additional calculations or comparisons to answer other questions of interest to them.

<u>Example</u>: A government report presents statistics on the inflation rate in their country for each of several years.

Readers could then use that numeric information to <u>compare</u> inflation rates with other countries or for other dates.

<u>Example</u>: A university website reports how many degrees it granted to men and women last year.

Readers who want to assess the size of the gender difference would be able to <u>calculate</u> various comparisons themselves, working from the numbers in the report.

Unless the sole purpose of a document is to make data available to potential users for their own analysis, however, authors should also **interpret** the numbers to help their readers make sense of the information. A number that has not been introduced or explained leaves it entirely to the audience to figure out what it means for the question under study. Those who are not familiar with the topic or setting are unlikely to know which comparisons to make or to have the information for those comparisons at hand. To help the audience understand what the numbers mean for that question and setting, authors should interpret (explain) the comparisons.

Example: A newspaper article reports last year's crime rate for a large city but does not describe whether that city's crime rate is trending up, down or is stable, or whether that city's crime rate is higher, lower, or similar to that in other cities.

> The writer did <u>not</u> **interpret** the crime rate, thus if readers want answers to those important questions, they would have to go to other sources to look up crime rates for other cities and years, and "do the math" themselves to compare them against the **reported** crime rate.

Example: A middle-school teacher is planning an end-of-year trip to an amusement park that has just opened a new ride that all her students are talking about. If she doesn't compare her students' heights against the minimum height needed to go on that ride, she might have a lot of disappointed students on her hands!

> Here, knowing just the students' heights isn't enough. The teacher also needs to assess (**interpret**) whether most of her students are tall enough to participate.

Reporting numbers means presenting their values and the associated W's in the text, table, or chart. **Interpreting** means explaining how those numbers answer a question of interest.

Although it is important to interpret quantitative information, it is also essential to report the numbers. If a researcher <u>only</u> describes a ratio or percentage difference, for example, they will have painted an incomplete picture.

Example: A website advertises a sale offering 25% off all its products but doesn't list the prices themselves. A 25% reduction can be taken off prices at any level: ¥1.00, ¥400, or ¥2,000,000, to name just a few possibilities.

> The percentage discount **interprets** price differences <u>without</u> **reporting** the associated prices. Lacking data on either the original or discounted price on a particular product, customers won't be able to tell whether they can afford it even with the discount or how that store's discounted price compared to what the same product would cost at a different store.

Example: Suppose a newspaper article reported that use of the Google Translate app doubled during the 2018 World Cup in Russia but did not report the amount translated either before or during that event. Doubling is consistent with many possible pairs of numbers: 100 translations before the World Cup versus 200 at the event, or 30,000 versus 60,000, or 2 million versus 4 million, for example.

"Doubling" **interprets** *the values by quantifying change over time. Unless the number of translations themselves are also* **reported***, the popularity of the Google Translate app couldn't be compared with other ways of translating such as hardcopy phrase books or live translators. Furthermore, without info on the number of translations, it is impossible to tell whether that app was rarely used during the 2018 World Cup or was an essential tool for non-Russian speakers. The first pair of numbers would show that the app remained fairly unpopular even after the increase, the last pair that an already popular app went viral. In fact, the well-written article <u>did</u>* **report** *that the Google Translate app had "some 500 million users and translates some 143 <u>billion</u> words a day, into and out of dozens of languages," pointing out that even with that high baseline usage, the increase (doubling) of the Google Translate app was surprisingly large (Smith, 2018).*

When numbers are intended as evidence to answer a question, they should be both reported and interpreted. When numbers are intended to mainly for others to use in their own calculations, the numbers may be reported but not interpreted.

Specify Direction and Magnitude

One of the most important aspects of interpreting a numeric comparison is describing both the direction and magnitude of that pattern.

Direction of Association

When comparing two or more values, **direction** identifies which of those values is higher. For change across time in the value of a variable, direction means conveying whether the trend is upward, level, or downward.

<u>Example</u>: "Today it is hotter in Vancouver than in Toronto,"

"Hotter" captures the **direction** *of the temperature difference between the two named locations.*

<u>Example</u>: "The average global temperature has risen steadily over the past few decades."

"Risen" expresses an <u>upward</u> temperature trend over time.

A relationship between two variables is called a **bivariate association**. There are two possible **directions of association** between quantitative variables. In a **positive association**, as the value of one variable increases, the value of the other variable also increases. A different way of explaining a positive association is that as the value of the independent variable decreases, the value of the dependent variable also decreases. Put differently, in a positive association, values of the two variables move in the <u>same</u> direction.

In a **negative association**, as the value of one variable increases, the value of the other variable decreases. In other words, in a negative association, the values of the two variables move in <u>opposite</u> directions. In math terms, direction specifies the **sign** (positive or negative) of the comparison.

<u>Example</u>: Children get taller with age.

*Age and height are **positively associated** because they move in the <u>same</u> **direction**, as in the blue line in Figure 2.4 that slopes upward from left to right.*

Figure 2.4   Positive and Negative Associations

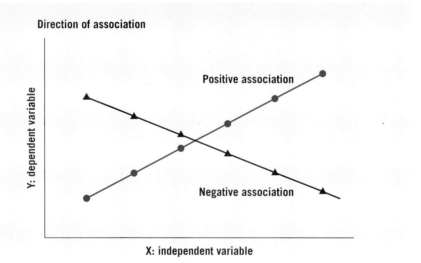

Direction of association

Y: dependent variable

Positive association

Negative association

X: independent variable

<u>Example</u>: As the price of an item increases, consumers buy less of that item.

*Price and quantity bought are **inversely** (**negatively**) associated because as one goes up, the other goes down, as in the <u>downward</u>-sloping black line in Figure 2.4.*

<u>Example</u>: The population of City A grew between 1960 and 2010, whereas that in City C decreased over that period (Figure 2.5).

*The **association** between time and population of City A is **positive**, while that in City C is **negative**.*

Figure 2.5   Illustration of Direction and Magnitude of a Trend

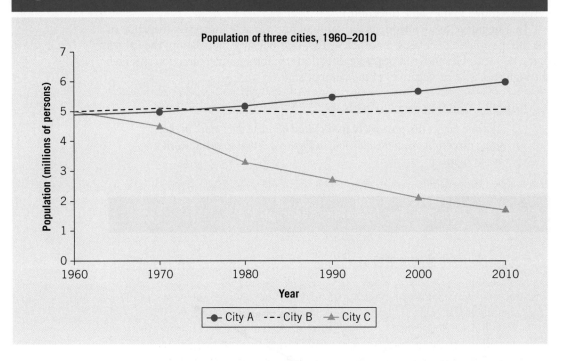

Population of three cities, 1960–2010

It is also possible to describe the shape of a **univariate** pattern, which looks at how values of one variable are distributed. You will learn more about univariate distributions in Chapter 10.

Example: In Figure 2.1, three of the listed students are male and three are female, so the two groups are equally common. One-third of the listed students transferred into School 1227 midyear, so they were less common than those who did not transfer in.

> Gender **composition** is **univariate** because it looks at how values of that <u>one</u> variable are distributed across the gender categories, <u>without</u> considering how it is related to any of the other variables in the data set. Likewise, the **transfer status** distribution conveys information about that one variable alone, so it is also **univariate**. "Less common" conveys **direction** by identifying which transfer status category is smaller than the other.

> A **univariate distribution** (also known as **composition**) portrays how values of one variable are spread across possible values; "uni" means one, "variate" refers to a variable. A **bivariate association** examines how two variables are related to one

another; "bi" means two. The **direction** of an association conveys which of the values being compared is larger. In a **positive association** (also known as a **direct association**), as the value of one variable increases, the value of the other variable also increases. In a **negative** (or **inverse**) **association**, as the value of one variable increases, the value of the other variable decreases.

Magnitude of an Association

Whereas direction identifies <u>which</u> value is bigger, **magnitude** captures <u>how much</u> bigger—in other words, the **size** of the difference between those values. We will learn various ways of calculating magnitude in Chapter 9 and how to use wording to express magnitude in Chapter 14.

> <u>Example</u>: Suppose a school district conducted an evaluation of whether a free breakfast program improves the nutritional status of students from low-income families. Half the elementary schools in the district were randomly assigned to provide free breakfasts to their low-income students and the other half to <u>not</u> provide free breakfast. Students were measured at the beginning and end of the school year and the average increases in height compared for the two groups of schools (Figure 2.6). At the end of the year, the researchers concluded that "children in the free breakfast program grew 0.6 centimeters more during the school

Figure 2.6   Illustration of Direction and Magnitude of an Association

Average change in students' height, schools with and without free breakfast program

2.7 cm – 2.1 cm = 0.6 cm

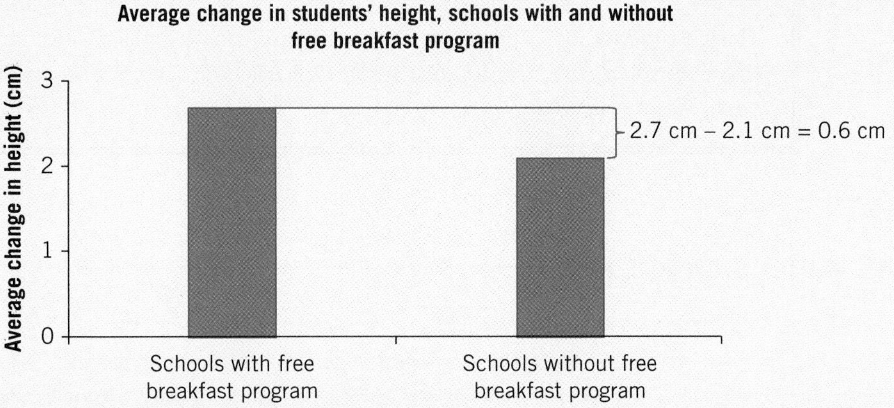

Change in height from beginning to end of the school year.

year than those who did not receive free breakfasts (2.7 cm. and 2.1 cm. growth, respectively; Figure 2.7)."

> Students in both groups grew taller (same **direction** of change over the course of the year), but the free-breakfast group grew faster (larger **magnitude** of change). The word "more" conveys the **direction** of the association between program participation and growth in height), whereas "0.6 centimeters" (shown with the blue bracket) conveys the **magnitude** of that difference. This description both **reports** the information (the average height change for each group) _and_ **interprets** how the differences in growth between those groups answers the key question underlying the study: whether poor children given free breakfasts grew faster than those who were not given free breakfasts.

Magnitude quantifies the **size** of the difference between two numbers.

A hypothesis should state the predicted direction of association between the independent and dependent variables.

<u>Example</u>: Hypothesis: That children from poor families who participate in a free breakfast program will grow faster than those who do not receive a free breakfast.

> The phrase "grow faster" conveys a hypothesized **positive association** between program participation (the **independent variable**) and growth in height (**dependent variable**).

The most effective descriptions of numeric patterns convey both the direction and size of the pattern. Hypotheses should state expected direction but typically do <u>not</u> predict exact magnitude.

TERMS AND CONCEPTS

Bivariate association 28	Dependent variable 20	Empirical 18
Case 14	Outcome (variable) 20	Evaluation research 23
Constant 15	Response variable 20	Explanatory research 22
Data 13	Direction (sign) of	Exploratory research 22
Data set 15	association 28	Hypothesis 19

HIGHLIGHTS

- A **data set** is composed of information on a consistent set of variables for all **cases** in a sample or population. **Variables** are characteristics that can take on different **values** for different cases in the data set, whereas **constants** are attributes that are the same for all cases in a data set.

- The **research circle** connects inductive (from **data** to **theory**) and **deductive** (from theory to **hypothesis** to data) research strategies. Depending on the research objective, a study can start at any point on the research circle.

- Research can pursue any of four main **goals**: **descriptive**, **exploratory**, **explanatory**, and **evaluative**. The choice of a research goal for a particular research project does <u>not</u> depend on the topic but rather on the question or perspective that is the aim of that research.

- The **W's** include **what** topics or concepts were measured, **where**, **when**, and **from whom** those data were collected, and "**how**" they were collected and analyzed. The W's provide a good mental checklist of the information needed to make sense of the results of a quantitative study.

- For quantitative research documents intended to answer a research question, numbers should be both **reported** and **interpreted**. For research documents intended to provide data mainly for others' use, the numbers may be reported but not interpreted.

- Interpretation of a numeric pattern should describe both the **direction** and **magnitude** of that pattern.

RECOMMENDED READINGS

Ghose, T. (2013, April 2). "Just a theory": 7 misused science words. *Scientific American*. https://www.scientificamerican.com/article/just-a-theory-7-misused-science-words

Utts, J., & Heckard, R. (2014). Turning data into information. *Mind on statistics* (5th ed., pp. 14–67). Cengage, Brooks Cole.

EXERCISES

Individual Exercises

Quantitative Reasoning in Everyday Life

1. Plan a data set about restaurants so that you and your friends have a consistent set of information to help you decide where to eat out. Specify (a) what constitutes a case; (b) a characteristic that is a constant across all cases; and (c) the topics of several variables (things you will measure for each case). (d) Sketch a grid of your data set like that in Figure 2.1, showing (i) what goes in the rows (fill in four or five possible items); (ii) what goes in the columns (fill in four or five possible items); and (iii) possible values for each variable for each case (in the interior cells of the grid).

2. Find a newspaper article or website that compares two or more numeric values on a topic of interest to you. Determine whether the authors described the direction and magnitude of differences between those numbers or left it to readers to do the mathematical comparison.

Identifying and Interpreting Research

3. On the website for the Inter-University Consortium for Political and Social Research (ICPSR; https://www.icpsr.umich.edu), identify a study on a topic of interest to you, either from their list of thematic collections or browse by topic. On the web page for that study, identify (a) the name of the data set and its acronym (e.g., "Civil Rights Data Collection [CRDC]") and (b) the W's (when, where, and from whom data were collected). **Save the URL for the ICPSR website for that data set study to use in exercises for later chapters.** From the tab titled "Data & Documentation," preview or download the codebook or documentation. (c) Use it to identify what constitutes a case in their data set (e.g., type of entity). (d) On the tab titled "Variables" find information on (i) a characteristic that is a constant across all cases in that data set and (ii) the topics of several variables.

4. For each of the following articles or reports, identify (a) its research **goal** (descriptive, exploratory, explanatory, or evaluative) and (b) which research **strategy** it employed (inductive, deductive, or descriptive): Klapper et al. (2015), Chapman et al. (2016), and Crowley (2011). References are in the list of references at the end of the book. Specify the sentences and page numbers in each article that conveyed the information needed to answer each question.

5. Use information from the article by Williams et al. (1997) to identify the following: (a) what constitutes a case in their analysis; (b) the W's (when, where, and to whom the data pertain); (c) the dependent variable in their hypothesis; (d) the main independent variable in their hypothesis; and (e) the hypothesized direction of association between those two variables. For each step, specify the page and paragraph number where you found that information.

6. Repeat the instructions to Exercise 2 but for a journal article or research report.

Planning Research

7. Repeat the instructions to Exercise 1 but for a data set about students' current employment.

Group Exercises

Interpreting Research

8. Discuss the following aspects of the article by Chapman et al. (2016): (a) Identify the process by which they developed their theory or theories (e.g., from what data or other types of information). (b) Write a hypothesis about the relationship implied by their theory, including the expected direction of association. (c) Consider whether they also describe other theories of the same phenomenon. If so, write a hypothesis for each theory.

Planning Research

9. Compare the data sets you designed for Exercise 7 above (about employment), identifying similarities and differences in terms of (a) what constitutes a case in each of your hypothetical data sets; (b) a characteristic that is a constant in that data set; and (c) the topics of several variables. (d) Discuss how these differences could affect your ability to compare information across your data sets.

10. Decide on a social issue of interest. For each of the following types of research goals, discuss possible ways to conduct a study of that topic: (a) descriptive, (b) exploratory, (c) explanatory, and (d) evaluative. For each of those hypothetical projects, discuss whether you would use a descriptive, inductive, or deductive research strategy and why you would choose that strategy.

How Topic, Measurement, and Context Help Make Sense of Numbers

PART

II

As discussed in Part I, to make sense of numbers you must be able to identify the topic under study, how it is measured, and the context in which it is being studied. In Part II, I go into more depth on each of those facets. In Chapter 3, I explain what it means to define a concept and why that is an important aspect of planning and describing a quantitative study. In Chapter 4, I discuss several aspects of measuring a concept and why the measurement approach matters for making sense of numbers. In Chapter 5, I consider various dimensions of a study's setting, including place, time, and subgroups. In terms of the W's checklist, Chapter 3 covers "**what**" was studied, Chapter 4 discusses "**how**" it was measured, and Chapter 5 considers "**when**," "**where**," and "**who**" was studied.

Topic and Conceptualization

Identifying and defining the topic—**what** a study is about—are important first steps in undertaking or understanding a research project. In this chapter, I discuss what it means to define a concept and how that definition affects the scope of what is included. Finally, I discuss ways that perspective on a question affects the way numeric values are interpreted.

Conceptualization

The procedure by which researchers specify the concepts they plan to study is called **conceptualization**, which means providing a specific definition of what is encompassed by their topic. The topic of a research study clearly affects the level and range of numeric values that make sense, moving away from a number as an abstract measure to one that is attached to a particular quantifiable thing or dimension. Some concepts, such as height, have only one dimension, making those topics relatively straightforward to conceptualize.

> Example: Credible values of height are completely different for mountains (up to thousands or even tens of thousands of feet) than for buildings (from about 8 feet to 2,700+ feet for the world's tallest building—the Burj

Khalifa in Dubai; Valencia, 2019) than for people (from less than 2 feet for newborn infants up to 7 feet for extremely tall adults).

> For **plausibility** of numeric values to be assessed, the topic must be specified <u>not</u> just as "height" but as "height <u>of [mountains or buildings or people]</u>"

Other topics have several different variants, dimensions, or components, in which case conceptualizing involves deciding which of those aspects to include in the definition.

<u>Example</u>: Suppose a researcher is interested in how exercise affects health. There are many different aspects of exercise they could study, including type of exercise (e.g., running, swimming, or yoga), or its frequency, duration, or intensity. Likewise, there are many different aspects of health on which they could choose to focus.

> Before they can begin their study, the researcher must decide which of these dimensions to include in their **concept** of "exercise." Ditto for the concept of "health." If one study looks at how the <u>frequency</u> of exercise is associated with <u>heart rate</u>, whereas another study examines how the <u>type</u> of exercise is associated with <u>obesity</u>, the two studies are using different **conceptualizations** of exercise and health.

Conceptualization is the process of defining what is meant by a term.

Many research topics involve abstract concepts, rather than concrete, distinct phenomena such as height or chronological age. Before conducting research on an abstract topic, a researcher must carefully specify what they mean by that concept.

<u>Example</u>: Rubin (1970) defined romantic love as "an attitude held by a person toward a particular other person, involving predispositions to think, feel, and behave in certain ways toward that other person" (p. 265). He also specified that romantic love is multidimensional, encompassing "physical attraction, idealization, a predisposition to help, the desire to share emotions and experiences, feelings of exclusiveness and absorption, felt affiliative and dependent needs, the holding of ambivalent feelings, and the relative unimportance of universalistic norms in the relationship" (p. 266).

> Romantic love is an <u>abstract phenomenon</u>, not something that can be easily measured by a bathroom scale or a ruler! Rubin's **conceptualization** thus had to identify which dimensions to include in the definition of romantic love, in order to specify its scope and to differentiate it from platonic friendship. You might have other ideas of what "romantic love" encompasses, in which case we would say you have **conceptualized** it differently.

<u>Example</u>: The political theorist Karl Marx believed that a person's "social class" was defined by his or her relationship to the means of

production, distinguishing between the proletariat who work but do not own the means of production, and the bourgeoisie who invest and live off the surplus generated by the proletariat's operation of the means of production (Marx & Engels, 2002). In contrast, the sociologist Max Weber argued that "social class" included power and prestige in addition to property or wealth (Weber, 1921/2015).

> *Thus, Marx and Weber **conceptualized** (**defined**) "social class" in distinct ways, encompassing different aspects of individuals' social standing.*

SCOPE OF A DEFINITION

The **scope** of a definition refers to the range of cases that will be included in a concept by specifying the criteria used to include or exclude cases under that definition. In his landmark book *Damned Lies and Statistics: Untangling Numbers From the Media, Politicians, and Activists,* Joel Best (2001) pointed out that in defining a concept, the scope of the definition affects not only <u>how many</u> cases will be captured by that definition, but also <u>which</u> cases. If different studies use different definitions of the same general concept, it is difficult to compare their findings.

> <u>Example</u>: Suppose one study conceptualized the topic "crime" to include only felony crimes, another study focused on crimes against persons, and a third study included only crimes that resulted in convictions. Some felonies are crimes against persons (the overlap between the dark blue and gray circles in Figure 3.1), but many are not (the portion of the dark blue circle that does not overlap the gray). Some crimes against persons result in convictions (overlap between the gray and pale blue circle), but some do not. And some felonies lead to convictions (overlap between the dark blue and pale blue circles), but some do not. Still fewer are felony crimes against persons that result in convictions (the area where all three circles overlap one another.)

> *Felony crimes include crimes against <u>property</u> (e.g., arson) and crimes against <u>persons</u> (e.g., murder, rape, and kidnapping), and crimes against <u>society</u> (e.g., drugs/narcotics) (U.S. Department of Justice, 2012). Some crimes against persons are lower-level offenses such as vandalism or disorderly conduct that are <u>not</u> classified as felonies. Convictions occur for felonies, misdemeanors, and other less serious crimes, whether they are crimes against persons, property, or society. These <u>differences</u> in the **scope** of the three conceptualizations of "crime" are likely to lead to <u>different ways of</u> **measuring** crime, which in turn may result in <u>different conclusions</u> about levels and patterns of crime.*

A narrow, focused definition is likely to exclude some of the cases of interest, resulting in **false negatives**—cases <u>incorrectly</u> classified as <u>lacking</u> the trait of interest. For quantifiable phenomena, a numeric **cutoff** is specified to identify which cases are classified as meeting the definition and which are excluded. The definition should specify whether to include cases above or below that cutoff

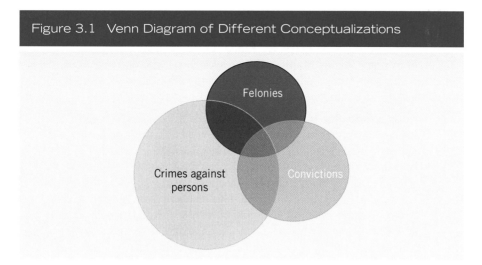

Figure 3.1   Venn Diagram of Different Conceptualizations

Felonies

Crimes against persons

Convictions

Note: Schematic diagram only. Sizes of circles do not represent any actual data.

value. A broad definition will encompass a larger number of cases, some of which might be beyond the scope of what we are trying to capture. Cases that <u>are</u> captured by a definition despite <u>not</u> having the desired trait are known as **false positives** because they <u>incorrectly</u> classify a case as <u>having</u> that trait.

The **scope** of a definition refers to the range or set of cases that will be included in a concept. A **cutoff value** is a **numeric criterion** used to define the scope of a concept measured along a quantifiable spectrum. **False negatives** are cases that are <u>incorrectly</u> classified as <u>lacking</u> the trait of interest. **False positives** are cases that are <u>incorrectly</u> classified as <u>having</u> the trait of interest.

<u>Example</u>: For diagnosing autism or autism spectrum disorder (ASD), clinical evaluations involving long-term histories of a child's behavior are the gold standard. However, they are expensive to administer and require more expertise, so they are typically conducted only after an initial screening test identifies which children appear likely to have the condition (Bestpracticeautism.com, 2016). Children who are suspected of having the condition can be screened using tests such as the Autism Diagnostic Observation Schedule (ADOS).[1]

Figure 3.2a compares the distribution of screening test scores against the clinical diagnostic ranges. The clinical ranges "normal," "?" (not sure),

---

[1]Although ADOS scores "can be used in an <u>inclusionary</u> fashion to help make a diagnosis of ASD if 'positive,' they cannot be used by themselves in an <u>exclusionary</u> fashion to negate a diagnosis of ASD" because (the ADOS) does not capture long-term behavioral histories—an important diagnostic criterion for ASD (Coplan, 2013).

and "abnormal" are shown on the x-axis and the number of cases that have each ADOS screening score would be on the y-axis. The distribution of scores on the screening test for children who have autism (dashed bell curve) overlaps the distribution of scores for those who don't have the condition (solid black bell curve), thus it is <u>not</u> possible to set a cutoff value of the screening score that will correctly classify everyone.

*If the **cutoff value** is set as shown by the dotted vertical line in Figure 3.2a, scores in the dot-filled area will be classified as having autism. However, with that cutoff value, some children who do <u>not</u> have autism would be classified as <u>having</u> the condition based on the screening scores: Those under the "healthy" curve who fall to the right of the cutoff are thus **false positives** (blue-shaded area). That cutoff value of the screening score would also misclassify some children who <u>do</u> have autism as <u>not</u> having the condition: Those under the "disease" curve who fall to the left of the cutoff line are thus **false negatives** (gray shaded area).*

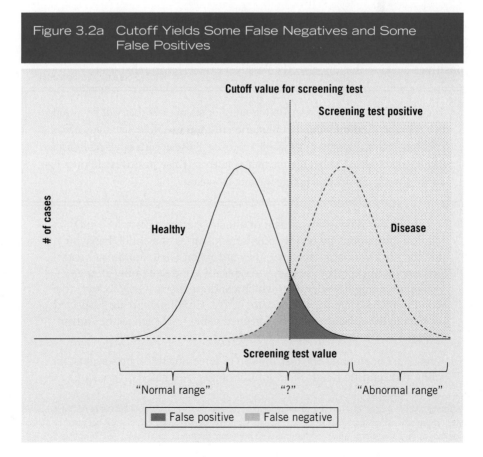

Figure 3.2a   Cutoff Yields Some False Negatives and Some False Positives

> The **definition of a concept** will affect how many and which cases will be included. Broad definitions will encompass more cases than narrow ones. Definitions that include differing criteria may overlap with one another but will include different sets of cases.

When distributions of the screening scores overlap between those who do and do not have the condition based on more thorough clinical criteria, no one definition is perfect—any cutoff value of the screening score will lead to some cases being misclassified.[2] Therefore, changing the **scope** of the definition of autism can reduce <u>either</u> the number of false negatives <u>or</u> the number of false positives, but <u>not both</u>: There is a trade-off between those two types of misclassification.

<u>Example</u>: Ruling out everyone who does <u>not</u> have autism by raising the cutoff value for classifying children as having ASD will exclude some children who actually have the condition (Figure 3.2b). On the other

Figure 3.2b   Revised Cutoff Yields No False Positives But Many False Negatives

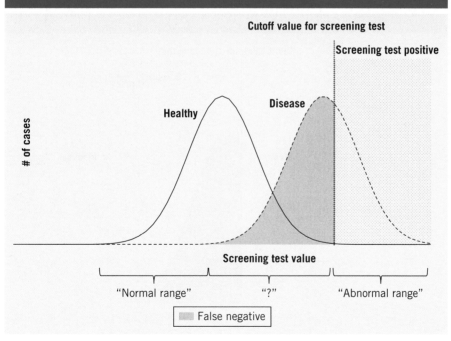

hand, identifying every case of autism by lowering the cutoff value will also capture children who <u>don't</u> have the condition (Figure 3.2c).

*Raising the cutoff value (Figure 3.2b) eliminates **false positives** (note the <u>lack</u> of blue-shaded area in that figure) but increases **false negatives** (gray shaded area). Conversely, lowering the cutoff value (Figure 3.2c) eliminates **false negatives** but increases **false positives**. In other words, revising the **cutoff value** amounts to changing the **scope** of the autism **definition**, which alters both the <u>number</u> of children diagnosed and the <u>composition</u> of those classified (rightly or wrongly) as having ASD.*

There is a trade-off between the number of false positives and the number of false negatives. A <u>broader</u> scope (or more generous threshold on the numeric cutoff value) will include more cases that <u>don't</u> fit the intended criteria, thus increasing the number of **false positives**. Conversely, a <u>narrower</u> scope (more restrictive numeric threshold) will exclude more cases that <u>do</u> have the trait of interest, thus increasing the number of **false negatives**.

Figure 3.2c Revised Cutoff Yields No False Negatives But Many False Positives

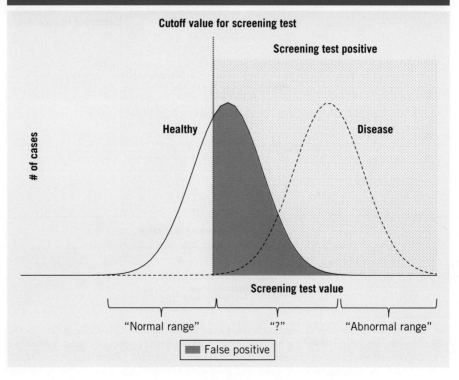

Note: ADOS: Autism Diagnostic Observation Schedule

How Change or Variation in a Definition Affects the Scope

Often, a given concept is defined differently in different locations, time periods, or for different groups. When that occurs, the scope of what is encompassed for that concept will vary in terms of the number and nature of cases included under those different definitions, making it difficult to compare numeric values across contexts.

> Example: U.S. states vary in terms of how they define a felony and how different types of felonies are classified (Portman, 2019). In Kansas, for instance, crimes are divided into nondrug and drug offenses; nondrug offenses are divided into severity levels 1 to 10, and drug offenses are divided into severity levels 1 to 5. In New Mexico, felony crimes are categorized into five classes: capital felonies (most serious crime) and first-degree to fourth-degree felonies (least serious felonies).
>
> > *These different **definitions** and **classification systems** mean that the same type of crime will be categorized differently depending on where it occurred. Both the <u>number</u> and <u>type(s)</u> of crimes will vary according to the definition of "felony."*

Definitions of a phenomenon also change over time, leading to changes in the breadth and scope of which cases or values are included.

> Example: In 1990, the U.S. Congress passed the Hate Crime Statistics Act, which required the attorney general to collect data "about crimes that manifest evidence of prejudice based on race, religion, sexual orientation, or ethnicity" (U.S. Department of Justice, 2017). Since then, the definition of hate crimes has since been revised several times, adding new types of bias motivation classifications (disability, sexual orientation, gender, and gender identity), new categories within several of the bias motivation types (e.g., Anti-Arab, Anti-Mormon), and increasing the number of bias types that can be reported for a single hate crime incident.
>
> > *Do <u>NOT</u> worry about absorbing the details of Table 3.1! Even a quick glance at that table reveals the number and variety of changes in the **scope** of how "hate crime" has been **conceptualized**. The number of gray shaded boxes has increased over time (left to right in the columns), reflecting changes in what falls under the U.S. definition of "hate crime." In addition, some rows (bias motivation classifications) that were shaded in the early years are not shaded in later ones due to **renaming** or **reclassification** of bias types. The sheer number of notes to the table hints at the many fine-grained changes in wording and scope of the changes in how "hate crime" was conceptualized.*

When the definition of a concept is revised, there may be a change in the level, steepness, or even the direction of a trend before and after the definition

Table 3.1 Changes in Scope and Detail of a Definition

Hate Crime Bias Motivation Classifications and Definitions, U.S. 1996–2017				
Bias Motivation Classification	Data Reporting Years			
	1990–96	1997–2013	2013–14	2015–17
Race:[a]				
Anti-White				
Anti-Black or African American[b]				
Anti-American Indian or Alaska Native				
Anti-Asian[c]				
Anti-Native Hawaiian or Other Pacific Islander				
Anti-Multiple Races, Group				
Anti-Arab				
Anti-Hispanic or Latino[d,e]				
Anti-Other Race/Ethnicity/Ancestry[e]				
Religion:				
Anti-Jewish				
Anti-Catholic				
Anti-Protestant				
Anti-Islamic (Muslim)[f]				
Anti-Other Religion				
Anti-Multiple Religions, Group				
Anti-Mormon				
Anti-Jehovah's Witness				
Anti-Eastern Orthodox (Russian, Greek, Other)				
Anti-Other Christian				
Anti-Buddhist				
Anti-Hindu				
Anti-Sikh				
Anti-Atheism/Agnosticism/etc.				
Sexual Orientation:[g]				
Anti-Gay (Male)[h]				
Anti-Lesbian[i]				

Hate Crime Bias Motivation Classifications and Definitions, U.S. 1996–2017				
	Data Reporting Years			
Bias Motivation Classification	**1990–96**	**1997–2013**	**2013–14**	**2015–17**
Sexual Orientation:[g]				
Anti-Homosexual[j]	■	■		
Anti-Lesbian, Gay, Bisexual, or Transgender (Mixed Group)[k]			■	■
Anti-Heterosexual	■	■	■	■
Anti-Bisexual	■	■	■	■
Ethnicity/National Origin:[l]				
Anti-Hispanic or Latino[d]	■	■	■	
Anti-Not Hispanic or Latino[e]			■	
Disability:				
Anti-Physical		■	■	■
Anti-Mental		■	■	■
Gender:				
Anti-Male			■	■
Anti-Female			■	■
Gender Identity:				
Anti-Transgender			■	■
Anti-Gender Nonconforming			■	■
Multiple-Bias Incidents[m]				

Source: Data from U.S. Department of Justice (2018). Retrieved from https://ucr.fbi.gov/hate-crime/2017/resource-pages/about-hate-crime.

Notes:

a. In 2015, the bias classification "Race" was renamed Race/Ethnicity/Ancestry, incorporating the previously separate "Ethnicity/National Origin" classification.

b. In 2013, "Anti-Black" was renamed "Anti-Black or African American" to match the U.S. Government's Office of Management and Budget wording for the collection of race and ethnicity (U.S. Department of Justice, 2018).

c. In 2013, "Anti-Asian/Pacific Islander" was divided into two categories: "Anti-Asian" and "Anti-Native Hawaiian or Alaska Native" to match the U.S. Government's Office of Management and Budget wording for the collection of race and ethnicity (U.S. Department of Justice, 2018).

d. In 2013, "Anti-Hispanic" was renamed "Anti-Hispanic or Latino."

e. In 2015, "Anti Not Hispanic or Latino" was changed to "Anti-Other Race/Ethnicity/Ancestry" and moved from the "Ethnicity/National Origin" category into the "Race/Ethnicity/Ancestry" bias motivation classification.

(Continued)

Table 3.1   (Continued)

f. In 2013, "Anti-Islamic" was renamed "Anti-Islamic (Muslim)."

g. In 2013, the hate crimes data collection's sexual-orientation bias types were revised based on recommendations from the Criminal Justice Advisory Policy Board and the Hate Crime Coalition (U.S. Department of Justice, 2018). See specific types for detail.

h. In 2013, "Anti-Male Homosexual" was revised to "Anti-Gay (Male)."

i. In 2013, "Anti-Female Homosexual" was revised to "Anti-Lesbian."

j. In 2013, "Anti-Homosexual" bias type was discontinued, replaced by revised other sexual-orientation types.

k. In 2013, "Anti-Lesbian, Gay, Bisexual, or Transgender (Mixed Group)" type was added.

l. In 2015, "Anti Hispanic or Latino" was moved from the "Ethnicity/National Origin" bias motivation classification to the "Race" bias type classification, which was renamed "Race/Ethnicity/Ancestry."

m. Beginning in 2013, law enforcement agencies could report up to five bias motivations per offense type.

change. The size and direction of the change in the number of cases captured by a definition depend on whether the scope of the definition increased, decreased, or shifted to encompass a different set of phenomena.

Example: After several more religions were added to the U.S. hate crime definition in 2015, the number of religious-motivated hate crime incidents increased nearly 50%, from just over 1,000 in 2014 to more than 1,500 in 2017 (gray line in Figure 3.3). In the first 2 years after the more detailed list of religions was added to the hate crime definition, between 90 and 100 incidents were reported in the newly listed religions, more than offsetting the decline of about 30 incidents per year from the "Anti-Other Religion" classification. Previously listed religions (especially Anti-Jewish and Anti-Islamic) also showed increases during that period (detail not shown).

Naming those additional religions in the hate crime criteria did not simply change the category in which such incidents were reported (from "Other religion" to a specific, newly listed religion), but the change was associated with an increase in the number of bias-motivation hate crimes being reported—overall and for most of the listed religions.

Example: In 2015, the Ethnicity/National Origin classification was combined with the Race classification to create a new bias-motivation classification named "Race/Ethnicity/Ancestry." The number of hate crimes related to race shifted upward after that change, in part because a group that had previously been classified separately was now included in that group.

*That **merging** and **reclassification** altered trends in two of the major categories: The dashed black line in Figure 3.3 that represented Ethnicity/ National Origin ceased in 2014, whereas the blue line depicting the number of incidents for Race/Ethnicity/Ancestry increased from 2014 to*

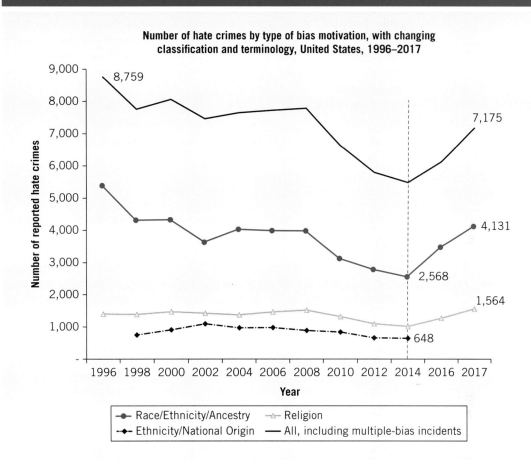

Figure 3.3 Effect of Changes in Scope and Definition of "Hate Crimes" Over Time

Number of hate crimes by type of bias motivation, with changing classification and terminology, United States, 1996–2017

Source: Data from U.S. Department of Justice, Uniform Crime Reporting, various years.

2017, substantially due to the inclusion of Anti-Latino and Anti-Other Race/Ethnicity/Origin incidents.

Example: After "Anti-Islam" was renamed "Anti-Islam (Muslim)," the number of reported incidents of that bias type increased nearly 80%. Likewise, adding the phrase "African American" to the "Anti-Black" category was associated with an increase of 25% in incidents classified as that bias type (not shown).

*Even a seemingly minor change in <u>labeling</u> can alter what people recognize as within a **definition**.*

However, caution should be applied when interpreting the effect of a definition change on observed levels because the <u>actual</u> number of events might have changed at the same time as the scope of the definition changed.

> <u>Example</u>: In 2016, Donald Trump replaced Barack Obama as President of the United States, resulting in a shift in the political and cultural climate that could account for changes in the number of hate crimes that occurred to, or were reported by, some of the groups listed in the hate crime definition.
>
> > *The observed changes in* **reported** *hate crimes between 2015 and 2017 might have reflected the <u>actual</u> change number of such crimes that took place, <u>not just</u> changes due to revised* **conceptualization** *and* **labeling** *of the bias types.*

Anecdotes Are <u>Not</u> Definitions

Anecdotes (descriptions of one or two selected cases) are <u>not</u> adequate substitutes for definitions because anecdotal examples are often chosen based on extreme, rather than typical, features (Best, 2001). Instead, a definition should specify the criteria for identifying cases that fall within the intended scope of that concept.

Using anecdotes to define a concept is known as **overgeneralizing**— extrapolating from one (or a few) cases to many. Choosing a specific anecdote because it supports a particular viewpoint is known as **selective observation**. Both overgeneralization and selective observation are reasoning errors that can lead to incorrect conclusions about the actual pattern of the phenomenon of interest. You will learn more about overgeneralization and selective observation in Chapters 5 and 11, respectively.

An **anecdote** is a short description of or narrative about some phenomenon based on one or two instances (cases). **Overgeneralization** occurs when someone unjustifiably concludes that what is true about <u>some</u> cases is true for <u>all</u> cases. **Selective observation** occurs when a researcher decides which cases to include in their analysis based on whether or not those cases support their prior opinion or hypothesis about the topic under study.

When anecdotes are used to illustrate boundaries or extremes of a phenomenon, researchers must be very clear that those examples are best- or worst-case scenarios as opposed to typical or average.

> <u>Example</u>: Although some violent crimes are committed by someone who has schizophrenia, most people who have schizophrenia are <u>not</u> violent; they "typically withdraw from social interaction and simply prefer to be left alone" (National Alliance on Mental Illness, 2008).

*In this example, an extreme **anecdote**—the rare person with schizophrenia who commits a violent crime—is being **overgeneralized** to paint an incorrect picture of what the condition looks like. If that anecdote was chosen to support an agenda against people with schizophrenia, it would represent **selective observation**. A correct **definition** of schizophrenia should be based on evidence related to the full range (**scope**) of people who have that condition, including clinical criteria used to diagnose it and a description of the symptoms, behaviors, and experiences of people with that disease.*

Anecdotes should <u>not</u> be used in place of definitions because they are often chosen based on <u>extreme</u>, rather than <u>typical</u>, features. Researchers should make clear if they are using anecdotes to illustrate best- or worst-case scenarios and should specify the criteria used to determine the scope of the definition.

How Topic and Scope Affect Plausibility

The topic and scope of a definition substantially affect which numeric values are plausible, meaning that the level and range of those values make sense for the topic—that they are realistic and believable. The topic also affects how a specific plausible value is interpreted.

<u>Example</u>: At your annual checkup, the nurse measured your systolic and diastolic blood pressure (BP), pulse rate, respiratory rate, and cholesterol. If you wrote down a bunch of numbers for your health test results but forgot to indicate which number went with which test, you wouldn't know which of them reflected excellent health and which indicated potential areas of concern.

> *A <u>systolic</u> BP of 115 mmHg is in the **normal** range, but a <u>diastolic</u> BP of 115 mmHg is classified as Stage 2 hypertension (American Heart Association, 2018). A resting <u>heart</u> rate of 60 beats per minute is in the **normal** range, but a resting <u>respiratory</u> rate of 60 breaths per minute would be highly **worrisome** (Cleveland Clinic, 2014). A <u>total</u> cholesterol of 130 mg/dl (milligrams per deciliter) is in the **healthy** range, but an LDL (low-density lipoprotein—the "bad" cholesterol) of 130 mg/dl might be a red flag (National Heart, Lung, and Blood Institute, n.d.).*

<u>Example</u>: A sociology department at a small liberal-arts college with a total of 2,000 students is trying to demonstrate demand for its courses. It reports that in the most recent semester, 30 students majoring in that field, a total enrollment of 250, and a total of 820 credit hours were taught. The first definition of "demand"—number of majors—counts individual students who are concentrating in sociology. Each of

them must enroll in <u>several</u> sociology courses per semester in order to complete their program of study. The second definition—enrollment—counts every student taking one or more courses in the department, including those that are open to nonmajors (e.g., a large introductory survey course or electives that satisfy general college distribution requirements) as well as advanced electives open to majors only. The third definition—credit hours—factors in that some courses are for three credits, others for four credits (e.g., lab courses), and others for six or more credits (e.g., internships or honors thesis courses).

> *Although each of these figures sheds light on some aspect of the demand for sociology courses, the different aspects have very different **levels** and **ranges**. Whereas 820 might be a believable number of credit hours taught in one semester, it would be an implausibly high number of majors in any one department at a small college. And although 30 might be an acceptable number of majors for a small department, no dean will be persuaded to give additional resources to a department that taught only 30 credit hours in a semester.*

Concepts With Limits on Their Possible Values

Many concepts have **limits** on the numeric values they can take on, including minimum and/or maximum values; whether values can be positive, negative, or both; whether they can be integers only or also include decimal places; and various other specifications such as intervals between values. Both the topic and the scoring system (measurement) affect interpretation of numeric values. We'll learn more about how measurement affects plausibility in Chapter 4 and about limits on values of different types of numeric measures in Chapter 9.

<u>Example</u>: Each exam on the SAT has a minimum scaled score of 200 and a maximum scaled score of 800 points. The aggregate SAT score—which combines scores on the Math and the Evidence-Based Reading and Writing (EBRW) sections—therefore has a theoretical range from 400 to 1600. The essay section is scored from 2 to 8 (College Board, 2019).

> *To make sense of a score, you must know which aspect (**topic** area) of the SAT you are evaluating. A value of 650 is quite good for <u>either</u> a math or EBRW subtest score, but very poor for the <u>combined</u> score. An 8 is a perfect score on the essay test, but is <u>less than</u> the **minimum** possible score for either the Math or EBRW sections.*

<u>Example</u>: Each <u>set</u> of a tennis match is scored in terms of the number of games won within that set, with the first player to win six games winning that set. However, the set must be won by at least two games. The overall <u>match</u> is scored in terms of the number of sets won within that match. The winner is the first player to win two sets (of three), although in men's Grand Slam play the winner is the first to win three sets (of five).

*Thus, the **minimum** number of <u>games</u> a player can win within a set is zero and the **maximum** is often six but can go higher in closely contested sets where the players alternate winning games. And although the **minimum** final <u>set</u> score for a player is 0 for both men and women, the **maximum** values are 2 for women and 3 for men (U.S. Tennis Association [USTA], 2017). Even within tennis scoring, the maximum possible values differ for the different components (<u>game</u>, <u>set</u>, and <u>match</u>), and—for Grand Slam match scores—by gender.*

Example: There is no ceiling (upper limit) on the number of runs in baseball, although some leagues invoke a "mercy rule" ending the game if one team is leading by 10 runs after the trailing team has played at least seven completed innings (Welsh, 2017).

*Still, that rule does <u>not</u> limit the **maximum** score—only the <u>difference</u> between the two teams' scores.*

Positive and Negative Values

For some topics, numeric values can be positive, zero, or negative, but for other topics, only some of those values can occur.

Example: A TV meteorologist showed a map with negative numbers on it but forgot to label what aspect of the weather was being reported. Negative values are valid for temperature level (current, previous day, or predicted for some day in the future), wind chill, <u>change</u> in the temperature since the previous day, or <u>difference</u> in temperature compared to the average for the same date, among other possibilities. However, numeric values for rainfall, snowfall, or wind speed must be 0 or higher.

Only by knowing which weather-related <u>topic</u> is shown on the map can you figure out which numbers are plausible, and for those that are, how to interpret the value. A temperature <u>change</u> of −1 °F degree has a very different meaning than does a <u>current temperature</u> of −1 °F. The former could occur in just about any season (e.g., from 55 °F to 54 °F); the latter would be reasonable only in the winter in certain locations.

Other Limits on Numeric Values

For some topics, only certain numeric values within the plausible range can occur.

Example: SAT scores on the Math or EBRW sections range from 200 to 800 in increments of 10 points.

SAT scores such as 470 and 650 are possible, but scores of 477 or 652 are not.

Example: Each <u>game</u> of tennis is scored love (zero), 15 (for the first point a player won within that game), 30 (second point won), 40 (third point won), so it is impossible to obtain a score in between those values or higher than 40 numeric points within a game. If the game is tied 40-40 (known as "deuce,"), players continue on with scores termed "ad-in" and "ad-out" instead of higher numeric scores (USTA, 2017).

These are the kind of funky, unique numeric systems that make it such a challenge to make sense of numbers for a new topic!

For some topics, measures have defined limits on their values, including the following:

- A **minimum** value (lowest possible, or "floor"), a defined **maximum** value (highest possible, or "ceiling"), or both

- Only **integer** values or also **decimal** or **fractional** values

- Only **positive** values or also including **zero** or **negative** values

- Other limits on specific values they can assume.

How Topic and Perspective Affect Optimal Values

For many numeric topics, certain values (or direction of change in values) are preferred or **optimal**. In some instances, perspective on that topic also influences which values are ideal.

An **optimal** value is the one that is the most favorable or desirable for the topic and measure at hand.

How Topic Affects Optimal Value

For some topics, higher numbers represent the optimal value, for other topics, lower numbers are preferred, and for yet other topics, the middle of the range is the most favorable.

Example: For SAT scores, the higher, the better.

*Higher SAT scores are **optimal** regardless of whether the score is a raw or scaled score, a percentile, a subtest score, or a composite score.*

Example: For crime rates, the lower, the better.

Figure 3.4   Middle of the Range Is Best

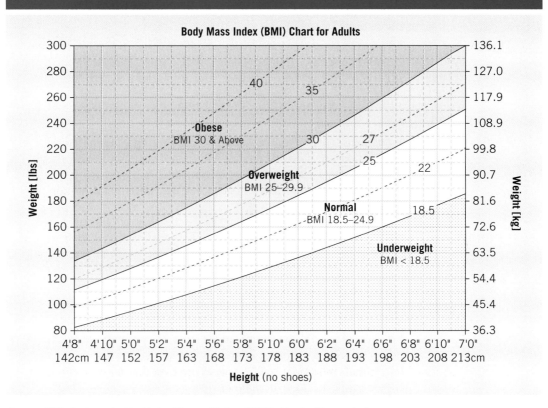

Body Mass Index (BMI) Chart for Adults

Source: BMI chart created by Vertex42.com (Vertex, 2009). Used with permission.

Example: For body mass index (BMI; a measure of weight-for-height), middle values are best. In Figure 3.4, the healthy (white) range is in between underweight (dotted fill), and gray (overweight/obese).

> *BMI less than 18.5 kg./m.² is considered underweight, between 18.5 and 24.9 to be a healthy weight, 25.0 to 29.9 overweight, and 30 or higher obese (Centers for Disease Control [CDC], 2017).*

How Perspective Affects Optimal Value

Identifying the topic and its definition is not always enough information to help us make sense of numbers; interpretation might depend on which perspective you are taking.

Example: "Savers and retirees seeking juicier yields will have an easier time finding savings accounts that pay more than 2 percent, a figure that looks attractive after they were starved of any interest for nearly a decade. But people trying to whittle down a pile of credit card debt, tap their home equity line of credit, or purchase a car may find that it will cost a little more" (Siegel Bernard, 2018).

> *Here, just knowing that the **topic** is interest rates isn't enough information to determine whether a high or a low value is "better" because the **preferred value** depends on whether you are a saver or a spender.*

Example: As noted earlier, for screening tests that have overlapping distributions between scores of those who do and do not have a condition, there is a trade-off between false positives and false negatives. In such situations, deciding where to set the cutoff depends on how the results of the screening test will be used (Coplan, 2013): Researchers studying autism want to include only children who have that condition in order to avoid "watering down" their study sample, so they want to minimize false positives. They can tolerate the fact that this will yield a lot of false negatives because their aim is research, not clinical care. However, clinicians' goal is to find as many affected individuals as possible, so they want to minimize false negatives. They can put up with the fact that this will result in some false positives because they will be following up on all of the positive screening results, thus allowing them to differentiate between the false positives and true positives based on further testing.

> *The choice of a **definition** (**cutoff value** for the screening test) will affect the number and characteristics of children who are identified as having autism. The preferred value of the cutoff for identifying cases depends on whether you are looking at it from the **point of view** of a researcher or a clinician.*

Optimal numeric values (or optimal direction of change) for a given topic can be the following:

- Higher is better, lower is better, or a middle value is preferred

- Affected by the **perspective** (or point of view) on the topic or question

---

TERMS AND CONCEPTS

HIGHLIGHTS

- Specifying how the topic under study is **defined** is essential to making sense of numbers used to describe that phenomenon.

- **Conceptualizing** a topic involves specifying the terminology to be used in research on that topic and providing a **definition** that identifies the **scope** of what is to be encompassed.

- The **scope** of a definition affects both the level and range of plausible numeric values for the phenomenon under study.

- **Definitions** often vary across **studies, locations,** and **dates,** making it difficult to compare findings across studies.

- There is a trade-off between **false positives** and **false negatives,** thus no one definition can eliminate both types of **misclassifications.**

- **Anecdotes** are not substitutes for **definitions,** often showcasing atypical values rather than spanning the full intended range of a concept.

- Topic affects which numeric values are **plausible,** including whether there are **minimum** and/or **maximum** values, whether the variable can take on **positive, zero,** and/or **negative** values, and other types of **numeric restrictions.**

- Topic and its conceptualization affect whether higher, lower, or midrange values are most favorable (**optimal**) for that topic.

- **Perspective** on a topic influences how numbers are interpreted, with high values preferred from some points of view but low values preferred from other perspectives on that same topic.

RESEARCH TIPS

- Consult and cite standard reference materials on your topic(s) to become familiar with the different definitions that others have used and why they chose them.

- Read articles, books, and other credible resources to learn what level and range of numeric values make sense for a topic and what values are optimal for that topic, definition, and measure.

RECOMMENDED READINGS

Best, J. (2001). *Damned lies and statistics: Untangling numbers from the media, politicians, and activists.* Berkeley: University of California Press.

Chambliss, D. F., & Schutt, R. K. (2018). Conceptualization and measurement. *Making sense of the social world* (6th ed., pp. 70–97). Sage.

EXERCISES

Individual Exercises

Quantitative Reasoning in Everyday Life

1. Thinking about hobbies or everyday tasks, identify measures that meet each of the following criteria (each criterion <u>alone</u>):

   (a) can include both negative and positive values (and zero), (b) can include only zero or positive values, (c) can include only whole numbers, or (d) can include both whole numbers and decimal values.

2. Identify two or three measures of the quality of performance in a favorite sport or other hobby. For each measure, specify (a) whether higher, lower, or middle values are better; (b) whether interpretation of "better" depends on perspective and, if so, list at least two different perspectives; and (c) for each of those perspectives, indicate whether higher, lower, or middle values are "better."

3. (a) Find a newspaper article or blog that uses an anecdote about a social issue to define the scope of that issue. (b) Look up information on that issue from an authoritative source such as a government agency or a professional association that specializes in that field. (c) Compare the scope of the definition from the authoritative source to the definition implied by the anecdote. (d) Identify ways that the anecdote limits or biases the definition of that issue.

Interpreting Research

4. Repeat the instructions to Exercise 1 but for measures of academic or economic performance.

5. For the same measure used in the preceding question, repeat the instructions to Exercise 2.

Group Exercises

Quantitative Reasoning in Everyday Life

6. Make a list of the sports or hobbies each of you discussed in Exercise 2, along with (a) the measures you identified, (b) what comprise optimal values for each measure, (c) whether a given measure is interpreted differently depending on perspective, and (d) what constitutes those perspectives.

7. Discuss your answers to Exercise 3, including (a) the issue each of you

investigated, (b) the anecdote you found, (c) the definition of scope from an authoritative source, and (d) what you learned about the limitations and biases that would be imposed if the anecdotes were used as definitions.

Interpreting Research

8. Identify a screening test used to identify a certain disease or other health condition. Consider what would constitute (a) a false positive and (b) a false negative. Discuss (c) the trade-off between false positives and false negatives for that condition—for example, the consequences of each type of incorrect classification—and (d) the circumstances under which one type of misclassification might be preferred to the other.

9. Read the description of definitions of cases on the *New York Times GitHub* site used to share data on the COVID-19 epidemic (https://github.com/nytimes/covid-19-data). (a) Discuss the implications for the number and severity of cases of different definitions (e.g., "confirmed" versus "suspected" cases) used by different sources of data. (b) Consider the repercussions of differences in those definitions for comparisons across locations and dates.

Planning Research

10. Decide on a social concept of interest. (a) Working individually, each student writes a definition of that concept. As a group, (b) make a Venn diagram to show ways that the set of group members' definitions (i) <u>overlap</u> one another and in terms of which dimensions of the concept, (ii) <u>include different</u> aspects and in terms of which dimensions. (c) Discuss the implications of those differences for the (i) number and (ii) types of cases that would be included based on each definition.

CHAPTER 4

Measurement

Learning Objectives

After reading this chapter, you will be able to do the following:

1. State the difference between conceptualization and measurement.
2. Identify factors that affect how a concept should be operationalized.
3. Recognize levels of measurement, units, and categories.
4. Explain how data collection relates to level of measurement.
5. Define unit of analysis, system of measurement, and scale of measurement.
6. Describe how measurement affects plausible and optimal values for a particular topic.
7. Define reliability and validity and their role in quantitative research.

The preceding chapter discussed the importance of conceptualization—of defining **what** you seek to study. However, conceptualization does not determine **how** the phenomena of interest is to be measured. The choice of how a concept will be measured can substantially affect which numeric values are plausible and how to interpret those values; therefore understanding some fundamental aspects of measurement is an essential step for making sense of numbers.

In this chapter, I start by distinguishing between conceptualization and measurement. I then discuss different levels of measurement and how they are influenced by the ways data are collected. I then cover how various aspects of units affect what numeric values make sense for a particular variable. Finally, I introduce reliability and validity of measures and explain why they are important considerations for quantitative research.

Measurement

Defining the concepts to be studied is the essential first step in conducting a research project. Once that has been done, the next step is to **operationalize** each concept, which refers to the procedure for identifying the value of a variable for each case. In other words, operationalizing involves specifying a concrete, specific procedure for how that abstract concept is to be measured.

> **Operationalization** is the process of specifying the approach that will be used to obtain the value of a particular variable for each case.

Example: As part of his project to measure romantic love, Rubin (1970) developed a set of survey questions, each of which asked respondents to rate the extent of one aspect of their feelings or behavior toward their partner, such as their physical attraction; how much they idealized that person, wanted to help them, wanted to share emotions and experiences with them; and other aspects of interpersonal relationships. He also developed a "mutual gazing" approach to assessing differences in the extent to which participants made eye contact with their romantic partners versus with their friends.

*The survey questions were one way Rubin **operationalized** the concept of "romantic love," providing a specific way to **measure** each of the dimensions he included in the scope of his definition (Chapter 3). He also **operationalized** romantic love a second way, observing participants' behavior rather than relying on self-reported attitudes and behaviors toward romantic partners and platonic (non-romantic) friends.*

> The way a research concept is <u>measured</u> is a distinct step from the way that concept is <u>defined</u>. Whenever possible, conceptualization should precede measurement so that researchers have specified the desired aim and scope of the concept before choosing how to measure it.

Often a given concept can be operationalized in any of several ways.

Example: Suppose a researcher has decided to conceptualize an individual's "social standing" as determined by their economic position. That definition alone does not tell us how to <u>measure</u> the concept. One widely used measure is the Duncan index, which is calculated based on each individual's educational attainment, income, and occupation (Duncan, 1961). For instance, someone in an occupation that pays well and requires a high level of education is assigned a higher Duncan index score than someone in a job that pays minimum wage and mainly employs people who did not complete high school. An alternative measure—the MacArthur Scale—measures social standing by presenting respondents with a picture of a "social ladder" and asking them to place an "X" on the rung they feel represents their social status (Figure 4.1; Adler & Stewart, 2007). Instructions for completing the MacArthur Scale do not specify the criteria respondents are to use to make their assessment.

> *The Duncan Index and the ladder of social standing are two different ways of* **operationalizing** *the abstract concept "social standing." The Duncan Index is an* <u>objective</u> *(fact-based)* **measure,** *based on average income and educational attainment for an occupation, using data from the U.S. Census. The MacArthur ladder is a* <u>subjective</u> *(opinion-based)* **measure,** *with respondents choosing the criteria they use to rate their own social standing in their community.*

Figure 4.1   MacArthur Scale of Subjective Social Standing

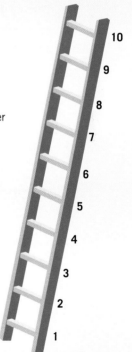

Think of this ladder as showing where people stand in their communities.

People define community in different ways. Please define it in whatever way is most meaningful to you.

At the top of the ladder are the people who have the highest standing in their community.

At the bottom are the people who have the lowest standing in their community.

Where would you place yourself on this ladder?

Place an **X** on the rung where you think you stand at this time of your life relative to other people in your community.

Source: Data from Adler and Stewart (2007).

Example: A systematic review of studies of childhood chronic health conditions found a wide range of definitions, some of which focused only on specific health conditions and others on duration of the condition or other factors. Even when researchers used the same definition of "chronic health conditions," they used different sources to collect data on that conceptualization, including surveys of parents, review of medical records, and review of school health records. Estimates of the prevalence of chronic conditions varied from less than 1% to 44% of all children (van der Lee et al., 2007).[1]

> Inconsistencies in both the **conceptualization** of "chronic health condition" and its **measurement** (definitions and data sources) made it difficult to compare results across populations and time periods.

The way a concept is operationalized affects how values of that measure are interpreted.

Example: From birth through age 23 months, infants' and toddlers' height (length) is measured with them lying down ("recumbent"). From age 2 years (24 months) and up, their height ("stature") is measured with them standing up. On average, recumbent length is approximately 0.8 cm (¼ inch) greater than standing height, based on U.S. national survey data (CDC, 2015).

> When assessing a child's height from their 2-year-old checkup against growth standards, it is important to know whether he or she was **measured** lying down or standing up, because the standards shift at that age. If recumbent length is compared against standing-height standards, it will <u>ove</u>restimate the child's percentile of height for age; conversely, if their standing height is compared against the recumbent-length standards, it will <u>unde</u>restimate their percentile. You will learn more about percentiles in Chapter 9.

Factors Affecting Operationalization

Several factors influence the decision of how to operationalize a concept, including audience, ease of measurement, and ease of comparing values.

Expected Audience and Use

The choice of how to operationalize a concept should reflect the study's anticipated audiences and how they are expected to use the data.

---

[1]Prevalence quantifies how common a particular characteristic or disease is in a population; see Chapter 9 for more on measures of prevalence.

Example: A researcher seeks to analyze how health is affected by brisk walking—a type of moderately intense exercise. Past studies have used many different ways of measuring "brisk walking." According to Reynolds (2018), researchers "may say, for instance, that it requires three metabolic equivalents of task, or METs, meaning that it uses about three times as much energy as sitting still. Or they might tell us that brisk walking occurs at a pace that increases our heart rate until it reaches up to 70 percent of our heart rate maximum. The U.S. Centers for Disease Control and Prevention defines brisk walking (and other moderate-intensity activities) as occurring at a pace at which people can talk but not sing."

> Scientists who study exercise probably have good reasons for using those technical approaches to operationalizing the **concept** of "moderately intense exercise;" they also have the tools to take the **measurements**. However, non-scientists will find these ways of measuring brisk walking too complicated and confusing: Most people don't know what a "MET" is, or even if they do, are unlikely to have the tools to measure it. Similarly, few people want to deal with the hassle of calculating 70% of their heart rate maximum even if they have a heart rate monitor. Thus. if researchers want their results to be used by <u>everyday people</u> who are trying to meet exercise guidelines, they need to translate their findings into terms that are easier for that **audience** to understand and measure.

Ease of Measurement

The choice of how to operationalize a concept should also take into account how difficult it will be to collect data using the specified measurement approach.

Example: To arrive at a consistent and easily operationalized way of measuring brisk walking, Tudor-Locke and her collaborators (2018) reviewed many studies and determined that "brisk walking involved a pace of about 2.7 miles per hour. Or put more simply, it required about 100 steps per minute" (cited in Reynolds, 2018).

> Reynolds (2018), citing Tudor-Lock et al. (2018), pointed out "This is a number that is very easy for any of us to **measure** on our own. . . . You do not need special equipment or expertise." Reynolds (2018) advises, "Just count how many steps you take in 10 seconds and multiply that number by six. Or count how many steps you take in six seconds and multiply by 10. Or count how many steps you take in a single minute and skip the multiplication altogether." In other words, it is a very <u>easy</u> way to **operationalize** the concept of brisk walking—a good choice for respondents who track their own exercise levels.

Example: According to the Criminal Justice Information Services (CJIS), "Because motivation is subjective, it is sometimes difficult to know with certainty whether a crime resulted from the offender's bias. Moreover, the presence of bias alone does not necessarily mean that a crime can be considered a hate crime. Only when a law enforcement investigation reveals sufficient evidence to lead a reasonable and prudent person to conclude that the offender's actions were motivated, in whole or in part, by his or her bias, should an agency report an incident as a hate crime" (CJIS, 2015).

> *Because hate crimes are stressful, emotional occurrences, the* **measurement approach (operationalization)** *must include specific criteria so that law enforcement officers can objectively assess whether a particular crime fits that definition.*

Example: The U.S. Criminal Justice Information Services (CJIS) provides a detailed training manual that specifies how to collect, report, assess, and classify information related to hate crimes (CJIS, 2015). It includes detailed definitions of each of the broad types of bias motivations (e.g., race, religion, or sexual orientation) and the categories within each.

> *By creating and disseminating a training manual and examples of crimes and how to classify them, the CJIS aims to* **standardize** *the agreed-upon ways of* **measuring** *and* **reporting** *hate crimes.*

Ease of Comparison

Another consideration is the consistency of measurement approaches across studies, locations, and dates. If different studies use different approaches, it is difficult to compare their findings.

Example: The U.S. Department of Justice Uniform Crime Reporting (UCR) Program collects statistics on the number of offenses for eight types of crime: murder and non-negligent homicide, rape, robbery, aggravated assault, burglary, motor vehicle theft, larceny–theft, and arson.

> *This choice of which types of offenses to collect data on was made to facilitate* *(consistent) statistics. They were selected because they are (1) serious crimes, (2) occur with regularity in all areas of the country, and (3) are likely to be reported to police (U.S. Department of Justice, 2017). All three of those criteria will affect the level and range of numeric values for crime reported through that system. The first is a* **conceptualization** *issue. The second and third are* **measurement** *issues.*

Example: How does a MET relate to 70% of someone's heart rate maximum?

> *Those two ways of assessing (**measuring**) whether exercise is "moderately intense" are difficult to* compare *with one another.*

Measurement Issues for Secondary Data and Non-Research Data Sources

When analyzing data that were already collected by other researchers (known as "**secondary data**"), people using those data don't have control over how each concept was measured, meaning that the measurement approach might not capture the concept they wish to study. This is especially the case for data that were not originally collected with research in mind, such as administrative records or "big data." In such situations, researchers should be especially thorough in discussing the strengths and weaknesses of that approach for capturing the underlying concept, such as whether the scope is broader, narrower, or simply different. You will learn more about the pros and cons of different data collection approaches in Chapter 11.

When deciding how to operationalize a concept, researchers should consider the following:

- Who will use the information (e.g., scientists or laypeople)

- Ease of conducting that measurement

- Ease of comparing it with other common ways of measuring the concept

- Other factors that help intended users make sense of the values produced by that approach

---

Levels of Measurement

One of the first decisions about how to operationalize a concept is **level of measurement**, which refers to the mathematical precision with which a variable is measured. Variables can be classified into one of four levels of measurement: **nominal, ordinal, interval,** and **ratio**, listed in order from least to most mathematically precise. Some concepts can be measured at only one of these levels; other concepts might be measurable at more than one level.

Variables can be either **quantitative** (numerical) or **qualitative** (nonnumerical). Qualitative variables capture attributes that differ in nature but not extent, so those attributes cannot be quantified.

Example: Height in centimeters is a quantitative variable. You can figure out who is taller and how much taller by comparing the values of height for different cases.

*Knowing the numeric **value** for a case, along with **units** in which it was measured **quantifies** "height" for each case.*

Example: Religious affiliation (e.g., Christian, Hindu) is a <u>qualitative</u> variable because it captures a characteristic that differs in nature (<u>quality</u> or type) but not in quantity. We cannot say someone who is Buddhist has a higher amount of "religious affiliation" than someone who is Muslim, Catholic, or any other type of religion.

*Other dimensions of religion such as <u>frequency</u> of attendance at religious services or <u>degree</u> of religiosity can be **quantified** using **interval**, **ordinal**, or **ratio levels of measurement.***

Level of measurement (sometimes known as **type of variable**) refers to how variables are defined and categorized, which determines the mathematical precision with which a variable is measured.

- **Qualitative variables** capture characteristics that differ in nature or quality but <u>not</u> in the extent or degree of that trait. They include variables at the **nominal** level of measurement.

- **Quantitative variables** capture characteristics that differ in the extent or degree of the trait being measured. They include variables at the **ordinal**, **interval**, or **ratio** levels of measurement.

Categorical Variables

Categorical variables are those whose values represent separate categories or classifications, including those that describe some kind of state (status), condition, or situation and those that group numeric information into ranges. There are two types of categorical variables: nominal and ordinal. **Nominal** variables capture some quality that can be <u>described</u> but <u>not quantified</u>, so they are considered **qualitative** variables. The characteristic being described is classified into named categories that do <u>not</u> have a natural order in terms of the extent or degree of the characteristics they are measuring.

Example: Marital status is a nominal variable with the named categories "never-married," "cohabiting," "married," "separated," "divorced," and "widowed."

*There is <u>no inherent order</u> to those categories in terms of "marital status-ness" (the amount of marital status); therefore, marital status is a **nominal** variable.*

Ordinal variables measure attributes that can be classified into categories that have an inherent rank order in terms of the trait they are measuring but for which the distance between categories cannot be quantified. Thus, ordinal variables are considered **quantitative categorical** variables.

<u>Caution:</u> In electronic databases, each category of a nominal or ordinal variable is assigned a numeric **code** as shorthand for that category to avoid having to type in or store a text label for the value of that variable for each case. However, those numeric codes do <u>not</u> have a mathematical interpretation; they are just abbreviations for the names of the categories.

> <u>Example</u>: The categories of a variable capturing a respondent's religious affiliation might be coded 1 = Jewish, 2 = Protestant, etc.
>
> > *Clearly, those **codes** <u>cannot</u> be treated mathematically. First of all, the assignment of specific numbers to particular religions was arbitrary. Second, it doesn't make sense to do computations such as Jewish – Protestant, or Baptist ÷ Atheist!*

There are two types of categorical variables: **Nominal** variables are those that are classified into <u>named</u> categories for which there is <u>no</u> inherent order in terms of the amount or extent of the concept (quality) being measured and no units of measurement. They are **qualitative** variables. **Ordinal** variables are classified into categories that can be placed in rank order in terms of the quantity or degree of the concept being measured. They are a type of **quantitative** variable. **Codes** are numeric values used in electronic databases as abbreviations for each category of a variable. They do <u>not</u> have a numeric interpretation.

A variable with "group," "range," or "category" in its name is often ordinal, especially if units are also specified. However, many ordinal variables do not have such terms in their names, so that criterion alone should not be used to assess whether a variable is ordinal. Ordinal variables may or may not have units attached to them.

> <u>Example</u>: A form asks respondents to check which of the following age groups reflects their current age: <18 years, 18–34, 35–49, 50–64, 65–84, or 85+ years.
>
> > *This variable is **categorical** because responses are grouped into ranges, with years as the **units**. Obviously, those categories have a <u>logical numeric order</u> (from youngest to oldest), so age <u>group</u> is an **ordinal** variable.*

> <u>Example</u>: A questionnaire at a doctor's office asks patients "How would you rate your health: Excellent, very good, good, fair, or poor?"
>
> > *Although **units** don't pertain to this question, the response categories clearly fall along a spectrum capturing the patient's rating of their own health <u>from most to least favorable</u>, so self-rated health is an **ordinal** variable.*

Don't be fooled into thinking that a variable with categories that are named with words is <u>necessarily</u> nominal. If its categories can be put into a logical order of lowest to highest amount of whatever is being measured, that variable is ordinal, not nominal.

Example: A survey asks respondents: "Choose the answer that best reflects your views about the following statement: 'Stricter gun control laws and limitations would decrease gun-related deaths and injuries.' Strongly disagree, disagree, neutral, agree, or strongly agree."

*The responses are distinct **categories** that have a natural <u>order in terms of extent of agreement</u> with the statement. The fact that those categories are labeled with names rather than numbers does <u>not</u> invalidate their ordered (**ordinal**) nature.*

A good test of whether a variable with categories labeled in words is nominal or ordinal is to consider whether it makes sense to list them in a different order.

Example: "Very good, poor, excellent, fair, good" would not be a sensible order in which to list responses to the self-rated health variable. However, either listing religions as "Catholic, Jewish, Protestant, Hindu, etc." <u>or</u> "Hindu, Jewish, Catholic, Protestant, etc." (or any other order) would make sense.

*The fact that both variables use words to label their categories does <u>not</u> mean that they are both nominal. Self-rated health is **ordinal** because there is a <u>logical, quantitative order</u> of the categories used to capture level of health. Religious affiliation is **nominal** because the order of categories doesn't matter in terms of capturing the concept.*

Continuous Variables

Continuous variables are quantitative variables with values spaced equally from one another along a spectrum, with the concept measured in the units specified for that variable. There are two types of continuous variables: interval and ratio. **Interval** variables quantify the extent of the characteristic being measured but <u>don't</u> have a fixed zero point, meaning that those variables can take on negative values.

Example: On Mars, the winter temperature near the poles can be as low as –195 degrees Fahrenheit (°F), equivalent to –125 degrees Celsius (°C). The summer daytime temperature near its equator can reach up to 70 °F (20 °C; Sharp, 2017).

*Temperature in degrees Fahrenheit (°F) and Celsius (°C) are **continuous variables** because each **one-unit** increment represents a difference of 1 degree. They are **interval variables** because they range from negative to positive values, meaning that zero is <u>not</u> the minimum value for either of those temperature scales. The **system of measurement** must be* *specified because the values of the Fahrenheit and Celsius scales are not equivalent. Water freezes at 0 °C but at 32 °F.*

Like interval variables, **ratio** variables are continuous variables that quantify the degree or amount of the characteristic being measured, with equally spaced numeric values in the units in which that variable is measured. However, ratio variables have a fixed zero point, meaning that negative values are not possible.

Example: In the physical sciences, temperature is measured on the Kelvin scale, which has an absolute zero point (0 K) at the temperature at which molecules would stop moving (Zimmerman, 2013).

*Kelvin temperature is a **ratio variable** because the lowest possible value is 0 K (equivalent to −459.67 °F or −273.15 °C).*

Interval and ratio variables are two types of **continuous variables**; values one unit apart are equally spaced in the units specified for that variable. **Ratio variables** have a fixed zero point (minimum), whereas **interval variables** can take on negative values (zero is not their lowest possible value).

Variables with numeric values can sometimes be ordinal rather than continuous.

Example: In the U.S., women's pants sizes are listed as numbers (e.g., size 6, 8, 10, etc.), whereas men's pants sizes measure waist circumference and inseam length in inches (e.g., 34" waist, 32" inseam).

*Women's sizes within a particular brand are **ordinal**: from the name of the size, you can tell which is bigger but not how much bigger in any measured dimension. As many women know from experience, a particular size name (e.g., a size 10) can have very different proportions from one brand or style to another. And clearly a size 0 doesn't literally have a value of 0 on any measured dimension (waist, hips, inseam, etc.)!*

*In contrast, men's pants sizes are ratio (**continuous**) measurements, because knowing the numeric value and its units conveys an actual measured quantity (e.g., a 34" waist). Thus, people buying men's pants can determine what size they need based on their own measurements and can more reliably compare across brands and styles.*

Units

To be able to make sense of the numbers for data you collect, calculate, analyze, and communicate, you need to know several different aspects of units: the units of observation and the system and scale in which the variable was measured.

Unit of Observation

The first aspect of units to identify is the **unit of observation**, also known as the **unit of analysis** or **level of aggregation**. For qualitative (nominal) variables, the unit of analysis is the only aspect of "units" that pertains because nominal categories don't have units.

> Example: A restaurant listed as Asian might include menu items from Japan, China, and Vietnam.
>
> *Restaurants are a different **unit of observation** than items on those restaurants' menus.*

> Example: In 2016, there were 40.6 million people but 8.1 million poor families in the United States (Semega, Fontenot, & Kollar, 2017).
>
> *If poverty is measured in number of persons with income less than some threshold, a person is the **unit of analysis**. If it counts the number of families with income below a threshold, a family is the unit of analysis. Poverty can also be measured at the census tract, county, state, or national **levels of aggregation**.*

When collecting, analyzing, or interpreting data, look for a consistent way of aggregating items.

> Example: Suppose a package of ten Brand Q tortillas costs $1.80 and a package of twenty Brand X tortillas costs $2.60.
>
> *Although the package of Brand Q is less expensive than the package of Brand X, the brands **aggregate** (group together) different numbers of tortillas per package. To determine which brand is the better value, their prices must be converted to a comparable level of aggregation. The price per tortilla (per individual **item**) is cheaper for Brand X ($0.13/tortilla) than Brand Q ($0.18/tortilla).*

System of Measurement

A **system of measurement** is a collection of units of measurement and rules relating them to each other, such as the metric system and the British system of measurement. You are likely familiar with many of them because many dimensions of our world can be quantified using any of several systems of measurement: money (e.g., rupees or Euros or other currency systems), mass (e.g., kilograms or pounds), length or distance (e.g., meters or yards), volume (e.g., liters or quarts), dates (e.g., Christian or Jewish or other calendar), and time (e.g., Greenwich mean time, military time, daylight saving time or standard time), among many other topics. The coexistence of these different systems of measurement means that to avoid making mistakes when collecting, reporting, or interpreting numbers, it is essential to pay attention to which is system being used.

> Example: Figure 4.2 shows height growth curves for boys in both centimeters and inches (U.S. NCHS, 2000), illustrating, for example, that

Figure 4.2 Growth Chart in Different Units of Measurement

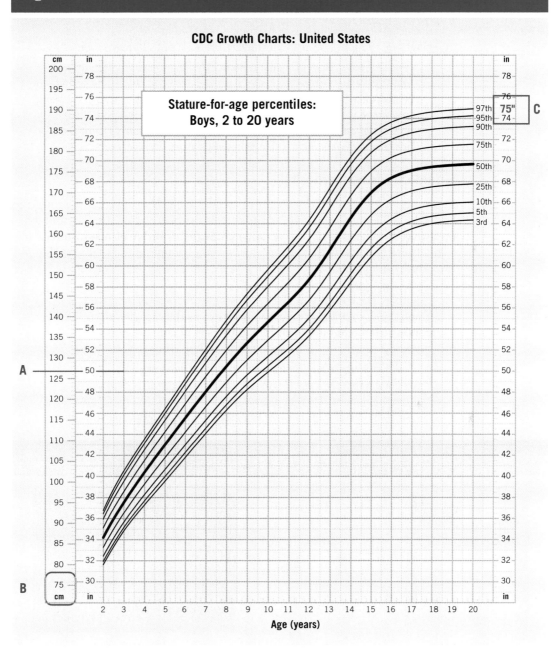

CDC Growth Charts: United States

Stature-for-age percentiles:
Boys, 2 to 20 years

Source: Developed by the National Center for Health Statistics in collaboration with the National Center for Chronic Disease Prevention and Health Promotion (U.S. NCHS, 2000).

50 inches is equivalent to approximately 127 centimeters (Point A). A particular numeric value means very different things in the two systems of measurement: A height of 75 centimeters (Point B) is so short that it doesn't even appear in the normal range for 2-year-old boys, whereas a height of 75 inches (Point C) is taller than 97% of full-grown men!

*Knowing the **system of measurement** helps flag values that simply don't make sense for the topic (height of a person) and context (age and gender; see Chapter 5). And even if you know the gender and age of the person being measured, you must know whether height is reported in inches (**British system of measurement**) or centimeters (**metric system**) to figure out whether a given numeric value represents a short, average, or tall value.*

Scale of Measurement

Even once you know which system of measurement is being used, you need to know the **scale** of measurement in order to assess plausibility of values and interpret what they mean for the topic at hand. **Scale**, or **order of magnitude**, refers to multiples of units, with each order of magnitude <u>ten times as large</u> as the next lower order of magnitude.

<u>Example</u>: The capacity of electronic storage media has increased dramatically over time (Figure 4.3). Whereas the capacity of a 1970s floppy disk might have been 80 kilobytes (kB), and a 1990s CD stored 80 megabytes (MB), at the time of this writing (2020) ads for smartphones and Cloud storage were advertising capacity in the tens to hundreds of gigabytes (GB).

*Each of these **scales** is approximately 1,000 times as large as the next smallest one (1,024 times, to be precise!). Obviously, you don't want*

Figure 4.3   Order of Magnitude of Electronic Storage Media

(a) Kilobytes   (b) Megabytes   (c) Gigabytes

Source: iStock.com/malerapaso, iStock.com/liangpv, iStock.com/Jirsak.

*to accidentally compare values without knowing which **scale** each measurement uses, because a GB is three **orders of magnitude** larger than a MB, which in turn is three powers of ten greater than a kB.*

<u>Example</u>: Even if you know that the distance of a running race is in metric units, that doesn't convey whether the scale is meters or kilometers (multiples of one thousand meters).

> *Whereas 100 meters is a sprint, 100 kilometers is an ultra-marathon (62 miles). Although many of us can probably run (or at least walk) 100 meters; few can manage a 100,000-meter race!*

A **unit of observation** is an individual entity about whom or which data are collected, such as a person, family, school, or country. These are also known as **units of analysis** or **levels of aggregation**. A **system of measurement** is a set of units and rules explaining how they relate to each other; common examples are the metric system and the British (Imperial) systems. **Scale of measurement**, also known as **order of magnitude**, refers to multiples of units. In most instances, one order of magnitude is one power of 10 (ten times) larger than the next lowest level.

All calculations and comparisons must involve consistent units. This point is covered in more depth in Chapter 8 and Appendix A.

When comparing quantitative measures, look for consistent units of analysis, system of measurement, and scale of measurement, or convert the data into comparable units.

Data Collection and Level of Measurement

For many quantitative concepts, the topic does <u>not</u> automatically determine whether the measure is ordinal (categorical) or continuous. Which level of measurement pertains depends on how the concept was operationalized and how the data were collected.

<u>Example</u>: A survey in India collecting information on income might ask respondents to report their income to the nearest rupee (₹) or could instead ask them to report into which of several ranges their income falls.

> *The first version of the question would yield a **continuous** measure of the concept (income), whereas the second would produce an **ordinal** (**categorical**) measure.*

Example: Shoe sizes are an interesting conundrum: Men's U.S. shoe sizes 8, 9, and 10 for one popular brand measure 26, 27, and 28 centimeters (cm) from heel to toe, respectively (Table 4.1; amazon.com, 2018), but the size names don't convey that information. Moreover, women's U.S. shoe sizes 8, 9, and 10 for the same brand measure 25, 26, and 27 cm. The shoe size names in the United Kingdom and Europe don't capture the underlying length measurement, either.

> _For each gender, the length of each shoe size is measured on a **continuous** scale, with a consistent difference of 0.5 cm. between successive U.S. sizes (e.g., between sizes 7 and 7.5). Although the shoe sizes are labeled with numbers, those numbers don't capture the underlying length measurement or its units; they are essentially abbreviations for **ordinal categories**. And a size "8" reflects different heel-to-toe lengths for men than for women. How much easier would it be if simply knowing the length of your foot told you the name of the size you needed to order?_

Table 4.1   Variation in Numeric Values for Different Measures of the Same Phenomenon

Shoe Size by Gender, Location, and System of Measurement									
Merrell Men's Shoe Sizes					Merrell Women's Shoe Sizes				
Shoe Size Measurement System			Heel to Toe Length		Shoe Size Measurement System			Heel to Toe Length	
U.S.	U.K.	Europe	Inches	Centimeters	U.S.	U.K.	Europe	Inches	Centimeters
8	7.5	41.5	10.24	26.0	8	5.5	38.5	9.84	25.0
8.5	8	42.0	10.43	26.5	8.5	6	39.0	10.04	25.5
9	8.5	43.0	10.63	27.0	9	6.5	40.0	10.24	26.0
9.5	9	43.5	10.83	27.5	9.5	7	40.5	10.43	26.5
10	9.5	44.0	11.02	28.0	10	7.5	41.0	10.63	27.0

Source: Data from Amazon.com (2018).

Ideally, data should initially be collected using the highest (most precise) level of measurement that is practical for that particular concept and method of data collection. Doing so allows those who later use those data the most flexibility in analyzing the information, including the option of creating a less precise level of measurement (see Appendix A). However, sometimes even quantitative phenomena cannot be collected using a continuous measure.

Example: Few of us can remember exactly how many hours we spend online on a typical day, so a survey might ask us to report our usage in ranges such as none, less than 1 hour, 1 to 4 hours, 5 to 9 hours, and so on. However, if our measure were based on electronic tracking of usage, it could be collected to the nearest second!

> *If respondents cannot be expected to report an exact numeric response to a question, either because they can't remember at that level of detail or are reluctant to provide detailed information, data should be collected at the **ordinal** rather than **continuous** level of measurement. On the other hand, the electronic tracking measure could be collected at the **ratio** level.*

How Question Format Affects Measurement

Data collection **instruments** (forms) such as survey questionnaires, vital registration documents, or insurance forms can use either closed-ended or open-ended question formats. The format used to collect data affects the level of measurement, categories, and units for the resulting variables.

Closed-Ended Questions

A **closed-ended question** provides respondents with a list of possible answers to choose among, accompanied by instructions about how many answers each respondent is to select. Responses to closed-ended questions are usually treated as categorical—either nominal or ordinal depending on whether the information being collected is qualitative or quantitative.

> Example: "What is your current marital status? Choose the best answer."
>   ___ *Never married*
>   ___ *Married*
>   ___ *Cohabiting*
>   ___ *Separated*
>   ___ *Divorced*
>   ___ *Widowed*
>
> *This is a **closed-ended question** because it lists a set of possible answers for respondents to choose among. The resulting variable will be **nominal**, with one category for each of the different marital statuses—a **qualitative**, not quantitative, concept.*

Attitudinal items that use an ordinal rating scale to measure attitudes or opinions such as the extent of agreement with a statement are called **Likert items** (Likert, 1932). Likert items also can be used to capture other concepts measured across an ordered spectrum, such as frequency of a certain type of experience (from never to always), quality (from very bad to very good), or likelihood of an event (from none to high).

> Example: "How would you rate the quality of service you received from our company today: Excellent, very good, good, fair, or poor?"

*This **closed-ended question** will create an **ordinal** variable with one category for each possible response. It is a **Likert item** because the response categories have a logical order reflecting <u>extent of agreement</u> with the statement.*

"True/false," "yes/no," and other types of multiple-choice questions are examples of other types of closed-ended question formats you have probably encountered many times.

Closed-ended questions rarely are used to collect continuous variables unless the range of responses is known to be very narrow and to include only integer values.

<u>Example</u>: A closed-ended question might be used to collect data on age for students in a school that spans kindergarten through third grade because that grade range would only require listing ages 5, 6, 7, 8, and 9 years. However, a closed-ended question would be a ridiculous way to collect ages of adults, which would require listing every single year of age from 18 to 108!

Open-Ended Questions

Open-ended questions collect data <u>without</u> providing a list of answers, instead asking respondents to fill in their own responses. They can yield either continuous or categorical variables depending on the nature of what they are measuring.

<u>Example</u>: "What is your current age? _____ (years)?"

*This question yields a **continuous** measure of age in years. Much more space-efficient than providing a list of possible ages for a sample of adult respondents to choose among!*

<u>Example</u>: "Fill in the main reason you chose your college major _____"

*This question yields a **nominal** variable, with a different named category for each reason or group of similar reasons. For instance, a researcher might decide that "financial reasons" and "to make a lot of money" are capturing the same idea and could be classified into the same category when analyzing the data.*

The document or form used to collect data is referred to as a **data collection instrument**. **Closed-ended questions** are those that provide a list of possible answers for respondents to mark. They are also known as **multiple-choice** or **fixed-choice questions**. **Open-ended questions** are those that allow respondents to answer in their own words.

Single-Response and Multiple-Response Questions

Both open-ended and closed-ended questions can be either **single-response** or **multiple-response**, depending on the topic under study. As their names suggest, single-response items are those for which each respondent is allowed to provide only one answer, whereas multiple-response questions permit each respondent to give anywhere from no answers to many answers, depending on how many pertain to them. The number of allowable responses is determined by the nature of the topic and does <u>not</u> affect whether a question is worded as open-ended or closed-ended.

<u>Caution</u>: **Multiple-<u>response</u>** questions are different from **multiple-<u>choice</u>** questions. The former dictates the number of <u>answers</u> each respondent can give (regardless of whether it is open- or closed-ended). The latter simply offers a list of several possible responses for participants to choose from and is a form of closed-ended question (regardless of whether it is single- or multiple-response).

> <u>Example</u>: Question: "How do you commute to work?" Mark all that apply.
>
> ___ Car
> ___ Ride-sharing
> ___ Bus
> ___ Train
> ___ Bike
> ___ Walk
> ___ Other
> ___ I work from home
> ___ I am not employed
>
> *This is a **multiple-choice** (**closed-ended**), **multiple-response** question, allowing respondents to choose varying numbers of responses depending on their commuting patterns. Some people will find exactly one answer that suits them, while others will mark several answers.*

> <u>Example</u>: "List here all the ways you commute to work.
> _____ "
>
> *This is an **open-ended** version of the same **multiple-response** question, allowing respondents to describe in their own words the different ways they commute, whether that is zero ways (they don't work or they work at home), one way, or several ways.*

Appendix A explains how variables are created to capture answers to multiple-response items.

Single-response questions allow only one answer for each respondent. **Multiple-response questions** permit respondents to choose the number of answers that suit them, which can range from none to many.

Mutually Exclusive and Exhaustive Categories

Writing response categories for closed-ended questions requires careful thought to ensure that those categories both are mutually exclusive and exhaustive. **Mutually exclusive** categories are those that "exclude" (do not overlap) one another in terms of the definition and scope of what they encompass. An **exhaustive** set of responses includes at least one response that would suit every possible case. To make a set of responses exhaustive, often an "other," or "other, specify ____" option is included so those to whom the other listed responses don't fit have a valid answer to select. If the set of responses to a closed-ended question is <u>not</u> mutually exclusive or exhaustive, respondents who can't find a valid answer are likely to either skip the question or give an answer that doesn't suit them, introducing bias into the data (Chapter 11)

Figures 4.4a, b, c   Mutually Exclusive and Exhaustive Categories

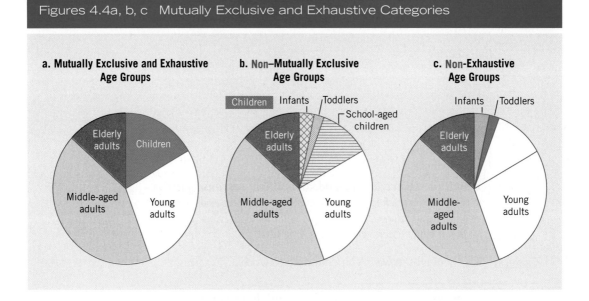

a. Mutually Exclusive and Exhaustive Age Groups

b. Non–Mutually Exclusive Age Groups

c. Non-Exhaustive Age Groups

<u>Example</u>: A questionnaire collects information on age using the categories shown in Figure 4.4a.

> *Those age groups are* **mutually exclusive** *because they don't overlap: each person is either a child, young adult, middle-aged adult, or elderly adult. They are* **exhaustive** *because every respondent can be classified into one of the groups listed. Those categories completely fill the "pie" without any slices overlapping.*

However, if respondents were asked to mark one age group from among "infant, toddler, school-aged child, child, young adult, middle-aged adult, elderly adult," some respondents would have a problem. For instance, a 2-year-old is both a toddler and a child, so whoever is filling out the form wouldn't be able to choose just one relevant answer.

*The infant, toddler, and school-aged child categories each overlap with the "child" category, so those categories are <u>not</u> **mutually exclusive**. In Figure 4.4b, those three age groups are each shown in a blue pattern, indicating overlap with the solid blue used to denote "children."*

If the question were to list the age groups as "Infant, toddler, young adult, middle-aged adult, elderly adult," those who are older than toddlers but not yet young adults don't fit in any of the listed categories.

*This set of responses is <u>not</u> **exhaustive** because it fails to provide a valid answer for some respondents (in this case, school-aged children); the listed response options don't fill the pie (Figure 4.4c).*

Mutually exclusive categories do <u>not</u> overlap one another in terms of scope of the values they include. A set of **exhaustive** categories together provide every respondent with at least one possible answer.

Regardless of whether the question is single- or multiple-response, a closed-ended question should be written with mutually exclusive and exhaustive categories. Answers to a closed-ended multiple-response variable should not overlap definitionally with one another—in other words, they must be mutually exclusive. However, many respondents will be able to find more than one answer that suits them, so giving a particular answer does <u>not</u> rule out giving one (or more) of the other possible responses as well.

<u>Example</u>: The list of responses to the above question "How do you commute to work?" includes "I work from home" and "I am not employed." Thus, every respondent can find at least one answer that fits them, even if they don't commute.

*Even though that question is **multiple-response**, it must have an **exhaustive** response set. The types of transportation are named in ways that also make them **mutually exclusive**. However, some respondents will correctly choose more than one of those responses.*

The list of responses for closed-ended questions must be mutually exclusive and exhaustive.

Missing Values

An important issue that affects variables of all levels of measurement is when information is missing on a particular variable for one or more cases. In such situations, the data set should include **codes** to identify **missing values**, to differentiate between reasons that a variable is missing, and to clearly distinguish codes for missing values from actual (valid) numeric values. As discussed in Chapter 1, although "9999" is well above the plausible range for birth weight in grams, if that **missing value code** is treated numerically along with the valid values, the 9999s will badly skew the apparent distribution of birth weight.

To avoid confusion between actual numeric values and missing values, missing value codes must be outside the range of plausible values for that variable. For instance, missing income could be denoted –99, because a value of +99 could have been someone's actual income (e.g., $99). Alternatively, some databases use letters instead of numbers to denote missing values.

Not Applicable

Some questions do not apply to some respondents, in which case the value of the associated variable should be denoted as **not applicable** rather than missing. Often, surveys use a **filter question** to identify respondents to whom a set of **contingent questions** pertain. Those for whom the contingent questions are <u>not</u> relevant skip over them and are given a code of "not applicable" to the contingent questions. In other words, whether a respondent is asked the contingent questions depends (is <u>contingent on</u>) their answer to the filter question. Thus, filter questions create what is called a **skip pattern** in the questionnaire because those to whom the contingent question(s) don't apply are not asked ("skip over") those questions, instead of being directed to a later section of the questionnaire.

Figure 4.5   Distinction Between Not Applicable and Missing

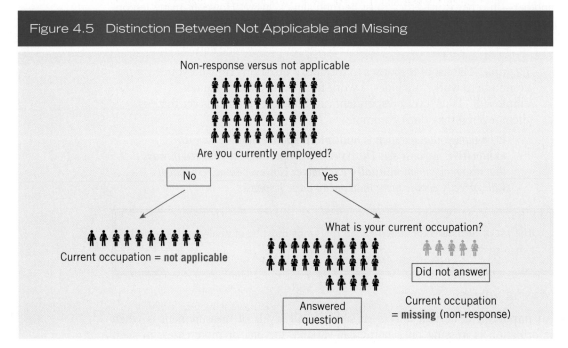

Not applicable is when information on a variable is not provided for a case because the item is not relevant for that case. "Not applicable" is different from a **missing value**, which arises when information on a question is <u>not</u> provided for a case to whom that question <u>does</u> apply. **Filter questions** are used to identify the subset of respondents to whom a set of questions on a particular topic pertains. Those questions are referred to as **contingent questions**. A **skip pattern** is generated by a filter question, determining which subsequent questions are asked of which respondents.

<u>Example</u>: As shown in Figure 4.5, Question 1 sorts respondents into those who were employed and those who were unemployed at the time the data were collected. Anyone answering "no" (unemployed) was not asked Question 2, because for them, current occupation is "not applicable." Anyone answering "yes" (employed) was asked Question 2. If an employed respondent didn't indicate their current occupation, they received a missing value on Question 2 as it <u>was</u> applicable to them.

> *Question 1 (employment status) is the **filter** question, determining which cases were asked the **contingent** question on current occupation (Question 2). The filter question created a **skip pattern** because those who said "no" to Question 1 skipped over (were not asked) Question 2. For the occupation variable, the data set might list a code of –98 for "not applicable" and –99 for "missing," along with **codes** for each of the various occupations for respondents who provided a valid answer.*

How Measurement Affects Plausibility

The choice of a measurement approach affects which numeric values are plausible and whether higher or lower values are considered optimal for that topic.

Level and Range of Possible Values

Different ways of measuring a concept can lead to different levels and ranges of plausible values.

<u>Example</u>: Although the Duncan Index and MacArthur Scale each measure social standing, valid values of the Duncan Index range from 0 to 100, but valid values of the MacArthur Scale of Subjective Social Standing range from 1 to 10. Obviously, it is essential know which of those ways a researcher operationalized "social standing" to make sense of the observed numeric values.

*Whereas a "10" on the Duncan Index reflects very <u>low</u> social standing, on the MacArthur scale, a "10" reflects the <u>highest possible</u> social standing. For the Duncan Index, a value of 70 is well within the **plausible** range, but for the MacArthur Scale, it is <u>not</u> a **valid value**.*

Optimum Values

As discussed in Chapter 3, topic often determines whether a higher, lower, or middle value is considered more favorable. Even knowing the topic, however, you can't identify which value(s) are optimal until you know the system and units in which it was measured.

Example: Fuel economy is measured in miles/gallon (mpg) in the U.S and Britain, but in liters/kilometer (L/km) in the metric system (Gershtein & Gershtein, 2018). A car that gets 30 mpg U.S. uses on average 7.84 L/km. A truck that gets 15 mpg U.S. uses 15.7 L/km.

*Thus, a <u>higher</u> value is **optimal** (better) using the U.S. measure because the <u>farther</u> the distance traveled for each unit of gasoline volume, the better the fuel economy. Conversely, a <u>lower</u> value is **preferable** when using the metric system, because the <u>lower</u> the volume of gas needed to travel a given distance, the better the fuel economy.*

Reliability and Validity of Numeric Measures

Another important aspect of measurement is whether the measure is both consistent and accurate. In research terminology, we want measures that are both **reliable** and **valid**. If those criteria aren't met, the data should <u>not </u>be used because you can't "count on" the quality of the resulting numbers (no pun intended!)

Reliability

A **reliable** measurement process is one that produces consistent values. If the concept being measured is not changing, the measurements of that phenomenon should not change. If the concept <u>is </u>changing across time (or varying across cases), a reliable measure will capture those differences or changes.

Example: If I step on my bathroom scale several times within a few minutes, the scale should tell me I weigh the same amount each time.

*My weight hasn't actually changed during that small time interval, so a **reliable** bathroom scale should be <u>consistent</u> in the weight it shows on the dial.*

Example: If I weigh myself in early December and then again in January after I have eaten a lot and not exercised much over the winter holidays, the scale should report that I weighed more in January than I did in December.

If my weight actually increased during the time between measurements, a reliable scale should capture that increase. If it were to tell me I weighed the same both times despite my actually having gained weight, it would be <u>un</u>reliable.

There are several types of reliability, including **test-retest reliability**, **inter-rater reliability**, **inter-item reliability**, and **alternate-forms reliability**. They differ in terms of the nature of the comparison made to assess reliability.

Example: If a professor accidentally graded two identical copies of one assignment and gave the same (or very similar) grades both times, it would suggest <u>high</u> **test-retest reliability**. On the other hand, if she was <u>inconsistent</u> in her grading because of fatigue or an erratic approach to assigning scores, that would represent <u>low</u> test-retest reliability.

*This is <u>**test–retest**</u> reliability because it compares the level of consistency between <u>repeated measurements</u> of the <u>same</u> phenomenon (in this case, scoring the same student's homework assignment).*

Example: If several different teaching assistants each grade a homework assignment separately, <u>high</u> **inter-rater reliability** would mean each of them came up with grades within a few points of each other for a given student. However, if they were poorly trained or some TAs were stricter than others, they might show <u>low</u> inter-rater reliability by assigning very different grades to the same student's work.

*"Inter" means "between," so **inter-rater** means comparing consistency between raters—in this case, whether different people gave similar scores to the same homework assignment.*

Example: A professor designs several different questions to test whether her students understand how to perform a specific statistical calculation. On the weekly quiz, each student is randomly assigned one of the questions on that skill. If the questions have <u>high</u> **inter-item reliability**, the distribution of scores on those items will be very similar to one another for students with similar levels of mastery. However, if one of those questions is much harder or more confusing than other questions about that skill, the items would show <u>low</u> inter-item reliability.

*This illustrates <u>**inter-item**</u> reliability because it considers whether students do about as well regardless of which version of the question (**item**) they are given to test their mastery of that statistical concept. In other words, it compares consistency of scores for different items, each of which aims to measure the same phenomenon.*

Example: A professor is trying to minimize cheating on a final exam for a large introductory course. He designs two versions (A and B) of the test form that include the same set of multiple-choice questions but lists them in different orders and hands them out so that students sitting next to each other don't have the same version. If the test has high **alternate-forms** reliability, the distributions of scores for students taking Version A and Version B will be very similar.

*This illustrates **alternate-forms** reliability because it assesses whether different versions of the exam (**form**) that is intended to test the same set of material yield scores that are consistent with one another.*

Reliability reflects the extent to which a measurement procedure produces consistent values. A reliable measurement approach will capture actual differences or changes in the values of the underlying concept.

Test-retest reliability of a measure assesses the extent to which similar values (scores) are obtained when we test the same phenomenon more than once when that phenomenon has not changed, or when the change in values reflects the actual change in what is being measured.

Inter-rater (also known as **inter-observer**) **reliability** evaluates the degree to which similar values are obtained from different observers who are rating the same cases.

Inter-item reliability assesses the extent to which similar values are obtained on each of several items used to measure the same concept. It is also known as **internal consistency**.

Alternate-forms reliability evaluates the degree to which similar scores are obtained when different versions of the same form are used.

Measurement Validity

Measurement validity occurs when the way a concept is measured accurately captures that concept. Think of a valid measure as one that is "on target," reflecting the concept you seek to measure.

Example: In the image on the left of Figure 4.6, the arrow hits the center of the target, landing squarely in the bull's-eye representing the concept we seek to measure. In the image on the right, the arrow landed in the outermost (black) circle on the target, portraying a measurement that is off-topic.

*The measure on the left is **valid**, whereas the one on the right is invalid (inaccurate).*

Figure 4.6 Valid and Invalid Measures

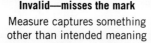

Valid—"on target"
Measure captures intended content

Invalid—misses the mark
Measure captures something other than intended meaning

Example: To measure respondents' health, a survey asks them how often they've been to the doctor in the past year. One respondent following general guidelines for annual checkups visited a doctor even though they were perfectly healthy, whereas another respondent who was very sick didn't visit the doctor because they couldn't afford the fees.

> *These two respondents' answers to the number of doctor visits capture influences <u>other than</u> health, so interpreting a higher number of visits as reflecting worse health is **invalid**. The first respondent's one visit reflects good health, whereas the second respondent's answer (zero doctor visits) doesn't capture their poor health, thus this question is <u>not</u> a **valid** measure of health.*

There are several ways to assess measurement validity, including face validity, content validity, criterion validity, and construct validity.

Face Validity

Face validity assesses the extent to which a measure appears "on the face of it" to be measuring what it is supposed to measure. The above example about using number of doctor's visits to measure health status illustrates <u>poor</u> face validity because even a quick appraisal shows that the measure (doctor's visits) doesn't match the desired concept (health status).

Face validity is the first aspect of validity to be tested: If a measure fails face validity, there is no need to evaluate the other types of validity—the measure shouldn't be used! However, even if a measure satisfies face validity, that measure could fare poorly on one of the other aspects of validity, so it is essential that those aspects be assessed as well.

Content Validity

Content validity considers the degree to which the items in a measure span the entire domain of concepts that the test aims to measure.

> Example: Williams and colleagues (1997) conceptualized "everyday discrimination" as encompassing chronic, routine, and relatively minor experiences of unfair treatment. They created a scale that collected data on items measuring frequency of being treated with less courtesy than others, receiving less respect than others, receiving poorer service than others in restaurants or stores, people acting as if you are not smart, people acting as if they are better than you, people acting as if they are afraid of you, people acting as if they think you are dishonest, being called names or insulted, and being threatened or harassed.
>
> > *Their everyday discrimination scale has <u>high</u> **content validity** because it includes at least one item to capture discrimination on each of the attitudes, behaviors, and situations that the researchers theorized were an important dimension of everyday discrimination.*

Criterion Validity

Criterion validity compares the values on a new measure against another measure of the same phenomenon that has already been shown to be accurate. There are two forms of criterion validity: **concurrent** and **predictive**.

> Example: Facing budget cuts, a school district suggests collecting data by asking parents to report their children's heights, allowing the district to reduce the number of hours they have to pay a school nurse to make those measurements. One of the school board members cites a study showing that parents' recall of height is frequently off by a couple of inches compared to measures taken with the standard ruler and measurement method used in the nurse's office.
>
> > *Although parents' reports of height pass the face validity test (they <u>do</u> measure children's height), the article cited by the school board member shows that such reports have <u>low</u> **criterion validity** because they compared poorly against a more direct, already validated other measure (the **criterion**) of the same characteristic (height). Parental reports are intended to replace nurse measurements for the <u>same time period</u>, so this is an example of poor **concurrent validity**.*

> Example: One way to estimate how tall a child will be as an adult is to double a boy's height at age 2 or a girl's height at age 18 months (Hoecker, 2017).

*If that method estimated heights that were very close to the child's eventual adult height, that measure would have <u>high</u> **predictive validity**, with the measure based on current height comparing favorably against actual future height (the **criterion**).*

Construct Validity

Construct validity is used to evaluate measures of "constructs"—ideas that don't have an obvious measurable dimension. Construct validity assesses whether the measure captures aspects of that phenomenon that are identified by theory.

<u>Example</u>: To develop a measure of romantic love, Rubin (1970) reviewed theories and talked to experts in the field, asking them to identify the dimensions of that concept. Having identified three components (affiliative and dependent need, a predisposition to help, and an orientation of exclusiveness and absorption toward one's romantic partner), he developed several items to measure each of those dimensions and added together the scores on those items to create an overall measure of romantic love.

> *Romantic love is an abstract **construct** rather than an event or physical object that could be measured by counting or using a ruler. To attain good **construct validity** for his new measure, Rubin designed it as a composite of multiple items that captured dimensions thought to be important aspects of romantic love, thus also satisfying **content validity**.*

Face validity is assessed by considering whether a measure captures the dimensions of interest "on the face of it." **Content validity** is assessed by the extent to which the items capture each dimension of the domain the test seeks to measure. **Criterion validity** is evaluated by comparing the values on a new measure against another measure of the same phenomenon that has already been shown to be accurate. There are two types of **criterion validity**: **Concurrent validity**, in which the measure and the criterion pertain to the <u>same</u> point in time, and **predictive validity**, in which the criterion occurs at a <u>later</u> time than the measure being validated. **Construct validity** is assessed for ideas that don't have an obvious measurable dimension, instead showing that the measure captures aspects of that phenomenon identified by theory.

Reliability is a prerequisite for measurement validity. If a measure isn't reliable, it shouldn't be used! However, even if a measure is reliable, it is <u>not</u> necessarily valid.

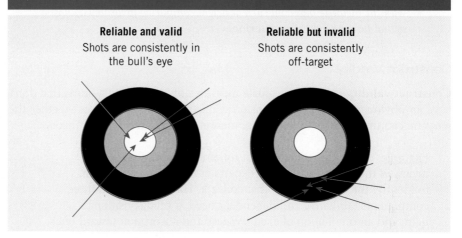

Figure 4.7 Distinction Between Reliability and Validity

Reliable and valid
Shots are consistently in the bull's eye

Reliable but invalid
Shots are consistently off-target

<u>Example</u>: In the image on the left of Figure 4.7, the arrows consistently land in the middle of the target, hitting the desired concept repeatedly. In the image on the right, the arrows are consistently off-target, all landing close together in the black outer circle of the target.

*The left-hand image illustrates a measure that is <u>both</u> **reliable** <u>and</u> **valid**, while the one on the right indicates a measure that is **reliable** (<u>consistent</u>) but <u>not</u> **valid** (is off-topic).*

<u>Example</u>: If my bathroom scale always tells me I weigh less than I actually do, that scale is producing invalid measurements.

*Even though that bathroom scale measures weight **reliably** (consistently), it is **invalid** because it always <u>understates</u> my weight.*

Reliability and validity of a measure must be assessed <u>before</u> it is used to collect data because there is no way to overcome unreliable or invalid data after the fact.

> For numbers to make sense, the measures that produce those numbers must be both reliable and valid. A reliable measure is <u>not</u> necessarily valid. Reliability and validity of a measure should be assessed before it is used to collect data. For existing data, measures of reliability and validity should be reported and interpreted.

TERMS AND CONCEPTS

HIGHLIGHTS

- The way something is **conceptualized** is distinct from the way it is **measured**. Often, there are several ways to measure a particular topic and concept. Choice of how to operationalize a concept should be based on the expected **audience** and their **intended use** of the measure, **ease of measurement**, and **comparability** across studies, context, or locations.

- **Level of measurement** refers to the precision with which variables are measured and affects how data are collected, analyzed, and communicated.

- Aspects of units to identify for each variable include **unit of observation**, **system of measurement**, and **scale of measurement**.

- Data can be collected using **closed-ended** or **open-ended questions**, which will determine the levels of measurement of the resulting variables. Either of those question formats can be **single-response** or **multiple-response**.

- **Missing values** on variables must be identified to avoid misinterpreting numeric information.

- The way a concept is measured affects the **level** and **range** of **plausible** variables as well as whether high, low, or midrange values are **optimal** for that concept.

- Measures should be assessed for **reliability** (consistency) and **validity** (accuracy) before they are used to collect data. Reliability and validity of measures should be discussed when results based on those measures are reported.

RESEARCH TIPS

- Read articles, books, and other credible resources to find out how the measurement approach for a concept affects the plausible level and range of numeric values for that variable and optimal values.

RECOMMENDED READINGS

Chambliss, D. F., & Schutt, R. K. (2018). *Making sense of the social world* (6th ed.) Thousand Oaks, CA: Sage.

Currie, C., et al. (2008). Researching health inequalities in adolescents: The development of the Health Behaviour in School-Aged Children (HBSC) Family Affluence Scale. *Social Science and Medicine, 66*, 1429–1436.

Lewis-Beck, M. S., Bryman, A., & Liao, T. F. (2004). *The SAGE encyclopedia of social science research methods*. Sage.

Rubin, Z. (1970). The measurement of romantic love. *Journal of Personality and Social Psychology, 16*(2), 265–273.

EXERCISES

Individual Exercises

Quantitative Reasoning in Everyday Life

1. Look up a recipe for one of your favorite foods that involves at least five different ingredients. For each ingredient, identify (a) the system of measurement (e.g., British, metric, or other) in which the amounts are listed and (b) the units of measurement (e.g., grams, teaspoons, cups). (c) List an amount of a particular ingredient that would make the recipe taste horrible if it were measured in the wrong units and explain why.

2. Use the chart at https://www.finder.com.au/shoe-size-conversion-guide to look up which size shoe would you need in (a) the UK, (b) Europe, or (c) Japan. (Be sure to specify men's or women's size!) (d) If you accidentally asked for your Australian shoe size in each of the following countries, indicate whether the shoes be too big, too small, or the salesperson wouldn't be able to fulfill your order in (i) the U.K., (ii) the United States, (iii) or Japan.

Interpreting Research

3. Working from the "Variables" tab on the ICPSR (https://www.icpsr.umich.edu/) website you chose for Exercise 3 for Chapter 2, identify at least one variable at each of the following levels of measurement: (a) nominal, (b) ordinal, and (c) continuous (interval or ratio). For each of those variables, specify (i) its units and/or categories, (ii) whether the data were collected using an open-ended or closed-ended question, and (iii) whether those questions were single-response or multiple-response.

4. In Table 1 from the World Bank Development Goals (http://wdi.worldbank.org/table/WV.1), look up the following aspects of units used for each topic: (a) system of measurement, (b) scale of measurement, and (c) unit of analysis.

5. For a topic of interest to you, write a question in each of the following formats, following the guidelines in this chapter: (a) closed-ended, single-response; (b) closed-ended, multiple-response. (c) Rewrite each of those questions in open-ended form.

Group Exercises

Quantitative Reasoning in Everyday Life

6. Identify issues that could affect the reliability and validity with which members of each of the following groups report hate crimes: (a) victims, (b) witnesses of a crime, (c) police officers, and (d) political figures. (e) Discuss differences that might occur in the levels and types of offenses reported by those different stakeholder groups.

Interpreting Research

7. Find three journal articles that study the same topic that you and your classmates used in Exercise 8 for Chapter 3. (a) Identify how each study measured that concept. Discuss how those different measures are likely to affect (b) the number of cases included, (c) the types of cases included in terms of (d) social and demographic factors, and (e) extent/degree of the concept you defined.

8. Review Currie et al. (2008), cited in Recommend Readings, to find information about the following: (a) which type(s) of reliability were assessed; (b) whether each of the following types of validity were assessed: (i) face validity, (ii) content validity, (iii) construct validity, (iv) criterion validity.

For each of the parts of this exercise, provide a direct quote in the Currie article that answers the question as well as the page and paragraph number where you found that information.

Planning Research

9. With the same group of students with whom you worked on the exercise for Chapter 3 on defining a concept, decide on one definition of that concept that you will all use. (a) Working independently, each student writes a description of one way to operationalize (measure) that concept, including the wording of a question to collect that information. (b) Discuss similarities and differences across the different measures of your concept and how any differences in your measures will affect the numeric values of data collected with those measures.

10. Agree upon a topic of interest to your group; avoid any sensitive or personal topics. Each student writes (a) an open-ended question to collect data on that topic and (b) a closed-ended question on the same topic. Include instructions on the number of allowable responses to each of those questions. (c) Each student answers the questions written by a different student. (d) Discuss any difficulties you had in answering their question(s), such as not finding a suitable answer or finding too many answers, and how that might affect quality of the data. (e) Discuss similarities and differences across your versions of (i) the closed-ended question, (ii) the open-ended question, and (iii) how any differences in wording or level of measurement might affect comparability of data collected using those questions.

Context

What Is Context?

The previous two chapters discussed how to define a research topic and determine how the pertinent concepts were measured. With those tasks accomplished, the next step is identifying the context in which a study will take place. Thinking back to our handy list of W's, if the **topic** is "what" those numbers provide information about and **measurement** is "how" they are being measured, the **context** refers to **when**, **where**, and to **whom** (or **which** cases) the data pertain.

In this chapter, I explain how to identify the different dimensions of context and illustrate how context can affect what numeric values make sense for a particular topic and measurement. I then introduce the distinction between a sample and a population and explain the importance of identifying the characteristics of a sample before drawing conclusions about a larger or different population based on results for that sample. Finally, I introduce levels of analysis and why they matter when interpreting and applying quantitative research results.

How Context Affects Plausibility

The **context** of a study encompasses the dates, locations, and environment (both physical and social) that characterize the data used in that study. Sometimes known as the **setting**, context is a critical consideration for making sense of numbers because values that are plausible for certain times, places, and groups may be totally unreasonable for other places, times, and groups.

Example: In 2014, the country with the tallest men on average was the Netherlands, with a mean height of 6' (or 182 cm; Table 5.1; Geggel, 2016). In the same year, the country with the shortest men was East Timor, with a mean height of 5'2" (162 cm). Although a height of 5'10" wouldn't have been the least bit unusual in the Netherlands, it would have been truly rare in East Timor.

The differences in average height are partly due to genetic differences and partly due to variations in nutritional and health status across countries—where the data are from.

Table 5.1 Trends in Average Human Height by Country, 1914 to 2014			
	Country	Value	
		British Units	Metric Units
Men			
Shortest average height, 2014	East Timor	5 ft., 2 in.	160 cm.
Tallest average height, 2014	Netherlands	6 ft., 0 in.	183 cm.
Largest **increase** in average height, 1914–2014	Iran	5 inch gain from 5 ft., 1 in. to 5 ft., 6 in.	6 cm gain from 157 cm. to 173 cm.
Women			
Shortest average height, 2014	Guatemala	4 ft., 8 in.	149 cm.
Tallest average height, 2014	Latvia	5 ft., 5 in.	170 cm.
Largest **increase** in average height, 1914–2014	South Korea	7 inch gain from 4 ft., 6 in. to 5 ft., 3 in.	20 cm. gain from 142 cm. to 162 cm.

Source: Data from Geggel (2016).

Example: Average human height has changed considerably over the past century: Between 1914 and 2014, average height for Iranian men increased from 5'1" to 5'6" (157 to 173 cm.)—the largest such increase in height among the countries studied (Geggel, 2106, Table 5.1). Increases in average height were observed over that period in most countries and for women as well as men. Thus, a height value that is quite reasonable for a particular country, gender, and date might be very unlikely for that same country and gender in a different time period.

> *Knowing in which year–1914 or 2014 (**when**)—the data were collected helps identify which height values make sense.*

Example: In the United States, a loaf of bread costing $2.00 in 2019 would have cost about $1.00 in 1989 (U.S. Inflation Calculator, 2019).

> *When inflation is occurring, the <u>same</u> numeric price has <u>different</u> meanings in different **times**. The amount of money that in 2019 would have paid for <u>one</u> loaf of bread could have bought <u>two</u> loaves of bread **30 years earlier**.*

Figure 5.1 is a growth chart, with the diagonal upward sloping curves showing how boys' height (on the y-axis) increases with age (x-axis) based on international data from 2007. The middle growth curve portrays the 50th percentile (also known as the **median**) height for boys at each age, and the top growth curve shows the 97th percentile—the value that is higher than that for 97% of boys that age; the bottom growth curve shows the 3rd percentile. You will learn more about percentiles in Chapter 9.

Example: Based on the 2007 international growth standards, a height of 127 centimeters (about 50 inches) would be quite typical for an 8-year-old boy (Point A in Figure 5.1) but far too tall for a 5-year-old (Point B) and very short for an 11-year-old (Point C) (WHO, 2007). A height of 70 inches (5'10", or 1.78 meters) is slightly taller than average for adult males in the U.S. but would be unusually tall for adult females.

> *People grow taller throughout childhood, and adult men are on average several inches taller than their female counterparts. Age and gender are examples of ways that **who** determines which numeric values are reasonable for this particular **topic**—height.*

Context (or **setting**) refers to when, where, and from whom (or which cases) data were collected.

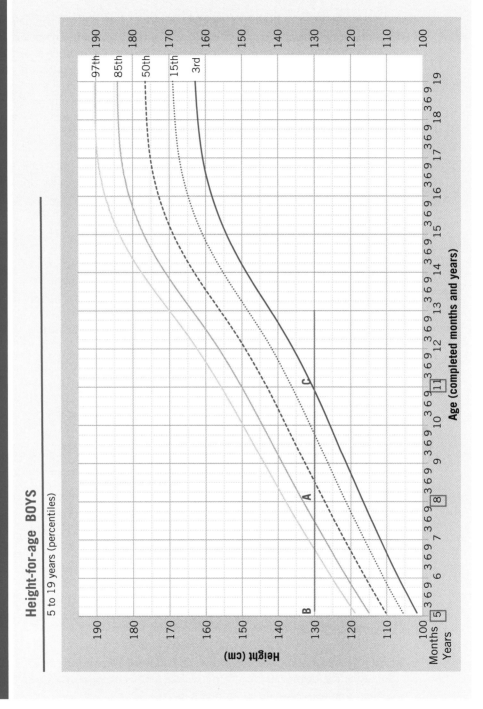

Figure 5.1 Percentiles of Height-for-Age Among Boys

Context as Limiting the Set of Cases Studied

Context can also refer to limits on which cases are included in a set of data, identifying criteria that have been specified for the time, place, and characteristics of the cases to be studied. These restrictions can be described either as **inclusion criteria** (which cases are <u>included</u> among those studied) or **exclusion criteria** (which cases are <u>excluded</u> from the data set).

Sometimes the **analytic sample** (set of data used for a specific analysis) are restricted to a particular subgroup because that is the set of cases to whom the question pertains.

> <u>Example</u>: Uterine cancer is studied only among females because males don't have a uterus, so it is impossible for them to develop cancer in that organ! Thus, it wouldn't make sense to calculate the uterine cancer rates for the entire population (both sexes).
>
> *<u>Female</u> sex is an **<u>inclusion</u> criterion** for this topic. Alternatively, <u>male</u> sex could be used as an **<u>exclusion</u> criterion**.*

> <u>Example</u>: The U.S. Supplemental Nutrition Assistance Program (SNAP)—formerly known as Food Stamps—provides nutrition benefits to supplement the food budget of eligible low-income individuals and families (U.S. Department of Agriculture, 2018). Thus, a study of enrollment rates into SNAP should include only people who meet eligibility criteria for that program.
>
> ***Inclusion criteria*** *for this study would be income, assets, age, and household size, which also determine eligibility for SNAP. If people who are <u>not</u> eligible for SNAP were included in the sample, enrollment rates would be underestimated because those who don't meet the eligibility criteria can't enroll.*

An **analytic sample** is the set of cases used to analyze a specific research question. **Inclusion criteria** specify the characteristics used to define which cases are <u>included</u> in the analytic sample, whereas **exclusion criteria** specify characteristics used to determine which cases are <u>omitted</u> from the analytic sample.

Other times, "who" is studied is limited to the set of cases for whom the information is available from a particular data set, which might or might not be due to the topic at hand.

> <u>Example</u>: Many surveys such as the U.S. National Health Interview Survey or the European Health Interview Survey collect only data on the civilian noninstitutionalized populations.

*Many people with dementia live in institutions such as long-term care facilities or nursing homes and are thus **excluded** from the survey sample; therefore, estimates based on those data sources are likely to understate rates of dementia.*

<u>Example</u>: Surveys of attitudes and interests that are sponsored by social media sites collect only data from people who access those sites. Such surveys will capture preferences of people who are media savvy and follow those particular platforms; thus, statistics based on those data are unlikely to reflect attitudes and interests among the broader population of adults.

*For these types of data sources, it may be difficult to identify limits on age, gender, or socioeconomic factors on **who** is included, other than specifying that data are available only for people who accessed that survey online.*

When, where, and **from whom** data were collected can affect which numeric values make sense for the topic under study.

Other Dimensions of Context

We've been using the "W's" (who, what, when, where) as a simple mental checklist for information to keep track of when assessing plausibility of a numeric value. When studying topics related to people, "who" is a handy way to remember to consider whether <u>all</u> people in a place or time are being studied or just a **subgroup** defined by age, race, or other human attribute. However, if the study concerns something other than people, there might be other criteria that limit whether all cases in that time and location are being (or should be) included—not really "who," but rather "which" cases are to be studied.

<u>Example</u>: Suppose you are about to visit a new city and want to compare ratings of restaurants. One of your travel companions doesn't eat meat so you decide to look only at reviews of restaurants that serve vegetarian food.

*__Inclusion criteria__ for your investigation are the location (**where**) and type of restaurant (**which** cuisines) to be considered.*

<u>Example</u>: A comparison of safety and effectiveness associated with different types of opioid-containing medications would include only those types of medications.

*__Exclusion criteria__ would specify which **classes of drugs** (those <u>without</u> opioids) would be <u>omitted</u> from the analysis.*

How Context Affects Measurement

Another reason to pay attention to the setting of a study is that systems of measurement and definitions of units vary by place, time, and for some topics, who (or what) is being measured.

Example: In much of the world today, people's height is measured in centimeters (metric system), but in the U.S. and Britain, height is usually measured in feet and inches (the Imperial—also known as British—system).

*Different locations use different **systems of measurement** for the same concept (height). If you read that someone's height was 72 but don't note the units used to measure height in that location, you might misinterpret the meaning of that value.*

Example: In Biblical times, the cubit (18", based on the distance from someone's elbow to fingertips) was used as a standard measure of length (Encyclopedia Britannica, 2016). China converted to the metric system during the early 20th century, but for the preceding 3,000 years had used *chǐ* (approximately 12.6 inches or 0.32 meters, originally derived from the distance spanned by a human hand, from the tip of the thumb to the tip of the forefinger) and *cùn* (the width of a person's thumb at the knuckle or one-tenth of a *chǐ*) to measure length. *Chǐ* and *cùn* units were originally derived as a system to find acupuncture points (TCM Student, n.d.).

*These **systems of measurement** for length or height vary by both **time** and **place**.*

Example: The height of a horse is conventionally measured in the number of hands (defined as 4") from the ground to shoulder when the horse is standing (Ministry of Agriculture, Food and Rural Affairs, 2011).

***Who** is being measured (horses versus people) affects the **units** used to measure height as well as the **scale** of values.*

Interesting how many different types of height measures used various body parts as the reference for these units – probably because they are always "handy" (pun intended). Variation in the ways things are measured in different times and places makes it crucial to note which units of measurement were used in a particular study so that if necessary, results from different studies can be converted into consistent units before they are compared. Inches to inches or cubits to cubits as the case may be! You will return to this aspect of numeric comparisons in Chapter 8.

Population Versus Study Sample

You might think that once you've specified the date, place, and any limits on groups or other cases, that would be all you need to know about context.

However, many data sets don't collect information on every single case in a given time, place, and group, which would be too time-consuming and expensive. Instead, a **sample** of cases is often studied and the results are used to infer patterns for the overall **population** (or **universe**) from which those cases are drawn.

In Figure 5.2, the **population** is depicted in the larger solid circle, with an "X" for each **element** (member of that population). The **sample** is depicted as a smaller dot-filled circle, also including an "X" for each element. The sample is a <u>subset</u> of the population—chosen from among the members of that population—as shown by the fact that the dot-filled circle is entirely enclosed in the larger circle.

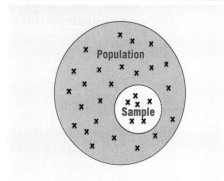

Figure 5.2   Population, Sample, and Elements

Example: Instead of talking to every voter in the country, a pre-election poll typically collects information from a few thousand voters drawn from the population.

> The **population** is all potential voters in the location of interest, the **elements** are the individual voters, and the **sample** is the subset of voters who participated in the poll.

In research methods, the term "population" doesn't have to refer to people. It could be a set of other **entities** such as corporations, countries, or whatever type of element is being studied. The sample will then be a subset of cases drawn from the larger set (the population).

Example: For a study of vehicle safety in a new model of car, a consumer protection agency tests half a dozen of the new cars.

> Here, the **population** (or **universe**) is all the units of that car model that were manufactured that year, the **elements** are the individual vehicles (each car), and the **sample** is the subset of cars that were actually tested.

A **population** (also known as a **universe**) is the entire set of cases or entities a study seeks to learn about. An **element** is an individual member of the population. An **entity** is the <u>type</u> of element used in a study. A universe encompasses all the elements that meet the inclusion criteria. A **sample** is the subset of cases used to study the population as a whole. It is the set of elements about whom data are collected.

Representativeness

The relationship between a population and a sample sounds straightforward enough, but it turns out to be very important to know whether the sample is **representative** of that population, meaning that its composition in terms of demographic, socioeconomic, and other characteristics mirrors that of the population. In other words, in a representative sample, the distribution of those characteristics is about the same as in the population. You will learn more about distribution and composition in Chapter 10.

> Example: In 2019, the total population of the Philippines was 101 million persons, of whom 32% were under age 15 years, 64% aged 15 to 64, and 4% aged 65 and older (Philippine Statistical Authority, 2019).
>
> *A **representative** sample of the Philippines population would have approximately the same shares of each of those groups as the population: about 32% <15 years old, 64% aged 15 to 64, and 4% aged 65 or older.*

An unrepresentative sample is one in which certain characteristics are present in higher proportions than in the population (<u>**overrepresented**</u>) and others in lower proportions than in the population (<u>**underrepresented**</u>). If one or more groups is overrepresented in a sample, one or more other groups defined by that characteristic <u>must</u> be underrepresented, because together those subgroups must total 100% of the sample.

> Example: If the age composition of a sample of the Philippine population was 25% under age 15 years, 65% aged 15 to 64, and 10% aged 65+, it would be an unrepresentative sample.
>
> *The hypothetical sample **underrepresents** people under age 15 years because the share of that age group in the <u>sample</u> (25%) is less than its share of the <u>population</u> (32%). Conversely, the sample **overrepresents** those aged 65+ (10% of the sample > 4% of the population). The age group 15 to 64 is present in approximately equal percentages in both the sample and population, so the sample is representative <u>of that age group</u>. By definition, the sum of the percentages in those three age groups in the sample must equal 100% because those three age groups are mutually exclusive and exhaustive (Chapter 4). Likewise in the population.*

In Chapter 11, you will learn more about different approaches to selecting cases for a study and how those methods affect representativeness.

> A **representative sample** is one whose composition is very similar to that of the population in terms of all characteristics that pertain to the study. If a subgroup is

present in a higher proportion of a sample than in the population, that subgroup is **overrepresented** in that sample. Conversely, if a subgroup comprises a lower proportion of a sample than of the population, it is **underrepresented**.

Generalization

When researchers study a sample of cases, they usually want to be able to **generalize** the findings of that study to beyond just the specific cases studied. The group to whom we want to apply the findings is called the **target population**.

> Example: Results of national pre-election poll provide estimates about how all voters will cast their ballots based on a sample of voters.
>
> *Results from the poll* **sample** *are* **generalized** *to the* **target population**: <u>all</u> *voters in the country where the election is taking place.*

Figure 5.3 illustrates the two types of generalization from a sample to a target population, which may differ from the sample in terms of size, composition, location, or other characteristics. **Sample generalization** involves extrapolating the conclusions based on a sample to the larger population from which that sample was drawn (Arrow 1). Note that Population A and the sample have the same characteristics: Both are denoted by circles filled with "X"s. The only difference is that the sample is smaller than the population from which it was selected.

Figure 5.3   Sample- and Cross-Population Generalizability

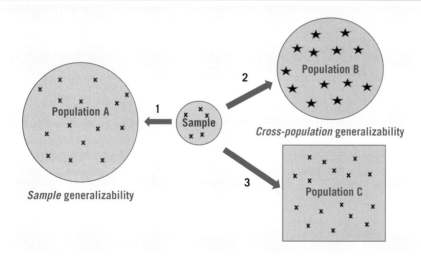

Cross-population generalization (shown by Arrows 2 and 3 in Figure 5.3) occurs when the conclusions based on a sample are used to draw inferences about a <u>different</u> population. Population B is symbolized by a circle but is filled with stars, whereas population C is symbolized by a square filled with "X"s. In other words, populations B and C have different characteristics than the study sample.

> A **target population** is the set of entities to whom researchers wish to apply (**generalize**) the findings. It may or may not be the same as the **universe** from whom the study sample was selected. **Sample generalizability** refers to the ability to apply results based on a sample to the larger population from which that sample was drawn. **Cross-population generalizability** refers to the ability to apply conclusions based on a sample to a population that has <u>different</u> characteristics than the population from which the sample was drawn. The extent to which the results of a particular study can be generalized is known as its **external validity.**

To get a more concrete idea of what these different types of generalization mean, imagine that the shape of the gray-shaded components signifies location and the symbols within those shapes denote characteristics of the elements, whether place, date, demographic traits, or other qualities.

<u>Example</u>: Suppose that in Figure 5.3, circles indicate urban areas and squares indicate rural areas. Further, suppose the "X"s are adults and the stars are children.

The sample and Population A are both made up of adults from urban areas, so **sample generalization** *implies taking results of a small number of urban adults and extrapolating them to <u>all</u> urban adults.*

*However, Population B is children from urban areas, so the generalization illustrated by Arrow 2 implies taking results obtained from urban <u>adults</u> and applying them to urban <u>children</u>. This inference might be **externally valid** for some topics (e.g., how close fast-food outlets are to where the respondents live) but not others (e.g., amount of daily exercise).*

*Population C is adults from rural areas, so the generalization shown by Arrow 3 means taking results obtained from <u>urban</u> adults and applying them to <u>rural</u> adults. Again, such a **cross-population generalization** might be reasonable for some topics (e.g., time spent on social media) but not others (e.g., time spent commuting to work).*

Cross-population generalization of research findings is more common than you might think, so get in the habit of critically evaluating whether a generalization is justified based on the context (time, place, and subgroups) of a study.

Example: Often, studies of human behavior are based on volunteers recruited on the university campus where the researcher happens to work, which means that many of the participants are highly educated young adults from that specific school.

*Before assuming that the numeric results of such studies can be **generalized** to the broader population, consider whether it makes sense to apply those conclusions to the behavior of people of ages, socioeconomic groups, or geographic locations that were <u>not</u> in the study sample.*

Example: Experiments to assess the benefit of exercise on health are frequently limited to only one gender or racial/ethnic group, a narrow age range, and a particular fitness level. In addition, they often test only one specific type of exercise and follow the respondents for a few hours or days.

*Think about whether it seems reasonable to conclude that findings for the sample of people who were actually studied also **apply** to people of <u>other</u> groups or fitness levels or to <u>long-term</u> health outcomes of that type of exercise.*

Results of studies frequently continue to be generalized well beyond the date they were conducted—a different kind of "cross-population" generalization.

Example: Imagine that the circles in Figure 5.3 represent the year 1990, the square denotes 2020, and the "X"s denote people who had at least a college degree.

*Based on Arrow 3, **cross-population generalization** involves assuming that results based on college-educated people in 1990 also apply to people with that education level 30 years later.*

To decide whether the numeric results of long-ago studies still pertain today, think carefully about what might have changed about the population since the date the study was done. If there have been substantial changes in the characteristics of the population (e.g., aging, ethnic or cultural diversification), context (e.g., pollution levels or economic conditions), or other factors that might influence the results, a more recent study might be needed to see whether the earlier statistics still pertain.

The **characteristics of a sample** affect the extent to which results based on those data can be applied (**generalized**) to another context.

Errors in Generalization

Overgeneralization is an <u>incorrect</u> form of generalization. As discussed in Chapter 3, overgeneralization occurs when someone assumes that a pattern that was observed in a few cases applies more broadly. **Stereotyping** is a form of overgeneralization, where assumptions are made about a <u>group</u> based on characteristics of an <u>individual</u> who is or appears to be a member of that group.

> <u>Example</u>: A man is arrested for shooting people who were attending prayer services in a mosque. After police learn that the perpetrator practices Fundamentalist Christianity, a news report implies that all Fundamentalist Christians are religious zealots who believe that violence should be used to eradicate Islam.
>
> *Here, a **stereotype** about members of a particular religious group based on one incident is being **overgeneralized** to draw conclusions about <u>all</u> individuals who follow that religion. A systematic study based on a **representative** sample of Fundamentalist Christians would reveal that very few of them advocate for the use of violence against those who practice Islam.*

Stereotypes are when <u>all</u> members of a group are overgeneralized as sharing the same set of characteristics.

Watch out for statements involving wording such as "always," "all," "never," or "none," which often signal overgeneralization, especially when they are based on a small number of observations.

> <u>Example</u>: After the grades on the midterm exam for his Research Methods class are released, several students come to Professor Herrera to ask how they can improve their grades. One of the students admits she hadn't done the assigned reading. In frustration, Professor Herrera thinks to himself, "Students are so lazy. They never do the readings."
>
> *The professor is **overgeneralizing** ("never") to explain why students didn't do well on the midterm based on what he learned about <u>one</u> student. Had he spoken to other students, he might have discovered different reasons for their poor performance, such as that they found the material to be very challenging despite having done the reading, or that they misunderstood the instructions on the exam. In addition, some students presumably (hopefully!) did well on the midterm, at least in part because they <u>did</u> do the readings.*

However, if a generalization about a pattern was actually based on a comprehensive evaluation of a representative sample, that statement may indeed be valid—in other words, <u>not</u> an overgeneralization!

> <u>Example</u>: Professor Herrera notices that every student who spent at least 2 hours reviewing material on the Learning Management Site for the

Research Methods course during the week before the midterm exam earned at least a B on that exam.

*This conclusion ("every") is <u>not</u> an **overgeneralization** because it is based on information about all the students who followed a certain study pattern.*

Level of Analysis and Fallacy of Level

Another aspect of context that affects the applicability of findings is the **level of analysis**, which refers to the extent of **aggregation** (grouping) of the elements being studied, such as individuals, families, schools, or cities. Different entities have different levels of aggregation. The lowest **level of aggregation** is often referred to as the **micro** level or unit, whereas those that combine individual entities into groups are referred to as more **macro** units.

To draw correct conclusions about patterns at one level of analysis, the data used must come from the same level of analysis. **Fallacy of level** occurs when inferences about patterns at one level of analysis are based on data from either a higher (more **macro**) or lower (more **micro**) level. There are two such types of fallacy: ecological fallacy and reductionism. Errors in drawing conclusions about one level of analysis based on data from a <u>higher</u> level of aggregation are referred

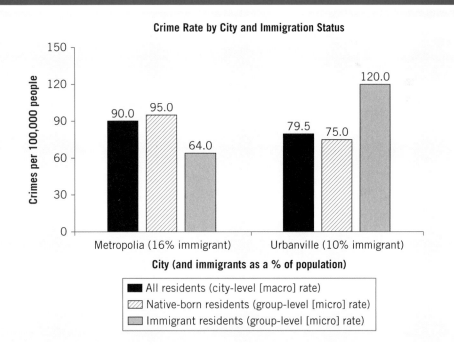

Figure 5.4   Crime Rates for Two Cities, Overall and by Immigrant Status

to as **ecological fallacy**, such as when inferences about individuals are deduced from findings about a group to which those people belong.

Example: A study found that Metropolia had a crime rate of 90 per 100,000 residents, whereas Urbanville had a crime rate of 79.5 per 100,000 (black bars of Figure 5.4). Immigrants comprised 16% of Metropolia's population but only 10% of Urbanville's population. A journalist for the *Metropolia Daily News* used that city-level information to conclude that immigrants were more likely to commit crimes. However, a closer look revealed the opposite pattern at the group level: in Metropolia the crime rate for immigrants was lower than that for native-born residents (64 per 100,000 and 95 per 100,000, gray and striped bars, respectively).

*The journalist's incorrect conclusion occurred due to **ecological fallacy**: the inference about criminal behavior at the **group level** (immigrant status) was based on a comparison of **city-level** data; solid arrow in Figure 5.5. Although the city with the higher crime rate higher had a higher percentage of immigrants, the group-level data within that city showed that the crime rate was higher among native-born than among immigrant residents. In Metropolia, the pattern at the group (**micro**) level was the opposite of the pattern at the city (**macro**) level.*

Figure 5.5 Ecological Fallacy and Reductionism

Level of aggregation	Level of analysis for data	Research findings	Conclusion (may be incorrect)	Level of analysis for conclusion
Most **macro**	State		States with higher average income are more likely to vote Republican	State
	City	Cities with high percentages of immigrants have higher crime rates		
	Group			
	Individual	Higher income individuals are more likely to vote Republican	Immigrant are more likely to commit crimes than non-immigrants	Individual
Most **micro**				

Notes: Solid arrow illustrates ecological fallacy; dashed arrow illustrates reductionism.

In Urbanville, however, crime rates were lower among native-born than immigrant residents (75 per 100,000 and 120 per 100,000 people, respectively, Figure 5.4).

> *In Urbanville, the group-level pattern <u>was</u> consistent with the conclusion based on the city-level data. The correct way to arrive at that conclusion was to use data at the <u>same</u> **level of aggregation** as the desired inference: **group-level <u>data</u>** to draw an inference about a **group-level <u>pattern</u>**.*

The other fallacy of level—**reductionism**—occurs when conclusions about one level of analysis are incorrectly inferred based on data on a <u>lower</u> (more micro) level of analysis.

<u>Example</u>: Concluding that because high-income <u>individuals</u> are more likely than lower-income individuals to vote Republican (Huang et al., 2016), high-income <u>states</u> will be more likely than lower-income states to vote Republican.

> *Reductionist logic, shown with dashed arrow in Figure 5.5, led to the incorrect conclusion about **macro** (state) level based on data at the **micro** (individual) level. In fact, evidence at the <u>state</u> level showed that in many U.S. presidential elections, high-income states were more likely than low-income states to vote Democratic (Gelman et al., 2007)—the opposite of the pattern observed at the <u>individual</u> level.*

Data can be collected at different **levels of analysis** such as individuals, families, schools, or countries. These are also known as **units of observation** or **levels of aggregation** (Chapter 4). **Ecological fallacy** occurs when conclusions about a <u>lower</u> (more **micro**, <u>less</u> **aggregated**) level of analysis are based on findings from a <u>higher</u> (more **macro**, <u>more</u> **aggregated**) level of analysis. **Reductionism** occurs when conclusions about a <u>higher</u> (more macro, more aggregated) level of analysis are based on findings based on data from a <u>lower</u> (more micro, less aggregated) level of analysis.

In some situations, a numeric pattern can be consistent between micro and macro levels of analysis. However, to make sure an inference about a particular level of analysis is correct, that conclusion should be based on analysis of data measured at that <u>same</u> level of analysis. Fallacy of level often arises if data are not available at the level of aggregation that matches the level at which the question is posed, so instead, researchers use data at a different level of aggregation than the question of interest.

<u>Example</u>: Lacking data on crime rates by immigrant status of individuals, the journalist used available data on city-level crime in cities that have different immigrant composition to assess whether immigrants are more likely to commit crimes.

As you read or write about research results, be aware of the potential for fallacy of level so you can think carefully about how great a risk is posed about drawing conclusions about the desired level of aggregation.

> To avoid **fallacy of level**, conclusions about a particular level of analysis (type of entity) should be based on data from the same **level of analysis** (equally-aggregated type of entity).

TERMS AND CONCEPTS

HIGHLIGHTS

- Identifying the **context** (time, place, and group) of a quantitative study is essential to making sense of the numbers produced by that study.

- Numeric facts that fit one **context** don't necessarily fit a different place, time, or group. The **scope** of a definition may also differ by location, date, and group (Chapter 3).

- **Inclusion criteria** specify which cases are included in the **universe** <u>for a study</u>. They may be based on the topic or aspects of data collection.

- The way a concept is measured can vary by **context** because systems of measurement change over time and differ from one culture or geographic location to another.

- A **representative sample** is one in which the distribution of characteristics is very similar to the distribution of those characteristics in the population.

- Characteristics of a sample and population affect the degree to which it makes sense to **generalize** a study's findings to other contexts. **Sample generalizability** involves applying results based on a sample to the population from which it was drawn. **Cross-population generalizability** involves applying results based on a sample to a population with different characteristics.

- **Overgeneralization** is an error in reasoning whereby information about a few cases is used to draw inferences about an entire group. **Stereotyping** is one form of overgeneralization.

- Statistics based on one **level of analysis** should not be used to draw inferences about more micro (smaller) or macro (larger) aggregations of elements.

RESEARCH TIPS

- Read articles, books, and other authoritative resources for information about ways the location, date, and which cases are included affect which numeric values make sense for that data and topic.

- When reading a study, pay attention to the characteristics of the sample and think about

how those traits affect the extent to which numeric results based on that sample can be generalized.

- To avoid fallacy of level when applying results of a study, be sure it is at the same level of analysis as the desired inference.

RECOMMENDED READINGS

Chambliss, D. F., & Schutt, R. K. (2018). *Making sense of the social world: Methods of investigation* (6th ed.) Sage. Chapters 2 and 6

Klass, G. (2008). *Just plain data analysis*. Rowman & Littlefield.

EXERCISES

Individual Exercises

Quantitative Reasoning in Everyday Life

1. For yourself, a same-age friend of a different gender, and a neighbor or relative over age 65 years, fill in information on year of birth,

gender, country of birth, and current height in feet and inches. Use the online calculator available at http://time.com/4423803/how-tall-100-years-height/ to calculate how tall you would have been 100 years ago for each of the scenarios shown in Table 5A:

Table 5A			
	You	Different-Gender Friend	Someone Over Age 65 Years
Year of birth			
Gender			
Country of birth			
Current height (feet and inches)			
Height if born 100 years ago in the same country			
Height if born 100 years ago in Cameroon			
Height if born 100 years ago in Pakistan			

2. You are going to study abroad for a semester. The university where you'll be studying says you'll need to purchase books on-site in the local currency. They estimate a cost of $200 for textbooks. Using the currency converter https://www.xe.com/currencyconverter/, calculate the equivalent cost in local currency if you will be studying in (a) Brazil, (b) Vietnam, (c) Italy, and (d) England.

Interpreting Research

3. Find a quantitative research article in your field. Read the methods section to determine (a) whether they analyzed data from a sample or population, (b) their inclusion or exclusion criteria, and (c) whether they discussed the representativeness of their sample.

4. Find a research article in your field that analyzed data from a sample. Read the discussion and conclusion section to determine (a) which type(s) of generalization(s) they made (sample and/or cross-population), and (b) if they generalized to a different population, specify on what dimensions (W's) that population differed from the sample. (c) Identify the wording they used to generalize the findings. HINT: Look for any recommendations they made about applying the results of their study.

Analyzing Data

5. At the U.S. Census website (census.gov), look up the U.S. Federal Poverty Thresholds for the most recent available year for each of the following sized households: (a) one adult aged less than 65 years, (b) one adult aged 65 or older, (c) one adult and two children, and (d) two adults and two children. (e) For each of those family compositions, look up information on the poverty threshold for ten years ago. (f) Calculate how much the thresholds vary according to family size, age composition, and date.

6. Using data from the sources listed after Table 5B, indicate which of the values in the table make sense for the specified date and location.

Table 5B

Topic and Context	Number of Persons		
Average family size, China, 2017	2	3	5
Average family size, Somalia, 2017	2	3	5
Population of China, 2017	4.5 million	4.5 billion	45 billion
Population of Asia, 2017	400 million	4.5 billion	45 billion
World population, 2017	7.3 million	73 million	7.3 billion

Sources: United Nations, Department of Economic and Social Affairs, Population Division. (2017). *Household size and composition around the world 2017—Data Booklet (ST/ESA/ SER.A/405).* http://www.un.org/en/development/desa/population/publications/pdf/ageing/household_size_and_composition_around_the_world_2017_data_booklet.pdf

Population Reference Bureau. (2018). *2017 World population data sheet.* https://assets.prb.org/pdf17/2017_World_Population.pdf

Group Exercises

Quantitative Reasoning in Everyday Life

7. Discuss the kinds of reasoning you have heard people use (or have used yourself) to create or justify stereotypes about people of different genders, cultures, or other characteristics. (b) Consider the extent to which they were overgeneralizing their experiences.

Interpreting Research

8. Rubin (1970) developed an indicator of romantic love that measured how much time members of a couple spent gazing into each other's eyes while in a laboratory setting; more gazing time was associated with higher scores on the survey measures of romantic love discussed in this chapter. Those measures were developed and validated for a U.S. sample of mostly white heterosexual dating couples in the mid-1960s. For this exercise, <u>assume that you agree that those measures were reliable and valid for that time, place, and group</u>. Discuss whether and why you think Rubin's gazing measure would be a reliable and valid measure of romantic love: (a) currently, (b) for homosexual couples, and (c) for people from other countries, and explain why or why not. Discuss what type of generalizability you are evaluating in each of the preceding questions.

9. Using the Poverty Risk Calculator (https://confrontingpoverty.org/poverty-risk-calculator/#), calculate the risk of falling into poverty within the next 5 years for people with each of the following combinations of characteristics: (a) unmarried white male aged 22 with a high school education or less, (b) unmarried white female aged 22 with a high school education or less, (c) unmarried white female aged 22 with beyond a high school education, (d) unmarried non-white male aged 52 with a high school education or less, (e) married non-white male aged 52 with a high school education or less, and (f) married non-white female aged 52 with beyond a high school education. Discuss how much age, gender, race, and educational attainment each affects poverty risk. Identify which combination of those four characteristics is associated with (i) the highest risk of falling into poverty and (ii) the lowest risk of falling into poverty.

10. Discuss whether each of the specified inferences in Table 5C represents ecological fallacy, reductionism, or neither, and explain your answer.

Table 5C Studies of Sixth-Grade Math Performance

Level of Analysis <u>Studied</u>	Level of Analysis <u>to Which</u> <u>Conclusions Were Applied</u>	Type of Fallacy of Level (one for each row)		
		Ecological Fallacy	Reductionism	Neither Fallacy (a <u>correct</u> inference)
Students in selected elementary schools	Classrooms in all elementary schools			
Classrooms in selected elementary schools	Students in all elementary schools			
Students in selected elementary schools	Students in all elementary schools			
Selected elementary schools	Classrooms in all elementary schools			
Selected elementary schools	All elementary schools			

Note: All studies occurred in the same location and date.

Exhibits for Communicating Numeric Information

To prepare you for the widespread use of tables and figures throughout the rest of this book, in Part III I take a necessary detour to explain and illustrate the structure, purpose, interpretation, and design of basic tables, charts, and other visualizations—collectively referred to as **exhibits**—for presenting numeric information.

> **Exhibit** is a general term encompassing tables, charts, figures, maps, visualizations, and other types of diagrams.

In Chapters 6 and 7, I introduce terminology for the components of tables, charts, and visualizations and explain conventions for using those elements effectively. I also provide guidelines on how to read and design exhibits, and I give examples of those exhibits for common quantitative reasoning tasks. In Chapter 14, I return to discuss how to use exhibits along with prose—the third main tool for presenting numbers –to communicate quantitative research.

Working With Tables

Learning Objectives

After reading this chapter, you will be able to do the following:

1. State the criteria for effective tables.

2. Name the parts of tables and guidelines for their use.

3. Describe the principles for organizing data in tables and how to choose among them.

4. Read and interpret data from tables.

5. Design tables with appropriate layout and numeric detail for specific tasks.

In this chapter, I cover the skills you need to become both an effective consumer and producer of tables—able to make sense of the numbers in tables you encounter and prepared to design tables that communicate the points you want to make about the numbers you need to present. In later chapters, I will go into more detail about how to use tables for specific research methods tasks.

Criteria for Effective Tables

Good tables present numbers in a concise, well-organized fashion that makes it easy for readers to find and understand numbers in the table, including their purpose, topic, context, and how they are measured. Table layout and labeling should be straightforward and predictable and should coordinate with the order and wording of the associated written description. To be effective, tables should be focused, self-contained, and well-organized.

Focused Tables

Many documents and websites include several tables, each of which addresses one aspect of the topic. A report on poverty might present information on the observed income distribution in one country (one table), how poverty rates vary by gender, race, and socioeconomic characteristics (a second table), and the health and social consequences of poverty (a third table). Each of those tables **focuses** on one aspect of the overall report and should be designed to accomplish that specific objective.

Self-Contained Tables

As we learned in Part II of the book, information on the topic, context, and measurement of the numbers at hand is crucial for making sense of numbers. Thus, one of the key principles for effective tables is that they should be **self-contained**— understandable <u>without</u> readers needing to look elsewhere in the text (or other documents) to find that information. Using the table's title, row and column headings, and footnotes, readers should be able to discern the following:

- The purpose of the table, including its topic
- The context of the data (the W's—when, where, and who)
- The meaning of each variable in the table
- Units of measurement or categories for every number in the table
- Data sources
- Definitions of pertinent terms and abbreviations

The units and sources of data can be specified in any of several places in the table depending on space considerations and whether the same information applies to all numbers in the table; see examples throughout the rest of this chapter.

> Tables should be **focused** to communicate the information needed for the specific objective and task of that table, and **self-contained** so that readers can interpret the context, meaning, and units or categories for every number within the table without reference to the text.

A section later in the chapter covers the third criterion for effective tables—that they should be well-organized—after you have learned vocabulary for parts of a table.

Anatomy of a Table

Tables use a grid to organize numbers in a predictable way, guided by the title, labels, and notes. To provide a consistent vocabulary for discussing table structure and design, in this section I define the names and features of each table component, or what I call "anatomy of a table."

Title

The **title** for each table should communicate the specific topics or questions addressed in that table. In documents that include several tables or charts, the titles should differentiate them from one another. Instead of itemizing every variable in the table as part of the title (which would lead to awkwardly long titles), table titles should use summary phrases or thematic labels such as "socioeconomic characteristics," "voting patterns," or "attitudes about immigration." The individual variables will be labeled in the rows or columns.

In the title to a table or chart, the word "by" or the phrase "according to" often helps differentiate the independent from the dependent variable or variables. The variable mentioned before "by" is usually the dependent variable, while the variables listed after "by" are the independent variables.

> Example: In Table 6.1, the title "Marital Status by Gender and Age Group" signals that marital status is the dependent variable, whereas gender and age group are the independent variables.
>
> *The concept listed before the word "by" is the **dependent variable** because the table is reporting how that outcome varies according to gender and age group (the **independent variables**).*

> Example: The title "Opposition to the Death Penalty by Demographic, Political, and Religious Characteristics" conveys that the (hypothetical) table shows how opposition to the death penalty differs according to each of several independent variables.
>
> *Here, the phrase after the word "by" indicates that the table presents information on how values of that outcome (**dependent variable**) differ according to each of several **independent variables**, organized into **themes** (demographic, political, and religious characteristics).*

Caution: Designers of numeric tables do not always use "by" in this way when writing their titles. Always think through which "cause-and-effect" order makes sense for the two concepts under study rather than relying on "by" to identify which is the independent and which is the dependent variable (Chapter 2). We will discuss cause-and-effect relationships in more detail in Chapter 12.

> Example: If you download a tabulation of sex and marital status from the American Community Survey (see U.S. Census Bureau, n.d.a), it will be labeled "sex by marital status."
>
> *Sex (gender) is clearly not the **dependent variable** (e.g., it is not caused by marital status), so here "by" is conveying simply that the table presents the relationship between those two variables.*

Table 6.1 Anatomy of a Table

		Marital status by gender and age group (years), United States, 2015					
		Number of persons (thousands)					
	Never married	Currently married[1]	Separated	Formerly married		Widowed	All
				Divorced			
Males							
All ages	46,031	63,278	2,172	12,070		3,300	126,850
<20 years	10,751	93	8	5		3	10,860
20 to 24	10,587	864	38	56		6	11,551
25 to 34	12,696	8,287	321	921		30	22,256
35 to 44	5,098	12,424	515	2,133		74	20,244
45 to 54	3,524	13,645	564	3,285		222	21,240
55 to 64	2,238	13,227	443	3,240		497	19,645
65 to 74	798	9,305	198	1,749		809	12,858
75 to 84	255	4,290	68	557		918	6,088
85+ years old	84	1,144	16	125		741	2,110
Females							
All ages	40,056	61,993	3,087	16,142		11,864	133,142
<20 years	10,207	131	12	6		4	10,359
20 to 24	9,407	1,354	83	98		9	10,951
25 to 34	10,147	9,772	543	1,260		66	21,788
35 to 44	4,078	12,674	785	2,684		192	20,413
45 to 54	2,832	13,598	794	4,029		598	21,851
55 to 64	1,967	12,838	558	4,145		1,595	21,103
65 to 74	874	7,983	227	2,619		2,943	14,646
75 to 84	361	3,047	67	989		3,536	7,999
85+ years old	183	596	17	313		2,922	4,032

Source: Data from U.S. Census Bureau (2018c).

Note:

1. Excludes separated.

The words or phrases **"by"** or **"according to"** in a title <u>often (but not always)</u> communicate which are the independent and which are the dependent variables in that table.

- The concept listed before the word "by" is the dependent variable.

- The concept(s) listed after "by" are the independent variable(s).

Context

A good table title should specify the context of the data by listing the **W's**: where and when the data were collected and, if relevant, limits on who (or which cases) is included. If the data are from a specific study (such as the Human Genome Project or the 2013 Dominican Republic Demographic and Health Survey) or institution (e.g., one corporation or university), its name should be included in the title. Abbreviations should be kept to a minimum; if they are necessary to avert overly long titles, the acronym or abbreviation should be spelled out in a note to the table.

Units

The **units of measurement**, **level of aggregation**, and **system of measurement** for every variable in the table should be specified within that table. Although that seems like a lot of information to pack into a table, it can usually be expressed in a few words such as "annual household income in thousands of $," or "mean height in centimeters." If the same units apply to most numbers in the table, they can be included as part of the title rather than repeated in each row and column.

If there isn't enough space in the title or if the units vary for variables in the different rows and columns within that table, units should be reported in the row and column headings or in a column spanner. For instance, the column spanner in Table 6.1 specifies that the units are number of people in thousands because every number in the table is reported in those units.

Types of Measures or Statistics

If only one type of measure or statistic is reported in the table, it can be named in the table title.

- The title of a table designed to report statistics on each of several variables <u>separately</u> (univariate statistics) should mention whether it reports distribution or composition, average values, or other descriptive statistics on each of the variables in that table.

- The title of a table showing relationships between pairs of variables (bivariate statistics) should convey whether it reports correlations, differences in means, cross-tabulations, or specific other measures of association.

For tables that report several different types of statistics, the concepts under study should be named in the title and the types of statistics identified in column, row, or panel headings. We will return to discuss these types of statistics and the associated table structures in more detail in Chapter 10.

Row and Column Labels

Each **row label** or **column label** should use a short phrase to convey the concept and units or category names for that specific part of the table. Avoid using acronyms from data sets as row or column labels, which are poor ways to communicate the meaning of a variable. Instead, write a short phrase that succinctly conveys the concept measured by that variable.

> Example: Table 6.2 includes information on mean height (in inches), weight (in pounds), and Body Mass Index (in kilograms per meter^2).
>
> *With different **units** for each **variable**, the units <u>cannot</u> be summarized for the table as a whole, so they are reported in the respective **row labels**. We <u>cannot</u> assume that the units of measurement will be apparent once the concepts are named: For instance, height and weight could have been reported in metric rather than British units.*

Table 6.2 Table With Different Units for Different Continuous Variables					
	n	Mean	5th Percentile	Median	95th Percentile
Weight (lbs.)	5,425	168.5	110.5	159.1	256.8
Height (inches)	5,547	63.7	59.0	63.7	68.3
Body Mass Index[a]	5,413	29.2	19.6	27.7	43.3

Source: Data from Fryar (2016).

Note:

a. Body Mass Index (BMI) = weight (in lbs.)/[height (in inches)^2] × 703, which converts it to the standard international units for BMI = weight (in kilograms)/[height (in meters)^2] (CDC, 2014).

Example: As a row label, "Supports abortion if the mother's health is in danger" is much easier to understand than Q117a (the variable name from a hypothetical data set). Likewise, "Hispanic" conveys the name of a category much more effectively than an acronym such as ETHCAT2.

Readers will not be working with the electronic data set from which the numbers came, so there is no reason to obscure the meaning of the variables and their categories by using acronyms or "alphabet soup" variable names or value labels.

Indenting

Indenting of row labels conveys how different categories of a variable are related to one another. Categories of a nominal or ordinal variable should be listed in consecutive rows under a single major row header with the subgroups indented. This convention dictates that counts or percentages for subgroups that are indented equally can be added together to give the total.

Example: In Table 6.1, the label "<20 years" is indented in the row below "All ages," showing that the former is a subgroup of the latter. The individual age groups listed in the rows are equally indented from the left margin, showing that they add up to the total number of people of each gender.

*Row labels that are **indented** farther indicate **subgroups** and should not be added with the more aggregated groups to avoid double counting. In the terminology of Chapter 4, "all ages" and "<20 years" are not mutually exclusive; thus, indenting is used to show that they are overlapping groups so readers don't make that error when calculating totals.*

Column Headings

Each **column heading** should be used to identify the variable or measure (e.g., count, mean, or percentage of a whole) in that column. The guidelines for labeling abbreviations, notes, and units and categories in rows also apply to columns: If most numbers in a large table are measured in the same units, a spanner can be placed across columns to generalize with a phrase such as "percentage unless otherwise specified." The units for variables measured differently (e.g., in mortality rate per 1,000 persons, or median age in years) should then be named in the pertinent column heading.

Column Spanners

In the same way that indenting shows how a set of rows is related, **column spanners** convey how a set of columns is related. The text for the column spanners is in a separate row, centered above the columns that list the subcategory headings like an umbrella covering all the related categories.

Example: In Table 6.1, marital status falls into three broad categories—never married, currently married, and formerly married. "Formerly Married" encompasses separated, divorced, and widowed.

> A **column spanner** shows which three marital status subgroups together comprise "formerly married."

Interior Cells

Interior cells are those in the inside (middle) of a table, where the numbers are reported. They do <u>not</u> need to contain concept labels or units; those pieces of information should be evident from the labels of the overall row and column in which a cell is positioned.

Example: In 2015, approximately 8.3 million 25- to 34-year-old males in the United States were currently married.

> The dark gray **cell** in Table 6.1 is the intersection of the lighter gray **row** and **column**, so its topic and categories can be found in the respective **row** and **column labels**: gender in the **major row heading** for each panel, age group from the **row label**, and marital status from the **column heading**. The scale of the number is specified in the **column spanner**, so 8,287 represents the number of <u>thousands</u> of persons, which I rounded to millions in the sentence above. The W's are identified in the table **title**.

In many fields, numeric estimates based on only a few cases will be intentionally omitted from tables, either because of the lack of statistical precision of those estimates or in order to protect confidentiality of human subjects (Ligon & Clements, 2008; U.S. Census Bureau, 2013, 2018d). If there is an insufficient number of cases to report data for one or more cells in a table, those cells will often include a symbol in place of the numeric estimate, with a footnote describing the minimum size criterion and providing a pertinent citation.

Example: Statistics Canada places an X when an estimate is suppressed to meet confidentiality requirements of the country's Statistics Act, and an F symbol if an estimate is considered too unreliable to be reported (Statistics Canada, 2019).

Notes to Tables

Information about topic, context, or measurement of variables that does not fit easily in the title, row, or column labels should be reported in notes to the table. Common uses of footnotes to tables include spelling out abbreviations, giving brief definitions of concepts, and providing citations for data sources or other background information.

Example: A **footnote** to Table 6.2 gives the formula for Body Mass Index, with the component concepts (weight and height) and their units spelled out. The note is keyed to the row label for that variable.

If a table reports numbers from measures based on long or complex wording of a question or a scale or index constructed from multiple items (see Appendix A), a footnote to that table should refer to an appendix or cite a reference that contains the pertinent part of the questionnaire so that readers can understand the meaning or source of that measure.

Tables that require more than one note should label them with different symbols or letters rather than numbers (which could be confused with exponents), with the notes listed in that order at the bottom of the table (Nicol & Pexman, 2010; University of Chicago Press, 2017).

More Advanced Table Features

Tables that involve several dimensions often take advantage of additional features to help organize and communicate the data.

Panels

Panels can be used in several ways: to introduce another concept to a table, to report several different measures of the relationship in the table, or to organize rows into thematically grouped blocks.

Panels are blocks of consecutive rows within a table separated by horizontal lines or an extra blank row that can be used to organize tables that have several dimensions or different measures. Typically, the panels will be arranged one above another with column headings shared by all panels.

Examples of tables that use panels to introduce an <u>additional dimension</u> of comparison to a table:

- Separate panels for different years. For example, the relationship between gender, age group, and marital status (Table 6.1) might be shown at 10-year intervals from 1990 through 2020, with each year in a separate panel, labeled accordingly. The panels introduce another variable—in this case, year—to a tabulation of marital status by gender and age group. The panels would share the column headings (marital status) but repeat the row headings (for gender and age group) for each panel.

- Separate panels for other characteristics. For instance, the relationship between gender, age group, and marital status might be shown for each of several countries or income levels.

Table 6.3 Use of Panels to Present Two Different Types of Measures

Observed and Projected Population, by Level of Development, 1970–2070

A. Billions of persons

| Year | More Developed Regions | Less Developed Regions | | | World |
		All	Excluding China	China Alone	
1970	1.0	2.7	1.8	0.8	3.7
1980	1.1	3.4	2.4	1.0	4.5
1990	1.1	4.2	3.0	1.2	5.3
2000	1.2	5.0	3.6	1.3	6.1
2010	1.2	5.7	4.3	1.4	7.0
2015	1.3	6.1	4.7	1.4	7.4
2020	1.3	6.5	5.1	1.5	7.8
2030	1.3	7.3	5.8	1.5	8.6
2040	1.3	7.9	6.5	1.5	9.2
2050	1.3	8.5	7.1	1.4	9.8
2060	1.3	8.9	7.6	1.3	10.2
2070	1.3	9.3	8.0	1.2	10.6

B. Percentage of the World's Population, Specified Year

| Year | More Developed Regions | Less Developed Regions | | | World |
		All	Excluding China	China Alone	
1970	27%	73%	50%	23%	100%
1980	24%	76%	53%	23%	100%
1990	22%	78%	56%	22%	100%
2000	19%	81%	59%	21%	100%
2010	18%	82%	62%	20%	100%
2015	17%	83%	64%	19%	100%
2020	16%	84%	65%	19%	100%
2030	15%	85%	68%	17%	100%
2040	14%	86%	70%	16%	100%
2050	13%	87%	72%	14%	100%
2060	13%	87%	74%	13%	100%
2070	12%	88%	76%	12%	100%

Source: Data from United Nations (2017).

Note: Shading indicates projected values.

Panels can also be used to organize a table that presents different measures of the same concept, such as number of cases or events, along with measures of distribution or rate of occurrence:

- A table might present <u>number</u> of persons by region and year in one panel and <u>percentage</u> of the world's population in another, as in Table 6.3.

- A table might present <u>number</u> of deaths by cause or other characteristics in one panel and <u>death rates</u> in another, as in many World Health Organization reports.

- A table might present <u>mean income</u> for several different demographic groups in one panel, and <u>poverty rates</u> for those same groups in a second panel.

For these types of applications, the row headings should be repeated within each panel with the names of the specific measures and their respective units specified in a separate header or column spanner for each panel.

Finally, when a table contains many related variables in the rows, panels can be an effective way to organize them into blocks of thematically similar items. If two small, simple tables have the same column headers and address similar topics, they can be combined into a single table with panels, one panel for the set of rows from each of the smaller tables.

<u>Example</u>: Table 6.4 presents results of six questions about circumstances in which respondents think abortion should be legal and how responses differ for males and females. Rather than putting all six circumstances into one block, they are arranged into two panels—the top panel on <u>health</u> reasons for seeking an abortion, the bottom panel on <u>social</u> or preference reasons—each labeled accordingly.

*Although Table 6.4 could have been constructed as two separate tables— one on health reasons for abortion, another on social or preference reasons—putting them into **panels within** a single, unified table makes it easier to compare within or across themes, such as pointing out that respondents were considerably more likely to agree that abortion should be legal for health than for social reasons.*

Appendix tables that organize data for reference use often include more panels and continue onto several pages. For multipage tables, the table number and column headings should be repeated on each page, and the panels should be labeled to specify the topics, units, or contexts that differentiate them.

Table 6.4 Use of Thematic Panels to Organize Data Within a Table

Extent of Agreement With Legal Abortion Under Specified Circumstances, by Gender, U.S., 2000			
"Please tell me whether or not you think it should be possible for a pregnant woman to obtain a legal abortion."	% of Respondents Who Agree or Strongly Agree		
	All	Males	Females
Health reasons			
If the woman's own health is seriously endangered by the pregnancy[a]	88.2	90.0	86.0
If she becomes pregnant as a result of rape.[a]	80.8	82.2	79.3
If there is a strong chance of defect in the baby.[a]	79.8	80.4	79.0
Social or preference reasons			
If she is married and does not want more children	44.4	44.4	44.4
If the woman wants it for any reason	43.5	43.4	43.6
If she is not married and does not want to marry the man	42.5	42.4	42.5

Source: Data from 2000 U.S. General Social Survey (National Opinion Research Center, n.d.).

Note:

a. Gender difference in rate of agreement is statistically significant at $p < .05$.

Panels within tables can be used to do the following:

- Introduce another variable to a comparison
- Present several different types of measures of the same concept
- Organize variables or items into themes

Organizing Data in Tables and Charts

Tables and charts are efficient tools for organizing numbers. Too often, however, authors don't give much thought to the order in which they present data in tables or charts. As a consequence, variables often are listed in an arbitrary order, in a sequence that doesn't correspond with the patterns the authors seek to describe, or in an order that makes it difficult for readers to find the numbers they need for their own calculations. Such lack of thought increases the amount of effort required for readers to make correct use of the information in the table; the level of effort is known as **cognitive load** (Chapter 7).

Cognitive load can be substantially reduced by applying several organizing principles, helping both researchers and their readers see patterns that might have gone unnoticed in a poorly organized table.

Level of Measurement

First, data should be organized to suit the level of measurement of the variables in the table. For ordinal variables, the order in which to arrange items in rows or columns will be obvious: The response categories should be listed in their inherent ranked order, from "Agree strongly" to "Disagree strongly," or from "Never" to "Always," for example, either in ascending or descending order. Information for each of several dates should be listed in chronological order.

Example: Table 6.3 presents data on population for the world as a whole and by level of development at 10-year intervals from 1970 to 2070.

Since eleven different dates are involved, they are organized **chronologically** *in the* **rows***, with the geographic regions labeled in the* **columns***. Rows for the years 2020 through 2070 are shaded to show that those values are projected, with shading explained in a* **note** *after the table. Units are specified in each* **panel***—billions of persons for the upper panel, percentage of the world's population for that year in the lower panel.*

When trend data include only two or three time points, the information can be organized with dates in the columns and topics, groups, or settings in the rows.

Example: Table 6.5 reports the prevalence of stunting (low height-for-age, an indicator of poor long-term nutrition) in each of two survey years for each of eight countries. Additional columns report the percentage change in stunting between those two dates and an average annual percentage change to correct for differences in the number of years between the earlier and later surveys in the countries studied.

The survey years are listed **chronologically** *from left to right in the* **columns***, with the countries organized in* **alphabetical** *order in the* **rows***. Columns for percentage change and average annual percentage change are labeled with those topics and units.* **Footnotes** *to the table provide a detailed definition of stunting, specify survey dates for each country, and explain the calculation of average annual percentage change.*

Although ordinal variables have an inherent numeric order to their categories, nominal variables such as race, region, or political party affiliation do <u>not</u>, so some other criterion must be used to organize their categories. The same issue arises for tables that encompass several different variables, such as health symptoms, barriers to accessing social services, or a series of attitudes about several different social issues, because there is no inherent order in which to organize those items.

Table 6.5 Outcome at Two Time Points, With Measures of Change Over Time

Prevalence and Change in Prevalence of Stunting Among Children Under the Age of 5 Years, Demographic and Health Surveys (DHS)				
	Prevalence of Stunting[a] (%)		Change in Prevalence of Stunting	
	Earlier DHS Survey[b]	Later DHS Survey	% Change	Average Annual % Change[c]
Democratic Republic of Congo (DRC)	45%	43%	4%	0.7%
Ghana	27%	18%	33%	5.6%
Haiti	29%	22%	24%	3.7%
Kenya	35%	26%	26%	5.1%
Liberia	39%	32%	18%	3.0%
Mali	37%	38%	–3%	0.4%
Nigeria	41%	37%	10%	2.0%
Zambia	46%	40%	12%	1.7%

Source: Data from Assaf and Pullum (2016).

Notes:

a. Stunting = height more than two standard deviations below the median height-for-age of the World Health Organization 2007 reference population.

b. Survey years: DRC: 2007 and 2013–2014; Ghana: 2008 and 2014; Haiti: 2005–006 and 2012; Kenya: 2008–2009 and 2014; Liberia: 2007 and 2013; Mali: 2006 and 2012–2013; Nigeria: 2008 and 2013; Zambia: 2007 and 2014.

c. Percentage change between earlier and later DHS surveys, divided by the number of years between survey dates.

Second, the criteria for deciding how to organize data are different when the table or chart will be accompanied by a written interpretation than when the main use is presenting data for researchers to use for their own calculations and presentations.

Organizing Data in Tables to Accompany a Written Description

When writing a narrative description of a pattern from data in a table, the designer of that table should decide in advance on the main point they want to make about the data using one or more of the principles described in this section and in Miller (2007). Two very common objectives are thematic and empirical patterns.

Thematic Criteria

Arranging items or nominal categories into **thematically** related sets can be very effective for assessing patterns because that organization will correspond to themes used to organize the associated narrative. Labels for these themes can then be used to organize data within a table, with related variables or categories reported in consecutive rows or adjacent columns.

Example: In Table 6.4, using panels to separate health and social situations for seeking an abortion reveals important distinctions between attitudes about those situations that would be obscured if they were listed in one indistinguishable block.

Major row headings name the two themes, with the situations that fit each of the themes arranged underneath the pertinent headings. Within each thematic block, items are listed in descending order of percentage agreement (the outcome). The accompanying description could use those thematic phrases to tie together the table and prose, without readers having to look all over the table to find the numbers for the respective themes.

Example: Table 6.6 reports variation in the socioeconomic and demographic characteristics of each of the world's continents.

Major row headings organize the measures by broad topic area (e.g., "Population Change Components"), with consecutive rows used to report related concepts and their units (e.g., births per 1,000 population, followed by total fertility rate). The column headers name the continents. Population is reported in millions (rather than billions) to accommodate the fact that Oceania is much smaller than the other continents. Footnotes define complex measures such as per capita (per person) GNI and PPP.

Table 6.6 Table Organizing Measures Within Several Thematic Areas

Demographic and Income Characteristics by Continent, 2018			Continent				
	World	Africa	Americas	Asia	Europe	Oceania
Population						
2018 Population (millions)	7,621	1,284	1,014	4,536	746	41
2030 Projected population (millions)	8,571	1,714	1,113	4,943	751	50
2050 Projected population (millions)	9,852	2,586	1,220	5,253	730	64
Population change components						
Births per 1,000 population	19	35	15	17	10	17
Total fertility rate[a]	2.4	4.6	2	2.1	1.6	2.3
Deaths per 1,000 population	7	9	7	7	11	7

Demographic and Income Characteristics by Continent, 2018						
				Continent		
	World	Africa	Americas	Asia	Europe	Oceania
Population change components						
Infant mortality rate per 1,000 live births	31	50	13	26	4	21
Rate of natural increase (%)	1.2	2.6	0.8	1.1	−0.1	1
Net migration rate (%)	0	−1	1	0	3	7
Age structure						
Percentage of population < 15 years	26	41	23	24	16	24
Percentage of population 65 years+	9	3	11	8	18	12
Income						
Per capita gross national income[b] (PPP units)[c]	16,927	4,965	31,140	13,714	35,501	33,668

Source: Data from Population Reference Bureau (2018).

Notes:

a. Total fertility rate: The average number of children a woman would have assuming that current age-specific birth rates remain constant throughout her childbearing years (usually considered to be ages 15 to 49).

b. Gross national income (GNI) in purchasing power parity (PPP) divided by midyear population.

c. Purchasing power parity is a way of equalizing the purchasing power of currencies for different countries by taking into account differences in cost of living and inflation; see Chapter 8.

Empirical Order

An important objective in quantitative research often is showing which variables or nominal categories have the highest and the lowest values and where other items fall in the overall ranking. To support such a description, the associated tables should organize the items in ascending or descending **empirical order** of numeric values or frequency. The *U.S. News and World Report* (2019) ratings of colleges lists them from highest to lowest overall rating and for specific types of schools (e.g., national universities, liberal arts colleges). Likewise, Yelp ratings of things to do in a particular city are listed in descending numeric order.

> **Thematic** or **theoretical criteria** can identify ways in which categories or items are conceptually similar to one another. **Empirical order** refers to the observed sequence of values. A table organized in empirical order will list the values in either **ascending** or **descending** numeric order of one of the measures reported in the table.

Organizing Variables by Their Role in an Analysis

Another useful consideration for organizing tables is that most quantitative research is about relationships between two or three <u>main</u> variables, with other variables playing less central roles. Ideally, the authors will discuss the key variables first; thus, those variables should be presented at the top of their tables so that the order of the writing matches the order of the items in the associated table. For instance, a table of descriptive statistics for a study of how educational attainment and gender relate to the rate of violent crime might put the dependent variable (crime rate) in the top row, followed by information on the main independent variables (educational attainment and gender), and then other characteristics considered in their analysis (e.g., other demographic, socioeconomic, or geographic factors).

Organizing Data in Tables Intended for Data Lookup

Some research reports and websites report data mainly for **data lookup**, whereby other researchers are interested in the numbers for their own calculations. For those situations, data should be organized in ways that make it as easy as possible for readers to find the numbers they seek without needing written guidance, using principles such as alphabetical order or the order in which the variables were listed on the data collection form.

Alphabetical Order

For appendix tables or other large data tabulations that are not accompanied by written guidance, **alphabetical order** is often the best way to organize data because readers will be finding their own way through the rows and columns. For such tasks, using a familiar convention helps them find specific information quickly. The daily stock market report of opening, closing, high, and low prices of thousands of stocks is a well-known example.

Order of Items as Collected From Source

The documentation provided with data sets from sites such as the Inter-University Consortium for Political and Social Research (ICPSR) often lists variables in the **order in which the items were collected** on a questionnaire. That order makes it easy for users who are familiar with that data source to find information on the variables in which they are interested.

However, very few substantively meaningful patterns occur alphabetically or in the order that items appear on a questionnaire; thus, those principles are <u>not</u> well-suited to organizing items within tables to be discussed in the text because the order in the table and description will not match.

To help drive home the respective advantages of these approaches, Figures 6.1a, b, and c use three different ways of organizing the same set of data on median income in the 25 largest U.S. metropolitan areas in 2016.

Example: By displaying the metro areas in **descending** order of median income, Figure 6.1a makes it evident which ones have the highest income and by how much, compared with the others in the chart. By organizing the metro areas by **region** and <u>then</u> **empirical order within region**, Figure 6.1b conveys that the West region has the most metro areas in the top 25 and also shows how the regions compare in terms of median income. With the metropolitan areas listed in **alphabetical** order, Figure 6.1c obscures both the regional and rank order patterns.

> Versions 6.1a or 6.1b would be preferred if they are to be <u>accompanied by narrative descriptions</u> of the shape and size of the pattern among metro areas. Which version to use would depend on the main point the author wants to make. Version 6.1c might be preferred for independent **data lookup**. See Chapter 7 for more on the design and interpretation of lollipop charts like Figure 6.1.

Figures 6.1a, b, c   Median Household Income, 25 Largest U.S. Cities, 2016

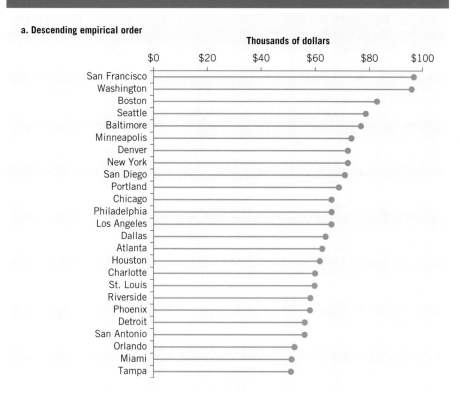

a. Descending empirical order

(Continued)

Figures 6.1a, b, c (Continued)

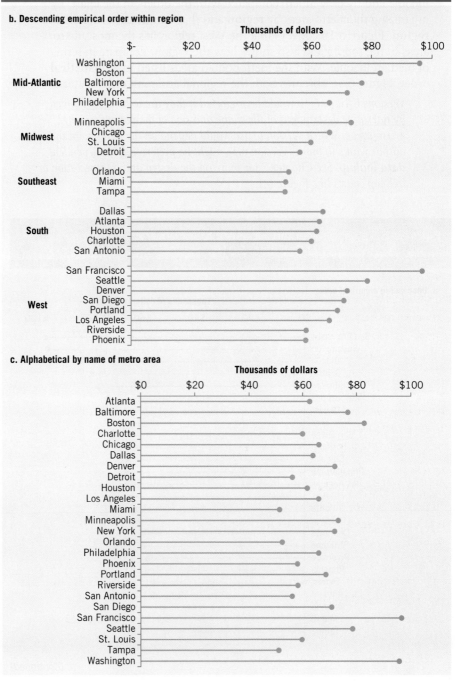

Source: Data from Guzman (2017).

Example: Table 6.7 reports the data in the same order as Figure 6.1c, illustrating the trade-offs between tables and charts for presenting numeric information:

> The **tabular** version makes it easy to look up _precise values_ of median income for one or more metropolitan areas of interest, such as if a reader needs _detailed_ numbers for their own calculations. The table also has space for a more complete name of each metro area than a chart can gracefully accommodate.

Table 6.7   Data Lookup Table in Alphabetical Order

Median Household Income for the 25 largest U.S. Metropolitan Areas, 2016	
Metropolitan Area	Median Household Income (dollars)
Atlanta–Sandy Springs–Roswell GA	$62,613
Baltimore–Columbia–Towson MD	$76,788
Boston–Cambridge–Newton MA	$82,830
Charlotte–Concord–Gastonia NC–SC	$59,979
Chicago–Naperville–Elgin IL	$66,020
Dallas–Fort Worth Arlington TX	$63,812
Denver–Aurora–Lakewood CO	$71,926
Detroit–Warren–Dearborn MI	$56,142
Houston–The Woodlands–Sugar Land TX	$61,708
Los Angeles–Long Beach–Anaheim CA	$65,950
Miami–Fort Lauderdale–West Palm Beach FL	$51,362
Minneapolis–St. Paul–Bloomington MN–WI	$73,231
New York–Newark–Jersey City NY–NJ–PA	$71,897
Orlando–Kissimmee–Sanford FL	$52,385
Philadelphia–Camden–Wilmington PA–NJ–DE–MD	$65,996
Phoenix–Mesa–Scottsdale AZ	$58,075
Portland–Vancouver–Hillsboro OR–WA	$68,676
Riverside–San Bernadino–Ontario CA	$58,236
San Antonio–New Braunfels TX	$56,105
San Diego–Carslbad CA	$70,824
San Francisco–Oakland–Hayward CA	$96,677
Seattle–Tacoma–Bellevue WA	$78,612
St. Louis MO–IL	$59,780
Tampa–St. Petersburg–Clearwater FL	$51,115
Washington–Arlington–Alexandria DC–VA–MD–WV	$95,843

Source: Data from Guzman (2017).

*On the other hand, the **chart** version quickly conveys the <u>direction and magnitude</u> of differences between metro areas' median incomes without readers having to do a lot of mental calculations to see those patterns. However, the chart version makes it hard to discern exact numeric values for each point.*

Multiple Criteria for Organizing Tables

For tables with more than a few rows or columns of numbers, a combination of approaches may be useful for organizing the data. Items might be grouped into thematic blocks, then arranged <u>within</u> those blocks in order of descending frequency or other empirical consideration.

> <u>Example</u>: In a packaging insert for a medication, side effects are classified first into (a) life-threatening ones and (b) less urgent symptoms, then from highest to lowest prevalence <u>within</u> each of those categories.
>
> *With that combination of **theoretical** and **empirical** organization, people can rapidly figure out whether they need to dial 911 if they are experiencing one of those symptoms—the critical question for readers of that informational insert.*

Sometimes it makes sense to apply the same organizing principle sequentially, such as identifying major themes and then minor themes within them. The U.S. Consumer Expenditure Survey organizes expenditures into "necessities" and "non-necessities." Among the necessity categories of consumer expenditures are items related to housing, food, and apparel, which are further divided into minor categories (such as shelter and utilities within the housing category).

A table organized into several thematically or empirically similar groups of items often uses alphabetical order to determine the order of items <u>within</u> those groups. For instance, information on the world's countries is frequently organized by continent, by regions within each continent, and in alphabetical order within those regions. Alphabetical order within conceptual or empirical groupings is also sometimes used if several items have the same value as the numbers reported in the table (such as number of cases or average value).

Tables should be **well-organized**

- Following standard conventions for using row and column headings, the title, and notes

- Organizing the variables and their categories in an intentionally chosen manner that suits the **levels of measurement** of the variables and the **likely use of the data by the intended audiences**

---

o Use thematic or empirical criteria to **coordinate with a written description** of that table (Chapter 14)

o Use alphabetical or order-of-data collection for **tables to be used independently by readers** to look up data for their own calculations or writing

Organizing Data in Three-Way Tables

Three-way tables are used to present data on a relationship between three variables, such as how a dependent variable varies according to values of two independent variables together. For three-way tables, researchers should consider the major points to be made by the data to help identify the most effective way to organize the variables in that table. Options include separate panels for each two-way comparison or the use of column spanners to organize two of the variables in the columns. We will learn more about how to interpret data from three-way tables in Chapters 10 and 13.

Example: Tables 6.8a and 6.8b are two variants of a table to present the same migration statistics for each of the four U.S. regions at three "mobility periods" spaced 10 years apart. In Table 6.8a, the fact that the Northeast region had net population losses from internal migration in each of the three periods is immediately evident because adjacent columns in the NE section all have bolded negative migration figures. Likewise, the overall gains in each of the three other regions in most years are easy to see. Those patterns are harder to identify in Table 6.8b because readers must look **across** the clustered columns to find the data for a given region in each year.

On the other hand, Table 6.8b makes it easier to notice which regions gained population and which ones lost population due to internal migration (to other U.S. regions) within a mobility period. For instance, in 2017–2018, the South was the only region to grow due to internal migration, as each of the other regions had negative net internal migration.

*Table 6.8 is a **three-way table** because it shows the relationship between three variables: region, date, and migration. The **row labels** are identical in the two versions of the table, identifying the various dimensions of migration (**dependent variables**: in- and out-, internal, and from abroad), and using bold numbers to convey which of the net flow statistics are statistically significant at $p < .10$; see Chapter 13.*

The difference between the two versions of Table 6.8 is in terms of how they <u>organize the two independent variables</u> (period and region),

Table 6.8a-b Two Variants of Three-Way Table With Column Spanners

a. In-Migration, Out-Migration, Net Migration, and Movers From Abroad, by Region and Mobility Period, United States, 1998–2018

Thousands of Persons

Region and Mobility Period

Type of migration	Northeast			Midwest			South			West		
	1997–1998	2008–2009	2017–18	1997–1998	2008–2009	2017–2018	1997–1998	2008–2009	2017–2018	1997–1998	2008–2009	2017–2018
In-migrants	504	409	243	873	464	518	1,335	1,038	1,227	660	569	566
Out-migrants	708	531	595	753	560	555	1,105	773	714	806	614	689
Net internal migration	−203ᵃ	−123	−352	120	−97	−38	230	265	512	−146	−45	−122
Movers from abroad	247	162	229	170	242	156	416	344	446	370	398	335
Net migration (incl. abroad)	43	39	−124	290	145	118	646	609	959	224	352	212

b. In-Migration, Out-Migration, Net Migration, and Movers From Abroad by Mobility Period and Region, United States, 1998–2018

Thousands of Persons

Region and Mobility Period[b]

Type of migration	1997–1998				1997–1998				1997–1998			
	NE	MW	S	W	NE	MW	S	W	NE	MW	S	W
In-migrants	504	873	1,335	660	409	464	1,038	569	243	518	1227	566
Out-migrants	708	753	1,105	806	531	560	773	614	595	555	714	689
Net internal migration	−203	120	230	−146	−123	−97	265	−45	−352	−38	512	−122
Movers from abroad	247	170	416	370	162	242	344	398	229	156	446	335
Net migration (incl. abroad)	43	290	646	224	39	145	609	352	−124	118	959	212

Source: Data from U.S. Census Bureau (2018a).

Notes:

a. **Bolded numbers** indicate net flow is statistically significantly different from zero at the 90% confidence level. See Chapter 13 for explanation of statistical significance.

b. NE: Northeast; MW: Midwest; S: South; W: West.

*which is communicated using the **column spanners**. Table 6.8a groups the columns by mobility period <u>within each region</u>, with four column spanners—one for each region—covering the three mobility periods. Table 6.8b groups the columns by region <u>within each mobility period</u>, with three column spanners—one for each mobility period—each encompassing the four regions. With 12 columns of numbers, column labels are abbreviated: the dates in Table 6.8a and the regions in Table 6.8b; see **footnote** to table.*

Reading Data From Tables

If the conventions described earlier in this chapter were followed when a table was designed, readers should be able to identify the topic, context, units, categories, and data source for every number in that table based on its title, row and column headings, and notes.

- The title, row, and column labels identify the topic and purpose of the table.

- The "by" convention often differentiates the independent variable(s) from the dependent variable(s).

- The indenting structure of row headings and the umbrella structure of column spanners clarify how categories make up a whole.

- The meaning of a number in the interior cells is conveyed by the phrases and units or category names in the associated row and column labels.

- The title, major row headings, and column spanners identify themes or other attributes used to organize items within the table.

- Notes provide definitions, spell out acronyms, and name the data source(s).

Percentaging of Tables

Another key skill in reading data from tables is being able to determine the direction in which percentages reported in that table were calculated. Using terminology we will learn in Chapter 9, readers need to know "percentage of what?" Sometimes that information is conveyed in a title or in row or column labels; other times, it can be determined by looking closely at the numbers in the table. Although "percentage of what?" might sound technical and trivial, it is extremely important for interpreting a percentage, as each of those possible ways of calculating a percentage has a completely different interpretation and answers a completely distinct question.

Direction of Percentage Calculations

A common type of table is one that reports how cases are distributed across two categorical variables <u>together</u>—called a **cross-tabulation** as we will learn in Chapter 10. In cross-tabulations, there are several possible definitions of the whole against which some part is being compared: the total within a <u>row</u>, the total within a <u>column</u>, or the total for the <u>overall table</u>.

<u>Example</u>: The 12.8 million children in the United States who were poor in 2017 can be interpreted in several ways: Depending on the question the table is intended to address, it might report the percentage of the <u>total population</u> that is in each of the six possible poverty/age group combinations (Table 6.9a), the percentage of <u>each poverty category</u> that falls into each age group (Table 6.9b), or the percentage of <u>each age group</u> that is poor (Table 6.9c).

In each of the subtables 6.9a, b, and c, the **numerator** *of the percentage calculation is the* **same** *12.8 million poor children (blue-bordered cell). However, the* **denominators** *("percentage of what?") are different for each of those subtables (dark gray fill, blue bordered cells). Blue arrows in each subtable indicate the direction in which the percentage was calculated. With different denominator values, the calculated percentages (dashed blue border, light gray fill) differ for each of the three ways of presenting the association between poverty status and age group:*

- *Percentage of the* **table total** *(Table 6.9a): 12.8 million poor children out of 322.5 million people of all ages and poverty statuses = 4.0%.* <u>*Meaning*</u>*: The 12.8 million poor children comprise 4.0% of the total U.S. population.*

- *Percentage of the* **column** *("*<u>*down*</u> *the column"; Table 6.9b): 12.8 million poor children out of 39.7 million poor people of all ages = 32.3%.*

- *Percentage of the* **row** *("*<u>*across*</u> *the row"; Table 6.9c): 12.8 million poor children out of 73.4 million children = 17.5%.*

In 2017, slightly less than one-third of the 39.7 million poor people in the United States were children (<18 years old; Table 6.9b), but 17.5% of the total 73.4 million children were poor (Table 6.9c).

These values have <u>*completely different meanings*</u>*, so the table* **titles** *help to differentiate their meanings: Table 6.9b is titled "Age Distribution* <u>*by*</u> *Poverty Status," whereas Table 6.9c is titled "Poverty Rate* <u>*by*</u> *Age Group." The* **"by" variable** *in each* **title** *conveys the whole to which the parts are compared: within poverty status in 6.9b, and within age group in 6.9c. Table 6.9a has no "by" variable in the title, so the percentages refer to a group's share of the entire population.*

Three Versions of the Same Cross-Tabulation: (a) Joint Distribution, (b) Composition Within Subgroups, (c) Rates of Occurrence Within Subgroups

a. Age Group and Poverty, United States, 2017

Age Group (years)	Millions of Persons (% of total population)		
	Poor	Nonpoor	Total
<18	12.8	60.5	73.4
	(4.0%)	(18.8%)	(22.7%)
18–64	22.2	175.9	198.1
	(6.9%)	(54.5%)	(61.4%)
65+	4.7	46.4	51.1
	(1.5%)	(14.4%)	(15.8%)
All ages	39.7	282.9	322.5
	(12.3%)	(87.7%)	(100.0%)

b. Age Distribution (%) by Poverty Status, United States, 2017

Age Group (years)	Poor		Nonpoor		Total	
	Population (millions)	% of All Poor	Population (millions)	% of All Nonpoor	Population (millions)	% of Total Pop.
<18	12.8	32.3%	60.5	21.4%	73.4	22.7%
18–64	22.2	55.9%	175.9	62.2%	198.1	61.4%
65+	4.7	11.8%	46.4	16.4%	51.1	15.8%
All ages	39.7	100.0%	282.9	100.0%	322.5	100.0%

c. Poverty Rates (%) by Age Group, United States, 2017

Age Group (years)	# Poor (millions)	Population (millions)	% Poor Within Age Group
<18	12.8	73.4	17.5%
18–64	22.2	198.1	11.2%
65+	4.7	51.1	9.2%
All ages	39.7	322.5	12.3%

Source: Data from Fontenot et al. (2018).

Percentages for Two-Category Variables

A specific situation in which "percentage of what" arises is when reporting results for categorical dependent variables that have <u>exactly two</u> categories (known as **dichotomous**, meaning "two categories"). Examples include "yes/no" variables (such as whether a case has a characteristic of interest), holds a particular attitude (e.g., <u>agrees</u> that abortion should be legal; Table 6.4), or is on one side of a numeric threshold (e.g., has income <u>below</u> the poverty level; Table 6.9c)

A **cross-tabulation** displays how values of two categorical variables are jointly distributed. **Dichotomous** variables are those that have exactly two categories. Either nominal or ordinal variables can be dichotomous.

When reporting information on dichotomous dependent variables, a table needs to present only the percentage of the sample that falls into <u>one</u> category of interest because the percentage <u>without</u> that characteristic is by definition 100% minus the percentage <u>with</u> that trait.

Table 6.10   Reporting Percentages for a Dichotomous Dependent Variable

Voter Participation Rates in Most Recent Nationwide Elections, Selected Countries	
Country	Voter Participation Rate (% of voting-age population)
Northern America	
Canada (2015)[a]	62.1
United States (2016)	55.7
Europe	
Scandinavia	
Denmark (2015)	80.3
Netherlands (2017)	77.3
Norway (2017)	70.6
Sweden (2014)	82.6
Britain	
Ireland (2016)	58.0
U.K. (2017)	63.3

Voter Participation Rates in Most Recent Nationwide Elections, Selected Countries	
Country	Voter Participation Rate (% of voting-age population)
Europe	
Western Europe	
Austria (2017)	68.8
Belgium (2014)	87.2
France (2017)	67.9
Germany (2017)	69.1
Luxembourg (2013)	55.1
Switzerland (2015)	38.6
Eastern Europe	
Czech Republic (2018)	63.4
Estonia (2015)	56.8
Latvia (2014)	51.7
Poland (2015)	53.8
Slovakia (2016)	59.4
Southern Europe	
Italy (2018)	65.3
Spain (2016)	61.2
Oceania	
Australia (2016)	79.0
New Zealand (2017)	75.7

Source: Data from DeSilver (2018).

Note:

a. Year of most recent nationwide election in parentheses.

Example: Table 6.10 reports the percentage of the voting-age population in each country that voted in their most recent national election.

*"Percentage of what" (voting-age population) is clearly conveyed in the column heading. The **percentage of** voting-aged persons who did not vote is (100% – the percentage who did vote). As a consequence, the table can omit the percentage who did not vote, saving an entire column of numbers while providing the information needed to compare voting patterns across countries and reducing cognitive load in the process.*

*The table reports the **percentage of the voting-age population** in each country (**row**) that voted, not the **percentage of all voters** who were from each country (**column**). Check: the sum of the reported percentages for all of the countries vastly exceeds 100%!*

The direction in which a percentage is calculated in a table affects the way that number is interpreted. To figure out which way a table was percentaged:

- Identify the "by" variable in a table title (e.g., "by race" should mean that the percentages are <u>within</u> each racial group).

- Look for a "total" row or column showing 100%. If a column shows that the total across that row = 100% (as in Table 6.3b), the percentages were calculated across each row (horizontally within the table). If a row shows that the total down the column = 100% (as in Table 6.9b), the percentages were calculated down in each column (vertically).

- Lacking that information, use the count (number of cases) in an interior cell and in the associated row and column to figure out which direction of calculation matches the percentage reported in the cell.

Considerations for Creating Tables

When you are responsible for creating tables, there are a few additional design issues to consider.

Portrait Versus Landscape Layout

Tables can be laid out either in **landscape** (with the long dimension horizontal, like Table 6.1 or Table 6.8), or **portrait** (with the long dimension of the page vertical, like Tables 6.7 or 6.10). Landscape layout is often preferred for slides or chartbooks, to match page layout for the rest of the document. Portrait layout is usually preferred for print documents and web pages or other social media because the accompanying text pages are usually vertical.

A key factor when planning a table is making sure the layout will accommodate the number of rows and columns needed to hold the needed set of numbers and the associated labels in a type size that is actually readable! Unless your column labels and the numbers in the associated interior cells are very narrow, four to five columns are the most that can fit in a portrait layout, and up to 12 narrow columns are the maximum that a landscape layout can accommodate (e.g., Table 6.8). If you must present information on a dozen or more values (e.g., categories or variables), use a portrait layout with many rows. There is no fixed rule that determines which variable must go in the rows, so assess various arrangements of variables in the rows and columns.

Which variable to put in the rows is determined by the number of variables (e.g., dimensions of migration), measures (e.g., count, percentage distribution, rate), or categories (countries or continents), <u>not</u> the concept being measured.

> <u>Example</u>: Suppose you are to design a table showing characteristics or outcomes of geographic entities. Names of the six populated <u>continents</u> easily fit within the columns of a landscape table, whereas the fifty United <u>States</u> are almost always listed in the rows because a fifty-column table would require several pages to fit all the data.

Alignment

There are standard ways to align the contents of different table components:

- **Left-justify** row labels, then use indenting to show subgroups.

- **Center** labels above the column to which they pertain, and center column spanners over the range of columns to which they apply.

- In the **interior cells** where numbers are reported, use **decimal alignment** to line up the numbers properly within each column, especially if symbols are used in some but not all rows (such as conveying statistical significance or note callouts). **Right alignment** can also work <u>if</u> all numbers in that column have a consistent number of decimal places and no symbols are needed.

Digits and Decimal Places

Many researchers report numbers with far more numerals than are necessary, cluttering up the table and overwhelming their readers. Just because the calculator or software used to do the calculation displays the result with six (or more) decimal places, doesn't mean they are either accurate or useful. Instead, researchers should consider the minimum number of digits and decimal places needed to accomplish the purpose of the table. The number of digits and decimal places should also be consistent with the type of measure (e.g., rate, percentage) and scale of measurement of the variables summarized in that table.

> <u>Example</u>: Table 6.11 is a <u>badly designed</u> version of a table intended to compare distributions across marital statuses for males and females. The upper panel of Table 6.11a reports that in 2015, an estimated 16,142,413 females aged 15 or older in the U.S. were divorced, and the lower panel reports that is a proportion of 0.121242 out of all females in that age group.
>
> *Table 6.11a reports the number of persons in each cell to the nearest individual person, while the lower panel shows the proportion of each*

a. Detailed Enumeration, Too Many Digits and Decimal Places

Marital Status by Gender, Persons Aged 15 Years or Older, United States, 2015

	Number of Persons					
	Currently Married	Currently Not Married				All Marital Statuses
		Never married	Separated	Divorced	Widowed	
Male	63,278,073	46,030,989	2,171,609	12,069,824	3,299,927	126,850,422
Female	61,992,726	40,056,147	3,086,556	16,142,413	11,864,395	133,142,237
All	125,270,799	86,087,136	5,258,165	28,212,237	15,164,322	259,992,659

	Proportion of Gender					
	Currently Married	Currently Not Married				All Marital Statuses
		Never married	Separated	Divorced	Widowed	
Male	0.498840	0.362876	0.017119	0.095150	0.026014	1.000000
Female	0.465613	0.300852	0.023182	0.121242	0.089111	1.000000
All	0.481824	0.331114	0.020224	0.108512	0.058326	1.000000

b. Rounded to Higher Scale With Fewer Digits and Decimal Places

Marital Status by Gender, Persons Aged 15 Years or Older, United States, 2015

	Number of Persons (millions)					
	Currently Married	Currently Not Married				All marital Statuses
		Never married	Separated	Divorced	Widowed	
Male	63.3	46.0	2.2	12.1	3.3	126.9
Female	62.0	40.1	3.1	16.1	11.9	133.1
All	125.3	86.1	5.3	28.2	15.2	260.0

	Percentage of Gender					
	Currently Married	Currently Not Married				All Marital Statuses
		Never married	Separated	Divorced	Widowed	
Male	49.9%	36.3%	1.7%	9.5%	2.6%	100.0%
Female	46.6%	30.1%	2.3%	12.1%	8.9%	100.0%
All	48.2%	33.1%	2.0%	10.9%	5.8%	100.0%

Source: Data from U.S. Census Bureau (2018c).

*gender that falls into each marital status, reported to <u>six</u> **decimal places**. The sheer number of **digits** in the table is not only visually overwhelming but also provides far more detail than is needed <u>to complement a description of the pattern</u>. Although people using the table as a data source for their own calculations might need that level of <u>detail</u> for population counts, no one needs that many **decimal places** for proportions! Furthermore, because the values are estimates based on a sample survey, reporting to the nearest individual person is actually misleading about the <u>precision</u> of the estimate[1].*

Table 6.11b is an improved version of the same table. The upper panel reports that in 2015 an estimated 16.1 million females aged 15 or older in the U.S. were divorced, and the lower panel conveys that that is 12.1% of all females in that age group. Among males, 12.1 million are divorced, which is 9.5% of males in that age group.

*In the accompanying **text**, the population counts would be rounded to the nearest million and the proportions converted into percentages, rounded to the nearest 10th of a percentage point. Why not report them in the **table** to the <u>same</u> **scale**, making them much easier to find and understand?*

See Miller (2015), Chapter 4, for more criteria for choosing an appropriate number of digits and decimal places for the topic and type of measure. For more guidelines on how to design and format tables, see Miller (2015), Chapter 6, or Nicol and Pexman (2010).

---

[1]In the Census Bureau table presenting these data, the population counts for each subgroup are associated with a margin of error because they were estimated from a sample. See Chapter 13 for an explanation of margin of error.

TERMS AND CONCEPTS

HIGHLIGHTS

- Designing and interpreting **tables** of quantitative information are fundamental skills for making sense of numbers.

- Each table should be **focused, self-contained**, and **organized** to suit the **objective** and **audience** of that specific table, bearing in mind that tables are best when **detailed numeric values** are needed.

- **Titles**, **row-** and **column labels**, **indenting**, **column structure**, and **footnotes** of a well-designed table provide all the information needed to interpret the numbers in that table, including the **topic, W's, units**, and **categories** for every **variable** in that table.

- For tables to be **accompanied by a written description**, nominal variables or multiple items should be organized **thematically** and/or **empirically** to coordinate well with the order of that description.

- For tables to be used **independently** by people seeking data for their own calculations or presentations, **alphabetical** order or a **standard sequence for that data set** are better ways to organize the numeric information.

- To correctly interpret percentages from a table, identify **in which direction percentages were calculated**.

- Considerations for designing tables include page **layout, alignment** of elements within a table, and how many **digits** and **decimal places** to report for different table usages.

- The decision about whether to use a **portrait** or **landscape** table **layout** depends on **the number of variables** to be presented as well as their **levels of measurement**.

RECOMMENDED READINGS

Nicol, A. A. M., & Pexman, P. (2010). *Presenting your findings: A practical guide for creating tables* (6th ed.). American Psychological Association.

Miller, J. E. (2015). *The Chicago guide to writing about numbers* (2nd ed.). University of Chicago Press. Chapter 6.

Miller, J. E. 2007. Organizing data in tables and charts: Different criteria for different tasks. *Teaching Statistics, 29*(3), 98–101. http://dx.doi.org/10.1111/j.1467-9639.2007.00275.x

EXERCISES

Individual Exercises

Quantitative Reasoning in Everyday Life

1. On a website or in a newspaper article or blog about popular culture, sports, the weather, or other "everyday" topic, find a chart that shows how values of one variable (e.g., characteristic, attitude, or behavior) are distributed. Sketch a table to present the same information, including complete title, row and column labels, and notes.

2. Find a newspaper or magazine article that includes one or more tables of numeric information. (a) Evaluate whether the tables in that article can stand alone without the text, using the guidelines in this chapter. (b) Suggest ways to improve labeling and layout. (c) Using information in the article, revise the table to correct those errors.

Interpreting Research

3. In a journal article from your field, find a table that presents the numeric relationship between a nominal independent variable with three or more categories and an outcome variable. (a) Identify the principle used to organize the categories of the nominal variable in the rows or columns of the table, referring to the criteria in this chapter. (b) Critique whether that organization coordinates with the associated narrative. (c) If the order of categories is not consistent with the narrative, describe how you would revise the organization of the categories in the table.

4. On the Bureau of Labor Statistics website (https://www.bls.gov/opub/reports/), find a report that includes a table in which percentages are reported. (a) Identify in which direction the table was percentaged and (b) specify how you confirmed whether your answer is correct.

Communicating Research

5. Pick a topic involving a two-category (e.g., yes/no) dependent variable and a nominal independent variable with more than two categories. (a) Design a table shell (without numbers filled in) to show the relationship between those two variables, following the guidelines in this chapter for designing effective tables. Include a complete, specific (i) title, (ii) row- and (iii) column labels. (b) Indicate in which direction you would percentage the table and why, given the roles of the variables in the analysis. (c) Specify which organizing principle(s) you would use to display the categories of the independent variable in the rows, referring to the criteria in this chapter. (d) Justify your choice of an organizing principle, with reference to the specific objectives of your analysis.

6. Design a table to report the data in Figure 7.9, following the guidelines in this chapter.

7. Design a table to report the data in Figure 7.12, following the guidelines in this chapter.

Group Exercises

Interpreting Research

8. On the New York Times Tracking the Global Epidemic site https://www.nytimes.com/ interactive/2020/world/coronavirus-maps .html?action=click&module=Spotlight &pgtype=Homepage scroll down to the table presenting information on number of cases, prevalence (cases per 100,000 people), number of deaths, and death rates. (a) Sort the data in descending order within a column by clicking on the column heading; clicking on the column heading a second time will sort in ascending order. Repeat for each of the columns of numbers. (b) As a group, agree on a country to focus on, then look up how the rank of that country changes based on (i) which criterion (column) you use and (ii) whether you sort the values in ascending or descending numeric order. (c) Identify a question for which each of those organizing principles (topic and ascending/descending) would provide the most useful perspective on the numeric information.

Communicating Research

9. With a classmate, exchange the table shells you designed in Exercise 5. (a) Review each other's tables for completeness and clarity. (b) Identify the principle they used to organize the nominal independent variable in their table. (c) Discuss whether you agree with that principle, based on the topic, categories, and other criteria in this chapter. If not, suggest and justify a different organizing principle.

10. Repeat the instructions to Exercise, 10 but do so for the table shells you designed in Exercise 6.

Working With Charts and Visualizations

Charts and visualizations are widely used to present research findings, whether showcasing a statistic about the prevalence or impact of a social problem, demonstrating trends over time, showing how subgroups make up a sample or population, or conveying a relationship between two variables. New approaches for presenting numeric data visually have emerged, moving away from what I will term "classic" charts, with their formal titles, axis labels, and legends. Taking their place are **visualizations** (AKA "**vizzes**") formatted with take-home points instead of titles that simply list the W's, increased use of color and shading and selected data labels in place of legends and axis labels, and other revisions to declutter charts and increase their friendliness to nonscientific audiences. Vizzes include modified versions of classic pie-, bar-, and line charts as well as newer forms such as short text presentations of numbers, icon arrays, and other types of diagrams. For an excellent introduction to a wide range of visualizations, see Evergreen (2017).

Innovative visualizations have begun to replace classic charts in infographics, dashboards, chartbooks, and fact sheets, especially in materials for non-research audiences. However, use of classic chart styles persists in journal articles, books, and reports in scientific and academic communities and is likely to do so for some time. In addition, the quantitative research literature that was conducted prior to the visualization revolution continues to provide relevant information for future studies; thus, you must be able to work with classic charts as well as newer viz formats.

In this chapter, I discuss criteria for using charts to present numeric information effectively based on what is known about how people perceive and interpret visual information. I then define the features of charts and visualizations and how to use them well. To prepare you to read and create classic chart styles and newer types of visualizations, I provide and annotate examples of both approaches, pointing out their similarities and differences and how they affect interpretation and design. Finally, I cover some common mistakes in designing charts and how to avoid such errors. In later chapters, I go into more detail about charts and visualizations for specific research and communication tasks.

Charts, otherwise known as **figures** or **graphs**, include pie charts, a variety of "XY" charts (those that include an *x*-axis and a *y*-axis), and maps to display patterns of quantitative information. **Visualizations**, also known as **"vizzes"** (the plural form of **"viz"**), are newer ways of presenting data to reveal trends, outliers, and patterns.

Criteria for Effective Charts and Visualizations

A well-conceived chart or viz provides a good general sense of the level of a numeric value or the shape and size of a pattern, conveying the key point or points that the designer wants to make. Conversely, a poorly designed figure can leave too much of the work for the audience, expecting them to know (or to look up) pertinent comparison values, perform mathematical calculations, and extract the take-home point for themselves. Those tasks are the responsibility of the researcher or person communicating the results, as discussed in Chapters 8 and 9.

As with tables, effective charts or vizzes should be focused, self-contained, and well-organized.

Focused Charts

Many infographics, chartbooks, slide sets, and other documents include several charts or visualizations, each of which addresses one question or task. Each of those vizzes should focus on one aspect of the overall topic and should be designed to communicate the numbers that address the specific task for that viz.

> Example: A report on educational attainment might present information on the number of people who haven't completed high school (one **viz**); how the high school graduation rates vary by gender, race, and family income (a second **chart**); and effectiveness of several different programs to increase graduation rates among high school dropouts (a third **viz**).

In addition, charts should <u>avoid</u> bells and whistles that distract from the main message that is the focus of that chart. Examples later in this chapter show how to avoid such clutter.

Self-Contained Charts

Each chart or visualization should be able to stand alone, designed so that readers can identify its purpose and interpret the data from the titles, labels, and notes <u>alone</u>, without having to turn to other parts of the document or other resources. Thus, each chart should include information on the topic, context, units, category names, data sources, and definitions of abbreviations—in other words, those familiar W's from Chapters 3, 4, and 5.

Well-Organized Charts

To facilitate interpretation of patterns, the items or categories presented in a chart or viz should be organized based on thematic similarity or empirical order (or both) to be consistent with the organization of the accompanying take-home point or prose description. See the section on organizing data in tables in Chapter 6 as well as examples throughout the rest of this chapter for illustration.

Charts and vizzes should have these features:

- **Focused** to communicate the information needed for the specific objective and task

- **Self-contained,** following standard conventions for using axis labels, data labels, and legends so that readers can interpret the meaning of every point on the chart without needing to refer to the text

- **Well-organized,** using **thematic** (theoretical) or **empirical** (ascending or descending numeric order) principles

---

Visual Perception Principles

An understanding of principles that affect how people perceive and interpret visual information provides valuable background for chart design, helping identify graphic design elements that make it as easy as possible for the intended audience to make sense of the numbers. Later in this chapter, I illustrate how good choices about those elements can enhance the effectiveness of a chart and, conversely, ways that poor design choices increase the risk that readers will misinterpret numeric information.

Perceptual Tasks

Charts and visualizations are made up of elements such as dots, lines, curves, and color- or pattern-filled shapes. For readers to make sense of charts, they must be able to correctly read and interpret those elements. A study by Cleveland and McGill (1984) revealed a hierarchy of basic visual perception tasks, from those that people are <u>most</u> likely to understand to those they are <u>least</u> likely to grasp (Figure 7.1). They found that people do best assessing numeric values from the position of dots next to a common scale and length; have more difficulty assessing direction, angle, and area; and perform least well at interpreting numbers based on volume and curvature. Hatching or shading are also challenging for many people to read accurately (Evergreen, 2017).

Those findings suggest that readers will have an easier time interpreting numbers from a dot plot (dots next to an axis scale, as in the "lollipop" display of median income; Figure 6.1) or a bar chart (which combines length and area) than from a pie chart (which combines angle, arc, and area).

Cognitive Load

An important consideration in chart and visualization design is minimizing the effort readers must exert to read and interpret the data from those exhibits. Scientists term the amount of mental effort needed to learn new information **cognitive load** (Nussbaumer Knaflic, 2015). The higher the perceived cognitive load associated with a chart or viz, the less likely readers are to be willing or able to correctly interpret the data in that chart. In other words, if readers anticipate a heavy cognitive load to understand a chart or visualization, they might either skip it or not believe they can comprehend it—clearly <u>not</u> what you are aiming for when you design a visualization!

Thus, a well-designed chart will include only those elements that were strategically identified based on ease of visual perception, taking into consideration the specific audience and objective of that chart. So-called "bells and whistles" such as jazzy font style or unnecessary use of color should be avoided because they create clutter and distract from the main point of the viz. For charts to be displayed as part of an oral presentation or via electronic media, sound and animation should be kept to a minimum, chosen only if they enhance communication rather than adding needless cognitive load.

Figure 7.1 Hierarchy of Chart Design Elements by Ease of Interpretation

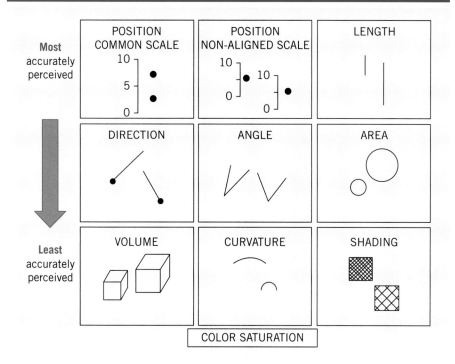

Source: Cleveland, W. S., & McGill, R. (1984). Graphical perception: Theory, Experimentation, and application to the development of graphical methods. *Journal of the American Statistical Association, 79*(387), 531–554. https://doi.org/10.1080/01621459.1984.10478080. Reprinted by permission of American Statistical Association. http://www.amstat.org.

Cognitive load is the amount of mental effort needed to grasp new information.

Example: Consider your own reaction and willingness to try to read (let alone make sense of) the data in Figure 7.2.

> *This viz attempts to convey both detail and shape of the pattern, leading to an extremely cluttered chart. With seven-digit **labels** on every data point overlapping one another, a long **title** that repeats information on units and countries that is found on the axes and in the legend, and far more **digits** than needed on the **units** of the population variable, readers are likely to ignore the chart and just take the authors' word for whatever points they choose to make! Contrast Figure 7.2 against the*

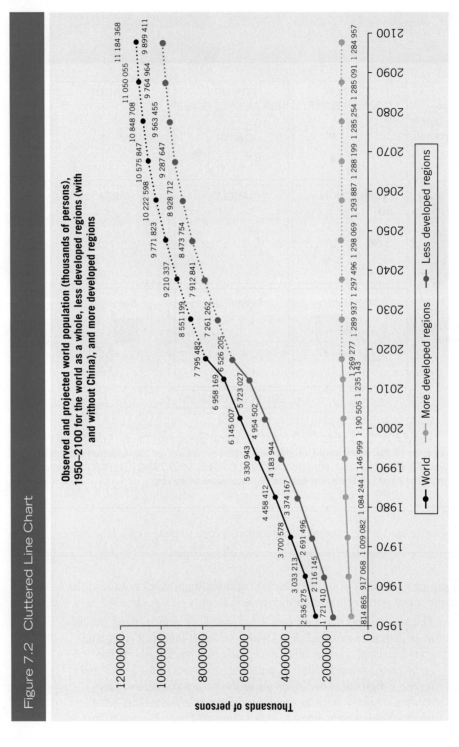

Figure 7.2 Cluttered Line Chart

Observed and projected world population (thousands of persons), 1950–2100 for the world as a whole, less developed regions (with and without China), and more developed regions

Source: Data from United Nations (2017).

improved versions (Figures 7.3a and 7.3b) to see how much it matters to designing with cognitive load in mind.

As you will learn in Chapter 14, if a designer anticipates that their readers will need precise numeric values for more than a few cases or time points, a **table** *is a better choice than a chart for presenting those numbers.*

Perceptions of cognitive load are often Gestalt reactions, both instantaneous—as soon as viewers see a chart—and subconscious (Nussbaumer Knaflic, 2015). There are six Gestalt principles of how people perceive visual images and perceive order from their elements. The most pertinent Gestalt principles for chart design[1] are as follows:

- **Similarity:** Objects that are alike in color, shape, size, or orientation (angle) are perceived to be related or part of a group. This principle suggests that line styles and marker shapes can be used to differentiate geographic areas in a trend chart (as in Figure 7.3), or color applied to distinguish between points, bars, or slices that belong to different groups (Figure 7.16).

- **Connection:** Objects that are physically connected tend to be perceived as more closely related to one another than to objects that are not connected. This principle suggests using lines to connect the points for a given group to show which ones belong to the same series (Figure 7.3).

- **Continuity:** Eyes seek the smoothest path and fill in (create **continuity**) between elements that are not explicitly connected. This principle allows a vertical axis line to be omitted when there is a consistent amount of white space between the data label and the left-hand side of a bar; viewers will detect that all the bars line up at the same vertical starting point (Figure 7.13).

- **Closure:** People tend to mentally fill in gaps between individual elements if they form an overall shape, such as perceiving a circle as a whole even when only segments of a circle are shown. Thus, a border is often not needed around a chart because readers will already perceive it as a single entity.

Cognitive load underscores the importance of minimizing clutter in charts, and the Gestalt principles provide guidance on ways to simplify "classic" designs into visualizations (Evergreen, 2017):

- Writing a short text take-home point title and moving the W's to a footnote

- Including data labels <u>only</u> on carefully selected points related to the main point of the chart

---

[1]Two other Gestalt principles are more pertinent for table design: **Proximity**: Objects that are physically close together tend to be perceived as belonging to part of a group. **Enclosure**: Objects that are enclosed together within a shape are perceived to belong to a group.

- Simplifying or removing axis titles, axis lines, and/or gridlines
- Using color for emphasis
- Replacing the legend with text data labels next to each series, often color coded

These issues are illustrated in examples throughout the rest of this chapter. See Muscatello et al. (2006), Cleveland and McGill (1984), and Evergreen (2017) for more on visual perception and how it affects the interpretation of charts and visualizations.

> Charts and vizzes should be designed to minimize cognitive load, using information about which features are easiest for readers to grasp and Gestalt principles for visual perception. Every element should be intentionally and strategically chosen to foster the audience's understanding of the main point or conclusion of the chart. So-called "bells and whistles" should be avoided because they clutter the chart and distract from its main point.

Anatomy of a Chart or Visualization

Like tables, charts organize information into a predictable format: the axes, labels, color scheme, and other features of a well-designed visualization facilitate an understanding of the numeric patterns being presented. Although "classic" charts and visualizations share some anatomical features such as titles, axes, and data labels, they frequently deploy them in different ways. In addition, some elements that are present in classic charts are omitted from vizzes and vice versa. In this section, I describe and illustrate the objectives and applications of those design elements and explain how they relate to the visual perception principles described above.

Title

As with table titles, the W's (what, where, when, and who) can often be included in the **title** of a chart or viz. The title should also differentiate the topic of a chart from those of other charts and tables in the same document.

Example: In the classic version (Figure 7.3a), the **title** lists all of the **W's**. In the "viz" version (Figure 7.3b), the title states a **take-home point** about the pattern in the chart naming the topic and dates. Both versions include a **subtitle** explaining the meanings of the solid versus the dotted line.

*The **classic version** is the form that has traditionally been required in scientific journals or other research publications, whereas the **viz version** might be used on a website or in a chartbook.*

Figure 7.3a Anatomy of a Chart: Classic Formatting

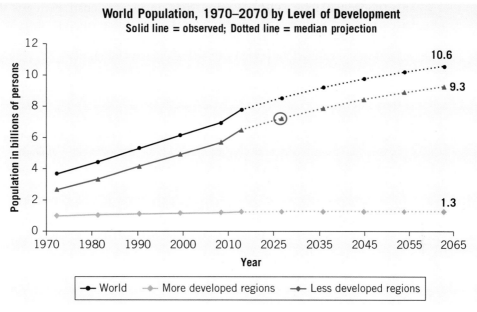

World Population, 1970–2070 by Level of Development
Solid line = observed; Dotted line = median projection

Source: Data from United Nations (2017).

Figure 7.3b Anatomy of a Chart: Visualization Formatting

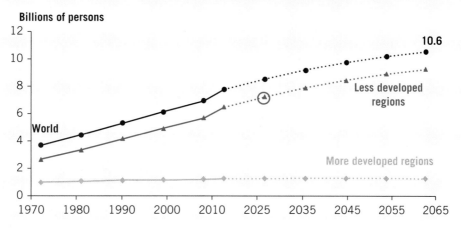

By 2070, the world population is projected to grow to 10.6 billion, with most of the growth in less developed regions
Solid line = observed; Dotted line = median projection

Note: Median projection assumes that the 2015 growth rate continues throughout the projection period.
Source: Data from United Nations (2017).

Axis Titles and Axis Labels

Charts that illustrate the relations between two or more variables usually have an x (horizontal) **axis** and a y (vertical) **axis**. In a classic chart, each axis should have a title that identifies its topic and units of measurement and labels for categories or values along that axis. In visualizations, numeric and text data labels are sometimes substituted for formal **axis titles** and **axis labels**. Axis titles and labels should be brief but informative, using short phrases or single words instead of acronyms whenever possible to minimize the cognitive load needed to make sense of the chart.

> Example: In Figure 7.3a (the "**classic**" version), the x-axis and y-axis titles name the overall concept (year and population, respectively), while the axis labels identify specific values along those axes. In Figure 7.3b (the **viz** version), a text box above the vertical axis specifies the units for that axis.
>
> *In both versions, the scale was changed to report population in billions (Figure 7.3) instead of thousands of persons (Figure 7.2), vastly reducing the number of digits in both the **y-axis labels** and **data labels**.*

Legend

Classic chart designs use **legends** to identify the series or categories of variables that are not labeled elsewhere in the chart. In visualizations, text labels frequently replace legends, reducing the cognitive load needed to interpret which category or series is represented by each line style or bar color.

> Example: In the classic version (Figure 7.3a), the **legend** below the chart specifies which line style corresponds to each of the three geographic regions, whereas in the viz version (Figure 7.3b), a **text series label** sits next to each line, with the **font color** matching the **line color.**

Data Labels

Data labels can be used to report the numeric value, category name, or series name of individual points or entire series. However, they should be used judiciously in order to avoid cluttering the chart.

> Example: In Figure 7.3a, only three data points are labeled, specifying the projected population for the year 2070 for each series. In Figure 7.3b, only one data point is labeled: the overall world population projection for 2070, highlighting the location of the number cited in the take-home-point title.
>
> *See how much easier it is to read Figure 7.3, with its <u>selective</u> use of **numeric data labels** than Figure 7.2? Data labels for the other points*

are not needed because both the classic and viz versions retain the
vertical axis labels *with* **units**, *giving readers the information they need
to identify the approximate values of observed or projected population for
any date and region.*

Notes to Charts

Notes to charts or visualizations can be used to specify W's, provide brief definitions of concepts, cite sources, or spell out acronyms or abbreviations, allowing that information to be omitted from titles, axes, or legends.

> <u>Example</u>: One **note** to Figure 7.3 identifies the **data source** with author and date of the publication; the full citation would be provided elsewhere in the document. A second **note** defines "median projection."

Charts later in this chapter provide other examples of ways that notes can be used to provide essential information for charts and visualizations.

Other Features

Other features such as symbols and annotations can be used to enhance interpretation of the data presented in charts. These features are illustrated throughout this and later chapters. More advanced elements such as reference lines and error bars are explained in Chapters, 8, 10, and 13.

Reading Data From a Chart or Visualization

If all the components of a chart or visualization are designed thoughtfully, that exhibit will be completely self-contained, providing readers with everything they need to make sense of each number in the chart without having to look elsewhere in the document for that information.

> <u>Example</u>: In Figure 7.3, the blue circled point shows that the population of the world's less developed regions projected to be about 7 billion persons by 2030.
>
> *The* **topic** *(population) is conveyed in the* **title**, *the meaning of the dotted line is explained in the* **subtitle**, *the* **date** *on the horizontal axis, the* **units** *for population on the vertical axis, and the region associated with the blue line is identified in the* **legend** *(in Figure 7.3a) or the blue* **text data label** *(in Figure 7.3b).*

The overall layout and labeling of the chart or viz should also foster quick interpretation of the overall patterns in the chart.

Example: Two patterns are immediately apparent from Figure 7.3: First, there is the upward trend in both observed and projected population in the world as a whole and each of the component regions, with much a more pronounced rise in the less-developed than in the more-developed regions. Second, the less-developed regions are much more populous than the more-developed regions in every year shown, with a rising gap by the end of the projection period.

The first pattern can be seen by tracing <u>left to right along each of the colored lines</u>, with the rate of increase depicted by the lines' <u>slopes</u>. The second pattern can be seen by <u>cutting through the four lines from top to bottom</u> to assess rank order of the regions and the vertical distance between the trend lines in any year.

*Either the **classic chart or viz** make it much easier to see the **direction and magnitude** of differences across regions and rates of change across time than a tabular presentation of the same data (Table 6.3). Working from the table, readers would have to do the math themselves to see "which is higher? How much higher?"—imposing unwelcome **cognitive load** to identify the patterns of population difference and change.*

If a chart or visualization is designed well, readers should be able to do the following:

- Determine the topic and context of the data.
    - In a "classic" chart, the title usually includes most of the W's (what, when, where, who).
    - In a visualization, the title is often written as a take-home point that might omit some of the W's, in which case the remaining W's should be included in a footnote to the visualization.
- Identify the units and/or categories for every variable in the exhibit.
- Quickly grasp the key points or patterns that the exhibit is intended to convey.

A warning: Both classic charts and visualizations can be made well or made poorly depending on the thought and care applied by the designer. Neither is inherently better for all audiences and tasks, nor is one type easier to make than the other.

Charts and Visualizations for Specific Tasks

Communicating the results of quantitative research involves several different tasks: presenting one number, showing how the parts make up the whole, comparing two or more numbers, describing trends, conveying how two variables relate to one another, and portraying spatial patterns (Evergreen, 2017). In this section, I review the features and interpretation of common types of charts and visualizations for each of those tasks.

The choice of a visualization type depends on how many variables are involved and their respective levels of measurement: Charts to portray nominal and ordinal (categorical) variables have different attributes and involve different design considerations than those depicting continuous variables.

> The appropriate type of chart or visualization for a particular task is determined by the number of variables involved, their level(s) of measurement, and the objective of the chart.

Presenting One Number

Presenting a single number is a common task in quantitative research, often used to persuade the audience either of how big, frequent, or important something is or, conversely, how small, rare, or otherwise trivial. That number might be a simple count of people or things, an average value, the cost of some phenomenon, a percentage, or a share of a whole. There are several different ways to present one number visually, including formatted text, pie charts, donut charts, and icon arrays. As always, the level of measurement determines which of these options makes sense.

Text Visualization for One Large Number

A **text visualization** uses only words (and a numeral or two!) to convey a fact—no axes, dots, lines, or slices. They can be used for any level of measurement, whether a level or mean for a continuous variable, percentage share of a categorical variable, or other type of numeric fact. The phrasing of a text viz should follow the guidelines from Chapter 14 for reporting one number, including reporting the topic, context, and units or categories. To avoid making the phrase too long, some of the W's can be reported in a footnote with smaller type and subtler color or shade. Figure 7.4 is an example of text formatted to convey one number, using font size and color to emphasize key aspects of the phrase.

Figure 7.4   Text Visualization of One Big Number

In 2018, **1.4 billion** people in
China **traveled home** to celebrate New Year.

Source: Data from Chan (2018).

The next three types of visualizations for presenting one number—**pie charts**, **donut charts**, and **icon arrays**—are best suited for values of nominal variables. They cannot be used for values of continuous variables.

Pie and Donut Charts

A common research task involves presenting information about dichotomous (2-category) categorical outcomes. Examples include whether someone has experienced an event (e.g., gotten married, received a particular medical diagnosis) or has a particular characteristic, attitude, or knowledge. As noted in Chapter 6, the percentage without that characteristic is by definition 100% – % with that trait; therefore, cognitive load can be kept to a minimum by simply presenting the share in only one of those categories. In such situations, the visualization should be designed to emphasize the category of greatest interest to the intended audience.

Example: Policymakers seeking support for their program to reduce homelessness will be more interested in conveying the percentage of their constituents who are homeless than the share who are not.

If, as in Figure 7.5, 10% of the target population is homeless, then by definition, 90% (= 100 – 10) are not homeless, so there is no need to report both of those percentages in the visualization.

Figures 7.5a and b are pie chart and donut visualizations of the same statistic: The percentage of public high school students in New York City who experienced homelessness in 2018.

*A **bright color** is used to fill the **slice of the pie** (or **section of the donut**) that represents the percentage homeless, while the rest of the area is filled in a pale gray shade. The **title** and **data labels** convey the take-home point and report the **W's** and **units**. **Blue text** ties the topic (homelessness) to the **contrast color** in the body of the chart, eliminating the need for a legend. The **pie chart** (Figure 7.5a) reports the key statistic as part of the title and data label, whereas the **donut chart** (Figure 7.5b) reports it in the donut hole. A **footnote** specifies the total number of students to whom that statistic pertains.*

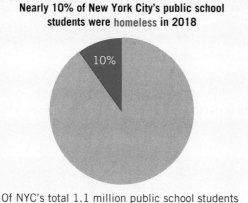

**Nearly 10% of New York City's public school
students were homeless in 2018**

Of NYC's total 1.1 million public school students

Source: Data from Shapiro (2018).

Figure 7.5b Donut Chart Emphasizing One Category of a
Two-Category Variable

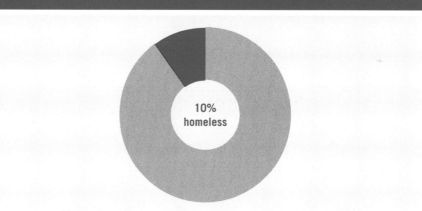

Of New York City's 1.1 million public school students, 2018

Source: Data from Shapiro (2018).

Icon Arrays

An **icon array** is a visually effective way to convey the share or percentage of cases
that falls into a category of interest. An **icon** can be a simple shape (e.g., a circle
or square) or a little picture chosen to illustrate some aspect of the topic. These

shapes are repeated in rows and columns to form an array (grid), with each individual icon representing a specified number of individual cases. Two contrasting colors or shades are used to convey the share of cases that have a particular trait, opinion, or behavior of interest (usually the darker shade or featured color) and the other cases (typically a lighter hue or a grayscale color).

Example: Figure 7.6 uses icons of people to show what percentage of current smokers favor raising the minimum age at which people can buy cigarettes to 21.

Seven of the ten people **icons** *are* <u>*shaded darker*</u> *blue to match the* **font color** *in the accompanying phrase, which also reports* **when, where, and to whom** *the statistic pertains.*

Figure 7.6   Icon Array

In 2015, **7** out of **10** U.S. adult cigarette smokers **favored** making 21 the minimum age of sale.

Source: Data from CDC, based on data from King et al. (2015).

An **icon array** is composed of multiples of small images—often chosen to reflect the topic—arranged in rows and columns. Color or shading is used to show the share of cases that have a characteristic of interest.

For percentages that are close to a multiple of 10, the array could have a total of 10 icons. To convey a more precise value of the percentage, the array might have 100 icons. A note to the figure would indicate how many cases each icon represents, as in Figure 11.3. Other multiples of icons can be used to present "round" shares of a whole, such as the following:

- One of every three cases (three total icons, one shaded a darker tone)
- Two of every five elements (five total icons, two shaded the featured color)

By using three contrasting colors or different shades of the same color family (or three icon styles), an icon array can also be used to show how values are distributed across three categories such as poor, near poor, and nonpoor. More than three colors would be visual overload, so to portray composition across four or more groups, one of the other approaches described in the section "Parts of a Whole" should be used.

Pie charts, **donut charts**, and **icon arrays** can only be used to present distributions of categorical variables. They are best suited for nominal variables, for which there is no inherent order to the categories.

Text visualizations can be used to report numbers based on a variable at any level of measurement.

Parts of a Whole

Another common research task is showing **composition** or **distribution**—how the values of a variable in a sample or population are distributed across the set of possible responses to that variable. Charts designed to show composition display what share of the entire sample (or population) falls into each category of either a nominal or ordinal variable. Put differently, such charts portray how categories of a variable fit together to make up (compose) the whole.

The types of charts or visualizations for displaying parts of a whole depend on the level of measurement of the variable. To display the composition of a categorical variable, options include pie or stacked bar charts. Both are designed using different colors for each response category and showing how those parts (responses) make up the whole. You will learn how to portray distributions for continuous variables in Chapter 10.

Pie Charts

In **pie charts**, the "whole" is represented by a circle, divided into wedges ("pizza slices") that together fill the entire pie. The slices are arranged radially from the center of the circle. For nominal variables with more than two categories, pie charts are best reserved for one of two situations: either when the categories are approximately equal in size or when one category is much larger than the others.

Example: In Figure 7.7a, the three leading coffee roasting companies have roughly the same share of the market, which is easily seen by the similar areas occupied by their respective slices.

The **take-home title** makes that point. No detailed numbers or percentages are needed to convey the overall pattern, keeping the visualization simple and uncluttered.

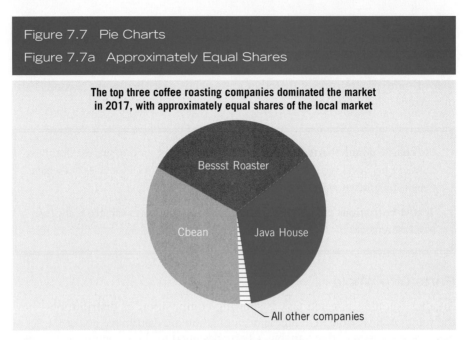

Figure 7.7   Pie Charts

Figure 7.7a   Approximately Equal Shares

The top three coffee roasting companies dominated the market in 2017, with approximately equal shares of the local market

Bessst Roaster

Cbean   Java House

All other companies

Source: Data from CDC, based on data from King et al. (2015).

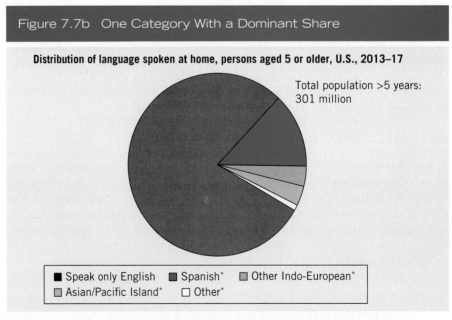

Figure 7.7b   One Category With a Dominant Share

Distribution of language spoken at home, persons aged 5 or older, U.S., 2013–17

Total population >5 years: 301 million

■ Speak only English   ■ Spanish*   ▨ Other Indo-European*
▨ Asian/Pacific Island*   ☐ Other*

*Includes those who speak English "very well" and "less than very well."

Source: Data from CDC, based on data from King et al. (2015).

Example: In Figure 7.7b, the dominance of English-only speakers in the United States is conveyed by the fact that its slice is much larger than the others. The second-place position of Spanish as a language spoken at home by U.S. residents is also apparent.

> The **slices of the pie** pie conveys the relative shares of each language, and a **text box** reports the overall <u>size of the population</u> to which those data pertain. A **footnote** explains the meaning of the categories. This chart would work well if the <u>main point was the dominance</u> of English-only speakers, and that the next most common language in the U.S. is Spanish. If the intended audience is expected to want to know the <u>relative sizes of several categories</u>, a viz that more clearly displays rank order and value for each of those categories, such as a **bar** or **lollipop chart** (below) would be preferable.

As discussed in the section "Presenting One Number," if a variable has only two categories, a text viz, icon array, or donut chart are more effective ways to focus on the share contributed by the category of main interest.

Stacked Bar Charts

Stacked bar charts are another way to show how the values of a multicategory variable fit together to compose the whole. As discussed in Chapter 6, categories of nominal variables should be organized either thematically or empirically so that the display will coordinate with the associated written description. Categories of an ordinal variable, such as Likert items, should be arranged in their natural order.

Example: The top horizontal bar in Figure 7.8 shows that in 2018, of U.S. adults who said they used Facebook, 51% used it "several times a day," 23% "about once day," and 26% "less often."

> Each **response category** of the **ordinal** variable (social media use) is represented by a **different slice color** (explained in the legend), with the **categories** organized left to right from highest to lowest level of use. The lengths of the bar segments convey the frequency of that response. The three response categories total 100%: in this case, everyone who said they used Facebook.

> Figure 7.8 consists of **five** sets of **stacked bars**, each showing the distribution of how often users visited <u>one</u> particular social media platform. See additional discussion under "Multiple Stacked Bars."

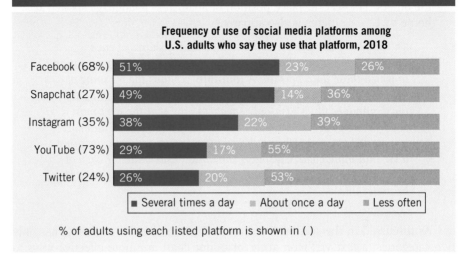

Figure 7.8   Stacked Bar Chart of Responses to Ordinal Items

Frequency of use of social media platforms among
U.S. adults who say they use that platform, 2018

Platform	Several times a day	About once a day	Less often
Facebook (68%)	51%	23%	26%
Snapchat (27%)	49%	14%	36%
Instagram (35%)	38%	22%	39%
YouTube (73%)	29%	17%	55%
Twitter (24%)	26%	20%	53%

■ Several times a day   ■ About once a day   ■ Less often

% of adults using each listed platform is shown in ( )

Source: Data from Smith and Anderson (2018).

Comparing Two or More Numbers

The charts and visualizations in this section are designed to portray both the direction and magnitude of a **bivariate association** between an independent and a dependent variable, which is a very common objective of quantitative research projects. By now, you won't be surprised to hear that the choice of a chart type depends on the levels of measurement of the two variables. Research has shown that bar charts lead readers to perceive a comparison of outcomes between distinct <u>groups or categories</u> of an independent variable, whereas line charts visually suggest <u>trends</u> (changes in the value of a dependent variable across values of a <u>continuous</u> independent variable) (Zacks & Tversky, 1999).

Categorical Independent Variables

As discussed earlier in this chapter, the length of a bar or position of dots next to a scale (axis) are easy for most readers to interpret correctly. The most common ways of portraying associations between one categorical independent and either a continuous or categorical dependent variable—simple bar charts and lollipop charts—include combinations of those elements.

Simple bar charts. In a **bar chart**, the length of each bar depicts the level of the outcome (dependent variable) for the category (value of the independent variable) represented by that bar.

Figure 7.9   Simple Bar Chart

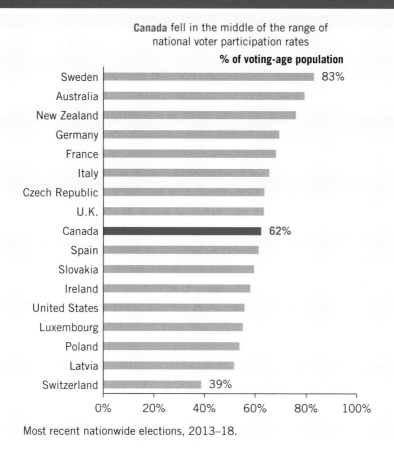

Canada fell in the middle of the range of national voter participation rates

Most recent nationwide elections, 2013–18.

Source: Data from DeSilver (2018).

Example: Canada's position in the middle of the range of voter participation rates in recent nationwide elections is clearly portrayed in Figure 7.9. The wide range of voter participation rates across countries is also immediately apparent: from 83% of the voting-age population (VAP) in Sweden (top bar) to only 39% of the VAP in Switzerland (bottom bar).

*The **lengths of the bars** convey the voter participation rate (**dependent variable**) for each country (**category** of the **nominal independent variable**), with countries organized in **descending empirical order** of voter participation rates because that order is a key point of the chart. This viz is designed to focus on Canada, communicated via the **take-home point** about its rank order and blue-**colored bar** and **text** to emphasize* *that country. A classic chart version would show all the bars in the same color and replace the title with generic wording listing the topic and W's.*

Lollipop charts. A **lollipop chart** is a variation of a bar chart that can be used to de-clutter a chart when comparing values of an outcome for an independent variable with many categories. The length of each lollipop "stem" (line) and position of its "head" (dot) conveys the value of the dependent variable for that category of the independent variable.

> Example: In Figure 6.1, the distance from the vertical axis to the lollipop "heads" presents median income (continuous dependent variable) for each of 25 cities (nominal independent variable).
>
> *That viz communicates the same information as a bar chart but with <u>less</u> **visual weight** because thin **lollipop stems** replace the thicker **bars** from a classic bar chart.*

Continuous Independent Variables

Charts and vizzes for associations involving quantitative independent and dependent variables include trend charts and scatterplots.

Trend charts. **Trend charts** are a form of **line chart** used to depict how values of a categorical or continuous dependent variable varies across values of a quantitative (ordinal or continuous) independent variable. Trend charts use the position of each point relative to an axis to convey level and angle of lines to show the amount of difference or change across values. Dots or other markers can be used to show specific points along each line, using different marker styles for each line—a useful feature on a black-and-white chart.

> Example: The age-specific mortality rate declines slightly between infancy and early childhood, rises very slowly until age 35 or so, and then rises more and more steeply into old age (Figure 7.10).
>
> *A **trend line** connects the mortality rates (**continuous dependent variable**, on the **y-axis**) for each age group ((the **ordinal independent variable**, on the **x-axis**), revealing the direction and magnitude of the **bivariate association** between those two variables.*

Scatter charts. **Scatter charts** show how values of two continuous variables are associated. One continuous variable is labeled on each axis, with a dot (or other marker) plotting the combination of values of those variables for each case. The regression line for the association can also be included to portray the direction and size of the overall pattern between those two variables.[2]

---

[2]A regression line is calculated to minimize the average distance from each observed point to that line (Salkind, 2016).

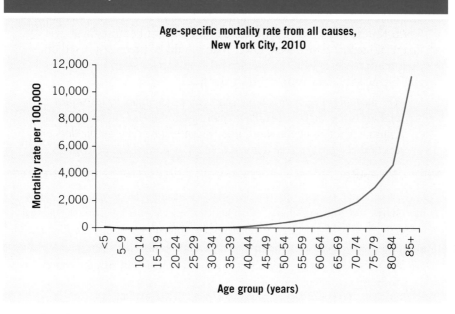

Age-specific mortality rate from all causes,
New York City, 2010

Source: Data from New York City Department of Health (2010).

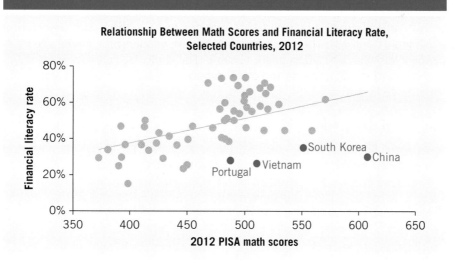

Relationship Between Math Scores and Financial Literacy Rate,
Selected Countries, 2012

Source: Klapper et al. (2015). Reprinted with permission.

Note: PISA = Programme for International Student Assessment.

Example: The upward-sloping line in Figure 7.11 reveals that in 2012, countries with higher math scores also had on average higher financial literacy rates. For instance, as math scores increase from 400 to 500, the financial literacy rate rises from about 37% to 49%. Portugal, Vietnam, South Korea, and China are identified on the chart because their financial literacy scores were lower than would be predicted based on their math scores, given the average relationship between math scores and financial literacy (portrayed by the line).

> The meaning of each **dot** on the chart can be identified by the **topics** and **units** on the two **axes**. Four countries are singled out based on their unusual positions on the chart, using a contrasting color for the **dots** and **text labels** that could be referred to in an associated text description.

Many charts and vizzes to portray bivariate associations are forms of XY charts. **Bar charts** and **lollipop charts** are suited for associations involving categorical independent variables because they encourage comparison of discrete (separate) categories. **Line charts** are appropriate for associations involving continuous independent variables because they foster comparison of trends. **Scatter charts** are used to portray combinations of two continuous variables for individual cases; they often also include a fitted line to show the average relationship between those variables in the overall sample.

More Complex Patterns

Many research questions aim to understand how an outcome varies according to two other factors simultaneously—referred to as a **three-way association** (Chapters 10 and 13). These patterns often involve relationships among two independent variables and a dependent variable. The choice of a chart type for three-way associations depends on the combinations of levels of measurement of the variables to be portrayed.

Clustered Bar Charts

A **clustered bar chart** can be used to depict relationships involving two categorical independent variables and either a continuous or categorical dependent variable. One independent variable is placed on the horizontal axis, the other independent variable in the legend (or differentiated by color or shading and labels), and the dependent variable on the vertical axis.

Example: In the United States in 2017, regardless of race/ethnicity, males had higher median incomes than females (Figure 7.12).

> Figure 7.12 portrays a **three-way association** because it examines a relationship between three variables: race/ethnicity, gender, and income.

Figure 7.12 Clustered Bar Chart

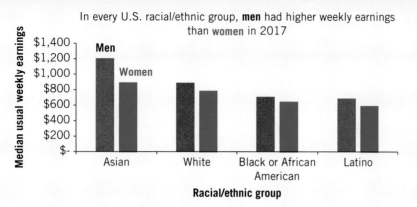

In every U.S. racial/ethnic group, **men** had higher weekly earnings than **women** in 2017

Among full-time employed wage and salary workers; excludes self-employed persons

Source: Data from Bureau of Labor Statistics (2018a).

> There is a **cluster** on the x-axis for each racial/ethnic group (**one independent variable**) and a **bar color** for each gender (the **other independent variable**, identified with colored text labels yielding eight bars—one for each combination of the four racial/ethnic groups and the two gender categories. The height of each bar shows median weekly earnings (a **continuous dependent variable**, labeled on the y-axis) for that group. The direction of association is evident because in each of the clusters (racial/ethnic groups) the black bar (males) is taller than the blue bar (females).

Multiple Stacked Bar Charts

When several **stacked bar charts** are displayed together, they can be used to compare distributions of several related items or variables.

Example: Figure 7.8 shows that Facebook had the highest share of users visiting it several times a day (51% of FB users), followed by Snapchat (49% of its users), Instagram (35%), YouTube (29%), and Twitter (26%).

> A separate **horizontal stacked bar** shows frequency of use of one type of platform, displayed top to bottom from highest to lowest percentage of "several times a day". The percentage of all respondents who used each platform is reported in parentheses next to the platform name. Each of the stacked bars totals 100%, conveying the distribution of frequency of use (the different colored segments) among all respondents who used that platform (explained in the subtitle).

A majority of Facebook, Snapchat, and Instagram users visit those platforms on a daily basis

Among U.S. adults who say they use __, the % who use each site . . .

	Several times a day	About once a day	Less often
Facebook (68%)	51%	23%	26%
Snapchat (27%)	49%	14%	36%
Instagram (35%)	38%	22%	39%
YouTube (73%)	29%	17%	55%
Twitter (24%)	26%	20%	53%

% of U.S. adults using platform in ( ). Data from 2018 survey by the Pew Research Center.

Source: Data from Smith and Anderson (2018).

Example: Figure 7.13 presents the same data as Figure 7.8, but separates the colored slices for each social media platform with white space so that each color has its own vertical axis. A higher share of Instagram and Twitter used those platforms "about once a day" (light blue) than Snapchat, although Snapchat users were more likely to use it several times a day (dark blue) than were Instagram or Twitter users.

*This design takes advantage of the **Gestalt principle of continuity** to facilitate comparing the size of the middle category across the different social media platforms: the left-hand sides of the light blue bars **line up vertically** with one another, allowing readers to assess the relative lengths of those segments. Likewise, the left-hand sides of the gray bars align with each other. Variation in the light blue and gray categories across the type of platform is harder to perceive when the different-colored segments are stacked right up against one another, as in Figure 7.8. In the "**separate baseline**" version (Figure 7.13), the slices still total 100% in each horizontal bar (for each social media platform).*

Diverging Stacked Bars

A variant of a stacked bar chart can be very useful when there are several ordered categories representing **diverging** (opposite) meanings, such as a spectrum from "strongly disagree" to "strongly agree." A central vertical axis is used to divide responses, emphasizing the opposing nature of the response categories. Lengths

Figure 7.14   Diverging Stacked Bar Chart

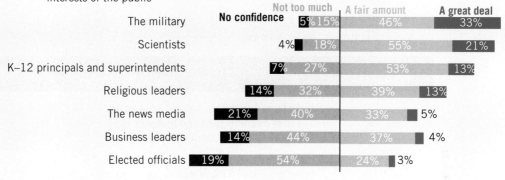

**In 2016, Americans' trust in military and scientists was relatively high
but trust in media, business leaders, elected officials was low**

Percentage of U.S. adults who say they have __ (of) confidence in these groups to act in the best interests of the public

	No confidence	Not too much	A fair amount	A great deal
The military	5%	15%	46%	33%
Scientists	4%	18%	55%	21%
K–12 principals and superintendents	7%	27%	53%	13%
Religious leaders	14%	32%	39%	13%
The news media	21%	40%	33%	5%
Business leaders	14%	44%	37%	4%
Elected officials	19%	54%	24%	3%

Source: Data from Funk (2017).

of the bars going to the left of that central axis can be compared with those going to the right, both for a given topic and across topics.

> Example: In 2018, U.S. adults were much more likely to be confident in the military, scientists, educators, and religious leaders than in the news media, business leaders, or elected officials (Figure 7.14).
>
> *A **vertical axis line** differentiates between the <u>unfavorable</u> responses (to the <u>left of that line</u>) and <u>favorable</u> responses (to its <u>right</u>). The **color-coded text labels** identify the meaning of the **segment colors**—black and gray for "no confidence" and "not too much," light and dark blue for "a fair amount" and "a great deal." The four colored segments in each **horizontal bar** add up to 100%, accounting for all respondents who replied to the question about that leadership group (labeled on the **vertical axis**). By organizing the leadership groups top to bottom in **descending order** of "a great deal" of confidence, the viz makes it very easy to perceive the rank order of that category of the dependent variable—coordinating with the order in which those groups are listed in the **take-home point title**.*

Although diverging bar charts can also be used for two-category (dichotomous) opposites such as "favor" versus "oppose," such patterns can be portrayed simply by presenting bars or lollipops for <u>one</u> of those categories, as noted in the section "Comparing Two or More Numbers."

Dumbbell Dot Plots

In a **dumbbell dot plot**, a horizontal line segment is used to connect two dots—one for each of two values of a quantitative independent variable, forming a "dumbbell." There is one dumbbell for each category of a second independent variable, which is arranged on the vertical axis. The numeric values of the dependent variable can be assessed by comparing the position of each dot and its distance from the other dot in its pair against the horizontal axis.

<u>Example</u>: Figure 7.15 shows how the prevalence of teen motherhood differs between the lowest and highest quintiles (fifths) of household

Figure 7.15 Dumbbell Dot Plot

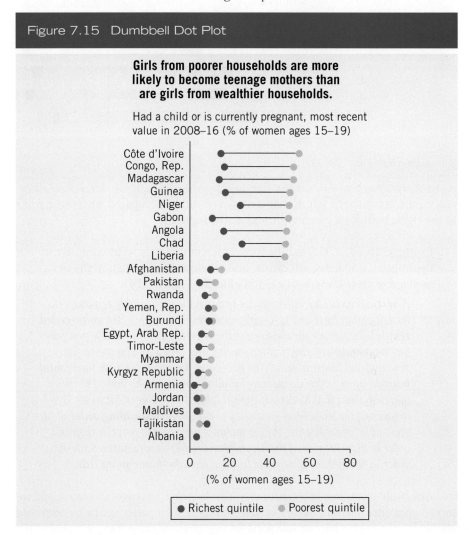

Source: Data from World Bank (2018). © World Bank. License: CC BY 3.0 IGO.

wealth in each of several dozen developing countries. Côte d'Ivoire not only has the highest teen motherhood rate (~55% of teens were mothers) but also one of the widest gaps in teen motherhood between the poorest and richest quintiles (more than 35 percentage points). In contrast, Afghanistan's rate for the poorest quintile is much lower (about 18%) than Côte d'Ivoire's, and the gap between the rates for the richest and poorest quintiles in Afghanistan is only about 5 percentage points.

> *The units of the **dependent variable** (teen motherhood) are identified on the **horizontal axis** and defined in the **subtitle**. The length of each **horizontal line segment** connecting a dark and light dot shows how much teen motherhood <u>differs</u> between the lowest and highest wealth quintiles (**ordinal independent variable**) <u>within</u> that country (**nominal category of the second independent variable**). The meaning of the dot colors is defined in a **legend**. By noticing that the light blue dots (poorest quintile) are to the right of the dark blue dots (richest quintile) for all but one country readers can confirm the pattern stated in the **title**.*

Multiple-Line Chart

Multiple-line charts are used to portray a relationship between a quantitative independent variable (on the *x*-axis) and a dependent variable (on the *y*-axis), with separate lines for each category of the second independent variable (defined in the legend or using text labels for each series).

<u>Example</u>: Figure 7.3 uses a multiple-line chart to show growth in population across time for the world as a whole and for each of several levels of economic development.

> *Time (the **independent variable**) and population (the **dependent variable**) are both **continuous**, with **topics** and **units** labeled on the respective **axes**. The geographic areas are **labeled** next to each line. **Data labels** on each line are used to show values for a specific region (**line color**) and time (**x-axis**).*

Multiple-line charts can also be used to convey relationships with categorical dependent variables by plotting the percentage of cases that fall into a particular category. For instance, the percentage of people who are poor (*y*-axis) could be graphed by age (continuous independent variable on the *x*-axis), with a separate line for each level of education (ordinal independent variable defined in the legend)—not shown.

Slopegraphs

A **slopegraph** is a variant of a multiple-line trend chart involving only two time points, using the angle of a line in combination with the position of dots to convey the size and direction of the trend. The dependent variable is placed on the vertical axis, with time treated as a two-category independent variable. The earlier of two time points graphed on the left-hand side of the *x*-axis and the later one on the right-hand side. For each category of the second independent variable, a line connects the values of the dependent variable for the earlier and later time points.

Example: The slopes in Figure 7.16 convey that in all but one country, the prevalence of stunting (very low height-for-age) among children under age 5 years declined over time. Stunting is an indicator of long-term nutritional deprivation.

*Stunting (the **dependent variable**) is defined in a note to the viz. The **left-hand dot** for each country is the percentage of young children*

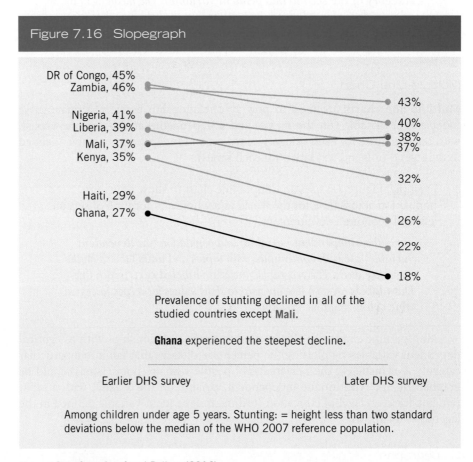

Figure 7.16 Slopegraph

Prevalence of stunting declined in all of the studied countries except **Mali.**

Ghana experienced the steepest decline.

Earlier DHS survey   Later DHS survey

Among children under age 5 years. Stunting: = height less than two standard deviations below the median of the WHO 2007 reference population.

Source: Data from Assaf and Pullum (2016).

who were stunted at the time of the earlier of two Demographic and Health Surveys (DHS) in that country, while the **right-hand dot** is the percentage stunted at the DHS survey conducted a few years later in the same country. The **angle of the line connecting the two dots** (another visual feature) portrays the direction and magnitude of change in stunting over time (**one independent variable**) in that country (the **second independent variable**), with <u>downward</u> sloping lines conveying a decrease in stunting and the one <u>upward</u> sloping line an increase. **Annotations** report two key take-home points from the chart, with the country names **color-coded** to match the colors of those two lines.

Choice of a chart or visualization to portray a **three-way association** depends on both the task at hand and the levels of measurement of the variables involved. Charts involving <u>categorical</u> **independent variables** include the following:

- A **clustered bar chart** shows how levels of a dependent variable differ according to two categorical independent variables simultaneously.

- A **multiple stacked bar** chart portrays how the distributions of responses to an ordinal dependent variable differ across topics or categories of an independent variable.

- A **diverging stacked bar** displays responses of an ordinal variable with categories that represent opposite directions of an attitude about each of several different topics (overall bar).

- A **slopegraph** portrays how the value of a dependent variable changes between two time points (one independent variable) for each of several categories (groups, locations, or outcomes defined by a second independent variable).

- A **dumbbell dot plot** displays the difference in the value of a dependent variable between two values of a quantitative independent variable for each of several groups, locations, or outcomes.

Three-way patterns involving a <u>continuous</u> **independent variable** and a categorical independent variable are portrayed using **multiple-line charts**.

Maps

Maps are often the most effective way of showing how some characteristic or outcome varies by location because they depict the geographic arrangement of the locations being compared. Likewise, they are useful for portraying distance to a specific feature such as the nearest train station or emergency room. In these tasks, the geographic units are the independent variable, and the characteristic being compared is the dependent variable. Maps can be used to portray geographic patterns for either categorical or continuous dependent variables.

> Example: Figure 7.17 conveys which regions of the world had the highest and lowest levels of income.
>
> *The **title** specifies the topic and the **legend** identifies the range of income levels associated with each **color** on the map, from low (blue shades) to high (gray shades). The **map** shows the geographic arrangement of the countries' income levels much more effectively than a table or chart could, even if geography were used to determine the order in which regions were listed.*

Heat Maps

Heat maps use grids of colored or shaded blocks to compare values of several ordinal outcomes for each of several items, cases, or time points. They are structured with one set of variables in the rows and the other dimension of the comparison in the columns. Colors of the blocks convey the value of an ordinal measure of the outcome for each of the attributes being rated.

> Example: From Figure 7.18, students registering for a Research Methods course could see how previous students rated five different professors on each of several dimensions of teaching quality. They might want to avoid Prof. Z, who received below-average ratings on preparedness and availability, and Prof. T, who was rated below average on ability to explain ideas clearly or make them interesting. Better choices might be Prof. J, rated at or above average on every dimension except easiness of grading, or Profs. A or R who were at or above average on each dimension.
>
> *The different aspects of teaching are named at the top of the columns, and the names of the professors (**cases**) in the **rows**. A **legend** defines the colors associated with an **ordinal** measure of teaching quality, classified as "above average" (blue), "average" (gray), and "below average" (black). By looking **down a column** for the blue squares, students can identify which professors were above average on a particular aspect of teaching. By looking **across a row**, they can see the ratings of a specific professor on each aspect of teaching.*

Figure 7.17 Map of Gross National Income per Capita Level by Country

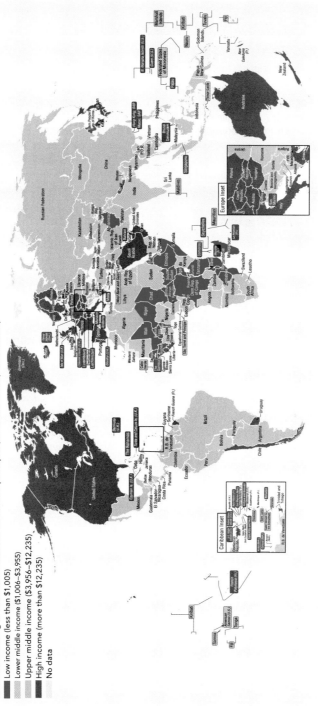

The world by income
Classified according to World Bank estimates of 2016 GNI per capita (current US dollars, *Atlas* method)

Low income (less than $1,005)
Lower middle income ($1,006–$3,955)
Upper middle income ($3,956–$12,235)
High income (more than $12,235)
No data

Source: Data from World Bank (2018). © World Bank. License: CC BY 3.0 IGO.

Note: The World Bank classifies economies as low-income, lower-middle-income, upper-middle-income or high-income based on gross national income (GNI) per capita. For more information see https://datahelpdesk.worldbank.org/knowledgebase/articles/906519-world-bank-country-and-lending-groups.

Figure 7.18   Heat Map

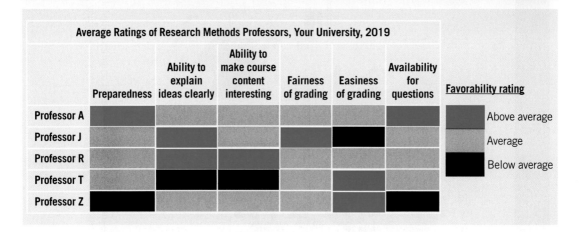

Average Ratings of Research Methods Professors, Your University, 2019

Design Issues

A couple of design issues affect the ease of making sense of numbers from charts.

Use of Color

Color is widely used in charts and visualizations for slides for speeches as well as online publications, websites, and dashboards. Until fairly recently, however, most documents were published in black and white. Even today, many scientific books (like this one!), journals, and reports are published with limited, if any, color. When you conduct a literature search to provide background for understanding a social research question, some publications that turn up are likely to include charts made without the use of color, so it is still important to learn how to interpret and design visualizations in grayscale.

Important visual perception considerations include avoiding combinations known to affect those with color blindness (e.g., the inability to differentiate red from green) and anticipating which color contrasts can be discerned if the chart or viz is copied into black and white. Too often, designers choose default colors imposed by software programs or use colors from a company logo that limit the range of available color contrasts. Many midrange colors will be almost indistinguishable from one another when printed in grayscale. In such instances, white, one dark and one middle shade and one (or at most two) different types of line styles (e.g., solid or dashed), hatching or shading should be used, as in Figure 7.7a.

If you are producing a figure in black and white and have more than a few categories, it is difficult to differentiate categories using colors alone. In those cases, "small multiples" (separate small charts) for each time, place, or group can be effective, each labeled with a title reflecting the name of the group (Figure 7.21). Alternatively, text labels adjacent to the pertinent bars or slices can be used instead of a legend to identify their meaning.

Linear and Logarithmic Axis Scales

When the range of values of the dependent variable covers more than one or two orders of magnitude (multiples of 10), a **logarithmic axis scale** is often used for scientific audiences. On a base-ten logarithmic scale, the distance between adjacent tick marks on the axis corresponds to a 10-fold <u>multiple</u> instead of the uniform difference (from subtraction) on a **linear axis scale**.

<u>Example</u>: When mortality rates are graphed on a linear axis scale (Figure 7.10), it is very difficult to see the 10-fold decrease in mortality between children under 5 years and those 5 to 9 years old or to notice that mortality rates rise from then through middle age because the y-scale has to accommodate the very high mortality rates among people age 75 and older. Plotted on a logarithmic axis scale (Figure 7.19), differences among the low-mortality age groups are easily perceived, yet the much higher mortality rates among the oldest age groups still fit on the chart.

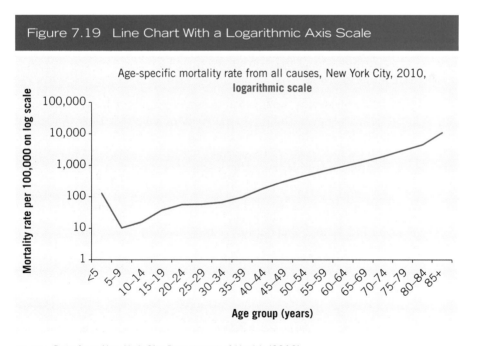

Figure 7.19 Line Chart With a Logarithmic Axis Scale

Source: Data from New York City Department of Health (2010).

*In Figure 7.19, the first three **tick marks** on the **y-axis** are for 1, 10, and 100 deaths per 1,000 persons, instead of the uniform 2,000-unit difference between tick marks in Figure 7.10, which portrays the same pattern on a **linear axis scale**. To reduce the chances of readers misinterpreting the values, a chart like Figure 7.19 should be annotated to point out the **logarithmic axis scale**. Logarithmic scales should generally be used only for scientific audiences because many laypeople will not know how to interpret them.*

Common Errors in Chart Creation

Certain design errors find their way into charts and vizzes, either accidentally, due to default programming in software programs, or intentionally by designers seeking to "lie with statistics." These issues can confuse or mislead readers as they try to make sense of numbers from the chart or viz. To prevent your making those types of mistakes when you are reading or producing charts and vizzes, I point out and illustrate several of the most common and deceptive errors. For more on errors in chart creation, see Evergreen (2017), Zacks and Tversky (1999), or Pandey et al. (2014).

Incorrect Chart for Level of Measurement

Some of the most frequent mistakes involve choosing a type of chart that does not suit the level(s) of measurement of the variables being portrayed—a point covered in Chapter 10 which explains how to display distributions and associations.

Incorrect Axis Scales

The range of values on an axis should span the set of <u>possible</u> values for that variable. A common mistake is including only a truncated (shortened) portion of the theoretically possible range for a variable, making even a trivially small difference appear massive if the axis scale begins at a sufficiently high value. For all variables that include 0 in their plausible range, the axis that portrays that variable should include 0 on the axis scale.

<u>Example</u>: In Figure 7.20, the heights of the bars make it appear that women's median income is about half of men's in each racial/ethnic group. However, calculations based on the actual values (read off the y-axis) show that women's median income is between 75% and 93% of men's—lower but not as egregious a disadvantage as the incorrect chart implies.

*This <u>exaggeration</u> of the actual difference occurs because the **y-axis scale** starts at $600. When the chart <u>correctly</u> starts the **y-scale** at 0, the size of the gender difference in income is accurately portrayed (Figure 7.12).*

Figure 7.20   Incorrect *Y*-Axis Starting Value

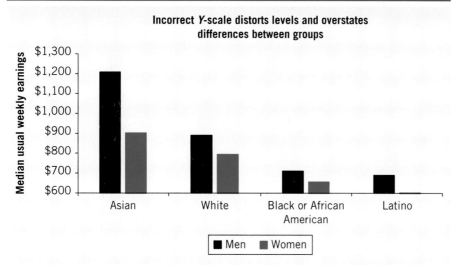

Incorrect *Y*-scale distorts levels and overstates differences between groups

Among full-time employed wage and salary workers; excludes self-employed persons.

Source: Data from Bureau of Labor Statistics (2018a).

If the range of theoretically possible values for a variable <u>doesn't</u> encompass zero, the axis scale of the chart should reflect that.

Example: The lowest possible SAT score on each test is 200 points, so the axis scale for that variable should start at that value, <u>not</u> at zero.

Likewise, the maximum value on a chart axis should be at or slightly above the theoretically possible maximum for that variable. This averts making differences between numeric values appear <u>smaller</u> than they are by including too wide a range on the axis.

Example: If the *y*-scale in Figure 7.8 ranged up to 120%, it would <u>understate</u> differences across the frequency of social media platform use by leaving room on the chart for values that, by definition, cannot exist.

The sum of the share of respondents who reported "several times a day," "about once a day," and "less often" <u>cannot</u> exceed 100% of respondents who reported ever using that platform.

Inconsistent Axis Scales

When several panels or subcharts are created to compare patterns across those panels, the range of *y* values should be consistent across panels.

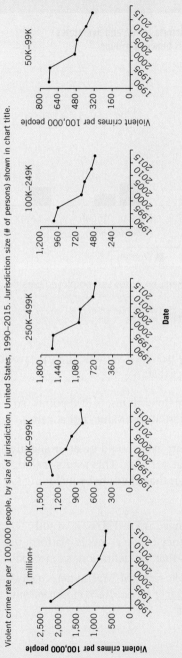

Figure 7.21a-b Importance of Consistent Y-Axis Scales for Related Charts

a. **Inconsistent** Y-Axis Scales

Violent crime rate per 100,000 people, by size of jurisdiction, United States, 1990–2015. Jurisdiction size (# of persons) shown in chart title.

b. **Consistent** Y-Axis Scales

Violent crime rate per 100,000 people, by size of jurisdiction, United States, 1990–2015. Jurisdiction size (# of persons) shown in chart title.

Source: Data from James (2018).

Example: Figure 7.21 portrays how violent crime rates in the United States changed between 1990 and 2015 and how that pattern varied by size of jurisdiction. A quick glance at underline incorrect Figure 7.21a, makes it appear that levels of violent crime are very similar for each of the jurisdiction sizes. In actuality, crime rates are much higher in the largest jurisdictions than in smaller ones.

> *Careful examination of Figure 7.21a reveals that the **maximum values** on the vertical axes <u>differ</u> for each of the five **subcharts**: 2,500 violent crimes per 100,000 for jurisdictions with 1 million or more people, 1,500 for those with 500K to 999K people, 1,800 for 250K to 499K, 1,200 for those with 100K to 249K, and 800 for jurisdictions of 50K to 99K persons. As with many charts created in Excel or other software, each chart is automatically scaled to maximize the visual difference between the highest and lowest values. Those <u>inconsistencies</u> in the **range of values** portrayed <u>hide</u> important differences in the levels across the respective charts.*

> *When the y-axes for <u>each</u> of the five subcharts are <u>corrected</u> to range from 0 (the **theoretical minimum**) to 2,500 violent crimes per 100,000 people (Figure 7.21b), the vast differences in the levels of violent crime by jurisdiction size are correctly portrayed. At the same time, the important point that violent crime rates declined in jurisdictions of all sizes is still evident.*

Even if consistent numeric axis ranges have been used, the subcharts (panels) must be printed in a uniform size on the page. A given level or change in level will appear lower on a small panel than on a larger panel, misleading readers as they visually compare them.

Incorrect Spacing of Values on an Axis

Another mistake frequently introduced by graphing software is when spacing of the values of a variable on a chart axis doesn't reflect the actual distance between those values. In a line chart, equal spacing of unequal distances between values misrepresents the true slope of the relationship between the variables on the *x* and *y* axes (Evergreen, 2017).

Example: In Figure 7.22a, the rate of population increase (slope of each line) appears far steeper for 1970 through 2015 than for the later years.

> *That <u>misleading</u> pattern occurs because the x-axis spaces the dates equally, overlooking the fact that the chart shows data at <u>10-year</u> intervals from 1970 to 2010, then at a <u>5-year</u> interval (to 2015), followed by <u>1-year</u> intervals for the projected populations through 2020.*

Figure 7.22a-b   Importance of Correct Date Spacing in a Chart

a. **Incorrect** date spacing

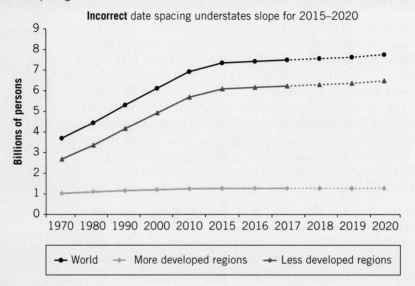

b. **Correct** date spacing

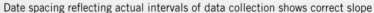
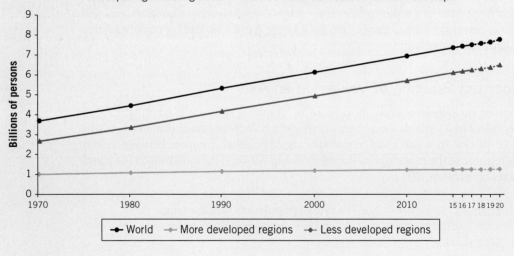

Source: Data from United Nations (2019).

In Figure 7.22b, the slope of each line is fairly consistent throughout the entire period shown.

> When the years are **spaced** <u>correctly</u> **on the x-axis**, the **slopes** accurately portray the rate of population increase across the entire time period.

Likewise, if ordinal categories are different widths, the y-value should be plotted above the <u>midpoint</u> of the ordinal category of the x variable, with those categories in increments that capture the true distance between values. For instance, the age groups <18 years, 18 to 64, 65 to 84, and 85+ each capture a different number of years, with spans of 18, 46, 20, and open-ended (depending on age of the oldest person) years. Thus, the spacing of those categories on a chart axis should reflect the widths of those respective categories (not shown).

Other Design Issues

Pie With Too Many Categories

With the ease of creating pie charts in many software programs, that type of chart is often misused to show how a large number of categories together make up a whole. And don't even get me started on the problems created by using a pie chart to show the distribution of a many-valued continuous variable.

> <u>Example</u>: In Figure 7.23, even though the 50 U.S. states are arranged from smallest to largest around the pie, the chart is truly overwhelming. Yes, the 50 states together make up the entire United States population, but a pie chart isn't needed to inform us of that.
>
> > Problems include the following: The **font size** of the data labels is necessarily microscopic to fit in all the state names and populations. Many of the **colors** are so <u>similar</u> that it is very difficult to differentiate them from one another. And the **number of digits** reported for each state's population is misleading since each is clearly taking the population to the nearest tenth of a million and inserting enough zeros to imply that it was a count to the nearest individual person. A **bar chart** would be more effective at conveying the rank order and relative sizes of the 50 states' populations. Or if the expected audience needs detailed population data for each state, a **table** would work better than a chart (Chapter 14).

Use of 3-D and Angled or Tilted Perspective

Designers sometimes create 3-D versions of two-dimensional charts, creating bars or pie slices that distort the relative sizes of values by inflating the apparent size of some components depending on the positions of those elements. Tilted or angled perspectives on charts also misrepresent relative shares of different categories.

Figure 7.23   Pie Chart With Too Many Categories

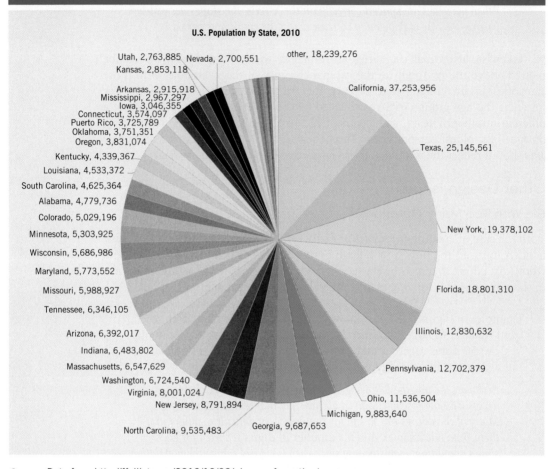

U.S. Population by State, 2010

Utah, 2,763,885   Nevada, 2,700,551   other, 18,239,276
Kansas, 2,853,118
Arkansas, 2,915,918   California, 37,253,956
Mississippi, 2,967,297
Iowa, 3,046,355
Connecticut, 3,574,097
Puerto Rico, 3,725,789
Oklahoma, 3,751,351
Oregon, 3,831,074
Kentucky, 4,339,367   Texas, 25,145,561
Louisiana, 4,533,372
South Carolina, 4,625,364
Alabama, 4,779,736
Colorado, 5,029,196
Minnesota, 5,303,925   New York, 19,378,102
Wisconsin, 5,686,986
Maryland, 5,773,552
Missouri, 5,988,927
Tennessee, 6,346,105   Florida, 18,801,310
Arizona, 6,392,017
Indiana, 6,483,802   Illinois, 12,830,632
Massachusetts, 6,547,629
Washington, 6,724,540   Pennsylvania, 12,702,379
Virginia, 8,001,024
New Jersey, 8,791,894   Ohio, 11,536,504
North Carolina, 9,535,483   Michigan, 9,883,640
Georgia, 9,687,653

Source: Data from http://ffolliet.com/2013/10/03/pies-are-for-eating/.

Example: In Figure 7.24a, Item C appears to be about the same size as Item A when in fact, it is less than half as large (see data labels on Figure 7.24b).

By positioning Item C toward the front of the figure, **tilting** *the figure, and making it* **3-D***, the size of that category is* <u>visually inflated</u> *compared with Item A with its position at the back of the diagram (Figure 7.24a). The* **2-D** *(flat) version (Figure 7.24b)* <u>correctly</u> *depicts the* **relative sizes** *of the categories.*

Figure 7.24a-b   Visual Distortion by Use of 3D

a. 3-D pie chart

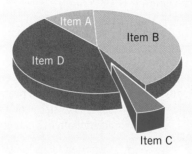

b. 2-D pie chart of the same data

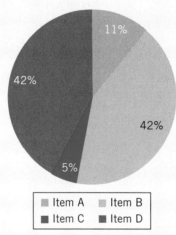

TERMS AND CONCEPTS

HIGHLIGHTS

- Knowing how to design and interpret **charts** and **visualizations** is an essential skill for both consumers and producers of numeric information.

- Charts and visualizations should be designed to be **focused, self-contained**, and **organized** to suit the specific **audience** and **objective**.

- Principles of **visual perception** and **cognitive load** suggest minimizing clutter and being strategic in the use of chart design elements.

- Charts are best used to **convey the general shape** and **size of a pattern**. If the audience is expected to want precise numeric values for their own calculations, a table should be used to organize the numbers.

- Charts are most effective when accompanied with a **text interpretation**—whether a short take-home title, brief annotation, or accompanying paragraph.

- Common tasks for charts include communicating **one numeric fact**, portraying **parts of a whole**, **comparing two numbers** or series of numbers, displaying **three-way associations**, and **mapping** numeric patterns that have a spatial component.

- The type of chart or viz is determined by the **task** and the **number** and **levels of measurement** of the variable(s) to be presented in that chart.

- Chart designers should avoid chart features such as 3-D or errors in axis scale that can **distort** numeric values and comparisons.

RECOMMENDED READINGS

Evergreen, S. D. H. (2017). *Effective data visualization: The right chart for the right data*. Sage.

Evergreen, S. D. H., & Emery, A. (2016). *Data visualization checklist*. http://stephanieevergreen

.com/wp-content/uploads/2016/10/DataViz Checklist_May2016.pdf

Nussbaumer Knaflic, C. (2015). *Storytelling with data*. John Wiley.

EXERCISES

Individual Exercises

Quantitative Reasoning in Everyday Life

1. Find charts or visualizations on a website or in a newspaper article or blog about popular culture, sports, the weather, or other "everyday" topic for each of the following tasks: (a) how the parts make up a whole, (b) a trend over time, and (c) comparing two or more values of a variable across groups. (d) For each of those charts, (i) discuss the strengths and weaknesses of

its design, using the criteria in this chapter, and (ii) describe how the chart or viz could be revised to make it easier to interpret.

Interpreting Research

2. On the Pew Research Center website (https://www.pewresearch.org/), find an article that includes a chart or visualization to present the relationship between a nominal independent variable with three or more categories and an outcome variable. Use that chart to provide the following information: (a) who is described by the data; (b) the date or dates to which the data pertain; (c) the location(s) where the data were collected; (d) the units of measurement and whether they are the same for all numbers displayed in the chart; (e) whether the chart includes all needed footnotes and, if not, what information is missing; (f) what criteria were used to organize the values of the variables on chart axes; and (g) whether that organization coordinates with the associated narrative. If the order of categories is not consistent with the narrative, describe how you would revise the organization of the categories in the chart and why.

3. On the U.S. Census Bureau website (https://www.census.gov/library/visualizations.html), find a chart or visualization on a topic of interest to you. (a) Evaluate whether the figures or visualizations can stand alone without the text, using the guidelines in this chapter. (b) Determine which of the perceptual elements (from Figure 7.1) are used in the chart. (c) If any of the elements are those that Figure 7.1 identifies as challenging for many readers, suggest a way to redesign the chart to use more straightforward design elements. (d) Evaluate whether the figures involve any of the types of design errors listed in this chapter. (e) If so, describe each such problem and suggest ways to redesign the chart to correct that error.

Communicating Research

4. Go to the State Health Compare site for the percentage of households that have access to a broadband Internet connection (http://statehealthcompare.shadac.org/map/232/percent-of-households-with-a-broadband-internet-subscription-by-total#a/25/266). Toggle among the different ways of displaying interstate comparisons (Map, Rank, Trend) and test out their capabilities for ordering the data. Identify which of those ways of presenting the data would make it easiest to see for gathering the following information: (a) geographic pattern in 2018, (b) most extensive Internet access in 2018, (c) least extensive Internet access in 2018, (d) change between 2016 and 2018.

5. Design "viz" versions of (a) Figure 7.7b and (b) Table 6.9c, using the guidelines in this chapter.

6. Design a "classic" black-and-white version of Figure 7.13, using the guidelines in this chapter.

7. In a journal article in your field, find a table that presents data on a relationship between two variables. (a) Draft a chart to present the same information, including complete title, axis labels, legend, and notes. (b) Explain your choice of chart type, based on (i) task, (ii) number of variables, and (iii) their levels of measurement.

Group Exercises

Interpreting Research

8. Discuss your answers to Exercise 3, with each student presenting a different chart or visualization. For each, discuss (a) whether that chart is self-contained, (b) which visual perception principles were used in that chart, (c) whether the chart included any of the design errors

discussed in this chapter and, if so, (d) how the chart could be redesigned to correct those errors.

Communicating Research

9. Each group member looks up the COVID-19 data dashboards for a different U.S. state (https://www.shvs.org/state-covid-19-data-dashboards/). (a) List how many different types of visualizations or charts were used to present the information. (b) Discuss alternative ways different states present information on a given topic (e.g., total number of deaths, total number of cases, trends in deaths or cases, geographic distribution of cases or deaths). (c) Identify the advantages and disadvantages of each approach.

10. With a classmate, exchange the draft charts you created for Exercise 7 and the table where you found the data. (a) Provide specific feedback to each other on the design of that chart based on the principles in this chapter. (b) Revise the design of your draft chart to correct any problems found by your peer reviewer.

Making Sense of Numbers From Mathematical and Statistical Methods

An important aspect of quantitative research is using numeric comparisons to quantify the shape and size of a pattern by calculating the direction and magnitude of differences between two or more values. In Part IV, I describe several decisions researchers need to make as they conduct their analyses and explain how those processes help determine the meaning and plausibility of numbers based on how they were measured and calculated. In Chapter 8, I discuss how to choose comparison values and contrast sizes to suit a specific research question and variables and explain the role of various types of numeric benchmarks. In Chapter 9, I review common numeric measures, comparisons, and mathematical computations, with an emphasis on how the formula for each type of calculation affects the plausible range of values of the results. In Chapter 10, I introduce the statistical methods used to describe the distributions of single variables and associations between two or three variables, again focusing on criteria to help make sense of those results.

Comparison Values, Contrast Sizes, and Standards

Despite the fact that almost all quantitative research requires comparing two or more numbers, many people put little effort into identifying which comparisons are best suited to answering the question at hand. However, the choice of a comparison value affects both the analysis and presentation of results, so knowing how to decide what comparisons to make is a key skill for conducting quantitative research. In this chapter, I start by defining comparison value and contrast size, and then I introduce different types of standards, thresholds, patterns, and benchmarks. I then discuss the criteria for choosing the group against which to compare other groups (for categorical variables), or the numeric value and size of the contrast (for continuous variables). Finally, I review how to ensure that numbers to be compared are in a form that can be correctly compared.

Reference Groups and Comparison Values

As discussed in Chapter 2, the purpose of many research studies is to show how values of a dependent variable (outcome) differ across values of an independent variable (predictor). In general terms, a **comparison value** is the value of the independent variable against which other values of that variable are to be contrasted. Depending on the topic being investigated, the comparison value (sometimes known as the **base-** or **reference value**) can be a time point, group, location, or other characteristic.

The level of measurement of a variable, which was covered in Chapter 4, determines which type of comparison value is needed: For nominal or ordinal (categorical) variables, the comparison value—termed the **reference category** or **comparison group**—will be the <u>category</u> of that variable against which the others will be compared. For interval or ratio (continuous) variables, the comparison value will be the <u>numeric value</u> of that variable against which other values are compared.

> <u>Example</u>: In a report on earnings among recent college graduates, a university compares earnings of other major areas of study to earnings of those who received engineering degrees.
>
> *The university chose engineering as the **reference group** of major (the **independent variable**) for the comparison of earnings (the **dependent variable**).*

For nominal or ordinal (<u>categorical</u>) independent variables, a **comparison group**, also known as a **reference group** or **reference category**, is the category against which other categories are compared. A **comparison value** is the numeric value of a <u>continuous</u> independent variable to which other values are compared. It is also known as the **base value** or **reference value**.

Criteria for Identifying Comparison Values

Choices about comparison values are <u>not</u> "one size fits all" and should be tailored to the specific phenomena under study, using the familiar "W's"—what, where, when, who, and how measured. A thorough quantitative study will include comparisons both within the researcher's own data and against external standards (discussed later in this chapter).

Researchers should use one or more of the following guidelines to decide on a reference value or group for comparisons <u>within their own data</u>.

Comparisons Across Groups

For many social research questions, **cultural norms** for the place, time, and group under study will suggest a sensible reference group. Statistical considerations often recommend using the **modal** (most common) category within a data set as the comparison group.

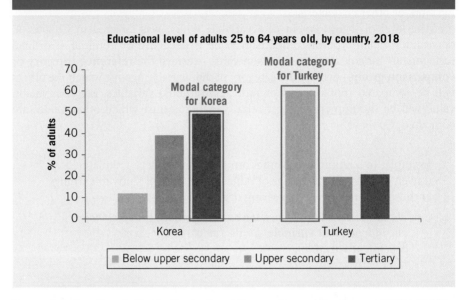

Figure 8.1   Different Modal Categories for Within-Country Comparisons

Educational level of adults 25 to 64 years old, by country, 2018

Modal category for Korea

Modal category for Turkey

% of adults

Korea   Turkey

■ Below upper secondary   ■ Upper secondary   ■ Tertiary

Source: Data from Organisation for Economic and Co-operation and Development (OECD, 2017).

Example: For a study of outcomes across levels of education within Korea in 2018, the highest level (tertiary education) would be a sensible reference group because data show that nearly half of Koreans aged 25 to 64 had attained that level (Figure 8.1). For a study of data from Turkey, however, a better choice of reference group would be the lowest educational attainment level ("below upper secondary") because more than 60% of adults in that country fell into that group (OECD, 2017).

> The **modal** (most common) educational attainment category in Korea was a higher attainment level than the modal group in Turkey. Thus, **empirical** criteria would suggest that a <u>within</u>-country study of Korea should use a different **reference category** of education level than a <u>within</u>-country study of Turkey.

Many health studies compare outcomes for people with and without a **risk factor**, which is a characteristic or behavior thought to increase chances of developing a disease or other health condition. In such studies, the risk factor is the independent variable, and the health condition is the outcome (dependent variable). For such studies, the group <u>without</u> that risk factor is often used as the reference category.

Example: In a study assessing whether second-hand smoke is a risk factor for sudden infant death syndrome (SIDS), the logical reference category would be infants who were <u>not</u> exposed to secondhand smoke.

*SIDS incidence (values of the **dependent variable**) would be compared for different levels of exposure to secondhand smoke (the **risk factor**, or **independent variable**). Those <u>without</u> the risk factor would be a sensible **reference category**.*

A **risk factor** is a trait or behavior believed to increase a person's chances of developing a disease or other condition.

When describing the results of an experimental study, the control condition is typically specified as the reference group. You will learn more about experimental studies in Chapter 12.

Example: In an evaluation of a new intervention program to reduce high school dropout rates, the logical **reference category** would be an existing program (or lack of a program).

*The new program is the **treatment**, and the old program is the **control** condition.*

Audience interests frequently suggest a logical comparison group or value.

Example: At a technology-focused university, comparing salaries of recent graduates for various majors to those of electrical engineering students would probably be of substantial interest. At a liberal arts college, psychology majors would be a better choice of a reference category.

*For each type of school, one of the most **popular** majors is chosen as the **reference category**, but which major is most popular differs considerably between tech and liberal arts schools.*

Geographic proximity often identifies reference locations for spatial comparisons. For instance, a report to the World Bank on a particular country might compare it to adjacent countries or against the entire continent where that country is located.

Criteria for selecting comparison groups include the following:

- Social or cultural norms for the topic and context (time, place, and group)

- Control group (in an experimental study)

- Group <u>without</u> a risk factor of interest

- Modal (most common) group or value

- Value of an independent variable with the highest (or lowest) value of some outcome of interest

- Interests of the intended audience

- Geographic proximity

Temporal Comparisons

Temporal comparisons (across time) are often made against the earliest value under consideration, sometimes against the most recent value. Alternatively, the timing of an important change related to the topic might suggest a comparison date or threshold for interpreting a time trend.

> <u>Example</u>: For a study of types of pain management used by cancer patients, comparing patterns before and after a state legalized medical marijuana would make sense.
>
> *Different U.S. states have legalized medical marijuana at different dates (National Conference of State Legislatures, 2019). The logical **comparison date** for each patient would be the date when medical marijuana was legalized in the state in which they were living at the time of their cancer treatment. That choice would allow researchers to identify whether that patient was studied pre- or post-legalization (or spanned the two time periods).*

Choice of a comparison date may be constrained by when data were collected. Most national censuses are conducted at 10-year intervals, and surveys are conducted periodically; thus, a study using secondary data (Chapter 12) might have to compare to the closest data collection date even if it doesn't exactly match the date of interest.

> <u>Example</u>: In Zambia, Demographic and Health Surveys were conducted in 2007 and 2014 (Assaf & Pullum, 2016).
>
> *Estimates for 2010 would have to be approximated by averaging the values for those two dates—one before and one after the year of interest.*

For trends across time, criteria for selecting a comparison date include the following:

- The earliest relevant value

- The most recent value

- The timing of a change in a cause or outcome under study

- Data collection dates

Standards, Thresholds, and Target Values

For many topics, comparison against standard patterns, thresholds, cutoffs, historical records, cyclical patterns, or target values can help place a number in context, revealing whether a particular value is typical or unusual for the topic and context under study. For many everyday topics, cutoffs and patterns are part of cultural literacy: Most people know the age at which they can be conscripted into the military in the country of which they are a citizen. That 50% or more constitutes a democratic majority, and cyclical patterns of temperature where they live are also familiar to most adults. However, for new topics, contexts, and variables involving unfamiliar or technical measures, researchers should consult the literature to identify appropriate standards, cutoffs, thresholds, and benchmarks.

Standards

A **standard** for a given topic is a value or pattern that is used as the basis of comparison or assessment for measures of that phenomenon. Examples include weather patterns and growth charts for children. Comparison against a standard helps make sense of numbers because it shows whether a particular value is high, low, or average relative to other data on the topic and setting (location, date, and group) or whether an observed trend follows that seen in other times or places.

Standard patterns or **norms** are often calculated from observed data for large populations or over a long period of time. For instance, average monthly rainfall in a given location is calculated from several decades of data, and growth standards for height and weight are based on international data on thousands of children. In addition to some measure of average value, standards often include information on range or other aspects of distribution. Weather standards mention record high and low temperatures as well as averages. Growth charts for children typically show the 3rd, 10th, 25th, 50th, 75th, 90th, and 97th percentiles to help pediatricians see how a child's size compares to others his age.

Thresholds and Cutoffs

Thresholds and **cutoffs** are numeric values used to define a change in status or classification based on the concept being measured. They are often related to the meaning of that variable in its social or other "real-world" context or based on theoretical criteria for that topic. A threshold can be either the <u>minimum</u> value needed (e.g., the value must <u>meet or exceed</u> that level), or the <u>maximum</u> value allowed (e.g., the value must <u>be below</u> the threshold to meet the definition).

For some quantitative variables, multiple cutoffs are used to define relevant ranges for the topic.

> <u>Example</u>: In the United States in 2018, a family of one adult and three children the poverty threshold was $25,554 (Table 8.1).
>
> *The federal poverty <u>threshold</u> is the **maximum** (ceiling) income that **classifies** a family as poor: those earning below that **cutoff** are classified as poor. The poverty threshold is derived from the cost of a minimum food diet multiplied by three to account for other family expenses (U.S. Census Bureau, 2017)—in other words, by looking at financial criteria for meeting basic family needs.*

> <u>Example</u>: Exemplar High School (EHS) participated in a citywide study of six school practices or conditions related to student achievement, shown on the horizontal axis of Figure 8.2. Parents rated each of those attributes on a scale from 0 to 4 (on the vertical axis). EHS exceeded the target for three of the school attributes (collaborative teachers, rigorous instruction, and trust), met the target for two others (effective school leadership and supportive environment), and was approaching the desired level for one (strong family-community ties).
>
> ***Cutoffs** at 1, 2, and 3 points are used to create **ordered ranges** that help interpret the scores, shown on the vertical axis. The black range of the stacked bars encompasses scores that do <u>not</u> meet the criterion (scores less than 1), dark gray means approaching the desired level (scores between 1 and 2), light gray means target scores met (scores between 2 and 3), and dotted fill means exceeding the desired level (scores between 3 and 4). The chart—called a "bullet chart"—shows how the actual score (white-filled bar) compares to both the minimum **target** value (blue line) and the substantive **ranges**.*

> <u>Example</u>: New Jersey's Children's Health Insurance Program (CHIP), called NJFamilyCare, serves uninsured children up to age 19 in families with incomes too high to qualify them for Medicaid. In 2019, families earning up to and including 150% of the Federal Poverty Level (FPL) did not have to pay premiums or co-pays, those earning between 151% and 200% of the FPL no premiums but a $5 to $10 co-pay per visit, and those with incomes between 200% and 355% of the FPL paid premiums and co-pays based on a sliding scale (Table 8.2).

Table 8.1 Poverty Thresholds by Size and Age Composition

	U.S. Poverty Thresholds ($) for 2018 by Size of Family and Number of Related Children Under 18 Years								
		Number of Related Children Under 18 Years							
Size of Family Unit	None	One	Two	Three	Four	Five	Six	Seven	Eight or more
One person (unrelated individual):									
Under age 65	13,064								
Aged 65 and older	12,043								
Two people:									
Householder under age 65	16,815	17,308							
Householder aged 65 and older	15,178	17,242							
Three people	19,642	20,212	20,231						
Four people	25,900	26,324	25,465	25,554					
Five people	31,234	31,689	30,718	29,967	29,509				
Six people	35,925	36,068	35,324	34,612	33,553	32,925			
Seven people	41,336	41,594	40,705	40,085	38,929	37,581	36,102		
Eight people	46,231	46,640	45,800	45,064	44,021	42,696	41,317	40,967	
Nine people or more	55,613	55,883	55,140	54,516	53,491	52,082	50,807	50,491	48,546

Source: Data from U.S. Census Bureau (2018f).

Figure 8.2 Multiple Cutoffs to Define Ranges

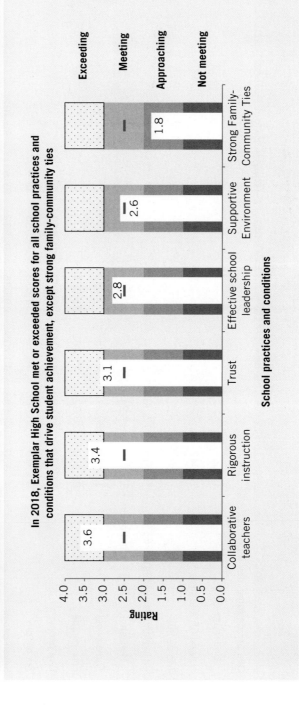

In 2018, Exemplar High School met or exceeded scores for all school practices and conditions that drive student achievement, except strong family-community ties

School practices and conditions

Source: Fictitious data from Mega City Public School District (2018).

Table 8.2 Multiple Cutoffs to Determine Program Eligibility and Cost

Family Size*	Adult(s) (Age 19–64)	Pregnant Women (Any Age)	Children (Under Age 19)					
			Federal Poverty Level % (FPL)					
	0–138%	0–205%	0–147%	> 147–150%	> 150–200%	> 200–250%	> 250–300%	> 300–355%
			Maximum Monthly Income					
1	$1,437	N/A	$1,531	$1,562	$2,082	$2,603	$3,123	$3,695
2	$1,945	$2,889	$2,072	$2,114	$2,819	$3,523	$4,228	$5,003
3	$2,453	$3,644	$2,613	$2,667	$3,555	$4,444	$5,333	$6,311
4	$2,962	$4,399	$3,155	$3,219	$4,292	$5,365	$6,438	$7,618
5	$3,470	$5,155	$3,696	$3,772	$5,029	$6,286	$7,543	$8,926
6	$3,978	$5,910	$4,238	$4,324	$5,765	$7,207	$8,648	$10,233
Each Additional	$509	$756	$542	$553	$737	$921	$1,105	$1,308
Monthly Premium	No premium	No premium	No premium	No premium	No premium	$44.50 per family	$90.00 per family	$151.50 per family
Copayments	No copay	No copay	No copay	No copay	$5–$10	$5–$35	$5–$35	$5–$35

*The size of your family may be determined by the *total number* of parent(s) or caretaker(s), and all blood-related children under the age of 21 who are tax dependent, as well as any other tax dependent residing in the home.

Source: Data from NJFamilyCare (2019).

*Eligibility for NJFamilyCare has several **cutoffs**: 150% of the FPL, 200% of the FPL, 250% of the FPL, 300% of the FPL, and 355% of the FPL. The cutoffs serve as **dividing points** between the **ranges** of family income that determine the level of premium and co-payments for each eligible family.*

Benchmarks, Targets, and Objectives

Another useful set of comparison values are **benchmarks** for the topic and context, which are often specified as **goals** or **objectives** for future levels of the phenomenon being measured. They can be the <u>minimum</u> desired level (when higher values of that variable are optimal) or the <u>maximum</u> desired level (if lower values are preferred). Comparisons against such benchmarks are used to assess whether values for particular cases, places, or times are above or below the target and whether a decrease or increase is desirable for that topic.

<u>Example</u>: Healthy People 2020 Objectives included a goal of increasing the percentage of middle and high schools that prohibit harassment based on a student's sexual orientation or gender identity from 88% (in 2010) to 92% by 2020.

*In 2011, the **target** for the year 2020 was set as a 4 percentage-point improvement over the **baseline rate** (88%), which was calculated as the median of state rates in 2010 (U.S. Office of Disease Prevention and Health Promotion, 2011).*

<u>Example</u>: Many countries have implemented standards to decrease emissions that must be met by new cars (Climate Change Authority, 2018).

*The **standards** provide a specific numeric **target** for evaluating the emissions level of each new car model.*

Note that each of these numeric goals is specific to the topic, context, and measurement.

A numeric **benchmark**, **standard**, or **threshold** is a value for a particular variable that can be used as a comparison value to help interpret the values of that variable. A **standard** (also known as a **norm** or **convention**) is a value or pattern considered by authorities in that field to be the usual basis of comparison for that phenomenon. A **threshold** (also known as a **cutoff**) is a level or value that creates a change in status or classification. **Benchmarks**, **target values**, **goals**, or **objectives** are values to be aimed for at some future date.

Historical Records

Another common basis of comparison for many topics is **historical data** on the lowest value, highest value, or rank order of values observed for that topic over time.

Example: "Drug overdoses killed about 72,000 Americans last year [2017], a record number that reflects a rise of around 10 percent, according to new preliminary estimates from the Centers for Disease Control. The death toll is higher than the peak yearly death totals from H.I.V., car crashes, or gun deaths." (Sanger-Katz, 2018).

> Drug overdose deaths for 2017 were compared against previous **historic highs** for that cause of death in the United States. By also comparing that

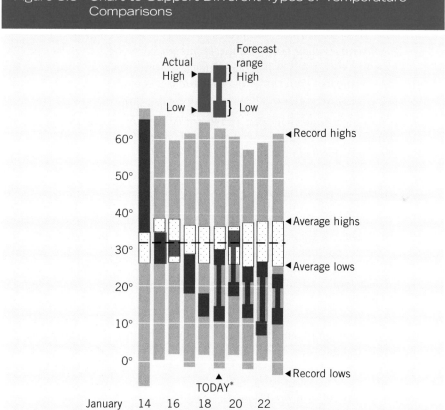

Figure 8.3   Chart to Support Different Types of Temperature Comparisons

Record, average, and actual or forecast high and low temperatures (°F), New York City, January 14–23, 2005

*"Today" is the day the chart was published.

*number against the **record number of deaths** ("peaks") for three other **major causes of death**, the article placed the 2017 statistic (72,000 drug overdose deaths in one year) into a broader social and health perspective.*

Example: Figure 8.3 depicts weather patterns for a week in 2005 when New York City saw its daily high temperature plummet from a near-record high (Jan. 14) to below average (Jan. 16 through the end of the week). Although several days remained below freezing the entire day, the 15th and 16th experienced a "freeze/thaw" cycle as their temperature was above 32 °F for part of the day but below freezing for the rest of the day.

> *The chart includes information to support <u>multiple</u> **comparisons**: Of <u>each day's actual</u> high and low temperatures (**blue slice**) to those of <u>previous and subsequent days</u>, to <u>average</u> highs and lows (**dot-filled slice**), and to <u>record</u> highs and lows (**gray slice**) for that place and date. Those comparisons give meaning to temperature in **context**: A temperature in the 60s (°F) would be interpreted very differently in New York City in <u>July</u> or in <u>Miami in January</u>, which would be captured in the **historical patterns** for those **locations** and **months**.*

> *The horizontal dashed line in Figure 8.3 identifies a **threshold** for that temperature (**topic**) in degrees Fahrenheit (**system of measurement**) that determines whether precipitation would be rain or snow—another useful question that the chart can answer.*

Cyclical Patterns

Cyclical patterns are those that repeat with regular periodicity, whether annually, monthly, daily, or according to some other interval of time. Depending on the topic, they occur due to factors such as human behavior or the weather. Comparing an observed data point or pattern against an established cyclical pattern for that topic and context can help reveal whether that point or trend is usual or atypical.

Example: Retail employment rises rapidly in the month or so before the winter holidays and drops off rapidly thereafter, as shown in the darker "not seasonally adjusted" line in Figure 8.4 (DeSilver, 2014). By factoring out the average seasonal pattern of employment (lighter smooth "seasonally adjusted" line), it is easier to see the overall decline in retail employment in 2008 and the slow increase over the subsequent few years. It is also apparent that the December 2008 hiring increase (Bracket A) was much smaller than the December rise in other years (Bracket B).

*Employment and unemployment statistics are often **seasonally adjusted** to measure and remove the influences of predictable **seasonal patterns** to reveal ways that a particular year diverged from what would be expected at that time of year (U.S. Bureau of Labor Statistics, 2001).*

Cyclical patterns are those that vary regularly according to some repeating cycle. **Seasonal patterns** repeat every year, **monthly** patterns every (calendar or lunar) month, and **diurnal** patterns every day.

Seasonal adjustment is a technique that measures and removes the influences of predictable patterns due to cyclical variation in some factor that affects the variable under study, making it easier to observe other, non-cyclical patterns such as spikes or long-term trends.

Figure 8.4 Cyclical Pattern of Employment

The Seasonal Peaks of Retail Employment

Monthly retail payrolls, Jan. 2004–Nov. 2014

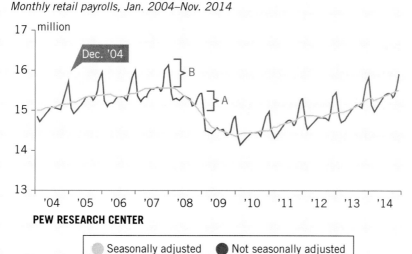

PEW RESEARCH CENTER

Seasonally adjusted   ● Not seasonally adjusted

Note: Figures for OCT. and Nov. 2014 are preliminary.

Source: Data from DeSilver (2014).

Figure 8.5 Daily and Weekly Patterns of Traffic Fatalities

a. Average weekly pattern

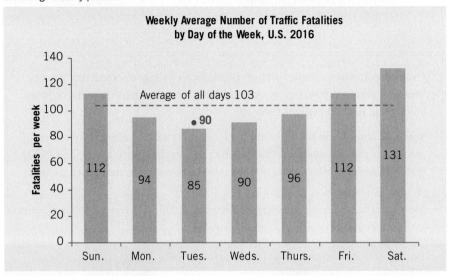

Source: Data from Carrig (2018).

b. Average daily pattern

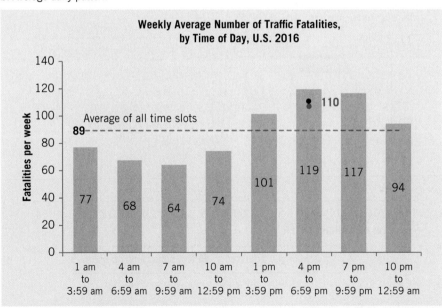

Source: Data from Carrig (2018).

Example: During an average week in 2016, there were 103 traffic fatalities each day in the United States; however, there is considerable variation by day of the week (Figure 8.5a). By knowing the typical **weekly pattern** of traffic fatalities, you could identify a Tuesday that had an unusually high number of fatalities <u>for that day of the week</u> (90 versus 85 on a typical Tuesday), even though that number would have been low for a Saturday (average value = 131). Likewise, you could detect an evening rush hour with an unusually low number of fatalities (110 compared to 119 for a typical 4 to 6:59 pm time slot; Figure 8.5b) by factoring out the typical **cycle by time of day**.

Criteria for Choosing External Comparison Values or Standards

External **standards** for a particular topic are based on information from outside the researcher's own data and are often based on long-term averages or values for several locations or groups.

Example: The cost of health care has been rising in the United States over the past few decades (CDC, 2020).

*Comparison against the **overall rate of inflation** would help assess whether the trend of rising <u>health care</u> costs is steeper or shallower than the trend in <u>other</u> costs.*

Example: A parent takes her 4-year-old to the doctor, concerned that he has not been growing as quickly over the past year as he had as a toddler.

*Comparisons against **international growth standards** for his age (such as Figure 4.2) will help the doctor learn whether that child is growing at the expected rate, is substantially below (or above!) the average size for his age, and if so, whether that gap is increasing, decreasing, or stable as he gets older.*

For many topics, there are well-established standards, patterns, thresholds, records, or benchmarks to help interpret the meaning of observed numeric values. To become familiar with comparison values used for a particular topic, review the scholarly and professional literature in related fields. This step is especially important when working with an unfamiliar topic, setting, or unit, a technical issue, or when precise values are needed.

Contrast Sizes for Quantitative Variables

When a comparison involves a quantitative independent variable, another key question concerns what sized contrast would be most helpful. The **contrast size** specifies how big of a <u>change or difference</u> in the independent variable is used in a comparison, measured in number of units of that variable. A contrast size can be less than a one-unit change (e.g., decimal or fractional value), a one-unit difference, or a multiple-unit contrast.

> <u>Example</u>: A study compares levels of consumer debt among 25-year-olds and 45-year-olds to that among 65-year-olds.
>
> *Here, the comparison **value** is 65-year-olds—the value of the **continuous independent variable** (age in single years) against which each of several other ages are compared. We would <u>not</u> expect much difference in consumer debt between 25-year-olds and 26-year-olds, so a one-unit difference in age is <u>too small</u> of a contrast to provide much insight about the association between age and debt. Instead, a **contrast size** of 20 years for age is chosen to be big enough to be associated with meaningful differences in debt (the **dependent variable**).*

For ordinal variables, which are quantitative variables already grouped into ranges, it might be necessary to combine several small categories into wider ranges to arrive at a comparison big enough to be of interest.

> <u>Example</u>: Given the very high market value of homes in her sales area, a real estate agent wants to compare sales of homes in price ranges of $20,000.
>
> *If prices of homes were originally collected as an **ordinal (categorical quantitative** variable) in ranges of $5,000, she would have to combine sets of four consecutive ranges of the original variable to arrive at the desired **contrast size**.*

> The **contrast size** specifies the number of units of change or difference in a quantitative independent variable used in a comparison.

The "Goldilocks" Problem

As Goldilocks discovered, no one chair fit all three members of the Bear Family equally well because Papa Bear, Mama Bear, and Baby Bear were completely different sizes. Likewise, for a particular variable, some contrast sizes are too big, some contrast sizes are too small, and some contrast sizes are just right. In other words, the same size contrast will <u>not</u> necessarily make sense for every quantitative variable because different variables have different levels, ranges, and distributions that depend on the topic (Chapter 3), measurement (Chapter 4), and context (Chapter 5). The good news is that many of the criteria discussed in those chapters can help determine a suitable choice of contrast size for a particular continuous variable.

Many researchers start by working with "easy" or "obvious" contrast sizes, such as seeing how values of a dependent variable change for each one-unit increase in the independent variable. In societies like ours that use a decimal (base 10) system of numbers, another frequently used contrast size is some multiple of 10.

Although one-unit contrasts are realistic or interesting for <u>some</u> topics (and contexts and systems of measurement), for other situations, that contrast size doesn't make any sense. The level and distribution of a quantitative variable help determine whether a one-unit contrast is too big, too small, or just right for that variable. Figure 8.6 shows the same bell-shaped distribution spanning different ranges of values (labeled on the x-axis).

Figure 8.6 When a One-Unit Contrast Size Is (a) Too Big, (b) Too Small, (c) Just Right

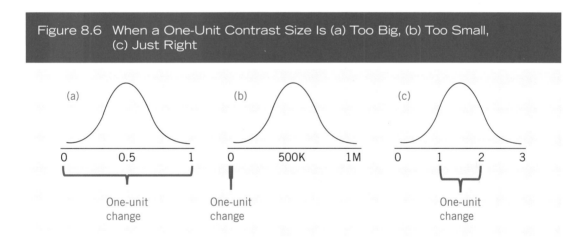

When a One-Unit Contrast Is Too Big

For independent variables whose values fall mostly between 0 and 1 or are clustered within a couple of units of each other in the data set, a one-unit increase will be <u>too large</u> of a contrast (Figure 8.6a).

> <u>Example</u>: Over the past few decades, the U.S. EPA has implemented stricter national air quality standards (NAAQS), lowering the limit below which ozone must fall from 0.085 parts per million (ppm) in 1997, to 0.080 ppm in 2008, to 0.070 parts per million in 2015 (U.S. Environmental Protection Agency, 2018).

*The policy changes in the NAAQS were in increments of 0.005 parts per million, so a change (**contrast size**) of 1.0 ppm would be <u>far too big</u> for comparing outcomes of the ozone reductions.*

Another common situation in which a one-unit contrast is too big occurs when the independent variable is measured as a proportion. The valid range for a proportion is 0.0 to 1.0, so a 1.0-unit increase would span the entire theoretically possible range of such a variable, representing upper and lower bounds rather than a reasonable change.

When a One-Unit Contrast Is Too Small

On the other hand, there are some variables for which a one-unit contrast is too small: Those whose values are very high or have a range many units wide (Figure 8.6b).

Example: If you were studying the United States in 2019, a $1 increase in weekly income would be trivially small. However, if you were studying the United States a century ago or one of the world's poorest countries today, a $1 increase in weekly income would be a suitable-sized contrast.

*With a median weekly income of about $900 in the United States in 2019 (U.S. Bureau of Labor Statistics, 2019), most people couldn't even report their income to the nearest $1, and few would even notice a $1 increase (**contrast size**) to their weekly take-home pay.*

Criteria for Identifying Contrast Sizes

There are two main types of criteria for choosing a contrast size for a particular research question and variables: first, **theoretical** considerations for the specific topic and, second, **empirical** information based on the context and method of measurement.

Theoretical Criteria for Contrast Size

When determining an appropriate contrast size for a variable, researchers should consider the kinds of topic-related thresholds, cutoffs, and standard patterns discussed earlier in this chapter, as well as historical or expected future changes that affect the concept under study.

Example: When comparing health outcomes for people with different levels of blood pressure, a contrast size of 10 mmHg (millimeters of mercury) makes sense because it aligns with the widths of the ranges clinicians use to distinguish between normal blood pressure (<120 mmHg), elevated (120 to 129 mmHg), hypertension Stage 1 (130 to 139 mmHg), and hypertension Stage 2 (140 mmHg or higher).

> *A 1 mmHg **contrast** is <u>too small to be clinically meaningful</u> (a **theoretical** consideration) or <u>measured accurately</u> (an **empirical measurement** issue). Reading the literature identified well-established ranges of systolic blood pressure used by clinicians to screen for health risks such as heart attack risk (American Heart Association, 2018), matching both the **topic** and its **units of measurement**.*

<u>Example</u>: In early 2019, proposed legislation called for the U.S. federal minimum wage to increase from $7.25 per hour to $15.00 by the year 2024 (Selyukh, 2019), so it makes sense to look at a $7.75 increase when studying the impact of that change on poverty and employment.

> *A $1 per hour increase would be <u>far too small</u> of a **contrast size**, given the size of the proposed change. Instead, the contrast size should match the proposed legislation.*

Empirical Criteria for Contrast Size

If theoretical criteria aren't available to guide the choice of a contrast size for the topic, researchers often use **empirical** information on the distribution of a variable or its association with other variables of interest to identify a suitable contrast. You will learn more about those measures in Chapters 9 and 10.

<u>Example</u>: An admissions counselor might compare college grades for students in the top quartile (top 25%) of SAT scores to those for students in the second-to-highest quartile.

A combination of theoretical and empirical considerations should be used to determine an appropriate contrast size for a given variable, context, and measurement approach.

- **Theoretical considerations** include whether there are standard patterns, thresholds, or target values or ranges used to analyze that topic or historical or impending changes to that variable in its real-world context.

- **Empirical considerations** include definitional limits on the values a variable can assume and the observed distribution or trend in the data at hand.

- Both empirical and theoretical criteria should take into account the topic, context (Ws), and method used to measure the variable.

Rescaling continuous variables to adjust contrast size. When a one-unit change is too big or too small of a contrast for a particular variable, researchers often rescale that variable so that a one-unit change is better suited to its level and range.

Example: Instead of analyzing today's annual family income in the United States in single dollars, researchers create a new version of that variable by dividing by 10,000.

> *With the revised **scale**, a "one-unit contrast" is a **$10,000** increase, which is much better suited to the **topic** (annual income) and **context** (United States today).*

Example: Instead of specifying the air quality standards in parts per million (ppm), the newer air quality standards are reported in parts per billion (ppb), by multiplying ppm values by 1,000. Thus, the 2015 standard becomes 70 parts per billion instead of 0.070 parts per million.

> *Whereas a 1-part per million decrease in ozone levels is **much too big** for the observed levels, a 1-part per billion decrease is much closer to the actual implementation.*

Considerations for Comparability

Before comparing numeric values of a variable, researchers must consider how topic, context, and measurement affect comparability.

Measurement

For numeric values to be compared with one another, they must be measured in consistent units and/or categories. The level of aggregation (e.g., person, family, community) must also be consistent.

Units

All values of continuous variables must be in the same system and scale of measurement before they can be compared. A **conversion factor** (or multiplier) can be used to convert measures from one set of units into another, or to change the scale within a system of measurement as in the income and air quality examples just used. See Appendix A for more on conversion factors.

Example: Rohan is 4 feet, 7 inches tall. Before his doctor can look up his height on a growth chart, it needs to be expressed in inches, not mixed feet and inches.

> *There are 12 inches in a foot, so his height in inches is (4 feet × 12 inches/ foot) + 7 inches, or 55 inches. When the **conversion factor** "12 inches per foot" is multiplied by "feet," the "feet" units cancel, **converting** that component of his height into inches.*

Example: A study seeks to compare heights of Bangladeshi and British children. The Bangladeshi children were measured in centimeters, whereas the British children were measured in inches.

> Using the **conversion factor** 2.54 centimeters per inch, either the Imperial units could be **converted** into metric (by multiplying) or the metric units converted into Imperial (by dividing). Then all the children's heights would be in a consistent **system of measurement** and could be directly **compared** with one another.

Example: An American student, Talia, went to study in Beijing for the fall 2019 semester. For her first few days of expenses there, she converted $200 (USD) into Chinese currency, obtaining 1,370 Yuan Renminbi (¥, abbreviated CNY; The Money Converter, 2019). The same semester, a Chinese student, Meili, was an exchange student at a university in New York City. For her first few days of expenses, she converted 2,000 ¥ into American currency, obtaining $292.

> The **currency exchange** rate is the **conversion factor**, translating prices from one **system of currency** to another. In June 2019, 1 U.S. dollar ($) was worth 6.85 ¥. Thus, Talia's calculation was $200 × 6.85 CNY/USD = 1,370 ¥. The **exchange rate** from CNY to USD was $0.146USD/CNY, so Meili's calculation was 2,000 CNY × 0.146 USD/CNY = $292.

A **conversion factor** is a multiplier that converts a quantity expressed in one set of units into the equivalent quantity expressed in another set of units.

Categories

If the categories used in one dataset are defined differently than the corresponding categories used to classify that characteristic in another dataset, they cannot be directly compared.

Example: One dataset classifies respondents into seven racial/ethnic groups: Non-Hispanic black, non-Hispanic White, Hispanic, Asian, Native American, Pacific Islander, and "other racial/ethnic groups." A second dataset classifies them into four groups: non-Hispanic black, non-Hispanic white, Hispanic, and "other racial/ethnic groups."

> The scope of "other race" is not consistent in the two data sets, so their distributions cannot be **directly compared**. However, a new variable

*could be defined in the first data set, combining Asian, Native American, and Pacific Islander with "other" to mimic the four-category classification in the second data set, allowing the values of the <u>equivalently classified</u> variables to be **compared** with one another.*

> To be compared, data must be in a **consistent set of units and/or categories**.

Context

For most quantitative research, an important objective is assessing whether an independent variable measuring some aspect of context such as date, location, or demographic group is associated with an outcome of interest. To do so, researchers should vary only one aspect of context at a time—either when <u>or</u> where <u>or</u> whom—<u>not</u> several of the W's at once. If more than one of those comparisons is important, a separate calculation should be performed for each of those independent variables to better understand how that specific W relates to the dependent variable.

> <u>Example</u>: A researcher compares the unemployment rate for 2018 among Montreal residents who did not complete high school against the unemployment rate for 2010 for all adults in Canada.
>
> *Here, the comparison changes the **date** (2018 versus 2010), **location** (one city versus the entire country), <u>and</u> **education level**. With all three of those W's (**independent variables**) being varied at the same time, it is impossible to figure out how much of any observed difference in unemployment rates (**dependent variable**) was due to date versus place versus educational attainment. Instead, the researcher should conduct <u>three</u> **separate comparisons**—one for <u>each</u> dimension.*

> When conducting a comparison, vary only one "W" or characteristic at a time—<u>either</u> the time, location, <u>or</u> group.

Comparison Across Time

When comparing monetary values across time within a particular country, the comparison should first correct those values for inflation by converting **current** units (e.g., in U.S. currency, current dollars) into **constant** units (e.g., constant dollars) (Bureau of Labor Statistics, 2020a).

> <u>Example</u>: In 2020, your 10-year-old kid brother told your grandfather that he receives $10/week in allowance. Your grandfather was shocked,

saying that when he was 10 (back in 1970), he received only $1.50/week. Your mom reminded them that there had been inflation over that 50-year period, so instead of comparing the <u>current</u> dollar value for the years when each of them received their allowance, they needed to first **convert** them to values for the <u>same</u> year—either 1970 or 2020.

Factoring in inflation, it turns out that your grandfather's allowance was actually worth slightly <u>more</u> than your brother's. $1.50 in 1970 dollars was worth $10.24 in 2020; $10 in 2020 dollars was worth $1.47 in 1970 (Bureau of Labor Statistics, 2020b).

Comparison Across Location

When comparing economic values across locations, another aspect of comparability is that a monetary unit in one context should have equivalent real-world value in another context. To make this kind of correction, a **cost-of-living index** is used to compare costs of goods and services in one location to those in another.

<u>Example</u>: Wanting to make sure she had planned a realistic budget for her semester abroad, Talia compared the cost of living in Beijing to that in New York City. Although she was used to paying $1,500 a month to rent an apartment in New York City, she learned that she would have to budget only about $605/month for rent in Beijing (Numbeo, 2019). Thus, she was able to reduce her overall budget for her time in Beijing.

*In late December 2019, the **cost of living** was only about 45% as high in Beijing as in NYC. In other words, simply converting the $1,500 she usually spent each month on rent in NYC into Chinese currency would <u>not</u> accurately reflect what Talia could purchase with that amount of money in Beijing because the cost of living was lower in Beijing than in NYC.*

Comparison Across Units, Place, and Time

To make monetary comparisons as consistent as possible across settings, international financial comparisons are based on purchasing power parity (PPP). **Purchasing power** of a currency refers to the amount of that currency needed to purchase a common basket of goods and services, such as food, clothing, and housing, and **parity** means equivalence or comparability (Economics Online, 2019). By adjusting for currency conversion, cost of living adjustment, <u>and</u> correction for inflation, PPP accounts for differences in units (measurement) as well as where and when (two aspects of context).

<u>Example</u>: Figure 8.7a shows the 2014 gross domestic product (GDP) of 11 countries when each was converted into nominal U.S. dollars. When price differences between countries were <u>not</u> taken into account, the United States had by far the highest GDP, more than $7,000 billion

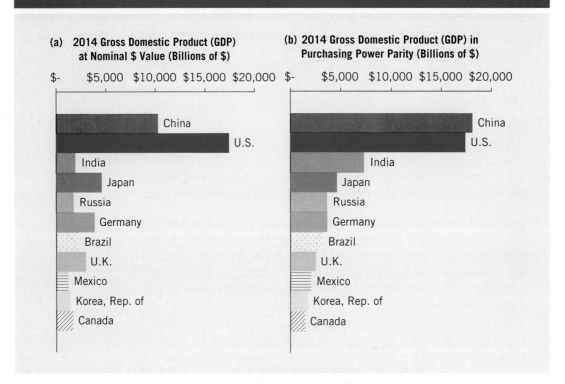

Figure 8.7   International Comparison of Gross Domestic Product With Two
             Different Measures of Monetary Value: (a) Nominal and
             (b) Purchasing Power Parity

Note: In the context of prices, "nominal" does not refer to a level of measurement but rather to the fact that GDP is evaluated at current market prices and does not take into account changes in prices due to inflation.

Source: Data from Economics Online (2019).

higher than second-place China and more than three times that of third-place Japan. In Figure 8.7b, where GDP is presented in PPP-adjusted rates, GDP in China (with its much lower cost of living) slightly exceeds that of the United States, India moves up from 7th to 3rd place, and Japan drops to 4th.

> ***Purchasing power parity*** (PPP) *equalizes the value of GDP in different currencies by converting them into the same **currency system** <u>and</u> factoring in **differences in prices** for a consistent set of goods. When PPP units were used, the gap in GDP between the richer and poorer countries was substantially reduced, and the rank order of the countries changed.*

Example: In 2008, prices in PPP units were much higher in Denmark or Ireland than in Romania or Bulgaria (OECD/Eurostat, 2012).

> Even though all those countries used the same **system of currency** (Euro; €), the purchasing power of that currency varied from country to country due to differences in their costs of living. Hence, **PPP** factors were needed to convert those expenditures into a <u>consistent</u> **scale** before their prices could be compared.

A **currency exchange rate** is used to convert the value from one system of currency to another. **Current dollars** (also known as **nominal dollars**) refers to the value in the prices for that year. **Constant dollars** (also known as **real dollars**) refers to monetary value after adjustment for inflation which is used to compare the purchasing power of currency across time. A **cost-of-living index** is used to compare costs of goods and services in different places and times. **Purchasing power parity** (**PPP**) takes into account (a) currency exchange rates, (b) differences in cost of living, and (c) inflation in different places and times. **Parity** means equivalence or comparability.

Comparability of Standards

Although the term "standard" implies consistency in scope and numeric value, in practice standards can vary substantially across time, place, and other factors. Researchers should confirm that all values to be compared were based on the same standard. For some topics and contexts, agreed-upon dates are the standards for comparisons.

Example: In 1988, the base period for the Consumer Price Index (CPI) was changed to 1982–1984 for calculating the rate of inflation.

> The base period has been updated periodically since 1890 (U.S. Bureau of Labor Statistics, 2018b). Any comparison in cost of living across time must use a <u>consistent</u> **base period** for all calculations.

Due to changes over time in the way something is defined or measured, various standards are updated periodically.

Example: "Across the United States, the heights of structures, landmarks, valleys, hills and just about everything else are about to change, at least with regard to <u>average sea level</u> [which has historically been used as the **reference point**]. Most will get shorter. Parts of the

Pacific Northwest will shrink by as much as five feet, and parts of Alaska by six-and-a-half feet" (Mitchell, 2020).

> *The **standard height reference** has been **adjusted** five times since 1900, most recently in 1988. As of the time of this writing, the United States and Mexico use the 1988 standard, which will be replaced with the new National Spatial Reference System in late 2022 or 2023.*

Standards also vary by location.

<u>Example</u>: Limits for 24-hour average levels of particulate matter (hazardous particles suspended in the air) range from a low of 50 micrograms per cubic meter ($\mu g/m^3$) in the European Union and residential areas of China to 100 $\mu g/m^3$ in Japan, 150 $\mu g/m^3$ in the United States, and 250 $\mu g/m^3$ in industrial regions of China (National Environmental Research Institute of Denmark, n.d.). Thus, a value of 130 $\mu g/m^3$ would be acceptable in the United States, but substantially above the allowable limit in the EU or Japan.

> *Complicating comparisons based on <u>different</u> **international standards** is that they often calculate averages over <u>different</u> **time intervals**: over a 1-hour, 8-hour, or even 24-hour period.*

Standards, patterns, or thresholds can also differ according to other characteristics.

<u>Example</u>: In 2018, the United States federal poverty threshold for a single elderly person was $12,043, compared to $16,815 for two adults under age 65 with no children, and $25,465 for a family with two adults and two children (Table 8.1) (U.S. Census Bureau, 2018f).

> *The **poverty thresholds** for a particular year <u>vary</u> by the total number of people in the household and their ages, with <u>differing</u> amounts for adults under age 65 years than those 65 and older, and for children under age 18.*

The initial choice of a reference group or value may have been arbitrary: it might not matter which location, time, or group was selected as the basis of comparison. However, once a reference value has been chosen, it should be used for most (if not all) calculations addressing a particular question. Researchers should consult the literature to ensure that their approach is consistent with existing conventions.

<u>Example</u>: With New York City as the reference city, the **cost-of-living index** (COLI) values in December 2019 were 45, 49, and 81 for Beijing, Prague, and Sydney, respectively (Numbeo, 2019). If instead, Berlin

had been used as the **reference city**, the corresponding values for those cities would have been 68, 78, and 123.

> *The results of a cost-of-living comparison differ depending on which city was used as the* **reference value**. *The cost of living was <u>lower</u> in Beijing, Prague, and Sydney than in <u>New York City</u>, reflected in COLI values <u>below 100</u> for all three cities. However, the cost of living was <u>higher</u> in Sydney than in <u>Berlin</u>, yielding a COLI <u>above 100</u> for Sydney when Berlin was used as the* **reference city**: *cost of living was 23% higher in Sydney <u>than in Berlin</u>.*

When comparing several values, researchers should choose one value of the independent variable against which <u>each</u> of the other values is compared, using criteria related to the research question and intended audience. Even when only two values are to be compared, one of those values should be identified as the comparison value because that choice determines where that value should be placed in the formula for the calculation (Chapters 9 and 13) and how the results should be phrased (Chapter 14).

The **topic**, the **ways in which a variable was measured and collected**, and the **context** in which it was studied can all affect whether values of that variable can be correctly compared with one another.

All comparisons of numbers for a given analysis should be based on a **consistent standard**, whether a set of norms, threshold, benchmark, or target value.

TERMS AND CONCEPTS

HIGHLIGHTS

- Understanding how to select and use appropriate **comparison values**, **contrast sizes**, and **standards** is an important step in conducting and understanding data analysis.

- Researchers use both internal and external **comparison values** to assess how values from their data compare to **standard patterns** or important **cutoffs** for the issue under study. These comparisons provide perspective on whether a given value is average or unusual, high or low, or meets some kind of **threshold** for the topic.

- **Standards** include a variety of **patterns, records, cyclical patterns**, and **benchmarks** or **target values**, based either on existing data or on associations with related characteristics or outcomes of the topic in its real-world context.

- **Theoretical criteria** for choosing comparison values include social or cultural norms, spatial and temporal factors, and interests of the intended audience for the work.

- **Empirical criteria** for identifying pertinent comparison values and contrast sizes include levels and distributions of values of the variables under study.

- The **topic**, the **context** in which it was studied and the ways in which it was **measured** are all important elements to consider when selecting appropriate comparison values and contrast sizes for quantitative research.

RESEARCH TIPS

- Read the literature to identify contrast sizes, thresholds, benchmarks, standards, targets, or other comparison values that are commonly used to analyze numbers for a particular topic, type of measure, and context.

- Pay attention to how measurement affects the choice of comparison values and contrast sizes.

- Check that numbers to be compared are in consistent units; if not, they must be converted to consistent units before comparisons can be conducted.

EXERCISES

Individual Exercises

Quantitative Reasoning in Everyday Life

1. Watch a live weather forecast on the Weather Channel or your local station for half an hour on a weekday morning to see whether they compared any weather data against a benchmark value. If so, describe what type of benchmark (e.g., record, topic-specific comparison value). For any comparisons, identify the (a) concept, (b) units, (c) location, and (d) time to which the reference value refers (e.g., yesterday or 10-year average).

2. For sports or other recreational activities, identify a measure that uses the following (one at a time): (a) a threshold, (b) a series of cutoffs to define ranges or categories, (c) a standard pattern (e.g., a trend or cyclical

pattern), and (d) a historical record. In an authoritative source of information on the numeric value of each of those measures, find (i) the numeric value of the pertinent threshold, cutoff, or pattern; (ii) its units; and (iii) how values above or below that value are interpreted.

3. Use the Bureau of Labor Statistics inflation calculator (https://www.bls.gov/data/inflation_calculator.htm) to figure out how much (a) your current income would have been worth 10 years ago, (b) your current income would have been worth 25 years ago; (c) an income of $20,000 from 50 years ago would be worth today.

Interpreting Research

4. In the Executive Summary of the UNESCO report "Migration, Displacement and Education: Building Bridges, Not Walls" (https://unesdoc.unesco.org/ark:/48223/pf0000266092), identify two or three numeric comparisons across categories (e.g., groups, institutions, or locations) in some outcome. (a) Specify what comparison group or value the authors used. (b) Determine whether the authors explained why they used that comparison group or value—for example, whether it was (i) benchmark or threshold for the topic, (ii) the most common group or value, (iii) another value of interest and, if so, (iv) chosen for what reason. (c) For each type of comparison or calculation (i) identify the reference value, (ii) specify whether it comes from within the data set used by the author or from some other source (e.g., a historic value or a reference population), and (iii) discuss whether the author provided a citation to the source of the comparison value.

5. In the same document used in the previous question, identify three numeric comparisons

across values of a continuous variable. For each such comparison, (a) identify what contrast size (how many units of that variable); (b) determine whether the authors explained why they chose that contrast size; (c) indicate whether the authors provide enough information for you to assess whether it is a realistic difference or change for the (i) topic, (ii) context, and (iii) units. (d) Discuss whether different or additional size contrasts would be useful for the intended audience, considering (i) plausibility, (ii) real-world application, and (iii) measurement issues discussed in this chapter.

Analyzing Data

6. Use information in Table 8A to calculate the difference (from subtraction) between Black households and the reference group, with (a) Asian households as the reference group, (b) Hispanic households as the reference group, and (c) White households as the reference group. (d) Write separate sentences to report the results of each of those calculations.

Table 8A	Median Income by Race and Hispanic Origin of Householder, United States, 2018
Race/Hispanic Origin	**Median Income**
White	$66,943
Black	$41,631
Asian/Pacific Islander	$87,194
Hispanic (can be of any race)	$51,450

Source: U.S. Bureau of the Census. (2020b). Table A-1. Income summary measures by selected characteristics: 2017 and 2018.

7. Use information in Table 8B to calculate the difference in world population between the specified year and 2020, with (a) 2015 as the reference year, (b) 2010 as the reference year, and (c) 2000 as the reference year. (d) Write separate sentences to report the results of each of those calculations.

Table 8B World Population, 2000 to 2020	
Year	Population (billions)
2000	6.1
2010	7.0
2015	7.4
2020	7.8

Source: United Nations (2019).

Group Exercises

Interpreting Research

8. Using information in the Program for the International Assessment of Adult Competencies report (https://nces.ed.gov/surveys/piaac/current_results.asp), perform the following steps based on Figures 1-A and 1-B about numeracy in the United States compared with other countries. (a) Identify the reference values and/or benchmarks used by the authors. (b) Determine whether the authors explained why they chose that reference value or values. (c) Discuss whether you agree with their choice(s) and, if not, (d) what other value(s) you would use instead or in addition.

9. Find a scholarly article or research report on how COVID-19 affected mortality, unemployment, travel, or shopping behavior or other outcome of interest. (a) Discuss how you think the authors chose the comparison dates, locations, groups, or other values they used in their analysis—for example, whether they identified historic highs or lows, averages, or some other type of threshold, pattern, or cutoff. (b) Consider how their point might have changed if they had used a different comparison value.

Analyzing Data

10. Exchange your answers to Exercise 6 with a classmate. Provide each other with feedback on whether (a) the numeric results are correct, (b) the sentences correctly convey the reference group, and (c) the sentences correctly convey the direction and magnitude of the difference. (d) Revise your description to correct any errors found by your peer reviewer.

Figure 1-A   Average Scores on PIAAC Literacy, Numeracy, and Digital Problem Solving for U.S. Adults Age 16 to 65: 2021/14 and 2017

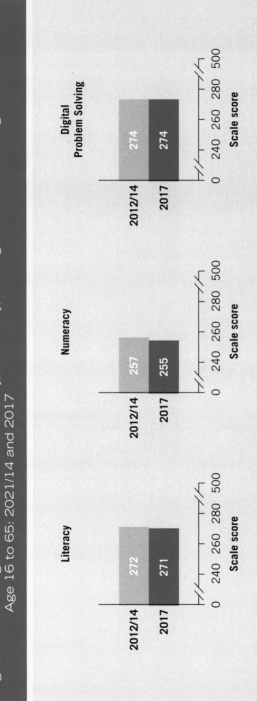

Note: LIT = Literacy, NUM = Numeracy, DPS = Digital problem solving. The PIAAC literacy, numeracy, and digital problem solving scales range from 0 to 500. Some apparent differences between estimates may not be statistically significant. Only statistically significant differences between years are marked with an asterisk. Users may explore other differences via the full data links and using the International Data Explorer tools.

Source: U.S. Department of Education, National Center for Education Statistics, Program for the International Assessment of Adult Competencies (PIAAC), U.S. PIAAC 2017, U.S. PIAAC 2012/2014.

Figure 1-B   Percentage Distribution of U.S. Adults Age 16 to 65 at Selected Levels of Proficiency on PIAAC Literacy, Numeracy, and Digital Problem Solving: 2012/14 and 2017

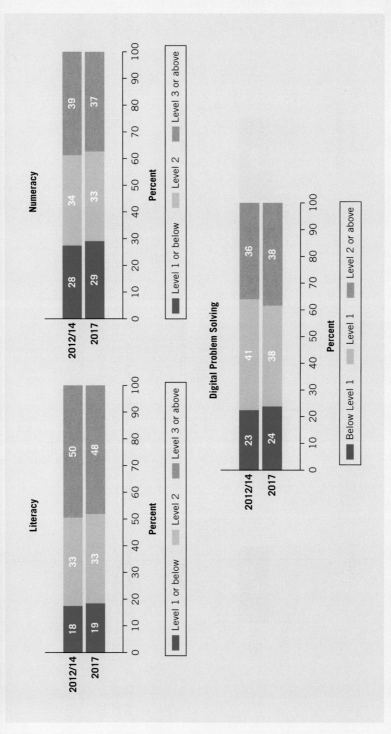

Note: LIT = Literacy, NUM = Numeracy, DPS = Digital problem solving. Detail may not sum to totals because of rounding. Only statistically significant differences between years are marked with an asterisk. Users may explore other differences via the full data links and using the International Data Explorer tools. In literacy and numeracy, higher, middle, and lower performance are denoted by "Level 3 or above," "Level 2," and "Level 1 or below," respectively. In digital problem solving, these are denoted by "Level 2 or above," "Level 1," and "Below level 1."

Source: U.S. Department of Education, National Center for Education Statistics, Program for the International Assessment of Adult Competencies (PIAAC), U.S. PIAAC 2017, U.S. PIAAC 2012/2014.

CHAPTER 9

Numbers, Comparisons, and Calculations

Learning Objectives

After reading this chapter, you will be able to do the following:

1. Identify frequently used measures of level or value.

2. Assess plausibility of values for measures of level.

3. Apply common measures of position in a list (rank).

4. Evaluate plausibility of values for measures of rank.

5. Use different types of mathematical calculations to compare numbers.

6. Assess plausibility of values for different types of numeric calculations.

7. Understand how a variable's level of measurement determines which types of comparisons and calculations can be conducted with values of that variable.

8. Choose comparisons and calculations to suit the research topic and field.

Not surprisingly, an essential part of quantitative research involves comparing numeric values such as information about individual cases, statistics for populations or subgroups, or trends across time. In this chapter, I start by reviewing common measures of level and then progress to discussing different types of numeric comparisons and calculations, focusing on the criteria for evaluating whether the results of a comparison or calculation make sense based on the procedure used to produce it. For a general reference on mathematical terms and formulas, see Vogt and Johnson (2011) or Kornegay (1999).

To help you learn how to decide which types of comparison to use, I discuss the kinds of questions each of those procedures can (and cannot) answer. I also explain how level of measurement of a variable determines which types of comparisons and calculations can be done with values of that variable. Finally, I discuss how choices about which measures and comparisons to use for a particular research project are affected by topic, field, and audience.

The material in this chapter is mostly "behind-the-scenes" information: vital to conducting and interpreting comparisons and calculations but <u>not</u> usually included in a research paper. (**<u>Exception:</u>** In class or for homework assignments, your instructor might ask you to explain the steps you took to arrive at your answers in order to have you demonstrate that you understand and can work with the concepts.) In this chapter, I use mathematical terminology and equations to convey the elements of each type of comparison or calculation. Then in Chapter 14, I demonstrate how to communicate quantitative results, focusing on how they answer the research question at hand rather than on how the numeric results were produced.

Numeric Measures of Level

Knowing the definition of a measure and the units in which it is measured are critical to making sense of numbers because that information helps one identify possible minimum and maximum values and determine whether a variable can take on decimal or fractional values. In this section, I review common measures of the level for a single case or summary statistic for a sample or population, how each is created, and limits on their values. Note that the **numeric level** (or **value**) of a variable is a distinct concept from its **level <u>of measurement</u>** (see Chapter 4; also see the section on "How Level of Measurement Affects Valid Types of Comparisons," later in this chapter).

Value or Level

The **level** is the numeric **value** of a quantitative variable for one case, population, location, group, or time. Depending on the concept under study, the value may be in integer, whole number, or real number form. **Integers** are numbers that do not have a fractional part or any digits after the decimal point; they can be positive, negative, or zero. Phenomena that exist as discrete (separate) countable items are measured with **whole numbers**, which include zero and the positive integers.

> Example: A family is applying for social benefits. On the application form, they report that their family consists of three adults and no children.
>
> *The counts of adults and children are measured in **whole numbers**. There <u>cannot</u> be a fractional or decimal number of people in a family, nor can that number be negative!*

> Example: An underground parking garage labels the floors −4, −3, −2, −1, and 0.

*Zero (0) denotes ground level, and the **negative integers** convey the number of levels <u>below</u> ground level. A fractional floor level is impossible.*

Variables measuring things that can take on partial units are measured in **real numbers**, which encompass integers as well as values with decimal or fractional values.

<u>Example</u>: A pancake recipe calls for 2 cups of flour, 1 teaspoon of baking powder, ¼ teaspoon salt, 1½ cups of milk, and 2 eggs.

*Eggs are counted with **whole numbers**, but the other ingredients are measured with **real numbers** because they can include **fractional** units. It makes sense to say 2.0 cups of flour or 1.0 teaspoons of baking powder, but <u>not</u> 2.0 eggs!*

Numeric values include **integers, whole numbers,** and **real numbers.** An **integer** is a number that has no fractional part and no digits after the decimal point. **Whole numbers** include zero and the positive integers. **Real numbers** can include **fractional** or **decimal** components.

Incidence and Prevalence

As you read statistics about disease patterns, you may encounter the terms "incidence" and "prevalence," which are two different measures of frequency. **Incidence** refers to <u>new</u> cases that were identified with the condition of interest during a specified time period, whereas **prevalence** refers to <u>all</u> (new and previously existing) cases at that time (Schneider & Lilienfeld, 2015). In economic terminology, incidence measures <u>flow</u> (introduction of new cases), and prevalence measures <u>stock</u> (total number of cases at a point in time). Incidence and prevalence can be reported as the number of cases (whole numbers), the affected percentage of the population (which can take on decimal values), or as a rate (see the following section). Incidence and prevalence can also be used to measure the frequency of other conditions or characteristics—not just health issues.

<u>Example</u>: In 2018, an estimated 1.7 million individuals worldwide became newly infected with HIV. In that year, approximately 37.9 million people had HIV/AIDS (HIV.gov, 2020a).

*Incidence (<u>new</u> cases) of HIV was 1.7 million cases; **prevalence** was 37.9 million (<u>all</u> surviving cases, whether newly or previously diagnosed). With the **scale of measurement** rounded to millions, the numbers can take on **decimal** values.*

<u>Example</u>: In 2017, there were 39.7 million poor people in the United States, comprising 12.3% of the total population (Fontenot et al., 2019).

*These statistics are measures of **prevalence** because they include both people who <u>became</u> poor in 2017 and those who <u>remained</u> poor from previous years. Anyone who <u>became</u> non-poor between 2016 and 2017 would be included in the 2016 poverty **prevalence** statistics but <u>not</u> in the 2017 prevalence figures. **Incidence** of poverty in 2017 (not reported here) would count people who became newly poor in that year.*

Incidence refers to <u>new</u> cases of a disease or status that were identified during a specified time period, whereas **prevalence** refers to all cases present within that time period (both new and cumulative remaining from previous time periods).

Rating

Ratings are used to capture assessments of the quality or extent of some attribute, often collected using Likert-type questions with responses along a spectrum such as strongly disagree to strongly agree or poor to excellent (see Chapter 4). Although the rating scale response options offered to individual respondents are often whole numbers, an <u>average</u> rating can include decimal values.

<u>Example</u>: Based on a total of 200 student evaluations, Professor Oh was rated 3.7 on a scale from 1 to 5.

*Each student could **rate** the professor 1, 2, 3, 4, or 5 (**positive integer** values). The professor's overall evaluation score was an average of the 200 students' ratings, resulting in a **decimal** value.*

When reporting results of ratings, the minimum and maximum possible values of the rating scale should be specified so that readers can assess the meaning of a particular value.

<u>Example</u>: A restaurant proudly advertises that it earned an average rating of 4.8 stars. Thinking that was a really strong rating, you were disappointed to discover that the food was just OK.

*Fine print on the restaurant's website revealed that the rating scale ran from 1 to 10, meaning that 4.8 stars represented only a mediocre rating, rather than the "excellent" you assumed it meant when you believed that 5 was the **maximum** possible rating.*

The conceptual meaning of each number on a rating scale should also be specified, along with whether higher values or lower values are favorable.

<u>Example</u>: A numeric scale to assess the challenge level of a task could rate either the difficulty or the ease of that task.

*If the scale measures increasing <u>difficulty</u>, **higher** numbers reflect harder tasks. However, if the **rating** scale measures increasing <u>ease</u>, **lower** numbers reflect harder tasks.*

Ratings are assessments of quality or degree along a numeric spectrum, reflecting low to high values for the attribute or phenomenon being rated.

Ratios

Ratios are calculated by dividing one quantity by another. Sometimes the topic and units are the same for the numerator and denominator of the ratio; other times, the concepts and units are different for the numerator than for the denominator. Units for the calculated ratio will be the number of units for the numerator per unit in the denominator, where **per** means "for each."

<u>Example</u>: In China in 2017, the sex ratio at birth was 1.119 males per female, which is equivalent to 111.9 males per 100 females (UNICEF, 2019).

*Sex **ratio** at birth = number of male births ÷ number of female births; thus, both the **numerator** and **denominator** measure the same **topic** (births) in the same **units** (number of cases). Clearly, the **scale of the units** matters: plausible values if the sex ratio is expressed **per** <u>100 female births</u> are 100 times as high as if it is in the original **scale** (**per** <u>female birth</u>).*

<u>Example</u>: In 2018, the world population density was 535 people per square kilometer of arable land (Population Reference Bureau, 2018).

*The concepts and units in the numerator and denominator of a density calculation are <u>different</u> from one another: the number of people in millions in a geographic area (in this example, the entire world) in the **numerator** and the number of square kilometers of farmable land in that geographic area in the **denominator**.*

Rates

A **rate of occurrence** is a form of ratio measuring how often a particular type of event takes place in a defined population in a specified period of time. The concepts in the numerator and denominator of a rate are measured in different units, with the numerator measuring number of events, and the denominator measuring the number of people or other entities at risk of experiencing that event. In other words, the denominator includes only those who are susceptible to that type of event. Common units for rates include percentage (out of 100), per 1,000, or per 100,000—chosen to reflect the scale of occurrence.

Example: In 2018, Honduras had the highest murder rate in the world, with 90.4 homicides per 100,000 people (WorldAtlas, 2019).

*Each country's murder **rate** is calculated as the number of murders in that country in 2018 ÷ number of people in that country in that same year × 100,000 to put it into the desired **scale**.*

Example: In Mexico in 2011, approximately half (50%) of secondary school students dropped out (Reuters, 2011).

*The secondary school dropout **rate** = (number of students who dropped out of secondary school ÷ number enrolled in secondary school) × 100. Only students who were enrolled in secondary school are "at risk of" (eligible for) dropping out at that level of schooling, so the **denominator** is limited to that group.*

Example: In 2018, the incidence of HIV was 13.3 per 100,000 persons in the United States (HIV.gov, 2020b).

*The **incidence rate** was calculated as the number of newly diagnosed cases in 2018 divided by the entire U.S. population in that year, multiplied by 100,000.*

Although the root of the terms is the same, do <u>not</u> confuse "rate" with "rating!"

Ratios and rates are measures of **level** when they are calculated for an individual entity (e.g., one group, place, or time point). Later sections cover how those measures can be used to compare two or more groups, places, times, or outcomes.

Risk

Risk is the probability that a particular type of event or outcome will occur, often expressed as a percentage. The risk of a future outcome can be estimated using the past rate of occurrence for that event, assuming that factors affecting that rate remain the same as in the period for which it was calculated.

Example: Allemani and colleagues (2018) found that in the United States, the 5-year survival **rate** for women diagnosed with breast cancer between 2010 and 2014 was 90.2%. When counseling a patient with a new diagnosis of breast cancer, a physician might inform her that she would have about that chance of living at least 5 years after her diagnosis.

A **ratio** is simply one number divided by another $= d \div c$. The units of a ratio will be units of the concept in the numerator (**d**) per (for each) unit of the concept in the denominator (**c**). A **rate** is a measure of occurrence in a defined population within a specified period of time = number of events in a population ÷ number of people "at risk of" that type of event in that population during the same time period × scale factor. **Risk** is the probability that a particular type of event will occur in the future. It is often projected based on the rate of occurrence for a similar context.

Plausibility Criteria for Measures of Level

Table 9.1 summarizes criteria for assessing the plausibility of values for numeric measures of level, including limits imposed by the definition of that measure, and whether the range and scale of its values are affected by the units in which it was measured or by the topic and context under study.

> Example: Although occasionally, infants are born weighing more than 5 kilograms (11 lbs.), the vast majority weigh less because most women's pelvises cannot physically hold a larger fetus.
>
> > Knowing the **topic** (infant birth weight) helps identify relevant criteria for upper limits on the value of that measure—in this case, anatomical constraints. The specific numeric value of that limit also depends on the **units** in which birth weight was measured: 5 <u>pounds</u> is a <u>low</u> birth weight, whereas 5 <u>kilograms</u> represents a very <u>high</u> one!
>
> Example: Number of persons in a <u>family</u> will have a much lower level and range than number of persons in a <u>town</u>, <u>nation</u>, or <u>continent</u>.
>
> > Although all are counts of people, the **level of aggregation** (family, town, or larger geographic unit) and **context** (where and when) affect the plausible **maximum** value.

As discussed in Chapter 8, many comparisons and calculations require choosing a comparison value, reference category, or standard distribution. To ensure that the results make sense for the topic, measure, context, audience, and objective of their study, researchers should decide on a comparison value <u>before</u> conducting the comparisons or calculations.

Measures of Position in a Ranked List

Measures of **position in a ranked list** pinpoint where an observed value falls in the overall ascending or descending order of the values of that list. They convey the direction but <u>not</u> the magnitude of differences between values. Measures of position do not involve mathematical computations, so they can be used to compare values of any quantitative variable—those at the ordinal, interval, or ratio level of measurement.

Rank

Rank is the position of the value for one case compared to other values in a numerically sorted list. Rank or position can be based on observed data at the same time or place (internal comparison), compared with a well-established standard, or compared with a historic high or low value (external comparisons) (Chapter 8).

The units of rank are the numeric position in that list, <u>not</u> the units of the characteristic that is being ranked. Possible values for rankings range from 1 to N,

Table 9.1 Criteria for Making Sense of Measures of Value (Level)

Type of Measure	Definitional Limits on Values	Other Criteria Affecting Scale and Range of Plausible Values	
		Topic and Context	Units of Measurement of Variable(s)
Integer	• Can be positive, zero, or negative • Cannot include decimal or fractional values	• Determine whether values can be negative, zero, and/or positive • Have a substantial effect on plausible values	• The system of measurement, scale of measurement, and level of analysis can each have a substantial effect on plausible values.
Count	• Can only be zero or positive • Cannot include decimal or fractional values	• Will have a substantial effect on plausible values	
Real number	• Can be positive, zero, or negative • Can include fractional and whole number values	• Determine whether values can be negative, zero, and/or positive • Have a substantial effect on plausible values	
Rating	• Lowest possible value is lowest value available in the scale used for rating • Highest possible value is highest value in the scale used for rating	• Minimal effect on plausible values	
Ratio = $d \div c$, where d and c are values for the concepts in the numerator and denominator, respectively.[a]	• Depending on the range of values of variables in the ratio, can be • Zero or positive (if both concepts are the same sign) • Negative (if either of the concepts can take on negative values) • Can include decimal values	• Topic and context of concepts in numerator and denominator will have a substantial effect on plausible values	• The system of measurement and level of aggregation of the variables in the numerator and denominator will have an effect on plausible values.
Rate = $ev \div pop \times$ scale factor, where ev is the number of events among cases in the population at risk, pop, during the specified time period.[c]	• Cannot be negative • Can include decimal values	• Topic and context of concepts in numerator and denominator will have a substantial effect on plausible values • Width of time period to which the rate pertains will also affect plausible values	• Scale (order of magnitude) at which the ratio or rate is reported will affect plausible values.[b]

Notes:

a. The units of a ratio will be units of numerator per unit of denominator.

b. For example, whether rate is per 100 (%), per 1,000, or per 100,000.

c. The unit of a rate will be unit of numerator per unit of denominator during the specified time period. Units are often expressed to higher orders of magnitude (scales), e.g., per 1,000 or 100,000

Table 9.2 Application of Basic Calculations to World Population Data

Geographic region	(1) Population (millions) 2005[a]	(2) Percentage of the world pop., 2005[b]	(3) Rank, 2005	(4) Ratio, 2005 (relative to Africa)[c]	(5) % difference, 2005 (rel. to Africa)[d]	(6) Population (millions) 2015	(7) Pop. change 2005 to 2015 (millions)[e]	(8) % change, 2005 to 2015[f]
World	6,542.2	100.0%	NA	NA	NA	7,383.0	840.8	12.9%
Africa	924.8	14.1%	2	1.00	0.0%	1,194.4	269.6	29.2%
Asia	3,964.3	60.6%	1	4.29	328.7%	4,419.9	455.6	11.5%
Europe	730.3	11.2%	3	0.79	−21.0%	740.8	10.5	1.4%
Latin America & the Caribbean	561.7	8.6%	4	0.61	−39.3%	632.4	70.7	12.6%
Northern America	327.5	5.0%	5	0.35	−64.6%	356.0	28.5	8.7%
Oceania	33.6	0.5%	6	0.04	−96.4%	39.5	6.0	17.8%

Source: Data from United Nations (2017).

Notes:

a. Columns 1 and 6: Level or value.

b. Column 2: Percentage of a whole. Percentage of the world's population in 2005 = (region's 2005 population ÷ world's 2005 population) × 100.

c. Column 4: Division. Ratio, **compared to Africa** in 2005 = region's 2005 population ÷ Africa's 2005 population.

d. Column 5: Percentage difference in population, **compared to Africa** in 2005 = [(region's 2005 population − Africa's 2005 population) ÷ Africa's 2005 population] × 100.

e. Column 7: Subtraction. Population change within region, 2005 to 2015 = region's 2015 population − region's 2005 population.

f. Column 8: Percentage change in population, 2005 to 2015 = [(region's 2015 population − region's 2005 population) ÷ region's 2005 population] × 100.

where N is the total number of items being rated unless there are tied values. Two or more identical values of whatever characteristic is being assessed share the same rank, just as two equal vote tallies or two identical race times constitute a tie.

Example: Asia was the most populous continent in 2005, and Oceania was the smallest continent, ranking sixth of the six continents being compared (Table 9.2, Column 3).

> *The phrase "most populous" reflects both the **rank** of 1 and the **topic** (population size). Although the units of the characteristic being ranked (billions of persons) are used to determine rank, those **units** do <u>not</u> pertain to the rank value itself.*

Figure 9.1   Ratings and Rankings of Hybrid Car Models

Car Model	Overall Consumer Rating		Ranking
2018 Toyota Prius	4.9 out of 5	★★★★★	1
2018 Hyundai Ioniq Hybrid	4.5 out of 5	★★★★☆	2
2018 Ford Fusion Hybrid	4.5 out of 5	★★★★☆	2
2018 Honda Accord Hybrid	4.3 out of 5	★★★★☆	3

Source: Data from Edmunds (2019).

Example: With an average consumer rating of 4.9 out of 5 stars, the Toyota Prius ranked #1 among 2018 hybrid car models (Figure 9.1), followed by the Hyundai Ioniq and Ford Fusion (tied for second place with 4.5 stars), and the Honda Accord (third place, with 4.3 stars).

> *Each car's **rating** was on a scale of 1 to 5, with the minimum and maximum rating limited by the range specified on the rating scale and a higher number of stars reflecting a more <u>favorable</u> **rating**. The average consumer rating was used to determine the **rank** order of the models.*

Example: In a poll of American voters prior to the 2018 midterm elections, economic issues were the most important social issue (identified as the top policy issue by 27% of respondents), followed by security issues (21%), and health care (17%; Figure 9.2). However, those rankings varied by political affiliation. For instance, health care issues (shaded blue) ranked second of all issues among Democratic voters, third among Independents, and fourth among Republicans.

> *In Figure 9.2, the bars for each issue are shaded a different color, showing how the **rank order** of the issues varied by political party affiliation. Within each political party affiliation, issues were **ranked** top to bottom in descending order of percentage of respondents who identified an issue as most important.*

Figure 9.2 Rankings of Social Issues by Political Party, U.S. Midterm Elections, 2018

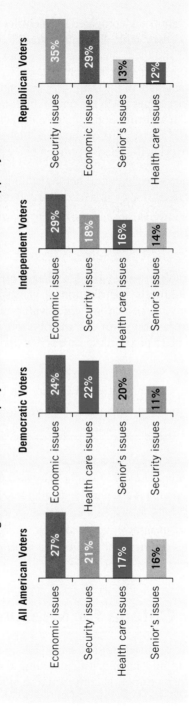

Percentages are of voters with that party affiliation who identified an issue as the top policy issue.

All American Voters

Issue	%
Economic issues	27%
Security issues	21%
Health care issues	17%
Senior's issues	16%

Democratic Voters

Issue	%
Economic issues	24%
Health care issues	22%
Senior's issues	20%
Security issues	11%

Independent Voters

Issue	%
Economic issues	29%
Security issues	18%
Health care issues	16%
Senior's issues	14%

Republican Voters

Issue	%
Security issues	35%
Economic issues	29%
Senior's issues	13%
Health care issues	12%

Source: Data from Golshan (2018).

239

Percentile

When many cases are being compared, **percentiles**, rather than position numbers, are often used to convey rank. Percentiles are calculated by ranking all the values as described above and then categorizing them into 100 groups each containing an equal share (1/100th) of the distribution (Utts & Heckard, 2014). Values that exceed 99% of all other values are in the 99th (top) percentile, whereas those that are lower than 99% of all other values are in the zeroth (bottom) percentile. Percentiles encompass all the values in a distribution, so they must fall between 0 and 99; it is impossible to be below the lowest value or above the highest value. Percentile is the unit of measurement, conveying the relative position of a value in the overall distribution.

> Example: Sophia's height placed her in the 38th percentile, meaning that she was taller than 37% of girls her age based on an international standard.
>
> *Her height was compared against an external* **standard distribution** *composed of thousands of girls her age, divided into 100 ranges (**percentiles**), each of which contained an equal share of the comparison sample.*

To describe rank in somewhat less detail, other forms of **quantiles** can be calculated by dividing the distribution of values in a sample into equal-width ranges, thus grouping percentiles into wider ranges: **deciles** (ranges of ten percentiles), **quintiles** (one-fifth of a distribution, encompassing 20 percentiles), **quartiles** (ranges of 25 percentiles), or **terciles** (the bottom, middle, and top third of a distribution) are often used.

> Example: Marco's quantitative GRE score put him in the top **quintile**.
>
> *His score was in the upper 20% (highest fifth) of all test takers nationally.*

Rank describes the position of a value in a list of values sorted in either ascending or descending numeric order; it can be calculated only for values of quantitative variables. A **percentile** is one one-hundredth (1/100th) of a distribution. The kth percentile is the value for which k% of values in the distribution are at or below that value. Other **quantiles**, such as **deciles** (tenths of a distribution), **quintiles** (fifths), **quartiles** (quarters), or **terciles** (thirds), convey the position of a value in broader groupings of the distribution.

Plausibility Criteria for Measures of Position

Table 9.3 summarizes criteria for assessing plausibility of measures of the position of a numeric value in a ranked list, including the total number of cases being ranked and whether position is conveyed as a simple position number or using percentiles or other grouped ranges of rank.

Table 9.3 Criteria for Making Sense of Measures of Position in a Ranked List

Measure of Position	Definitional Limits on Values	Other Criteria: Topic and Context	Other Criteria: Units of Measurement of Basis of Ranking	Comments
Rank = Position in an ordered list	• Lowest numeric value of rank is 1. • Highest numeric value of rank is determined by number of values being ranked. • Can be < total # of cases because of ties	Interpretation of a measure of position is affected by the following aspects of topic and context: • Whether higher positions are more favorable or more <u>un</u>favorable • Whether position from bottom or from top of list • Perspective on the issue • Topic and context affect which values comprise the list or were used to establish the percentiles	The system of measurement, scale of measurement, and unit of analysis do <u>not</u> affect measures of position.	Can have ties if two or more cases have identical ratings or scores on the measure being used as the basis for the ranking
Percentile = Position, out of 100 possible equal-width categories[1]	• Lowest value is 0th percentile • Highest value is 99th percentile			Can be based on distribution of values for (i) the sample being analyzed or (ii) an external standard
Quantile: decile, quintile, quartile, or tercile = Position, out of N possible ranges in the ranked list[2]	• Lowest value is 1st (bottom) • Highest value depends on number of ranges (N)			

Notes:

1. Each percentile is one one-hundredth (1/100th) of the overall distribution of cases ranked from smallest to largest observed values.

2. Where *N* is the number of ranges into which the distribution is divided (e.g., 3 equal-width ranges for tercile; 10 for deciles).

Example: A song was #1 on the Billboard top 100.

> *Rank* in the <u>list of all songs</u> for that date is conveyed as a simple *position* *number*, conveying that the song was the most popular.

Example: The fourth highest **quartile** is the <u>bottom</u> quartile, but the fourth highest **decile** is just above the <u>middle</u> of the distribution.

> *To be able to interpret what "fourth highest" implies, you need to know into* <u>how many ranges</u> *the values were grouped—**quartiles** (4) or **deciles** (10).*

Unlike measures of level, limits on numeric values of measures of position are <u>not</u> affected by the topic or context under study or the units of measurement for the variable used as the basis of the ranking.

Example: The highest is the highest, whether measuring height (e.g., tallest building), price (e.g., most expensive coffee), quality (e.g., best pizza), or ability (e.g., highest math test score).

Although measures of rank convey the **direction** of differences between values (<u>which</u> is higher), they do <u>not</u> capture the **magnitude** of differences between those values (<u>how much</u> higher) in the units of the original variable.

Mathematical Calculations

Mathematical calculations to compare numeric values include subtraction, division, and percentage difference or change, each of which captures both the direction and magnitude of differences between values. These types of computations can be conducted only on values of continuous (interval and ratio) variables.

Subtraction

Subtraction can be used to calculate the **difference** between two values of a variable or a **change** in the value of a variable over time. The result will be in the same units as the original variable.

Example: Gas costs $3.00 per gallon at the ABC station near your apartment, compared to $3.50 at the CleanGas station across the street, and $2.99 at the Quik Stop a mile away.

> *The **difference** in cost provides you with important information: Although Quik Stop is the least expensive (most favorable **rank**), you'd save only a penny per gallon by driving there instead of going to ABC. And CleanGas is $0.50 per gallon more expensive than the other options—probably enough to steer you away from them unless their gas is much better for the environment.*

To calculate **change over time**, conventionally the <u>earlier</u> value is subtracted from the <u>more recent</u> value: change $= V_2 - V_1$, where V_1 is the value at the earlier time point (Time 1) and V_2 is the value at the later time point (Time 2). When the values are subtracted in that order, a positive result implies an <u>increase</u> over time, and a negative result means a <u>decrease</u>.

> <u>Example</u>: In 2015, Oceania was home to 39.5 million people, an increase of 6 million over its population in 2005 (Column 7 of Table 9.2).
>
> > *2005 is the **base period** (Time 1). **Change over time** = 39.5 million in 2015 – 33.6 million in 2005 = an increase of 6 million people over that 10-year period.*

The difference or change is useful when the difference itself is of interest.

> <u>Example</u>: How many more students are expected in the local public school district over the next 10 years?
>
> > *That information helps planners anticipate whether additional classrooms and teachers will be needed to accommodate the increased number of students.*

However, the difference does not address all questions well.

> <u>Example</u>: Is a population increase of 10,000 people big? For a town with a total of 30,000 inhabitants prior to that increase, an increase of 10,000 people could overwhelm existing housing, schools, and other infrastructure. For the continent of Asia (with more than a billion people), a population increase of 10,000 would hardly be noticeable.
>
> > *A comparison such as a **rate** or a **percentage change** that takes the level of the values into account would be a better choice than subtraction for making that point. See the sections that follow.*

Division

Values of a variable for different cases can also be compared using a **ratio**: dividing the number of interest (d) by the comparison value (c), chosen as explained in Chapter 8. If d is greater than c, the ratio ($d \div c$) is greater than 1.0; if the numerator is smaller than the denominator, the ratio is less than 1.0.

> <u>Example</u>: In 2005, Asia had 4.29 times as many people as Africa (Table 9.2, Column 4).
>
> > *The **ratio** of the Asian population to the African population was 3.96 billion ÷ 0.9 billion = 4.29. Here, the comparison is across places for a specific topic and date.*

> <u>Example</u>: In the same year, Europe had 0.79 times the population of Africa (0.7 billion and 0.9 billion persons, respectively).

*0.7 billion ÷ 0.9 billion = 0.79. The **ratio** is <u>less</u> than one, meaning that the continent in the **numerator** (Europe) was <u>less</u> populous than the one in the **denominator** (Africa; the **reference category**).*

By dividing one value by the other, a ratio adjusts for the fact that a given size difference (from subtraction) has very different interpretations depending on the level of the base value (denominator).

<u>Example</u>: A hypothetical increase of 33 million people between 2005 and 2015 would yield very different ratios of old to new population in Oceania than in Asia.

*For either continent, the **difference** (from subtraction) would be 33 million. However, the **ratio** of old to new population is nearly twice as high in <u>Oceania</u> as in <u>Asia</u>. In Oceania, the 2005 population was only 33.6 million, so the **ratio** of new to old populations = (33.6 million + 33.0 million) ÷ 33.6 million = 1.98. In Asia, the 2005 population was 3,964.3 million, so the corresponding ratio is (3,964.3 million + 33.0 million) ÷ 3,964.3 million = 1.01.*

Recall that for interval variables, zero is <u>not</u> the lowest possible value; thus, variables at that level of measurement can assume either positive or negative values. Although it is mathematically possible to divide positive and negative values, for many real-world applications, it is difficult to interpret the meaning of a negative ratio.[1]

<u>Example</u>: If the temperature in Yourtown was 2 degrees below zero (–2° F) yesterday and it is 5 degrees above zero (+5° F) today, it is very awkward to say that it is –2.5 times as hot today as it was yesterday.

Calculating –2 ÷ +5 = –2.5 doesn't produce a sensible comparison because a negative multiple of temperature doesn't have an intuitive interpretation.

Relative Risk

A **relative risk** (abbreviated **RR**) is a specific type of ratio that is used to compare the risks of some outcome for two groups. It is calculated by dividing the value of that outcome (the dependent variable) for cases that <u>have</u> a particular risk factor by the value of that outcome among those who do <u>not have</u> that risk factor (independent variable) of interest. In epidemiology-speak, those who have the risk factor are referred to as the **exposed** group, and those without the risk factor as the **unexposed** (Schneider & Lilienfeld, 2005). As with other types of ratios for which the numerator and denominator are measured in the same units, the units "cancel" during the division process, so the ratio is no longer in the original units of the risk measures.

<u>Example</u>: Researchers found that the relative risk of subsequently developing autism was 0.92 for children who received the measles,

---

[1]Division would be a sensible approach to comparing values of interval variables that assume either only positive <u>or</u> only negative values, resulting in positive ratios.

mumps, rubella (MMR) vaccine compared to those who were not vaccinated (Hviid et al., 2019). Because this value was very close to 1.0 (which indicates no difference in chances of that outcome between the exposed and unexposed groups), they concluded that vaccination against measles is <u>not</u> a risk factor for autism.

> The **risk factor** was the MMR vaccine, so the **relative risk** of autism (the outcome, or dependent variable) was calculated: RR (autism) = rate of autism among vaccinated children (the **exposed** group) ÷ rate of autism among <u>un</u>vaccinated children (the **unexposed** group, which is the **reference category** for this comparison).

A **relative risk** (**RR**) is the ratio of risks for two groups with different values of an independent variable (often those with and without exposure to some **risk factor**). It is also known as a **risk ratio**. Relative risk = risk in exposed group ÷ risk in unexposed group

---

Percentage or Proportion of a Whole

A **percentage of a whole** expresses the value in the numerator as a percentage of the value in the denominator, where the concept in the numerator (denoted s) is a subset of that in the denominator (w, for whole). To express s as a percentage of the whole, compute $(s \div w) \times 100$. If you do <u>not</u> multiply by 100 (e.g., $[s \div w]$), the result is a **proportion** of a whole.

If s is a subgroup of a whole (w):

To express the numerator (s) as a **proportion** of the denominator (w) = ($s \div w$)

To express the numerator (s) as a **percentage** of the denominator (w) = ($s \div w$) × 100

> <u>Example</u>: In 2005, Asia's population comprised about 61% of the total world population (Table 9.2, Column 2). Put differently, the proportion of the world's population that lived in Asia in 2005 was 0.61.

> *Asia's population (s) is a subset of the entire world's population (w). 3,964.3 million people ÷ 6,542.2 million people × 100 = 60.6%. That **percentage** is equivalent to a **proportion** of 0.606. Be careful to label (or read) units: a proportion of 0.61 equals 61%, <u>not</u> 0.61%!*

As emphasized in Chapter 6, it is very important to know "percentage of what?" In other words, what "whole" was used to calculate a specific percentage.

> Read for and report units carefully to avoid mixing or mislabeling percentages and proportions, which have scales that differ by two orders of magnitude (a factor of 100). Also pay attention to what "whole" is in the denominator, which affects how the percentage is interpreted.

A **percentage of** expresses the value in the numerator as a percentage of the value in the denominator. It can be calculated from the ratio: numerator as a percentage of the denominator = ratio × 100.

> Example: According to Young and Nestle (2002), cookies sold at some popular fast-food and family restaurants have 800% of the calories of the USDA portion size, equivalent to eight times the calories of a "standard" cookie.
>
> *Here, calories in fast-food cookies are in the **numerator**, and calories in "standard" cookies are in the **denominator**. To convert from **numerator as a percentage of the denominator** to **ratio**: (800 ÷ 100) = 8.0. From **ratio** to **percentage of denominator**: 8.0 × 100 = 800%.*

> Example: The ratio of the Northern American to the African population is 0.35 (Column 1, Table 9.2), so the population of Northern America 35% as large as that of Africa (Column 3).
>
> *The **ratio** of those two continents' populations can be expressed as a **percentage of the denominator** (population of Africa). Note that this value is not a percentage **of a whole** because Northern America is not a subset of Africa!*

Percentage Difference

Percentage difference compares values for two cases, groups, or locations at the same point in time. It expresses the difference between two values as a ratio compared to a specified **base** (or **reference value**). A percentage difference is calculated by dividing the difference ($d - c$) by the reference value (c), then multiplying the result by 100 to put it in percentage terms: percentage difference = $[(d - c) \div c] \times 100$, with the results in units of **percentage points.**

Researchers often calculate percentage difference by subtracting the smaller from the larger value; therefore, such comparisons often yield positive percentage differences. Negative percentage differences usually occur only when each of several values is being compared against the same reference value, with some falling below and some above that comparison value.

> Example: In 2005, Latin America's population was 39% smaller than Africa's (percentage difference = −39.3; Column 5, Table 9.2), whereas Asia was 328.7% more populous than Africa.

*Africa is the continent against which each of the other continents is compared (**reference value**; shown in bold in Table 9.2). Latin America compared to Africa: ([(561.7 million – 924.8 million) ÷ 924.8 million] × 100 = –39.3%). Asia compared to Africa: ([(3,964 million – 924.8 million) ÷ 924.8 million] × 100 = 328.7%).*

Relationship between Ratio and Percentage Difference

A percentage difference is a mathematical transformation of a ratio: if you know either the **ratio** of two values <u>or</u> the **percentage difference** between their values, you can calculate the other measure. Percentage difference = (ratio – 1) × 100. Conversely, ratio = (percentage difference ÷ 100) + 1. See Chapter 14 for more on how to phrase results of percentage difference or ratio calculations to match the order in which the calculation was done.

<u>Example</u>: From the information above, we can calculate that cookies sold at those fast food restaurants have 700% <u>more</u> calories than the USDA portion size.

*To convert from **ratio** to **percentage difference**: (8.0 – 1.0) × 100 = 700%, so the value in the numerator (calories in cookies at those restaurants) is 700% <u>larger than</u> the denominator (calories in the USDA portion).*

<u>Example</u>: The ratio of the 2005 European to African populations was 0.79 (Column 1, Table 9.2), thus Europe was 21% <u>less</u> populous than Africa (Column 5).

***Percentage difference** = (0.79 – 1) × 100 = –21%. The <u>negative sign</u> means that Europe (numerator) is <u>smaller</u> than Africa (denominator).*

The numerator as a percentage of the denominator, the ratio between those two numbers, and the percentage difference between numerator and denominator are mathematical transformations of one another:

- Numerator **as a percentage of the denominator = ratio** × 100, and ratio = numerator **as a percentage of the denominator** ÷ 100.

- **Percentage difference** between numerator and denominator = (**ratio** – 1) × 100. Conversely, ratio = (percentage difference between numerator and denominator ÷ 100) + 1.

Percentage Change

A **percentage <u>change</u>** compares values for two different points in time: the convention is to subtract the earlier value (V_1) from the later value (V_2), then divide that difference by the initial value and multiply by 100: $[(V_2 – V_1) ÷ V_1] × 100$.

If the quantity increased over time, the percentage change will be positive. If the quantity decreased over time, the percentage change will be negative.

Example: From 2005 to 2015, the population of Northern America increased by 8.7% (Column 8; Table 9.2).

*The earlier date (2005) is used as the **base** (**reference value**) in the **percentage change** calculation. $[(V_{2015} - V_{2005}) \div V_{2005}] \times 100 = [(356.0$ million $- 327.5$ million$) \div 327.5$ million$] \times 100 = [28.5$ million $\div 327.5$ million$] \times 100 = 8.7\%$.*

Example: The population of Eastern Europe declined from 298 million persons in 2005 to 293 million persons in 2015, a decrease of 1.7%.

*[(293 million in 2015 − 298 million in 2005) ÷ 298 million in 2005] × 100 = (−5 million ÷ 298 million) × 100 = −1.7%. The **percentage change** is <u>negative</u>, reflecting the <u>decrease</u> in population over the period.*

A **percentage <u>difference</u>** compares two values measured at the same point in time.

Percentage difference = $[(d - c) \div c] \times 100$, where c and d are two different values.

A **percentage <u>change</u>** compares values at two points in time.

Percentage change = $[(V_2 - V_1) \div V_1] \times 100$, where V_1 and V_2 are the values at earlier and later time points, respectively.

Percentage of Versus Percentile
Versus Percentage Difference or Change

A common mistake in interpreting numbers concerns the phrases "percentage difference," "difference in percentage points," and "difference in percentiles." Although they all have "difference" and "percent" in their names they are <u>not</u> comparable measures. If c and d are expressed as percentages, their units of measurement are percentage points; hence the difference between their values is reported as a **difference in percentage points**.

Example: If the interest rate on a credit card from Bank A is 18%, whereas that from Bank B is 20%, Bank B's rate is 11% higher than Bank A's.

*The **difference** (from subtraction) = 20% − 18% = 2.0 **percentage points**, <u>not</u> a 2.0% difference. The **percentage difference** between those interest rates is [(20% − 18%) ÷ 18%] × 100, or 11%.*

Percentages and percentiles calculate the share of a whole and the rank within a distribution, respectively. By definition, neither can be less than zero or greater than 100: no case can have less than none of the whole or more than all of it, nor can any case have below the lowest possible value or above the highest! Likewise, the minimum possible value for a proportion (an alternative way of expressing share of a whole) is 0 (none of the whole), whereas the maximum value is 1.0 (all of the whole).

In contrast, percentage change and percentage difference measure relative size against some reference value and are <u>not</u> constrained to fall between 0 and 100. If a value is more than twice the size of the reference value, the percentage difference will be greater than 100%. Likewise, if a quantity more than doubles, the corresponding percentage change will exceed 100%.

<u>Example</u>: In 2005, the population of Asia was 333% larger than that of Africa (Table 9.2, Column 5), with 3.9 billion and 0.9 billion persons, respectively.

> *The **percentage difference** between Asia's and Africa's populations is calculated [(3.9 billion − 0.9 billion) ÷ 0.9 billion] × 100 = 333%.*

If a quantity shrinks over time, the corresponding percentage change will be less than 0% (negative), as in the example of Eastern Europe.

Table 9.4 shows how percentage, percentile, and percentage change relate to one another.

Table 9.4 Raw Scores, Percentage, Percentile, Percentage Difference, and Percentage Change

Comparison of Standardized Test Scores, Sana Patel, 2019 and 2020		
	2019	2020
Number of questions correct **(V)**	38	44
Total number of questions	50	50
Percentage of questions correct **(P)**	76%	88%
<u>Difference</u> in % correct (vs. 2019) **(D)**	NA	12 percentage points
Percentile (compared to national norms) **(R)**	73	81
Percentage <u>change</u> in % correct (vs. 2019) **(C)**	NA	16%

<u>Example</u>: As shown in Table 9.4, in 2019, Sana Patel correctly answered 38 of 50 questions (76%). Compared to national norms for the exam, she placed in the 73rd percentile for the standardized test. The next year, she improved her score by 12 percentage points [from 76% of questions correct to 88% correct], placing her in the 81st percentile. That change represented an 16% improvement in her score. Her rank improved by 8 percentiles [relative to her 2019 rank of 73rd percentile].

> *The letters in parentheses in Table 9.4 are shorthand for the type of measure for each number: the number of questions asked and number answered correctly are denoted "V". From those values, it is possible*

*to calculate the **percentage of questions** she answered correctly (P) and her **rank** (R) in **percentiles**, compared with national norms. With information on her performance 1 year later, you can subtract to calculate the **change** in her scores between 2019 and 2020 (D) or compute the **percentage change** in her scores over that period (C).*

Plausibility Criteria for Results of Calculations

Table 9.5 summarizes criteria for assessing the plausibility of results of calculations used to compare two or more numeric values, including limits imposed by the formula for the calculation and whether the numeric results are affected by the topic and context under study or the units in which the variable was measured.

> The criteria involved in determining **position in a distribution** and the **formulas for calculations** impose limits on whether those measures can take on positive, zero, or negative values; whether they can have a decimal value or only whole number value; and whether there are definitional limits on their minimum and/or maximum values.

How Level of Measurement Affects Valid Types of Comparison

As discussed in Chapter 4, level of measurement refers to the mathematical precision with which a variable is measured, whether nominal, ordinal, interval, or ratio. That precision in turn determines which kinds of calculations and comparisons can be conducted with values of that variable.

The four levels of measurement are listed in the column headings of Figure 9.3. The top four rows list the types of mathematical comparison or calculation, and the bottom two rows convey which levels of measurement are qualitative and which are quantitative (and among the quantitative levels, which are categorical and which are continuous). The interior cells of the grid indicate which of the comparisons and calculations can be conducted with variables at each level of measurement.

Qualitative Variables

As described in Chapter 4, nominal variables are those with named categories that capture differences in a quality but not a quantity. When comparing two values of a nominal variable, all that can be determined is whether those values are the same as or different from each other.

Table 9.5 Criteria for Making Sense of Results of Mathematical Calculations

Type of Calculation	Definitional Limits on Results of Calculation	Other Criteria Affecting Level and Range of Plausible Values		Comments
		Topic or Context	Units of Measurement	
Difference* = $d - c$ Change over time = $V_2 - V_1$, where V_1 is the value at the earlier time point and V_2 is the value at the later time point.	• No definitional limits • Can be positive, zero, or negative • Can result in decimal values if values being compared include decimal values • If one value is positive and the other is negative, the **absolute value**† of the difference will be larger than the absolute value of either value.	• Topic and context affect scale and range of minimum and maximum values being compared, which can affect plausible values of the result.	• Units of result will be the same units as those for the variable; thus, the scale and range are affected by the system of measurement, scale, and unit of analysis of the variable whose values are being compared.	• Cannot be calculated for values of nominal or ordinal variables. • Can be calculated for frequency of occurrence of values for variables at any level of measurement
Ratio† = $d \div c$	• Can be negative if either the numerator or denominator value is negative • Can be zero if the numerator is zero		• Units of the original variable cancel during calculation; thus, the results of the ratio are not affected by system of measurement, scale, or unit of analysis of that variable.	• Cannot be calculated for values of nominal or ordinal variables. • Denominator cannot be 0. • Can be calculated for frequency of occurrence of values for variables at any level of measurement

Relative risk‡ = $\text{risk}_A \div \text{risk}_B$, where A and B are different groups, places, or time periods.	• Must be positive because both risk_A and risk_B must be positive
	• Can be
	  ○ >1.0, if risk_A > risk_B,
	  ○ 1.0 if risk_A = risk_B,
	  ○ <1.0, if risk_A < risk_B,
				• Denominator cannot be 0

(Continued)

Table 9.5 (Continued)

Type of Calculation	Definitional Limits on Results of Calculation	Other Criteria Affecting Level and Range of Plausible Values		Comments
		Topic or Context	Units of Measurement	
Percentage of a whole[§] $= (s \div w) \times 100$, where s is a subset of the whole (w)	• Minimum = 0 • Maximum = 100			
Proportion of a whole $= (s \div w)$, where s is a subset of w	• Minimum = 0 • Maximum = 1.0	• Topic and context affect scale and range of minimum and maximum values being compared, which can affect plausible values of the result.	• Units of the original variable cancel during calculation; thus, the results are not affected by system of measurement, scale, or unit of analysis of that variable.	
Percentage difference $= [(d - c) \div c] \times 100$	• Can be positive (d is bigger than c), zero ($d = c$), or negative (d is smaller than c) • No limits on minimum or maximum values			• Percentage difference between two values measured at the same point in time
Percentage change over time $= [(V_2 - V_1) \div V_1] \times 100$, where V_1 is the value at the earlier time point and V_2 is the value at the later time point[¶]	• Can be positive (increase over time), zero, or negative (decrease over time) • No limits on minimum or maximum values			• Percentage difference between two values measured at different points in time

Notes:

*Subtracting two values measured in percentage units yields a difference in percentage points, <u>not</u> a percentage difference (see formula for percentage difference below).

†Absolute value: the magnitude of a real number without regard to its sign; in other words, the distance between a value and 0.

‡Both numerator and denominator are measured in same units, thus units of original variable cancel during calculation. The result is expressed as a multiple <u>of the base value.</u>

§Both numerator and denominator are measured in same units, thus units of original variable cancel during calculation. The result is expressed as a percentage of the whole (denominator)

¶Both numerator and denominator are measured in same units, thus units of original variable cancel during calculation. The result is expressed as a multiple <u>of the value at the base time period</u> (T_1).

Figure 9.3 Types of Mathematical Operations for Different Levels of Measurement

		Level of measurement			
Comparisons that make sense with values of variables[a]		Least precise ---→ most **precise** Lowest **level** of measurement ----------------------------→ highest **level**			
Type	**Math**	**Nominal**	**Ordinal**	**Interval**	**Ratio**
Same or different	= or ≠	Yes	Yes	Yes	Yes
Greater or less than	< or >	No	Yes	Yes	Yes
Subtraction	−	No	No	Yes	Yes
Division	÷	No	No	No[b]	Yes
		Categorical[c]		**Continuous**	
		Qualitative		**Quantitative**	

Notes:

a. All four types of comparisons can be conducted on measures of <u>frequency of occurrence</u> (counts or percentage distribution) of values of variables at <u>any</u> level of measurement. See Figure 10.13.

b. See footnote regarding the use of division for interval-level variables.

c. Numbers used as codes (abbreviations) for categories of nominal and ordinal variables <u>cannot</u> be used for calculations; see Chapter 4.

<u>Example</u>: Suppose one of your classmates is from Canada, another from Morocco, and you are from the United States.

> *Nationality is a **nominal**, **qualitative** variable, capturing a characteristic that <u>cannot</u> be quantified. The nominal level of measurement is the least mathematically precise: The only valid comparison is whether you and your classmates are of the same nationalities (top row of Figure 9.3). We <u>cannot</u> say which of you has more "nationality-ness" (**rank**), and we certainly cannot **subtract** (Canada − Morocco makes no sense) or **divide** (Morocco ÷ United States has no meaning) values of the nationality variable. Thus, neither the rank order (**direction**) nor size (**magnitude**) of the difference between those values in the quality "nationality" can be determined.*

Quantitative Variables

On the other end of the spectrum, variables measured at the ratio level (the most mathematically precise) can be compared using rank, subtraction, division, and other mathematical computations that combine those operations.

<u>Example</u>: If you have completed 100 academic credits and your friend has completed 50, you can say all of the following: (1) each of you has

a different number of credits under your belt; (2) you have more credits than your friend; (3) you have completed 50 more credits than your friend; and (4) you have completed twice as many credits as your friend.

> *The variable measuring number of academic credits is at the **ratio level of measurement**, supporting all four types of mathematical comparisons (4th row of Figure 9.3), and allowing calculation of both **direction** and **magnitude** of the difference in how many credits you and your friend have completed.*

Example: Although Starbucks' Tall, Grande, and Venti beverage cups are each 4 fluid ounces (oz.) larger than the one-size-smaller cup, the Trenta is 11 oz. larger than the one-size-smaller cup (Venti) (Figure 9.4).

> *The named cup sizes are **ordinal** rather than **continuous** because the names can be listed in order from smallest to largest, but the "distances" between measured volumes across the spectrum of cup sizes are <u>not</u> equal numbers of units so you <u>cannot</u> treat the **named categories** mathematically. Thus, although a Starbucks barista (and many customers!) can rattle off the **order** of the cup size names (<u>which</u> is bigger), doing so does <u>not</u> convey the <u>size</u> of the differences in how much the cups hold (<u>how much</u> bigger).*

> *A **continuous** measure of coffee cup volume would report the number of ounces in each cup size, instead of the Starbucks name for that size.*

Figure 9.4   Illustration of Ordinal and Continuous Levels of Measurement

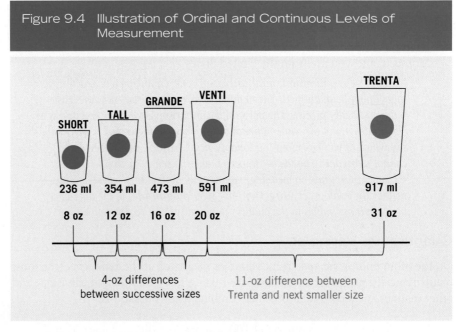

Source: Data from Starbucks.com.

Amusingly, although the 20 oz. cup is aptly named "Venti" (the Italian word for "20"), the 31 oz. cup is named "Trenta," which means "30" in Italian!

A variable's level of measurement determines the types of mathematical comparisons and calculations that make sense for the values of that variable.

- "Same or different" can be assessed for variables at any level of measurement.

- Rank can be determined for all quantitative variables, but <u>not</u> for nominal (qualitative) ones.

- Subtraction can be performed on all continuous variables, but <u>not</u> on categorical ones.

- Division can only be performed on ratio-level variables.

As discussed in the early chapters of this book, a key objective of quantitative research is identifying the direction and magnitude of the difference between numeric values. Because a variable's level of measurement governs the types of comparisons that can be made with that variable, it also affects when direction and magnitude of a pattern can be determined (Figure 9.5).

Figure 9.5 Direction and Magnitude by Type of Mathematical Comparison

Comparisons			
Type	Math	Captures direction?	Captures magnitude?
Same or different	= or ≠	No	No
Greater or less than	< or >	Yes	No
Subtraction	−	Yes	Yes
Division	÷	Yes	Yes

Direction of association between two values of a given variable can be assessed for all **quantitative** variables (ordinal, interval, or ratio) but <u>not</u> for **qualitative** (nominal) variables. It can be determined from rank, subtraction, division, or percentage change/difference.

(Continued)

> (Continued)
>
> **Magnitude** of differences between values can be assessed for **continuous** (interval or ratio) but not **categorical** (nominal or interval) variables. It can be calculated using subtraction, division, or percentage change/difference.

Choosing Types of Comparisons

For variables where several types of contrasts are possible, researchers often present results of more than one type of comparison to make distinct points about the same set of numbers. When doing so, they should report the value (**level**) to set the context and to provide data for other calculations and then interpret one or two types of comparisons to give a more complete sense of the pattern.

To help readers make sense of both the **level** and the **difference** between values, researchers should report the highest and lowest possible values along with the range observed in their own data.

> Example: A 1-point increase in the Nikkei (Japan) stock market index would be microscopically small—equivalent to less than a 0.005% change compared to its level of about 21,700 points in mid-2019. On the other hand, a 1-point increase on a 4-point Likert scale is huge—equal to one-third of the theoretically possible variation.
>
> *The **difference** (1 point) is the same in both examples, but the interpretation of that difference depends substantially on the **level** of the measure.*

> Example: Suppose a marketing firm reports that a new product is three times as popular as its predecessor. A very low market share for both products (e.g., 1% versus 3%) has very different implications than high shares for both (e.g., 15% versus 45%).
>
> *The same **ratio** has very different meanings depending on the **level** of the base value.*

> Example: A 100% increase (doubling) in the number of suicides over a 5-year period might be considered alarming if the suicide rate in the baseline period was already high but is less worrisome if there were initially only a handful of suicides.
>
> *Reporting the **percentage change** without also reporting the **base value** can be misleading.*

Influence of Topic and Field

Conventions for which calculations to include depends on the research topic and field.

- Results of elections, marketing studies, and sports competitions often present a measure of position (**rank**), complemented by **difference** (to capture direction and magnitude).

- Time trends are often described in terms of **difference** and **percentage change**, substituting **ratios** to express large changes such as doubling, tripling, or being cut in half.

- Variations in risks across groups or places are frequently reported as **relative risks** (a form of **ratio**).

TERMS AND CONCEPTS

HIGHLIGHTS

- Knowing how measures of **level**, **rank**, and **mathematical comparison** are produced provides essential information for assessing whether the numeric results make sense.

- The type of measure of **level** determines whether its values can be **positive, zero**, or **negative**, and whether values can only be **whole numbers** or also include **decimal** values. Likewise, the **procedure** used to calculate measures of **position in a list** and the formula for a mathematical computation to **compare values** determine the range of plausible values for those comparisons.

- The **topic, context**, and **units** of the variables involved often substantially influence the **scale** and **range** of numeric values that make sense for measures of level, position, and mathematical comparison.

- **The level of measurement** of a variable determines which types of comparisons and calculations make sense to use for the values of that variable.

- **Conventions** for which type(s) of comparisons and calculations to use when presenting research results vary somewhat by topic and field of study.

RECOMMENDED READINGS

Chambliss, D. F., & Schutt, R. K. (2018). Conceptualization and measurement. *Making sense of the social world* (6th ed., pp. 70–97). Sage.

EXERCISES

Individual Exercises

Quantitative Reasoning in Everyday Life

1. Watch a weather forecast on the Weather Channel or your local station for half an hour on a weekday morning. List all the different types of topics and measures for which they report numeric information (e.g., temperature, precipitation, wind, etc.). For each, specify its (a) topic, (b) numeric value(s), (c) units and/or categories, and (d) whether it is a measure of level, rank, difference, ratio, or other type of comparison or calculation.

2. Repeat the instructions from the previous Exercise but for a website that presents rankings of videos (e.g., https://www .digitaltrends.com/web/most-viewed-youtube-videos/) or music (e.g., https://www .billboard.com/charts/hot-100).

Interpreting Research

3. In a report about recent patterns in population, health (https://www.cdc.gov/ nchs/index.htm) or unemployment (www.bls .gov), find an example of each of the following measures: (a) level, (b) rank, (c) difference from subtraction, (d) ratio, (e) percentage difference, and (f) percentage change over time. For each, (i) copy a sentence from the report specifying the topic and units; (ii) specify how you knew it was that type of comparison, using the criteria in this chapter; (iii) identify the reference value; and (iv) specify whether the reference value comes from within the data set used by the author or from some other source (e.g., a historic value or an external reference population).

Analyzing Data

4. Use the information in Table 9A to perform the following: List the groups in descending numeric order of median income. Using white households as the comparison group, calculate the following comparisons with Asian households: (a) subtraction, (b) division, and (c) percentage difference.

Table 9A	Median Income by Race and Hispanic Origin of Householder, United States, 2018
Race/Hispanic origin	**Median income**
White	$66,943
Black	$41,631

Race/Hispanic origin	Median income
Asian/Pacific Islander	$87,194
Hispanic (can be of any race)	$51,450

Source: U.S. Census Bureau. (2020). Table A-1. Income summary measures by selected characteristics: 2017 and 2018.

5. Use the information in Table 6.5 to perform the following for stunting at the end of the study period: List the countries in descending numeric order of that outcome, using the country with the highest level of stunting as the reference value. Compare its level of stunting at the end of the study period with that of <u>one</u> other country using each of the following types of calculations: (a) subtraction, (b) ratio, and (c) percentage difference. For each calculation, (d) write the formula, including (i) the W's, (ii) units, (iii) mathematical operations, and (iv) numeric answer.

Group Exercises

Quantitative Reasoning in Everyday Life

6. Make a list of the different topics you identified for Exercise 1. Discuss each other's answers about whether they correctly identified the type of measure or comparison.

7. Repeat the instructions to the previous Exercise but for your answers to Exercise 2.

Interpreting Research

8. With a classmate, exchange your answers to Exercise 3, including a link to the report you used for that question. (a) Provide feedback to each other on whether you correctly identified (i) examples of each of the measures (ii) the reference group or value. (b) Revise your answers to correct any errors identified by your peer reviewer.

Analyzing Data

9. With a classmate, exchange your answers to Exercise 5. Provide feedback to each other on the following: (a) whether you can tell which group they used as the reference value; (b) whether their equation is complete (all W's, units, category names, and mathematical symbols); (c) whether the elements of the equation are in the correct order; and (d) whether the numeric answers are correct (values, units). (e) Revise your answers to correct any errors identified by your peer editor.

CHAPTER

10

Distributions and Associations

Learning Objectives

After reading this chapter, you will be able to do the following:

1. Choose and interpret basic statistics to describe distribution of values of a single variable (univariate statistics).

2. Assess plausibility of univariate statistical results.

3. Design and read tables and charts to display distributions.

4. Select and interpret statistics to describe the relationship between two variables (bivariate statistics).

5. Design and read tables and charts to display bivariate associations.

6. Identify methods used to describe associations among three variables.

7. Assess plausibility of bivariate and three-way results.

Two of the quantitative research tasks you will encounter most often include describing how values of a variable are distributed in a sample (**distribution**) and investigating how two or three variables are related to one another (**association**). In terms of our W's checklist, the methods of portraying distributions and associations are an "honorary W": **how** researchers get to know the numeric patterns in the data with which they are working.

In this chapter, I provide an overview of the basic statistical methods used to describe distributions and associations in a sample and explain how to choose the correct method based on levels of measurement. I then illustrate how to design tables and charts to display the results and how to interpret and assess the plausibility of numeric measures of distribution and association. For a more detailed treatment of specific statistical methods, consult a standard statistics textbook, such as Utts and Heckard's *Mind on Statistics* (2014) or Salkind's *Statistics for People Who (Think They) Hate Statistics* (2016).

As in Chapter 9, I use technical terminology and equations to convey the components of statistical calculations. Again, much of the material in this chapter is "behind the scenes" information that is typically not included in a research paper but that your instructor might ask you to explain in your course assignments, to demonstrate mastery of the statistical concepts. Examples here and in Chapter 14 will illustrate how information about distributions and associations can be presented to focus on the topic and the numeric results, not the process of obtaining those results. For a non-technical reference on statistical formulas, see Vogt and Johnson (2011).

Statistical methods refer to the approaches used to describe, organize, and interpret data. **Descriptive statistics** pertain only to the sample or population from which data have been collected, describing patterns but <u>not</u> generalizing the results beyond the set of cases that were actually analyzed. Chapter 13 will explain how statistics are used to draw inferences about numeric patterns from a sample to a population.

Statistical methods are used to describe, organize, and interpret data.

Distributions of Single Variables

Univariate statistics are used to summarize data on one variable at a time ("uni" means "one"). **Summary statistics** for single variables include measures of central tendency, variability, and shape. **Central tendency** measures the typical value of a particular variable in a data set. **Variability** measures how much the observed values of a variable differ from one another within that sample. **Shape** refers to whether a variable's values are distributed symmetrically or are skewed. A variable's level of measurement determines which types of univariate statistics make sense for that variable.

Univariate statistics are used to describe the distribution of values of <u>one variable at a time</u> within a data set. Univariate **summary statistics** include measures of central tendency, variability, and shape.

Measures of Central Tendency

There are three measures of central tendency: **mean**, **median**, and **mode**.

Mean

A variable's **mean** value (denoted $\bar{x}$) is the **average** of the values in a sample, calculated by adding together all the values of a variable in that sample and dividing that sum by the number of cases in the sample (denoted **n**). Strictly speaking, the mean can be calculated only for continuous (interval or ratio level) variables, although you will sometimes see a mean reported for Likert (a form of ordinal) items.

> Example: Scores for a midterm exam in a class of 13 students were 74, 68, 82, 88, 76, 49, 90, 83, 76, 72, 94, 90, and 76.
>
> *The **mean** exam score for that class is calculated by dividing the **sum** of the exam scores (= 1,018) by the **number of values** (students; **n** = 13), or 1,018 ÷ 13 = 78.3.*

Median

The **median** is the middle value when all of the observed values of a variable are listed in ranked order from lowest to highest. It is the 50th percentile (Chapter 9), with half of all observed values of that variable lower and half higher than the median. If there is an even number of cases in the sample, there is no "middle" value; so, in such situations, the average of the two middle categories is chosen as the median. The median can be calculated only for <u>quantitative</u> variables.

> Example: The **median** exam score in the previous example is 76.
>
> *Sorted into **ascending** order, the exam scores are 49, 68, 72, 74, 76, 76, 76, 82, 83, 88, 90, 90, and 94. The middle value of 13 values will be the seventh value—in this instance, 76.*

Mode

The **mode** is the most common value—the value observed the most frequently of all values in the sample. A distribution with two modes (equally common values) is termed **bimodal**, whereas a distribution with three or more modes is called **multimodal**. Mode can be identified for all levels of measurement.

> Example: The modal exam score was 76.
>
> *Three students scored 76, making it the most common (**modal**) score in the class.*

The mode can be used with nominal variables, because it does not require the values of the variable to have a meaningful numeric order.

> Example: If five of the students were majoring in sociology, three in economics, and five in psychology, the distribution of college majors would be **bimodal**.
>
> *Sociology and psychology are both **modal** majors in this sample, because they share the highest frequency in this set of students—they are <u>equally common</u>.*

The mode is most useful when used with categorical (nominal, or ordinal) variables or for continuous variables when the sample size is 100 cases or more. A variable can only have one median and one mean value for a given data set but can have more than one mode.

Measures of **central tendency** include the **mean**, **median**, and **mode**. The **mean** ($\bar{x}$) is the average of the values of a variable, calculated by dividing the sum of all the values of that variable by the number of cases. $(\bar{x}) = \Sigma(x_i) \div n$, where Σ denotes sum, and the x_i are the values of the variable, x, for each of the n cases in the sample. The **median** is the <u>middle</u> value when all values of a variable are ranked in order from lowest to highest. It can be identified for continuous or ordinal variables. The **mode** is the <u>most common</u> value.

Figure 10.1 Computations and Levels of Measurement for Measures of Central Tendency

Measure of central tendency	Comparisons and computations required to calculate measure of central tendency			Suitable level(s) of measurement of variables
	Ranking	Addition	Division	
Mean	No	Yes	Yes	Continuous
Median	Yes	Sometimes*	Sometimes*	Ordinal, continuous
Mode	No	No	No	Nominal, ordinal, continuous

Notes:

*If there are an odd number of values, the middle two values are averaged to calculate the median, requiring addition and division.

Figure 10.1 summarizes which measures of central tendency suit each level of measurement, based on the types of mathematical comparison and computation required to calculate them.

Measures of Variability

Measures of **variability** are used to show how the observed values of a variable are distributed and—for continuous variables—to quantify the extent of **spread** or **dispersion** around the mean value.

Frequency Distribution

A **frequency distribution** is a measure of variability, showing how often each value of a variable appears in a data set, either as the number of cases (**count**) or **percentage** of cases. The frequency distribution shows how the parts (values) make up the whole (overall distribution); therefore, the sum of the counts for each of the values (n_i, where i is a specific value of the variable) must add up to the overall sample size (n), and the sum of the percentage of cases for each of the values must add up to 100% of that sample. When one sample is to be compared against another sample or against an entire population, the <u>percentage</u> distribution is needed because it corrects for sample size.

> <u>Example</u>: Eleven students in the hypothetical class passed the exam by earning a score of 70 or higher. In a class of <u>13</u> students, that represents a passing rate of 85% (11 out of 13). In a class of <u>50</u> students, however, 11 passing scores would be only 22%. An 85% passing rate in the class of 50 would mean that 43 students passed, but that number passing would obviously be impossible in the class of 13.
>
> > *Although the same <u>number</u> of students passed the exam in both classes, that **count** has a very different meaning for class of 50 than for the class of 13. The **percentage** of students who passed provides the information in a form that allows us to compare success **rates** (percentage who passed) across different-sized classes. This analysis could be conducted on a **new indicator** variable, created from the original exam score to classify pass versus fail (see Appendix A).*

As we'll discuss further in Chapter 13, it is also important to know how many cases were analyzed; thus, most tables presenting frequency distributions report <u>both</u> the number of cases (counts) and the percentage of the sample with each value; see "Tables and Charts for Presenting Distributions," later.

A **frequency distribution** portrays how the observed values of a variable are **distributed**, or **spread**, across its possible values. It can be reported as either the **count** (number of cases, n_i) or the **percentage of cases** that have each value of the variable (i). The sum of n_i for all observed values of the variable equals the overall sample size, n.

A frequency distribution can be calculated for variables at any level of measurement. Although the output of statistical programs often includes the frequency distribution of a continuous variable that has many distinct values, in order to save space in written research documents, the complete frequency distribution of such variables is usually presented in a chart rather than in tabular form.

Both **distribution** and **composition** measure how many and what share of cases have a given value of that variable, so those terms are often used interchangeably. For instance, "age distribution" and "age composition" both refer to how the ages of the set of cases in a sample are spread across possible values. These concepts are illustrated in the section titled "Tables and Charts for Presenting Distributions."

> **Distribution** refers to how the values of a variable in a data set are **spread** (distributed) across the possible categories (for <u>categorical</u> variables) or numeric values (for <u>continuous</u> variables).
>
> **Composition** refers to how the categories or values together compose (make up) the entire sample.

For nominal variables, a frequency distribution is the only way to show spread of values, as the quantitative measures of variability (below) cannot be calculated based on nominal categories.

Minimum and Maximum

Other aspects of variability concern the lowest and highest <u>observed</u> values and the difference (distance) between them. The **minimum** value is the lowest observed value in a distribution, whereas the **maximum** is the highest observed value. They can be identified for variables at any of the <u>quantitative</u> levels of measurement.

> <u>Example</u>: In the hypothetical class discussed earlier, the worst score was 49 of out a possible 100 points, while the best score was 94 points.
>
> *The **minimum** score was 49, and the **maximum** score was 94. When referring to a distribution, the minimum and maximum pertain to observed, <u>not</u> to theoretically possible, values. For instance, thankfully no one scored the lowest possible score on the exam (0 points), but none of the students attained a perfect score (100 points) either.*

Range

The **range** is the difference between the highest and lowest observed scores, plus 1 to count the endpoints of that range. It can be calculated for continuous variables.

> <u>Example</u>: The observed exam scores spanned a range of 46 points.
>
> *The **range** of scores on the midterm was (**maximum − minimum**) + 1 = (94 − 49) + 1 = 46.*

For a distribution of a continuous variable with many values, the **interquartile range** can also be calculated. It is the difference between the 25th percentile (top of the lowest quartile) and the 75th percentile (bottom of the highest quartile), thus capturing the middle 50% of the overall distribution. Recall from Chapter 9 that percentiles are based on dividing the ranked list of all observed values into one hundred ranges, each encompassing 1/100th of the overall distribution.

> The **minimum** is the lowest observed value in a distribution; the **maximum** is the highest observed value. The **range** of a distribution is = (maximum observed value – minimum observed value) + 1. The **interquartile range** spans the values from the 25th percentile to the 75th percentile of an observed distribution = (75th percentile value – 25th percentile value) + 1.

Example: In 2017–18, the interquartile range on the verbal Graduate Record Examinations (GRE) was 13 points: from the 25th percentile (145 points) to the 75th percentile (157 points; MBA Crystal Ball, 2019).

*The **interquartile range** tells us that the **middle 50%** of all GRE scores fell into the 13-point range between (and including) 157 and 145 points.*

Variance

The **variance** (denoted s^2) of a distribution measures the average distance of each value in a sample from the mean value in that sample. It can be computed only for continuous variables. Distributions in which values are more spread out have higher variances than those in which values are more clustered.

There are several steps to calculating the variance: First, the **deviance** of each value from the mean of the distribution (Column B of Table 10.1) is calculated by subtracting the mean from each observed value (Column A). Next, the deviance is squared (Column C) to avoid having positive and negative deviances "cancel" each other out when they are added together. Next, the squared deviances are summed (bottom row of Column C).

Example: The variance of the hypothetical exam-score distribution shown in Table 10.1 is 130.1.

*Exam scores that were close to the mean of 78.3 contribute smaller amounts to the **variance** than those that are farther away. For instance, the score of 77 (light gray row in Table 10.1) was only 1.3 units below the mean (Column B), contributing a **squared deviance** of 1.7 (Column C). On the other hand, the score of 49 (black shaded row) was 29.3 points below the mean, contributing 858.9 points to the squared deviance.*

Outliers are values that are unusual compared to the rest of the data—either much lower or much higher than the next lowest or next highest observed values of that variable. Outliers increase the variance of a distribution because they are far from the mean value.

Table 10.1 Example Calculations of Descriptive Statistics on a Continuous Variable

Case ID	(A) Exam score (x)	(B) Deviance $x_i - \bar{x}$	(C) Squared deviance $(x_i - \bar{x})^2$
1	74	−4.3	18.6
2	68	−10.3	106.2
3	82	3.7	13.6
4	88	9.7	93.9
5	77	−1.3	1.7
6	49	−29.3	858.9
7	90	11.7	136.7
8	83	4.7	22.0
9	75	−3.3	10.9
10	72	−6.3	39.8
11	94	15.7	246.2
12	90	11.7	136.7
13	76	−2.3	5.3
Sum	1,018		1,690.8

Number of cases (n) = 13

Mean ($\bar{x}$) = 1,018 ÷ 13 = 78.3

Median = 76

Mode = 76

Variance (s^2) = 1,690.8 ÷ 13 = 130.1

Standard deviation (s) = $\sqrt{130.1}$ = 11.4

Example: In the distribution shown in Table 10.1, the test score 49 is 19 points lower than the next lowest score. All the other values are within a few points of the next highest and next lowest scores.

The score 49 is an **outlier**. Without that distant value, the variance of the distribution would be 69.3, or almost 50% lower than the variance when that case _is_ included.

Standard Deviation

The **standard deviation (abbreviated s or SD)** is the square root of the variance, putting the measure of spread back in the same scale as the original scores. It can be computed only for continuous variables.

The **variance** and **standard deviation** are measures of **spread**, calculating average distance of the individual values of a distribution from its mean. The **variance** (s^2) is a measure of the average distance of the values of a variable from the sample mean: Variance = $\Sigma\ (x_i - \overline{x})^2/n$, where Σ indicates a sum, x_i are the individual observed values of the variable, $\overline{x}$ is the sample mean, and n is the number of cases in the sample. The **standard deviation** (s) is the square root of the variance, providing a measure of distribution in the same scale (units) as the original measure. Standard deviation = $\sqrt{\text{variance}}$. **Outliers** are values of a variable that are much higher or lower than adjacent observed values of that variable.

Example: The standard deviation of the exam scores in Table 10.1 is 11.4.
> *Standard deviation* (*s*) *is the square root of the* *variance* = $\sqrt{130.1}$ = *11.4 points.*

Example: The standard deviation of height for 8-year-old boys in the 2015–16 U.S. National Health and Nutrition Examination Survey (NHANES) was 6.45 cm, meaning that the average distance of the heights of individual boys from the sample mean (132 cm) was 6.45 cm.

As discussed in Chapter 9, level of measurement determines which types of mathematical comparisons or calculations can be performed on that variable; thus, the measures of spread (variation) that suit a variable depend on whether it is nominal, ordinal, or continuous (see Figure 10.2).

A frequency distribution can be performed for variables at any level of measurement. The other measures of variance require mathematical computations on values of the variable; thus, they can be used only for quantitative variables.

Level of measurement determines which measure(s) of central tendency and spread suit each variable.

Measure of variation	Comparisons and computations required to calculate measure of variation			Suitable level(s) of measurement of variables
	Ranking	Addition/ subtraction	Multiplication/ division	
Frequency distribution	No	No	No	Nominal, ordinal, continuous
Minimum and maximum	Yes	No	No	Ordinal, continuous
Range	Yes	Yes	No	Continuous
Variance or standard deviation	No	Yes	Yes	Continuous

Shape

The **shape** of a distribution may be symmetrical, skewed (tilted to one side), or some other form. The easiest way to portray the shape of a distribution is by using a chart, with the values of the variable on the x-axis and the frequency with which each value appears shown on the y-axis. The higher the point on the frequency distribution curve, the more common that x value is in the data set.

A **normal distribution** is often referred to as a **bell curve**, because of its shape (see Figure 10.3a). When a normal distribution is perfectly symmetrical, the mean, median, and modal values are the same. In a **negatively skewed distribution** (Figure 10.3b), the mean (average) is lower than the median, which in turn is lower than the mode. Conversely, in a **positively skewed distribution**, the mean is higher than the median, which in turn is higher than the mode (see Figure 10.3c). A **bimodal distribution** (Figure 10.3d) has two peaks—one at each of two values that both appear often in the data set.

A **normal distribution** (also known as a **bell curve**) is a form of symmetrical distribution of values on either side of the mean. A **skewed** distribution is one in which the values are more spread out on one side than the other. In a **left-skewed** (**negatively skewed**) distribution, the values of the variable below the mean are more spread out than the higher values. In a **right-skewed** (**positively skewed**) distribution, the values above the mean are more widely distributed than the lower values.

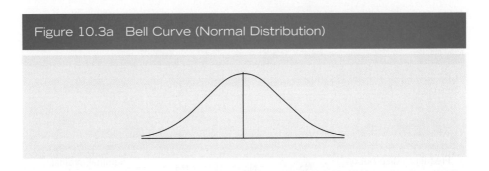

Figure 10.3a   Bell Curve (Normal Distribution)

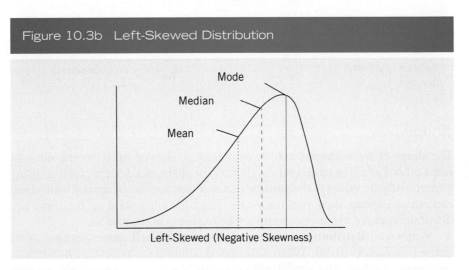

Figure 10.3b   Left-Skewed Distribution

Mode

Median

Mean

Left-Skewed (Negative Skewness)

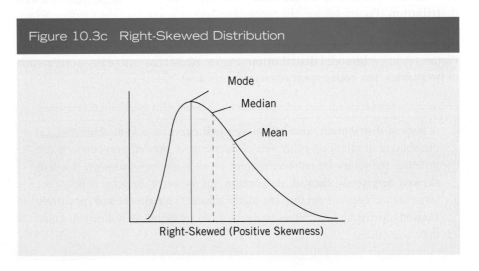

Figure 10.3c   Right-Skewed Distribution

Mode

Median

Mean

Right-Skewed (Positive Skewness)

Figure 10.3d   Bimodal Distribution

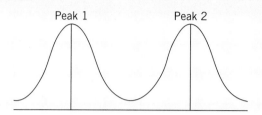

Which measures of central tendency can be used to characterize the distribution of a quantitative variable depend, in part, on the shape of the overall distribution.

- The **mean** is usually the best measure of central tendency for a continuous variable that has a fairly symmetrical distribution, such as when the data are normally distributed.

- The **median** is usually preferred to other measures of central tendency if the distribution of a variable is skewed, or for ordinal data.

- The **mode** is the only pertinent measure of central tendency for nominal variables; it can also be used for skewed continuous variables or for ordinal variables, but it is not as widely used as the median.

Position in a Distribution: Standardized Score or Z-Score

When a distribution of a continuous variable encompasses many cases, the position of an individual value of a continuous variable can be described numerically using either a percentile (discussed in Chapter 9) or a z-score.

Standardized scores, also known as *z-scores*, are a way of measuring how a particular value of a continuous variable compares to the average, taking into account the extent of spread in a reference population (Utts & Heckard, 2014). A z-score is computed by subtracting the mean from the value of interest, then dividing that difference by the standard deviation. The original units in which the variable was measured "cancel" during the calculation; thus, the units of a z-score are <u>number of standard deviations</u>. Z-scores are most suitable for variables that have approximately normal (bell-shaped) distributions.

A **z-score** (also known as a **standardized score**) quantifies the position of a given value of the variable in the overall distribution in terms of <u>multiples of standard deviations</u> above or below the mean. It is calculated as z-score = $(x_i - \bar{x}) \div s$, where $\bar{x}$ is the mean, x_i is the value for the case of interest, and s is the standard deviation.

Z-scores express whether a particular value was above or below the mean, and by how many standard deviations. A <u>positive</u> z-score corresponds to a value above the mean, a <u>negative</u> z-score corresponds to a lower-than-average value. In addition to correcting for level by subtracting the mean value, z-scores adjust for the fact that a given difference (from subtraction) is interpreted differently depending on the amount of variation in the values of that variable (the standard deviation).

Example: Taylor scored a 65 on a test that had a mean of 70 and a standard deviation of 5, placing her one standard deviation below the national average.

Filling in the formula with Taylor's score as x_i, *the national **average** as* $\bar{x}$, *and the **standard deviation** as s, Taylor's z-score = (65 − 70) ÷ 5 = −1.0 **standard deviation**. The negative sign indicates that her score is <u>below</u> the national average.*

Example: An 8-year old boy, Mike, measuring 138.5 cm tall, has a z-score of +1.0, meaning that he is one standard deviation (6.45 cm) taller than average for his age (132 cm; Figure 10.4). His classmate, Mason, at 119.1 cm tall, has a z-score of −2.0, equivalent to two standard deviations shorter than average.

*Instead of merely showing that Mike is 19.4 cm taller than Mason (**difference**, <u>measured in the original units of height</u>), **z-scores** reveal how each of the boys compares to the <u>mean for his age</u>, measured in **number of standard deviations** <u>above or below the mean</u>. The z-scores show that Mike is moderately taller than the average 8-year-old boy (z = +1.0), while Mason is considerably shorter than average (z = −2.0).*

Standardized scores allow variables with very different levels and ranges to be compared with one another by expressing position of a given value in terms of the mean and standard deviation for that variable. Likewise, z-scores can be used to compare values for subgroups that have different distributions.

Example: Using z-scores allows us to see how a particular girl's height compares with that of others her age. A 2-year-old girl, Olivia, who is 2.54 cm (1 in) taller than average would have a z-score of 0.7, indicating

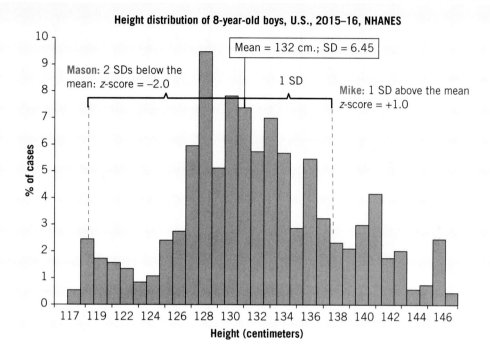

Height distribution of 8-year-old boys, U.S., 2015–16, NHANES

Mean = 132 cm.; SD = 6.45

Mason: 2 SDs below the mean: *z*-score = –2.0

1 SD

Mike: 1 SD above the mean *z*-score = +1.0

% of cases

Height (centimeters)

Source: Author's calculations based on data from the 2015–16 U.S. National Health and Nutrition Examination Survey.

Notes: Weighted to population level using sampling weights provided by the Centers for Disease Control and Prevention (CDC, 2018a).

Unweighted *N* = 121.

she is 70% of a standard deviation taller than average. A 12-year-old girl, Mariel, who is 2.54 cm taller than average, would be only about 30% of a standard deviation above the norm for her age ($z = 0.3$).

> The two **subgroups**—in this case, age groups—have very different means and standard deviations for height, reflecting how much children grow between ages 2 and 12 years. According to the World Health Organization standards (2006), **mean** height ($\overline{x}$) for 2-year-old girls is 90.4 cm, with a **standard deviation** (s) of 3.8 cm; whereas, for 12-year-old girls, the respective values are both larger ($\overline{x}$) = 153.5 cm; s = 7.6 cm). Thus, although Olivia and Mariel are both 2.54 centimeters taller than average for their age, that same distance from the mean is a smaller **fraction of a standard deviation** for Mariel (the older girl) than it is for Olivia ($z = 0.3$ and $z = 0.7$, respectively).

Univariate statistics can be performed either on variables as they were collected from the original source or on new variables created specifically to answer the research question of interest (see Appendix A).

Plausibility Criteria for Univariate Statistics

Knowing the math behind each of the measures of central tendency and spread helps identify criteria for assessing the plausibility of values for each of those measures. The formula for calculating each type of statistic places definitional limits on minimum and maximum values, sign (positive or negative), and other aspects of plausibility for each type of univariate statistic.

All the measures of central tendency and spread <u>except</u> frequency distribution and variance are in the same units as the original variable (see Table 10.2). That information provides initial guidelines on upper and lower limits on their values, based on the criteria in previous chapters about how topic, context, and units affect plausibility. Whether the measures of central tendency, the minimum, and the maximum can take on negative values depends on whether the original variable can be negative. The frequency distribution for a variable is reported in either number of cases (counts) or percentage of the sample that takes on each value of the variable, neither of which can be negative. Counts for each value cannot exceed the total sample size (n), and percentages of the whole must fall between 0% and 100%.

Range and interquartile range must also be positive, reflecting the number of units between (and including) the minimum and maximum for range and capturing the number of units between the first and third quartiles for interquartile range. Variance is in a <u>different scale</u> than the original variable, because the difference between each value and the sample mean is squared during calculation of the variance. Neither variance nor standard deviation can be negative, as they measure the average distance of the values from the mean; if all values are at the mean, the variance and standard deviation will be zero.

The measures of position of a particular value in the overall distribution, however, have different units and limits than the values of the variable on which they are based. Percentiles must fall between 0 and 99. Z-scores for a sample of cases, by definition, must include some negative and some positive values, because some cases must fall below the mean and others above the mean for that sample, unless all cases are at the mean (in which case all z-scores would be 0). However, if an external standard is used as the source of the comparison mean and standard deviation (Chapter 8), it is possible for z-scores for a sample to be skewed.

> <u>Example</u>: When World Health Organization standards are used to assess weight-for-height among children from a highly impoverished setting, z-scores for all cases in the sample could be negative.
>
> *Due to malnutrition and disease, children from impoverished populations could <u>all</u> have weight-for-height <u>below the mean</u> (producing **negative z-scores**), because that mean value was calculated from an international sample that also included children with normal diet and growth patterns.*

Table 10.2 Criteria for Assessing Plausibility of Values of Univariate Statistics

Type of statistic	Definitional limits on values	Other criteria for assessing plausibility of values	
		Topic and context	**Units of measurement of variable**
Central tendency			
Mean ($\overline{x}$)	Must fall between the lowest and highest observed values in the sample (inclusive).	See Chapters 3 and 5	Same units as variable
Median			
Mode			
Spread (variation: dispersion)			
Frequency distribution			
Number of cases (count) with each value of the variable (n_j)	The count with a given value must fall between 0 and the total number of cases in the sample. Sum must equal the total sample size [$\sum(n_j) = n$].	Not relevant	Not relevant
Percentage of cases with each value of the variable[a]	The percentage with a given value must fall between 0% and 100%. Sum of percentages across all values must total 100%.		Numerator and denominator are measured in same units, so the units of original variable cancel during calculation.
Proportion of cases with each value of the variable[a]	The proportion with a given value must fall between 0 and 1.0. Sum of proportions across all values must total 1.0.		

(Continued)

Table 10.2 (Continued)

Type of statistic	Definitional limits on values[b]	Other criteria for assessing plausibility of values		Units of measurement of variable
		Topic and context		
Spread (variation; dispersion, cont.)				
Minimum observed value	Must be greater than or equal to the lowest theoretically possible value for the variable.			Same units as variable
Maximum observed value	Must be less than or equal to the highest theoretically possible value for the variable.	See Chapters 3 and 5		
Range	Must be positive.			
Interquartile range	Must be less than or equal to the range.			Squared units of variable
Variance	Must be positive.			
Standard deviation (s) or SD	Must be positive.			Same units as variable
Position of a specific value in the overall distribution[b]				
Percentile	Must fall between 0 (lowest percentile) and 99 (highest percentile).	Can affect values used to establish the percentiles		Not relevant
z-score (standardized score)	Can be positive or negative. For most normal distributions, 99.7% of values fall between −3 SD and +3 SD.[c]	Determine the pertinent mean and SD		Affect the mean and SD used to calculate the z-score

Notes:

a. See Table 9.5 for formulas to calculate percentage and proportion of a whole.

b. Can be compared against the distribution of the sample or an external standard.

c. Z-scores lower than −3 or greater than +3 are more likely to occur when comparison is against an external standard.

Tables and Charts for Presenting Distributions

Tables and charts to present distribution are designed differently for categorical variables than for continuous ones, both because the pertinent types of univariate statistics differ by level of measurement and because displaying the units or categories of those variables requires different layouts.

Portraying Distribution of Categorical Variables

For categorical variables, distribution is portrayed by the frequency with which the values occur—either as number of cases, as percentage of cases, or both. Central tendency should be reported in the text as the modal and—for ordinal variables—median values. As discussed earlier in the chapter, means and mathematical measures of variation don't make sense for categorical variables.

> Example: The top few rows of Table 10.3 show that in 2019, out of the total 101 million people in the Philippines, the modal age group was persons between the ages of 15 and 64 years, with just over 64 million people (about 63%; Philippine Statistical Authority, 2019).
>
> *The **frequency distribution** reports both the **count** (**number** of people) and the **percentage** of the population in each age group. It shows how the three age groups together composed the entire population (100%) of the Philippines in 2019. The **modal** category can be identified by looking for the age group with the most (and thus highest percentage of) cases.*

Distributions of several categorical variables can be summarized in one table, reporting both the counts and the percentage distributions for each of those variables.

> Example: Table 10.3 presents the distributions of six categorical variables: one ordinal (age group), two nominal (gender and class of worker), and four yes/no indicator variables.
>
> ***Column headings** report the name of the measure, along with its units and scale. For instance, number of persons is reported in millions to save digits, labeled accordingly. Percentage <u>of population</u> is stated so that "percentage of what" (see Chapter 6) is clear. The **row labels** specify who is included in each measure, reflecting different restrictions on the population to whom each variable pertains. For example, literacy is defined only for persons aged 10 years or older, and employment is defined only for adults who are in the labor force (Philippine Statistical Authority, 2019). The row labels also convey the **unit of observation** for*

Table 10.3 Frequency Distributions of Several Categorical Variables

Demographic and socioeconomic characteristics of the Philippines, 2019 unless otherwise noted	Number of persons (millions)	Percentage of population
All	101.0	100.0
Age group		
< 15 years	32.2	31.8
< 5 years	10.8	10.7
15–64 years	64.0	63.4
65+ years	4.8	4.7
Gender		
Male	51.1	50.6
Female	49.9	49.4
Labor force participation rate (% of persons aged 15+)	41.4	60.2
Employment rate (% of labor force)		94.8
Employed persons by class of worker (% of employed persons)		
Wage and salary workers	27.2	65.8
Self-employed without any paid employee	10.8	26.2
Employer in own family-operated farm or business	1.4	3.3
Unpaid family workers	1.9	4.7
Literacy rate (% of persons aged 10+)		98.3
2015 poverty rate (% of families)		16.5

Source: Data from Philippine Statistical Authority (2019).

each measure. For instance, the poverty rate is for <u>families</u>, whereas the other statistics are for <u>individuals</u>. For each of the **indicator** variables, only one category (e.g., being poor) is needed to convey the distribution (see Chapter 6).

Although it is possible (and efficient) to report univariate statistics for several variables in one <u>table</u>, as in Table 10.3, a separate <u>chart</u> must be created to portray the distribution of each variable.

Nominal Variables

Traditionally, pie charts have been used to display the distribution of nominal variables, showing how the shares of the sample with each value fit together to make up the entire sample.

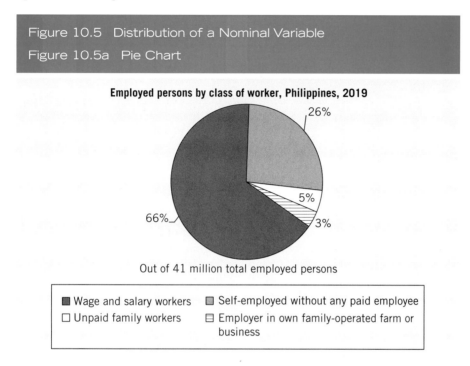

Figure 10.5   Distribution of a Nominal Variable

Figure 10.5a   Pie Chart

Employed persons by class of worker, Philippines, 2019

26%

5%

3%

66%

Out of 41 million total employed persons

◼ Wage and salary workers   ▨ Self-employed without any paid employee
☐ Unpaid family workers   ▤ Employer in own family-operated farm or business

Source: Data from Philippine Statistical Authority (2019).

Example: Figure 10.5a depicts how the four categories of class of worker made up the entire employed population in the Philippines in 2019.

> *The frequency distribution is reported as a **percentage** of all employed persons, with a note specifying the total **number** of persons to whom those percentages apply. The sizes of the slices convey the sizes of the categories, making it easy to identify the **modal** category as the one that occupies the largest portion of the pie (black slice). **Median** and **mean** do not apply, because class of worker is a **nominal** variable.*

However, as discussed in Chapter 7, pie charts combine three of the visual elements that many people have difficulty interpreting: angle (between the sides of each slice), arc (the length of the segment of the pie's border), and area (the amount of space filled by the slice). To overcome these perceptual challenges, the distribution of a nominal variable can be displayed using a histogram (a form of a bar chart), where the height of each bar conveys the frequency of one category of the variable, either as counts or as percentage of cases.

Figure 10.5b   Histogram

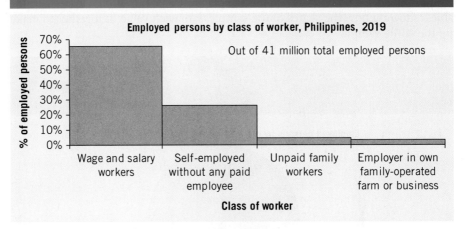

Employed persons by class of worker, Philippines, 2019

Out of 41 million total employed persons

(y-axis: % of employed persons, 0% to 70%)

(x-axis categories: Wage and salary workers; Self-employed without any paid employee; Unpaid family workers; Employer in own family-operated farm or business)

Class of worker

Source: Data from Philippine Statistical Authority (2019).

Unlike an ordinal variable, for which the order of the categories will be obvious (based on the quantity of whatever is being measured), for a nominal variable the categories have no inherent numeric order. Thus, either thematic or empirical criteria should be used to determine the order in which the categories appear in the histogram (see Chapter 6).

Example: Figure 10.5b shows how the four classes of workers together make up the entire population of employed persons, using the same data as in Figure 10.5a.

*The x-axis of the **histogram** lists the classes of workers, and the y-axis specifies the units (%). Class of workers (a **nominal variable**) is organized in **descending empirical** order of frequency in this population. A note reports the number of persons to whom the distribution applies. The **modal** category is the one with the tallest bar.*

Ordinal Variables

As noted previously, a chart or table presenting the distribution of an ordinal variable should preserve the inherent order of the categories.

Example: Table 10.3 shows the age distribution of the Philippine population in 2019.

*Age group is **ordinal**; thus, its categories are listed in consecutive rows in their **natural numeric order** (youngest to oldest age group). **Subgroups** are **indented** using the conventions explained in Chapter 6, communicating that children under age 5 years (preschoolers) are a subset of those under age 15 (all minors).*

Figure 10.6   Distribution of an Ordinal Variable

Figure 10.6a   Histogram

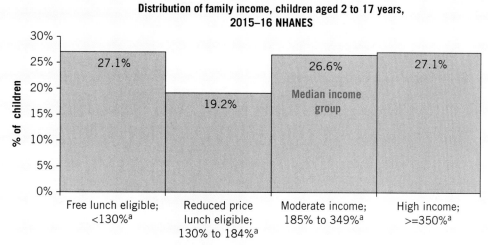

Distribution of family income, children aged 2 to 17 years, 2015–16 NHANES

Source: Author's calculations based on data from the 2015–16 U.S. National Health and Nutrition Examination Survey.

Notes: Weighted to population level using sampling weights provided by the Centers for Disease Control and Prevention (CDC, 2018a). Unweighted $N = 3,115$.

a. Family income as a % of Federal Poverty Threshold.

Example: Figure 10.6a shows the distribution of family income among children in the 2015–16 U.S. NHANES sample.

> The income categories have a logical, **ranked numeric order**, so they are shown in that sequence on the x-axis of the **histogram**, with units specified in the **axis title**. The y-axis reports the units (percentage of children) in which frequency is reported. The **bimodal** nature of the distribution is evident, because the bars for two of the groups are equally tall and are taller than the bars for the other income groups. The **median** income group can be identified as the category that spans the **50th percentile** of the distribution. The mean <u>cannot</u> be calculated, because income <u>group</u> is **categorical**, not continuous.

A stacked bar chart is a different way to portray the distribution of an ordinal variable.

Example: In Figure 10.6b, the four ordinal categories of family income stack together to total 100% of the sample.

> The income groups are presented bottom to top <u>from lowest to highest</u> income. The **modal** category is the one with the thickest slice, whereas the **median** is the category that crosses the 50% line on the vertical axis.

Figure 10.6b Stacked Bar Chart

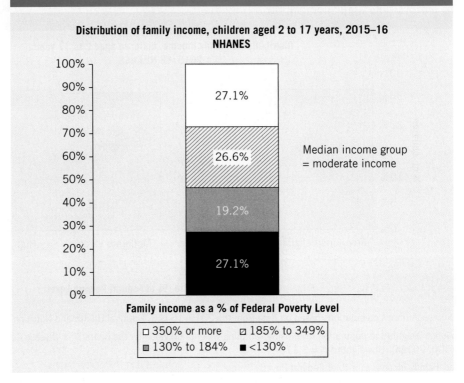

Source: Author's calculations based on data from the 2015–16 U.S. National Health and Nutrition Examination Survey.

Notes: Weighted to population level using sampling weights provided by the Centers for Disease Control and Prevention (CDC, 2018a). Unweighted $N = 3,115$.

Pie charts should <u>not</u> be used to present distributions of ordinal variables, because the slices are arranged radially (spreading out like rays from the center of the pie), making it difficult to see the order of the categories.

<u>Example</u>: Figure 10.6c is a pie chart of the same income distribution as in Figures 10.6a and 10.6b.

> *To understand the pattern from the **pie chart**, readers would have to notice that the **rank order** of the income categories is conveyed in the **legend**, locate the starting point for the lowest income group on the circle, then find the respective slices by color and read them clockwise around the pie. Much easier to see the ordered nature of the categories in the **histogram** (Figure 10.6a) or **stacked bar chart** (Figure 10.6b) versions.*

Figure 10.6c   Incorrect Use of Pie Chart

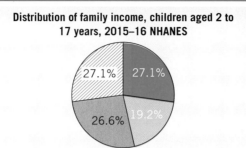

**Distribution of family income, children aged 2 to
17 years, 2015–16 NHANES**

27.1%   27.1%

26.6%   19.2%

Family income as a % of Federal Poverty Level

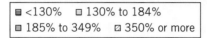

| ■ <130%   □ 130% to 184% |
| ■ 185% to 349%   ▨ 350% or more |

Source: Author's calculations based on data from the 2015–16 U.S. National Health and Nutrition Examination Survey.

Notes: Weighted to population level using sampling weights provided by the Centers for Disease Control and Prevention (CDC, 2018a). Unweighted $N = 3,115$.

Portraying Distribution of Continuous Variables

To present information on the distribution of a continuous variable, typically a table is used to organize summary statistics on central tendency and spread, sometimes complemented by a chart to show the entire distribution. Descriptive statistics for several continuous variables can be combined into one table, because the types of measures of central tendency and spread are the same for all continuous variables. Descriptive statistics for each variable are in the same units as the original continuous variable, and they are labeled accordingly in the table and the associated write-up.

Example: Table 10.4 reports descriptive statistics on the height, weight, and BMI of 8-year-old U.S. boys.

*Each **variable** occupies its own row, with the **row label** specifying the **topic** and **units**, which are different for each of the three variables. The **column headings** convey the types of statistics, including three **measures of central tendency** (mean, median, and mode) grouped under one column spanner and five aspects of **variation** (min, max, standard deviation, and first and third quartiles) grouped under a second **column spanner**. These are **univariate** statistics, because information is on each variable by itself, not in association with the other variables in the table. The table **title** specifies the **W's** (who, when, and where), and **footnotes** define abbreviations and report **sample size**.*

Table 10.4 Univariate Statistics on Several Continuous Variables

Descriptive statistics on child weight, height, and body mass index, 8-year-old boys, 2015–16 NHANES	Central tendency					Variation		
	Mean	Median	Mode	Minimum	Maximum	Standard deviation	Q1	Q3
Height (cm)	132.0	131.3	132.5	116.5	151.5	6.45	127.9	135.9
Weight (kg)	31.4	29.7	34.7	18.1	55.8	7.52	26.4	34.7
Body mass index (BMI; kg/m²)	17.9	17.00	17.4	12.7	27.9	3.29	15.6	19.6

Source: Author's calculations based on data from the 2015–16 U.S. National Health and Nutrition Examination Survey.

Notes: Weighted to population level using sampling weights provided by the Centers for Disease Control and Prevention (CDC, 2018a).

Q1: 1st quartile. Q3: 3rd quartile. Unweighted *n* = 121.

Rarely is a table used to display the frequency distribution of a continuous variable, unless it has only a handful of values, because separate rows would be needed for each observed value of the variable.

Example: The shortest 8-year-old boy in the 2015–16 NHANES was 116 cm tall; the tallest was 151 cm. Thus, a table to present the frequency distribution of height would require 35 rows—one for each height (in centimeters) observed in the data set!

> Imagine how many rows would be needed to report the height distribution in centimeters for the full sample of children in the NHANES, who range from 2-year-old toddlers to 17-year-olds who have reached their adult height.[1] This would not be an efficient way to display the data!

Figure 10.7   Histogram to Portray Distribution of a Continuous Variable

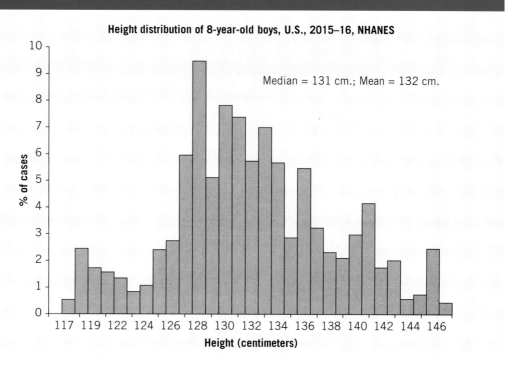

Height distribution of 8-year-old boys, U.S., 2015–16, NHANES

Median = 131 cm.; Mean = 132 cm.

Source: Author's calculations based on data from the 2015–16 U.S. National Health and Nutrition Examination Survey.

Notes: Weighted to population level using sampling weights provided by the Centers for Disease Control and Prevention (CDC, 2018a).

Unweighted *n* = 121.

---

[1]Height changes rapidly during childhood and differs for boys and girls, so I have restricted the analysis in this chapter to one age/gender group.

To present the frequency distribution of all values of a continuous variable in a sample, a histogram is often used, sometimes with a bell curve superimposed to summarize the shape.

Example: Figure 10.7 is a **histogram**, showing the height distribution of 8-year-old in boys the NHANES sample.

> *Height values are listed in **ascending** order on the x-axis, with a bar portraying the percentage of cases that have that height value, with units (% of sample) specified in the **y-axis title**. Annotations to the chart report the **mean** and **median** heights. The **modal** height can be identified as the value with the tallest bar.*

An alternative way to present summary statistics on the distribution of a continuous variable is with a **box-and-whisker plot**.

Example: Figure 10.8 shows that the height of 8-year-old boys ranged from 116 to 151 cm, and the middle half of cases were between 128 and 136 cm tall.

Figure 10.8 Box-and-Whisker Plot to Portray Distribution of a Continuous Variable

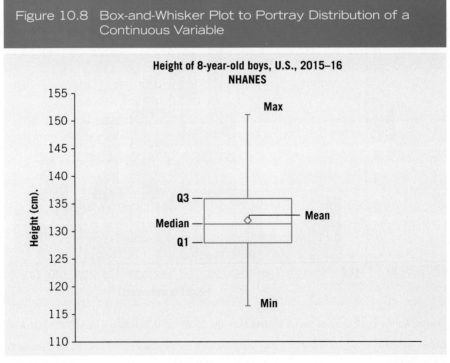

Source: Author's calculations based on data from the 2015–16 U.S. National Health and Nutrition Examination Survey.

Notes: Weighted to population level using sampling weights provided by the Centers for Disease Control and Prevention (CDC, 2018a).

*The "whiskers" portray the **minimum** and **maximum** values, for a range of 46 cm (the distance from the lower to upper whiskers). The lower and upper edges of the "box" show the **first quartile** (Q1) and **third quartile** (Q3), respectively; the **interquartile range** is the distance between those values. The **median** is conveyed by the horizontal line in the middle of the box, and the **mean** is identified by a diamond symbol.*

Associations Between Two or More Variables

Quantitative research often investigates questions about relationships (associations) between variables, such as how an outcome differs across groups or how some phenomenon changes over time. In other words, **associations** consider how two variables are <u>related to each other</u> (bivariate), rather than how each of them <u>alone</u> is distributed (univariate).

The relationship between two variables is called a **bivariate association**, where "bivariate" means "two variables." An association can be analyzed either by using variables in their original forms or by creating new variables to look at different aspects of that association, such as income in groups instead of income in continuous monetary units (see Appendix A).

> A **bivariate association** describes how values of two variables in a data set relate to each other.

Typically, one of the variables is identified as the independent variable (the hypothesized cause or predictor) and the other is identified as the dependent variable (what we think is the outcome or consequence; see Chapter 2). Thus, a bivariate method is often used to investigate how values of the dependent variable differ or vary across values of the independent variable.

<u>Caution:</u> As you may have learned in a statistics course, "Association does not necessarily mean causation." In other words, just because two variables are numerically associated with each other does <u>not</u> mean that one caused the other. In Chapter 12, we will cover the criteria for assessing whether a relationship can be interpreted as cause and effect.

> The presence of a numeric association between the values of two or more variables does <u>not necessarily</u> imply a cause-and-effect relationship between those variables.

The type of statistics used to quantify a relationship between two variables depends on the levels of measurement of those variables. In other words, different statistical methods suit different combinations of levels of measurement of the independent and dependent variables. In this section, I describe different types of bivariate methods, show how to present the results in tables and charts, and explain how to interpret those results, including the pertinent units in which they are measured.

Heat maps can be used to convey the strength of associations among pairs of variables.

Figure 10.9 Heat Map of Strength of Association

Relative strength and statistical significance of each factor as a predictor of attitudes about climate change and energy

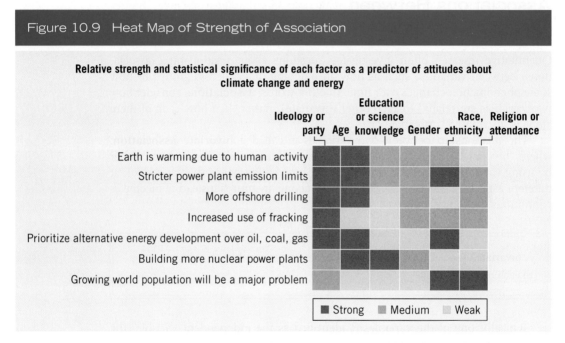

Source: Pew Research Center (2015).

Example: Figure 10.9 portrays how each of several ideological, demographic, and social characteristics relate to individuals' opinions about climate change and energy issues based on a 2015 survey of U.S. residents. Ideology/political party and age have the strongest associations with public opinion on several different climate change and energy issues, while race/ethnicity and religion are most strongly associated with concerns about the growing world population. Education or science knowledge has a weak or medium association with most issues.

In the **heat map**, *each of the colored squares shows the* **bivariate association** *between one of the ideological, social, or demographic factors (**independent variables**; in the <u>columns</u>) and one climate change or energy issue (**dependent variables**, in the <u>rows</u>). A **legend** defines the*

288   Part IV | Making Sense of Numbers From Mathematical and Statistical Methods

*colors associated with an **ordinal** measure of strength and the statistical significance of each association, classified as "strong," "medium," and "weak." By looking down a column for concentrations of the dark color, readers can identify which issues are strongly associated with the characteristic in that column. By looking across a row, they can find which traits are most strongly associated with a specific issue. However, because numeric values are <u>not</u> reported and the categories of variables are <u>not</u> named, the heat map does <u>not</u> communicate either the direction or the magnitude of the associations. For instance, we cannot tell which political party is least likely to believe that "Earth is warming due to human activity" or how much those attitudes differ by political party.*

We will delve into statistical significance in Chapter 13.

Correlation

Bivariate correlations are used to measure the relationship between two continuous variables.[2] If two variables are positively associated, the **correlation coefficient** (r) will be between 0 and 1.0. If they are negatively associated, the correlation coefficient will be between −1.0 and 0. Negative values of r indicate an **inverse** association (as x increases, y decreases), whereas positive values of r indicate a **direct** association (as x increases, y also increases). A correlation coefficient of 1.0 or −1.0 is termed a **perfect correlation**, meaning that knowing the value of one variable precisely predicts the value of the other variable.[3] When the correlation coefficient = 0, x and y are uncorrelated—the values of the two variables do not move with one another. We will go over using tables to present correlations in Chapter 13.

> Example: In the 2015–16 U.S. NHANES, family income and height-for-age percentile were positively correlated ($r = .054$), meaning that as income rose, so did height-for-age.
>
> *Family income (the **independent variable**) and height-for-age percentile (**dependent variable**) are both **continuous** variables, so a **correlation** was used to assess the strength of their association with each other.*

The **coefficient of determination**, calculated by squaring the correlation coefficient, measures the proportion of variation in one variable that is accounted for by variation in the other variable. Values of r must fall between −1.0 and +1.0;

---

[2]Correlations can also be used to measure strength of association between variables at other levels of measurement (Utts & Heckard, 2014). However, other approaches are preferred for conveying the <u>size</u> of patterns involving categorical variables. See other bivariate methods listed in this chapter.

[3]In a perfect correlation, the change in value of one variable is exactly proportional to the change in value of the other.

thus, r^2 must fall between 0 and 1.0, where 0 indicates that the two variables don't share any variance and 1.0 denotes complete (100%) shared variance.

> **Correlations** are used to measure the strength of association between two continuous variables, x and y. A **correlation coefficient** (r) can range from -1.0 for a **perfect negative correlation** to $+1.0$ for a **perfect positive correlation**. For **inverse (negative)** associations, $r < 0$; for **direct (positive)** associations, $r > 0$. The **coefficient of determination** (r^2) is a measure of the strength of an association between two variables, calculated by squaring the correlation coefficient (r).

Example: Variation in family income accounts for about 2% of the variation in BMI percentile (BMIP) among children in the 2015–16 NHANES.

*The **correlation coefficient** for income and BMIP was −0.131, so their coefficient of determination* ($\mathbf{r^2}$) = $(-0.131)^2$ = 0.017, *or about 2%.*

Cross-Tabulation

When both the independent and dependent variables are categorical, a **cross-tabulation** is used to show how they are associated with each other. Any combination of nominal and ordinal variables can be analyzed using a cross-tabulation.

> **Cross-tabulations** (abbreviated **cross-tab** or **x-tab**) are used to portray the association between a categorical independent variable and a categorical dependent variable.

Results of cross-tabulations are usually reported as the <u>percentage</u> of cases in each category of the independent variable that fall into a specified category of the dependent variable. As discussed in Chapter 6, a table or chart reporting information on a dichotomous (two-category) dependent variable can convey the pattern by presenting information only on the percentage of cases that fall into the category of interest; the percentage <u>without</u> that trait is, by definition, 100% minus the percentage <u>with</u> that trait.

Example: Figure 10.10 uses a bar chart to portray the percentage of U.S. respondents at each educational attainment level who opposed the death penalty in 2018.

*A **cross-tabulation** was used to investigate how opposition to the death penalty (a **nominal dependent variable**) varied by educational attainment (**ordinal independent variable**), because both of those variables are categorical. Categories of educational attainment are presented in ascending order on the x-axis, with the heights of the bars showing the **percentage***

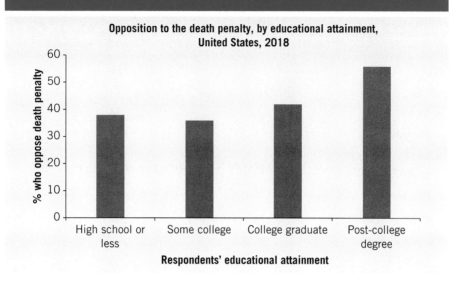

Source: Data from Oliphant (2018).

of each educational attainment group *that opposed the death penalty. Since*
the dependent variable is **dichotomous**, *the chart needs only to present* one
category of that outcome ("oppose") to show the pattern.

Output from several bivariate procedures that share either the independent
or the dependent variable can be combined into tables based on type of statistical
procedure, instead of creating a separate table for each pair of variables.

Example: Table 10.5 summarizes how opposition to the death penalty in
the United States in 2018 varied according to each of six demographic
and social characteristics of respondents.

The table reports results of six **cross-tabs**, *all involving attitudes about*
the death penalty. Each of the independent variables is listed in the **rows**,
*while the outcome (*opposing *the death penalty) is in the* **column**. *The*
categories of each **nominal** *independent variable (gender, race/ethnicity,*
political party, and religion) are organized under a row heading for that
variable in **ascending order** *of* percentage opposing the death penalty.
Categories of each **ordinal independent variable** *(age group and*
educational attainment) are listed in their **inherent numeric order**.

See Chapter 13 for examples of tables to present results of cross-tabulations
involving multi-category dependent variables.

Table 10.5 Cross-Tabulations of Several Independent Variables With a Dichotomous Dependent Variable

Opposition to the death penalty by demographic, political, and religious characteristics; United States; 2018	% who oppose death penalty
All	39
Gender	
Men	34
Women	45
Race/ethnicity	
White	34
Hispanic	49
Black	52
Age group (years)	
18 to 29	46
20 to 49	38
50 to 64	38
65+	35
Educational attainment	
High school or less	38
Some college	36
College graduate	42
Post-college degree	56
Political party affiliation	
Republican	17
Independent	40
Democrat	59
Religion	
White evangelical Protestant	19
White mainline Protestant	30
White Catholic	35
All Catholic	42
Unaffiliated	45

Source: Data from Oliphant (2018).

Difference in Means or ANOVA

When the independent variable has exactly two categories and the dependent variable is continuous, the association between them is characterized using a **difference in means**, which is shorthand for "difference in the mean value of a continuous dependent variable across categories of a two-category independent variable." When the independent variable has at least three categories, the association is captured using an **ANOVA** (**AN**alysis **O**f **VA**riance). For either of those procedures, the independent variable can be nominal or ordinal. Other summary statistics for continuous dependent variables, such as the median, can also be reported in place of, or in addition to, the mean. The result will be in the units of the dependent variable.

When the dependent variable is continuous and the independent variable is categorical, their bivariate association is analyzed using

- a **difference in means,** if the independent variable is <u>dichotomous</u> (two-category), or

- an **ANOVA (ANalysis Of VAriance),** if the independent variable is <u>multichotomous</u> (three or more categories).

Example: Figure 10.11a shows how median age varied across selected countries in 2018.

> *There is one **bar** for each country (**horizontal axis**), and the height of the bar reflects its median age (a **continuous dependent variable**, labeled with its units on the vertical axis). Country (a **nominal independent variable**) is organized in **ascending** order of median age (the dependent variable).*

Caution: As emphasized in Chapter 7, line charts should <u>not</u> be used to present difference in means or cross-tabulations involving nominal variables, because the line connects values of the dependent variable (on the y-axis) for adjacent values of the independent variable (on the x-axis), implying a trend (Zacks & Tversky, 1999). The line misleads readers to perceive a "slope" (e.g., an increase in the y variable for a one-unit increase in the x variable). However, a "one-unit increase" doesn't make sense for a nominal variable, because its categories have neither units nor an inherent numeric order.

Example: The apparent slope of a line connecting pairs of countries in Figure 10.11b implies a "one-unit increase" in country-ness between each of the adjacent pairs of countries (e.g., between Brazil and Canada, or between Mexico and Monaco), which makes no sense.

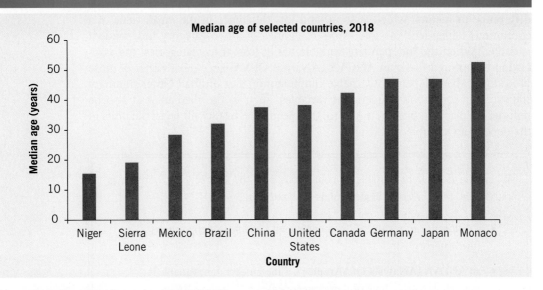

Figure 10.11a   Bar Chart to Show Bivariate Association Between a Nominal Independent Variable and a Continuous Dependent Variable

Source: Data from World Population Review (2019).

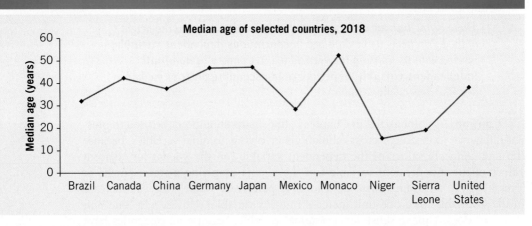

Figure 10.11b   Incorrect Use of Line Chart for Nominal Independent Variable

Source: Data from World Population Review (2019).

*In Figure 10.11b, the countries (**categories of a nominal variable**) are organized in **alphabetical** order. The slopes of the line segments between adjacent bars would change substantially if the countries were, instead, organized in **descending** order in of the dependent variable (median age) or using some other principle to sequence them.*

*For associations involving nominal independent variables, a **bar chart** (Figure 10.11a) is the better choice, correctly inviting readers to judge differences in the outcome by comparing heights of the bars for each country.*

Levels of measurement for the variables under study determine which types of bivariate methods are appropriate. Methods differ for different <u>combinations</u> of nominal, ordinal, and continuous independent and dependent variables. It is best to use

- correlation when both the independent and dependent variables are continuous,

- cross-tabulation when both the independent and dependent variables are categorical, and

- difference in means or ANOVA when the independent variable is categorical and the dependent variable is continuous.

Three-Way Associations

For many research questions, an important issue concerns how a dependent variable varies according to values of two independent variables <u>simultaneously</u>. These relationships are known as **three-way associations**, because they examine a relationship among three variables. They are often conducted to reveal patterns between an independent and a dependent variable within subgroups defined by a third variable or to test whether one variable explains an association between two other variables.

A three-way association involves a relationship among three variables.

The combination of levels of measurement for the three variables determines the type of statistical procedure and the design of tables or charts to report the results. Two common types of associations among three variables are two-way differences in means and three-way cross-tabulations. See "Multiple Regression" in Chapter 13 for additional methods used to analyze relationships among more than two variables.

Two-Way Difference in Means or Two-Way ANOVA

Two-way difference in means or **two-way ANOVA** procedures are used to show how the value of a continuous dependent variable varies across values of two categorical independent variables at the same time. The categorical variables can be any combination of ordinal and nominal variables. The results (mean values) will be expressed in the same units as the dependent variable.

Figure 10.12   Clustered Bar Chart to Display a Two-Way ANOVA

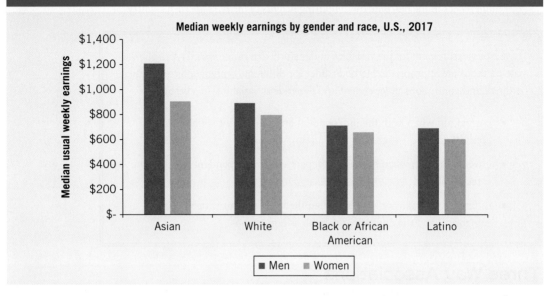

Median weekly earnings by gender and race, U.S., 2017

Notes: Among full-time employed wage and salary workers; excludes self-employed persons.

Source: Data from U.S. Bureau of Labor Statistics (2018a).

Example: Figure 10.12 shows how 2017 median income in the United States varied by race and gender together.

*The **title** lists two "by" variables: race/ethnicity and gender, thus identifying them as the **independent variables** as explained in Chapter 6. Categories of one independent variable (race/ethnicity) are displayed on the **x-axis** in **descending order of the outcome** (median earnings); categories of the other independent variable (gender) are identified in the **legend**. The height of each bar shows the median value of weekly earnings (a **continuous dependent variable**) for each of the eight possible combinations of race (four categories) and gender (two categories). **Units** on the **y-axis** are those of the dependent variable.*

Three-Way Cross-Tabulations

Three-way cross-tabulations are used to investigate relationships among three categorical variables. A cross-tabulation of a two-category dependent variable by two categorical independent variables produces information about how many (and what percentage of) cases in each combination of the two independent variables had the outcome of interest.

Table 10.6 Three-Way Cross-Tabulation

Agreement Between Urine Test and Self-report, Adult Male Arrestees, by City and Type of Drug, 2013 (% of arrestees)				
	Type of drug			
City	Marijuana	Cocaine	Opiates	Methamphetamines
Atlanta	78.5%	82.6%	95.0%	98.2%
Chicago	86.7%	87.4%	94.9%	100.0%
Denver	83.9%	88.5%	94.4%	92.2%
New York	81.4%	82.7%	94.4%	99.7%
Sacramento	84.8%	93.2%	89.1%	82.7%
All cities	83.2%	86.9%	93.6%	94.6%

Source: Office of National Drug Control Policy (2014, p. 56).

Example: Table 10.6 presents the association among three categorical variables: city, type of drug, and whether or not an arrestee's urine test agreed (concurred) with his self-report of whether he used that type of drug. For instance, 78.5% of men arrested in Atlanta in 2013 had urine-test results consistent with whether they said they had used marijuana—either both the respondent and the test indicated yes, or both the respondent and the test indicated no.

> The **dependent variable** is classified as whether or not the urine test was concordant with (gave the same result as) the self-report. One **nominal independent variable** (city) is listed in **alphabetical** order in the rows; the **other nominal independent variable** (type of drug) is listed from left to right across the columns in ascending order of concordance for all cities combined. The **percentage of concordant cases** for each combination of city and type of drug is reported in the **interior cell** at the intersection of a row and column.

> The **dependent variable** is dichotomous (concordant or not), so reporting information on extent of concordance is sufficient to illustrate the pattern.

Plausibility Criteria for Bivariate and Three-Way Statistics

Knowing what kinds of calculations are involved in each type of bivariate or three-way calculation provides guidance for assessing the plausibility of values for those statistics and for identifying the units in which they are measured.

Table 10.7   Criteria for Assessing Plausibility of Values of Bivariate Statistics

Type of statistic	Definitional limits on values	Other criteria for assessing plausibility of bivariate results	
		Topic and context	Units of measurement of independent and dependent variables
Correlation			
Correlation coefficient (r)	Must fall between −1.0 and +1.0, inclusive.	N/A	N/A
Coefficient of determination (r^2)	Must fall between 0.0 and +1.0, inclusive.		
Difference in means or ANOVA			
Mean of the dependent variable for each category of the independent variable	Must fall between lowest and highest observed values of the dependent variable.	See Chapters 3 and 5	Units of the dependent variable
Cross-tabulation			
Number of cases in each combination of categories of the independent and the dependent variable	Must fall between 0 and the total number of cases in the sample. Sum of counts within each row must equal the total number of cases in that row. Sum of counts within each column must equal the total number of cases in that column. Sum of counts in all cells must equal the total sample size.	N/A	N/A
Percentage of cases within a category of the independent variable that fall within each category of the dependent variable	Must fall between 0% and 100% for each cell. Sum of percentages within each row or column must total 100% of that row or column. Sum of percentages in all cells must total 100% of the overall sample.	N/A	N/A

A correlation coefficient is constrained to fall between −1.0 (a perfect negative correlation) and +1.0 (a perfect positive correlation), regardless of the topic, the context of the data, or the original units of the continuous variables being analyzed.

The results of a difference in means or an ANOVA are reported as the mean value of the dependent variable for each of the subgroups defined by categories of the independent variable. The mean values are in the original units of the dependent variable, with the level and range of values influenced by the topic and context under study, as discussed in Chapters 3 and 5. As with limits on mean values in general, the means for each subgroup must fall between the minimum and maximum observed values of the dependent variable for the overall sample.

The results of a cross-tabulation are reported as either the number or the percentage of cases that have each of the possible combinations of the categories of the independent and the dependent variable. Consistent with our discussion about results of frequency distributions, the counts for each cell of the cross-tab (n_i, where i is the number of cases in a cell) must be between 0 and the total sample size (n), and the sum of the counts across all cells must equal the overall sample size. The percentage of cases in each cell (<u>out of the overall sample</u>) must be between 0% and 100%, and the sum of the percentages for all interior cells must equal 100%. The <u>percentage of a row's</u> cases that fall in each cell of that row must total 100% of its subgroup size; likewise for column percentages. (See Chapter 6 for more on "percentage of what?") Neither topic nor context affects the units or limits on numeric results of cross-tabs (n_i or percentage).

Comparisons by Level of Measurement, Revisited

Recall from Chapter 9 that the types of comparisons that can be conducted for each level of measurement relate only to comparing one <u>value</u> of a variable with another <u>value of that variable</u>.

> Example: If one student is Muslim and another is Jewish, we can say only that they have different religions, not that one has more religion-ness or how much more religion-ness.
>
> *"Muslim" is the name of one category of the variable "religious affiliation," while "Jewish" is the name of another category of that variable. Because religious affiliation is a **nominal** variable, we can assess whether the **values** for two cases are the same or different, but we <u>cannot</u> rank, or calculate the difference (from subtraction) or ratio (from division) those values (**names** of religions).*

However, calculations on the <u>frequency of occurrence</u> of values—counts or percentage of cases with each value—can be performed for variables at any level of measurement. These calculations can then be used to describe the direction and magnitude of differences in how often specific values occur.

Figure 10.13 Calculations Using Frequency of Occurrence vs. Value of Variable, by Level of Measurement

Level of measurement	Can compare frequency of occurrence of values?*	Can compare values of variable?			
		Same or different	Rank	Difference (from subtraction)	Ratio (from division)
Nominal	Yes	Yes	No	No	No
Ordinal	Yes	Yes	Yes	No	No
Interval	Yes	Yes	Yes	Yes	No
Ratio	Yes	Yes	Yes	Yes	Yes

Note: *Frequency reported either as number of cases (counts) or as a percentage of cases.

Example: Suppose your university has a total enrollment of 10,000 people, of whom 1,400 (14%) are Muslim and 700 (7%) are Jewish. From those numbers, we can see that there are twice as many Muslim as Jewish students at your school.

> The **frequency** of each nominal category is measured at the **ratio** level; thus, division **can** be used to compare <u>which</u> religion is more common among students and <u>how much</u> more common. Rank or subtraction of the sizes of those religious groups could also be calculated, either from the number of cases or from their percentage share of total enrollment.

For quantitative variables, both the values of the variable <u>and</u> how frequently those values occur in a sample or population can be compared numerically.

Example: In a university, some students are 19 years old, some are 20 years old, and so on. The latest roster shows that 2,300 of the students are aged 19, whereas 2,700 are aged 20.

> <u>All four types</u> of calculation (same/different, rank, subtraction, and division) can be used <u>both</u> for the **values** of the age variable and to compare the **frequency** with which those values occur in the sample. Twenty-year-olds are one year older than 19-year-olds (based on subtraction involving **values of the ratio variable** age). Moreover, there are 400 fewer 19-year-olds than 20-year-olds (based on subtraction involving the **number of cases** of each age).

Mathematical comparisons (subtraction and division) can be conducted on the **frequency distributions** (count or percentage of cases) for variables at <u>any</u> level of measurement. However, the types of mathematical computations that can be conducted on the **values** of a variable differ by level of measurement.

TERMS AND CONCEPTS

HIGHLIGHTS

- Identifying the correct type of **statistical method** to address a specific research question is an important aspect of making sense of the results.

- **Univariate statistics** describe how values of one variable at a time are distributed in a data set. They include measures of **central tendency**, **spread (variation)**, **shape**, and the **position** of a particular value in the overall distribution. Choice of appropriate types of univariate statistics depends on a variable's **level of measurement.**

- The range of **plausible values** of **univariate statistics** is determined by the types of **computations** or **comparisons** required to calculate the statistic, the **units** in which the variable was measured, and the topic and context of the data.

- **Bivariate statistics** describe associations between two variables, while **three-way methods** examine associations among three variables. Association between two variables

does <u>not</u> guarantee that the independent variable caused the dependent variable; see Chapter 12.

- Choice of an appropriate bivariate or three-way procedure depends on the combination of **levels of measurement** of the independent and dependent variables.

- Limits on the scale and range of bivariate statistics are completely different for **correlations, cross-tabulations,** and **differences in means**. Plausible values of each of those statistics are also affected differently by the units, topic, and context.

- Calculations to compare quantitative **measures of distribution** and **association** can be performed on variables at any level of measurement, even those whose <u>values</u> cannot be compared numerically.

- Distributions and associations can be presented in either **tabular** or **chart** form, with the correct design of those exhibits determined by the **number of variables** and their **levels of measurement.**

RESEARCH TIPS

- When planning a bivariate statistical procedure, pay careful attention to the level(s) of measurement of the independent and

dependent variables, to ensure that you choose the method that suits the specific variables that fulfill those roles in your analysis.

- When setting up a cross-tabulation, pay careful attention to where you place the independent variable before determining in which direction to have the software calculate the percentages; see "Percentaging of Tables" in Chapter 6.

RECOMMENDED READINGS

Golnick, L., & Smith, W. (1993). *The cartoon guide to statistics* (Chapter 2). Harper Perennial.

Salkind, N. J. (2016). *Statistics for people who (think they) hate statistics* (6th ed., Part IV). SAGE.

Utts, J., & Heckard, R. (2014). *Mind on statistics* (5th ed., Chapter 2). Cengage, Brooks Cole.

EXERCISES

Individual Exercises

Quantitative Reasoning in Everyday Life

1. Use information in Figure 10A to identify the (a) minimum, (b) maximum, and (c) modal number of calories in a Chipotle food order.

(d) Identify the approximate percentage of orders that had (i) 700 calories, (ii) 1,600 calories, and (iii) the modal number of calories. (e) Determine the purpose of the reference line at 2,000 calories.

Figure 10A Distribution of Calories From Chipotle Food Orders

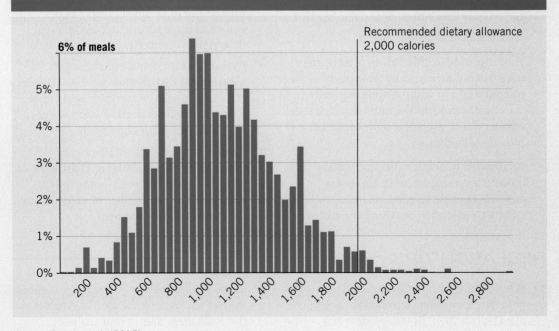

Source: Quealy et al. (2015).

Interpreting Research

2. Answer the following questions for the data set you selected from the ICPSR Website (Chapter 2, Exercise 3). On the "Variables" tab or in the codebook for that data set, find examples of each of the following: (i) a nominal variable, (ii) an ordinal variable, and (iii) two continuous (interval or ratio) variables. (a) Specify the concept measured by each variable and (b) its units and/or categories. (c) For each variable, name the pertinent measure(s) of (i) central tendency and (ii) spread or variability. (d) Explain why those univariate methods suit the particular variable, with reference to its levels of measurement.

3. Working with the same variables you described in your previous answer, identify pairs of variables for which each of the following bivariate methods would be appropriate for characterizing the association between those variables: (a) correlation, (b) cross-tabulation, and (c) difference in means or ANOVA. (d) For each, explain why that bivariate method suits those variables, with reference to their levels of measurement.

4. Find a journal article in your field that reports results of bivariate associations. Identify (a) the dependent variable and independent variables in the authors' analysis; (b) the types of bivariate statistical methods they used; (c) whether they explained their choice of methods, given the levels of measurement of their variables; and (d) whether that method was a correct choice.

Analyzing Data

5. Buy a small package of plain M&Ms (or any other kind of candy that has small pieces of varying colors). (a) Identify the level of measurement of candy color. (b) From the package of candy, pour 10 pieces of candy onto your desk, and sort them by color. Create a histogram like that in Figure 10B. Identify the modal color. **Note**: Your color distribution is likely to be different than in the figure.

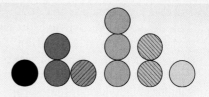

Figure 10B   Colors of Candy

Red Orange Blue Yellow Brown Green

6. Keep eight pieces from your candy sample from the previous exercise. (b) From a small package of a <u>different</u> type of small-piece candy that also has pieces of varying colors, such as peanut M&Ms or Skittles, pour two pieces of the second kind of candy onto your desk; sort the sample by color. (c) Within each color of candy (row), create a separate column for each type of candy, as in Figure 10C. **Note**: Your color distribution is likely to be different than in the figure. (d) Identify the level of measurement of candy type (e.g., plain vs. peanut M&Ms). (e) Identify the name of this type of display, and (f) explain why it is suitable for this bivariate procedure, given the levels of measurement of the two variables (color and candy type).

Figure 10C   Colors of Two Types of Candy

Color	Candy type	
	Candy 1	Candy 2
Brown	◎	◎
Yellow	◯ ◯	◯
Red	●	
Orange	◉ ◉	
Blue	◍	
Green	◯	

Group Exercises

Analyzing Data

7. As a class (or in groups of at least 20 students), discuss the steps to figure out univariate statistics on height. (**Hint**: Take advantage of the fact that height is very visually apparent, so you can sort yourselves standing up!) (a) Identify the level of measurement for height in inches. (b) List the pertinent measures of central tendency for height, using the guidelines in this chapter. (c) Discuss how you would go about calculating each of those measures. (d) Create a frequency distribution by height, with students standing in the position indicated by their height. (e) Divide the class into quartiles by height; (f) determine the numeric values of the cutoffs for those quartiles.

8. Discuss the steps to figure out univariate statistics on an indicator of who already drank coffee today (yes or no). (a) Identify the level of measurement for coffee-drinking status. (b) List the pertinent measure(s) of central tendency for that variable. (c) Create a frequency distribution based on coffee-drinking status. (d) Identify the modal value. (e) Tabulate the number of people with each value of coffee-drinking status. (f) Calculate what percentage of those present are in each category.

9. Discuss how you can visually display the association between age group (< 20 years old, 20–24, 25 or older) and coffee-drinking status by sorting yourselves into groups. (a) Identify the level(s) of measurement for (i) age group and (ii) coffee-drinking status. (b) Identify the type of bivariate method to observe the association between those two variables, based on their levels of measurement. (c) Tabulate the number of people in each combination of the two variables. (d) Calculate the percentage of each age group who drank coffee already today. (e) Calculate the percentage of each coffee-drinking group that is in each age group. (f) Discuss why the answers to parts (e) and (f) were different from each other, with reference to the material in Chapter 6 on percentaging a table.

10. Discuss how you can calculate the bivariate association between height and coffee-drinking status. (a) Identify the level(s) of measurement for (i) coffee-drinking status and (ii) height. (b) Identify the type of bivariate method to observe the association between those two variables, based on their levels of measurement. (c) Figure out what information you need about the height distribution to perform the comparison. (d) Calculate the mean height within each coffee-drinking group.

Assessing the Quality
of Numeric Estimates

In **Part V**, I introduce several factors that affect the accuracy and precision of quantitative research results. In Chapter 11, I cover how study design and data collection can introduce bias—an important issue to consider when evaluating the quality of the numeric results. In Chapter 12, I explain the principles for assessing whether a relationship between two variables can be interpreted as cause-and-effect, and why that is an important consideration for determining how results of a study can be applied to solving real-world problems. In Chapter 13, I introduce the concept of statistical uncertainty, how it is calculated, and what it means for interpreting numeric results based on samples rather than populations.

CHAPTER 11

Bias

Learning Objectives

After reading this chapter, you will be able to do the following:

1. Define bias and why it is important for making sense of numbers.

2. Describe the time structure of different types of study design.

3. Recognize different types of probability and non-probability methods of selecting a sample and how they affect sampling bias.

4. Define study nonresponse and understand how it relates to external validity.

5. Describe types of item nonresponse and how they can introduce bias.

6. List sources of measurement bias and how they affect reliability and measurement validity.

7. Itemize common sources of data collected for research and for non-research purposes, and how those sources are affected by different types of bias.

B ias concerns whether the data used for a study are valid, and, if not, in what direction they might be incorrect. As a consequence, evaluating bias and its causes is an essential part of interpreting the results of quantitative studies. Continuing through our checklist of W's for making sense of numbers, in this chapter we consider ways that bias can be introduced by **how** a study was designed and **how** data were collected, with "how" once again granted honorary "W" status.

I begin by providing an overview of some of the main ways study design and data collection can introduce bias into quantitative studies. I describe the different time structures of major types of study designs, and I compare approaches to selecting a sample of cases for analysis—both of which can affect the types and extent of bias in a study. I then explain how bias can occur due to nonresponse, data-collection strategies, and sources of data. Throughout, I discuss how bias relates to information from earlier chapters about representativeness of samples (Chapter 5), reliability, and measurement validity (Chapter 4).

What Is Bias?

Bias is a systematic error resulting from the way a study was designed, or how data were collected or analyzed, which can lead to incorrect estimates of the values of a variable or the direction or size of an association between variables (Gordis, 2009).

> Example: If a bathroom scale has a positive reading even when there isn't anything on the scale, it will overestimate the weight of anyone who steps on that scale.
>> The scale is **biased** *upward, because its estimate of a person's weight will exceed their actual weight.*

Bias occurs when the estimated value of a variable or the size of a relationship between variables is consistently incorrect in the <u>same</u> direction.

Unlike **random error**, where some measured values are higher than their actual values and some are lower, **bias** occurs when measurements are consistently wrong in the <u>same</u> direction. You will learn more about random error and its importance for making sense of numbers in Chapter 13.

> Example: On the left side of Figure 11.1, all the arrows hit above the bull's-eye.
>> *The pattern suggests that the archer's aim was* **biased**, *because they consistently missed in the same direction (high) with every shot.*

> Example: On the right side of Figure 11.1, each of the arrows misses the bull's-eye, but some were too high, some too low, some off to the right, and some off to the left. Some barely missed the bull's-eye; others were further off-target.
>> *The archer exhibited* **random error**, *because the arrows were off-target in different directions and by varying distances, with no consistent pattern. Although there was error in the shots, they were* <u>not</u> **biased**.

There are three major types of bias that occur at the study design and data-collection phase: sample selection bias, nonresponse bias, and biased responses (Utts & Heckard, 2014). **Sample selection bias** and **nonresponse bias** occur

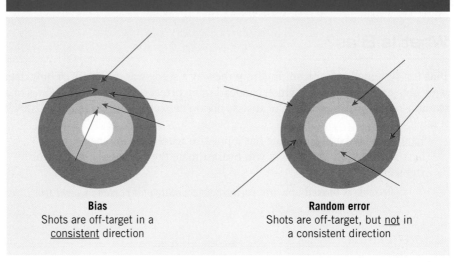

Figure 11.1   Bias vs. Random Error

Bias
Shots are off-target in a
<u>consistent</u> direction

Random error
Shots are off-target, but <u>not</u> in
a consistent direction

due to <u>incomplete</u> data at either the study level or the question level, while **biased responses** are due to <u>inexact</u> (inaccurate) data (Michael et al., 1984). Before turning to details about each of those types of bias, we need to be familiar with different time structures of study design, which determine which types of bias could affect data from a particular study.

Time Structure of Study Designs

The **temporal (time) structure** of studies has to do with the timing and sequencing of data collection. The first basic distinction in terms of the time structure of studies is between **cross-sectional** and **longitudinal** studies.

Cross-Sectional Studies

Cross-sectional studies are like a still photo of a population (see Figure 11.2a), collecting data on all variables for a given study participant at one point in time. Read the description of a study's design carefully, because even those that list a range of dates can be cross-sectional if the study collected information from each element only once.

> <u>Example</u>: The 2015–16 National Health and Nutrition Examination Survey (NHANES) collected information about each respondent at only one time point (CDC, n.d.-b).

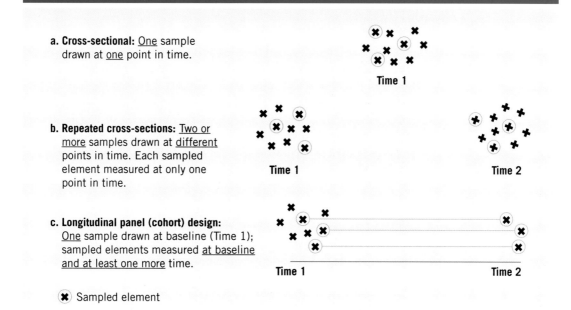

Figure 11.2   Cross-Sectional and Longitudinal Study Designs

a. Cross-sectional: <u>One</u> sample drawn at <u>one</u> point in time.

Time 1

b. Repeated cross-sections: <u>Two or more</u> samples drawn at <u>different</u> points in time. Each sampled element measured at only one point in time.

Time 1   Time 2

c. Longitudinal panel (cohort) design: <u>One</u> sample drawn at baseline (Time 1); sampled elements measured <u>at baseline and at least one more</u> time.

Time 1   Time 2

(✖) Sampled element

Source: Adapted from Chambliss & Schutt (2019).

> *Although the title of the survey mentions the 2-year period during which respondents were enrolled into the study, <u>each respondent was studied only once</u>, so the NHANES was **cross-sectional**.*

Cross-sectional studies collect data for each case at one point in time, so all the variables are measured concurrently.

Longitudinal Studies

Longitudinal studies are like a video—collecting data at two or more points in time—making it possible to observe change over time in the variables under study. There are several types of longitudinal studies.

Repeated Cross-Sectional Studies

Repeated cross-sectional studies collect data on a given set of variables at several points in time, but based on different samples from the same population at each time point (see Figure 11.2b). The set of cases that are observed will, thus, be different at each **round** (time point) of a repeated cross-sectional study. Repeated cross-sectional studies are often used to analyze trends across time in the level of a variable in a population.

Example: Assaf and Pullum used data from the Demographic and Health Surveys to examine trends in the prevalence of stunting (low height-for-age) among children in seven countries (see Figure 7.16).

*Each country conducted surveys in two <u>different</u> years, drawing separate random samples in each year; thus, the observed trends were based on data from **repeated cross-sections**. For instance, the 2008 Ghana sample included a different set of children than the 2014 Ghana sample.*

Longitudinal studies collect data at two or more points in time. Each of those data-collection time points is sometimes referred to as a data-collection **round**. **Repeated cross-sectional studies** collect data about the same population at several points in time, but based on <u>different</u> samples at each round. **Prospective studies** follow cases from one sample forward in time from the initial round to at least one subsequent round. **Retrospective studies** collect information from cases about their past characteristics and experiences.

Prospective Studies

Prospective studies collect information on a set of elements starting at a **baseline** (the initial data-collection point) and into the future.

Example: Weisburd et al. (2004) used data on "street segments" (the two sides of a street block between two intersections) to reveal that the overall decline in crime in Seattle between 1989 and 2002 was primarily explained by strong declining crime trajectories in a small number of areas rather than by uniform declines throughout the city.

*The researchers used data from police incident reports on crime within small geographic areas (the **elements of the sample**) of the city to analyze the time trend in crime rates for each street segment and the city as a whole. The <u>same</u> set of geographic units was included in each year throughout the study period; thus, the data were **longitudinal**.*

Cohort studies follow individual cases across time (see Figure 11.2c), collecting data on those cases at two or more time points. The **cohort** is often defined in terms of a common starting point or event, such as year of birth, date of entry into college, or date of diagnosis with a particular illness.

In **prospective studies**, the first data-collection time point is called the **baseline**, while later time points are referred to as **follow-up rounds**. A **cohort** (or **panel**) is a group of cases whose members share a significant experience in the same time period. **Prospective cohort studies** (also known as **fixed-panel studies**) follow a set of cases forward in time, collecting data from those same individual cases at two or more time points.

Example: Using data from the NHANES I Epidemiological Follow-up Study (NHEFS), Arrieta and Russell (2008) showed that non-leisure physical activity (e.g., transportation to work, school, or errands; and chores around the house) was associated with a 25% to 35% reduction in mortality during the 2-decade follow-up period. They concluded that it is important to take into account all physical activity—not just leisure-time (recreational) physical activity—when studying health.

> *The NHEFS is a prospective* **cohort study**, *following the participants from the NHANES I* **baseline round** *(in 1971–75) to collect data from those* *same people* *again in 1982–84, 1986, 1987, and 1992 (CDC, n.d.-a).*

Retrospective Studies

Retrospective studies identify the study sample and then collect information about participants' current and past characteristics and experiences. They include case-control studies and retrospective surveys. A **case-control** design is a form of retrospective cohort study used to study outcomes that are rare in the general population. For a case-control study, researchers identify the set of **cases** who have the condition of interest and a set of **control** subjects who do not have that condition. They then collect information on the subjects' history of exposure to the hypothesized risk factor (independent variable), and the association between the risk factor and outcome is analyzed.

Two cautions: First, the meaning of "case" in a case-control study is different than the more general research meaning of case (respondent, study subject, or participant; see Chapter 2). Second, the meaning of "control" in a case-control study is different from the way that term is used in experimental studies, as you will learn in Chapter 12.

Case-control studies are a form of retrospective cohort study in which investigators identify and enroll study subjects after the outcome of interest has already occurred. **Cases** are the study subjects who have the outcome of interest, whereas **controls** are those who do not have that outcome. Information on past characteristics is collected for both cases and controls.

Example: To investigate whether highly religious people are more likely to commit hate crimes, researchers obtained a roster of hate-crime perpetrators from the police. They matched them with people who committed other types of felonies in the same jurisdictions but who were similar to the cases in terms of their socioeconomic and demographic traits. They asked both the cases and the controls to fill out a questionnaire about their religious beliefs and behaviors; they then analyzed whether people with high past levels of religiosity had been more likely to perpetrate hate crimes.

> *Fortunately, hate crimes are very rare! Thus, to obtain enough **cases** (hate-crime perpetrators) for this hypothetical study, the sample included <u>everyone</u> who committed that type of crime during a specified period. Researchers chose **controls** from among those who committed equally serious crimes that did <u>not</u> involve hate. **Retrospective** (past) information was collected on sociodemographic characteristics and religiosity.*

Retrospective surveys draw a sample of the population of interest and then collect information on their past characteristics.

Example: The Demographic and Health Surveys collect information on adult participants' current health and socioeconomic status, along with information on their marital and reproductive histories (National Population Commission & ICF International, 2014).

> *The data on marital and reproductive experiences were **retrospective**, because they predated the survey.*

Retrospective designs can suffer from **survivor bias,** which arises because the cases that are present at the time the sample is drawn are <u>not</u> representative of all members of the relevant cohort; obviously those who die before the baseline time point cannot be included in the study. As a consequence, the results of such studies are biased in favor of characteristics of those who survived until the date the sample was selected.

Example: A study sought to identify characteristics of successful financial companies. The researchers collected data from companies that exceeded the market average over a 40-year period and then searched for shared characteristics among them (Shermer, 2014).

> *By looking backward (**retrospectively**) at <u>only</u> the companies that did well over such a long period of time, the researchers imposed **survivor bias** by excluding companies that did <u>not</u> last for at least 40 years. By omitting less-successful companies from the study sample, they produced a biased picture of characteristics that predict financial success.*

> **Survivor bias** occurs because a sample for a retrospective study cannot include those who were lost from the cohort before the baseline time point.

Sampling Methods

The first major type of bias related to study design occurs due to **sample selection bias**, which occurs when a sample is not representative of the **target population** to whom researchers want to generalize the results due to the way cases are chosen for the sample (Utts & Heckard, 2014). As noted in Chapter 5, data for many quantitative research studies are collected on a **sample** (subset) of cases rather than from the entire **population** of interest. Sampling may be done either because it isn't necessary to study every element or because collecting data on fewer cases is more feasible.

When a population is **homogeneous** (all elements have identical characteristics), there is no need to collect data on every element.

Example: You are making soup for supper. After it has been bubbling away for an hour, you want to check the seasoning, so you taste one spoonful.

> *By the time the soup has been cooking that long, flavorings will have been uniformly distributed throughout the pot, so it is <u>not</u> necessary to taste every single spoonful to determine whether you need to add salt or other seasonings. The spoonful is your **sample** of the **population** (entire batch of soup).*

Even when a population is **heterogeneous** (elements differ from one another on one or more characteristics), a carefully selected sample can provide fairly precise estimates of patterns in an entire population—an important advantage, because the effort and cost of collecting data increase as sample size increases. Chapter 13 discusses how sample size affects precision of numeric estimates.

However, in order for estimates based on a relatively small sample to be generalizable to a population, that sample must be selected using a process that yields a representative sample. As explained in Chapter 5, a representative sample is one that has a very similar distribution of characteristics to that found in the overall population. When the composition of a sample differs from that of the target population, that sample suffers from **sample selection bias**. The following sections describe how different sampling methods affect the extent of sample selection bias.

In a **homogeneous** population, all elements are the same in terms of the characteristic(s) of interest, whereas in a **heterogeneous** population, elements differ from one another on one or more traits. **Sample selection bias** (also known as **sampling bias**) occurs when the composition of the sample chosen for a study differs from that of the population it is intended to represent, known as the **target population**.

A **sampling method** is the procedure used to determine which elements are selected from the population to be included in the study sample—those from whom data are to be collected. Sampling methods can be classified into probability sampling methods and non-probability sampling methods.

Probability Sampling Methods

Probability sampling methods are designed to draw samples that are representative of the populations from which they were selected. They use a **random selection** process, such as a coin flip or lottery, to determine which elements of a population are selected for the study. Although in everyday, informal use, the word "random" means arbitrary, haphazard, or capricious, in research methods terms, random selection means that whether a specific case is chosen for the sample is based solely on chance and that each element in the population has a specified probability of being selected.

Probability sampling begins by assembling a **sampling frame**, which is a complete list of all the elements in the population for which the limits and membership can be defined. Then random selection techniques are used to choose a fraction of elements from that list. The type of entity that constitutes an element (e.g., person, family, or specific type of institution) is known as the **sampling unit**.

Sampling is the process by which elements are selected from the population to be included in a study sample. In **probability sampling methods**, every element of the population has a specified probability of being chosen at random to be included in the sample. A **sampling frame** (also known as the **sample universe**) is a list of all the elements in the population from which the sample is to be drawn. A **sampling unit** is the type of element that is listed in the sampling frame.

<u>Example</u>: For a survey of hospitals, researchers make a list of all hospitals in the location and date under study.

*The sample was drawn from the complete list (the **sampling frame**); thus, every hospital in the area has a chance of being included. Hospitals are the **sampling unit**.*

Example: Many telephone surveys use random-digit dialing to select a sample.

> The **sample universe** is constructed by listing all the phone numbers in the population of interest. A computer then randomly dials phone numbers from that list until the desired sample size is reached. Nothing other than random chance determines which numbers are dialed.

The chance that a given element is included in a sample is called the **probability of selection**. It is calculated as the number of elements selected to participate in a study (*n*) divided by the total number of elements in the population from which the sample is drawn (*N*). By definition, the probability of selection must fall between 0 (no cases are selected for the sample) and 1.0 (all cases in the sample universe are selected, as in a census).

The **probability of selection** (also known as the **sampling fraction**) = # elements selected into the sample ÷ # elements in the population = $n \div N$.

Simple Random Sampling

In **simple random sampling**, every element of the population has the same chance of being selected for the sample.

Figure 11.3   Simple Random Sampling

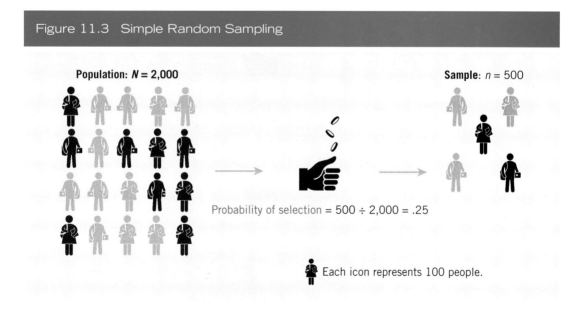

Population: *N* = 2,000

Sample: *n* = 500

Probability of selection = 500 ÷ 2,000 = .25

Each icon represents 100 people.

Example: The University of X wants to survey 500 of its 2,000 students, so researchers randomly select one out of every four students.

*For this study, the **probability of selection** = n ÷ N = 500 ÷ 2,000 = .25 (Figure 11.3). This is a **simple random sample**, because each of the **elements** in the population has the same probability of being selected (.25): Each student has a 25% chance of being selected for the sample. The university's roster is the **sampling frame.***

Stratified Random Sampling

When researchers want to make sure that their sample includes elements from each of several population subgroups, they use **stratified random sampling**. Under this process, researchers divide the overall sampling frame into **strata** ("layers," or subgroups of the population) that share a characteristic, such as income or race. They then sample separately from each stratum.

Example: The University of X has two schools, a liberal arts school and an engineering school, each of which has 1,000 students. The university wants its study sample to include 500 students from each school, so it draws separate random samples from each of those academic units.

Figure 11.4 Stratified Random Sampling

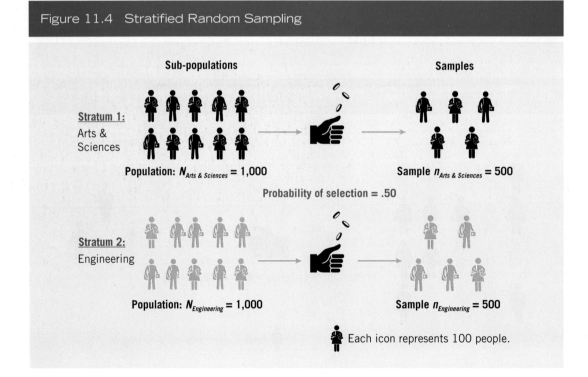

Sub-populations   Samples

Stratum 1:
Arts &
Sciences

Population: $N_{Arts\ \&\ Sciences}$ = 1,000   Sample $n_{Arts\ \&\ Sciences}$ = 500

Probability of selection = .50

Stratum 2:
Engineering

Population: $N_{Engineering}$ = 1,000   Sample $n_{Engineering}$ = 500

Each icon represents 100 people.

The academic units (the school of arts and sciences and the school of engineering) are separate **strata** *for the study. The* **probability of selection** *for elements in each* **stratum** *is* n ÷ N = 500 ÷ 1,000 = .50 *(Figure 11.4). Each student in the school of arts and sciences and each student in the school of engineering has a .50 probability (50% chance) of being selected.*

Disproportionate Sampling

Disproportionate random sampling is used to select higher proportions from small subgroups of particular interest, to increase the reliability and precision of estimates for those subgroups.[1] The process of selecting higher proportions of elements from some strata than from others is known as **oversampling**.

Example: The nursing school at the University of Y has 200 students, and its school of arts and sciences has 2,000 students. To obtain a sample that includes 100 students from each of those schools, researchers oversample nursing students.

Figure 11.5 Disproportionate Random Sampling

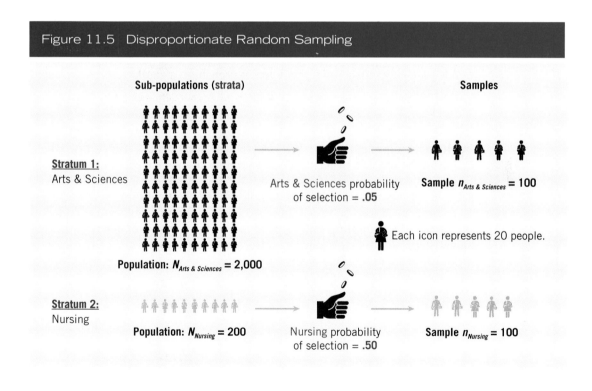

---

[1]Determining the appropriate size of a probability sample is determined by statistical power, money and time cost of data collection, and other practical considerations. Sample size determination is beyond the scope of this book; for additional information, see Utts & Heckard (2012) or another statistics textbook.

*To ensure an adequate number of nursing students in the sample, elements in the nursing school were **oversampled** by applying a higher **probability of selection** for them than for elements in the larger **stratum** (the school of arts and sciences). For the nursing school, the **probability of selection** is .50 (number of nursing students selected ÷ total number of nursing students = $n_{Nursing} \div N_{Nursing}$ = 100 ÷ 200; Figure 11.5). For the liberal arts school, it is .05 (number of arts and sciences students selected ÷ total number of arts and sciences students = $n_{Arts\ \&\ Sciences} \div N_{Arts\ \&\ Sciences}$ = 100 ÷ 2,000).*

Example: The 2015–16 U.S. NHANES oversampled people from the following sociodemographic groups: Hispanic, Non-Hispanic black, Non-Hispanic Asian, low-income Non-Hispanic white and other persons, and older adults (CDC, n.d.-b).

*In order to support statistical comparisons of those small groups with larger racial/ethnic, age, and income groups, the NHANES **disproportionately sampled** the listed groups, using higher **sampling fractions** for the small than for the large groups.*

When data from a sample chosen using disproportionate sampling methods are analyzed, sampling weights are used to bring the patterns back to the population level, taking into account the different probabilities of selection, as explained in Appendix B.

Cluster Sampling

In **cluster sampling**, the population is divided into **clusters** (subgroups), often based on the physical or institutional proximity of the elements to one another. First, a random sample of clusters is drawn, and then elements only from those selected clusters are included in the sample. Either all elements of selected clusters or a randomly chosen subset of those selected clusters' elements are included in the sample. The **sampling unit** (type of entity that is being sampled) in the first **stage** (step) of cluster sampling is larger (more aggregated) than the sampling unit(s) used in later stage(s) of cluster sampling.

Example: Alpha University offers 20 sections of its Introduction to Expository Writing course. Rather than studying all the students in that course, researchers randomly selected five sections and then randomly picked half of the students in each of those five sections.

*In the first **stage** of sampling, the **sampling unit** was a course section, and each section (**cluster**) of the course had a 25% probability of selection (5 ÷ 20 = .25). In the second **stage**, the **sampling unit** was students, and a sampling fraction of 0.5 was used to select individual students (**elements**) only from those enrolled in the selected course sections.*

The main distinction between <u>cluster</u> sampling and stratified sampling is that the sampling units are different: In cluster sampling, the cluster is the sampling unit, whereas in stratified sampling, the individual <u>elements within each stratum</u> are the sampling unit.

Multistage Random Sampling

In **multistage sampling**, researchers use several steps (stages) to sample progressively smaller units within the population (e.g., large geographic areas or institutions, then smaller areas or units, then individuals) to reach individual elements. Multistage sampling often combines two or more of the probability sampling methods described above.

In **simple random sampling,** all elements of the population have an equal probability of selection. **Strata** are homogeneous subgroups of a population defined based on elements' shared attributes, such as income and race. In **stratified random sampling**, the overall sampling frame is divided into strata, and random samples are drawn from each **stratum** (the singular form of "strata"). In **disproportionate sampling**, the probability of selection varies across strata, with elements of some strata sampled at higher rates than others. In **cluster sampling**, elements are selected in two or more **stages** (steps in the sampling process). The first stage involves random selection of naturally occurring **clusters**, such as geographically close elements. Later stage(s) then use random selection procedures to choose which elements within the selected clusters are included in the sample. In **multistage random sampling**, several stages (steps) are used to sample successively smaller levels of aggregation.

<u>Example</u>: The National Health and Nutrition Examination Survey (NHANES) conducts the physical examinations component in a mobile examination center, so it would be very inefficient to use a one-stage method to draw a sample of individuals from all over the United States. Instead, the NHANES uses a strategy to select locations that are close together yet still represent the population as a whole. First, all the counties in the United States are divided into 15 groups based on their characteristics, and then one county is selected from each of those groups (Figure 11.6). Within each of the 15 selected counties, 360 smaller groups, called "area segments," each with a large number of households, are formed. Second, from those 360 area segments, 20 to 24 are selected. Third, from all the households within each selected area segment, about 30 households are selected. Fourth, a

Figure 11.6 Multistage Cluster Sampling

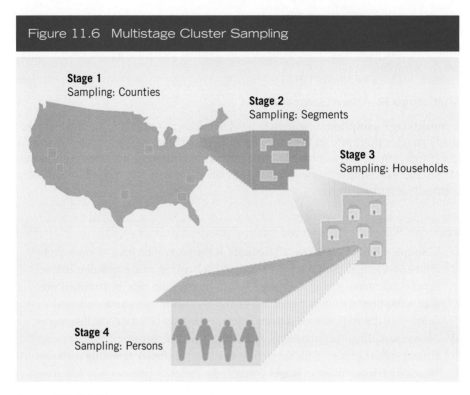

Stage 1
Sampling: Counties

Stage 2
Sampling: Segments

Stage 3
Sampling: Households

Stage 4
Sampling: Persons

Source: CDC (2018b).

computer randomly selects some, all, or none of the members of those households to create the final sample of individuals for the study. Finally, interviewers collect information about age, race, and gender of the selected individuals (CDC, 2018b).

> *The NHANES sampling strategy is multistage cluster sampling: The first **stage** is the selection of **primary sampling units** (PSUs) from a **sampling frame** of all U.S. counties. Random selection of area segments (census blocks or combinations of census blocks) is the second **stage**, random selection of households is the third **stage**, and random selection of persons is the fourth **stage**.*

Non-probability Sampling Methods

Non-probability sampling methods do <u>not</u> use a random process to select study participants. As a consequence, the probability of selection for a given element is not known. Non-probability sampling methods that are sometimes used for quantitative research include availability sampling and quota sampling. Except for case-controls designs, non-probability sampling methods are poorly suited for quantitative research because they typically do <u>not</u> produce samples that are representative of any specifiable population. Thus, their results have poor generalizability. For case-control studies, however, it is often possible to characterize the population from which participants are drawn—and, thus, the groups to whom results can be generalized.

Case-Control

As noted in the section on Retrospective Studies above, **case-control studies** are used to select cases in situations when a random sample from a general population would <u>not</u> provide enough cases who have experienced the outcome of interest, such as a rare disease or a condition due to exposure to an uncommon risk factor. For case-control studies, sampling is conducted on the <u>dependent</u> variable, taking all (or at least many) **cases** that have the outcome of interest and pairing them with **controls** who do not have that condition. **Matching** is performed based on possible causes of the outcome <u>other than</u> the risk factor under study. The goal is to ensure that the controls are as similar as possible to the cases, in order to test whether the risk factor is the cause of the rare condition. We will explore assessing cause-and-effect relationships further in Chapter 12.

Matching involves pairing cases with controls based on characteristics <u>other than the risk factor of interest</u> that are known to be associated with the outcome under study.

<u>Example</u>: In the hypothetical study of religiosity and hate crimes (above), researchers matched hate-crime perpetrators with people who committed other types of felonies in the same jurisdiction and who had similar socioeconomic and demographic traits.

> Each **case** (hate-crime perpetrator) was **matched** to a **control** (perpetrator accused of a different type of felony) based on age, gender, and education level—factors that might explain the association between religiosity and committing a hate crime. The sample was thus limited to people who committed some type of felony.

Other types of non-probability methods, including convenience and quota sampling, are not well-suited to quantitative research but are often appropriately used for <u>qualitative</u> research (see Chambliss & Schutt, 2019).

Convenience Sampling

Convenience sampling (also known as **availability sampling**) is a non-probability method in which participants are selected for a study because they are easily available to the researchers. Convenience samples often differ substantially in terms of demographic and other traits from the population to whom researchers seek to generalize the results.

Example: Your research methods professor is conducting a study of a proposed law to restrict the use of single-use plastic bags at grocery stores. He assigns each student in your class to collect data from 20 adults about their attitudes regarding that law. The homework assignment is due in 2 weeks, so you decide to hand out questionnaires at the train station on your way home.

> A sample obtained in this way will exclude people who don't ride the train or who take it at other times. Also, if (like many people) you are more likely to approach people who are similar to you in terms of gender, race, and other factors, your **convenience** sample will be **biased** in terms of those traits.

Studies based on a group of **volunteers**, such as those who apply to participate in clinical trials or psychology experiments, also use non-probability sampling methods. Samples obtained in this way suffer from self-selection that can bias the results.

Example: For a survey of cannabis use and exercise, participants were recruited through Websites, dispensaries, and clinics in several U.S. states where the drug was legal as of 2017, including Colorado, California, Washington, and Oregon (YorkWilliams et al., 2019). Many people who reported using cannabis shortly before their workout believed that it made their exercise more enjoyable and might have helped motivate them to be active.

> The researchers point out that "the results are severely limited because they are by self-assessments from self-selected volunteers." In addition, "the states that have legalized cannabis also happen to be the states that we know are the most physically active," so the study does not address whether "people in less-active states would respond similarly to cannabis if and when it is legalized there" (Reynolds, 2019). In other words, the **cross-population generalizability** of this study's findings is unknown.

Example: For a clinical trial of a new headache medication, researchers enrolled patients who came to their weekly headache clinic.

> Their sample would be highly **self-selected,** consisting only of people who heard about the study and were able to go to the clinic. It would not represent those who weren't motivated to go to the clinic because they had fewer or less-severe headaches, and it would also exclude those who didn't have the time for or health insurance to cover the cost of a clinic visit. Consequently, the results of this study would not be **generalizable** to all headache sufferers.

Quota Sampling

To address some of the drawbacks of convenience sampling, **quota sampling** establishes allocations for selecting elements to ensure that a few specified characteristics are represented in the sample in the same proportion in which they occur in the population of interest. Although quota sampling imposes representativeness with regard to the characteristics used to set the quotas, it will <u>not</u> ensure representativeness on any other characteristics. Practically speaking, it is difficult to impose quotas on more than two or three variables at a time.

> <u>Example</u>: Your research methods professor tried to publish a peer-reviewed journal article regarding attitudes toward a proposed law to restrict the use of single-use plastic bags at grocery stores based on the sample collected by last year's class, but reviewers pointed out that the convenience sample didn't adequately represent the composition of the local voting population. The professor changed this year's assignment to specify that each student is to collect data from 20 people, making sure to include 10 men and 10 women, at least 7 Democrats, at least 7 Republicans, and at least 2 Independents.
>
> > <u>Quotas</u> were set at 50% male, 50% female, with minimum criteria for political party distribution. Although the **quota sampling** method will improve representativeness of the sample for gender and party affiliation, it <u>won't</u> ensure that it is **representative** in terms of <u>other</u> characteristics, such as income or educational attainment, that might affect people's opinions on the proposed single-use plastics law.

Non-probability sampling methods do <u>not</u> use a random method to select a sample from the intended population. They include volunteer, convenience, and quota sampling. In **volunteer** sampling, participants self-nominate to participate in a study. In **convenience** (or **availability**) **sampling**, elements are selected based on the ease of collecting data from those elements. In **quota sampling**, elements are selected to represent a few characteristics in proportion to how common they are in the population. A **quota** is the share of the sample that is allocated for cases with a particular characteristic.

The way a set of cases is selected, and the characteristics of that sample, affect the extent to which numeric results based on those data can be applied (generalized) to other sets of cases. **Probability sampling methods** are designed to produce samples that

(Continued)

are representative of the population because elements are chosen based solely on random chance, with a specified probability of selection for each element in the sampling universe. If they have high response rates (see below), samples chosen using random sampling methods can have very good generalizability (external validity). **Nonprobability sampling methods** are <u>not</u> well-suited to quantitative research, because they generate samples that are not representative of the target population and thus cannot be generalized beyond the scope of the included cases. Researchers should describe the approaches used to select cases for their analysis and specify the strengths and limitations of their sample in terms of representativeness and generalizability.

Selective Observation

Before we conclude this section on sampling methods, it is important to point out a reasoning error related to which cases are used to arrive at conclusions about a group or population. **Selective observation** occurs when researchers analyze only cases that are consistent with their prior beliefs or hypotheses, ignoring other cases that do not support their position, leading to incorrect inferences about the actual pattern of that phenomenon. In some occurrences of selective observation, the researchers might have arrived at a conclusion after finding one or two instances that confirm their preexisting beliefs. In more egregious instances, researchers intentionally exclude instances that contradict their desired conclusion.

> <u>Example</u>: David's parents divorced when he was a child, and his father neglected to pay court-ordered child support. When he writes a research paper on "deadbeat dads," David only summarizes results of articles that support the conclusion that divorced fathers fail to meet their child-support obligations.
>
> *Here, **selective observation** occurred when David chose (sampled) which articles to include in his literature review. His conclusions about the experiences of children of divorced parents are likely to be flawed, because he systematically excluded any article that showed that some (or many, or all) fathers paid their required child support. To arrive at valid conclusions about his topic, he should have summarized a range of articles about child-support payment, regardless of the conclusions of those studies.*

Selective observation occurs when researchers choose which cases to include in their analysis based on whether those cases support their prior views about the topic.

Selective observation and **overgeneralization** (see Chapter 5) are two different forms of incorrect reasoning about patterns from a sample.

Example: Mara didn't start writing her course paper about child support until the night before it was due. In a hurry, she skimmed the first article that appeared in her literature search about child support. That study presented evidence that very few divorced fathers paid their court-ordered child support. In her paper, Mara implied that there was consensus in the literature that divorced dads fail to pay child support.

> *This is an instance of **overgeneralization**, because Mara read only one article but implied that her conclusions were based on agreement across multiple studies. Had she chosen that article solely based on its conclusion, it would <u>also</u> have been **selective observation**.*

Study Nonresponse

A second major source of bias in quantitative research is **study nonresponse**, which occurs when only some of the intended study subjects participated. In other words, the data are incomplete because some sampled cases were not actually studied (did not respond). The **nonresponse rate** is the percentage of those selected for the study who did <u>not</u> participate.

Baseline Nonresponse

The **baseline nonresponse rate** measures what percentage of those selected for a study participate in the first round of data collection. For a cross-sectional study, data are collected only once for each participant; thus, the "baseline" response rate is the only relevant response rate.

Example: Of the people in more than 15,000 cases selected for the 2015–16 NHANES, about 9,970 (just over 60%) participated in the interview portion of the study (CDC, n.d.-c).

> *The <u>**nonresponse rate**</u> for the interview component = 100% − **response rate**; in this instance = 100% − 60% = 40%.*

Example: Between 1997 and 2016, the response rate to random-digit dialing (RDD) telephone surveys conducted by the Pew Research Center declined from 36% to 9% (Keeter et al., 2017).

> *Caller ID and call blocking have made it easier to avoid calls from unrecognized numbers. Thus, the potential for **nonresponse bias** has increased over time, because the people who agree to participate in a study are different in terms of various demographic and social traits from those who can't be reached or who refuse to participate.*

In many studies of people and the institutions and geographic areas they populate, those with certain characteristics are less likely to respond than others, resulting in **differential nonresponse**. Members of groups with higher <u>non</u>response rates will be **underrepresented** in the sample of cases from whom data is actually collected.

<u>Example</u>: The nonparticipation rate for the physical examination components of the 2015–16 NHANES was much lower for infants (30.6%) than for persons aged 80+ (58.6%).

> Among people selected for the NHANES, the **nonparticipation (nonresponse) rate** increased substantially with age (CDC, n.d.-c). **Differential nonparticipation** by age meant that the set of cases from whom data were collected **underrepresented** older persons and was biased in favor of younger members, compared to their shares of the overall U.S. population.

<u>Example</u>: For a longitudinal survey of workplace satisfaction, researchers drew a stratified random sample of 2,000 employees, of whom 1,700 responded to the initial survey, for an overall response rate of 85% (Figure 11.7; Arrow A). Although 900 of the 1,000 blue-collar workers chosen for the sample participated, only 800 of the 1,000 selected white-collar workers did.

Figure 11.7   Baseline Nonresponse, Attrition, and Bias

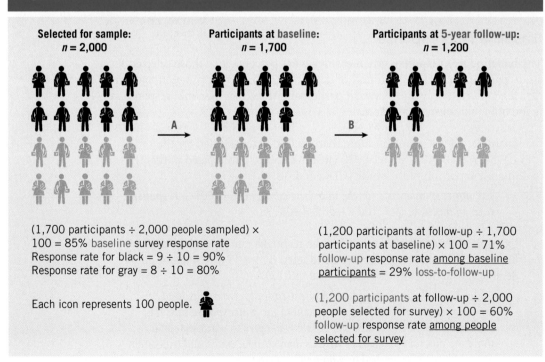

Selected for sample:
n = 2,000

Participants at baseline:
n = 1,700

Participants at 5-year follow-up:
n = 1,200

A

B

(1,700 participants ÷ 2,000 people sampled) × 100 = 85% baseline survey response rate
Response rate for black = 9 ÷ 10 = 90%
Response rate for gray = 8 ÷ 10 = 80%

Each icon represents 100 people.

(1,200 participants at follow-up ÷ 1,700 participants at baseline) × 100 = 71% follow-up response rate <u>among baseline participants</u> = 29% loss-to-follow-up

(1,200 participants at follow-up ÷ 2,000 people selected for survey) × 100 = 60% follow-up response rate <u>among people selected for survey</u>

*The response rate was 90% among the blue-collar workers (black icons), versus 80% among white-collar workers (gray icons). That **differential response rate** resulted in a baseline sample that **underrepresented** the white-collar employees.*

The <u>study</u> **response rate** (also known as the **participation rate**) is the share of cases selected for a study from whom data are actually collected, usually expressed as a percentage of those selected for the study: Response rate = (# study participants ÷ # persons sampled) × 100. **Nonresponse rate** = 100% − response rate. The **baseline response rate** is the response rate for the first round of a longitudinal study or the only round of a cross-sectional study. **Differential nonresponse** occurs when the response rate varies by characteristics of the sampled elements.

Attrition From Longitudinal Studies

Attrition from longitudinal studies introduces another form of nonresponse that occurs as participants drop out between rounds of the study. Depending on the topic and nature of a study, reasons for attrition (also known as **loss-to-follow-up**) might include moving out of the area, death, or lack of interest in the study. Attrition results in a decreasing sample size as the study progresses and often leads to increasingly <u>non</u>representative samples over time. The **retention rate** is the percentage of those present at baseline who remain in the study at follow-up; thus, retention + attrition = 100% of the baseline sample.

Attrition (**loss-to-follow-up**) occurs when cases that were included in the baseline round of a longitudinal study drop out of the study over time. **Retention rate** = (# elements present at <u>follow-up</u> ÷ # elements present at <u>baseline</u>) × 100. **Attrition rate** = 100% − retention rate.

<u>Example</u>: Of the 1,700 employees who participated in the baseline survey, only 1,200 participated in the follow-up 5 years later (Figure 11.7, Arrow B). Thus 29% of baseline participants were lost to follow-up during the intervening years. In terms of the overall design of the study, only 1,200 of the 2,000 originally selected for the survey participated at the 5-year mark, for a 5th-year response rate of 60%.

*The **retention rate** = (1,200 participants at follow-up ÷ 1,700 participants at baseline) × 100 = 71%. Since the **attrition rate** = 100% − retention rate, 100% − 71% = 29% <u>of baseline participants</u> were lost between rounds.*

As with baseline nonresponse, attrition frequently increases bias, because elements with certain characteristics are more likely than others to drop out of the study, meaning that, over time, some strata of an overall sample become less representative of the subgroup to whom the results are to be generalized.

> Example: The rate of attrition was higher among white-collar workers (37.5%) than among blue-collar workers (22%; Figure 11.7). By the follow-up round, only 50% of the initially sampled white-collar workers remained in the study, compared with 70% of the blue-collar workers.
>
> > Higher **attrition** among white-collar than blue-collar workers means that the sample of white-collar workers who remained in the study at the 5-year follow-up may have been **less representative** of all white-collar workers than the remaining sample of blue-collar workers was of all blue-collar workers.

Item Nonresponse

Item nonresponse occurs when some cases who participated in the overall study did not provide an answer to a particular item (question). Item nonresponse can introduce bias into numeric results, because the cases for whom information on a variable is missing are often different in important ways from those with complete information on that variable. Any cases for which the independent or dependent variables are missing cannot be included in the analysis of that research question, meaning that the sample for that analysis will be smaller and potentially less representative of the target population.

> Item nonresponse is the percentage of elements from whom data were collected for a study but who did not provide data on that specific item (question, or variable). The item nonresponse rate = (# elements missing information on an item ÷ # elements participating in the study) × 100.

> Example: In 2010, 13% of respondents to the General Social Survey (GSS) did not provide information about family income, although they answered most other questions on that survey. Older, female, married, and self-employed respondents were less likely than others to answer the income question (Kim et al., 2012).
>
> > **Item nonresponse** to the income question differed by age, gender, marital status, and employment, increasing the chances of biased estimates of income distribution based on the GSS data.

Several issues related to question wording, data sources, and data-collection methods increase the risk of item nonresponse.

Question Wording

By making it difficult for respondents to understand what a question is trying to ask, ambiguous, overly technical, or confusing wording makes it more likely that some respondents will not provide an answer.

> Example: Item on a survey: "Do you have problems with drugs? Yes or no?"
>
> *The phrase "problems with drugs" is ambiguous (unclear), because it could be interpreted to refer to abuse of prescription or over-the-counter drugs, use of illicit drugs, experiencing side effects of a medication, or difficulty paying for prescription medications. If respondents recognize that they don't know which of several interpretations to use, they are more likely to skip the question.*

> Example: Question on an emergency room intake form: "Have you ever had a transient ischemic attack (TIA)? Yes or no?"
>
> *If the respondents were physicians, that technical wording would make sense. However, many people visiting an ER will not know what "TIA" means, increasing the chance that they will leave the answer blank.*

Double-negative questions and double-barreled questions are two forms of questions that are hard to understand or to answer correctly because of the way they are worded. **Double-<u>negative</u> questions** are those that include two negative words or phrases.

> Example: Question on a teaching evaluation form: "Don't you think Research Methods should not be a required course? Yes or no?"
>
> *You probably had to read that question at least twice to figure out what it is asking! Both "don't" and "should not" are negatives, so this is a **double-negative question**. **Item nonresponse** is much more likely based on such wording than on more straightforward phrasing like "Do you think Research Methods should be a required course?"*

Double-<u>barreled</u> questions are those that ask two questions but allow only one response. They are also known as **compound questions**, reflecting the fact that they are made up of two or more parts. Use of "and" or "or" separating distinct concepts in a single survey question often signals the presence of a double-barreled question. A double-barreled question should be replaced by separate items for each question.

> Example: Question on a teaching evaluation form: "Do you think your Research Methods professor is interesting and knowledgeable? Yes or no?"
>
> *This is a **double-<u>barreled</u> question**, because it asks about <u>two</u> different attributes of the professor in <u>one</u> question. Only students who think the professor is both boring and ignorant (or both fascinating and brilliant) can*

*answer the question as worded! Any students who think the prof is interesting but not knowledgeable (or vice versa) <u>cannot</u> find an answer that suits their opinion, leading them to skip the question, aka **item nonresponse**.*

A **double-<u>negative</u> question** is one that is worded with two negative words or phrases, making it difficult to understand the intended meaning. A **double-<u>barreled</u> question** (also known as a **compound question**) is one survey item that includes two distinct questions but allows each respondent to choose only one answer.

Item nonresponse can also arise if the list of responses for a closed-ended question is not exhaustive, meaning that some respondents cannot find an answer to suit them, as in Figure 4.4c.

Respondents Who Lack Knowledge

Item nonresponse can also be introduced if some respondents are asked questions they are not competent to answer or lack confidence about their answers.

<u>Example</u>: If young children are asked about their parents' educational attainment or income, they might skip the question because they don't know, or aren't sure, about the answer.

*To decrease **item nonresponse** about family socioeconomic status in surveys of children, alternative ways of measuring family SES should be used (Currie et al., 2008).*

A related issue occurs with **proxy reporting**, which is when someone else serves as a stand-in or "proxy" for the sampled respondent, providing information when that respondent isn't available or is incapable of participating.

Proxy respondents are people who provide information about some other person who was selected for the study, often because the sampled person is not available or is unable to provide that information.

<u>Example</u>: For a case-control study of how the age at which people started smoking cigarettes affected their risk of lung cancer, Hegmann and colleagues (1993) obtained retrospective smoking histories from respondents, or—for those who had died before the start of the study—from their spouses or other family members. They then

compared smoking patterns among those who developed lung cancer
("cases") to those who did not have lung cancer ("controls").

> *Data on age of smoking initiation, amount smoked, and whether and when
> someone quit smoking is less likely to be known by a **proxy** than by the
> person themselves. In this study, proxies were used for more than 40% of
> people with lung cancer (because many of them had died before the data were
> collected) but only 4% of those who did not have cancer. As a consequence,
> **item nonresponse** was higher among cases than among controls.*

However, proxy respondents can, and often do, provide valid information if
they are chosen specifically for their knowledge of the topics under study.

Example: The Fragile Families Study sought to learn about social, health,
and educational outcomes of children born to low-income, unmarried
parents. The researchers collected data from parents and primary caregivers
for children from birth through age 15 years. When the children reached
age 5 years, the study also collected data from teachers. Starting when the
children were 9 years old, the study collected data on some topics directly
from the children (Fragile Families and Child Wellbeing Study, n.d.).

> *Parents, caregivers, and teachers served as **proxies** for the children,
> providing information that the children were not yet old enough to give. In
> this situation, the proxy respondents were chosen specifically for their ability
> to report valid information about various aspects of the children's health,
> behavior, and education, thus decreasing the chances of **item nonresponse**.*

Missing Values vs. Not Applicable

Recall from Chapter 4 that **missing** values (**item nonresponse**) are different from "not
applicable." Unlike missing values, which can lead to bias, **not applicable** responses
to contingent questions will <u>not</u> create bias, because respondents who <u>validly</u> skip
those questions are not part of the subgroup to whom those topics pertain.

> <u>Item</u> nonresponse and <u>study</u> nonresponse are two different phenomena, each of
> which introduces the possibility of bias in the completeness and composition of
> the study sample.

In summary, three forms of bias at the study-design and data-collection phases
contribute to a sample being nonrepresentative of the target population: sampling
bias, <u>study</u> nonresponse bias, and <u>item</u> nonresponse bias.

Example: A researcher used random-digit dialing to conduct a telephone
survey. The intended sample of 1,000 thus included only people who had
cell phones (Arrow A in Figure 11.8). Of those dialed, only 600 answered the

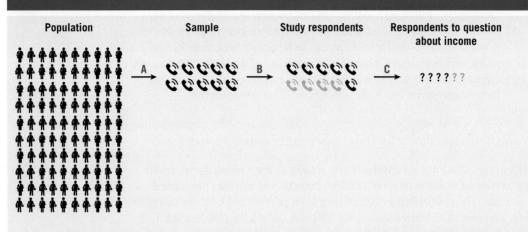

Figure 11.8   Sampling Bias, Study Nonresponse, and Item Nonresponse

| Population | Sample | Study respondents | Respondents to question about income |

A. 1,000 people randomly selected from 10,000 in the population using random-digit dialing. Sampling fraction = 1,000 ÷ 10,000 = 0.10

B. 600 people interviewed ÷ 1,000 people sampled × 100 = 60% survey response rate

☏ Completed interview
☏ Did not respond to interview

Each icon represents 100 people.

C. 400 people answered income question ÷ 600 people who responded to survey × 100 = 67% item response rate among survey participants

? Answered income question
? Did not answer income question

phone and participated in the survey (Arrow B). Of those who participated in the survey, only 400 answered the question about their income (Arrow C).

*People who have cell phones have different characteristics than those who do not, introducing **bias** at the **sampling** phase due to the process used to draw the sample (random-digit dialing). People who answered the phone were socioeconomically different from those who did not, introducing bias at the **study-response** phase of the study. People who answered the income question were socioeconomically different from those who refused to answer, introducing bias at the **item-response** phase.*

> Sample selection bias, study nonresponse, and item nonresponse can all affect the external validity of a study if the sample of cases for whom the data are available is not representative of the target population.

In addition, people who respond to public opinion polls often have strong opinions about the topic of the poll, so results of studies based on such data will underestimate the prevalence of less extreme opinions or experiences because of higher survey and item nonresponse among those with more neutral opinions.

Measurement Bias

Another major type of bias, introduced at the data-collection phase of a study, is **measurement bias**, also known as **question response bias**. It occurs when the measured values of a variable are systematically wrong, at least for some cases. In other words, measurement bias is a form of invalid measurement; see Chapter 4. **Question response bias** (<u>inaccurate</u> data) is distinct from **nonresponse bias** (<u>incomplete</u> data; above).

> **Measurement** (or **question response**) **bias** occurs when at least some of the measured values of a variable are consistently wrong in the <u>same</u> direction.

Measurement bias can arise due to the topic or wording of questions used to collect the data, and it can occur due to other aspects of study design.

Social Desirability Bias

Social desirability bias occurs when respondents' answers reflect what they think is a normative or socially acceptable answer. It is most common for sensitive or stigmatized topics. Social desirability bias can also lead to higher item nonresponse.

Example: A study in California found that, between 2003 and 2011, the percentage of respondents who self-identified as a "sexual minority" (lesbian, gay, or bisexual) increased, while the **non**response rate to that question declined (Jans et al., 2015).

> *In the past, <u>stigma</u> associated with identifying as LGBTQ raised concerns that members of this group would have higher **item nonresponse** to questions about gender identity and sexual orientation and might be more likely to give a response that did not reflect their true answers (**biased response**). Increasing acceptance of LGBTQ persons has reduced both item nonresponse and biased responses to questions about these topics.*

Example: Social norms in some cultures suggest that women should be shorter than their male partners. On dating apps, some people feel pressure to describe themselves in ways that conform to those norms.

> *Social values about relative heights of male/female partners encourage short men to overstate their height and tall women to understate theirs—a form of **social desirability bias**.*

> **Social desirability bias** is a form of measurement error in which respondents shape their answers to suit social norms.

Biased Wording

Measurement bias can also be introduced if the wording of a question hints that one of the answers is somehow preferable or more normative. Two common forms of biased wording are leading questions and loaded questions. Either can arise inadvertently (when question-writers don't realize that they are introducing bias) or intentionally (when question-writers seek to influence response patterns). A **leading question** is one that uses non-neutral wording to encourage respondents to favor a particular perspective.

> Example: Survey question: "Don't you think the president is a moron?"
>
> *This question is **leading** because it uses <u>non-neutral wording</u>: "moron" has a very powerful negative connotation. By opening the question with "don't you think," the wording pressures respondents to agree with the statement—introducing **social desirability bias**.*

A **loaded question** incorporates a false or questionable assumption and is thus "loaded" with that premise in ways that constrain respondents to give answers that, often, do not reflect their situation or views. Loaded questions put respondents in a disadvantageous position, since the built-in assumption might reflect badly on them or induce them to choose an answer that they would not otherwise choose.

> Example: Survey question: "Have you stopped cheating on exams?"
>
> *This question is **loaded** because it implies that respondents previously cheated on exams. If respondents answer "no," it implies that they are still cheating. If they answer "yes," it implies that they used to cheat. Someone who had never cheated on exams would either have to skip the question (**item nonresponse**) or give a response that didn't capture their true answer.*

To avoid loaded questions, researchers should use a **filter question** to separate the implicit assumption from the **contingent question** so that respondents who answer "no" to a question behind the "loaded" assumption skip over the question that delves further into the situation for those who answer "yes" to the initial question. See Chapter 4 to review filter and contingent questions.

Leading questions use non-neutral wording to influence respondents to favor one of the responses. **Loaded questions** contain an assumption that does not pertain to at least some respondents and does not provide them with a valid response, instead forcing them into responses that do not accurately capture their views or situation.

Measurement bias can also arise if a question about a topic that should allow a respondent to mark more than one answer is written as a single-response question.

Example: Multiracial individuals will not be able to give an accurate answer if a question about their racial identity allows them to give only one answer.

*Faced with a **single-response question**, anyone who is multiracial would have to choose only one of the racial groups of which they are a part (an <u>incomplete</u> response for them). Alternatively, they might opt to skip the question (**item nonresponse**).*

Recall Bias

Recall bias is another form of measurement bias that occurs when respondents are asked to retrospectively report information pertaining to events of weeks, months, or even years ago. It can affect both the completeness and accuracy of reporting about the past. Recall bias is usually less problematic for events or characteristics that are very severe or otherwise memorable than for things that are more trivial. Extent of recall bias increases with the length of the recall period.

Example: When filling out a health history form, you might forget to mention a mild cold you had a year ago, but you would be unlikely to omit a bout of the flu that landed you in the hospital during that time.

*Here, **recall bias** results in an <u>incomplete</u> health history that includes the more serious illness but omits the less serious one.*

Example: While you might be able to remember what you weighed last month within a couple of pounds, if asked about your weight from several years ago, the best you could probably report is within 5 or even 10 pounds.

*Here, **recall bias** results in <u>inaccurate</u> reporting. The longer the recall period, the cruder (more approximate) the estimate is likely to be.*

> **Recall bias** is a form of measurement error that occurs when respondents do not remember past events, characteristics, or behaviors accurately, either recalling details incorrectly or omitting information.

A related issue is **time-lag bias**, which arises when collecting retrospective data on something that might have <u>changed</u> since it was last measured. For some topics, the direction of the time-lag bias might be predictable, but it may be difficult to assess the size of the bias.

Example: On back-to-school health forms due in mid-September, parents are asked to report their child's height.

*If some kids had their checkup in May and others in early September, the heights of those who were measured several months ago will be understated by a greater amount than the heights of those who were measured more recently. The children who were last measured in May have had three months to grow since their checkup, whereas those measured in September have had no **time lag** between measurement and reporting.*

Several of the causes of item nonresponse discussed in this chapter can also introduce measurement bias.

Poorly Worded Questions

Poorly designed questions can lead to measurement error.

Example: An emergency-room intake form provides a list of several health conditions, including "Transient ischemic attack (TIA)," "neoplasm," and "hypercholesterolemia." Instructions state: "Have you ever experienced these conditions? Check all that apply."

*If someone has had one (or more) of those conditions but isn't familiar with those technical terms, they might not mark the pertinent box(es). However, researchers analyzing the data would interpret the lack of a "check" as indicating that the person did <u>not</u> have the condition. Such omissions would lead to **downward bias** in estimates of the prevalence of those conditions.*

Responses to double-negative and double-barreled questions are also likely to have measurement bias, due to misunderstanding of what the question was asking or respondents being forced to choose among answers that do not suit them.

Respondents Who Lack Knowledge

Asking people questions they are not qualified to answer can increase measurement bias and reduce reliability (see Chapter 4).

Example: Professors are not a good source of information about whether their students think they are effective teachers.

__Bias__ (or wishful thinking!) might lead to professors overstating the effectiveness of their teaching.

Example: In the case-control study by Hegmann and colleagues (1993) described earlier, information about smoking history might be less accurate when provided by a proxy than by the person themselves.

*The researchers should consider whether **proxy** respondents were more likely than someone reporting on their own smoking history to systematically **under-** or **overestimate** how much the person had smoked. Even if there wasn't systematic bias, proxy reporting is likely to have lower <u>reliability</u> (higher random error).*

The time structure of a study determines which types of bias could pertain to that study.

The following types of bias can affect studies <u>regardless of whether a study is cross-sectional, retrospective, or prospective</u>.

- **Sample selection bias**
- <u>**Study**</u> **nonresponse** at **baseline**
- <u>**Item**</u> **nonresponse**
- **Measurement bias**

The following types of bias can affect only **longitudinal studies**.

- **Attrition** affects studies that collect data from the same set of cases more than once.
- **Recall bias** and **time-lag bias** pertain to questions collecting data about the past.
- **Survivor bias** affects only retrospective studies.

Data Sources

An important factor to consider when evaluating potential bias is the sources from which data were obtained. In this section, I briefly describe some of the most common types of data sources and discuss ways they can be affected by various sources of bias.

Primary and Secondary Data

Primary data are those collected by the researchers themselves, usually designed to answer a specific research question (or set of related questions) of interest to them. The researchers determine which sampling methods to use, design the data-collection instruments, and collect the information.

Secondary data are those that were collected by persons other than the researcher conducting the current project. For instance, government agencies and other research institutions, such as the U.S. Census Bureau, the Centers for Disease Control and Prevention, and the Pew Research Foundation, collect data for others to analyze. Sample surveys, censuses, and surveillance data are common forms of secondary data. Researchers who are analyzing secondary data often benefit from large, representative samples with enough cases to analyze small subgroups and with diverse sets of questions. However, they do not have control over the sampling strategy, data-collection methods, or wording of the questions.

> **Primary data** are those collected by researchers themselves (or a member of their team), whereas **secondary data** were previously collected and then made available to other researchers to analyze.

Example: Chapman and colleagues (2016) conducted a field experiment to test whether automatically scheduled appointments increase flu vaccination rates. They randomly assigned some patients to have automatically scheduled appointments and others to only receive a general reminder to get a flu shot. They then collected data on vaccination rates in both groups. They found that those who had automatically scheduled appointments were 10 percentage points more likely to be vaccinated than those who were just encouraged to do so.

> *Their study used **primary data**, because the researchers designed the intervention, drew the sample, and collected the data used to test their hypothesis.*

Example: The Survey of Income and Program Participation (SIPP) provides information on many social programs and the demographic and social characteristics of their participants. Those data have been used to write hundreds of research papers on economic well-being, family dynamics, education, assets, health insurance, child care, food security, and other topics, using different combinations of the variables available in the SIPP data (U.S. Census Bureau, n.d.-b).

> *Since many of the analyses using the SIPP data were conducted by researchers who were <u>not</u> involved in designing the study, they were using **secondary data**.*

Some quantitative research is conducted using data collected specifically for the purpose of research; other research takes advantage of data collected for other purposes. The distinction between data for research and non-research purposes can be important, because methods used to select cases, collect data, and phrase questions can introduce one or more types of bias.

Data Collected for Research Purposes

Data sources for research studies include survey questionnaires, surveillance systems, physical examinations, lab tests, and a variety of other sources.

Questionnaires

Questionnaires are widely used to collect research data, whether as part of a sample survey, a census, or part of a psychology lab experiment. Some questionnaires are self-administered (filled out by respondents themselves on a hard copy or online); others are administered through interviews with a researcher in-person or by telephone or other mode of communication. Types of potential biases depend on the design of the study, the nature of the questions, and the way the questionnaire was administered.

> Example: The National Health and Nutrition Examination Survey (NHANES) uses questionnaires to collect data on participants' demographic and social characteristics, nutritional intake, and health (Johnson et al., 2014).
>
> *The NHANES sample was selected using a sampling frame based on the U.S. Census and is corrected for study nonresponse using sampling weights (Appendix B), so both* **sampling bias** *and* **study nonresponse bias** *are relatively low for this type of source. However, self-reports of diet, exercise, and health are subject to* **measurement bias***.*

> Example: The U.S. Census is intended to count everyone in the nation and obtain information on their demographic characteristics. That population count is then used to determine how many seats each state will have in the House of Representatives and for other planning purposes. The Trump administration sought to add a question about citizenship to the 2020 Census. U.S. Supreme Court Justice Sotomayor argued that adding such a question would undermine the fundamental purpose of the census, stating "There is no doubt that people will respond less. That has been proven in study after study" (Liptak, 2019).
>
> *The presence of a question on citizenship might discourage noncitizens and other immigrants from filling out the Census questionnaire at all (***study nonresponse***) or encourage them to skip that question (***item nonresponse***). Sotomayor argued that the political sensitivity of that question would lead to an* <u>undercount</u> *of immigrants, affecting both the tally of the overall population and its demographic composition.*

Surveillance

Surveillance is the continuous, systematic collection, analysis, and dissemination of data, often on health topics such as death, disease, or exposure to risk factors for disease. Surveillance systems aim to collect data on all pertinent cases.

> **Surveillance** involves continuous and systematic collection of data for a defined population, usually seeking to collect information on <u>all</u> cases that meet a particular definition rather than only on a subset (sample) of such cases.

<u>Example</u>: The U.S. Centers for Disease Control and Prevention (CDC) tracks flu season by assembling weekly reports from healthcare providers about the number of outpatient, emergency-room, and inpatient visits among people with flu symptoms, as well as results of flu tests by clinical and public health labs.

> *These are **surveillance data**, because they are collected using a continuous nationwide process that seeks to record <u>all</u> cases. The data are collected from the CDC and its partners in state, local, and territorial health departments, public health and clinical laboratories, vital statistics offices, healthcare providers, clinics, and emergency departments who are charged with diagnosing and treating the flu; thus, both **sampling bias** and **nonresponse bias** should be minimal (CDC, 2018b). The flu data are reported by health experts; thus, **measurement bias** should also be relatively low.*

Other Sources of Research Data

Other sources of data collected for research purposes include health examinations, laboratory tests, and observations from psychology and other types of research labs.

<u>Example</u>: To complement information collected by questionnaires, the NHANES uses trained medical personnel to conduct physical examinations, providing data on height, weight, blood pressure, and other aspects of physical health, and to administer blood and urine tests to people selected for the NHANES sample (Johnson et al., 2014).

> *The **physical exams** and **lab tests** were undertaken specifically for research on population health, not to diagnose or treat individual patients. Probability sampling methods were used to ensure **representativeness**. Data were collected by health professionals using standard protocols and instruments to maximize **reliability** and **validity**.*

<u>Example</u>: A psychology study collects data on the trade-off between how quickly respondents complete a sorting task and the accuracy of their responses.

> *The outcomes are measured for all participants, so both **study** and **item nonresponse** should be minimal. However, participants in this type of study are often volunteers, so **sampling bias** may be present. By using a standard stimulus/response box that has been validated for measuring speed and accuracy, **measurement bias** is minimized.*

Data Collected for Non-Research Purposes

Researchers often analyze data that were originally collected for other purposes.

Administrative Data

Administrative data—such as insurance records; land titles and deeds; birth, marriage, and divorce certificates; and other types of registration—have long been used to conduct research.

> Example: For the 1988 National Maternal and Infant Health Survey (NMIHS), data on infants' gender, race, birth weight, and gestational age, and mother's age, education, and other characteristics were collected from birth certificates of sampled children (Sanderson et al., 1991). Those data were used to study social, demographic, and other differences in fertility and infant health.
>
> > Although birth certificates are produced for every child born in the United States, they are <u>not</u> specifically generated for **research purposes**. The NMIHS used probability sampling methods and a universe of all birth certificates for children born in the United States in 1988, so **sampling bias** should be minimal. Birth certificates are required for all children in the United States, minimizing **study** and **item nonresponse**.

> Example: For the Longitudinal Follow-up (LF) to the NMIHS, information on children's health for their first 3 years of life was collected using questionnaires to be completed by healthcare providers from the children's medical records (Sanderson et al., 1991). The data were used to analyze how healthcare utilization, health behaviors, and health outcomes varied by health insurance and characteristics of the child and family.
>
> > Medical records were originally intended for clinical and billing purposes, <u>not</u> for research. Consent to obtain information from the medical records was granted by parents of most of the children in the NMIHS sample, so **nonresponse** for this data source was minimal. The original medical records were completed by trained medical professionals, thus minimizing **measurement error**. However, inconsistency in how staff from different doctors' offices transferred information from medical records onto study forms might have reduced **reliability** and **validity** and introduced **differential item nonresponse**.

"Big Data"

Big data refers to the vast amounts of digital (electronic) information generated through sources such as GPSs (global positioning systems), social media, search engines, "smart devices," and records of economic transactions. Although the data sets collected in this way are indeed big (and growing rapidly!), the term "big data" in current usage refers to the ways the data are collected and analyzed, rather than to the actual size of a data set (Marr, 2013).

> **"Big data"** refers to the collection and analysis of data from digital sources that track human (and other) activities, such as remote sensing, social media, purchasing records, and internet activity.

Big data have several advantages for research. First, they provide information on a wide variety of topics for large numbers of cases, often in "real time" with continuous updating. Second, big data capture actual behavior of individuals and firms, rather than self-reports such as those collected by surveys. Third, sampling error is averted, because all cases (the "population") are included in the analysis. Fourth, big data support analysis of subgroups that wouldn't have enough cases in a traditional survey sample of a few thousand total cases (Maker-Schoenberger & Cukier, 2013).

Disadvantages of big data for research purposes include poorer generalizability and greater measurement error, because the variables were not collected using strategies to ensure reliable or valid measurement approaches such as those described in Chapter 4. The variables also might have been defined differently than the researcher would ideally have conceptualized them; see Chapter 3.

Example: Data from the LinkedIn professional networking site are used to produce a monthly report on employment trends in the U.S. workforce, including insights into hiring, skills gaps, and migration trends across the country.

With profiles on more than 190 million workers in the United States as of 2019, and more than 30,000 companies in the United States posting over 3 million jobs on the site every month, LinkedIn provides massive amounts of real-time data that can be analyzed by time, occupation, geography, and other factors (LinkedIn Economic Graph Team, 2019). However, many jobs are <u>not</u> posted on LinkedIn, and lots of workers either don't have a LinkedIn profile or don't keep it up to date, so the data are **biased** because they do <u>not</u> capture all employment activity in the United States.

Example: Data from Kinsa "smart thermometers" have been used to track the date and location of people with fevers, with almost 1 million U.S. households submitting about 40,000 readings a day in 2018–19 (McNeil, 2019). By using information on how long the fevers lasted (and information some users reported on other symptoms, such as vomiting), Kinsa's founder concluded that most people who had fevers during the 2018–19 winter season had colds (2 to 3 days of fever) rather than the flu (3 to 7 days of fever).

> These data were collected as a by-product of individuals' use of Internet-connected thermometers, which they purchased to monitor their own health, _not_ for **research purposes**. When data from all users were pooled, it allowed much more rapid tracking and mapping of colds and flu than the CDC's flu surveillance system. However, although the monitoring provided data on temperature for all users, only _some_ people provided information on their other symptoms, leading to **item nonresponse**. In addition, the lack of standard protocol for how often or for how many days users were to take their temperatures introduced possible **measurement bias**.

Some data are collected for research purposes; other data are collected as by-products of travel, purchasing behavior, social media, and other activities. The sources of data can affect the quality of numeric estimates produced from those data. When using data that were originally collected for non-research purposes, researchers should be especially thorough in discussing the strengths and weaknesses of those data in terms of sampling bias, study and item nonresponse rates, and measurement error.

TERMS AND CONCEPTS

HIGHLIGHTS

- Many aspects of study design and data collection can introduce bias to numeric estimates based on those data. Understanding the sources and implications of **bias** is an essential part of making sense of numbers from quantitative research.

- **Bias** affects the accuracy of study results and affects the extent to which results can be generalized beyond the sample that was analyzed.

- Bias related to <u>**incomplete**</u> **data** can be introduced when cases are chosen for a study (**sampling bias**), when some of the selected cases do not participate or drop out of a study (**study nonresponse**), and when some cases are missing information on specific questions (<u>**item**</u> **nonresponse**). Each of these forms of bias affects the representativeness of a study sample.

- **Probability sampling methods** are designed to create samples that are representative of the population. If they have a high response rate, the results of such studies often have good sample generalizability.

- **Non-probability selection methods** are <u>not</u> well-suited to quantitative research, because they produce samples that are not representative of the target population and thus cannot be generalized beyond the scope of the included cases.

- **Selective observation** is an incorrect form of selecting cases for analysis that leads to incorrect conclusions.

- Bias related to <u>**incorrect**</u> **data** can occur as individual variables are measured, leading to unreliable or invalid information. Common sources of **measurement bias** include confusing wording, social desirability bias, recall bias, time-lag bias, and use of proxy respondents.

- Studies of any time structure can be affected by **sampling bias**, <u>**study**</u> **nonresponse**, <u>**item**</u> **nonresponse**, and **measurement bias**. Longitudinal studies can also be affected by **attrition, recall bias**, and **time-lag bias**.

- Some data used in quantitative studies were collected with research in mind; these include experimental studies and observational studies, such as sample surveys. Other data come from sources that weren't originally designed for research purposes. Different sources of data are affected differently by each of the major types of bias.

RECOMMENDED READINGS

Chambliss, D. F., & Schutt, R. K. (2019). *Making sense of the social world* (6th ed., Chapters 5 and 7). SAGE.

Maker-Schoenberger, V., & Cukier, K. (2013). *Big data: A revolution that will transform how we live, work, and think*. Eamon Dolan/Mariner Books.

Utts, J., & Heckard, R. (2014). *Mind on statistics* (5th ed., Chapter 5). Cengage, Brooks Cole.

EXERCISES

Individual Exercises

Quantitative Reasoning in Everyday Life

1. In the weekly Well section of *The New York Times* (https://www.nytimes.com/section/well), find a description of a study about an association between a behavior or treatment and a health outcome. (a) State the topic under study. (b) See whether the author specified how the set of cases used was selected, and (c) specify the wording in the article that helped you figure out the sampling method. (d) Determine whether the author discussed to whom the results could be generalized, and, if so, (e) which type(s) of generalizability they implied. (f) Discuss whether you think their generalizations were justified, with reference to the (i) topic, (ii) sampling method, and (iii) target population of the study.

Interpreting Research

2. On the ICPSR Website, find an article or report that analyzed data from the study you used in Chapter 2, Exercise 3. Use information in that article to determine whether (a) the authors reported the study response rate; (b) described the composition of their sample in terms of age, gender, race, and/or socioeconomic status; and (c) whether and to whom the authors generalized the results of their study. Specify the page and paragraph number where you found the information to answer each of those questions. (d) Discuss whether and why you think their generalizations were valid, based on criteria in this chapter and your work on the earlier parts of this exercise.

3. Using the same article as in the previous exercise, investigate whether the authors (a) reported item-response rates for the main variables used in their analysis among those who responded to the overall survey and (b) discussed factors that might have influenced who did and did not respond to those items. Specify the page and paragraph number where you found that information.

Planning Research

4. For each of the following topics and populations, indicate what you would use as a sampling frame for drawing a probability sample: (a) post-graduation plans among undergraduates from a large state university, (b) level of preparation for an infectious disease outbreak among public health agencies for an international comparison, and (c) crime-reduction strategies among police departments in the country where you reside.

Analyzing Data

5. Based on the data in Figure 11.7, (a) calculate the percentage of baseline respondents represented in gray and compare that to the percentage gray among those selected for the initial sample; (b) calculate attrition rates separately for the (i) black and (ii) gray groups. (c) Describe the representativeness of the color composition of the set of cases at follow-up compared to those selected for the initial sample.

Group Exercises

Quantitative Reasoning in Everyday Life

6. Make a list of sources of "big data" that have been used to collect information on the

health, social, and economic repercussions of the COVID-19 epidemic. (b) Discuss the implications for (i) measurement validity and (ii) generalizability of the use of those data sources. (c) Consider how conclusions based on big data might differ from those based on data designed with research in mind, such as sample surveys or surveillance systems.

Interpreting Research

7. In Franzini et al. (2003) (https://dx.doi.org/10.2105%2FAJPH.2007.128702), find the following information: (a) whether the authors used a probability or non-probability method to draw their sample, (b) how many stages were involved in their sampling plan, (c) the sampling units at each stage of their sampling plan, (d) the sampling frame for their study, (e) the number of cases initially selected for the study, and (f) the response rate as a percentage of those selected. (g) Assess whether participants differed from nonparticipants, and, if so, (h) in terms of what characteristics. Determine to whom the authors generalized their results. Cite a specific page number where you found the information needed to answer the question. (j) Discuss whether you think the authors' generalizations were justified, based on criteria in this chapter and your work on earlier parts of this exercise.

Planning Research

8. (a) Describe a quota sampling approach for one of the topics and populations in Exercise 4. (b) Discuss the potential biases that might be introduced by that approach.

9. (a) Working individually, (each student) write (i) a question with double-negative wording, (ii) a double-barreled question, and (iii) a loaded question. (b) Exchange those questions with a classmate, and rewrite each other's questions to fix the errors in wording, using the guidelines in this chapter.

Analyzing Data

10. Buy a "sharing size" package of plain M&Ms (or any other kind of candy that has small pieces of varying colors). (a) From the nutrition information on the package, calculate the total number of pieces of candy in the package ("population size"). (b) Each student pour 10 pieces of candy out of the package onto your desk. (c) Calculate the probability of selection for any element (individual piece of candy) being selected from the population into one specific student's sample. (d) Identify which type of "sampling method" you used to draw samples from the population.

CHAPTER 12 — Causality

Learning Objectives

After reading this chapter, you will be able to do the following:

1. Define causality and why it is important in quantitative research.

2. List the criteria used to assess whether an association can be interpreted as cause-and-effect.

3. Understand the design features of true experiments.

4. State the differences between experimental and observational studies, and how those differences affect internal validity.

5. Recognize confounding and how it can be addressed in quantitative research.

6. Describe the difference between random sampling and random assignment, and how those processes affect different aspects of study validity.

7. Identify ways that internal validity affects interpretation of quantitative research results.

Many explanatory and evaluative research projects seek to identify causes of some phenomenon of interest, often with the goal of identifying a solution to a social, health, or other problem. In this chapter, I define what is meant by a causal relationship and why assessing causality is often an important aim of quantitative research. I then discuss the criteria used to evaluate causality and describe how those criteria are affected by study design, data collection, and analysis. I draw the distinction between random <u>sampling</u> (from Chapter 11) and random <u>assignment</u> (one of the features of an experimental study covered in this chapter) to underscore differences in how those aspects of study design affect study validity. Finally, I explain why assessing the internal validity of a study is critical for understanding how the results can be interpreted and applied. In Chapter 15, we return to consider how causality should be used along with other criteria for determining the "importance" of a research finding.

Causality Defined

Many quantitative research studies examine whether some characteristic, policy, or behavior is a cause of a particular social or health outcome. We say that a relationship between an independent variable (x) and a dependent variable (y) is **causal** if changing the values of x leads to a change in the values of y, all else equal. In other words, if a relationship is cause-and-effect, then altering the variable that we hypothesize is the **cause** will produce a response in values of the variable that we think is the **effect**. Studies that investigate causality ask, "If we were to change x, would y change in response?"

> Example: Does a new mentoring and support program increase students' chances of graduating from college?
>
> *The independent variable (the **hypothesized cause**) is whether someone participated in the program, and the dependent variable (the **hypothesized effect**) measures whether they graduated. If the mentoring program really **causes** a better college graduation rate, then implementing that program should increase the graduation rate.*

The phrase **all else equal** conveys that we seek to compare cases that are as similar as possible on all characteristics <u>other than</u> the specific independent variable (x) that is thought to be the cause. In social science research, holding all other characteristics constant is difficult, because many social, economic, and behavioral characteristics are highly correlated with one another. See the following sections "Non-spuriousness," "Experimental Studies," and "Observational Studies" for approaches to addressing that issue.

A **causal** (or **causative**) **relationship** between an independent variable (x) and a dependent variable (y) occurs when <u>changes</u> in the values of x lead to (cause, induce, or produce) <u>changes</u> in the values of y, all else equal. A hypothesized causal (**cause-and-effect**) **relationship** implies that x is the **cause** and y is the **effect**. **All else equal** (also written "holding everything else constant," or *ceteris paribus*) describes the process of comparing cases that are similar to one another on all variables <u>other than</u> the hypothesized cause.

Why Does Causality Matter?

Investigating whether an association between an independent and a dependent variable (outcome) can be interpreted as causal is a crucial step for any study whose results are intended to inform decisions, programs, or policies to affect that outcome or to advance a theory about that relationship. Before applying research results in those ways, researchers must assess whether it is reasonable to conclude that the intervention or other hypothesized cause is what produced change in the outcome.

<u>Example</u>: The rate of lung cancer is higher among gamblers than among non-gamblers. If we convince people to stop gambling, will it reduce their chances of developing lung cancer?

> *If gambling (the **independent variable**) <u>isn't</u> an actual **cause** of lung cancer (the **dependent variable**), then changing gambling behavior won't affect lung-cancer chances (Michael et al., 1984).*

For permanent characteristics, the implications of causality are somewhat different: Is the difference across groups defined by that characteristic causal, such that **targeting** (focusing on) cases based on those traits would be an appropriate strategy for improving the outcome (effect)?

<u>Example</u>: Women who have certain inherited mutations of the BRCA gene are at increased risk of developing breast cancer or ovarian cancer (American Cancer Society, n.d.).

> *Although it isn't possible to change someone's BRCA genes, screening for those mutations among women who have a personal or family history of cancer allows clinical interventions to be **targeted** (directed specifically) to those with the harmful mutations (**cause**) to reduce their risk of developing or dying from cancer (**effect**).*

Association Does not Equal Causation

Demonstrating that a relationship between two variables is cause-and-effect is tricky. As you might have heard in a statistics or research methods course, "Association does not equal causation" or "Correlation does not necessarily imply causation." In other words, the fact that values of one variable differ according to values of some other variable does <u>not, by itself</u>, prove that the independent variable actually caused change in the dependent variable. An observed association between variables *x* and *y* can arise due to **causality**, **reverse causality**, **confounding**, **bias**, or simple coincidence.

Those possibilities mean that, before we can conclude that an observed association is causal, we must assess the **internal validity** of the study that produced the results. Internal validity pertains to whether an association observed in the study sample can be interpreted as cause-and-effect. It depends on several aspects of study design, as we discuss later in this chapter.

Just because two variables are observed to be associated with each another does <u>not necessarily</u> mean that one caused the other. Before interventions involving the hypothesized independent variable are designed to improve the outcome, it is

(Continued)

(Continued)

important to rule out other possible explanations for how that association could have occurred, including

- reverse causality,
- confounding,
- bias, or
- coincidence.

Internal validity refers to the degree to which a particular study is able to demonstrate that variation in the dependent variable ("effect") can be explained by variation in the independent variable (intervention or treatment).

Criteria for Assessing Causality

There are three main criteria for assessing whether an association between variables is causal: empirical association, time order, and non-spuriousness (Chambliss & Schutt, 2019). Each of those criteria is <u>necessary</u>, but <u>none *alone* is sufficient</u> to demonstrate causality, so a good strategy for evaluating whether an observed association can be interpreted as causal is to consider the criteria <u>in the order listed</u>. If <u>any</u> of them is <u>not</u> satisfied, causality can be ruled out. Two other criteria—mechanism and dose-response—can be used to strengthen the case for causality (Schneider & Lilienfeld, 2015).

Empirical Association

An **empirical association** between two variables is the first criterion for assessing causality. If values of the hypothesized dependent variable <u>don't</u> differ according to values of the hypothesized independent variable, then there cannot be a causal relationship between those two variables. Researchers should consider both the **strength** and the **consistency** of an observed association between *x* and *y* when evaluating whether that relationship is causal. **Strength of association** refers to the size of the difference in values of the dependent variable across values of the independent variable (see Chapters 9 and 10) and to its statistical significance (see Chapter 13). The stronger the association, the better the evidence for causality.

   Consistency of association refers to whether the association between *x* and *y* has been observed in several samples or populations and demonstrated based on several types of study design. The more well-designed studies that demonstrate the same association, the better the evidence for causality.

> Example: A study by Wakefield and colleagues (1998) reported that vaccinating children for measles, mumps, and rubella increased their chances of developing autism. However, many later studies using stronger study designs found no such association (Taylor et al., 2014).
>
> > *The findings of the Wakefield et al. study were <u>not</u> **consistent** with those of other studies. The fact that Wakefield et al.'s results were based on observational data in one small clinical study increased the chances that their findings were a <u>fluke</u>, rather than conclusively demonstrating a real, **causal** relationship. See below for more on observational studies.*

A **meta-analysis** is a technique for combining the results of many studies, selected for high-quality research methods, to arrive at a summary of findings (Himmelfarb Health Sciences Library, 2019). A meta-analysis evaluates whether the direction, size, and statistical significance of the empirical associations observed in that set of studies are consistent with one another. The conclusions of a meta-analysis are statistically stronger than the findings of any single study, because they are based on larger numbers of study participants, wider varieties of participants and types of study designs, and results. In other words, if many well-conducted studies all observe an empirical association between x and y, that bolsters the evidence of a relationship between those variables.

> Example: Ousey and Kubrin (2018) reviewed 51 studies of the association between immigration and crime in the United States, including a variety of study designs, geographic units of analysis, measures of immigration, and measures of crime. They found that the higher the share of immigrants in an area, the lower its crime rate.
>
> > *The authors conducted a **meta-analysis** that summarized the results of many studies, <u>consistently</u> finding an overall small negative association between immigration and crime. That **consensus** of findings across several contexts and study designs provides good evidence for an inverse relationship between those variables.*

An **empirical association** occurs when values of the dependent variable (y) are observed to vary for cases with different values of the independent variable (x). A **meta-analysis** is used to combine the results of multiple studies to assess consistency of findings about the size, shape, and strength of the relationship between the variables under study.

Occasionally, an association between variables will be observed in only <u>some</u> locations or subgroups, but that finding has been confirmed using several types of studies, suggesting that the result is not an anomaly. In that case, we say that the pattern is **context-dependent.**

<u>Example</u>: Several studies have demonstrated that low-dose aspirin reduces the risk of stroke in women who are at high risk of heart disease but not in low-risk women or in men. On the other hand, low-dose aspirin reduces the risk of heart attack in men but not women (Wolff et al., 2009).

> *The findings were replicated using different study designs, increasing the confidence that the gender-specific findings were not aberrations. Here, the **context dependence** is based on gender, because the associations between aspirin and cardiovascular outcomes were different for men than for women and for stroke than for heart attack.*

An empirical correlation <u>alone is *not* sufficient</u> to infer that a relationship between two variables is cause-and-effect.

Time Order

Once an empirical association has been demonstrated, researchers should consider the next criterion for assessing causality—time order. **Time order** (also known as **temporal order** or **causal order**) refers to the sequence in which the hypothesized independent and dependent variables occur and are measured. A cause must precede its effect!

<u>Example</u>: A study by Werner and colleagues (2007) showed that low parental socioeconomic status (SES) at the time of a child's birth was associated with an increased risk of the child developing schizophrenia by early adulthood.

> *Using SES <u>at birth</u> allowed researchers to sort out the causal order between schizophrenia and SES, because they knew that their measures of SES (the hypothesized **independent variable**, in the unshaded box in Figure 12.1a) <u>predated</u> the schizophrenia diagnosis (the **dependent variable**, in the gray-shaded box). The solid arrow pointing from SES to schizophrenia conveys the **direction of causation**.*

Reverse causation occurs when what was thought to be the cause is actually the effect—that the direction of causality is "backward"—the <u>opposite</u> of the hypothesized causal order. It is also known as the "cart before the horse" bias. In other words, the supposed independent variable (cause) is actually the dependent variable (effect): *y* causes *x*.

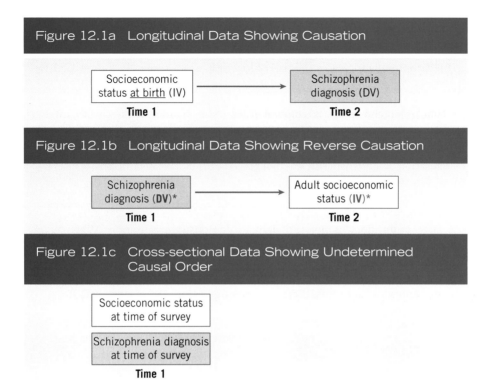

Figure 12.1a   Longitudinal Data Showing Causation

Socioeconomic status at birth (IV)
Time 1

Schizophrenia diagnosis (DV)
Time 2

Figure 12.1b   Longitudinal Data Showing Reverse Causation

Schizophrenia diagnosis (**DV**)*
Time 1

Adult socioeconomic status (**IV**)*
Time 2

Figure 12.1c   Cross-sectional Data Showing Undetermined Causal Order

Socioeconomic status at time of survey

Schizophrenia diagnosis at time of survey
Time 1

<u>Example</u>: Schizophrenia is more common among people living in low-income areas. However, people with schizophrenia are less likely to be able to work, causing them to have lower incomes than people without the condition (Dohrenwend, 1990).

> *This is a classic example of **reverse causation**, in which schizophrenia (the hypothesized dependent variable, shown in the gray-shaded box) causes low income (the hypothesized independent variable, in the unshaded box; Figure 12.1b). Note that the causal arrow points from schizophrenia (as the **cause**) to low SES (as the **effect**): the opposite (**reverse**) of the **hypothesized direction**.*

<u>Example</u>: Keith et al. (2017) found that among African Americans, darker skin tone was associated with greater levels of experiencing everyday discrimination, such as being treated with less courtesy, receiving poor restaurant service, being perceived as dishonest, or being insulted.

> *Someone's skin tone (the independent variable) was determined <u>prior to</u> their experience of discrimination (the dependent variable), so the **causal order** is unambiguous. Put differently, discrimination cannot cause permanent changes in skin tone; thus, **reverse causation** is <u>not</u> a plausible explanation for the association.*

For many research questions, causality can run in both directions.

Example: Low SES increases the risk of schizophrenia, <u>and</u> schizophrenia increases the risk of low SES, as illustrated in Figure 12.1.

Time order (also known as **temporal order** or **causal order**) refers to which came first: the independent or the dependent variable. For a variable (x) to be a cause of another (y), change or variation in x must precede change or variation in y. **Reverse causation** occurs when what was thought to be the independent variable (cause) is actually the dependent variable (effect).

Time order alone is <u>not</u> sufficient to demonstrate causation. When people incorrectly conclude that one event must have caused a later event simply because the first event occurred before the second, they have committed an error of reasoning called a **post-hoc fallacy**. "Post hoc" is short for "post hoc, ergo propter hoc," which is Latin for "after this, therefore because of this" (Nordquist, 2020).

Example: Autism was often diagnosed in young children a year or two after they received vaccines to prevent diseases such as measles, leading some people to conclude that the vaccines caused autism because they closely preceded the diagnosis (Nordquist, 2020).

*As noted earlier, the hypothesis that vaccinations cause autism has been refuted by many well-executed scientific studies (Taylor et al., 2014); thus, the time-order reasoning represents a **post-hoc fallacy**.*

A variation of the post-hoc fallacy called the **inflated causality fallacy** occurs when reasoning about a particular cause is oversimplified to imply that it is the <u>only</u> cause instead of one of several causal factors. The proposed cause is partially true, which is why this error is called <u>inflated</u>.

Example: A political commentator declared that a candidate won the presidential election solely because she performed better in one televised debate.

*If the candidate truly dominated the debate, her performance might <u>partially</u> account for her victory, but it is unlikely that the debate <u>alone</u> determined the election outcome. Although the debate might have been one reason for the victory, the reporter used **inflated causal** reasoning by implying that it was the <u>only</u> determinant of voters' choices.*

A **post-hoc fallacy** occurs when x is believed to cause y <u>solely</u> because x preceded y. The **inflated causality** version of the post-hoc fallacy occurs when a valid cause of some outcome is interpreted as the <u>only</u> cause, even though other factors also influence that outcome.

Study Design and Time Order

When both the hypothesized independent and dependent variables are changeable, time order helps identify instances of reverse causation: Which of the two variables occurred (or was measured) first? As discussed in Chapter 11, **longitudinal** studies collect data at two or more points in time, allowing information on the independent variable to be measured before the dependent variable, and allowing direction and extent of change over time to be determined for both variables.

> Example: A longitudinal study found that volunteering improved people's subjective well-being, with larger benefits among those with lower baseline well-being than those with higher initial well-being (Magnani & Zhu, 2018). After an increase during the year they volunteered, people's well-being returned to its original level within a year.
>
> > By taking advantage of the **longitudinal** nature of the Household, Income and Labour Dynamics in Australia (HILDA) survey, the authors were able to <u>rule out</u> that the observed correlation was due to people with higher subjective well-being being more likely to volunteer (**reverse causation**) and to demonstrate that the boost to well-being from volunteer activity was temporary.

Cross-sectional studies measure all variables at the same time, meaning that such data <u>cannot</u> be used to determine time order of changes in the hypothesized independent and dependent variables.

> Example: Data from a cross-sectional study show a positive correlation between dietary fat intake and blood pressure.
>
> > A correlation between two variables <u>measured at the same</u> time <u>cannot</u> be used to rule out the possibility of **reverse causation**—that the purported cause (diet) changed after the purported outcome (heart disease risk). Thus, cross-sectional data are weaker at establishing causal order than data from a prospective study showing higher blood-pressure levels among those with higher <u>prior</u> fat intake. A **longitudinal** study showing that blood pressure <u>increased</u> more over time among people with higher-fat diets at baseline would make an even stronger case that diet was the cause.

Repeated cross-sectional studies are also poor for demonstrating causality, because even when the dependent variable is measured at a later date than the independent variable, those measures are taken on different sets of cases (different cross-sectional samples), so change in an outcome for <u>specific individual</u> cases cannot be established.

> Study designs that measure the independent variable before observing differences or changes in the dependent variable are stronger at demonstrating causal order than are cross-sectional study designs. However, time order alone cannot establish causality.

Non-spuriousness

If both empirical association and time order have been established, the next criterion for assessing causality is whether the association between an independent and a dependent variable can be considered **non-spurious**, meaning that it <u>cannot</u> be explained by some other variable. If the association between the first two variables is due to a third variable, it is termed **spurious**, implying that what was thought to be the cause (the hypothesized independent variable) is <u>not</u> the real reason for the observed variation in the dependent variable. In other words, in a spurious relationship, the association between the first two variables is "not what it appears to be" based on the observed bivariate relationship, but instead occurs due to that third variable.

A variable that accounts for the observed association between the hypothesized independent and dependent variables is called a **confounding factor**. Also known as the "possibility of alternative explanations" (Michael et al., 1984), **confounding** refers to the fact that the third variable is the actual cause of variation in the dependent variable. To be a confounding factor, a variable must be associated with both the dependent variable <u>and</u> the hypothesized independent variable.

> A **spurious** relationship is an association between two variables that actually results from variation in a third variable (characteristic). The variable that explains (leads to) the observed association between the two variables in a spurious relationship is called a **confounding factor**, or **confounder**. A relationship between an independent and a dependent variable is termed <u>**non**</u>**-spurious** when that association is <u>not</u> confounded by some other variable.

<u>Example</u>: A hypothetical study found that people who gamble have a higher prevalence of lung cancer than people who don't gamble (22% vs. 14%; bivariate association in Figure 12.2a). However, further investigation revealed that gamblers are more likely than non-gamblers to smoke cigarettes (60% vs. 20%), and smoking is associated with higher cancer prevalence (Figure 12.2b). Since smoking is the cause of the higher cancer risk among gamblers, convincing them to stop gambling <u>won't</u> reduce their chances of getting lung cancer.

*In Figure 12.2b, the solid arrow from smoking to lung cancer denotes that the former is a **true cause** of the latter. The positive-signed two-way arrow between gambling and smoking conveys that gamblers were more likely than non-gamblers to smoke, although neither is considered a "cause" of the other and thus no causal order is specified. The arrow is dashed because the relationship between the two variables is an association, <u>not</u> causal.*

*Once the association between gambling and smoking is taken into account, the "effect" of gambling (the **hypothesized independent variable**) on lung cancer (the **dependent variable**) becomes zero. In other words, the association between gambling and lung cancer was **spurious** rather than causal—completely explained by the fact that both were associated with smoking (the **confounding factor**; Michael et al., 1984).*

<u>Example</u>: You take an umbrella with you on your way out the door. Later it starts to rain. You superstitiously conclude that you should not take an umbrella if you don't want it to rain.

Just because your grabbing the umbrella preceded the rain does <u>not</u> mean that it caused the rain! Rather, your observation of looming rain clouds caused both your decision to take the umbrella and the fact that it rained

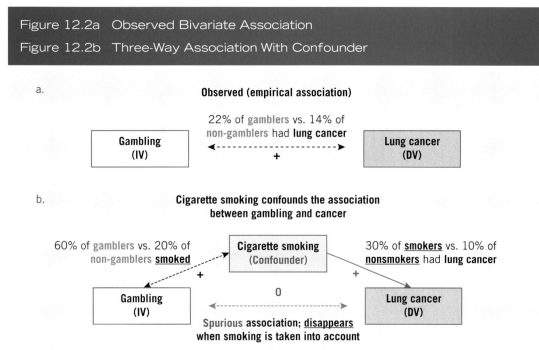

Figure 12.2a   Observed Bivariate Association

Figure 12.2b   Three-Way Association With Confounder

a.

Observed (empirical association)

22% of gamblers vs. 14% of non-gamblers had **lung cancer**

Gambling (IV)

+

Lung cancer (DV)

b.

Cigarette smoking confounds the association between gambling and cancer

60% of gamblers vs. 20% of non-gamblers **smoked**

Cigarette smoking (Confounder)

30% of **smokers** vs. 10% of **nonsmokers** had **lung cancer**

+

+

Gambling (IV)

0

Lung cancer (DV)

Spurious association; <u>disappears</u> when smoking is taken into account *later. The rain clouds **confounded** the observed association between umbrella and rain, disputing your **post-hoc fallacy** conclusion about ways to prevent rain in the future.*

In some associations, taking into account one or more confounding factors <u>reduces</u>, but <u>does</u> <u>not eliminate</u>, the association between an independent and a dependent variable. In such instances, the original association is not completely spurious, because the independent variable still partially explains variation in the dependent variable.

<u>Example</u>: Both obesity and a lack of exercise are associated with elevated risk of heart attack, but obesity and exercise are correlated with one another. When both of those risk factors are considered simultaneously as predictors of heart attack, the size of the association between each predictor and heart-attack risk is reduced but remains greater than zero.

*Each of those variables <u>partially</u> **confounds** the relationship between the other predictor and heart attacks, and both retain a role in explaining heart-attack risk.*

Once an empirical association, time order, and non-spuriousness have been established, two additional criteria can be used to strengthen the case for a cause-and-effect relationship.

Mechanism

If researchers can identify a **mechanism** by which the independent variable could affect the dependent variable, that increases the credibility of a causal argument. Depending on the topic under study, the mechanism might be a physical, an environmental, a behavioral, or another process connecting the hypothesized cause (independent variable) to the outcome (dependent variable).

A **mechanism** is a process that causally links two variables, explaining <u>how</u> variation in an independent variable generates or produces variation in the dependent variable.

<u>Example</u>: A substantial body of biomedical research shows that chemicals and particulates from cigarette smoke cause changes to the cells in the lungs—an early step in cancer development.

*The physical changes to the lungs after exposure to components of cigarette smoke reveal a plausible **mechanism** linking smoking to lung cancer, helping solidify the case that smoking **causes** cancer. On the*

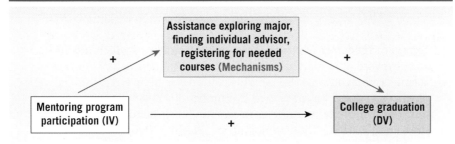

Figure 12.3   Mechanism for an Association Between an Independent and a Dependent Variable

other hand, it is difficult to come up with a process by which gambling per se would lead to the physical changes involved in lung cancer, except perhaps exposure to secondhand smoke in a casino, in which case the cause is still smoking, not gambling!

<u>Example</u>: An evaluation report shows that a mentoring program for students who were in the first generation of their family to attend college ("first-gen students") improved their graduation rate by providing them with more support, providing them with information about choosing a major area of study, and finding them an advisor in their chosen major.

*Those who were in the program received several types of advising tailored to their needs (blue-filled box in Figure 12.3), which were associated with a higher graduation rate. Identifying those **mechanisms** (aspects of advising) through which program participation (the **independent variable**; unshaded box) affected the graduation rate (the **dependent variable**; gray-shaded box) strengthens the argument that the higher degree-completion rate can be attributed to the program itself, rather than to other factors such as motivation or preparation.*

To increase confidence in an assertion of a causal relationship, researchers should describe theories and findings of prior studies that identify mechanisms that explain how the hypothesized independent variable could affect the dependent variable.

Dose-Response

Another criterion that helps improve the argument for causality is called a **dose-response relationship**, where the size of the response in the dependent variable changes according to the dose (amount or intensity) of exposure to the independent variable.

A **dose-response** relationship occurs when the size of the change in the dependent variable varies with the size of the dose (amount of the independent variable).

Example: The larger the dose of secondhand smoke to which infants were exposed at home, the larger the increase in their risk of Sudden Infant Death Syndrome (SIDS). This pattern was observed regardless of whether "dose" was measured by number of smokers in the home, number of cigarettes per day, or number of hours per day of cigarette-smoke exposure (Office on Smoking and Health, 2006).

*The risk of SIDS (the **dependent variable**) was positively associated with the amount (**dose**) of infants' environmental exposure to cigarette smoke (the **independent variable**).*

Summary of Assessing Causality

To build the case that an association can be interpreted as cause-and-effect, empirical association, time order, and non-spuriousness must <u>all</u> be established for the study upon which that conclusion was based; none of those criteria by itself is sufficient for establishing causality. Although causality can be <u>refuted</u> by demonstrating that even one of the causal criteria is <u>not</u> true, it is much more difficult for any single study to simultaneously establish that all the criteria <u>are</u> true. It may be impossible to determine from the available data whether change or variation in the hypothesized independent variable occurred before or after observed variation in the hypothesized dependent variable. In addition, often there are several possible confounders and biases that cannot be measured or taken into account.

> For an association to be interpreted as cause-and-effect, empirical association, time order, and non-spuriousness must <u>all</u> be demonstrated for the study upon which that conclusion was based; <u>none of those criteria alone is sufficient for establishing causality</u>. Researchers should describe how their study can or cannot provide information to address each of the criteria for establishing causality, working through them <u>in the order listed</u>:
>
> - Empirical association between the independent and dependent variables
> - Independent variable preceded the dependent variable (time order)
> - Non-spuriousness
>
> If even one of those criteria is <u>not</u> true, it disproves the case for causality.

Two additional criteria strengthen the case for a causal association, once the above criteria have been met:

- Mechanism linking the independent and dependent variables
- Dose-response

An important factor in assessing whether an association is causal is whether it is based on data from an experimental study or an observational study, because differences in those study designs affect researchers' ability to evaluate each of the criteria for causality.

Experimental Studies

Experimental studies (also known as **randomized controlled trials** or **randomized clinical trials**; **RCTs**) are considered the gold standard, because they allow each of the three required criteria for evaluating causality—empirical association, time order, and non-spuriousness—to be directly evaluated. As their name suggests, RCTs use a random procedure to decide which participants go into each of two (sometimes more) groups: (a) a **treatment group** that receives a treatment or intervention and (b) a **control group** that receives either no treatment or an alternative treatment (often an existing program or medication). Put differently, in an RCT, the researchers manipulate which study subjects have which values of the independent variable (treatment or control group). They then measure and compare values of the dependent variable for the two groups, which differ only in terms of whether they receive the treatment. Some studies involve more than one treatment group or more than one control group, allowing multiple comparisons.

> Example: A new medication is tested against both an older drug and a placebo (no medication).
>
> The **treatment group** is given the new drug, and there are two separate **control groups**: (1) cases who receive the old drug and (2) those who receive the placebo.

RCTs are also known as **true experiments**, to differentiate them from natural experiments (discussed later).

In **true experiments**, also known as **randomized controlled trials**, **randomized clinical trials** (**RCTs**), or sometimes just **clinical trials**, participants are assigned randomly into either a treatment group or a control group at the beginning of

(Continued)

the study, and the outcome is measured after the treatment has occurred. Participants in the **treatment group** receive the treatment or **experimental intervention**, whereas those in the **control group** do not.

Randomization Into Treatment and Control Groups

In a true experiment, participants are **randomly assigned** into treatment and control groups based entirely on chance, using techniques such as flipping a coin, a lottery, or using a random number table. **Randomization** is the process by which researchers manipulate the independent variable. It is <u>not</u> the same as random <u>selection</u>, as explained later, under "Random Sampling vs. Random Assignment."

Randomization, also known as **random assignment**, is a procedure used to determine which participants are placed in the treatment group and which are placed in the control group. That assignment uses a process that allows nothing but chance to influence which participants go into which group.

Random assignment is used to ensure that other characteristics or behaviors are approximately equally distributed between the treatment and control groups in order to reduce the chances that those other factors could **confound** the association between the independent and dependent variables. In other words, randomization into experimental and control groups strengthens the argument that the association between the independent and dependent variables is **non-spurious**.

Example: Suppose advisers at the University of X randomly assigned first-gen college students who applied to the mentoring program to either (1) receive mentoring and support tailored to students who don't have friends or families who have attended college or (2) receive the usual advising and support services available to all students, regardless of family educational background. The study found a higher graduation rate among students in the mentoring program.

*Only first-gen students were eligible for the program, and only those who applied to the program were included in the study sample. Applicants were assigned into either the **treatment** (mentoring program) or the **control** (regular advising) group using a **randomization** process (illustrated by the coin flip in Figure 12.4a). Randomization thus removed **potential confounders** of the association between advising group and graduation rate, because the treatment and control groups had very similar demographics and academic preparation and motivation, as shown by the similar composition of black (better-prepared) and gray (less well-prepared) icons in the two groups.*

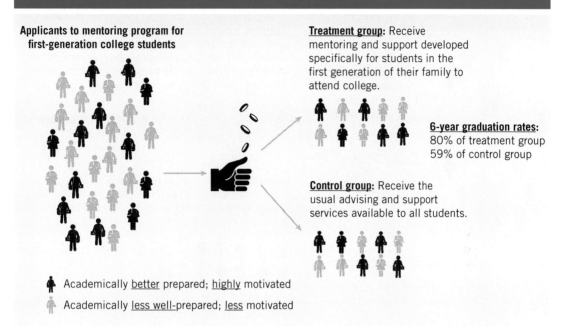

Figure 12.4a   Random Assignment Into Treatment and Control Groups

Applicants to mentoring program for first-generation college students

Treatment group: Receive mentoring and support developed specifically for students in the first generation of their family to attend college.

6-year graduation rates:
80% of treatment group
59% of control group

Control group: Receive the usual advising and support services available to all students.

👤 Academically <u>better</u> prepared; <u>highly</u> motivated

👤 Academically <u>less well</u>-prepared; <u>less</u> motivated

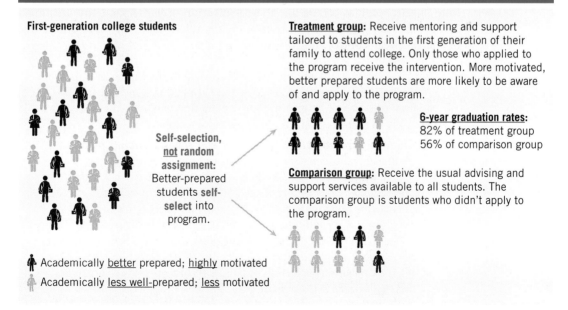

Figure 12.4b   Self-selection Reinforcing Difference Between Groups

First-generation college students

Self-selection, <u>not</u> random assignment: Better-prepared students **self-select** into program.

Treatment group: Receive mentoring and support tailored to students in the first generation of their family to attend college. Only those who applied to the program receive the intervention. More motivated, better prepared students are more likely to be aware of and apply to the program.

6-year graduation rates:
82% of treatment group
56% of comparison group

Comparison group: Receive the usual advising and support services available to all students. The comparison group is students who didn't apply to the program.

👤 Academically <u>better</u> prepared; <u>highly</u> motivated

👤 Academically <u>less well</u>-prepared; <u>less</u> motivated

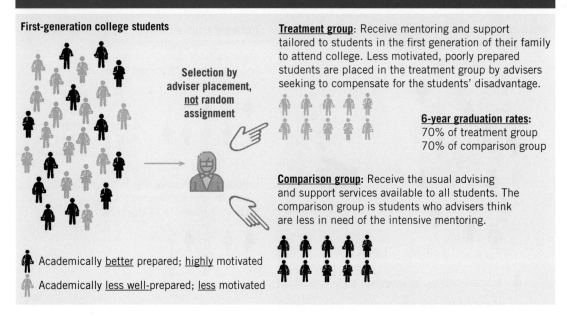

Figure 12.4c Adviser Selection Offsetting Difference Between Groups

First-generation college students

Selection by adviser placement, not random assignment

Treatment group: Receive mentoring and support tailored to students in the first generation of their family to attend college. Less motivated, poorly prepared students are placed in the treatment group by advisers seeking to compensate for the students' disadvantage.

6-year graduation rates:
70% of treatment group
70% of comparison group

Comparison group: Receive the usual advising and support services available to all students. The comparison group is students who advisers think are less in need of the intensive mentoring.

Academically <u>better</u> prepared; <u>highly</u> motivated

Academically <u>less well</u>-prepared; <u>less</u> motivated

Source: Adapted from Chambliss & Schutt (2019).

Randomization of subjects into treatment and control groups is intended to eliminate **selection bias**, which can introduce the possibility of confounding. One form of selection bias occurs due to **self-selection** of participants into treatment and comparison groups. See "Observational Studies," later, for more on the distinction between control and comparison groups.

Example: A hypothetical observational study found a higher graduation rate among first-gen college students who applied to a mentoring program (the treatment group) than among first-gen students who did not apply to that program (the comparison group).

> This **non-experimental** design allowed for **self-selection** to produce treatment and comparison groups that were different <u>prior to the intervention</u>, because students who were better connected with support services and more highly motivated (black icons) were more likely to apply to the program than their less-motivated peers (gray icons). Note the <u>absence</u> of a **randomization** process (coin flip) in Figure 12.4b. This self-selection introduced **confounding** of the association between program participation and graduation rate, because the students who received the intensive mentoring had traits that made them more likely to graduate, even <u>without</u> the extra support.

Selection bias can be introduced in other ways, such as by people implementing a program, prescribing a treatment, or conducting the research.

> <u>Example</u>: Advisers at the University of X put students whom they perceived as in greater need of services into the mentoring program, and they assigned other first-gen students whom they thought more self-sufficient into the comparison group (Figure 12.4c). They found no difference in graduation rate between the treatment and the comparison group.
>
> > *The advisers introduced* **confounding**, *because the students' need for the mentoring program differed between the* **treatment** *and* **comparison groups** *even <u>prior to the intervention</u>. The students in the treatment group were at higher risk of failing to graduate than those in the comparison group, due to their initial characteristics (the* **confounders**). *The fact that they graduated at the same rate as the students who were better prepared from the get-go suggests that the mentoring program <u>did</u> have a beneficial effect, because it raised the graduation rate among the disadvantaged (treatment) group to the same level as the advantaged (comparison) group.* **Selection bias** *thus obscured the effect of the program, which ran in the opposite direction of the selection bias.*

Selection bias occurs when characteristics of treatment and comparison group members differ in ways that are correlated with the outcome. **Self-selection** is a form of selection bias in which study participants choose their own value of the independent variable (treatment or comparison group).

Pre/Post Measurement

Another feature of a true experiment is its longitudinal nature: The independent variable is manipulated <u>before</u> the dependent variable is measured at a **posttest**. Some experimental studies also include a **pretest**, measuring the dependent variable before the intervention is administered. The posttest is exactly the same "test" as the pretest but is administered at a later time. Experiments that include both pretests and posttests often compare the extent of <u>change</u> in the dependent variable over the study period rather than simply comparing posttest values for the experimental and the control group. By using a longitudinal design whereby the intervention precedes measurement of the dependent variable, a true experiment clearly demonstrates that the hypothesized cause preceded the hypothesized effect, thus establishing time order—the second key criterion for assessing causality.

A **pretest** measures the outcome (dependent variable) <u>before</u> an experimental intervention, whereas a **posttest** measures the outcome <u>after</u> that intervention.

The length of time between randomization and the posttest depends on the nature of the process under study. It can be as short as a few minutes or hours, or it can be as long as years (or even decades).

<u>Example</u>: Infants 4 to 11 months old who were at high risk of developing a peanut allergy were randomly assigned either to (1) be regularly fed food that contained peanuts or (2) or be denied such food. These feeding patterns continued until the children were 5 years old. Less than 2% of children who were fed peanuts developed an allergy to them, compared with nearly 14% of those who did not consume peanuts (Figure 12.5).

None of the children had peanut allergies at **baseline** *(start of the experiment, denoted O_1 for "observation 1" in Figure 12.5), providing a* **pre-intervention measure** *of the outcome.* **Random assignment** *(R) into the* **treatment** *group (fed peanuts, shown with the T) or the* **control**

Figure 12.5 Diagram of a True Experiment

General design of a true experiment

		Baseline	Treatment period	Follow-up
Treatment group	R	O_1	T	O_2
Control group	R	O_1		O_2

R = randomization
O_1 = first observation point; baseline
T = treatment or intervention
O_2 = second observation point; follow-up

Design of the peanut allergy experiment

		Enrollment into study: Aged 4 to 11 mos.	Baseline to follow-up	% of cases with peanut allergy at age 5 years
Treatment group	R	No peanut allergies	Intervention: Fed peanut foods	1.9%
Control group	R	No peanut allergies	<u>No</u> intervention: <u>Not</u> fed peanut foods	13.7%

Source: Data from DuToit et al. (2015).

group (<u>not</u> fed peanuts) prevented either parents or physicians from deciding which children were in which group. The time between baseline and the follow-up (**posttest**; O_2) assessment was approximately 4 years.

<u>Example</u>: Five randomly assigned groups of participants watched a film showing a traffic accident. At the conclusion of the film, they were given a questionnaire, in which one group was asked, "About how fast were the cars going when they hit into each other?" The other groups were questioned with different verbs replacing the word "hit." Respondents' estimates of speed declined from an average of 41 miles per hour (mph) for "smashed," to 39 mph for "collided," 38 mph for "bumped," 34 mph for "hit," and 32 mph for "contacted" (Loftus & Palmer, 1974).

> *Here, the **posttest** measurement of the **outcome** (estimated speed) took place only a few minutes after watching the film, with the **intervention** (wording of the question) serving as the **independent variable** manipulated by the researchers. This **experiment** compared five groups: one for each of the different verbs used in the descriptive phrase for the accident scenario.*

Blinding

To reduce conscious or unconscious bias in how an experiment is designed and executed, experiments are often **blinded** so that the participants and/or researchers cannot tell who is receiving the experimental treatment. In a **single-blinded** study, the <u>participants</u> don't know whether they are in the treatment or the control group. In a **double-blinded** study, the <u>researchers</u> also don't know which participants are in which group, to ensure impartiality in the way they conduct the experiment and interpret the results.

To measure the true effect of a treatment, experiments are often blinded by using **placebos**—fake pills or other treatments given to the control group. The placebos are designed to resemble the actual treatments as closely as possible but do not include the medication or other intervention being tested. Use of placebos is intended to reduce the **placebo effect**, whereby participants' outcomes change because they <u>expect</u> an effect, rather than from the treatment itself.

<u>Example</u>: Clinicians testing a new medication regimen gave monthly shots to all children enrolled in a clinical trial to treat dwarfism disorder. Those in the treatment group received injections containing the new medication, whereas those in the control group received injections that were the same color as the actual treatment but did not include any medication. The researchers filled the syringes and noted in the children's charts whether they were in the "A" or "B" group, but the clinicians administering the shots did not know whether A or B was the treatment group. The children's height was measured before they were randomized into the treatment and control groups and at 6-month intervals throughout

the duration of the 3-year trial. All aspects of their treatment and monitoring followed a prescribed regimen that was the same for both groups.

> The injections that did <u>not</u> contain the medication were the **placebo**, given so that the children and their parents could not tell that they were in the **control group**. The clinicians were also unaware of which children received the **treatment** and which of them received the **placebo**, so this study was **double-blinded**. By double-blinding the experiment, the researchers in this hypothetical study reduced the chances that children in the new-medicine group would be treated or monitored differently than those in the control group due to bias in favor of (or against!) the new medication.

A change in the dependent variable (outcome) in the absence of any actual treatment is called a **placebo effect**, and it occurs in a substantial share of cases in the control group for many experiments. It can be positive (an improvement in the outcome) if participants expect the treatment or intervention to have a beneficial effect, or it can be negative (a worsening of the outcome) if participants expect the treatment or intervention to have harmful effects.

> This [placebo] effect is not deception, fluke, experimenter bias, or statistical anomaly. It is, instead, a product of expectation. The human brain anticipates outcomes, and anticipation produces those outcomes. The placebo effect is self-fulfilling prophecy, and it follows the patterns you'd predict if the brain were, indeed, producing its own desired outcomes.

(Brynie, 2012)

Blinding is a process in which one or more parties in an experiment are kept unaware of which participants have been assigned to treatment and which to the control group. In **single-blinded** studies, the <u>participants</u> do not know whether they are in the treatment or the control group, but the researchers know. In **double-blinded** studies, neither the <u>participants</u> nor the <u>people conducting the experiment</u> know who is receiving the treatment. A **placebo** is a dummy (fake) pill or treatment used in blinding so that participants cannot tell whether they are in the treatment or the control group. A **placebo effect** is a change in the dependent variable that occurs in the control group despite the fact that members of that group are not receiving the actual treatment.

For some experiments, blinding is not possible.

<u>Example</u>: In the study of peanut allergies, parents were clearly aware of whether they were serving their children peanut foods.

*This study could not be **blinded**; therefore, parents knew whether their children were in the **treatment** or the **control** group and might have reported subjective outcomes (such as perceived allergy symptoms) differently. Lab testing for peanut allergies at the end of the study period provided an objective measure of the outcome.*

Although many experimental studies are conducted in clinical settings or psychology laboratories, true experiments also can be conducted in real-world settings, in which case they are known as **field experiments**.

Example: During the 2006 election, researchers conducted a field experiment of voting behavior in low-income neighborhoods in Los Angeles. They randomly assigned volunteers into two groups: (1) People from the same zip code as the voters they visited—the "neighbors"—and (2) people from other zip codes—the "strangers." The volunteers in each of those groups used the same script to make a nonpartisan pitch (nudge) to encourage voting. The researchers found that turnout increased by 9 percentage points among voters who spoke with neighbors, more than 1.5 times as much as the 5.5 percentage point increase in voter turnout among those nudged by "strangers" (Sinclair et al., 2013).

*The study included **treatment** (neighbors as nudgers) and **control** (strangers as nudgers) groups, as well as **random assignment** to determine which residents interacted with which version of the nudge intervention, thus making it a **true experiment**. It was a **field experiment** because it took place in a community setting.*

Colloquial vs. Research Meaning of "Experiment"

When referring to study design, the term **experiment** has a specific meaning that is much more precise than the colloquial (everyday) use of the word. Whereas, in informal conversation, "experiment" often means simply to "try" something, in a research context, experiments include randomization into treatment and control conditions, posttest measurement of the dependent variable, and, often, blinding.

Example: Suppose you wanted to see whether a new shampoo worked better than the one you've been using. First, you take notes on how clean, shiny, and full your hair is after washing it with your old shampoo. Then you switch to the new one and, after a few weeks, observe whether you think your hair is cleaner, shinier, and fuller than it was with your original shampoo.

*Although you might tell your friends you were "experimenting" with the new shampoo, this comparison is not a **true experiment**: You knew* *exactly which shampoo you were using when, allowing for possible bias in your observations based on what you expected or wanted to happen. In addition, other factors—such as changes in the weather or your stress level between the periods when you used the old and new shampoos (the **independent variable**)—could have been responsible for (**confounded**) any differences you observed in how your hair looked and felt (the **dependent variables**).*

Example: A company that manufactures hair products wants to compare a shampoo it is developing to another brand, so it intentionally makes its new shampoo the same color, texture, and scent as the comparison brand. It packages the two types of shampoo into identical-looking bottles—one labeled "left-hand side," the other "right-hand side." It conducts a study in which participants are asked to wash their hair for the next few weeks with both types of shampoo, making sure to use each one on its assigned side of their head. Participants fill out daily forms to rate the cleanliness, shine, and body of the hair on each side of their head.

*This study is a **true experiment**, because it includes both **treatment and control conditions** (old and new shampoos), **randomization** (a coin flip to decide which shampoo is to be used on which side of the head), **blinding** (participants don't know which shampoo is which), and **posttesting**. Since participants tested both shampoos simultaneously throughout the study period, trends in the weather or their stress levels could <u>not</u> explain (**confound**) any observed differences in the shampoos' performance. Each participant effectively served as their own **control**, because each person used both types of shampoo.*

Observational Studies

Unlike in experimental studies, in **observational studies** researchers do <u>not</u> determine which participants have which values of the independent variable. Instead, observational studies collect data on the values of the independent and dependent variables for each participant. For some topics, observational studies are conducted because of ethical or practical factors that preclude an experimental study (Michael et al., 1984).

Example: To assess the effects of domestic violence, researchers compare mental health outcomes among people who have experienced domestic violence and people who have not.

*Studies of whether domestic violence affects mental health are **observational**, because it would be **unethical** to randomly assign people to be victims of such violence.*

Example: The study of how skin tone was associated with respondents' experience with discrimination (Keith et al., 2017) was based on an observational study design.

> *Researchers could <u>not</u> randomly assign skin tone (the **independent variable**) to participants, so they observed how discrimination (the **dependent variable**) varied for African Americans with darker versus lighter skin tones.*

In **observational studies**, researchers do <u>not</u> determine or manipulate the independent variable.

This rest of this section reviews how observational studies do (or do not) meet the criteria for establishing a causal relationship.

Variation in the Independent Variable

As noted earlier, in observational studies, researchers measure the variables but do <u>not</u> manipulate or influence the independent variable. In other words, values of the independent variable differ across cases due to voluntary actions or natural variation rather than having been assigned randomly by researchers. Thus, a **comparison** group (from an **observational** study) is <u>not</u> the same as a randomly assigned **control** group (from an **experimental** study). Since values of the independent variable are <u>not</u> randomly assigned to participants in observational studies, such studies are more susceptible than true experiments to selection bias (see Chapter 11) and confounding.

Example: The Epidemiologic Followup Study (NHEFS) to the first National Health and Nutrition Examination Survey (NHANES I, 1971–1975) tracked deaths of NHANES I participants through 1992. Arrieta and Russell (2008) compared adults in the NHEFS who had low levels, those who had moderate levels, and those who had high levels of non-leisure physical activity with one another, taking into account a range of other health characteristics that might explain mortality differences.

> *The researchers did <u>not</u> determine the participants' physical activity (the **independent variable**), instead analyzing data on whatever level of physical activity each respondent pursued. As part of their statistical analysis, the researchers took into account factors that were associated with level of physical activity and mortality (the **dependent variable**), such as baseline health. However, it is unlikely that they could have accounted for <u>all</u> **potential confounders**, so their use of **observational data** makes a <u>weaker</u> case that exercise level could be interpreted as a **cause** of mortality.*

Time Order

Observational studies can be prospective, retrospective, or cross-sectional, thus affecting how well a particular study is able to demonstrate causal order. Data from **longitudinal observational studies** can establish time order if the independent variable (or change in the independent variable over time) is measured prior to the dependent variable.

> Example: Children of fathers who held positive parenting beliefs when the child was 9 months old and who frequently engaged in creative play with the child at age 5 years were at lower risk of developing problem behaviors by age 7 (Kroll et al., 2016).
>
> *The researchers used data from the **longitudinal** UK Millennium Cohort Study of children born from 2000 to 2001 and followed up at ages 3, 5, and 7 years. Fathers' parenting beliefs and practices (the **independent variables**) were measured <u>before</u> child behavior problems (the **dependent variable**) were assessed, thus confirming that the **time order** was consistent with the hypothesized **causal order.***

However, if a prospective study did not measure the independent variable before the dependent variable, those data cannot be used to determine whether the hypothesized cause preceded the hypothesized effect.

> Example: If researchers had analyzed data on parental engagement and problem behavior, both of which had been measured when the children were 7 years old, they wouldn't have been able to tell whether "difficult" children caused their parents to engage with them less or whether low parental engagement induced more child behavior issues.
>
> *Data from a <u>single</u> round of a **longitudinal** survey are essentially **cross-sectional** and, thus, <u>cannot</u> be used to ascertain the **time order** of changes in the values of the variables.*

Before-and-after studies are a form of longitudinal study that compare the outcome prior to and following a change in the independent variable but do <u>not</u> include a separate control group or comparison group. Instead, the pre-change value for each location or group serves as the comparison, establishing causal order by measuring the outcome after the change in the dependent variable. Before-and-after studies are observational (<u>not</u> experimental), because the researcher does not randomly assign cases into treatment and control groups.

> Example: In 2010, Michigan introduced a law restricting text messaging while driving. Researchers compared crash types, crash rates, and crash fatality rates before and after implementation of that restriction. They hypothesized that outcomes among younger drivers would be most affected by the restriction, because younger drivers were most likely

to have texted prior to the law and thus most subject to changes in texting behavior while driving (Ehsani et al., 2014). The researchers used drivers aged 65 to 99 years as a comparison group, because those drivers were least likely to have used texting prior to the restriction. They found that, overall, the most severe crash types increased slightly after the restriction on texting, whereas the least severe crash types decreased somewhat.

> This is a ***before-and-after design***, <u>not</u> a ***true experiment***. The population composition of Michigan (those affected by the law) did not change appreciably during the observation period, so differences in other characteristics or behaviors were unlikely to **confound** the association between texting while driving (the **independent variable**) and crashes or fatalities (the **dependent variables**). The researchers included the comparison against older drivers to rule out the influence of extraneous factors, such as weather (which would have affected drivers of all ages but could have explained trends in the outcomes).

Like true experiments, **natural experiments** include both a treatment and a comparison group or condition. However, which cases (or locations, or groups) experience each of those conditions is determined by "natural" conditions (e.g., a policy change) or an externally caused disruption (e.g., a natural disaster), rather than being artificially manipulated (assigned) by researchers. Time order can be established, because outcome is observed after the change in the independent variable has taken place. Like true experiments, natural experiments often include pre-intervention measures of the outcome.

Before-and-after studies are a type of longitudinal design that compares values of the dependent variable prior and subsequent to a change in the independent variable. Instead of a separate comparison group, the "before" value serves as the comparison against each case's "after" value. **Natural experiments** are a form of observational study in which an event or a situation effectively randomly assigns study subjects to different groups or conditions (values of the independent variable). The dependent variable (outcome) is measured after the change has been introduced by those "natural" conditions.

Natural experiments are often used in situations in which a true experiment is not possible, such as when an intervention cannot be practically or ethically assigned using randomization. They have the advantage of randomly introducing change and variation in the hypothesized cause, reducing the chances of confounding due to self-selection, because participants do not choose whether they are in the treatment or the control condition.

Example: Policymakers had long argued that increasing the minimum wage would cause employers to hire fewer people. Card and Krueger (1994) took advantage of the fact that in 1992, the minimum wage increased in New Jersey but not in adjacent Pennsylvania, creating natural treatment and comparison groups. They showed that an increase in the minimum wage was not associated with a reduction in employment at fast-food restaurants.

> *The study was a **natural experiment**, because the variation in the independent variable (the minimum wage) was <u>not</u> assigned by researchers but was also <u>not</u> subject to **self-selection** by those studied. Researchers compared changes in employment at places that employed a lot of minimum-wage workers, looking at levels of employment before and after the change, in the "**treatment**" (New Jersey) and "**comparison**" (Pennsylvania) groups.*

Retrospective studies can be used to establish causal order <u>if</u> data on the independent variable was collected referring to an earlier time period than that for the dependent variable.

Example: A study that related participants' smoking history over the 20 years preceding the date of data collection to their health at the time of the survey could demonstrate causal order.

> *Knowing for how many years each participant smoked over the 20-year **retrospective** recall period, the number of cigarettes they smoked per day over that period, and how long it had been since they quit smoking provides information on the **independent variables** <u>prior</u> to the date their health (**dependent variable**) was assessed.*

Cross-sectional studies are the weakest at determining whether the independent variable preceded the dependent variable.

Example: A survey that collected data about smoking behavior and health status at the time of the survey cannot establish causal order.

> *Concurrent measures of smoking and health at the time of the survey <u>cannot</u> rule out **reverse causation** (e.g., that some people quit smoking after their health declined).*

Mechanism

Data from observational studies can be used to test possible mechanisms through which the independent variable affects the dependent variable if those data include measures of the hypothesized mechanism.

Example: Magnani and Zhu (2018) showed that the positive effects of volunteering occurred because participants in their study reported that volunteering led to more frequent socializing, increased feelings of being part of the local community, and greater satisfaction with the neighborhood in which they lived.

> *By measuring respondents' frequency of socializing and satisfaction with being part of their community and neighborhood, the researchers were able to demonstrate that those aspects were the **mechanisms** through which volunteering (the **independent variable**) led to a higher sense of well-being (the **dependent variable**).*

Data from either a true experiment or an observational study can be used to assess the empirical association between an independent and a dependent variable. However, true experiments are better than observational studies for assessing causality, because they include design features to address temporal order, non-spuriousness, and (often) a mechanism linking the independent and dependent variables.

<u>Caution</u>: The term "research **study**" refers to both observational and experimental designs, each of which has a specific set of study design elements. Be careful <u>not</u> to use "experiment" as a synonym for "study."

Other Threats to Internal Validity

As explained in Chapter 11, sampling bias, study nonresponse, and item nonresponse can lead to bias in the sample of cases available for analysis, reducing <u>external</u> validity. Those same factors can also threaten the <u>internal</u> validity of a study by creating what are termed **noncomparable groups**. In other words, sampling bias, study nonresponse, and item nonresponse can result in differences between groups to be compared in terms of characteristics in addition to the independent variable of interest. These differences between groups, also known as **nonequivalent groups**, introduce potential confounders, as in the situation portrayed in Figure 12.4b. These issues can affect both experimental studies and observational studies.

In longitudinal studies, even if groups to be compared had similar characteristics at baseline, different rates of attrition can mean that those groups no longer have equivalent composition by the follow-up round. See Chapter 11 for a review of attrition.

<u>Example</u>: In a randomized clinical trial of a new medication for allergies, 22% of those in the treatment group dropped out before the end of the study due to severe headaches that were a side effect of the medication. Only 9% of the control group dropped out of the study. Women were more likely than men to experience that side effect.

*There was higher **attrition** from the **treatment** group than from the **control** group, much of which occurred among women. Thus, differential participation in the study (a form of **study nonresponse**) resulted in unequal gender composition of the two groups by the end of the clinical trial. Gender could, thus, **confound** any observed benefit (or detriment) of the new medication, compromising the study's **internal validity**.*

Noncomparable groups (also known as **nonequivalent groups**) occur when treatment and control (or comparison) groups differ on characteristics other than the key independent variable, introducing potential confounding.

Research Strategies for Assessing Confounding

Many studies—especially observational studies—run the risk that the associations they demonstrate are confounded by other factors, thus reducing the internal validity of those studies. This is particularly true of studies that include social and behavioral characteristics as independent variables, because so many of those traits are correlated with one another.

Example: In virtually every country in the world, there are vast differences in the SES of different ethnic and cultural groups.

*Any study of cultural differences in outcomes—such as income, occupation, or health—is likely to be **confounded** by differences in access to education and other resources that also affect those outcomes.*

Example: People who apply for a social program often have more information, motivation, and social support than those who are eligible for that program but do not apply.

*In **observational studies** of such programs, differences in those traits could explain (**confound**) observed difference in outcomes for those who do and do not participate in the program. That **self-selection** process makes it difficult to assess whether the program leads to improvements in (**causes**) health, education, or economic outcomes.*

There are several approaches to reducing or eliminating confounding, including during the design of the study, during data collection, and during analysis.

Randomize to Remove Confounders

In experimental studies, random assignment during the design phase equalizes the distributions of potential confounders in the treatment and the control group, so that differences in other characteristics cannot explain observed differences in outcomes across those groups.

> Example: The hypothetical mentoring program that randomly assigned first-gen students into either the treatment or a control condition eliminated self-selection, creating two sets of people with similar levels of preparation, motivation, and social support (Figure 12.4a).
>
> > *The **experimental design** reduced the possibility of **confounding** by equalizing those characteristics, strengthening the case that any observed difference in graduation rate was due to the mentoring program itself.*

Measure and Take Into Account Potential Confounders

In observational studies, data on potential confounders can be used to strengthen the argument that an association is non-spurious. By collecting data on other factors that could explain that association and including that information in the analysis, researchers can come close to mimicking experimental conditions. By holding those other factors constant, they essentially compare outcomes for cases that differ only on the independent variable of interest. This approach is known as creating a **quasi-experiment**, where "quasi" means "sort of" or "approximately." However, because it is impossible to measure all potential confounders, evidence of causality from quasi-experimental studies is weaker than evidence from randomized experiments.

A **quasi-experiment** is a research design in which subjects are not randomly assigned to the comparison and experimental groups, but the comparison group is made as comparable as possible to the experimental group by taking into account (holding constant) one or more characteristics known to be associated with the dependent variable.

A stratified (three-way) analysis is one way to remove the effect of a suspected confounding factor. See Chapter 10 for a review of three-way associations.

> Example: A hypothetical study investigates how much of the observed relationship between gambling and lung cancer can be explained by smoking. Consistent with the statistics reported in Figures 12.2a and 12.2b, the bivariate (two-variable) relationship shows that the lung-cancer rate is 8 percentage points higher among gamblers (22%) than among non-gamblers (14%; gray-shaded cells in Table 12.1a). The bivariate tabulation of smoking by gambling (Table 12.1b) reveals that

gamblers were three times as likely to smoke as non-gamblers (60% vs. 20%). The three-way analysis of lung-cancer rates by smoking status separately for gamblers and non-gamblers (Table 12.1c) shows that 30% of smokers have lung cancer and 10% of nonsmokers have lung cancer, <u>regardless of whether they gamble</u>. The higher rate of lung cancer among gamblers is completely explained by the difference in the prevalence of smoking between people who gamble and those who do not gamble.

> The **three-way analysis tabulates** lung-cancer rate (the **dependent variable**) by smoking status (the **confounder**) separately for strata[1] of gamblers and non-gamblers (the **independent variable**). The dark blue-shaded cells in Table 12.1c show that lung-cancer rates by smoking status are identical for gamblers and non-gamblers. Note that the number of persons by smoking and gambling status are the same in Tables 12.1b and 12.1c (black-bordered cells in those two sub-tables) and add up to the total number of gamblers and non-gamblers.

<u>Example</u>: An observational study of the hypothetical mentoring program for first-generation college students (e.g., Figure 12.4b or 12.4c) compared the graduation rate among students in the treatment group to the graduation rate among students in the comparison group who had the same level of academic preparation, as measured by SAT decile.

> **Stratification** by SAT decile created a **quasi-experiment** that eliminated **confounding** by that background characteristic, because, within each **stratum**, SAT scores were the same ("held constant"). Thus, stratification removed differences in academic aptitude as a possible explanation for observed differences in graduation rate between the groups. Of course, to be able to rule out confounding by controlling statistically for academic aptitude during analysis, researchers have aptitude data (e.g., SAT scores) on each of the participants.

In case-control studies, matching is another way to reduce spuriousness.

<u>Example</u>: By matching cases and controls based on educational attainment, the hypothetical case-control study of religiosity and hate crimes (see Chapter 3) makes it less likely that educational attainment could confound the association between religiosity and crime.

> Again, the study would need to have measures of the **potential confounder** (educational attainment) as well as the main **risk factor** (religiosity) and **outcome** (hate-crime incidence) of interest.

---

[1] Recall from Chapter 11 that "stratification" means looking separately at different subgroups in a population or sample—in this case, separate strata for gamblers and non-gamblers.

Table 12.1 Stratified Analysis to Assess Confounding

a: Bivariate analysis of lung-cancer prevalence (DV) by gambling status (IV)

	Number of people			Prevalence of lung cancer (%)
	No lung cancer	Lung cancer	Total	
Gambler	78	22	100	22%
Non-gambler	172	28	200	14%
Total	250	50	300	17%

b: Bivariate analysis of smoking status (confounder) by gambling status (IV)

	Number of people			Prevalence of smoking (%)
	Smoker	Nonsmoker	Total	
Gambler	60	40	100	60%
Non-gambler	40	160	200	20%
Total	100	200	300	33%

c: Stratified (three-way) analysis of lung-cancer prevalence (DV) by smoking (confounder) and gambling status (IV)

	Number of people			Prevalence of lung cancer (%)
	No lung cancer	Lung cancer	Total	
Gambler	78	22	100	22%
Smoker	42	18	60	30%
Nonsmoker	36	4	40	10%
Non-gambler	172	28	200	14%
Smoker	28	12	40	30%
Nonsmoker	144	16	160	10%
All	250	50	300	17%

Notes: IV: independent variable; DV: dependent variable.

Other, more advanced statistical techniques, such as multiple regression analysis, are able to take into account several potential confounders at once (Allison, 1999). See Chapter 13 for more on regression analysis.

Example: To estimate the effect of the mentoring program on graduation rate based on observational data (Figure 12.4b), researchers use a statistical method that takes into consideration students' high school grades, class rank, and SAT scores.

Multiple regression allows researchers to adjust statistically for those three measures of academic preparation that might **confound** *the association between program participation and graduation. That method estimates the difference in graduation rate between the mentoring and comparison groups,* **holding constant** *those three factors* simultaneously.

> Whenever possible, potential confounders or mechanisms for an association should be measured and included in the analysis of that association. Researchers should discuss whether they were able to remove the influence of those factors during their data collection or analysis, cite other studies of the associations between those factor(s) and the independent and dependent variables, and discuss the implications for their results. These steps will provide readers with the information they need to assess the extent to which results can be interpreted as nonspurious.

Random Sampling vs. Random Assignment

A common mistake involves confusing random sampling with random assignment. Although they both have the word "random" in their names, they refer to distinct aspects of study design. **Random sampling** refers to the procedure used to select study respondents from the population (Figures 11.3 through 11.6). It is intended to ensure **generalizability** of findings from the sample to the population from which it was drawn, otherwise known as **external validity** (see Chapter 11). However, external validity (representativeness) does not determine whether an observed association can be interpreted as causal.

Random assignment refers to situations in which the procedure used to determine which cases—among those already chosen to be in the study—are placed in the treatment group versus the control group is based on **randomization** (chance), thus avoiding self-selection (as in Figure 12.4a). Randomization is intended to ensure **internal validity**: that the groups to be compared are as similar as possible before the intervention (treatment) is administered. A purpose of random assignment is to strengthen the case that the intervention is the true cause of variation in the dependent variable. However, internal validity does not determine whether results can be generalized beyond the study sample.

In practice, very few studies include both random sampling and random assignment; thus, there is often a trade-off between the external validity (generalizability) and internal validity (ability to draw a causal inference) of any one study (see Figure 12.6).

Example: A psychology graduate student advertised on campus message boards to recruit participants for her thesis project. She randomly assigned half of those who signed up for the study into the experimental condition and half into a control condition.

> This study fits in the upper right-hand (lightly shaded) cell of Figure 12.6 (**random assignment** but *not* **random sampling**): Participants in the experiment were volunteers, *not* a random sample of the general population, so the study has poor **external** *validity*: the results cannot be generalized to people beyond those with traits similar to traits of the participants—in this case, students, faculty, and staff of that university. However, *randomization* into treatment and control groups enhanced **internal** *validity* (ability to interpret the association between the treatment and outcome as causal).

Figure 12.6 Random Sampling vs. Random Assignment

		Random <u>sampling</u> used to select cases?	
		Yes -> Sample represents population for question of interest.	No -> Sample does <u>not</u> represent population.
Randomization (random assignment) used to assign study subjects into treatment and control groups?	**Yes** -> Study is a true experiment.	• Cause-and-effect inferences are possible. (**Good** internal validity) • Can generalize results from sample to the population. (**Good** external validity)	• Cause-and-effect inferences possible for sample. (**Good** internal validity) • <u>Cannot</u> generalize findings from sample to population. (**Poor** external validity)
	No -> Study is observational.	• Can generalize results from sample to the population. (**Good** external validity) • <u>Cannot</u> draw inference about cause and effect. (**Poor** internal validity)	• <u>Cannot</u> draw causal inference. (**Poor** internal validity) • Can describe sample results but <u>cannot</u> generalize them to the population. (**Poor** external validity)

Source: Adapted with permission from Utts & Heckard (2014).

Example: Researchers selected participants for a pre-election poll using random sampling techniques, and they collected data on their occupation and attitudes about healthcare policy by means of a questionnaire.

> *This study fits in the lower left-hand (moderately shaded) cell of Figure 12.6 (**random _sampling_** but _not_ **random _assignment_**): Participants were chosen using techniques that ensured that the sample was representative of the voting-age population in that geographic area; therefore, the study findings can be generalized to that population (there is _good_ **external** validity). However, the study was **observational**: Occupation was _not_ assigned at random, allowing the possibility of confounding by educational attainment, age, or other characteristics (there is _poor_ **internal** validity).*

<u>Example</u>: A survey conducted via Twitter collected data about occupation and attitudes about healthcare policy from whoever chose to participate.

> *This study fits in the lower right-hand (darkly shaded) cell of Figure 12.6 (<u>neither</u> **random _sampling_** <u>nor</u> **random _assignment_**): Participants were volunteers and data were observational, so this study is weak on <u>both</u> internal and external validity. The results can be neither interpreted as cause and effect nor generalized to a specifiable population.*

- The combination of good internal validity and poor external validity characterizes many clinical trials, because they involve random assignment but <u>not</u> random sampling.

- The combination of good external validity and poor internal validity is true of many population-based sample surveys, because they involve random sampling but <u>not</u> random assignment.

- The combination of poor external and internal validity, unfortunately, characterizes any study that <u>did not use either</u> random sampling or random assignment.

> Random sampling and random assignment are two distinct aspects of study design. Random sampling is used to ensure <u>external</u> validity (representativeness of a sample), whereas random assignment (randomization) is intended to ensure <u>internal</u> validity (ability to assess cause and effect).

Implications of Causality for Quantitative Research

Assessing internal validity is an important step for any study whose results are intended to inform decisions, programs, or policies to affect the outcome under study—a key objective of many explanatory and evaluative studies. If confounding, bias, or reverse causation explains an observed correlation between variables, that association is <u>not</u> a good basis for policies or interventions aimed at changing the outcome, no matter how big the association appears to be! Put differently, if a study hasn't identified a true cause of a dependent variable, it won't matter how many resources are invested in changing that independent variable; doing so won't affect the outcome.

Example: If our goal is to reduce lung-cancer incidence, an anti-gambling program isn't likely to accomplish that objective. Rather, an anti-smoking intervention is the better choice.

*Gambling was associated with higher incidence of lung cancer only because both were elevated among smokers (Figure 12.2b). Because the relationship between gambling and cancer is **spurious**, changing the independent variable (gambling) won't affect the dependent variable (cancer). Instead, the **confounder** (smoking) is the true **cause** of cancer and, thus, is the appropriate intervention point.*

Unless a relationship between an independent and dependent variable can be plausibly shown to be causal, it should not be used as the basis for interventions intended to change the dependent variable (outcome) by manipulating that independent variable.

Research cannot definitively prove that a relationship between variables is causal. Rather, the best we can (and should!) do is assess the internal validity of a study: the extent to which information about a study's design and results supports the case that an observed association can be reasonably interpreted as cause and effect.

Research does not "prove" causality; it examines whether causality can be reasonably inferred from a particular research study, based on the study design and variables used. To aid in interpreting their results and how they can be applied, researchers should discuss strengths and weaknesses of the study design and their implications for inferring causality.

TERMS AND CONCEPTS

HIGHLIGHTS

- Knowing whether an association between an independent and dependent variable can be considered to be **cause-and-effect** affects how results of a study can be interpreted and applied. The ability of a study to provide evidence of causality is known as its **internal validity**.

- The main criteria for assessing causality are **empirical association**, **time order**, and **non-spuriousness**. All three of those criteria must be satisfied in order to establish causality, but none of them alone is sufficient. Of those criteria, only empirical association has to do with the size of the numeric results. The other criteria are determined by study design and data-collection methods.

- **Experimental studies** are stronger than **observational studies** at establishing whether an association is cause-and-effect, because experimental studies randomly assign cases into treatment and control groups, thus reducing the potential for confounding.

- For some topics, there may be ethical or practical issues that prevent experimental studies from being conducted. In such situations, careful consideration of the design of an observational study can be used to evaluate the extent to which its findings can be interpreted as causal.

- **Longitudinal designs** are stronger than **cross-sectional designs** at assessing causality, because time order of the independent and dependent variables can be specified.

- True experiments establish **time order** by measuring the outcome after the intervention. Observational studies that collect longitudinal data can also demonstrate time order of the independent and dependent variables.

- **Random assignment** is intended to ensure internal validity (the ability to assess cause and effect), whereas **random sampling** is used to ensure external validity (the representativeness of a sample).

- If **confounding**, **bias**, or **reverse causality** explains a correlation between an independent and a dependent variable (outcome), that association is not a good basis for policies or interventions aimed at changing the outcome.

RESEARCH TIPS

- Read the literature on the topic to become familiar with theories and findings of previous studies about
  o mechanisms linking the independent and dependent variables and
  o possible confounders.

- Consider whether researchers or their readers are interpreting a relationship as causal (e.g., as a way to identify a solution to a problem), and, if so, whether that inference is justified based on how aspects of their study do (or do not) satisfy each of the criteria for causality.

RECOMMENDED READINGS

Brynie, F. (2012, January 10). The placebo effect: How it works. *Brain Sense*. https://www.psychology today.com/us/blog/brain-sense/201201/the-placebo-effect-how-it-works

Chambliss, D. F., & Schutt, R. K. (2019). *Making sense of the social world: Methods of investigation* (6th ed., Chapter 6). SAGE.

Du Toit, G., Roberts, G., Sayre, P. H., Bahnson, H. T., Radulovic, S., Santos, A. F., Brough, H. A., Phippard, D., Basting, M., Feeney, M., Turcanu, V., Sever, M. L., Gomez Lorenzo, M., Plaut, M., &

Lack, G., for the LEAP Study Team. (2015). Randomized trial of peanut consumption in infants at risk for peanut allergy. *New England Journal of Medicine, 372*, 803–813. https://dx.doi.org/10.1056/NEJMoa1414850

Schneider, D., & Lilienfeld, D. E. (2015). *Lilienfeld's foundations of epidemiology* (4th ed., Chapter 4). Oxford University Press.

Utts, J., & Heckard, R. (2014). *Mind on statistics* (5th ed., Chapters 6 and 8). Cengage, Brooks Cole.

EXERCISES

Individual Exercises

Quantitative Reasoning in Everyday Life

1. Identify an association in "everyday life" that many people consider to be cause-and-effect. (a) Specify (i) which variable is hypothesized to be the independent variable (IV) and (ii) which is thought to be the dependent variable (DV). (b) Identify a possible mechanism linking them (e.g., how the IV could cause change in the DV). (c) Identify factors that might confound the relationship. (d) Design a hypothetical study to test the causality of the relationship, including (i) the nature of the treatment (intervention) and control conditions; (ii) the process by which cases would be assigned into those groups; (iii) the time structure of the experiment; and (iv) whether and how blinding would be used.

2. In the weekly Well section of *The New York Times* (https://www.nytimes.com/section/well), find a description of a study about how diet or exercise is associated with a health outcome. (a) State the topic under study, then (b) specify the phrase(s) in the article that provided you with the following information: (i) the time structure of the study, (ii) whether the study was observational or experimental, whether the *Times* article discussed (iii) other factors that might explain the observed pattern, and (iv) whether the results could be interpreted as cause and effect. (c) Discuss how you would (or would not) apply the findings of the study to your own health or wellness decisions and (d) why, based on criteria in this chapter and your work on the earlier parts of this exercise.

Interpreting Research

3. Answer the following questions for the data set you selected from the ICPSR Website (in Chapter 2, Exercise 3). Cite where on the Website or documentation you found information on whether the study was (a) observational or experimental and (b) cross-sectional or longitudinal.

4. Find and read an article from the research literature about a study to evaluate the effectiveness of a new vaccine against COVID-19. (a) Identify how the experiment

met (or did not meet) each of the criteria for assessing causality: (i) empirical association, (ii) time order, (iii) non-spuriousness, (iv) mechanism, and (v) dose-response. Specify the page and paragraph number where you found that information. (b) Discuss the internal validity of the study based on criteria in this chapter and your work on the earlier parts of this exercise.

Group Exercises

Quantitative Reasoning in Everyday Life

5. List the topics and reasons each of you did (or did not) think the results of the study described on the *New York Times* Well site applied to you personally, based on your work for Exercise 2.

6. Make a list of patterns in everyday life that could be due to <u>reverse</u> causation. For each: (a) identify the hypothesized independent variable and dependent variable, and (b) explain why the relationship illustrates reverse causation, referring to the mechanism linking the two phenomena. (c) Discuss how that reverse causation affects the way you would (or would not) interpret that relationship and apply it to your life.

Interpreting Research

7. Discuss the relationship between income and educational attainment, including (a) timing of when each of those variables was measured, (b) direction of causation, (c) possible confounding factors, and (d) possible mechanisms.

8. In DuToit et al. (2015) cited in this chapter, find information about (a) whether the article described the experimental and control conditions; (b) whether the study

used random assignment; (c) whether the authors discussed potential confounders and, if so, what they were; (d) whether blinding was used in the study, and why or why not; (e) whether the authors discussed whether their results could be interpreted as causal; and (f) to whom the authors generalized their results. Specify the page and paragraph number where you found that information. (g) Discuss whether you think that generalization was valid, and explain why or why not, based on criteria in this chapter and your work on the earlier parts of this exercise.

Planning Research

9. Design a hypothetical experimental study to test whether taking Ritalin before taking an exam improves students' performance. Specify (a) the nature of the treatment and control conditions, (b) how you would assign subjects to the treatment and control groups, (c) what you would measure at the pretest and posttest, (d) whether and how you would include blinding, and (e) why or why not.

10. (a) Describe an observational study to study the same relationship as in the previous exercise. (b) Identify factors that might affect the internal validity of your proposed study, including lists of (i) potential confounders and (ii) self-selection processes. (c) Discuss differences in the internal validity of the observational and experimental studies you designed and (d) the implications of those differences for which type of study you would trust when making decisions or recommendations about a possible strategy for improving performance on exams.

Uncertainty of Numeric Estimates

Learning Objectives

After reading this chapter, you will be able to do the following:

1. Define statistical uncertainty and why it is important for making sense of numbers.

2. Understand the basic concepts behind inferential statistics.

3. Recognize measures of uncertainty and how they are affected by sample size.

4. Distinguish between uncertainty and bias.

5. Understand the objectives behind statistical significance (hypothesis) testing.

6. List some disadvantages of traditional ways of reporting statistical significance.

7. Interpret results of bivariate and three-way inferential statistical tests.

Many quantitative studies are based on samples, which introduces uncertainty about the exact values of numeric estimates from those studies. As a consequence, an important aspect of making sense of quantitative research involves understanding what that uncertainty implies for interpreting and applying the results. In this chapter, I define the statistical meaning of "uncertainty" and explain why it arises for numeric estimates based on samples. I then explain what it means to draw an inference about a population from data on a sample, and I discuss how researchers measure the amount of uncertainty in numeric estimates. I then draw the distinction between uncertainty and bias. I provide an overview of the steps involved in traditional hypothesis testing, and I discuss some drawbacks of that approach to assessing and reporting statistical significance. Finally, I illustrate how to interpret results of bivariate and three-way inferential statistical tests.

If you are new to statistics, you might be relieved to hear that software can calculate all these statistics for you, so you might not have to crank through the formulas yourself! However, to be able to make sense of the resulting numbers, you must understand why inferential statistical tests are run and what the numeric results mean.

In this chapter, I aim to provide an intuitive explanation of the ideas behind statistical measures and tests so that when you run across them while reading about research results or analyzing data, you will recognize them as part of the process of dealing with uncertainty of numeric estimates. As this is not a statistics textbook, my treatment of these topics is necessarily short. Appendix C includes a brief summary of some of the more technical aspects of statistical significance testing, to help you relate the ideas in this chapter to material covered in most introductory statistics courses. See Vogt and Johnson's *Dictionary of Statistics & Methodology* (2011) for definitions of these concepts as they are used in the social sciences, and see a statistics textbook such as Salkind's *Statistics for People Who (Think They) Hate Statistics* (2016) or Utts and Heckard's *Mind on Statistics* (2014) for more detail about the derivation and use of the concepts and methods.

To convey how uncertainty affects the way we make sense of numbers, I introduce and illustrate concepts using the expected technical vocabulary. In Chapter 14, I demonstrate how to explain the results in more user-friendly language, which can help reinforce your grasp of the statistical concepts.

What Is Statistical Uncertainty?

As discussed in Chapters 5 and 11, many numeric facts are estimated based on a sample (subset) of cases rather than the full population of all cases. Using data from samples introduces **uncertainty** into those estimates because of variation in the samples drawn from that population, as I will explain and illustrate. Uncertainty means we can't be sure (certain) that a statistic estimated from a sample captures the <u>exact</u> value of that measure for the entire population. To convey that lack of precision, researchers provide information that expresses the degree of uncertainty attached to their numeric estimates. By definition, uncertainty and **precision** are inversely related to each other: The higher the uncertainty of an estimate, the lower the precision of that estimate—in other words, the less confident we can be about the exact numeric value we seek to measure.

> Estimates of numeric values for populations based on samples are associated with **uncertainty**. The higher the uncertainty, the lower the **precision** of an estimate.

<u>Example</u>: The 2015–16 National Health and Nutrition Examination Survey (NHANES) sample of about three thousand children can be used to estimate mean body mass index (BMI) for all 74 million children in the U.S. population at that time.

> *The true mean BMI in the population of <u>all</u> U.S. children could be higher, lower, or the same as the **estimate** of the mean calculated from the NHANES **sample**. NHANES reports include information on the extent of variation (**uncertainty**) around such estimates.*

Inferential Statistics

Descriptive statistics, which were covered in Chapter 10, pertain only to the sample of cases about which data have been collected. In contrast, **inferential statistics** involve using data from a sample to reach some conclusion (**inference**) about the characteristics of the <u>larger</u> population that a sample is intended to represent. As discussed in Chapter 5, the **population** is the entire set of elements about which inferences are to be made, and the **sample** is the subset of elements from whom data were collected. The number of cases in a population is denoted with a capital N, whereas the sample size is abbreviated with a lowercase n.

The value of a summary statistic such as a mean, proportion, or measure of association between two variables in a <u>population</u> is referred to as the **population parameter**. In research based on samples, the population parameter is unknown because data aren't available on the full population, so instead data from a sample are used to estimate that parameter. The estimate of that parameter based on a <u>sample</u> is referred to as a **sample statistic**, **sample estimate**, or **point estimate**.

Inferential statistics refer to the use of sample data to draw a conclusion about the characteristics of the larger population that the sample is intended to represent. The **population** is the entire set of elements about which inferences are to be made, and the **sample** is the subset of elements from whom data is collected. A **population parameter** is a numeric measure that characterizes a population, such as a measure of central tendency or an association between variables in that entire population. A **sample statistic**, also known as a **sample estimate** or **point estimate**, is the value of the statistic calculated based on a sample.

Sampling error estimates how a sample statistic is expected to differ from one randomly drawn sample to another. It refers to inaccuracies in inferences about a population that occur because the results are based on a sample rather than all elements in the population (Vogt & Johnson, 2011). The higher the sampling error, the lower the precision of the estimate and the greater the uncertainty about the value of that statistic. In other words, a large sampling error implies a greater chance that the sample statistic will differ substantially from the true value in the population.

> **Important:** Inferential statistics are based on the assumption that the sample is representative of the population in terms of the variables of interest. As discussed in Chapter 11, samples drawn using probability sampling methods (random sampling) are more likely to produce representative samples than those using non-probability methods such as convenience sampling and quota sampling. Therefore, conducting inferential statistics on data collected using <u>non</u>-probability sample methods is problematic, and care should be taken in applying those conclusions to the larger population.

Different samples drawn from a particular population will differ from each other due to random variation in which elements are included in each sample. This is known as **sampling variation**. Because different subsets of the population each include different sets of cases, sampling variation will lead to different estimates of the sample statistic.

<u>Example</u>: Figure 13.1 shows three random samples drawn from the same population. The Xs represent employed people, triangles represent unemployed people, and dots represent those who are not in the labor force. Each of the samples includes seven elements ($n = 7$). However, Sample 1 (circle with solid border) encompasses 4 Xs, 2 triangles, and 1 dot; Sample 2 (dashed border) captures 4 Xs (one of which also happened to be in Sample 1), 2 <u>different</u> triangles, and 1 <u>different</u> dot than those in

Figure 13.1   Repeated Random Samples From the Same Population

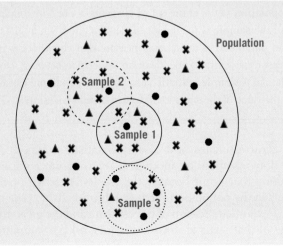

Sample 1. Sample 3 (dotted border) includes 3 Xs, 1 triangle, and 3 dots, none of which are shared with either of the other two samples.

*Although all three of the randomly selected **samples** are the same size (n = 7) and were drawn from the same **population**, the specific elements differ from one sample to another. **Sampling variation** implies that **sample statistics** about employment (such as the percentage unemployed) will vary from one sample to another due to random fluctuation in which elements of the population were included in each sample.*

Example: The sample statistic measuring average child height is likely to vary somewhat across different random samples drawn from the U.S. population.

***Sampling variation** reflects differences in estimates of mean height that arise, because different sets of children would be included in each randomly selected subset of the U.S. population.*

Sampling error is the numeric difference between the sample statistic and the population parameter. **Sampling variation** is the variation in a statistic across different samples drawn from the same population.

Figure 13.2 illustrates the relationship between the population parameter, sample estimate, sampling error, and sampling variation.

Figure 13.2 Relationship Between Population Parameter, Sample Statistic, Sampling Error and Sampling Variation

C: **Sampling error** = difference between population parameter and point estimate

E: Probability of observation

Mean height for all 8-year-old boys in U.S. population
A: **Population parameter**

Estimated mean height for 8-year-old boys based on NHANES sample
B: **Point estimate (sample statistic)**

Estimated mean height for 8-year-old boys based on repeated random samples from U.S. population
D: **Sampling variation**

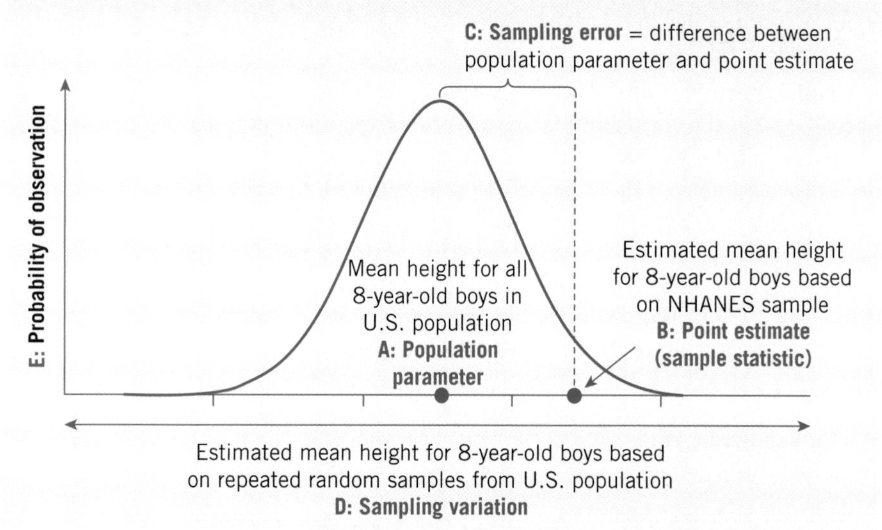

Example: An estimate of the mean height of all 8-year-old boys in the United States can be calculated based on data from the 2015–16 NHANES sample.

> The true value of mean height of _all_ 8-year-old boys in the United States is a **population parameter** (marked A in Figure 13.2). It is unknown, because it would be it would be very expensive and time-consuming to collect height information on all 2 million children in that age/gender group. Instead, data about the 121 boys in that age group in the 2015–16 NHANES **sample** were used to calculate a **point estimate** of mean height (marked B). The NHANES sample was drawn using a **probability sampling method** (CDC, 2018c), so it is appropriate to use inferential statistics to analyze those data.

> The _difference_ between the **population parameter** and the **sample statistic** is the **sampling error** (bracket C in Figure 13.2) for that specific value of the sample statistic. **Sampling variation** (D) in the estimate of mean height across different samples drawn from the same population is shown on the horizontal axis, with the **probability** of each point estimate (based on the true value in the population) plotted on the vertical axis (E). Different point estimates of the mean height (along the x-axis) would result in different values of the sampling error.

Measures of Uncertainty

Sampling variation means that there is uncertainty about how close an estimate from a given sample is to the true value in the population. There are several ways to quantify the extent of uncertainty associated with a sample statistic, including measures of variation around that estimate, calculation of a range of values associated with that estimate, and measures of how likely it is that the true value of the population parameter falls within that range.

Standard Error

A **standard error** is a measure of sampling error, quantifying the sampling variation around a sample statistic that arises due to random fluctuations across different samples from the same population. The smaller the standard error, the lower the uncertainty about the value of the population parameter. When reporting the standard error of a point estimate, the type of statistic is included in the name of that standard error, such as "standard error of the mean" or "standard error of the proportion." Standard errors are in the same units as the sample statistic: units of the original continuous variable for standard error of sample means; percentage points or proportion units for categorical variables.

> The **standard error** around a sample statistic is an estimate of the variation in that statistic from different random samples drawn from the same population.

Example: The mean height of 8-year-old boys in the 2015–16 NHANES was 132 cm, with a standard error of 0.73 cm.

> The **standard error of the mean** measures the extent of variation around the **point estimate** of mean height based on the NHANES sample. The **sample** mean cannot be interpreted as the <u>exact</u> value of the **population parameter** (mean height for <u>all</u> 8-year-old boys in the U.S. population), because of **sampling variation**.

Standard errors are affected by both the sample size and the extent of variation in the values of the estimate. For a given amount of variation, the larger the sample size on which the statistic is based, the smaller the standard error. This occurs because sample size is in the denominator of the standard error calculation for all types of sample statistics (whether means, proportions, or other statistics), and, by definition, the bigger the number we divide by, the smaller the result. (See Appendix C for more on how standard errors are calculated.) For a particular sample size, the wider the variation in the estimates of the sample statistic, the greater the standard error.

Standard errors are determined by the amount of variation in the point estimate and by the sample size.

- The greater the variation in the values of the sample statistic, the higher the standard error.

- The larger the sample size, the smaller the standard error.

Margin of Error and Confidence Level

Uncertainty around estimates from public opinion polls or surveys is often reported using the **margin of error**, which is a multiple of the standard error. The larger the margin of error, the more uncertainty about how close the sample statistic is to the population parameter. The size of the margin of error depends on the **confidence level** chosen by the researcher, specifying how likely it is that the true value of the population parameter falls within one margin of error on either side of the point estimate.

Although ideally researchers want to be very confident that the population parameter falls within the margin of error, the trade-off is that choosing a higher confidence level results in a wider margin of error. In other words, to increase the chance that the population parameter falls within the calculated margin of error, researchers have to be willing to tolerate a wider range of possible values for the statistic they seek to estimate. (See Appendix C for more details about how a margin of error is calculated.)

Figure 13.3   Margin of Error Around Election Poll Results

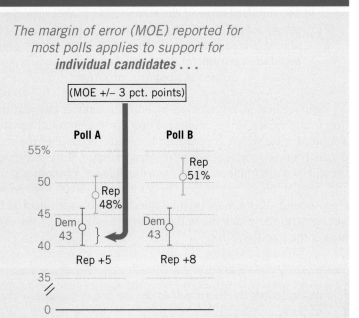

The margin of error (MOE) reported for most polls applies to support for **individual candidates** . . .

(MOE +/– 3 pct. points)

Poll A   **Poll B**

55%

50   Rep
                                      51%

          Rep
          48%

45
     Dem   Dem
      43   43

40

          Rep +5   Rep +8

35

0

Source: Mercer (2016).

Example: A newspaper reports that in Poll A, the percentage of voters who favor the Democratic candidate is 43% plus or minus 3 percentage points.

*Figure 13.3 portrays that uncertainty using vertical bars extending above and below the **point estimate** for the Democratic candidate (43%) by one **margin of error** (3 percentage points at the 95% confidence level) in each direction. In other words, the poll (**sample**) data suggest that the percentage of the entire voting **population** that supports the Democratic candidate is between 40% and 46% based on a 95% **confidence level**.*

The difference between the sample estimate and the population parameter is less than the margin of error about X% of the time, where X is the confidence level. With a confidence level of 95%, we conclude that the difference between the sample estimate and the population parameter is <u>smaller than</u> the margin of error about 95% of the time: in about 19 of every 20 estimates based on random samples drawn from the same population. Thus, the difference between the estimate based on the sample and the true value of that statistic for the overall population will <u>exceed</u> the margin of error only about 5% of the time, or in about 1 out of every 20 sample estimates.

A **margin of error** measures the precision of a sample estimate, calculated as a multiple of the standard error. A **confidence level** specifies how likely it is that the true value of the unknown population parameter falls within one margin of error on either side of the point estimate.

Like the standard error, the margin of error decreases with increasing sample size (see Figure 13.4).

Figure 13.4 Relationship Between Sample Size and Margin of Error

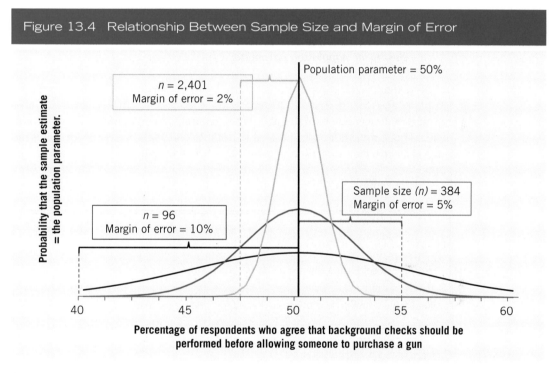

Source: Data created by Denise-Marie Ordway (2018) from Journalist's Resource. Reprinted with permission.

Example: A fictitious public opinion poll estimates that 50% of respondents agree that background checks should be performed before allowing someone to purchase a gun. The low, flat black curve in Figure 13.4 shows that if only 96 people were polled, the 95% confidence level margin of error around that estimate would be 10 percentage points (black bracket). That means that with such a small sample, we can be highly confident that the true population value is between 40% and 60% agreement with background checks (50% ± 10%)—a very wide range of values. If the sample size had been four times as large (n = 384), the margin of error would be cut in half, to 5 percentage points (blue bracket). If the sample had instead been 2,401 people, the margin of error would drop to 2 percentage points, allowing us to be 95% sure that the true value is between 48% and 52% (gray bracket)—a much more precise (less uncertain) estimate than that based on the smallest sample size in the diagram.

> *Each bell curve in Figure 13.4 shows the probability (on the y-axis) of each value of the **sample estimate** (on the x-axis). Each of those bell curves is centered on the **population parameter**: 50% of the entire voting population agrees with background checks. The **95% confidence level margin of error** declines substantially as the **sample size** (n) increases, as reported in the text boxes and illustrated by the successively narrower bell curves. As the sample size increases, the height of the bell curve's peak also rises, conveying the higher probability that the **sample estimate** falls close to the **population parameter**.*

Note that even for populations with millions of elements, a randomly selected sample of just two thousand elements can produce an estimate that is within a couple percentage points of the population parameter, with a high degree of confidence. This is crucial for social research, because collecting data on a few thousand cases is clearly far more affordable and feasible than collecting data on an entire population of millions (or even billions) of cases every time we want to answer a research question!

A representative sample of a few thousand cases yields a margin of error of less than 2%, implying that we can be highly confident that estimates based on those data are very close to the value for an entire population. Thus, well-conducted surveys based on randomly selected samples are a valuable approach to estimating statistics for a large population without sacrificing too much precision.

Confidence Intervals

As discussed, an estimate of a summary statistic based on data from a sample is a **point estimate**, so named because it is a single (one point) numeric estimate of the population parameter. To reflect the uncertainty of that estimate, researchers often calculate a **confidence interval** (abbreviated **CI**) around that point estimate. The confidence interval provides an **interval estimate**: the range (interval) of values within which the true population parameter falls, with the degree of confidence specified by the confidence level.

A confidence interval around a sample statistic is calculated as follows: point estimate ± margin of error. The bottom end of that range is called the <u>lower</u> **confidence limit** (**LCL**); the top end is called the <u>upper</u> **confidence limit** (**UCL**). Statistical software will calculate the confidence interval for an estimate—typically, based on a 95% confidence level unless the researcher specifies otherwise.

A **confidence interval** (**CI**) is a range of values calculated based on sample data that is likely to include the unknown value of a population parameter, with the confidence level specified by the researcher.

Confidence interval = sample estimate ± margin of error

The lower and upper values of a confidence interval are known as the **lower confidence limit** (**LCL**) and **upper confidence limit** (**UCL**).

LCL = point estimate − margin of error

UCL = point estimate + margin of error

The confidence interval spans the values between the LCL and the UCL.

Figure 13.5   Relationship Between Standard Error, Margin of Error, and Confidence Interval

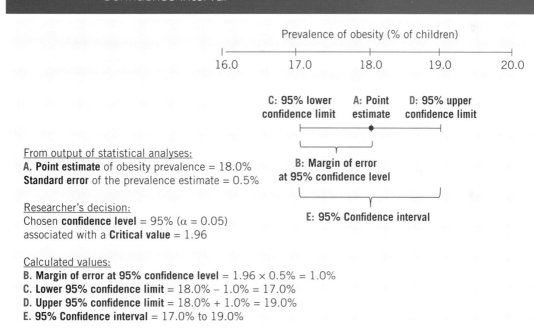

Notes: Weighted to population level using sampling weights provided by the Centers for Disease Control and Prevention (CDC, 2018c). Unweighted $n = 3,111$. See Appendix C for information about critical values.

Source: Author's calculations based on data from the 2015–16 U.S. National Health and Nutrition Examination Survey.

Example: The estimated prevalence of obesity among U.S. children based on the 2015–16 NHANES sample was 18.0%, with a margin of error of 1.0 percentage points. Thus, we can be 95% sure that the true prevalence of obesity among all U.S. children was between 17.0% and 19.0% (Figure 13.5).

*The **standard error** of the estimated child obesity rate from the NHANES sample is 0.5%. The associated **margin of error** with a **confidence level of 95%** = 1.0%, yielding a **95% confidence interval** around the **point estimate** of 18.0 ± 1.0, or 17.0% to 19.0%.*

Example: In Figure 13.3, the 95% confidence interval around the Republican estimate in Poll B is from 48% to 54%.

*With a **point estimate** of 51% and a **margin of error** of 3 percentage points, the **95% confidence interval** is 6 percentage points wide, from an LCL of 51% − 3% = 48% to a UCL of 51% + 3% = 54%.*

Confidence regions can be used to portray the interval estimate for trends.

Figure 13.6   Trend Line With Confidence Region

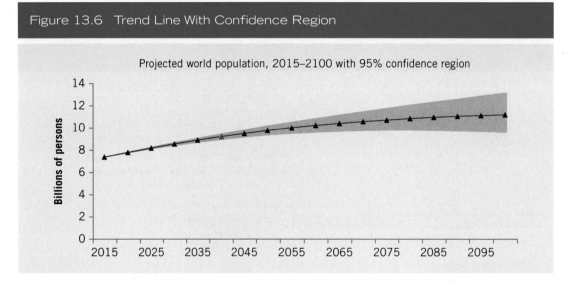

Projected world population, 2015–2100 with 95% confidence region

Source: Data from United Nations (2019).

Example: In 2015 (1 year after the most recent actual measurement used in the calculations), the confidence limits around the median projection of world population are almost indistinguishable from the point estimate (Figure 13.6). By the year 2100 (75 years after the initial projection date), the confidence interval around the median projection is very wide: from approximately 9.6 billion people to 13.2 billion.

*The shaded cone is the **95% confidence region** around the median projection line (**point estimate**). In 2015, the **upper and lower limits of the 95% confidence interval** (edges of the cone) are very close to the median projection, indicating <u>low</u> **uncertainty** of the estimate for that date. By the year 2100, the estimate is much more uncertain, with an **interval estimate** 3.6 billion people <u>wide</u> around the median projection* *(**point estimate** = 11 billion), revealing how even a small difference in the growth rate over a 75-year period can result in a large difference in projected population.*

> Standard errors, margins of error, and confidence intervals are common ways of conveying variation of sample statistics. The larger the standard error, the wider the confidence interval and, thus, the greater the uncertainty (and the lower the precision) of an estimate.

Criteria for Making Sense of Measures of Uncertainty

Table 13.1 summarizes criteria for making sense of measures of uncertainty for sample estimates, including whether and how the values of each of those measures are affected by units in which a variable is measured, its level of measurement, and the number of cases involved in the calculation. Like the standard error, the margin of error and confidence interval are measured in the same units as the associated sample statistic. Regardless of the variables involved in an analysis, a confidence level is specified in percentage units and, therefore, must fall between 0% and 100%. Sample size is inversely related to the standard error, margin of error, and confidence interval around an estimate, but it does <u>not</u> affect selection of a confidence level.

Important: If data for an <u>entire population</u> are analyzed, sampling error is 0, because the estimate is based on all the elements from the population; thus, the estimate equals the population parameter. In such situations, sampling variation is also 0, because only one "sample" was drawn: the entire population ($n = N$). Thus, for studies that analyze data for all the elements in a population, measures of uncertainty are by definition 0 and, thus, are not relevant to interpretation of the results.

> Standard errors, margins of error, and confidence intervals are each in the same units as the original variable; thus, criteria in Chapters 3, 4, and 5 for assessing plausibility for a particular topic, way of measuring, and context can be used to interpret those measures of uncertainty.

Uncertainty vs. Bias

Although random error and bias are both types of measurement error, they arise for different reasons and have different implications for making sense of numbers. **Random error**—a form of **uncertainty**—implies that chance fluctuation

Table 13.1　Criteria for Making Sense of Measures of Uncertainty

	Definitional limits on value	Affected by		
		Units of variables?	Level of measurement of variable(s)?	Sample size?
Confidence level	Must be between 0 and 100.0	No	No	No
Standard error	Must be positive	Same units as associated sample statistic[a]	Different formulas for measures related to continuous than categorical variables[b]	Inversely related to sample size
Margin of error				
Confidence interval = point estimate ± margin of error	Can span negative values, positive values, or a combination of negative and positive values		Through effect on standard error	

Notes:

a.　For continuous variables, measures of uncertainty will be in the same units as the original variable. For categorical variables, measures of uncertainty will be in percentage points or proportion units.

b.　Formulas for standard errors sample differ for continuous and for categorical variables. Consult a statistics textbook.

400

produces some numeric estimates that are higher and some that are lower than the true population values. The amount of random error in an estimate is affected by measurement **reliability** (see Chapter 4) and sample size. **Bias**, on the other hand, is a systematic error in which estimates are consistently wrong in the <u>same</u> direction. The extent of bias is affected by sampling procedures (which influence sample composition; see Chapter 11) and measurement **validity** (which influences accuracy with which specific variables are measured; see Chapters 4 and 11). Bias is <u>not</u> affected by sample size.

<u>Example</u>: Consider a hypothetical set of estimates of mean income based on a series of survey samples. Random error would lead to variation in those sample estimates around the true population mean, as in Figure 13.7a. The black circles are more widely dispersed than the gray circles, but both sets of estimates are centered on the true value ($30K), and both sets include values scattered to either side of the true value.

*Although the black set of circles exhibits more **random error** (higher **uncertainty**) than the gray (perhaps due to smaller sample size for the black set), both sets of estimates are **unbiased**. They could result from sampling and data-collection methods that yielded **representative** samples of the population. The variability across estimates could occur due to **sampling variation** or to **unreliable** (inconsistent) procedures to measure income.*

In Figure 13.7b, the gray circles are mostly to the left of the true population value (again, $30K), showing a tendency to systematically underestimate mean income. The black circles are all to the right of the true value—a consistent overstatement of income.

Figure 13.7 Distinction Between a. Random Error and b. Bias

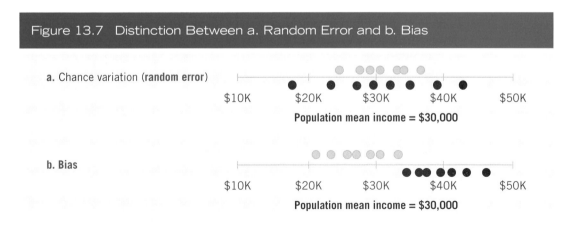

Note: Each circle represents a point estimate of mean income from one sample.

*Both sets in Figure 13.7b exhibit **bias**: The gray circles portray <u>downward</u> **bias**, which could occur if the sampling and data-collection methods produced samples that underrepresented higher-income households (**sampling bias**) or if respondents understated their incomes (**measurement bias**). The black circles depict <u>upward</u> **bias** that could arise if lower-income households were underrepresented in the sample or if respondents exaggerated how much they earned.*

The extent of **random error** in a sample statistic is affected by sample <u>size</u> and measurement <u>reliability</u>. The extent of **bias** is affected by the degree to which sample <u>composition</u> reflects population composition (representativeness or <u>external validity</u>) and by <u>measurement validity</u>.

Basics of Hypothesis Testing

To acknowledge the uncertainty associated with numeric estimates based on samples, the field of statistics developed a set of procedures called **hypothesis testing**, also known as **statistical significance testing**. Hypothesis testing consists of the following steps:

1. Write a hypothesis.

2. Calculate the statistical estimate and find the associated *p*-value.

3. Specify a significance level.

4. Assess statistical significance based on the *p*-value.

The objective of this section is to help you learn to identify and interpret the relevant numeric information to arrive at a conclusion about statistical significance, whether you are interpreting others' work or conducting statistical analysis yourself. If you are reading about others' statistics, their tables or text should include the numbers you need to see how they came to a conclusion about the results of their hypothesis tests. If you are estimating statistics using an electronic data set, you can program the software to calculate the information you need for Step 2; see Chapter 10 for information on how to identify the type of statistical test that suits the levels of measurement of your variables.

The explanations of hypothesis testing in this section are written for readers who have not yet have had a statistics course. For students who have already taken a statistics course, Appendix C provides more details about the logical and mathematical steps involved in inferential statistics and hypothesis testing, to help tie the "uncertainty" framing from this book to conventional ways of explaining statistical methods.

Step 1: Write a Hypothesis

The first step in statistical significance testing is to state the research question as a **hypothesis**, putting it into a form that can be tested using statistical methods. A hypothesis can be about the value of a summary statistic pertaining to one variable (a univariate statistic), or it can be about a measure of association between independent and dependent variables (bivariate or multivariate) (see Chapter 10).

Everyday use of the term "hypothesis" refers to an "educated guess" about the pattern under study; however, in research, a hypothesis is developed more formally. A hypothesis should be based on theory about the topic of interest and informed by results of previous studies of that phenomenon (Ghose, 2013).

> Example: In the evaluation of a "boot camp" to teach prospective applicants for a microloan program how to plan a 2-year budget for their proposed business, researchers conduct an experiment to test whether that training increases the percentage of businesses that remain in operation at the end of that period. Half of the applicants are randomly assigned to receive the budget training (the treatment group); the other half receive no special training or assistance (the control group). Researchers hypothesize that those who participate in the boot camp will be more likely than those who did not undertake that training to remain in business 2 years later.
>
> *The **independent variable** classifies whether each microloan applicant was in the treatment or the control group, and the **dependent variable** measures success or failure of the business. This **hypothesis** predicts the direction of the association between the independent and dependent variables; see Appendix C for more about directional hypotheses and Chapter 12 for a review of experimental design.*

Hypothesis testing, also known as **statistical significance testing**, uses data from a sample to assess whether a hypothesis about the value of the population parameter is supported or refuted by the data.

A **hypothesis** is a statement about the expected value of a sample statistic that can be tested using statistical methods.

Step 2: Obtain a *p*-Value

A sample statistic, such as a mean or measure of association, is calculated from the sample data and is reported along with the associated *p*-value. The **p-value** is the probability of obtaining a result at least as large as the sample statistic if the true population value (the population parameter) is equal to 0 ("no effect"; also called the **null** value). Appendix C provides more detail about the null value for different types of numeric comparisons and the steps involved in obtaining a *p*-value for an inferential statistical test.

Step 3: Specify the Significance Level

The next step in hypothesis testing is to select the **significance level** (α), which is the probability of <u>incorrectly</u> concluding that the population parameter is <u>not</u> equal to 0, based on the estimate from the sample. The significance level is equal to (100 – the **confidence level**) ÷ 100. Thus, the higher the confidence level, the lower the significance level. A significance level of .05 is the conventional cutoff for assessing statistical significance and is the default setting for most statistical software.

> <u>Example</u>: If a researcher selects a 95% confidence level, the corresponding significance level = .05.
>
> *The **significance level** associated with a **95% confidence level** is calculated as follows: (100 – 95) ÷ 100 = .05. It corresponds to accepting a 5% risk of <u>falsely</u> concluding that the **population parameter** is <u>not</u> equal to 0.*

Step 4: Assess Statistical Significance Using the *p*-Value

In a twist of reasoning that many people find confusing, the next step involves trying to <u>reject</u> the "no effect" hypothesis by posing the question "If the true value of the statistic in the <u>population</u> is 0, how likely would it be to obtain a value as large as, or larger than, the one observed in the <u>sample</u>?" To assess whether the probability of the sample estimate is as likely as, more likely than, or less likely than would be expected by chance, the calculated *p*-value is compared to the chosen significance level. If the *p*-value is less than the significance level, we conclude that the result is **statistically significant** (McLeod, 2019). In other words, a statistically significant result is one that has a very low probability (*p*-value) that the sample estimate could be as big as it is solely due to chance associated with how the sample was drawn.

To paraphrase Utts and Heckard (2014, p. 465):

> The logic of statistical hypothesis testing is similar to the "presumed innocent until proven guilty" principle of the U.S. judicial system. In hypothesis testing, we assume that the "nothing is happening" (e.g., no relationship between the independent and dependent variables) hypothesis is a possible truth until the sample data conclusively demonstrate otherwise. The "something is happening" hypothesis is chosen only when the data show that we can reject the "nothing is happening" hypothesis.

In a criminal trial, the standard of evidence is "beyond a reasonable doubt" (Hill & Hill, 2020), which is consistent with a 95% confidence level: high, but not 100% certain. In other words, although it is tempting to say that we have "proven" that a hypothesis is true, we cannot come to that firm of a conclusion because of the uncertainty attached to estimates based on samples. Likewise, we cannot definitively say that a hypothesis is false based solely on the p-value. Instead, researchers test a hypothesis and interpret their results in terms of whether those results support (or refute) a hypothesis at the selected level of significance. Put differently, the hypothesis-testing approach reflects that when sample data are used, there is always a chance of arriving at an incorrect inference about population parameter based on the value of the sample statistic. (See Type I and Type II errors in Appendix C).

A **p-value** is the probability of obtaining a result at least as large as the sample statistic if the population parameter is equal to 0. A **significance level** is selected by the researcher to express the level of risk they are willing to tolerate of concluding that the population parameter is not 0 when its true value is 0. Significance level = (100 − confidence level) ÷ 100. A **statistically significant** result is one for which the p-value calculated based on sample data is less than the chosen significance level.

Example: Based on the 2015–16 NHANES sample, mean body mass index (BMI) for 2-to-17-year-old children was 2.1 kg/m² lower among those who watched less than 1 hour of TV per day than among those who watched 4 or more hours per day. That difference in mean BMI across TV-watching groups was statistically significantly different from 0, at $p < .001$.

> The **sample estimate** of the mean difference in BMI by amount of daily TV-watching is associated with a **p-value** of .001, well below the **threshold for statistical significance** (significance level = .05). Therefore, with a very high degree (95%) of confidence, we reject the idea that there is no difference in children's BMI according to how much time they watched TV.

Example: In the 2015–16 U.S. NHANES sample of children aged 2 to 17 years, mean BMI for boys was 20.0 kg/m², versus 20.3 kg/m² for girls; $p = .29$.

> Comparing the **p-value** for the sample estimate against the **significance level**, .29 > .05, we conclude that the observed gender difference in mean BMI in the sample could be explained by sampling variation (chance) alone. In other words, that difference is not **statistically significant at the .05 level**.

Use of Confidence Intervals for Hypothesis Testing

Confidence intervals can also be used to assess statistical significance of differences in values of the dependent variable across values of an independent variable.

Statistical software will calculate confidence intervals for you, so the key thing to understand is how to interpret confidence intervals to evaluate the statistical significance of differences between two or more estimates.

Example: Figure 13.3 shows results of two hypothetical polls, each of which has a 3% margin of error. In Poll A (left-hand side of the figure), the 95% confidence interval (95% CI) for the percentage of all voters in favor of the Democratic candidate is 40% to 46%. The corresponding 95% confidence interval for the percentage who support the Republican is 45% to 51%. The confidence intervals for the two candidates overlap; thus, the poll results suggesting a Republican lead aren't very reassuring to members of that party.

*The 95% **confidence intervals** for <u>both</u> candidates include the range of values from 45% to 46%. As a consequence, there is a chance that the percentages of the <u>population</u> supporting each of the two candidates are <u>equal</u>, or even that support for the Democrat exceeds support for the Republican. For instance, the Democrat could have 46% and the Republican 45% based on the margin of error for Poll A. Therefore, we <u>cannot</u> conclude based on the poll (**sample**) results that the Republican candidate is leading in the **population**; that candidate's apparent lead could be solely due to **random error** (**sampling variation**). In other words, based on Poll A, the difference between the levels of support for those two candidates is <u>not</u> **statistically significant**, at* **p < .05**.

For Poll B, however, the 95% confidence intervals are 40% to 46% for the Democratic candidate and 48% to 54% for the Republican (right-hand side of Figure 13.3). Thus, the Republican can breathe a sigh of relief that the poll's estimate of her advantage over the Democrat probably reflects a genuine lead among <u>all</u> voters.

*The entire **95% confidence interval** for the Republican candidate is above that for the Democratic candidate, so her campaign manager can conclude with **95% confidence** that the Republican is leading in the entire **population** of voters, based on the **sample** data from Poll B. The level of support for the Republican candidate is **statistically significantly** higher than that for the Democratic candidate; p < .05. The word "probably" conveys that we <u>cannot</u> be completely sure of the inference about the population based on the sample data.*

To summarize, the hypothesis-testing process includes a mixture of tasks that must be conducted by the researcher and those that can be done by a computer. A human being must write the hypothesis, decide on a significance level, and assess statistical significance (Steps 1, 3, and 4), using information on the *p*-value provided by statistical software or extracted from someone else's research results (Step 2). However, even the calculations that the computer will conduct require correct instructions from the researcher—therefore, it is important to understand the logic behind each step of testing a hypothesis, as well as criteria for making sense of the resulting numeric information.

Criteria for Making Sense of Hypothesis-Testing Results

Table 13.2 presents criteria for making sense of numeric results of hypothesis tests. Significance levels and p-values must fall between 0 and 1 and are inversely related to sample size, no matter what topic is being studied and no matter where, when, or how the data were measured.

Table 13.2 Criteria for Making Sense of Hypothesis Test Results

			Affected by	
	Definitional limits on value	Units of variables?	Level of measurement of variable(s)?	Sample size?
p-value	Must be between 0.0 and 1.0	No	No	Yes, through effect on standard error
Significance level = (100 − confidence level) ÷ 100				No

Example: When the confidence level is set at 95%, the standard threshold for statistical significance is $p < .05$ whether the hypothesis concerns changes in voter-participation rates between the 2016 and 2020 presidential elections or differences in average BMI by social class in India in 2015.

> Significance level and p-values are in completely different units and levels of values than the sample estimates to which they pertain. Thus, the criteria for assessing the plausibility of hypothesis-testing results do not depend on the topic or context; rather, they are determined by the sample size, the level(s) of measurement of the variables, and other aspects of inferential statistical test (see Appendix C).

Drawbacks of Traditional Hypothesis Testing

Although applications of inferential statistics to social science and other research have a long history, over the past few decades statisticians have debated the appropriateness of traditional hypothesis testing in which the results are reported as either "statistically significant" or "not statistically significant" (Ziliak & McCloskey, 2008). They call attention to the fact that despite its widespread use, the choice of $p < .05$ (a 95% confidence level) is an arbitrary convention that has led to incorrect or misleading interpretation of statistical test results.

In a 2019 article in the journal *Nature* that was signed by more than 800 leading statisticians, Amrhein et al. called for a "stop to the use of *P* values in the conventional, dichotomous [yes/no] way—to decide whether a result refutes or supports the null hypothesis" [usually of a value of 0 for the population parameter; see Appendix C]. Instead, they recommended reporting and interpreting an interval estimate as a way of conveying the uncertainty of numeric estimates. Further, they encouraged replacing the term **confidence interval** with **compatibility interval**, to reflect the fact that any of the values within that interval are compatible (consistent) with the data used to calculate the estimate and that, therefore, focusing on just one particular value (such as 0) in that interval can be deceptive. However, they emphasized that the point estimate is the most compatible with those data and that values near the point estimate are more compatible than those near the upper or lower compatibility limit.

> Statisticians have recommended using the term "**compatibility interval**" as a replacement for the term "**confidence interval**." Any value within a confidence interval is <u>compatible</u> (consistent) with the data from the sample used to produce that estimate, given the specified confidence level.

In addition, Amrhein and colleagues (2019) pointed out that classifying results into "statistically significant" versus "<u>not</u> statistically significant" has led to several misleading practices. First, statistically significant estimates are <u>biased upward</u> in magnitude, because, for a given-sized standard error, the confidence interval around a high point estimate is less likely to include the null [no difference] value than the confidence interval for a lower point estimate. Conversely, non–statistically significant results are <u>biased downward</u> in magnitude. In combination with the historical bias in favor of statistically significant results based on the conventional $p < .05$ cutoff, the use of a yes/no approach to conveying conclusions about statistical significance leads to an upward bias in the effect sizes that are reported in the published literature, often referred to as **publication bias**.

Figure 13.8   Interpreting Compatibility Intervals Around Point Estimates

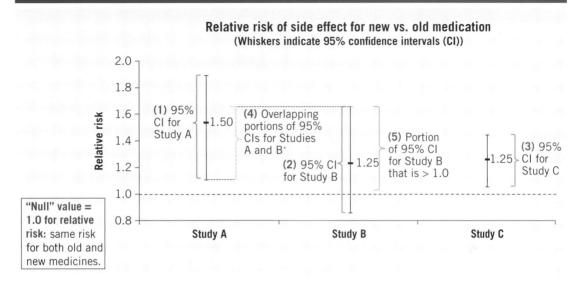

Relative risk of side effect for new vs. old medication
(Whiskers indicate 95% confidence intervals (CI))

*Bracket **(4)** encompasses values between the <u>lower</u> 95% confidence limit (CL) (shown with light dashed line) for Study A through the <u>upper</u> 95% CL for Study B, which comprises the overlapping portions of their respective 95% CIs.

<u>Example</u>: Study A estimated that patients taking a new medication were 1.5 times as likely to experience a particular side effect as those who took an established medication for that health condition. Study B attempted to replicate that result with a different sample of patients, obtaining a relative risk of 1.25. Both studies estimated a standard error of 0.2.

*The 95% **confidence intervals** for Study A's and Study B's estimates were the same width (± 0.39), shown with Brackets (1) and (2) in Figure 13.8. However, the confidence interval for Study B <u>overlapped</u> the "no difference" value (relative risk of 1.0 for those on the new vs. old medication),[1] but the confidence interval for Study A did not. When the researchers submitted their findings to a peer-reviewed journal that publishes only statistically significant results, only Study A was accepted for publication. Thus, despite the fact that the extent of uncertainty around the two estimates was identical, the higher **point estimate** of the relative risk became part of the published literature, but the lower point estimate was omitted, resulting in **publication bias** that favored larger **effect sizes**.*

---

[1]Recall from Chapter 9 that a relative risk of 1.0 corresponds to equal risk in the two groups being compared. the "null" value of no difference between groups.

A second problem occurs when effect size is interpreted solely based on whether it meets conventional cutoffs for statistical significance.

Example: Studies B and C both obtained point estimates of 1.25 for the relative risk of developing the side effect of the medication. However, the 95% confidence interval for Study C (Bracket 3 in Figure 13.8) was narrower than that for Study B (Bracket 2) and did not overlap the dashed black line (indicating a relative risk of 1.0). Study C researchers concluded that the drug increased the chances of experiencing that side effect, whereas Study B researchers interpreted their finding as showing that the drug did not increase that risk and stated that their finding contradicted that of Study C.

*The relative risk **point estimates** were identical for Studies B and C, and a substantial part of their 95% confidence intervals overlapped, so it is misleading to imply that their findings were not consistent with each other. Confidence intervals for both studies spanned values greater than the "no difference "value (Bracket 5); thus, both Studies B and C are **compatible** with the conclusion that the new drug is associated with a higher risk of the side effect than the old drug. Thus, although Study B is also **compatible** with no difference in the risk of side effects for the new and old medications because its confidence interval overlaps a relative risk of 1.0, it is incorrect to interpret Study B as definitively showing "no effect."*

Classifying numeric research results as either statistically significant or not statistically significant based on criteria like $p < .05$ can lead to

- incorrect conclusions about whether there is a null effect,

- upward biases based solely on published effect sizes (**publication bias**), or

- misleading conclusions about differences in results across studies based solely on statistical significance.

To minimize these problems, when presenting inferential statistical results, researchers should report the interval estimate (**compatibility interval**) along with the **point estimate** and interpret the direction and size of the point estimate as well as information about uncertainty of that estimate.

Interpreting Inferential Statistics for Bivariate and Three-Way Procedures

In this section, I cover how to apply and interpret inferential statistical tests for different types of bivariate and three-way procedures, building on Chapter 10's discussion of selecting a statistical method to suit the levels of measurement of the independent and dependent variables. To integrate concepts related to uncertainty and hypothesis testing, I will use technical wording in the examples. In Chapter 14, I show how to convey those ideas in language that does not require familiarity with the details involved in the statistical procedures. Several of the illustrative examples involve the use of sampling weights, which are explained in Appendix B.

Bivariate Statistical Results

Correlation

To review, an association between two continuous variables is measured by their correlation coefficient (r). Statistical significance is assessed by comparing the p-value against the chosen significance level. Results of correlations among all possible pairs of several continuous variables can be summarized into one table, called a **correlation matrix**. A correlation matrix will have one row <u>and</u> one column for each variable. The **correlation coefficient** (r) between any pair of variables is reported in the interior cell at the intersection of the pertinent row and column, along with the p-value for that correlation. Each correlation coefficient in the table is **bivariate**, because it measures how those two variables are associated with one another <u>without</u> taking into account their association with other variables in the table.

In a correlation matrix, variables are listed in the same order left to right in the columns and top to bottom in the rows; thus, the **diagonal cells** contain the correlation of each variable with itself. A p-value does not pertain to the diagonal cells, because the correlation coefficients in those cells are <u>not</u> sample statistics (estimates): by definition, a variable is perfectly correlated with itself ($r = 1.0$).

A **correlation matrix** presents **correlation coefficients** between pairs of variables organized in the rows and columns of the matrix (table). **Diagonal cells** in a correlation matrix show the correlation between each variable and itself, which is by definition = 1.0: a perfect correlation.

<u>Example</u>: Table 13.3 shows pairwise correlations among four continuous variables based on data from the 2015–16 NHANES sample of 2-to-17-year-old children: family income-to-poverty ratio (IPR),[2] family size, height-for-age percentile, and BMI percentile-for-age (BMIP).

---

[2]IPR = family income divided by the Federal Poverty Level for a family of that size and age composition.

Table 13.3 Bivariate Correlations Among Continuous Variables

Correlations among family sociodemographic characteristics, height-for-age, and BMI-for-age, Children Aged 2 to 17 Years, 2015–16 NHANES

Characteristic	Pearson Correlation Coefficient (r) [p-value]			
	Family income-to-poverty ratio (IPR)	Family size	Height-for-age percentile	BMI-for-age percentile (BMIP)
Family income-to-poverty ratio (IPR)	1.0 NA			
Family size	−0.160 [<.0001]	1.0 NA		
Height-for-age percentile	0.054 [.02]	−0.036 [.13]	1.0 NA	
BMI-for-age percentile (BMIP)	−0.131 [<.0001]	−0.025 [.43]	0.210 [<.0001]	1.0 NA

Source: Author's calculations based on data from the 2015–16 U.S. National Health and Nutrition Examination Survey.

Notes:

Unweighted n = 3,115.

Weighted to population level using sampling weights provided by the Centers for Disease Control and Prevention (CDC, 2018a).

IPR and BMIP are negatively correlated with one another ($r = -.131$), meaning that, as family income increases, BMIP decreases. The associated p-value is $< .0001$, indicating that the association is highly unlikely to be due to chance. Although family size is also inversely correlated with BMIP ($r = -.025$), that correlation is not statistically significantly different from 0 ($p = .43$).

> The four variables are organized from left to right in the **columns** of the **correlation matrix** in the same order they are listed from top to bottom in the **rows**. The **correlation coefficient** between IPR and BMIP, along with the **p-value** for that estimate, is at the intersection of the shaded row (for BMIP) and column (for IPR) in the black-bordered interior cell. Correlations of BMIP with <u>each</u> of the other three variables are in the **row** labeled "BMI-for-age percentile," while correlations between family IPR and each of the other three variables are in the **column** for family IPR.

Cross-Tabulation

A **cross-tabulation** shows how the distribution of a categorical dependent variable varies across categories of the independent variable, with statistical significance assessed by a chi-square (X^2) test.

> <u>Example</u>: The obesity rate among children in the 2015–16 NHANES declined from 22.7% among children from the lowest-income families, to 20.6% in the next-lowest income group, to 17.0% in the moderate-income group, and to 12.9% in the highest-income group (Table 13.4). With a p-value $< .001$, that large of a difference in obesity rates across income groups has less than a 0.1% chance of being due to random sampling alone.

>> A **cross-tabulation** was used to test whether obesity differed across levels of the categorical (ordinal) measure of family income. Obesity is a **dichotomous** (two-category) dependent variable; thus, only the percentage that fall into the category of interest (obese) needs to be presented (see Chapter 6). A footnote to the table reports the **p-value** used to assess **statistical significance**. The second sentence conveys the very small probability that the conclusion about the hypothesis is incorrect, reinforcing the idea that the hypothesis has <u>not</u> been definitively (100%) proven.

When a dependent variable is **multichotomous** (has more than two categories), a table or chart must report the percentages that fall into each of the categories, to convey the overall pattern.

Table 13.4   Bivariate Prevalence by an Ordinal Independent Variable

Prevalence of Obesity by Family Income Group, Children Aged 2 to 17 Years, 2015–16 U.S. NHANES		
Family income group (unweighted *N*)	Weighted % of sample	% obese
All income levels (*n* = 3,111)	100.0	18.1
Free lunch eligible (*n* = 1,155)	27.1	22.7
Reduced price lunch eligible (*n* = 703)	19.2	20.6
Moderate income (*n* = 682)	26.3	17.0
High income (*n* = 571)	27.4	12.9

Source: Author's calculations based on data from the 2015–16 U.S. National Health and Nutrition Examination Survey.

Notes:

Weighted to population level using sampling weights provided by the Centers for Disease Control and Prevention (CDC, 2018a).

Free lunch eligible, < 130% of Federal Poverty Level (FPL); reduced price lunch eligible, 130%–184% of FPL; moderate income, 185%–349% of FPL; high income, 350% + of FPL.

Obesity: BMI >= 95th percentile for age.

Unweighted *n* = 3,115.

Pearson X^2 = 22.8 with 3 degrees of freedom; p < .001 based on a one-sided (directional) test; see Appendix C.

Example: Free-lunch-eligible (low family income) children in the United States were twice as likely as those from high-income families to be in the highest TV-watching group (20% vs. 10%) and somewhat less likely to be in the lowest TV-watching group (34% vs. 47%; Table 13.5). The difference in the distribution of TV-watching by income group was statistically significant, at p < .001.

The NHANES classified TV/video watching time into three categories: 0–1 hours per day, 2–3 hours per day, and 4+ hours per day—making it a **multichotomous ordinal dependent variable***. By including* **columns** *for those three TV-watching levels, the table reveals that all the action is in the highest and lowest time categories; there is very little variation in percentages in the middle TV-watching category by income range (***ordinal independent variable***, shown in the* **rows***).*

Difference in Means or ANOVA

An association between a categorical independent variable and a continuous dependent variable can be assessed using a **difference in means** (for a two-category independent variable) or an **ANOVA** (**AN**alysis **O**f **VA**riance, for independent

Cross-Tabulation of Multi-category Independent and Dependent Variables

Daily TV/Video Watching by Family Income Group, Children Aged 2 to 17 Years, 2015–16 NHANES				
	% of income group			
	Hours/day watched TV or videos			
Family income group (% of FPL)	<1	2–3	4+	Unweighted *n*
All income levels	38%	45%	17%	3,104
Free lunch eligible (< 130%)	34%	46%	20%	1,159
Reduced price lunch eligible (130%–184%)	38%	44%	18%	702
Moderate income (185%–349%)	37%	47%	16%	673
High income (350%+)	47%	43%	10%	570

Source: Author's calculations based on data from the 2015–16 U.S. National Health and Nutrition Examination Survey.

Notes:

Weighted to population level using sampling weights provided by the Centers for Disease Control and Prevention (CDC, 2018a).

FPL: Federal Poverty Level.

Pearson X^2 = 24.8 with 6 degrees of freedom. p-value < .001.

variables with at least three categories; see Chapter 10); *t-statistics* and *F*-statistics are used to evaluate the statistical significance of difference in means and ANOVA procedures, respectively.

Example: In the 2015–16 NHANES child sample, mean BMI was positively associated with time spent watching TV or videos, rising from 19.6 kg/m² among those watching up to 1 hour/day to 19.9 kg/m² among those watching 2 or 3 hours per day, to 21.7 kg/m² among those watching 4+ hours per day (Table 13.6). The difference in mean BMI between the highest TV-watching group and the two lower groups was statistically significant at $p < .05$ as denoted by the asterisk next to the mean value in the row for the 4+ hours per day group. However, the difference in mean BMI between the two lower groups was not statistically significant (no asterisk for the 2–3 hours per day group).

*An **ANOVA** was conducted to assess whether the **mean value of the continuous dependent variable** (BMI, in kg/m²) varied across categories of the **ordinal independent variable** (TV/video-watching time per day, classified into three ranges). A **95% confidence interval** for*

Table 13.6   ANOVA Results

Mean Body Mass Index (BMI) by Hours/Day of TV and Video Watching, Children Aged 2 to 17 Years, United States, 2015–16					
				95% confidence interval	
Hours of TV or video watching per day	Unweighted *N*	Mean BMI (kg/m²)	Standard error of the mean	Lower 95% CL	Upper 95% CL
0 to 1	1,162	19.6	0.19	19.3	20.0
2 or 3	1,386	19.9	0.25	19.4	20.4
4 or more	517	21.7*	0.28	21.2	22.3
All	3,111	20.1	0.18	19.8	20.5

*Denotes difference compared to 0 to 1 hours/day is statistically significant, at $p < .05$.

Source: Author's calculations based on data from the 2015–16 U.S. National Health and Nutrition Examination Survey.

Notes:

Weighted to population level using sampling weights provided by the Centers for Disease Control and Prevention (CDC, 2018a). Unweighted $n = 3,111$.

F-statistic = 28.93 with 2 degrees of freedom; $p < .001$.

> *the **point estimate of the mean** for each group is reported in the table, along with the **standard error of the mean** from which it was calculated. Interpretation of the asterisk (*) is explained in a **footnote** to the table.*

Three-Way Associations

As discussed in Chapter 10, three-way associations are used to examine whether the relationship between one independent and one dependent variable differs according to values of a second independent variable. Two common types of three-way associations are three-way cross-tabulations and two-way ANOVAs.

Three-Way Cross-Tabulations

If all three variables are categorical, a **three-way cross-tabulation** shows how the distribution of the dependent variable differs for each combination of the two categorical independent variables. Any of those variables can be either nominal or ordinal, and any of them can be either dichotomous or multichotomous.

> A **three-way cross-tabulation** shows the relationship between two categorical independent variables and a categorical dependent variable.

Table 13.7   Three-Way Cross-Tabulation

Prevalence of Obesity (%) by Income Group and TV/Video-Watching, Children Aged 2 to 17 Years, 2015–16 U.S. NHANES					
	Average hours/day watching TV or video				*p*-value for difference across TV within income group
Income group	<= 1 (*n* = 1,162)	2 to 3 (*n* = 1,386)	4 or more (*n* = 517)	All (*n* = 3,065)	
Free lunch eligible (*n* = 1,145)	24.2	22.0	21.0	22.5	.31
Reduced price lunch eligible (*n* = 690)	15.9	19.6	34.9	20.7	*.0003*
Moderate income (*n* = 665)	10.1	19.6	26.6	16.9	*.0019*
High income (*n* = 565)	11.4	13.6	26.6	13.0	.22
All	14.9	18.7	24.9	18.1	*.0001*
p-value for difference across income groups within TV[a]	*< .0001*	*.024*	.05	*< .0001*	NA

a. Based on a one-sided (directional) test; see Appendix C.

Source: Author's calculations based on data from the 2015–16 U.S. National Health and Nutrition Examination Survey.

Notes:

Weighted to population level using sampling weights provided by the Centers for Disease Control and Prevention (CDC, 2018a). Unweighted *n* = 3,115.

Obesity: BMI >= 95th percentile for age.

Free lunch eligible, < 130% of Federal Poverty Level (FPL); reduced price lunch eligible, 130%–184% of FPL; moderate income, 185%–349% of FPL; high income, 350%+ of FPL.

Example: As shown in Table 13.7, in each of the three TV-watching categories, the obesity rate declines with increasing family income level. In three of the four income groups, obesity is more than twice as common in the highest as in the lowest TV-watching groups, but the difference across TV-watching levels is statistically significant only in the two middle income groups. In the free-lunch-eligible (lowest income) group, there is almost no variation in obesity by time spent watching TV.

*The results of the **three-way cross-tabulation** are organized with one **ordinal independent variable** (income group) in the **rows**, the other ordinal independent variable (TV-watching range) in the **columns**, and the value of the **dependent variable** (obesity rate) in the **interior cells**. The **p-value** for the increase in obesity as income level increases within a TV-watching level is reported at the bottom of the column for that TV-watching level, whereas the **p-value** for the increase in obesity as TV-watching level increases within an income level is reported at the* *right-hand side of the row for that income group. This analysis reveals that the size of the association between <u>one</u> **independent variable** (TV-watching time) and the **dependent variable** (obesity) varies according to the value of a <u>second</u> **independent variable** (income group).*

Within the three-way table, the results for two component bivariate associations are shown in the **marginals** (edges) of the table: The association between the column variable and the dependent variable is reported in the bottom gray shaded row, and the association between the row variable and the dependent variable is presented in the gray shaded right-most column. The value of the dependent variable for the entire sample (all categories combined) is reported in the cell at the intersection of the "All" row and the "All" column.

In a three-way cross-tabulation, each of the **marginals** (bottom row and right-most column) report the association between <u>one</u> of the independent variables and the dependent variable, without taking into account the second independent variable.

<u>Example</u>: For all levels of income combined, obesity rates rise from 14.9% among those who watch the least TV to 24.9% among those who watch the most, and the difference is statistically significant, at $p < .0001$. For all TV-watching levels combined, the prevalence of obesity declines from 22.5% among the lowest income group to 13.0% among the highest; $p < .0001$.

*The **bivariate association** between TV-watching (columns) and obesity (<u>regardless of income level</u>) is shown in the "All" **row** (**marginal**) of Table 13.7—the same pattern of obesity by TV-watching level in Table 13.4 with minor differences due to a smaller sample for Table 13.7. The bivariate association between family income group (rows) and obesity (<u>regardless of TV-watching time</u>) is shown in the "All" (**marginal**) **column**.*

Two-Way ANOVA

When both of the independent variables are categorical but the dependent variable is continuous, a **two-way ANOVA** can be used to estimate the mean value of the dependent variable for each of the possible combinations of the two categorical independent variables. The independent variables can be either nominal or ordinal and can be either dichotomous or multichotomous.

A **two-way ANOVA** is used to show how mean values of a continuous dependent variable differ across all possible combinations of the categories of two independent variables.

Table 13.8 Two-Way ANOVA Results

Mean Body Mass Index (BMI) by Income Category and Gender, Children Aged 2 to 17 Years, United States, 2015–16			
	BMI (kg/m²)		
Income group	Boys (n = 1,579)	Girls (n = 1,532)	All (n = 3,111)
Free lunch eligible (n = **1,145**)	*20.3*	*20.5*	*20.4*
Reduced price lunch eligible (n = **690**)	20.1	*21.0*	*20.6*
Moderate income (n = **517**)	20.1	20.1	20.1
High income (n = **3,065**)	19.4	19.6	19.5
All levels	20.0	20.3	20.1

Source: Author's calculations based on data from the 2015–16 U.S. National Health and Nutrition Examination Survey.

Notes:

Weighted to population level using sampling weights provided by the Centers for Disease Control and Prevention (CDC, 2018a). *n*s are unweighted.

Free lunch eligible, < 130% of Federal Poverty Level (FPL); reduced price lunch eligible, 130%–184% of FPL; moderate income, 185%–349% of FPL; high income, 350%+ of FPL.

Bold italic denotes difference compared to the high-income group in the same column is statistically significant at $p < .05$ based on a one-sided test; see Appendix C. Gender difference is not statistically significant in any income group or overall.

Example: Mean BMI declines with increasing family income among both boys and girls (see Table 13.8). Among girls, the difference in mean BMI compared to the high income group is statistically significant for the lowest two income groups; for boys, only the difference between the lowest and highest income groups is statistically significant.

> *The results of this **two-way ANOVA** are organized with the **ordinal independent variable** (income group) in the **rows**, the **nominal independent variable** (gender) in the **columns**, and the value of the **dependent variable** (mean BMI) in the **interior cells**. A footnote to the table explains that bold italic formatting conveys **statistical significance at the .05 level**. The dashed-line outlined **marginal row** reports the **bivariate association** between gender (one independent variable) and mean BMI (the dependent variable) for all income levels. The shaded **marginal column** reports the **bivariate association** between family income group (one independent variable) and mean BMI for both genders combined.*

Results of a three-way association can also be presented graphically, as in Figure 10.12. To convey uncertainty around the estimates, confidence intervals could be added to the chart (as in Figure 13.8), or the results of inferential statistical tests could be reported in a footnote (as in Table 13.8).

Multiple Regression

Two other common statistical methods that you might encounter as you read research articles are forms of **multiple regression**. **Ordinary least squares (OLS) regression** is used to analyze the relationship between one or more independent variables and a <u>continuous</u> dependent variable (Allison, 1999). <u>Multiple</u> regression means that more than one independent variable is included, often to investigate potential confounders or mechanisms linking an independent variable to a dependent variable; see "Research Strategies for Assessing Confounding" in Chapter 12. When the dependent variable is <u>categorical</u>, **logistic regression** is used for the same purpose (Miller, 2013, Chapter 9).

Output from a multiple regression includes estimates of effect size for each independent variable in the model, accompanied by p-values or other indicators of statistical significance. The estimated effect on an independent variable conveys both the direction and the magnitude of the relationship between that variable and the dependent variable when the other variables in the model are taken into account, while the p-value is interpreted as explained earlier for other inferential statistical methods (Miller, 2013, Chapter 9).

Multiple regression (also known as **multivariate regression** or **multivariable regression**) is used to estimate the direction and size of associations between each of two or more independent variables and a dependent variable. **Ordinary least squares (OLS) regression** (also known as **linear regression**) is used when the dependent variable is <u>continuous</u>; **logistic** (or **logit**) **regression** is used when the dependent variable is <u>categorical</u>.

TERMS AND CONCEPTS

HIGHLIGHTS

- Much quantitative research is based on analysis of **samples** rather than entire **populations**, introducing **uncertainty** to those estimates because of **variability** in the samples drawn from a population. For studies that analyze data on an entire population, the "sample" equals the population, so measures of uncertainty are not relevant.

- Making sense of numeric estimates based on samples requires understanding that those estimates cannot be treated as exact (precise) measures of the true value in the population. To convey the effects of sampling variation, researchers using data from samples should report results of **inferential statistical tests** and **measures of uncertainty**.

- The higher the **uncertainty** of an estimate, the lower the **precision** of that estimate. Uncertainty around a point estimate can be expressed using the **standard error** of the estimate, the **margin of error**, or a **confidence interval (interval estimate)**, each of which is inversely related to sample size.

- A representative sample of a few thousand cases can yield fairly **precise** estimates; thus, sample surveys are a practical way to draw inferences about patterns even for large populations.

- **Inferential statistics** assume that a sample is representative of the population in terms of the variables under study and, thus, are suited to samples drawn using **probability (random sampling) methods**. Results of inferential tests of data from samples drawn using non-probability sampling methods (e.g., convenience or quota sampling) should be interpreted with caution.

- **Random error (uncertainty)** and **bias** are different types of **measurement errors**. Although sample size affects uncertainty, it does not determine the extent of bias, which is affected by external validity and measurement validity.

- The probabilistic nature of hypothesis testing means that researchers do not "prove" hypotheses based on sample data; they "test" them at a specified level of significance.

- To avoid misleading conclusions about whether findings are consistent across studies, and to minimize **publication bias**, statisticians recommend using **compatibility intervals** instead of the traditional "yes or no" approach to reporting statistical significance.

RESEARCH TIPS

- Pay careful attention to the level(s) of measurement of independent and dependent variables, to ensure that the choice of inferential statistical method suits the variables for a particular research question.

RECOMMENDED READINGS

Ghose, T. (2013, April 2). "Just a theory": 7 misused science words. *Scientific American*. https://www.scientificamerican.com/article/just-a-theory-7-misused-science-words

McLeod, S. (2019). What a *p*-value tells you about statistical significance. Simply Psychology. https://www.simplypsychology.org/p-value.html

Salkind, N. J. (2016). *Statistics for people who (think they) hate statistics* (6th ed., Chapter 9). SAGE.

Utts, J., & Heckard, R. (2014). *Mind on statistics* (5th ed., Chapter 12). Cengage, Brooks Cole.

EXERCISES

Individual Exercises

Quantitative Reasoning in Everyday Life

1. Find an article in a local or national newspaper that reports results of a recent pre-election poll, including the margin of error. (a) For each candidate, calculate the 95% confidence interval around the estimated share (%) of the vote. (b) Write an interpretation about whether any of the candidates can state with 95% confidence that they were in the lead at the time of that poll, and (c) explain why or why not.

Interpreting Results

2. Find a journal article in your field that reports results of inferential statistical tests from an analysis of survey data. (a) Identify (i) the dependent variable and (ii) independent variable in the authors' analysis; (b) the types of bivariate statistical methods they used; and (c) whether they explained why, given the levels of measurement of their variables. (d) List the ways they presented information on the uncertainty of numeric estimates in tables or charts (e.g., margin of error, confidence interval, *p*-value).

3. Find a journal article in your field that presents results of an inferential statistical test in a table reporting *p*-values for each of several bivariate associations. For results of at least three different bivariate associations, explain how you identified which were statistically significant (a) at a .05 significance level and (b) at a .01 significance level.

Planning Research

4. Write a hypothesis specifying the expected direction of association between the independent and dependent variables in each of the following: from Chapter 12 (a) the hypothetical study of Ritalin and student exam performance from Chapter 12 exercises, (b) the hypothetical evaluation of a mentoring program, and (c) the study by Du Toit et al. (2015).

Analyzing Data

5. (a) Using the data in Table 13A, calculate the 95% confidence interval around the point estimate of the percentage of households that had access to a broadband internet connection in 2018. (b) Explain which states' (or districts') estimates are statistically significantly different <u>from one another</u> and (c) how you know, with interpretation of the confidence intervals.

Table 13A	Percentage of Non-group Quarters Households That Had a Broadband Internet Subscription, 2018, by State				

Location	Point estimate	Margin of error	Lower 95% confidence limit	Upper 95% confidence limit
Delaware	88.3%	1.3%		
District of Columbia	86.7%	1.5%		
Maryland	88.1%	0.5%		
Virginia	85.5%	0.5%		
West Virginia	79.0%	1.2%		

Source: SHADAC (n.d.).

Communicating Research

6. Sketch a chart to show how mean BMI varies by TV-watching, based on the information in Table 13.6. Include (a) axis titles and labels to specify categories and units, (b) point estimates, (c) 95% confidence intervals, and (d) symbols to show statistical significance at $p < .05$ and $p < .01$.

7. Write an interpretation of the meaning of the confidence interval around the point estimate of mean BMI for those who watched 2 to 3 hours per day of TV (Table 13.6), following the criteria in this chapter.

8. (a) Sketch a chart with 95% confidence bands around the trend line of the percentage of persons who were in families having problems paying medical bills in the past 12 months in the United States, 2011–2018, using information from the data table

for Figure 2 at https://www.cdc.gov/nchs/data/databriefs/db357_tables-508.pdf#page=2. (b) Identify which years can be considered to have (i) statistically significantly lower values from those for the year 2011 or (ii) statistically significantly higher values from those for 2018.

Group Exercises

Communicating Research

9. With a classmate, exchange your draft charts from Exercise 6. (a) Provide feedback about the content and design of each other's charts, based on the guidelines in this chapter. (b) Revise your draft chart design to correct any problems found by your peer reviewer.

10. Do the same for your written interpretation from Exercise 7.

VI

Pulling It All Together

This final part of the book integrates ideas from all the earlier chapters, explaining how you can use them together to make sense of numbers. Chapter 14 discusses how to use prose, tables, and charts in complementary ways to present numeric information, and it shows how to apply general expository writing techniques along with guidelines specifically related to writing about numbers. Chapter 15 describes how to assess the "importance" of a numeric result, linking together criteria covered in earlier chapters. It also summarizes how to apply the principles and skills from throughout the book to each of the four main quantitative research tasks: reading about, collecting, calculating, and communicating numeric information.

CHAPTER 14

Communicating Quantitative Research

Learning Objectives

After reading this chapter, you will be able to do the following:

1. Choose among tables, charts, and prose for different quantitative research tasks.

2. Use expository writing approaches to communicate numeric information.

3. Apply principles specific to writing about numbers.

4. Identify the type of measure or calculation based on wording, units, sign, and other clues.

5. Write a description of how values of a variable are distributed.

6. Write a description of an association between two variables.

7. Organize and write a summary of a pattern involving many numbers.

8. Describe the general structure and contents of documents used to present quantitative research to scientific, applied, and general audiences.

Quantitative research often tackles questions of interest to diverse audiences, including people who are interested in the answers to those questions but not necessarily interested in the gory details of how the results were obtained. As a consequence, an essential aspect of quantitative research is communicating that work so that readers can understand the findings and how to interpret them, regardless of whether they have training in research methods or statistics. Whereas Chapters 9, 10, and 13 presented "behind-the-scenes" steps for conducting and understanding the results of mathematical and statistical methods using the necessary technical language, in this chapter I teach how to avoid jargon about the calculation process, instead using clear, accessible language to write complete, correct descriptions of the numeric results.

I describe criteria for deciding among prose, tables, and charts for different situations and explain how to use those tools together when presenting quantitative research. Next, I review some fundamental expository writing approaches and show how to use them in conjunction with principles specifically related to presenting numeric evidence. After explaining how wording and units convey what kind of measure or calculation is being presented, I demonstrate how to combine these principles to perform common tasks for communicating quantitative research. I close the chapter with a brief summary of the format and structure of documents used to present research results to different audiences.

These communication skills will be useful to you, whether you are reading others' descriptions of research or writing about quantitative research for others to read.

Tools for Presenting Quantitative Research

There are three main types of tools for presenting numeric information: prose, tables, and charts. **Prose (text)** can be used to present numbers in a variety of ways: Single sentences can be used to report and interpret a numeric fact or compare a couple of facts, while paragraphs are needed to describe more complex patterns. In the body of a paper, journal or newspaper article, book, or blog, numbers are incorporated into full sentences. On slides for a speech, on Websites, on research posters, and in infographics, numbers are often reported in a bulleted list of short phrases rather than as complete sentences. Ditto for tweets about numeric facts.

Researchers often use text footnotes or appendixes to provide background information on their data or calculations.

> Example: The Census Bureau report on income and poverty in the United States (Fontenot et al., 2018) includes text appendixes that explain how income and poverty are defined and measured.

> Example: All the tables and charts in this book that report results using data from the NHANES include the footnote: "Weighted to population level using sampling weights provided by the Centers for Disease Control and Prevention (CDC, 2018a)."
>
> *Those footnotes use **prose** to explain the use of sampling weights (see Appendix B) and provide a citation to their source.*

Prose (also known as **text**) includes sentences and paragraphs in the body of a document or **appendix**, as well as **footnotes**. Shorter forms include **bulleted text** and tweets.

The other two types of tools used to communicate numbers are **charts** (also called **graphs**, **figures**, or **visualizations**) and **tables**. Which of those three tools is best suited to a particular quantitative research task depends on several factors, including the specific objective; how many numbers are to be presented; how much time readers have to absorb the information; and whether the focus is on conveying the general shape of a pattern or providing precise values for readers to use in their own calculations (see Table 14.1).

Table 14.1	Strengths and Weaknesses of Tools for Presenting Quantitative Information	
Tool	**Strengths**	**Weaknesses**
Prose	Is the easiest way to describe numeric patterns Is the easiest way to ask and answer research questions	Is a poor way to organize a lot of numbers
Table	Is a good way to store and organize lots of numbers Has a predictable structure via row and column labels Makes it easy to read detailed numbers	Is a poor way to convey shape and size of pattern
Chart or visualization	Is a good way to store and organize lots of numbers Has a predictable structure via axis labels and legend Makes it easy to see shape and size of numeric contrasts and patterns	Is a poor way to report detailed numeric values

What Is the Objective?

When the **objective** is to introduce a research question, define terms, or convey the role of a table or figure in the overall scheme of a research project, prose is the best choice. It is also the most effective tool for describing theories used to generate a hypothesis, explaining how data were collected and analyzed, interpreting numeric findings, and relating findings to those of other studies. On the other hand, if a particular task involves reporting numbers for others to analyze, or portraying the general shape of a pattern, a table or chart is often preferred.

How Many Numbers?

A second consideration is **how many numbers** are to be presented as part of the specific task. If just one or two numbers are needed, a simple sentence or bulleted phrase will do; a table or chart would be overkill.On the other hand, a table or chart is far more efficient than text for organizing and labeling a large set of numbers. As discussed in Chapter 6, well-designed tables make it easy to find and interpret a specific number by using clear, complete row and column labels. Well-designed charts or visualizations make it easy to locate and understand a particular value by using the axis titles, axis labels, and legend (see Chapter 7).

> Example: On August 21, 2019, the Standard and Poor's (S&P) 500 Index opened at $2,922.04 and closed at $2,924.43, with daily highs and lows of $2,983.73 and $2,917.91, respectively (Yahoo! Finance, 2020).
>
> > This **sentence** reports only <u>one</u> day's worth of data for the overall S&P 500. To report the corresponding information for <u>each of the 500</u> stocks in that index would require many sentences, each labeled with the stock name, date, and whether each number was the high, low, opening, or closing value. Trying to find a specific number of interest amid the long, cluttered block of text would be frustrating and time-consuming for a reader.

General Shape or Precise Values?

Another criterion for choosing tools is whether the main point an author wants to make concerns the **general shape** of a pattern or the reporting of **precise values**. Charts and diagrams can depict the shape of a relationship more effectively than a table can. However, it is difficult to read exact values from a chart. Thus, tables are preferred for reporting detailed numbers, as when readers need to extract data for their own calculations.

> Example: Detailed information for the daily stock market report is usually reported in tabular format, as in Table 14.2.
>
> > With the date range and units ($) specified for the overall **table**, and with **columns** labeled for "Open," "Close," "High," and "Low" stock prices, readers can easily find prices to the nearest penny for whichever dates (**rows**) they want. However, to assess the **direction** and **magnitude** of trends, they would have to do their own mental calculations with the numbers provided, so a **chart** would be a more effective tool for conveying those patterns.

> Example: Time trends in the value of a stock or stock index are often presented using a line chart like Figure 14.1.
>
> > With date on the **horizontal axis** and price on the **vertical axis**, readers can easily see **trends** over a long period of time, identifying when

Table 14.2 Table for Organizing Many Numeric Values

| Date | Standard and Poor's 500 Stock Index Price in U.S. dollars, May 20–Aug. 22, 2019 | | | | Volume (1000s of w) |
	Open	High	Low	Close	
Aug. 22, 2019	$2,930.94	$2,939.08	$2,904.51	$2,922.95	2,890,880
Aug. 21, 2019	$2,922.04	$2,983.73	$2,917.91	$2,924.43	3,011,190
Aug. 20, 2019	$2,919.01	$2,923.63	$2,900.51	$2,900.51	3,066,300
. . .					
July 22, 2019	$2,981.93	$2,990.71	$2,976.65	$2,985.02	3,003,720
. . .					
June 21, 2019	$2,952.71	$2,964.15	$2,946.87	$2,950.46	5,000,120
. . .					
May 20, 2019	$2,941.94	$2,953.86	$2,831.29	$2,840.23	3,288,870

Source: Data from Yahoo! Finance (2019).

Figure 14.1 Chart for Organizing Many Numeric Values

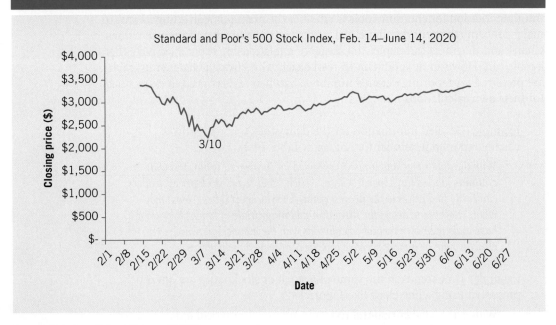

Source: Data from Yahoo! Finance (2019).

*stock prices were rising versus falling (**direction**) and how steeply those changes occurred (**magnitude**). However, it is difficult to identify the <u>exact</u> price for any date, and labels on each data point would make the chart unreadable, so, if readers need to perform calculations with those numbers, a **table** would make their life a lot easier.*

How Much Time?

Another consideration for choosing tools is **how much time** the expected audience will have to read and understand the information. When time is limited, large, complicated tables or intricate visualizations are too much for readers to scan and absorb. For brief presentations or automatically rotating electronic media, simple charts or short phrases help the audience grasp the numeric point quickly. For a memo or executive summary, one bullet for each fact or pattern gets the point across. However, readers can take as much time as they want to read formats such as journal articles, reports, or books—so, for those formats, detailed tables or charts can be used if they suit the objective and task.

Who Is the Audience?

A final criterion for choosing which tool to use to present numbers is the intended **audience**: Scientific audiences are accustomed to reading and interpreting tables and relatively complex types of charts and visualizations. The general public, on the other hand, may be intimidated by too many numbers or a chart with multiple axes, stacking, or error bars. For such audiences, small, straightforward tables and simple, familiar types of visualizations are better options.

Knowing that tables, figures, and prose have different advantages and disadvantages, quantitative research documents should use a combination of those tools, each chosen for its specific strengths for organizing and presenting numeric information for each task within the document.

> <u>Example</u>: A government report on unemployment patterns might use a **sentence** to report the current unemployment rate, a short **paragraph** to compare unemployment rates for people of different education levels, a **table** to show how current unemployment levels and rates vary by detailed occupational category, and a **visualization** to illustrate 10-year trends in unemployment for the entire country and by region. **Prose** would be used to introduce the topic, describe patterns in the tables and charts, and relate them to the main purpose of the report.

For oral presentations, chartbooks, or automated slide shows, researchers often accompany each table or chart with bulleted phrases to summarize the key points. See recommended readings at the end of this chapter for illustrative examples.

When presenting numeric information, use tables, charts, and prose to complement one another, taking advantage of their respective strengths for <u>each task</u> within a research project.

Criteria for choosing which tool(s) to use to present numbers include the following:

- The **objective** of the particular task:
  - reporting numbers
  - portraying patterns
  - asking and answering questions with numeric evidence

- **How many** numbers are to be presented

- Whether expected readers need **precise values** or to see the **general shape of a pattern**

- How much **time** readers have to read and process the information

- The intended **audience** and their expected use of the numbers

Expository Writing Techniques

Several fundamental writing techniques can be used to present quantitative research in much the same way they are used for other expository writing tasks. These approaches include using paragraphs to organize ideas; specifying the context of the work; and writing topic, evidentiary, and transition sentences.

Using Paragraphs to Organize Ideas

The material in the body of a research paper, report, or issue brief should be organized into separate paragraphs, each of which introduces and presents numeric information for one aspect of the research question or set of closely related questions.

> Example: A study of childhood obesity might start with a paragraph reporting the overall prevalence of obesity in the United States and how it varies by family income (describing the numbers in Table 13.4), then include a second paragraph on how the amount of time children spend watching TV differs across family income groups to accompany Table 13.5, a third paragraph presenting how body mass index (BMI) differs by

TV-watching time (Table 13.6), and a fourth paragraph discussing how obesity varies by income level and TV-watching together (Table 13.7).

> *This **set of paragraphs** organizes a series of <u>logically sequenced analyses</u>, building from a simple summary statistic on the obesity rate among <u>all</u> children (a **univariate** statistic on the dependent variable) to **bivariate associations** among two independent variables (income group and TV-watching level) and the dependent variable, to a **three-way association** between those two independent variables and the dependent variable. Each step in the overall analysis is the subject of a <u>separate paragraph</u>, linked by topic and transition sentences.*

Setting the Context

As mentioned throughout this book, a critical aspect of presenting quantitative research is specifying the context—conveying what, when, where, and who were studied. Each of those **W's** typically requires only a few words that can be easily included in the topic sentence for a paragraph or the sentence reporting the numbers.

> <u>Example</u>: Childhood obesity is a serious problem in the United States, affecting 18% of children aged 2 to 17 years in 2015 and 2016.
>
> *This sentence would work well to open a results section, introducing the overall topic (**what** = obesity), specifying **when** (2015–16), **where** (the United States), and **to whom** (children aged 2 to 17 years) the data pertain.*

In the body of a paragraph, the W's for individual facts or comparisons should be incorporated into the sentences that present the numbers, as shown in the examples throughout this book. Once the W's have been introduced, they do <u>not</u> need to be repeated in every sentence, <u>as long as they do not change</u>.

> <u>Example</u>: All the material in the childhood obesity analysis described earlier pertains to 2-to-17-year-old children in the United States in 2015 and 2016; thus, once those W's have been specified, they don't need to be included in every sentence about those patterns. However, when an analysis focuses on a subset of cases, such as 8-year-old boys (e.g., Figure 10.4), the associated paragraph must identify the pertinent W's because they are different than the W's used to introduce the overall analysis. Or, when subgroups are contrasted (e.g., income level, as in Table 13.4), the description of that pattern should convey the W's that define those subgroups.

With that said, in a long results section you should repeat the W's every few paragraphs, and when you are summarizing results in a discussion section you should restate them. Ditto for comparing findings against other studies of the same topic, to point out ways in which the W's differ across studies. As noted in Chapters 6 and 7, the W's also should be included in titles, labels, or footnotes for every table, chart, or visualization.

Using Topic Sentences

As with other types of expository writing, in documents describing quantitative research, **topic sentences** should be used to introduce the issue to be addressed in each paragraph.

> Example: The prevalence of childhood obesity is inversely related to family income.
>
> *This sentence introduces the **key independent variable** (income) and conveys the **direction** of its association with the **dependent variable** (obesity). Evidentiary sentences would then **report** and **interpret** numbers to illustrate that pattern and to convey magnitude.*

Rhetorical questions can also be effective as topic sentences, especially in documents for lay audiences or in oral presentations.

> Example: Are sedentary activities like watching TV or videos associated with higher rates of childhood obesity?
>
> *This **topic sentence** specifies the question to be addressed in a **new paragraph**, this time investigating how a <u>different</u> **independent variable** (TV-watching) is related to the **dependent variable** that is the focus of the overall study (obesity).*

Using Evidentiary Sentences

Just as writers use quotations from literary texts as evidence for their thesis statements, quantitative researchers present numeric facts as evidence to demonstrate a pattern or investigate a hypothesis. **Evidentiary sentences** should report the numbers and interpret how they address the question raised in the associated topic sentence, describing the direction, magnitude, and (for scientific audiences) statistical significance of the pattern. Any W's that were not mentioned in the topic sentence should also be specified. To tie the prose to the accompanying table or chart, it should be referred to by name in either the topic sentence or an evidentiary sentence.

> Example: In 2015, the obesity rate in the United States declined from 22.7% among children from the lowest-income families to 20.6% in the next lowest income group, to 17.0% in the moderate-income group, and to 12.9% in the highest-income group (Table 13.4;

$p < .001$). Thus, obesity was nearly twice as common among children from the lowest-income families as in the highest-income families.

> These **evidentiary sentences** present the numeric facts that address the question introduced in the **topic sentence** about income group and obesity. The first sentence specifies the **W's**, **reports** the value of the dependent variable (obesity rate) for each category of the independent variable (income group), states the p-value for the inferential test (p < .001), and names the **table** that presents the detailed information. The second sentence _interprets_ the evidence, conveying the **direction** and **magnitude** ("twice as common") of the association based on some behind-the-scenes math.

See Chapter 13 and Appendix C for a refresher on the more technical aspects of interpreting results of statistical significance testing. See also Chapter 15 about the importance of distinguishing between _statistical_ significance and _substantive_ significance (practical importance).

Using Transition Sentences

Transition sentences should guide the reader from one major point to another, introducing new angles on the overall research question such as different independent or dependent variables, changes in the W's (date, location, or subgroup), or next steps in the analysis. Transition sentences can be placed at the end of a paragraph to anticipate the next step, or they can be used as a topic sentence for a new paragraph.

> Example: One possible explanation for the higher obesity rates among children from lower income groups is that children from lower-income families spend more time on sedentary activities like watching TV or videos. The results in Table 13.5 confirm that, indeed, children who are eligible for free school lunches are twice as likely to be in the highest TV-watching group as those from high-income families (20% vs. 10%).

> > This **sentence transitions** to a _new_ **paragraph**, where it introduces a _new question_ to be addressed by evidence on the bivariate association between income group (a _different_ **independent variable**) and TV-watching (the **dependent variable** for _this step of the overall analysis_ of factors affecting childhood obesity). The _second_ **sentence** reports and interprets the relevant numeric evidence and names the **table** where it can be found.

> Example: Might those differences in TV-watching explain the higher obesity rates among children from lower-income families?

> > Here, a rhetorical question is used to **transition** to a new paragraph, asking whether one independent variable (TV-watching) might be the

mechanism by which another independent variable (family income group) affects the dependent variable (obesity). The topic sentence, thus, introduces all the variables involved in a **different type of analysis** (three-way association) that will provide the evidence to answer that question. Supporting **evidentiary sentences** would report and interpret the numeric results of the associated **table** (Table 13.7).

Transition sentences can be used to convey a change in the contrast of W's (e.g., where, instead of when or who).

Example: To assess whether the observed relationship between income group and BMI in the United States differs by gender, Table 13.8 presents evidence on that pattern separately for boys and girls.

Example: To determine whether childhood obesity shows a similar relationship with family income in other countries, we analyzed 2015 data from Germany, Japan, Nigeria, and Argentina.

Example: Has the income gradient in childhood obesity been consistent over time in the United States? To investigate that question, we compared results from 1995, 2005, and 2015.

*These three examples would be distinct facets of an overall analysis of how family income relates to childhood obesity: the first by subgroup (**who**); the second by country (**where**); the third by date (**when**). Each topic sentence states the **topic** (obesity by income) and the pertinent **W's**, clearly <u>differentiating the steps</u> in the hypothetical analysis.*

Numbers can be used as evidence to address a research question, using standard expository writing techniques:

- Organizing the material into **paragraphs**, each focusing on one aspect of the analysis

- Setting the **context** by specifying when, where, and to whom the data pertain

- Using **topic, evidentiary,** and **transition sentences** to keep readers oriented to where they are in the overall analysis and how numeric information answers the questions at each step of that analysis

---

Writing About Numbers in Particular

Several expository writing principles pertain specifically to presenting numeric information. In this section, I briefly describe those principles. In later sections, I illustrate them, to show how those principles are used <u>together</u> to present numeric information effectively.

Specifying Units

The importance of specifying units for all numeric measures and contrasts has been discussed and illustrated throughout this book, so I repeat it here simply for the sake of completeness.

Reporting and Interpreting Numbers

As noted in Chapter 2, an essential part of communicating quantitative information is to both report and interpret the numbers. For government reports and other published data that are intended mainly for others to use for their own analysis, merely reporting the numbers might be sufficient. By **reporting** the numbers in the text, table, or chart, researchers provide readers with the raw data, so that they can see the basis of the calculations or compare the data with values from other sources.

However, when those numbers are intended to characterize a pattern or test a hypothesis, researchers should convey that objective, **report** the associated numbers, <u>and</u> **interpret** them to show how they address the research question at hand. An isolated number that has not been introduced or explained leaves it entirely to the readers to make sense of that number. Readers who are not familiar with the topic or context are unlikely to know which comparisons to make or to have the necessary information (such as **benchmark** values) to make those comparisons (see Chapter 8). That behind-the-scenes work is the researchers' job, not the readers'! In other words, when describing a pattern or addressing whether a hypothesis is supported, researchers should avoid "just writing the <u>problem set</u>" [**reporting** the numbers], by <u>also</u> "writing the <u>answer</u>" [**interpreting** those numbers, by explaining results to show how they address the specific research question.]

Expressing Direction and Magnitude

An essential part of interpreting numeric comparisons involves conveying both the direction and the magnitude of a pattern. As Figure 10.13 showed, it is <u>always</u> possible to describe the direction and magnitude of a **distribution** of a variable (univariate statistic) or of an **association** between variables (bivariate or multivariate), regardless of the levels of measurement of the variables. However, the wording and nature of the comparison are different for nominal variables than they are for quantitative (ordinal, interval, or ratio) ones: For **nominal (qualitative)** variables, values are classified into categories with no inherent numeric order; thus, direction must be described by naming the categories being compared. For **quantitative** variables, the values have a natural numeric order that can help convey directionality of the distribution or association.

Specifying the Comparison Value

As covered in Chapter 8, often there are several possible comparisons (e.g., comparison across places, times, groups, or thresholds), making it crucial that researchers specify which comparison group or value they used, so that their readers can interpret the results.

> When presenting quantitative results, researchers should <u>both</u> **report** and **interpret** the numbers. Numbers can be reported in a table or chart and then interpreted in the associated text. Researchers must identify the **comparison group** or **reference value**, so that readers can make sense of the numeric comparisons.

Using Vocabulary and Calculations to Express Shape and Size

Not surprisingly, **numeric evidence** is a central part of quantitative research, so results of mathematical and statistical calculations are an expected part of describing direction and magnitude. However, researchers can enhance the power and precision of their writing by using **vocabulary** and **analogies** to describe a pattern and relate it to the specific topic (Miller, 2015, Chapter 8). Well-chosen adjectives, verbs, and adverbs can enhance descriptions of numeric patterns by conveying topic, level, direction, and magnitude. Adjectives such as "chilly," "expensive," and "sparse" express both the topic and the approximate numeric value, while other adjectives like "minuscule" and "steep" communicate the size of a difference between cases or the slope of a trend line. Verbs such as "eked" and "dominated" portray the size of differences, while "skyrocketed" and "plunged" communicate the direction and size of trends. Adverbs such as "narrowly" depict the size of changes or differences across values, while "consistently" implies either a steady, unchanging value, or that a pattern does not vary across the specified places or groups.

> Example: Candidate Q won the recent election by a landslide, with a 30,000-vote margin of victory out of the roughly 200,000 total votes tallied.

*"Victory" conveys **direction** (who won), and "landslide" conveys* *magnitude (by how much), using **vocabulary** commonly associated with* *competitions. The numeric information on the margin of victory and vote* *total quantify "landslide."*

Example: Plants that were fed "worm tea" compost grew rapidly over the course of the experiment, whereas those that were given only water grew more modestly. The "worm tea" plants grew on average 17 cm per week, versus 10 cm per week for the water-only plants.

*All the plants in the experiment grew (same **direction** of trend). The* *adverbs "rapidly" and "more modestly" communicate the <u>difference</u> in* *the rate (**magnitude**) of that change between plants grown under the* *two conditions. Growth rates reported in the second sentence provide the* *numbers used to arrive at those descriptors.*

Phrases and analogies, such as "J-shaped" and "bell-shaped,"can communicate the general shape of a pattern, which can then be fleshed out with comparisons such as rank, difference, ratio, and percentage difference to convey level and size of contrasts across values.

However, verbal descriptions <u>alone</u> should <u>not</u> be used to convey level or comparisons between values, because people's interpretations of descriptive words for numeric concepts differ substantially. Mauboussin and Mauboussin (2018) conducted a study of the numeric probability people associate with words and phrases that communicate the likelihood that something will happen. They found that although terms like "always" and "never" are widely understood to mean 100% and 0%, respectively, there is wide variation in how people interpret other terms. For instance, respondents associated "probably" with values ranging from about 40% to 75%, and the phrase "a real possibility" was associated with a nearly flat distribution of values spanning almost the entire range from 0% to 100%!

To avoid this kind of misunderstanding, researchers should also report the numbers associated with verbal descriptions, in order to provide a more precise sense of level, likelihood (chance), or size of a difference than words alone can provide.

Prose can be used to interpret the **shape (direction)** and **size (magnitude)** of a numeric pattern. The most effective descriptions of numeric patterns combine **vocabulary** or **analogies** with **results of calculations**, providing both a general sense of shape or level (wording) and precise value (numbers).

Conveying the Type of Measure or Calculation

As you read or write about numeric information, the units and wording provide important clues to which measures or calculations are presented. Descriptions should also mention the topic, and—for any comparison—identify the comparison group. Tables 14.3–14.5 summarize the types of information needed to report different measures of level, rankings, and comparisons, including units, sign (positive or negative) of possible values; commonly used wording; and other elements that should be included when that type of number is reported.

Measures of Level

The wording and units for specific types of measures of level differ somewhat from one another. Later in this chapter, I provide examples and point out common pitfalls in writing about each type of measure or comparison.

Specific Level or Value

Reporting the **level** or **value** for one case is simply that: just one number, conveying how <u>many</u> (for countable things) or how <u>much</u> (for concepts measured in continuous form, with decimal values possible) of whatever is being measured. No description of direction or magnitude is needed, because no comparison is involved. The sentence reporting the number should name the topic and specify the context and units if they have not yet been presented.

> <u>Example</u>: How many apples? How much flour?
>
> *Each apple is a discrete item, so "how <u>many</u>" is the appropriate phrasing. Flour, on the other hand, can be used in any amount, so we ask "how <u>much</u>?"*

> <u>Example</u>: How much beer? How many kegs of beer?
>
> *The second version specifies **countable units** (kegs), so the word "<u>many</u>" can be used.*

> <u>Example</u>: The new movie *Stars in Cars* was rated three out of five thumbs-up.
>
> *The sentence reports **type of measure** (rating), **units** (# of "thumbs-up"), <u>highest possible</u> **rating** (five), **topic** (movie quality), and **specific case** being rated (the named movie).*

Table 14.3 Criteria for Identifying a Type of Measure

Type of measure	Units	Sign	Wording	Other required elements
Level or value	Units of measurement of original variable	Can be positive or negative, depending on topic and system of measurement.	Level Value How much	
Count	Whole numbers of items that match the topic	Cannot be negative.[a]	Count Number Tally How many	Level of aggregation
Rating	Points, stars Rating for an individual case must be a whole number. Average ratings can have fractional values.	Cannot be negative unless rating scale offers negative values.	Rating Score	Maximum possible rating
Proportion of a whole	Proportion	Cannot be negative.	Proportion of Share of Portion of	What constitutes the whole ("proportion of [what]")
Percentage of a whole	Percentage points	Cannot be negative.	Percentage of Share of	What constitutes the whole ("percentage of [what]")
Ratio of variables measured in *different* units	Units in numerator per units in denominator	Can be positive or negative, depending on range of values for numerator and denominator variables.	# per # for each # for every	If units do not convey topic, specify topics of numerator and denominator.
Rate of occurrence[b]	Units in numerator per units in denominator per time period		# per [scale #] (e.g., deaths per 1,000 live births)	Time period to which rate pertains (e.g., daily, annual)

Notes:

a. *Change* or *difference* in a count can be negative but is the result of subtraction or percentage change. See pertinent entries in Table 14.5.

b. For rate of *change*, see entry on percentage change in Table 14.5.

Percentage or Proportion of a Whole

For the value of a percentage of a whole to be interpretable, researchers must specify the identity of the whole. In other words, "percentage <u>of what</u>?" Likewise for proportion of a whole.

> <u>Example</u>: The percentage <u>of children</u> who are obese has a completely different meaning (and likely a different numeric value) than the percentage <u>of obese people</u> are who are children.
>
> *Without the phrase "of ___," the **percentage** cannot be interpreted correctly. A review of the behind-the-scenes calculations from Chapters 6 and 9 reveals the issue: In both cases, the **numerator** is number of obese children, but the **denominators** (the whole, out of which the percentage is calculated) are completely different: the first version implies that the denominator was <u>all children</u> (regardless of obesity status); the second implies that the denominator was <u>all obese people</u> (regardless of age).*

Ratio Between Two Concepts

Some measures of level are results of a ratio of two concepts, each measured in different units. The reported value must convey both the concepts and their respective units, with wording such as "per" or "for every" between the units of the numerator and denominator (see Chapter 9).

> <u>Example</u>: "Fuel economy for the latest model of Hotshot Hybrid was 54" cannot be interpreted.
>
> *As noted in Chapter 4, fuel economy is measured in diametrically opposite ways in the <u>metric</u> (volume of gas/distance traveled) and <u>British</u> (distance/volume) **systems of measurement** (Gershtein & Gershtein, 2018). The units are not specified in this example; thus, it does not convey whether <u>distance</u> was in the **numerator** (the British measure; correct in this case) or the **denominator** (the metric measure)—a critical distinction, because it determines whether a <u>higher</u> (true in this case) or <u>lower</u> number represents better fuel economy.*

When reporting a rate of occurrence, in addition to naming the concepts and their units, researchers must specify the time period to which the rate pertains—which could be a year, a decade, or some other interval. Recall that some rates are expressed per 100 (%), per 100,000, or on some other scale, so it is also essential to convey the **scale** of the rate.

> <u>Example</u>: In 2018, the marriage rate in Big City was 7.0 per 1,000 people.
>
> *This sentence conveys the **concepts** and **units** for the numerator (marriages) and denominator (people), the **scale** (per 1,000), and the **period** (one specific year) to which the rate pertains.*

Measures of Rank

Rank and percentile do not involve units of their own; rather, they are based on the position of the values being compared (see Chapter 9). Measures of rank capture the <u>direction</u> of differences between values; so, rank should be reported using words that describe relative position, state whether that position is from the lowest or highest value in the list, and indicate whether higher is better or worse for that topic (Table 14.4). In addition, the description should specify what set of cases are encompassed in the list against which the value of interest is being compared—whether from within the data set used in the analysis or to an external standard (see Chapter 8). However, rankings do <u>not</u> capture the distances between values on the list, so the description should not imply any quantification of <u>magnitude</u> in the original units of the concept upon which the rank is based.

For many topics, phrasing for rank can reflect both the position and concept being compared, avoiding generic wording such as "[Case X] ranked #X in terms of [topic]."

> <u>Example</u>: "BASE jumping is the most dangerous sport in the world."
>
> *This sentence captures **topic** (danger), **identity of the specific case** (the sport of BASE jumping), **position** ("most"), and **comparison** (against all other sports). Although ranking tells us that BASE jumping is the most dangerous sport (**direction**), it <u>cannot</u> tell us <u>how much</u> riskier BASE jumping is than the next most dangerous sport (**magnitude**).*

If the values and units of the variable involved in the ranking have already been reported, they can be omitted from the description. If not, rank and value can be incorporated into the same sentence.

> <u>Example</u>: Anye's verbal reasoning GRE score of 155 points placed him in the second-highest quartile nationwide.
>
> *Without the word "highest," this sentence wouldn't convey whether the quartile was second <u>from the bottom</u> or second <u>from the top</u> of the list of students who took the exam.*

Results of Calculations

As mentioned throughout this book, the results of mathematical calculations should (a) identify the reference (comparison) value and (b) portray the direction and magnitude of the difference across groups, times, or places, following the guidelines in Chapters 8 and 9, respectively. Table 14.5 shows words and phrases that are widely used to report each type of calculation, with notes about which ones communicate direction (denoted D in the wording column), magnitude (M), and which do not and should therefore be rephrased (N). Wording that includes the symbol "#" must also include a numeric measure to convey magnitude.

Table 14.4 Criteria for Identifying a Type of Ranking Measure

Type of ranking	Units	Sign	Wording	Other required element[a]
Rank	Position of individual case in a numerically ordered list	Cannot be negative.	Rank Position number Standing Seeding	Total number of cases being ranked (optional but useful)
Percentile	Percentiles	Cannot be negative.	Xth percentile (e.g., 73rd or 22nd percentile)	
Decile; quartile; tercile etc.	Decile, quartile, tercile—whichever is being used	Cannot be negative.	Xth [_]cile or [_]tile (e.g., 2nd lowest tercile, 4th highest quintile) Nth portion (e.g., top fifth, bottom fourth)	

Note:

a. All measures of rank should include information on (1) identity of the list used for the ranking (e.g., what cases are encompassed); (2) whether high or low values are optimal; and (3) whether ranked position is from bottom or top of list.

Table 14.5 Criteria for Identifying a Type of Calculation

Type of calculation	Units	Sign	Wording[a]	Other required elements
Difference in values for continuous variable (subtraction)	Units of measurement of original variable[b]		#-unit[c] difference (M) Gap (N) Margin (N) Disparity (N) Discrepancy (N) # units higher/lower (D, M) # units fewer, less, more (D, M) #-unit advantage/disadvantage (D, M) Benefit/penalty (D)	Identity of reference value or comparison category
Change over time or other continuous variable (subtraction)	Units of measurement of original variable[d]	Can be positive, zero, or negative.	#-unit change (M) Trend (N) Upward/downward trend (D) # increase/decrease (D, M) #-unit decline (D, M) #-unit rise (D, M)	
Ratio (division) of values measured in the _same units_	Units from numerator and denominator "cancel," so units of original variable are _not_ associated with the ratio result.		# times as (D, M) # times more/less likely than[d] (D, M) #-fold (D, M) Fractional multiple (e.g., "half of," (D, M) # percentage of denominator[e] (D, M)	
Percentage difference	Percentage difference versus comparison value		# percentage difference (M) # percentage higher/lower (D, M) # percentage more/less likely (D, M)	
Percentage change	Percentage change versus value for comparison time point		# percentage change since [reference time point] (D, M) # percentage increase/decrease (D, M)	Identity of reference time point
Rate of change	Percentage change per unit time		[Time unit] percentage change (e.g., annual, monthly) (M) # percentage change per [time interval] (D, M)	Identity of reference time point Width of time interval

Notes:

a. D: conveys direction; M: conveys magnitude; N: does not convey direction.

b. If variable was measured in percentage point units, the calculated difference from subtraction is in "percentage points," not "percentage difference." See Chapter 9 for formula and explanation.

c. "#" is the measure of size of the difference/change; without that number and unit wording, wording does not convey magnitude.

d. "Likely than" wording is used for comparisons of a yes/no or other two-category outcome across values of an independent variable.

Subtraction

Subtraction calculates the size of a difference as well as its direction, measured in the original units of the variable. The order in which the two groups, places, or time periods are named in the sentence must reflect the order in which the subtraction was done.

Example: "Recipe A contains 1 cup more milk than Recipe B" has the same meaning as "Recipe B includes 1 cup less milk than Recipe A."

The first sentence implies A − B = +1; the second implies B − A = − 1. Both accurately capture which recipe uses more milk (A), because the <u>items are named in the same order as in the equation</u>, and the sign (+ or −) conveys which recipe has the larger amount.

Example: In 2018, Asia's population was 3,039 million people larger than Africa's.

Topic *(population),* **W's** *(when and where),* ***units*** *(millions of persons), and* ***direction*** *and* ***magnitude*** *of the difference (from* ***subtraction****), all in one short, simple sentence.*

<u>**Caution:**</u> As explained in Chapter 9, when the values being compared are measured in percentage units, subtraction results in a <u>difference in percentage points</u>, not a percentage difference.

Example: The interest rate for a 15-year fixed mortgage is 0.8 percentage points lower than that for an adjustable-rate mortgage (3.2% annual percentage rate and 4.0% APR, respectively).

The ***units*** *on the variable (interest rate) happen to be percentage points, so the* ***difference*** *(from subtraction) is also in* ***percentage*** <u>***points***</u>*.*

Phrasing such as "margin" or "gap" expresses that the results are from subtraction but does <u>not</u> convey either the direction or the magnitude of the difference. "Surplus" or "disadvantage" communicates direction but must be accompanied by a numeric measure of amount (size). "Fewer" implies lower counts (in whole numbers), whereas "less" indicates smaller amounts of things for which decimal or fractional quantities are possible. The word "more" can be used for either whole or fractional values.

Example: Recipe C uses <u>fewer</u> eggs and <u>less</u> butter, but more milk than, Recipe D.

Division

Results of division (a **ratio**) should be worded to reflect both the direction and the magnitude of the difference between the values being compared. As you learned in Chapter 9, when a ratio of two values measured in the same units is calculated, those units "cancel" during the division process, so the ratio should be reported as either a multiple or a percentage of the denominator value, <u>without</u> the units of the original variable.

> <u>Example</u>: In 2018, Asia was 4.3 times as populous as Africa.
>
> *The **ratio** of Asia's population to that of Africa = 3,964 million people in Asia ÷ 924 million people in Africa = 4.3 (Table 9.2). The **units** (million people) are the same for the numerator and denominator, so the ratio of their values is 4.3, <u>not</u> 4.3 million!*

The order in which the two groups, places, or time periods are named in the sentence must reflect which of those values was in the numerator and which one was in the denominator (the reference group).Common phrasing for units include "# X **per** Y," "#X **for each** Y," or "#-to-#." Note that the concept in the numerator (X) is named before that phrase, and the concept in the denominator (Y) is named after that phrase.

> <u>Example</u>: "Recipe A uses twice as many eggs as recipe B" has the same meaning as "Recipe B uses half as many eggs as Recipe A."
>
> *The first sentence implies A ÷ B = 2; the second implies B ÷ A = ½. Both accurately capture which recipe uses more eggs (Recipe A), because the **numerator** item is named <u>first</u>, and the **reference group** (denominator) is specified <u>after</u> the phrase "as many as."*

> <u>Example</u>: Voters favored Herrera's tax proposal 2 to 1 over that proposed by Walker.

Many writers struggle to present results of ratios without using jargon like "numerator," "denominator," "division," and even "ratio(!)," which keeps the focus on the computation process rather than on the substantive meaning of the result. Although I use those technical terms to guide the "behind-the-scenes" computations in Chapters 9 and 13 and to explain the writing guidelines here, writers should <u>avoid</u> those terms when presenting results, following the guidelines in Table 14.6 for more user-friendly wording.

If a ratio is close to 1.0, the key point is that that the values in the numerator and denominator are very similar to each other.

Table 14.6 Phrases for Describing Ratios and the Numerator as a Percentage of the Denominator

Value of ratio	Ratio example	Rule of thumb[a]	Writing suggestion[b]
<1.0 (e.g., 0.x) *Numerator as a percentage of the denominator =* ratio × 100	0.76	[Group] is only x% as ___ as the reference value.	"Students from poor families were only 76% as likely as those from non-poor families to graduate from high school."
Close to 1.0	0.98	Use phrasing to express similarity between the two groups' values.	"Average heights were similar for poor and non-poor children (ratio = 0.98 for poor compared to non-poor)."
>1.0 (e.g., 1.y) *Percentage difference between numerator and denominator =* (ratio − 1) × 100	1.32	[Group] is 1.y times as ___ the reference value. *or* [Group] is y% ___er than the reference value.	"Low-income people were 1.32 times as likely to have asthma as non-poor individuals." *or* "Low-income people were 32% more likely than non-poor people to have asthma."
	2.71	[Group] is (2.71 − 1) × 100, or 171% ___er than the reference value.	"On average, debt among recent college graduates from low-income families was 171% higher than that of students from non-poor families."
Close to a multiple of 1.0 (e.g., z.00)	3.97	[Group] is (about) z times as ___.	"Residents of low-income neighborhoods were nearly four times as likely to live in a 'food desert' as their non-poor peers."

Notes:

a. Fill in each blank with an adjective, verb, or phrase to convey the aspect being compared—e.g., "tall," "likely to graduate."

b. Non-poor people are the reference group (denominator) for all ratios in Table 14.6.

Example: Average heights were virtually identical for poor and non-poor children (ratio = 0.98 for poor compared to non-poor children).

The sentence conveys that the **ratio** *was* <u>*very close to 1.0*</u>*, reporting the precise value in parentheses.*

For ratios below 1.0, the sentence should convey that the numerator value is smaller than the reference value (denominator), expressed either in terms of multiples or with the numerator as a percentage of the denominator, which is an easy transformation of a ratio: As explained in Chapter 9, the numerator as a percentage of the denominator = ratio × 100.

Example: Two versions: (A) "The ratio of high-school-graduation rates for poor versus non-poor students was 0.76." (B) "Students from poor families were only 76% as likely as those from non-poor families to graduate from high school."

*Although both versions specify the **concepts**, the **groups** being compared, and the **direction** and **magnitude** of the difference, Version A uses off-putting <u>technical language</u> by reporting the **ratio** (0.76). Version B reports the result in **percentage** terms, using more familiar language to convey which group had higher graduation rates and by how much.*

For ratios above 1.0, the sentence should express that the numerator value is larger than the reference value (denominator).

Example: Low-income people were about 1.3 times as likely as more affluent individuals to have asthma—10.6% and 8%, respectively.

*This sentence conveys **direction** (which group is more likely to have asthma), **magnitude** (how much more likely), and the **identity of the reference group** (named after the second "as" in the comparison phrase).*

Alternatively, the size of the difference can be measured using the percentage difference between the numerator and denominator = (ratio − 1) × 100. (See the example under the next subheading.) When a ratio is close to an integer greater than 1, the result can be expressed as a simple multiple.

Example: Use of ride-sharing services increased threefold over the past 2 years.

*This sentence covers the **topic** (use of ride-sharing services), **direction** ("increased"), **magnitude** ("threefold" implies a **ratio** close to 3.0), and **reference time point** (2 years ago).*

Percentage Difference or Change

When reporting a percentage difference or change, the cases, groups, or places (for percentage <u>difference</u>) or the time periods (for percentage <u>change</u>) must be listed in the same order as in the calculation.

Example: Low-income people were 32% more likely than more affluent people to have asthma.

> The phrase "than more affluent people" specifies the **comparison group** and "more likely than" conveys that the comparison is a **percentage** _difference_.

Example: Enrollment increased 15% since last year.

> The phrase "since last year" conveys the **reference (baseline) time point**, whereas "increased" conveys that the comparison is a **percentage** _change_.

For information on units and wording to identify types of bivariate statistics, see Chapter 13.

> Always check whether the presentation of numeric results makes sense for the type of calculation reported, using the definitional or contextual limits on that type of calculation. Word order, units, and vocabulary all provide clues about the type of calculation used, the direction of, and the magnitude of comparisons.

<u>**Caution:**</u> Many authors are sloppy or incorrect when presenting results of calculations, whether in prose, tables, or charts. <u>Always</u> check whether the labeling of tables and charts, or the description of results, is consistent with the type of calculation reported, using the principles in Chapter 9 for definitional or contextual limits on that type of calculation and the guidelines in Table 14.5. Frequent mistakes when interpreting calculation results include naming the groups in subtraction "backward," reversing the order of the numerator and denominator (explaining a ratio upside-down), explaining subtraction as if it were division (or vice versa), and reporting incorrect units or scale.

Errors in interpretation of percentages and percentage change or difference are especially common. Be careful not to confuse the phrases "d is 80% <u>as high as</u> c" and "d is 80% <u>higher than</u> c." The first phrase suggests that d is <u>lower</u> than c ($d \div c = 0.80$); the second suggests that d is <u>higher</u> than c ($d \div c = 1.80$). When you encounter a description of a percentage **of a whole**, a percentage **difference**, or a percentage **change**, always check it against the original numbers to make sure the text correctly conveys which is bigger.

The next few sections integrate general expository writing principles with those for presenting numeric evidence, to illustrate how to perform common writing tasks for quantitative research.

Writing About Distributions

Often, researchers need to describe how the values of a variable are spread across its possible values, sometimes termed **distribution,** or how the parts (values for individual observations) fit together to make up the whole (**composition**). Key elements of such descriptions include the topic, units, direction, and magnitude of the distribution. As explained in Chapters 6, 7, and 10, level of measurement of the variables influences how variables and values are organized in tables and charts presenting the numbers; that order should guide how the narrative description is organized, so that the exhibit and associated prose are consistent with one another.

Nominal Variables

To describe the distribution of a **nominal** (**qualitative**) variable, researchers usually either identify which category is most common or identify a category of particular interest and then discuss how the sizes of other categories compare. As discussed in Chapters 6 and 7, categories of a nominal variable should be organized in the associated tables or charts either thematically or in empirical order of occurrence, which is how the text will, ideally, describe them.

Table 14.7 Nominal Distribution Organized Thematically	
Marital status distribution of persons aged 15 or older, United States, 2015	
Marital status	% of people aged 15 years or older ($N = 260$ million)
Currently married	48%
Currently not married	
Never married	33%
Separated or divorced	13%
Widowed	6%

Source: Data from U.S. Census Bureau (n.d.-b).

Example: In 2015, the most common marital status in the United States was currently married, comprising nearly half (48%) of the 260 million persons aged 15 years or older (Table 14.7). Among those who were not married, never-married adults were the largest group (33% of all adults, but nearly two thirds of the not-married), followed by separated or divorced (about one fourth of the not-married), and widowed.

*The description refers to the **thematic organization** (currently married versus <u>not</u> currently married), reports the percentage share for the <u>largest</u> group, and presents the subgroups among the unmarried in **descending order**—all consistent with the order of the categories in the rows of the associated **table**.*

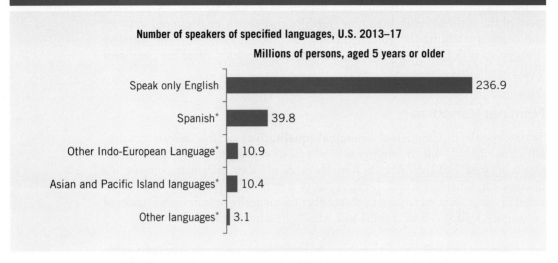

Figure 14.2 Histogram of a Nominal Variable, Descending Order of Occurrence

Number of speakers of specified languages, U.S. 2013–17

Millions of persons, aged 5 years or older

Speak only English	236.9
Spanish*	39.8
Other Indo-European Language*	10.9
Asian and Pacific Island languages*	10.4
Other languages*	3.1

*Includes those who speak English "very well" and "less than very well."

Source: Data from U.S. Census Bureau (n.d.-a).

Example: Estimates from 2013 to 2017 show that nearly 237 million people in the United States spoke only English, encompassing 80% of those aged 5 years and older (Figure 14.2). Those who spoke other languages included both those who spoke English "very well" and those who spoke English "less than very well." Spanish was the second most common language in the United States, accounting for 62% (39.4 million) of those who spoke languages other than English, followed by speakers of other Indo-European languages and Asian languages—each comprising about 16% of the other-language speakers.

> The description names which language is **most common** and reports the **frequency** as both a **count** and a **percentage**, then lists **rank order** of the other categories and their relative frequencies out of those who spoke languages other than English. The accompanying chart uses the same principle (**descending frequency**) to determine the order in which to display the categories.

Quantitative Variables

When describing distributions of **quantitative** variables (**ordinal**, **interval**, and **ratio**), researchers can take advantage of the ordered nature of those numeric values, complemented by vocabulary and analogies to convey the overall shape of the distribution. In tables and charts, distributions of such variables should always be presented with values in their inherent numeric order: chronological order (for dates) or ascending order (for other quantitative variables).

Ordinal Variables

For an **ordinal** variable with only a few categories, researchers can compare the relative sizes of most of the categories—either in ascending order, by identifying the largest category, or by focusing on a category of particular interest, then reporting rank order and size of differences between categories.

> Example: In the 2015–16 U.S. NHANES, just over one fourth of children were from families with income below 130% of the Federal Poverty Level (FPL), qualifying them for free school lunches (Figure 10.6). An additional 20% were income-eligible for reduced-price school lunches. The remaining children were about equally divided between moderate- and high-income families.
>
> > This description presents the **percentages** for the income categories in **increasing order of income level**, reporting the size of **two categories of particular interest**, explaining how those categories map into eligibility for free- or reduced-price school lunches and **naming the figure** where the numbers can be found. Rather than reporting the percentages for the two highest income groups in the text, the description simply points out that they each account for about half of the rest of the income distribution.

For ordinal variables with more than a handful of cases, researchers should identify the key point they want to make and present contrasts selected to illustrate that point. Readers interested in other comparisons could conduct them based on the numbers in the accompanying table or chart.

Continuous Variables

As discussed in the chapters about tables and charts, rarely do researchers report the frequency of every observed value of a continuous variable in the text—there are simply too many different values. Instead, distributions of such variables are often characterized using analogies and descriptive vocabulary for overall shape, complemented with information on summary measures of central tendency and spread.

> Example: The distribution of height among 8-year-old boys in the United States is roughly bell-shaped, but it is skewed slightly to the right (Figure 10.7). Mean height was 132 cm—slightly higher than the median (131 cm) and modal values (129 cm)—with a range from 118 to 148 cm.

*The description uses an **analogy** to depict the **overall shape** of the distribution rather than reporting the prevalence of each of the more than 25 specific height values observed in the data. The right-hand **skew** is evident from the diagram and is documented by reporting the measures of central tendency in **descending order**.*

Writing About Associations

As with descriptions of single variables, descriptions of relationships between two variables should include the topics and units or categories of both variables and the direction and magnitude of the association. Before writing a description of an association, researchers should organize the table or chart of results to reflect the main points they want to make—whether oriented around thematic patterns (for categories of a nominal independent variable, or a set of conceptually similar independent or dependent variables), empirical patterns, or a combination of those approaches.

Cross-Sectional Comparisons

Comparisons of values of a dependent variable across groups, places, or other-raits are referred to as **cross-sectional** comparisons, to distinguish them from time **trends** (discussed later in this chapter). The independent variable in a cross-sectional comparison is usually categorical (either nominal or ordinal), while the dependent variable can be either categorical (e.g., having a particular trait or outcome) or continuous (e.g., a mean value of the dependent variable).

Nominal Independent Variables

To convey direction of association for a nominal independent variable, the description must name which categories are being compared.

Example: In 2018, the median age of national populations varied more than threefold: The median age in Monaco (52 years) was more than triple that in Niger (15 years; Figure 10.11a). China—the world's most populous country—had a median age of about 38 years, placing it slightly above the median age for the entire world (30 years).

*The description reports the size of the difference between the **lowest and highest observed** values of the **dependent variable** (median age) by interpreting a ratio, **naming the two countries** (categories of the independent variable). It then singles out the **largest** country in the world and describes how it fits in the overall pattern.*

Ordinal Independent Variables

For **quantitative** variables, researchers often can describe direction of association in terms of positive (direct) or negative (inverse) associations, using either that wording or other phrasing that conveys an increase across values of the independent variable. Recall from Chapter 2 that, in a positive association, values of the dependent variable increase as the independent variable increases; in a negative association, the outcome decreases as values of the predictor increase.

> Example: The prevalence of obesity among U.S. children declined with increasing family income. For example, children from the lowest income category (free-lunch-eligible families) were nearly twice as likely as those from the highest income category to be obese (23% and 13%, respectively; Table 13.4).
>
> *The first sentence portrays the **direction** of the relationship between the dependent variable (obesity) and the **ordinal independent variable** (family income group) using the phrase "declined with increasing income." The second sentence conveys the **size** of that difference using a ratio ("twice as likely") and reports the values of the dependent variable for the groups being compared.*

Trends

To describe change over time in either a continuous or a categorical variable, the description should name the time points involved, as well as the topic, the W's, the units, and the direction and magnitude of the trend.[1]

> Example: Between 2015 and 2070, the world population is projected to rise by 2.8 billion people, reaching a total of 10.6 billion (Figure 7.3). Over that period, the population of the less-developed regions of the world is predicted to increase by 52%, versus only a 3% increase in the more-developed regions. That differential growth would result in a 4-percentage-point increase in less-developed countries' share of the world's population, from 84% in 2015 to 88% in 2070.
>
> *The topic sentence conveys the **topic**, **direction**, and **size** of population trends, specifying the **location** and **dates** of the projected change. **Direction** and **magnitude** are expressed with a combination of vocabulary ("rise," "increase," and "growth") and math (**subtraction** and **percentage change**).*

An alternative way to convey change over time or difference between groups is to report the extent of <u>change</u> (or <u>difference</u>) in a table or chart—instead of, or in addition to, the measures of <u>level</u> from which that change (or difference) is calculated.

---

[1] The word "trend" is also sometimes used to describe a difference across other continuous independent variables, such as age in years or income in monetary units.

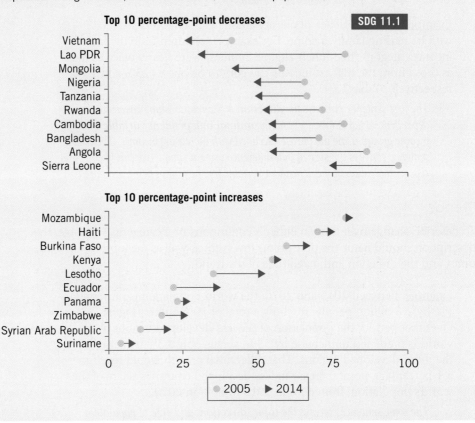

Despite increasing urbanization, many countries have reduced the share of urban dwellers living in slums.

Population living in slums, 2005 and 2014 (% of urban population)

Top 10 percentage-point decreases

SDG 11.1

Vietnam
Lao PDR
Mongolia
Nigeria
Tanzania
Rwanda
Cambodia
Bangladesh
Angola
Sierra Leone

Top 10 percentage-point increases

Mozambique
Haiti
Burkina Faso
Kenya
Lesotho
Ecuador
Panama
Zimbabwe
Syrian Arab Republic
Suriname

0   25   50   75   100

● 2005   ▶ 2014

Source: Data from World Bank (2018). © World Bank. License: CC BY 3.0 IGO.

<u>Example</u>: Despite increasing urbanization, between 2005 and 2014, many countries reduced the share of their urban-dwellers who lived in slums. Countries with the largest percentage-point decrease included Lao (from 80% to 30%), Angola (from 85% to 55%), and Cambodia (80% to 55%; upper panel of Figure 14.3). Among countries with a top-10 decrease, however, the percentage of the urban population living in slums varied substantially even at the end of the period, with a threefold higher prevalence in Sierra Leone (75%) than in Vietnam (25%).

Over the same period, some countries saw an increase in the share of their urban residents who lived in slums, with sizeable increases in Ecuador (from 20% to 35%), Lesotho (from 35% to over 50%), and the Syrian Arab Republic (from 10% to 20%; lower panel of Figure 14.3). Among countries with a top-10 increase, the percentage of urban residents living in slums in 2014 ranged from less than 5% in Suriname to nearly 80% in Mozambique.

> *The description is **organized into two separate paragraphs**: one for the countries that experienced a <u>decrease</u> over time in the percentage of urban residents who lived in slums (dependent variable) and another for those that experienced an <u>increase</u>. **Topic sentences** convey that the purpose of the chart is to show change over time (the independent variable) in slum-dwelling. The **evidentiary sentences** report the **direction** and **size** of <u>change</u> in the share of slum-dwellers for the top three countries and then discuss variation in the **level** of the dependent variable at the end of the study period.*

A **cross-sectional comparison** involves a categorical independent variable with either a continuous or a categorical dependent variable. A **trend** involves change over time in the values of either a continuous or a categorical variable.

Comparison Against a Benchmark

When comparing values to a **benchmark**, **threshold**, or **target**, researchers should report the value of that benchmark (including its units), explain what it means for values to fall above or below that threshold, and provide a citation to an authoritative source of the benchmark value and its interpretation. They should also describe any contextual factors—such as time, place, and group—that affect the numeric value of the threshold, discussing them in the methods section of a scientific paper or report, or a footnote to a document for a more general audience.

> <u>Example</u>: Families were classified as poor if their income was less than the U.S. Federal Poverty Threshold for that household size and age composition, adjusted for differences in cost of living for the respondents' residential location (U.S. Census Bureau, 2018e).

> *This sentence **interprets** the meaning of the **threshold**, explaining that values <u>below</u> the threshold are **classified** as poor. It also states that U.S. Federal Poverty Thresholds differ by the size and age composition of the household and the year [aspects of **who**), date (**when**), and location (**where**)] and provides a **citation** to the source of detailed thresholds.*

Having defined the meaning of the benchmark or threshold, researchers should then report observed statistics on the outcome based on that threshold, describing the direction and size of variation in that outcome across groups, places, or dates.

Figure 14.4 Distribution Compared to a Benchmark

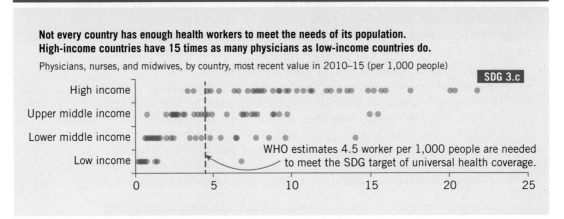

Not every country has enough health workers to meet the needs of its population. High-income countries have 15 times as many physicians as low-income countries do.

Physicians, nurses, and midwives, by country, most recent value in 2010–15 (per 1,000 people)

SDG 3.c

WHO estimates 4.5 worker per 1,000 people are needed to meet the SDG target of universal health coverage.

Source: Data from World Bank (2018). © World Bank. License: CC BY 3.0 IGO.

<u>Example</u>: The World Health Organization estimates that at least 4.5 healthcare workers per 1,000 people are needed to meet the Sustainable Development Goals target of universal health coverage (World Bank Group, 2018). Although many high-income countries surpass that target—some having three or even four times that level—all of the low-income countries fall far short of the recommended staffing levels (Figure 14.4). About half of middle-income countries meet the target—but, again, there is wide variability across countries in whether they meet that minimum target and, if not, how much of a deficit they face in healthcare workers per capita.

> *The topic sentence introduces the **target** value of the **outcome** (number of healthcare workers per capita), placing it in the **substantive context** of universal health coverage and citing the **authoritative source** for that target value. The evidentiary sentences **interpret** the level and range of observed values of that outcome by comparing them to the target value using phrasing such as "surpass" and "fall short" to convey the **direction** of the differences between the observed and target values. A ratio ("three or four times the level") conveys the **size** of the excess in high-income countries, and "<u>how much</u> of a deficit" conveys both the direction and the size of that difference in middle-income countries.*

Writing About Complex Patterns

One of the more challenging tasks in writing about numeric results is describing patterns involving three or more variables. Common examples include how a relationship between an independent and a dependent variable changes over time or differs across locations; how an independent variable differs according to two independent variables at the same time; and how several dependent variables are each related to the same independent variable.

These tasks can involve dozens of numbers, often causing researchers to write ineffective descriptions that either (a) lose the forest for the trees by presenting every number in the text or (b) provide a very incomplete picture of the overall pattern by describing only a few, arbitrarily chosen numbers from that pattern. A better approach is to organize the full set of numbers in either a table or a chart and then describe the pattern in prose, using a technique I developed called "Generalization, Example, Exception" (Miller, 2015). The idea is to identify and describe the general shape of a pattern, give a representative numeric example from the associated table or chart to illustrate that pattern, and then explain and illustrate any exceptions.

The first step is to identify the major questions to be addressed by the data. In many complex patterns, there are two or three relationships of interest: the association between <u>each</u> pair of variables and whether that pattern is consistent across values of the third variable. The second step is to organize the data in a table or chart in a way that makes it easy to see and describe how the set of numbers answers those questions. For quantitative independent variables, the ordered nature of their values will dictate how the variables are organized.

> <u>Example</u>: In Figure 14.5, the first major question is whether the relationship between TV-watching and obesity was observed in all family income categories, and the second major question is whether the relationship between family income and obesity was consistent across levels of TV-watching.
>
> *The <u>first</u> **question** concerns how obesity (the **dependent variable**, on the **y-axis**) varied by TV-watching (an **ordinal independent variable**; on the **x-axis**) within one sub-chart (income group, the **other independent variable**) and whether that pattern also fits the other income groups (**sub-charts**, arranged in ascending order of income group, which is also **ordinal**).*
>
> *The <u>second</u> **question** considers how obesity (**y-axis**) varied across income groups (**sub-charts**) for a given TV-watching level (point on the **x-axis**) and whether that pattern also fits the other TV-watching levels.*

Generalization

For each generalization, researchers should aim to describe a pattern that captures a relationship among most of, if not all, the numbers. If a pattern fits most of the groups (or times or places), it is a **generalization**. The cases that don't fit are **exceptions**. A generalization captures **consensus** in the direction of association and, possibly, also in terms of the magnitude of the relationship between two of the variables for each value of the third variable. In other words, the same general shape and size pattern occurs in many of the times, places, or groups involved in the relationship.

Figure 14.5   Chart for "Generalization, Example, Exception"

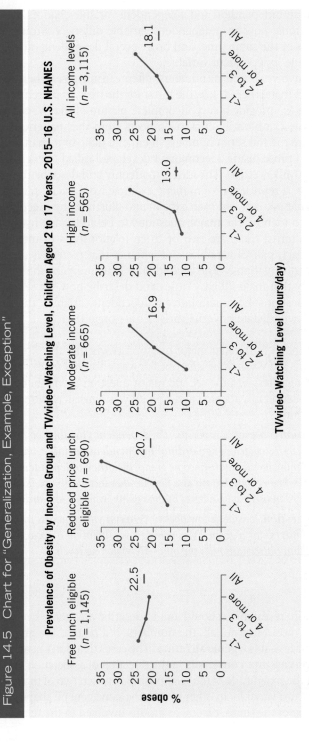

Notes: Weighted to population level using sampling weights provided by the Centers for Disease Control and Prevention (CDC, 2018a). Obesity: BMI >= 95th percentile for age. Free lunch eligible, <130% of Federal Poverty Level (FPL); reduced price lunch eligible, 130%–184% of FPL; moderate income, 185%–349% of FPL; high income, 350%+ of FPL.

Source: Author's calculations based on data from the 2015–16 U.S. National Health and Nutrition Examination Survey for children aged 2 to 17 years.

A **generalization** occurs when a description characterizes <u>many</u> or <u>all</u> parts of a numeric association among variables in terms of direction, magnitude, and (for scientific audiences) statistical significance.

Generalizations about each of the major patterns in a table or figure can serve as topic sentences for separate paragraphs, introducing the specific aspects of the topic involved in that pattern and painting a verbal picture of its overall shape. Phrases such as "throughout most of the period shown," "in most [locations,]" and "regardless of [trait measured by the third variable]" express that the pattern is a general one, <u>not</u> just for one time, place, or group. Such phrases also help differentiate between a pattern that is **universal** and one that characterizes <u>many, but not all,</u> cases.

Example

Although the topic sentences with those generalizations should convey the direction of association, they often don't include any numbers to capture the size of a pattern. That can be accomplished in the **example** step, which also should refer to the accompanying exhibit that reports the numbers. By using evidentiary sentences to describe a numeric example from the table or chart, this step links the generalization to the specific numbers upon which it is based. It helps tie the prose and the table or chart together, showing readers where in the table or chart those numbers come from and interpreting the results of calculations or comparisons to illustrate the direction and size of the pattern. Using other numeric information from the table or chart, readers can then check for themselves whether the pattern applies to other times, places, or groups.

Exception

For many social research questions, it is unusual for one general description to capture all relevant aspects of a pattern, thus creating one (or more) **exceptions** to the generalization. Exceptions occur when one or more numeric values depart from, or even contradict, the pattern among the other values. Having already described and illustrated the generalization, researchers should convey an exception by explaining how that value or set of values <u>differs</u> from the generalization. Is the exception higher or lower? By how much? If a trend, is it moving toward or away from the pattern they are contrasting it against? In other words, researchers should describe both the direction and the magnitude of the <u>difference</u> between the generalization and the exception.

Exceptions (also known as **inconsistencies** or **anomalies**) to a general pattern occur when one or more values do <u>not</u> conform to that generalization. They can occur when the direction, size, or statistical significance of a pattern for some places, times, or groups is different from a generalization that fits other places, times, or groups.

Phrases like "conversely" and "on the contrary" express that one part of a pattern is the <u>opposite</u> of the **direction** described in the generalization—such as a rising rather than a falling trend, or a negative instead of a positive difference between values. Phrases such as "on the other hand" and "however" distinguish an exception from a generalization in terms of the **size** of a difference or trend.

> <u>Example</u>: In the three highest family income groups, the child obesity rate increased with increasing amount of TV-watching time (Figure 14.5).For instance, among children from moderate-income families, those who watched 4 or more hours of TV per day were nearly three times as likely to be obese, and those who watched 2 to 3 hours per day were twice as likely to be obese, as those who watched up to 1 hour per day (26.6%, 19.6%, and 10.1%, respectively). In contrast, in the free-lunch-eligible (lowest-income) group, obesity declined slightly with increasing TV-watching time, although the variation was very small and not statistically significant.
>
> > *The topic sentence introduces the* **generalization** *with the phrase "in the three highest family income groups,"signaling that the pattern is true for <u>most, but not all</u>, of those income groups (one* **independent variable***). The rest of the topic sentence names the topic—how obesity (the* **dependent variable***) is related to TV-watching time (the other* **independent variable***)—and describes the <u>positive</u> association between those variables, naming the* **figure** *in which the overall pattern is depicted. The evidentiary sentence provides specific numeric* **examples** *from the chart, and it portrays the size of the difference across groups, using results of behind-the-scenes calculations.*
> >
> > *The last sentence introduces the* **exception** *using the phrase "in contrast,"pointing out that the association between obesity and TV-watching time among children from low-income families is in the <u>opposite</u>* **direction** *of the general pattern ("obesity <u>declined</u> with increasing TV-watching time") and characterizing its* **magnitude** *("slightly").*

For more guidance on how to use the "Generalization, Example, Exception" technique to summarize a complex pattern, see Chapters 2 and 10 and Appendix A in *The Chicago Guide to Writing About Numbers*, 2nd Edition (Miller, 2015).

Researchers should portray a pattern involving many numbers by addressing the overarching questions behind the table or figure. In other words, they should aim to describe the forest (big picture) rather than reporting each of the trees (individual numeric values) in the text.

- Detailed numbers involved in that pattern should be presented in a table or chart, organized thematically or empirically to coordinate with the accompanying written description.

- The "Generalization, Example, Exception" technique should be used to summarize the overall pattern, describing the direction and size of a relationship that fits most or all of the numeric values; illustrating that pattern with specific numbers from the table or chart; and pointing out exceptions from that general pattern.

- The description should be organized into paragraphs, with topic sentences to identify the major point and shape of the general pattern for each paragraph.

Content and Structure of Research Formats

The length, content, and structure of quantitative research documents vary substantially depending on whether they are intended for a research audience, a general audience, or an "applied" audience such as policymakers or clinicians.

Research Audiences

Articles, reports, and posters for **research audiences** have a standard structure, typically divided into an introduction, a review of the published literature on the topic, a description of data and methods, a results section with tables and charts, a discussion and conclusion section, and a complete list of the references that were cited in the text (Pyrczak & Bruce, 2016). Footnotes and technical appendixes are also common. Books for research audiences have the same elements as research articles but are organized into chapters, to provide room for more depth and detail.

Lay Audiences

Formats used to communicate to **lay audiences** (the "general public") include blogs, newspaper or magazine articles, and fact sheets or infographics. These formats are not divided into the formal parts that characterize a scientific paper. Instead, researchers should focus on writing a logical, coherent story line with numeric facts or patterns as evidence, incorporating information about context, data, and methods into the body of the narrative using the expository writing guidelines. Numeric facts are often used to highlight the importance of the topic, to provide other background information, or to illustrate patterns such as trends or relationships between variables. Especially for lay audiences, researchers should communicate the direction and size of patterns rather than simply reporting numbers and expecting readers to do the math needed to see the patterns in the data or to figure out how those numbers answer the question of interest. Technical language should be kept to a minimum, and vocabulary should be chosen with the education level of the specific audience in mind. Tables or charts, if used at all, should be kept simple and focused, and they should be referred to by name or number as examples are interpreted in the text or a sidebar.

> Example: The Urban Institute and the Brookings Institution created the *Briefing Book* to provide "A citizen's guide to the fascinating (though often complex) elements of the US tax system" (Urban Institute Tax Policy Center, 2017). On the Website, charts that portray patterns are alternated with short paragraphs that define terms and describe patterns.

> Example: An article in the online version of *The Independent* is titled "Ten Countries Host More Than Half of the World's Refugees." An accompanying visualization shows those countries in descending order of number of refugees, along with a map to show their locations (Osborne, 2016).

Fact sheets, infographics, and Websites for lay audiences frequently use headings to organize subsections, each of which focuses on one key question with an associated visualization. Vizzes for such audiences are often written with "take-home message" titles that capture the topic, direction, and magnitude of the association, thus reducing the amount of text needed to communicate the main point about each viz; see examples in Chapter 7.

Applied Audiences

So-called **applied audiences** for quantitative research are made up of policymakers, educators, health service providers, or other professionals who are interested in how the research answered a question related to their work so they can translate the results into real-world actions. Formats for such audiences include reports, chartbooks, and issue or policy briefs, which provide less detail and technical information than a research article but more depth and detail than materials for lay audiences.

When writing for an applied audience, researchers should portray results using types of visualizations or charts that are familiar to members of that profession, aiming to convey the overall shape and size of a pattern. Each chart or viz should include a take-home-point title. The written descriptions of those exhibits will be longer than for lay audiences, written either as a series of bulleted annotations or in short paragraphs that explain how those numbers address a specific aspect of the research question. Tables should be reserved for when a report or chartbook is intended mainly to organize detailed numbers for others' use. Such tables are often placed in an appendix rather than in the body of the document.

Typically, formats for applied audiences place information on the research process or analytic methods into sidebars, glossaries, and (for reports or chartbooks) appendixes for readers who need the technical details.

> Example: The American Community Survey Brief on Household Income (Guzman, 2017) is organized into sections, with bold headings to identify subtopics. Within each subtopic are charts to show patterns, descriptions of those patterns, and tables of detailed values for readers to use in their own calculations and comparisons. Sidebars are used to define terms.

The length, content, and organization of a presentation of quantitative research should differ depending on whether the intended **audience** is

- **researchers** (also known as a **scientific** or **academic** audience),

- a **lay audience** (the general public), or

- an audience of professionals who want to apply the research results.

If there is more than one intended audience, researchers should create separate documents, each designed to match the intended use of the results and the particular needs of a specific audience.

See Chapter 13 of *The Chicago Guide to Writing About Numbers*, 2nd Edition (Miller, 2015), for guidelines on writing about numbers for lay and applied audiences, and see the recommended readings at the end of this chapter for links to illustrative examples.

TERMS AND CONCEPTS ——————————————————

HIGHLIGHTS

- Being able to **communicate numeric results** clearly and correctly is a key aspect of making sense of the numbers, whether one is a producer or a consumer of research.

- **Tables, charts,** and **prose** should be used in complementary ways to take advantage of their respective strengths for presenting quantitative research results.

- **Standard expository writing approaches**, such as **paragraph structure**, and **topic, evidentiary,** and **transition sentences** should be used in combination with principles specifically related to presenting numeric information.

- Numeric evidence should be both **reported** and **interpreted**, specifying the **direction** and **size** of patterns.

- **Units** and **wording** provide clues to the **type of measure or calculation** being presented

and, thus, how to interpret what those results mean and whether the reported values are plausible.

- Conclusions about the statistical significance of results should convey that they are associated with a chance of being incorrect, where that chance is measured by the associated p-value (see Chapter 13).

- The "**Generalization, Example, Exception**" **technique** can be used to describe complex relationships involving many numbers, summarizing the main patterns and conveying the extent to which they capture all, many, or only some of the overall relationship.

- The organization, level of detail, and other aspects of formatting and style of communicating about research results should differ depending on the intended **audience** and the **objective**.

RECOMMENDED READINGS

Booth, W. C., Colomb, G. G., Williams, J. M., Bizup, J., & FitzGerald, W. T. (2016). *The craft of research* (4th ed., Chapters 14 and 15). University of Chicago Press.

Miller, J. E. (2015). *The Chicago guide to writing about numbers* (2nd ed.). University of Chicago Press. See Chapters 2 and 9 and Appendix A (on

"Generalization, Example, Exception"); Chapter 8 (on analogies); Chapters 11 and 12 (writing for research audiences); and Chapter 13 (writing for applied and lay audiences).

Pyrczak, F., & Bruce, R. R. (2016). *Writing empirical research reports: A basic guide for students of the social and behavioral sciences* (8th ed.). Routledge.

RESOURCES

Guzman, G. (2017). *Household income: 2016. American Community Survey briefs.* U.S. Census Bureau, U.S. Department of Commerce. https://www.census.gov/content/dam/Census/library/publications/2017/acs/acsbr16-02.pdf

McCarthy, N. (2015, January 23). *Air pollution: Chinese and American cities in comparison* [Infographic]. *Forbes.* https://www.forbes.com/sites/niallmccarthy/2015/01/23/air-pollution-chinese-and-american-cities-in-comparison-infographic/#3bcc32652362

Osborne, S. (2016, October 5). Ten countries host more than half of world's refugees – and the UK urgently needs to do more, says Amnesty. *The Independent.* https://www.independent.co.uk/news/uk/home-news/refugee-crisis-amnesty-international-10-countries-host-more-half-uk-needs-to-do-more-a7344171.html

Urban Institute Tax Policy Center. (2017). Briefing book. https://www.taxpolicycenter.org/briefing-book/what-are-sources-revenue-federal-government

EXERCISES

Individual Exercises

Quantitative Reasoning in Everyday Life

1. Find a newspaper article or blog entry about popular culture, sports, the weather, or another "everyday" topic. (a) List the major tools (text, tables, charts) used to present numbers. (b) For one example of each type of tool, identify its intended purpose (e.g., presenting detailed numeric values, conveying a general pattern). (c) Use the criteria in this chapter to evaluate whether it is an appropriate choice of tool for that task and audience. (d) If so, explain why. If not, suggest a more effective tool for that context.

2. (a) In a general-interest newspaper article, identify all instances where the authors report a single number (<u>not</u> a comparison of two or more numbers). (b) For each, indicate whether the author conveys whether that value is typical or unusual for the (i) topic, (ii) context, and (iii) units.

3. In the same article you used in the previous exercise, (a) identify a few instances in which two values are compared to one another. (b) For each, evaluate whether the authors specified (i) the direction of the difference between those values and (ii) the magnitude of that difference. (c) If they conveyed magnitude, specify (i) what kind of calculation they used to compare the values and (ii) what clues you used to determine what kind of math they used.

Interpreting Research

4. Do the same as for Exercise 1, but for a research article or report.

5. In that same research article or report, (a) find descriptions of univariate distributions for variables at each of the following levels of measurement: (i) nominal, (ii) ordinal, and (iii) interval or ratio variables with many possible values. (b) Critique those descriptions, using the guidelines in this chapter. (c) Identify the criteria the author used to choose which value(s) to highlight in each description. (d) Discuss whether those values match the research question and introduction to the article. (e) If all values of that variable

are described with equal emphasis, assess whether one or more values should be featured and why. (f) Rewrite the descriptions to correct any shortcomings you find.

6. Regarding that same article or report, evaluate the authors' use of the following expository writing principles in the methods and results sections: (a) headings and subheadings to organize material, (b) topic sentences to introduce the objective of each paragraph, (c) evidentiary sentences to present numeric information related to that objective, and (d) transition sentences to tie steps in the analysis to one another and to the overall purpose of the study.

Communicating Research

7. On the Pew Research Center Website (https://www.pewsocialtrends.org), find a chart accompanied by a description of how knowledge or attitude about an issue varies by a categorical trait, such as political affiliation. (a) Critique the description in terms of how clearly the authors convey the following elements: (i) the topic, (ii) the W's, (iii) the categories and units of each variable, and (iv) the direction and (v) the magnitude of observed differences. (b) Rewrite the description to correct any shortcomings you find.

8. Use information in the **Program for the International Assessment of Adult Competencies** report Figure 4-A on trends in digital problem solving by race/ethnicity: 2012/14 and 2017 (https://nces.ed.gov/surveys/piaac/current_results.asp) to perform the following steps. (a) Critique the description using the criteria in this chapter for writing about three-way associations. (b) Rewrite it using the "Generalization, Example, Exception" approach.

GROUP EXERCISES

Communicating Research

9. (a) Make a list of how each type of tool was used to present numbers in research articles, using your work for Exercise 4. (b) Discuss suggestions for different tools for those research tasks, and discuss the reasons for those suggestions.

10. With a classmate, exchange your written description of a bivariate pattern from Exercise 7, including the link to the page where you found the data. (a) Provide feedback on each other's drafts, referring to guidelines in this chapter about

(i) topic sentence, (ii) W's, and (iii) conveying direction and magnitude. (b) Revise your description to correct any problems found by your peer reviewer.

11. (a) Do the same as for the previous exercise, but using your "Generalization, Example, Exception" drafts from Exercise 8. (b) Provide feedback on (i) paragraph organization, (ii) choice of examples, (iii) whether the written narrative complemented the information reported in the associated chart, and (iv) whether the order of the description coordinated with the design of that chart.

CHAPTER 15

The Role of Research Methods in Making Sense of Numbers

Learning Objectives

After reading this chapter, you will be able to do the following:

1. State the importance of the W's for making sense of quantitative research.

2. Distinguish between the practical meaning and statistical significance of a numeric finding.

3. Identify the four dimensions of "importance" of a quantitative research result.

4. Differentiate which aspects of research methods determine practical meaning, statistical significance, internal validity, and external validity.

5. Describe how the quantitative reasoning principles from throughout this book are used for each of the four major types of research tasks.

This chapter builds on and ties together what you've learned throughout this book about making sense of numbers. After a quick refresher on the importance of the W's, I define what is meant by the "practical meaning" of a research result and discuss how (and why) researchers should assess that aspect of their findings. I then explain how practical meaning is distinct from the other perspectives on the importance of a research finding, including statistical significance, internal validity, and external validity. I then differentiate how each is affected by various aspects of study design and measurement. Finally, I describe how principles from throughout this book should be used for each of the four major types of research tasks: interpreting others' numeric information, collecting data, analyzing data, and communicating about quantitative research.

The W's Revisited

In Chapter 2, I introduced the W's as a checklist for identifying the types of information needed to make sense of numbers from quantitative research. As discussed in Chapters 1 and 3, **what**—otherwise known as the topic—is a crucial piece of information, because a numeric value that is completely reasonable for one topic might be utterly ridiculous for another. As discussed in Chapter 5, knowing the context of a study (which encompasses **when, where**, and **who/which** cases) is also essential for making sense of numbers, because a number that fits one time, place, or group can be far too high or too low for a different time, place, or group.

What at first appears to be a single "honorary W"—**how**—turns out to have several dimensions, including the approach used to measure the concept of interest (see Chapter 4); the type of study design, sampling methods, and data sources that produced the data (Chapter 11); the aspects of study design that affect whether a relationship between two variables can be interpreted as cause and effect (Chapter 12); and the mathematical and statistical methods used to analyze the data (Chapters 8, 9, 10, and 13). Each of those aspects of "how" the research was conducted affects the ways that the resulting numbers can be interpreted and applied.

As mentioned in Chapter 13, another "honorary W"—**how many** (sample size)—also has implications for making sense of a numeric estimate based on samples.

Practical Importance

What Is Practical Importance?

So far, we haven't considered another honorary W that is central to making sense of numeric results: **so what**? In quantitative research, "so what?" refers to the **practical importance** of a numeric estimate. Practical importance—also known as **substantive significance**—is concerned with whether an observed level, difference, or change is big enough to matter for that topic, context, and way of collecting data. Put differently, substantive significance pertains to whether the numeric result is meaningful clinically, politically, or educationally—or in whatever real-world domain the topic fits.

> Example: Is a proposed increase in the minimum wage large enough to lift workers out of poverty and help them pay for better housing, transportation, or child care?
>
> *Here, <u>substantive significance</u> relates to whether the increase in the minimum wage will have a <u>meaningful impact</u> on the incomes of those who earn that wage.*

> The **practical importance** (also known as **substantive significance** or **practical meaning**) of a quantative research finding concerns whether it is numerically large enough to matter for the topic, context, and measures under study.

Practical Significance vs. Statistical Significance

Often, researchers, journalists, and others describing results of quantitative studies are not very precise in their use of the term "significant" or "significance," failing to specify whether they mean <u>statistical</u> significance or <u>substantive</u> significance. Both are valuable aspects of the "importance" of a numeric result, and each provides a different perspective on what that finding means and how it can be applied.

Like many students who have recently learned about inferential statistics, you might believe that statistical significance is the <u>only</u> determinant of whether a research result (e.g., a mean value, difference across groups, or change across time) is "important." Although it is a <u>necessary</u> part of conveying the uncertainty associated with results based on a sample instead of an entire population (see Chapter 13), statistical significance alone is <u>not</u> a <u>sufficient</u> basis to assess the importance of a numeric estimate. As mentioned in Chapter 13, the standard error of an estimate decreases with increasing sample size; thus, with a large enough sample, even teeny-weeny effect sizes can be statistically significant. However, really small effects are unlikely to be meaningful in a practical sense.

> <u>Example</u>: If 1 million 8-year-old boys in the United States participated in a study of height, even a 0.1-inch difference in height might be statistically significant.
>
> *It is hard to envision a situation in which a one-tenth of an inch difference in children's height would be **big enough** for anyone to care about. That size difference (**effect size**) is also probably smaller than most rulers used to measure height could detect. And that small of a difference might even be due to measurement error related to whether a child has straight or curly hair!*

What Questions Can Statistical Significance Answer?

To clarify the distinction between statistical significance and practical importance, let's review what questions inferential statistics can and cannot answer. Inferential statistics assess how likely it would be to obtain an estimate at least as large as that based on the sample if the true value of that statistic was 0 in the population from which that sample was drawn (see Chapter 13). The *p*-value measures the probability of incorrectly concluding that the population parameter is 0 based on the sample estimate, so we want p to be as small as possible.

> Example: Based on an analysis of observational data from a large representative sample of teenagers in the United States, Cummings and Vandewater (2007) found that for every hour boys played video games per day, they read on average <u>just 2 minutes less</u> ($p < .01$).
>
>> $p < .01$ means simply that the 99% confidence interval around the point estimate of the effect of gaming time on reading time did not include 0. However, because of the large sample used in in the gaming study ($n = 1,400$), the standard error of that estimate was very small, meaning that even the trivially small effect (2 additional minutes spent reading for every hour less a boy played video games) reached conventional levels of **statistical significance**.

> Example: The same study found that each hour teenagers spent alone playing video games was associated with a 15-minute decrease in time spent with friends in activities other than video games. Although the association between time spent playing video games and time with friends <u>was</u> statistically significant for boys, the same size effect was <u>not</u> statistically significant for girls.
>
>> The 95% confidence interval for girls was −38 to +7 minutes. Simplifying the conclusion to "not statistically significant" overlooks the fact that a large part of the **interval estimate** (from −38 to 0) is **compatible** with the conclusion that, as for boys, time spent playing video games among teenage girls was inversely associated with time spent with friends.

The statistical significance (or lack thereof) of those two results merely tells us the probability that the patterns of time use observed in the sample could have arisen based solely on chance—if, in fact, there were no difference between groups in the population. That is important information, but it is <u>not</u> the only thing we need to know about those results.

What Questions <u>Can't</u> Statistical Significance Answer?

Although information about the degree of uncertainty of a numeric estimate is an expected part of analysis of data from a random sample, inferential test results <u>cannot</u> answer several other equally important questions for making sense of the results. First, statistical significance of an association between two variables does <u>not</u> tell us whether that relationship can be interpreted as **cause and effect**. Recall from Chapter 12 that if an observed association between an independent variable (x) and a dependent variable (outcome, y) is really due to a third variable (z), the association between x and y is **spurious**—it is **confounded** by that other variable. In other words, the hypothesized independent variable isn't the real cause of the outcome.

> Example: Would getting boys to cut down on playing video games <u>cause</u> them to increase the time they spend reading? Suppose that further investigation revealed that an increase in time spent participating in drama club or school government was associated with <u>less</u> time playing video games but <u>more</u> time reading.
>
> > *In this hypothetical situation, video-game-playing time (x) is <u>not</u> a real **cause** of (influence on) reading time (y); that association is **confounded** by time spent on those extracurricular activities (z). In other words, the observed inverse association between video-game-playing time (the independent variable) and reading time (the dependent variable) is **spurious**—explained entirely by the association of each of those variables with a third factor (time spent on those extracurricular activities). As a consequence, inducing boys to reduce their video-game-playing time would <u>not</u> yield the desired increase in reading time. A better intervention to increase reading time might be to encourage boys to spend more time on those extracurricular activities (the true cause).*

However, you might be skeptical about this case for confounding, because you remember from high school that students choose their own extracurricular activities. If so, comparing **observational** data on students who participated in drama club or school government to those who did not might still be confounded by other traits that were the cause of higher reading time, such as level of interest in reading literature or material about politics.

> > *To test whether drama and student government participation really **cause** an increase in reading time, you could attempt to conduct a **true experiment**, randomly assigning students to participate in those activities (treatment group) or not (control group). Doing so would rule out non-comparable groups due to self-selection. However, getting teenagers to participate in the activity to which they were assigned might be challenging (see the discussion about whether a characteristic is modifiable a little later in this chapter), so such an experiment might not be feasible.*

Second, statistical significance of an association does <u>not</u> help us determine **causal order** of the variables x and y: whether what we think is the cause is actually the effect, otherwise known as **reverse causation** or the "cart before the horse" problem (see Chapter 12).

> Example: What if boys who became more interested in reading cut back on video-game-playing to make more time for their reading? That would

also produce an inverse association between reading and playing video games, but with the <u>opposite</u> of our hypothesized causal order.

> *If video-game-playing time depends on reading time, then what we <u>thought</u> was the **independent variable** (cause) is really the **dependent variable** (effect). If **reverse causation** is occurring, then intervening to decrease what we believed was the cause (video-game-playing time) would <u>not</u> have the desired positive impact on what we thought was the effect (reading time).*

Third, the statistical significance of an association does <u>not</u> tell us whether that association is in the **expected direction**. The dependent variable could show statistically significant variation with the independent variable, but in the <u>opposite</u> of the hypothesized direction—a very important point about that numeric result!

<u>Example</u>: What if the study had found that—contrary to what was expected—less video-game-playing time was statistically significantly associated with <u>less</u> reading time?

> *If the goal is to increase reading time, we certainly wouldn't want to encourage teenagers to cut back on playing video games if doing so would also <u>reduce</u> the amount of time they spent reading.*

Fourth, statistical significance of an association does <u>not</u> tell us whether the size (magnitude) of the effect is practically meaningful—**large enough to matter** in the real-world context.

<u>Example</u>: As noted previously, teenage boys read <u>just 2 more minutes</u> for each 1-hour reduction in time spent playing video games. Is that a big enough difference to attract serious interest from parents or teachers who seek to increase boys' reading time?

> *Would <u>2 additional minutes</u> of reading per day appreciably improve boys' cognitive function or enjoyment of literature? It is difficult to imagine that an intervention to decrease time spent playing video games would be a worthwhile approach to increasing reading time, based on such a **small effect**.*

Standard deviations and other empirical measures of **distribution** are useful **benchmarks** for assessing whether an observed change in the outcome is big enough to matter.

<u>Example</u>: A 2-minute increase in reading time might be educationally meaningful if the standard deviation for that outcome was 4 minutes, but it would be trivially small if the standard deviation were 20 minutes.

*The same size effect is considered more **practically important** if it is equivalent to a substantial **share of a standard deviation** of the dependent variable than if it corresponds to only a small fraction of a standard deviation (see Chapter 10). A one-half standard deviation increase in reading (2 minutes ÷ 4 minutes) is <u>substantial</u>, whereas a 1/10th of a standard deviation increase is quite <u>small</u>.*

Finally, the statistical significance of an association does <u>not</u> tell us whether the independent variable is **modifiable**. If it cannot be changed, then even an effect that is statistically significant, causal, in the expected direction, and big enough to matter is <u>not</u> a good basis for an intervention to change the dependent variable in the desired direction.

<u>Example</u>: How easy is it to get teenage boys to substantially cut back on playing video games and to sustain that change?

*Prying a gaming device out of the hands of a teenage boy for an <u>hour every day</u> will probably require so much effort on the part of his parents, and to generate so much conflict, that such a strategy is not likely to succeed in the long run. Better to find a different cause of increasing reading time that is **easier to change and maintain**.*

Alternatively, if a realistic-sized change in the independent variable is small, it might not produce enough of a change in the dependent variable to be worthwhile.

<u>Example</u>: Many studies have shown that obesity is associated with a large, causal, and statistically significant increase in mortality, suggesting that weight loss would be an effective approach to reducing mortality risk among obese individuals. Although, in theory, body weight can be changed, in practice, most dieters find it very hard to lose a substantial amount of weight and keep that weight off.

*Research on weight loss has repeatedly shown that it is very difficult for many people to <u>achieve and maintain</u> a big-enough weight reduction to cause a meaningful reduction in mortality. In other words, that independent variable (weight) is <u>not</u> very **changeable**, so an intervention that addresses a different risk factor might be more effective at reducing mortality.*

The standard deviation of an independent variable can be used to evaluate whether a given-sized change in that independent variable is **realistic** (plausible) in the context of the study topic and setting.

<u>Example</u>: A 10-pound weight loss would be more believable if the standard deviation for weight loss is 15 pounds than if the standard deviation were 2 pounds.

> *The same size change in the predictor (10-lb. weight loss) is more realistic if it is equivalent to a <u>small share</u> of a **standard deviation** than if it corresponds to several <u>multiples</u> of a **standard deviation**.*

Statistical significance is **necessary** but <u>not</u> **sufficient** for assessing the importance of an association between an independent variable and a dependent variable based on data from a sample. Researchers should <u>also</u> discuss other pertinent aspects of that association, including whether

- it can be interpreted as **cause and effect** (see Chapter 12);

- the **causal order** is as predicted—in other words, that **reverse causation** is <u>not</u> occurring;

- the association between values of the independent and dependent variables is in the **hypothesized direction**;

- the effect is **practically meaningful** (big enough to matter) for the topic, context, and measurement approach; (Chapters 3, 4, and 5);

- the independent variable **can be modified** by enough to induce a meaningful impact (and that change in the independent variable can be **sustained**); and

- the direction and size of the association is consistent with other research on the topic.

As part of an ongoing debate among quantitative researchers, Ziliak and McCloskey (2004) and Thompson (2004) underscored that the failure to distinguish between practical importance and statistical significance has an unfortunately long history in many fields, including sociology, economics, psychology, education, and health. As a consequence, some top peer-reviewed journals have strengthened requirements for reporting and interpreting effect size (practical meaning) as well as statistical significance (Amrhein et al., 2019).

Researchers should be clear about which aspect of "significance" they are discussing, either by specifying <u>statistical</u> **significance** or <u>substantive</u> **significance** or by substituting a synonym, such as "**practical importance**," to clarify which aspect they mean.

Importance of a
Numeric Finding: The Big Picture

To illustrate how to integrate and balance the set of factors that determine the "importance" of a numeric finding, consider an evaluation of a hypothetical intervention to improve math skills: Six schools were randomly selected from a list of all middle schools in a large metropolitan area. Classes of seventh-graders in each of the selected schools were randomly assigned to either receive a new math curriculum or continue to follow the existing (old) one. Students' math skills were tested at the beginning of the school year and again at the end. The independent variable captured which curriculum the students followed, while the dependent variable measured change in math scores over the course of the year. Researchers hypothesized that students following the new curriculum would show a larger improvement in math scores over the course of the year than their peers who learned under the old curriculum.

The impact of the intervention was measured by, first, calculating the average change in math scores separately for those following the new and old curriculum and then subtracting the average score change for the "old" from that for the "new" within each study site. Thus, a positive impact means that students who received the new curriculum improved their math skills more than did those at the same school who followed the old curriculum, whereas a negative impact means that those following the old curriculum improved more than did those learning under the new one. Inferential statistics were needed, because the researchers want to draw conclusions about the effectiveness of the new curriculum among <u>all</u> seventh-graders, not just those in the six schools that constituted the study sample.

Figure 15.1 portrays the effect size, direction, and statistical significance of the impact of the intervention at each of the six study sites. The chart was designed based on concepts and skills discussed in Chapter 7 (charts), Chapter 8 (benchmark values), Chapter 10 (measures of variation), and Chapter 13 (statistical significance). Point estimates of impact on math scores are shown with a small bold horizontal marker for each school, with the associated 95% confidence intervals shown with the "whiskers." A reference line at $y = 0$ differentiates between positive (above the dashed line) and negative (below that line) impacts. A footnote to the figure reports the standard deviation in math scores, to provide a numeric basis for assessing the practical meaning of impact size.

> <u>Example</u>: Figure 15.1 shows that findings varied considerably across the six study sites in terms of the size and direction of the association between curriculum and change in math scores over the course of the study. All the schools except Counterculture School experienced larger improvements in math scores among students who received the new curriculum than among those who used the old one. The positive point estimates of impact ranged from +0.25 at MS 354 and Elite Prep to +2.0 at ABC Charter School and MS 110. In contrast, Counterculture School

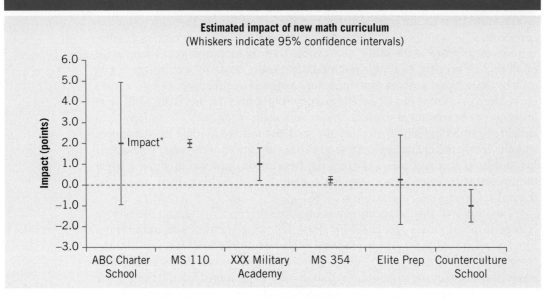

Figure 15.1 Distinguishing Between Statistical Significance and Practical Meaning

Estimated impact of new math curriculum
(Whiskers indicate 95% confidence intervals)

Notes:

*Impact = (post – pre-implementation scores for new curriculum) – (post – pre scores for old curriculum)

Standard deviation of impact was 2.0 points; exams were scored out of 100 points.

observed a <u>negative</u> impact: Students using the new math curriculum improved a full point <u>less</u> than those learning based on the old one.

> *The 2-point advantage to the new curriculum is equivalent to 1 standard deviation in the exam score—a **large effect size for any topic and context**. However, the 0.25-point differences are tiny—not enough of a difference to translate into meaningfully better advancement in math skills <u>regardless of whether they are</u> **statistically significant**. And although the impact on math learning at Counterculture was **statistically significant**, it was in the <u>opposite</u> of the **predicted direction**.*

There was also substantial variability across the six study sites in the amount of uncertainty around the point estimates of impact. The 95% confidence interval for MS 110 is very narrow around a point estimate well above 0, supporting the conclusion that the new math curriculum had a large, positive (+2.0), statistically significant effect on acquiring math skills, compared to the old curriculum. MS 354 also has a narrow 95% confidence interval that does not include 0, but the size of the positive impact is very small (+0.25).

> The impact was in the **expected direction** (the new curriculum had a positive impact) and **statistically significant** at both MS 110 and MS 354, but the size of the effect was big enough to represent an **educationally meaningful difference** _only_ at MS 110.

The confidence intervals for ABC Charter School and Elite Prep are each 6 units wide. However, the point estimate of the impact at ABC Charter is substantial (+2.0), whereas the point estimate at Elite Prep is very low (+0.25), and its confidence interval spans nearly equal numbers of positive and negative values.

> _Neither_ ABC Charter's nor Elite Prep's results meet conventional cutoffs for **statistical significance**, because their 95% confidence intervals cross the reference line at Impact = 0. However, the different **effect sizes** and range of values in their respective confidence intervals mean that researchers should discuss the results for those two study sites differently from one another: For ABC Charter, evaluators should report and interpret the **large positive point estimate** and draw attention to the fact that, although its confidence interval includes 0, the data are also **compatible** with the conclusion that the new curriculum had a favorable impact on math learning. For Elite Prep, they should point out that although the estimate of impact is _not_ **statistically significant**, that that hardly matters because the **effect size** is very small. In addition, they should note that the estimates for Elite Prep and ABC Charter are also compatible with non-trivial _negative_ effects of the new curriculum.

Researchers should also tie their findings back to their original hypothesis and discuss whether their results are consistent with those of previous studies on the topic. They might also present benchmarks to help readers interpret the practical importance of their numeric results (see Chapter 8) and provide other information on the repercussions of proposed changes or interventions based on their findings.

Example: Evaluators could explain how the observed greater improvement in math scores associated with the new curriculum translates into mastery of specific seventh-grade math skills or into chances of passing a national math-proficiency test. They could also provide estimates of the costs of textbooks and teacher training needed to implement the new curriculum nationwide.

> Presenting both the **benefits** and **costs** of the new curriculum would give readers perspective on whether the proposed intervention is a worthwhile investment for improving students' math skills—an important facet of the "importance" of the study findings.

Finally, the evaluators should emphasize that because the results were obtained from a true experiment, the observed association between curriculum and math-score change can be interpreted as causal (see Chapter 12). To enhance the argument that the new curriculum is responsible for (i.e., caused) the better learning, they should describe the mechanisms for that improvement: training teachers in the new instructional methods and providing textbooks that incorporate more effective learning materials.

> With **random assignment** of students in each school to either the old or the new curriculum, the results provide strong evidence that the curriculum (hypothesized independent variable) can be interpreted as the **cause** of (reason for) the observed difference in math-score changes (change in the dependent variable). The fact that schools can choose which curriculum to use satisfies the **changeability** criterion for the **real-world value** of the intervention.

In their book *The Cult of Statistical Significance* (2008), Ziliak and McCloskey argued that for urgent health, social, environmental, or other issues, it can be appropriate to act on a substantively significant effect size despite lack of statistical significance, rather than waiting to collect a larger sample that might increase the statistical significance of the finding.

How Study Design, Measurement, and Sample Size Affect "Importance"

Different aspects of context, study design, and methods of data collection and analysis affect the **practical meaning**, the **statistical significance**, whether an association can be interpreted as cause and effect (**internal validity**), and the extent to which findings can be generalized (**external validity**). That means that, even if one of those criteria for "importance" is satisfied for a particular study, one or more of the other criteria might <u>not</u> be.

To provide a systematic comparison of influences on the different dimensions of importance of a numeric finding, Table 15.1 includes separate panels for each of those dimensions. The W's and other criteria are listed in the columns, with specific aspects of each dimension of "importance" in the rows. The right-most column identifies the chapter(s) in which the pertinent concepts were introduced.

Practical Importance

As shown in Panel A of Table 15.1, evaluating the practical importance of a numeric result involves **quantitative criteria** that depend on the **level of measurement** of the variables and on the **units** in which they were measured. The

Table 15.1 Criteria for Assessing the Practical Meaning, Statistical Significance, Internal Validity, and External Validity of Quantitative Research Results

Aspect of "importance"	Quantitative criteria	Study design	Do criteria depend on?			Related chapters
			Units of variables	Sample size	Topic and context under study	
A. Practical meaning (substantive significance)						
Value (level)	Depends on type of measure	No	Yes—same units as variable	No	Distributions, thresholds, and cutoffs for the topic and context	Chapter 8 (comparison values)
Effect size (difference in value of DV across values of an IV)[a]	Size of effect compared to measures of spread	No	Depends on type of effect size[b]	Inversely related to some measures of spread,[c] which are often used to interpret meaning of an effect size	Distributions of IV and DV for the topic and context	Chapter 10 (standard deviation)
B. Statistical significance of an association						
Standard error						
Margin of error	Must be positive		Yes—same units as variable			
Confidence limits	Can be positive, zero, or negative depending on the topic, context, and units	Inferential statistics assume that probability methods were used to draw sample.		Inversely related to sample size	Yes	Chapter 13 (uncertainty of numeric estimates) Appendix C
p-value	Must be between 0.0 and 1.0		No	Through effects on test statistic and critical value	No	

(Continued)

Table 15.1 (Continued)

C. Internal validity (causality) of a study

Aspect of "importance"	Quantitative criteria	Study design	Do criteria depend on? — Units of variables	Do criteria depend on? — Sample size	Do criteria depend on? — Topic and context under study	Related chapters
Empirical association	**Size** and **strength** (statistical significance) of association establish practical meaning of association between IV and DV	**Consistency** of direction and size of association across **different types of study designs** strengthens the case for a non-spurious association.	Yes; see effect size in Panel A.	Can affect statistical significance of association between IV and DV	**Consistency** of effect size across **places, times, and subgroups** strengthens conclusions about empirical association.	
Time order: Cause (IV) precedes effect (DV)	No	**Longitudinal** studies are stronger than **cross-sectional** for establishing causal order.	No	No	No	Chapter 12 (causality)
Non-spuriousness	Practical meaning and statistical significance of: • association between potential confounder and key IV and DV • association between key IV and DV, once confounder has been taken into account	• **Experimental** studies are better than **observational** studies, because **random assignment** equalizes the distribution of potential confounders in treatment and control groups. • **Observational** studies can assess non-spuriousness if they have **measure(s) of potential confounders.**	No	Can affect statistical significance of associations between IV, DV, and **confounder** or mechanism	• The form and extent of confounding are affected by the topic. • The nature and extent of confounding are affected by the context.	

Aspect of "importance"	Quantitative criteria	Study design	Do criteria depend on?			Related chapters
			Units of variables	Sample size	Topic and context under study	
Mechanism	Practical meaning and statistical significance of associations among mechanism, key IV and DV	• **Experimental** studies may be able to explicitly test the mechanism via **randomization.** • **Observational** studies can test the role of a mechanism if they have a **measure** of that mechanism. • Longitudinal designs are stronger than cross-sectional ones at establishing **temporal order** of key IV, mechanism, and DV.	No	Can affect statistical significance of associations between IV, DV, and **mechanism**	The nature of the mechanism is determined by the topic and context.	Chapter 12
Dose-response	Practical meaning of the association between dose of the IV and value of the DV	No	Yes; see effect size in Panel A.		Yes; see effect size.	
D. External validity (generalizability) of a finding						
	Whether distributions of variables are similar in the sample and target populations	• **Probability methods** are stronger than **non-probability methods** at obtaining a representative sample. • Representativeness of a sample is often inversely related to **nonresponse rates.** • Samples from **longitudinal** studies may become less representative over time, due to **attrition.**	No	No	Yes. Consider differences between sample and target population in when, where, and who.	Chapter 5 (generalizability) and Chapter 11 (sampling)

Notes:

a. IV: independent variable; DV: dependent variable.

b. See Table 9.5 for information about units for results of different types of mathematical comparisons; see Table 10.7 regarding units for results of different types of statistical computations.

c. Sample size is inversely related to variance and standard deviation; it does not affect range or interquartile range.

topic and **context** of a study will affect the distributions of the variables and can determine the values of cutoffs or benchmarks used to assess the meaning and practical importance of an effect size (see Chapter 8).

> Example: The World Health Organization's definition of low birth weight is < 5.5 pounds, which is equivalent to 88 ounces, or 2,500 g (WHO, 1950). However, a male infant born 5 weeks early who weighed 2,499 g would be considered a normal size for a baby born that far in advance of his due date, because of the shorter amount of time he had to grow before being born (Chou, n.d.).
>
>> *Clearly, the **units** of measurement matter: an 88 <u>gram</u> infant would be far too small to survive, but a 2,500-<u>ounce</u> (156 pounds) one would be heavier than many mothers! Although 2,500 g is small for a full-term infant (born after a 40-week pregnancy), it is average for those born 5 weeks prematurely. Thus, the **threshold** for interpreting the meaning of a particular birth weight value <u>varies by</u> **context** (how long the pregnancy lasted).*

Although **sample size** does not influence the size of an effect, it is inversely related to some measures of spread (variation), which are often used to interpret the practical meaning of an effect size.

The **design of a study**—including its sampling methods, its time structure, and whether it was experimental or observational—does <u>not</u> determine whether a given effect size is big enough to be practically important.

Statistical Significance

Panel B of Table 15.1 summarizes Chapter 13's discussion about the relationship between **sample size**, the uncertainty of numeric estimates, and the statistical significance of a result. Smaller sample sizes are associated with greater standard errors around point estimates and, therefore, with larger margins of error and wider confidence intervals. Sample size is also inversely associated with p-values for hypothesis testing, because of its effect on the test statistic and associated critical values (see Appendix C).

> Example: In the Cummings and Vandewater (2007) study, the sample included nearly four times as many boys as girls who played video games ($n = 425$ and 109, respectively).
>
>> *Although the **point estimates** of time spent playing video games on time spent with friends were virtually identical for boys and for girls (~15 minutes per hour of video-game-playing per day), the larger **sample size** for boys yielded a smaller **standard error** of that estimate (5 minutes for boys, 11 for girls). That, in turn, resulted in a narrower **confidence interval** and lower **p-value** for boys than for girls, which led to the conclusion that the 15-minute difference was **statistically significant** among boys but not among girls.*

Standard errors, margins of error, and confidence intervals are in the same **units** as the dependent variable. **Topic** and **context** can affect those measures of uncertainty, through their effects on distributions of values of variables (see Chapters 3 and 5). However, interpretation of *p*-values is the same regardless of the topic, the context, or the units in which the variables were measured.

In terms of **study design**, all the inferential statistical tests assume that data are representative of the population from which they are drawn, so samples selected using probability methods (e.g., random sampling) are more likely to meet that criterion. Neither the time structure of a study nor whether it is experimental or observational affects measures of uncertainty or conclusions about statistical significance.

Internal Validity

As noted in Chapter 12, **internal validity** concerns the extent to which a study satisfies each of the criteria for evaluating whether an observed association between an independent variable and a dependent variable can be interpreted as cause and effect. **Quantitative** attributes of an association contribute to all of the criteria for assessing causality <u>except</u> whether a study can determine the timing of the independent and dependent variables (causal order; see Panel C of Table 15.1).

Establishing the presence of an **empirical association** involves quantitative criteria related to the practical meaning and statistical significance of that association. Larger effect sizes and lower *p*-values increase the degree to which a study meets the empirical association criterion. Assessing whether there is a **dose-response** relationship between the independent and dependent variables also has clear quantitative criteria: Does the effect size either increase or decrease in concert with the size of the "dose" of the risk factor?

> <u>Example</u>: The higher the dose of cigarette smoke to which infants are exposed, the higher their risk of Sudden Infant Death Syndrome (SIDS; Office on Smoking and Health, 2006).
>
> *Here, the **quantitative criterion** for a cause-and-effect relationship involves a **clinically meaningful** increase in the incidence of SIDS in response to increasing exposure to cigarette smoke. The **dose-response** relationship provides evidence that secondhand smoke is a **cause** of SIDS, rather than a phenomenon that is merely correlated with SIDS due to random chance.*

The two other criteria for evaluating causality—**non-spuriousness** and **mechanism**—involve more complex **quantitative criteria**. The effect of a non-spurious association will remain approximately the same size even after a potential confounder has been taken into account; whereas, in a relationship involving **confounding** or an explanatory **mechanism**, the effect size will shrink appreciably when that third variable is factored in. In other words, the estimate that does <u>not</u> take the confounder into account is marred by spurious correlation. Controlling for the potential confounder removes the spurious component from that association.

> Example: The inverse association between how much someone exercises and their risk of heart attack becomes smaller but is still statistically significant and big enough to be clinically meaningful even after their obesity status is taken into account.
>
> > *Here, **quantitative criteria** to demonstrate **confounding** require that the size of the association between exercise and heart attack decrease when obesity is taken into account. Exercise remains inversely associated with heart attack even after obesity has been statistically controlled, so the results suggest that the association is <u>not</u> completely **spurious**—both exercise and obesity retain a **causal** relationship with risk of heart attack.*

Most of the criteria for evaluating the internal validity of a study have to do with aspects of **study design**, including which methods were used to select the cases, whether the study is cross-sectional or longitudinal, and whether it is observational or experimental. Longitudinal studies are stronger than cross-sectional ones at establishing **time order**, because they make it possible to assess whether changes in the independent variable preceded changes in the dependent variable, thus determining whether reverse causation can be ruled out. Likewise, longitudinal studies are preferable for assessing possible **mechanisms** linking an independent and a dependent variable, because the time sequence of those variables can be determined.

As explained in Chapter 12, experimental studies are better than observational ones for establishing **non-spuriousness** because they equalize potential confounders between the treatment and control groups. In studies based on observational data, measuring and analyzing potential confounders can help improve internal validity.

In addition, if multiple well-conducted studies using <u>several types</u> of **study designs** find the same (or similar) direction and size of association between a particular independent and a particular dependent variable, it makes a stronger case for an **empirical association**. Likewise, if the same direction and size of association between the independent variable and the dependent variable are observed in multiple contexts (locations, subgroups, and/or time periods), that **contextual** information strengthens the **empirical association** criterion. As always, assessment of whether a study is "well-conducted" involves evaluating measurement validity, external validity, and internal validity of the study design and measures used; see "Garbage in, Garbage Out" later in this chapter.

The context of a study can influence the form and extent of **confounding**, the nature of causal **mechanisms** linking the independent and dependent variables, and the extent of a **dose-response** relationship. Context (where or who was studied) does <u>not</u> affect whether a study can be used to establish **time order**.

Contrary to what many novice researchers believe, **sample size** does not influence most of the criteria for assessing internal validity. The exception is that sample size can affect the statistical significance of an association (see Chapter 13), which is one aspect of the **empirical association** criterion.

External Validity

Panel D of Table 15.1 summarizes factors that affect the **external validity** of a study—the last major criterion for "importance" of a research result. As discussed in Chapters 5 and 11, external validity refers to whether and to which other populations the results of a specific study can be generalized. A key **quantitative criterion** for assessing external validity is whether the distributions of the variables of interest are similar in the sample and target populations—in other words, the extent to which the sample is representative of the population.

> Example: The teenagers who were studied in the analysis of video-game-playing and reading time were selected using random sampling methods (Cummings & Vandewater, 2007), yielding a nationally representative sample of 10-to-19-year-olds in the United States from 2002 to 2003.
>
> *In terms of **external validity**, the study has good **sample generalizability**, meaning we can have high confidence about extrapolating the findings to all U.S. teenagers in those years. The plausibility of **cross-population generalizability**, such as to other age groups or countries, would depend on whether those other populations differed substantially in terms of characteristics related to video-game-playing and reading.*

The composition of a study sample is substantially affected by several aspects of **study design**. As discussed in Chapter 11, samples selected using probability (random sampling) methods are much better for obtaining representative samples than studies that use non-probability sampling methods.

> Example: Yelp restaurant reviewers are diners who use the Yelp app or website and were motivated to submit a review.
>
> *Yelp reviews have poor **external validity**, because samples of volunteers (a non-probability way of selecting a sample) are often not **representative** of the restaurant-visiting population: People who provide reviews via social media channels tend to be younger than those who do not submit that type of rating, and people who submit voluntary ratings tend to have either strongly favorable or strongly unfavorable opinions. Thus, the ratings that appear on Yelp are not **generalizable** to all restaurant diners.*

Random sampling methods are more commonly used for observational than for experimental studies, meaning that results of observational studies often have better external validity. Low response rates (which are often beyond the control of researchers) threaten the external validity of a study, because those who respond are typically quite different from those who do not, resulting in a sample that has very different characteristics than the <u>intended</u> sample. It is also more difficult to determine external validity of samples drawn using non-probability methods, because the amount and pattern of nonresponse cannot be determined. The time structure of a study can affect external validity, because samples from longitudinal studies may become less representative over time due to differential attrition—an issue that does not affect cross-sectional studies.

Sample size and the **units** in which the variables were measured do <u>not</u> affect generalizability, because they don't determine the representativeness of a sample.

The four dimensions of "importance" of a numeric research result include **practical meaning**, **statistical significance**, **internal validity**, and **external validity**. Each of those dimensions is affected by <u>different combinations</u> of the following:

- quantitative criteria

- study design (sampling methods, time structure, experimental vs. observational design)

- sample size

- topic

- context

- units of measurement

Researchers should discuss how those attributes affect their conclusions about the importance of their findings.

Relationships Among Dimensions of "Importance"

Statistical significance, practical importance, internal validity, and external validity are four distinct phenomena, each influenced by different aspects of study design, measurement, and analysis. As a consequence, just because a study meets criteria for one of those dimensions of "importance" does <u>not</u> guarantee that it will meet criteria for the other dimensions. Conversely, just because a study fares poorly on one of those dimensions does <u>not</u> necessarily mean that it will also fare poorly on the others.

- **Statistical significance** does <u>not</u> necessarily translate into **practical importance**: The association between video-game-playing and reading was statistically significant, but the increment to reading time associated with a reduction in video-game-playing time was extremely small.

- Conversely, **practical importance** does <u>not</u> ensure **statistical significance**: A large effect might not be statistically significant, due to wide variation in the values of the variable in the sample or to small sample size, as in the math-curriculum impact at ABC Charter School (Figure 15.1).

- In **observational** (<u>nonexperimental</u>) studies, a **statistically significant** association does <u>not</u> necessarily imply **causation**: Gambling and cancer could be correlated at the 99% confidence level, but that does <u>not</u> make gambling a cause of cancer (see Chapter 12). In true experiments, where cases are randomized into treatment and control groups, however, the possibility of **confounding** is reduced, so statistically significant findings are typically interpreted as causal.

- Conversely, a **causal relationship** does <u>not</u> guarantee **statistical significance**: Random error can overwhelm the effects of the new curriculum on math learning, as at ABC Charter School.

<u>Caution</u>: If researchers don't specifically mention a <u>lack</u> of statistical significance, many readers will interpret their findings to validate theories or as the basis for developing solutions to problems, even if the effect is small. This is especially true if the association has already been shown to be causal.

- Evidence that an association is **causal** does <u>not</u> automatically mean that it is of **practical importance**: A new curriculum might improve math learning, but that change could be so tiny as to be unworthy of investment, as with the findings from the MS 354 study site (Figure 15.1).

- **Practical importance** (a "big effect") does <u>not</u> necessarily mean that an association is **cause-and-effect**, as in the example of gambling and cancer.

- **Inferential statistics** assume a **representative sample**, but a representative sample does <u>not</u> ensure statistical significance: The gender difference in mean body mass index among children in the nationally representative NHANES sample was not statistically significant (Table 13.8).

- **Practical significance** does not automatically translate into **external validity**: An estimated high level of support for a ban on single-use plastic bags based on a **convenience sample** <u>cannot</u> be generalized to the population (see Chapter 11). And large effects can be **context-specific**, implying <u>low</u> **cross-population generalizability**, as in the finding that aspirin is protective against stroke among women but not men (see Chapter 12).

- **External validity** does <u>not</u> guarantee **practical importance**, because an estimate based on a representative sample might be very small, as in the study of video-game-playing and reading.

- **Internal validity** does <u>not</u> guarantee **external validity**, and vice versa (see Figure 12.6).

> To give readers a well-rounded perspective on the importance of a quantitative research finding, a description of research results should pull together information about each of the four aspects of importance—**practical meaning, statistical significance**, **internal validity**, and **external validity**. By integrating information about the topic, context, and design of the study, along with the direction, size, and statistical significance of numeric effects, researchers can provide readers with the information they need to truly make sense of the results and perceive how they can (and cannot) be applied.

Garbage In, Garbage Out

To summarize why it is so important to evaluate data quality, "**garbage in, garbage out**:" Numeric results based on data from a poorly conducted study are <u>not</u> a good basis for arriving at sound conclusions about the pattern or relationship under study (Knowles, 2016). "Garbage" data might be a consequence of poor measurement validity (e.g., badly designed data-collection instruments), low external validity, or poor internal validity. Once data have been collected, such flaws often <u>cannot</u> be overcome, which is why we take validity so seriously when making sense of numeric results—and, ideally, when planning data collection!

> The phrase "**garbage in, garbage out**" (abbreviated **GIGO**) is used to express the idea that incorrect or poor-quality data will always produce faulty results.

Making Sense of Numbers
in Quantitative Research Tasks

Throughout the rest of your formal education, your career, and your everyday life, you will need to make sense of numbers in several ways—including interpreting numeric information that others have presented, collecting and analyzing numeric data, and communicating numeric information. Table 15.2 summarizes the principles for making sense of numbers for each of those common tasks (in the columns), organized in the order of the chapters in which those principles were introduced (in the rows).

Conceptualizing and defining the topic under study (Chapter 3) is an essential step for most of the major research tasks, including how you interpret others' numbers, plan for your own data collection, and communicate the results of a quantitative study. Reading the literature about a topic is an important way to become familiar with how it has been studied in the past. The research literature also provides information about reasonable minimum and maximum values; whether high, low, or middle values are best; benchmarks or cutoffs for the topic; and other clues about how to collect and analyze data and interpret the meaning of a particular numeric value for the concepts or variables of interest.

Obtaining information on units of observation, categories or units of measurement, and system and scale of measurement (Chapter 4) is also crucial for identifying the approximate level and range of plausible values; choosing appropriate data-collection, mathematical, and statistical methods; and correctly interpreting the findings—whether others' or your own.

Identifying when, where, and to whom (or which cases) data pertain is a key aspect of every one of those tasks (Chapter 5). Whether you are reading about, collecting, analyzing, or communicating numbers, make note of those W's and consider how they affect other steps, such as selecting relevant benchmarks (Chapter 8) and generalizing findings.

Reviewing example tables, charts, and vizzes (Chapters 6 and 7) can help you identify ways to collect and analyze data and communicate the results for similar types of measures or comparisons. Armed with your new knowledge of measurement, analysis, and communications, you can determine which aspects of those exhibits would fit your task—or you can devise ways to revise their contents, layout, and labeling to improve clarity and completeness.

Identifying criteria used to assess causality affects how you interpret and apply quantitative research findings (Chapter 12), whether you are reading others' research, planning and executing your own data collection and analysis, or describing conclusions of a quantitative study. This is especially true when you are considering whether a particular set of findings can be used to confirm a theory about a relationship between different phenomena or translated to create a solution to an existing problem.

Expository writing (Chapter 14) also plays an important role in each of the four major tasks for making sense of numbers—contributing essential strategies

Table 15.2 Principles for Making Sense of Numbers for Common Quantitative Research Tasks

Principle	Chapter(s)[a]	Research task			
		Interpreting others' use of numbers	Collecting data	Analyzing data	Communicating research results

Conceptualization and definition of key elements of research question	Ch. 3	Read for conceptualization and definition in published literature (I; M).[b] Watch for variation in conceptualization and definition across studies and its implications for interpretation of findings (I; D).	Use to guide
			• design of questions and
			• choice of
			  ○ unit of analysis (level of aggregation),
			  ○ target population,
			  ○ respondent, and
			  ○ data source.
					Specify topic and how it was conceptualized and defined (M). Explain implications of conceptualization and definition for interpretation of findings (I; D).

Units and categories • Unit of observation • Units of measurement • Level of aggregation • Definitions or numeric limits for categories	Ch. 4	Read for units and categories (M; R).	Read prior literature for commonly used units and categories before designing data-collection instrument. Justify use of different units or categories, if applicable.	Confirm that formulas and comparisons are based on the units and categories in your data set. If not, convert units or categories to suit the formula.	Specify units and categories (M; R).
The W's: when, where, and to whom (or which cases) the data pertain	Ch. 5	Read for the W's (M; R).	Make note of the W's. Consider how they affect categories and cutoffs used in data collection.	Consider how the W's affect categories and cutoffs used in data analysis.	Specify the W's (M; R).

Principle	Chapter(s)[a]	Research task			
		Interpreting others' use of numbers	Collecting data	Analyzing data	Communicating research results

Table structure and labeling	Ch. 6				Consider
					• the audience and
					• the objective:
					  o detailed numeric values (table preferable)
					  o overall shape of a pattern (chart or viz preferable)

Chart or visualization structure and labeling	Ch. 7	Review (R) for • complete labeling; • appropriate layout for levels of measurement of all variables; and • consistency of prose interpretation of results with the numbers presented in the table or chart.	If a chart or table template exists to present data or analytic results, design data collection accordingly.	If a chart or table template exists for the desired analysis, plan data analysis accordingly.	Design for • completeness and • clarity of interpretation.
Benchmarks, standards, and cutoffs (**BSorC**) for the topic, context, and measurement	Ch. 8	Read for • definitions, values and use of benchmarks and cutoffs (M); • pertinent citations; and • interpretation of findings relative to benchmarks, standards, or cutoffs (R).	Identify pertinent benchmarks or cutoffs for the topic, context, and measures. Consider whether benchmarks or cutoffs affect the design of questions for data collection.	Use **BSorC** for the topic, context, and measures to guide analysis.	Explain reasons for use of benchmarks or cutoffs based on topic and study objectives (M). Specify values of any **BSorC**, and their sources, with citations (M). Refer to **BSorC** in interpretation of findings (R).
Types of mathematical calculations and comparisons used	Chs. 9 and 14; App. A	Read for type(s) of calculations and comparisons used (M). Check that presentation of results is consistent with that type of calculation or calculation (R).	Anticipate desired type(s) of calculations or comparisons; design question formats accordingly.	Create new variables if needed to support desired analysis. Apply the correct formula or comparison for the level(s) of measurement.	Convey the type(s) of calculations, either explicitly (for complex calculations; M) and/or through the wording of the results (R).

(Continued)

Table 15.2 (Continued)

Principle	Chapter(s)^a	Research task			
		Interpreting others' use of numbers	Collecting data	Analyzing data	Communicating research results
Types of statistical method used	Chs. 10, 13, and 14; Apps. B and C	Read for type(s) of statistical methods used (M). Check that presentation of results is consistent with type of statistical method (R).	Anticipate desired type(s) of statistics; design question formats accordingly.	Create new variables if needed to support desired analysis. Consider appropriateness of statistical methods to match <ul><li>the level(s) of measurement of variables,</li><li>the sampling approach, and</li><li>the use of sampling weights.</li></ul>	Convey the type(s) of statistical method, both explicitly (M) and through the wording of the results (R). Report assumptions behind the method (M).
How cases were selected (sampling)	Chs. 5 and 11; App. B	Read the methods section (M) for <ul><li>sampling method,</li><li>target population, and</li><li>response rate.</li></ul> Read the discussion section (D) for <ul><li>whether and to whom results are generalized and</li><li>implications for interpretation of results.</li></ul>	Consider the appropriate sampling method for your <ul><li>objective;</li><li>target population;</li><li>subgroups (strata), and whether disproportionate sampling is needed; and</li><li>available time and resources.</li></ul>	Consider the appropriateness of statistical methods to match the sampling approach. Apply sampling weights if appropriate.	In the methods section (M), specify <ul><li>sampling method,</li><li>target population, and</li><li>response rate.</li></ul> In the discussion section (D), explain implications for generalizability of results.
Whether the study is cross-sectional, retrospective, or prospective	Ch. 11	Read for <ul><li>the temporal design of the study (M) and</li><li>implications for causal interpretation of the results (D).</li></ul>	Consider an appropriate temporal design for your <ul><li>objective and</li><li>available time and resources.</li></ul>		Specify <ul><li>the temporal design of study (M) and</li><li>implications for causal interpretation of the results (D).</li></ul>

Principle	Chapter(s)[a]	Research task			
		Interpreting others' use of numbers	Collecting data	Analyzing data	Communicating research results
Whether the study is observational or experimental	Ch. 12	Read for • whether the study is a true experiment or observational (M) and • implications for causal interpretation of the results (D).	Consider an appropriate study design for your • objective and • available time and resources. Collect information on potential confounders or mechanisms.	Control for potential confounders or mechanisms, if measures are available.	Specify • whether the study is a true experiment or observational (M) and • implications for causal interpretation of the results (D).

Use of expository writing approaches	Ch. 14	Read for
		• identification of key questions of the study (I);
		• interpretation of findings (direction and magnitude; R); and
		• a cohesive story line tying
		  ○ evidence to the research question (R),
		  ○ steps in the analysis to one another (M; R), and
		  ○ the findings to prior literature (D).
			Organize the description of data-collection methods (M) into paragraphs and sections on
			• the target population,
			• sampling,
			• the temporal design of the study,
			• data sources, and
			• measurement (wording of items on data-collection instrument).
				Organize the description of analytic methods (M) into paragraphs on
				• univariate statistics and
				• bivariate, three-way, or other inferential statistics.
					Use to convey
					• key questions of the study (I);
					• interpretation of findings (direction and magnitude; R); and
					• a cohesive story line tying
					  ○ evidence to the question (R),
					  ○ steps in the analysis to one another (M; R), and
					  ○ the findings to prior literature (D).

Notes:

a. Chapters of this book in which principle is introduced and illustrated.

b. Section(s) of a research paper, report, or book for a scientific audience in which this information can be found: I: introduction; M: methods section; R: results section; D: discussion section.

for (a) posing questions, (b) interpreting numeric values or patterns, (c) summarizing conclusions based on the numeric evidence, and (d) organizing longer pieces into paragraphs and sections such as descriptions of data collection and analysis in a methods section and explication of findings in a results section of a quantitative research paper.

The role of study design and data analysis (Chapters 8–11 and 13) varies across the four major research tasks, so I discuss them individually in the sections below.

Reading About and Assessing Others' Use of Numeric Information

As shown in the second column of Table 15.2, when **interpreting or applying others' use of numeric information**, a key step is to read for their description of the various principles—whether the W's, units, aspects of measurement or study design, or types of mathematical and statistical calculations—many of which should be described in the methods section of a paper or report for a research audience. Also, you should critically inspect their presentation of results for the direction and magnitude of patterns, as well as how values compare to benchmarks or cutoffs in the field.

> Example: A government report about marital patterns provides detailed information in a table, labeled with all the W's, units, and categories, and with footnotes about how concepts were defined and measured.
>
> *The writers' careful work makes it easy for you to **find the numbers you need** and to **perform additional calculations** to investigate trends in marital patterns using additional data from earlier reports.*

Reading about how the cases were selected, the time structure of the study, and the methods and sources used to collect the data will help you assess important aspects of the numeric results, such as whether and to whom they can be generalized, whether cause and effect can be inferred based on the results, and possible biases in the measures.

> Example: A study reports that people who eat spicy foods are less likely than those who do not eat such foods to have acid indigestion. The authors make the recommendation that indigestion can be prevented by eating spicy foods more often. Reading the methods section, you realize that their study was cross-sectional, so you don't give it as much credibility as studies that show that people who ate spicy foods at the beginning of the study period were <u>more</u> likely to develop indigestion.
>
> *Armed with your new awareness that **longitudinal** studies are better for inferring **cause and effect** than are **cross-sectional studies** that*

measure both variables at the same time, you are able to identify which studies present stronger evidence for causation.

Example: Your mother sends you a link to a tourism blog that rates the activities on offer at a place you're planning to visit. Recognizing that the blog is one person's opinion, and that the blogger is much older and wealthier than you are, you reject that source of information in favor of a "frugal traveler" app that shows ratings by thousands of people of a similar age and income level as you.

> *Even before taking this course, you might have decided to ignore the blog your mother recommended, but now you can pinpoint the scientific reasons why you did so! The blog gave the opinion of one person with very <u>different</u> **W**'s (age and income) than yours, rather than being based on responses of a* **representative sample** *of many people like you.*

Collecting Numeric Data

As shown in the third column of Table 15.2, when your task is to **collect numeric data,** many of the principles explained throughout this book can guide you toward sensible choices about how to define and measure the concepts of interest; how to choose the target population (whom to study), sampling methods, and time structure of the study; and how to write questions to collect the information. Thinking carefully about those concepts <u>before</u> you collect the data can spare you a lot of frustration by helping you make sure the sample includes the set of cases you need and that the questions cover the concepts you want and are measured in ways that allow you to address the goals of your study.

Example: While searching for a place to live after graduation, you look up rents in the city where you've obtained a new job. You don't yet know anyone in that city, so you decide against having a roommate, and you investigate only studio and one-bedroom apartments.

> *The* **W**'s *for your search include the location and size of apartments for rent.*

Example: Having been told that a client at your new job wants to be able to calculate average age for each of several geographic areas, you design the questionnaire to collect age in single years.

> *If you had collected data on age <u>group</u>, you would <u>not</u> be able to conduct the statistical analysis the client requested.*

Identifying standard benchmarks and cutoffs in the field, and anticipating the types of mathematical and statistical analyses for which the data will be used, will help you design data-collection instruments to provide the data in the needed form.

Example: You are conducting a needs assessment for an after-school program at a local public elementary school. Knowing that many people have difficulty reporting their exact income, you instead design a question asking parents/guardians to mark whether their child qualifies for free lunch, reduced-price lunch, or neither.

> *Even if they don't know the* **standard income thresholds** *that are used to classify children into those categories, parents or guardians probably know whether their child is eligible for free or reduced-price lunch, providing the needed socioeconomic data. For this* **target population** *and* **intended use of the data***, collecting data with a simple* **closed-ended question** *is likely to yield a higher* **response rate** *and more* **valid** *information than an* **open-ended** *one asking about income to the nearest dollar.*

Identifying the goals of a research project (see Chapter 2) is a key step in planning for data collection.

Example: Your department at a nonprofit agency has been asked to describe the demographic characteristics of its clientele. With that in mind, you recommend using random sampling methods to obtain a representative sample using the agency's client list as a sampling frame. A different department at your agency has been asked to assess the impact of an intervention program. Your colleague in that department recommends conducting a randomized controlled trial, to reduce the chances of confounding due to self-selection of participants into intervention and control groups.

> *A year later, both of you receive promotions based on the correct alignment of data-collection and study-design strategies with the goals of your respective projects: Your project was* **descriptive research** *and needed to prioritize* **generalizability***, whereas your colleague's was* **evaluative** *and needed to assess* **causality***.*

Recognizing limits on the available time and resources can help you choose among data-collection strategies, including sample size, sampling methods, and whether a longitudinal study is feasible.

Example: During her senior year of college, Natalie joins her psychology professor's lab for a one-semester independent study about students' experiences of adjusting to college. She analyzes pilot data on a few dozen students that other lab members collected last year, and she creates a research poster to present her findings. Mahalia—a second-year doctoral student in that same professor's lab—writes a proposal for a small, externally funded grant, including the associated human subjects' research plan and a strategy for collecting and analyzing data from several hundred participants over their first 2 years of college.

> *Natalie designed a project that fits the **amount of time** she has and her current research **skill set**. With only one semester to complete her project, she doesn't have time to collect data. Mahalia, in contrast, planned her project to reflect that she has more time (several years), a higher skill level, a larger base of knowledge about the topic, and higher expectations about what she should produce (in order to earn her PhD).*

Conducting Mathematical and Elementary Statistical Analysis

Another common task in quantitative research is **analyzing numeric data** (second column from the right in Table 15.2). By now, you are probably painfully aware that to plan and conduct such an analysis, you need to know the levels of measurement for each of your variables, which will help you choose the appropriate kinds of comparisons and mathematical and statistical calculations. Knowing the relevant units and categories and identifying standard measures, benchmarks, and cutoffs in the field will prepare you to create new variables (see Appendix A) or limit the set of cases to address the questions of interest.

> Example: For your apartment search, you've created a budget to help you identify the maximum rent you can afford based on your income, student loan repayments, and other anticipated expenses.
>
> > *That limit on what you can afford becomes the **threshold** that helps you identify which apartments to cross off your list.*

> Anticipating the types of mathematical and statistical analyses for which the data will be used will help you prepare the variables and conduct and interpret results of those analyses.

> Example: A client asks you to analyze how the need for a variety of services to support aging-in-place differs across three subgroups of the elderly: "young-old," "old-old," and "oldest old" individuals.
>
> > *She provides you with **standard cutoffs** used to define those age groups, which you use to create a <u>new</u> **age-group variable** from the original continuous age measure. Based on what you learned in Chapter 13, you know to conduct **cross-tabulations** with chi-square tests to evaluate whether the need for each of those services (a yes/no **dependent variable**) differs across age group (an **ordinal independent variable**).*

Communicating Quantitative Information

When tasked with **communicating about quantitative research** (see the right-hand column of Table 15.2), your approach will be the flip side of that for interpreting others' presentation of numbers: The same things you had to <u>read for</u> you will now <u>write about</u>, so that others can interpret and use your numbers! As noted in Chapter 14, you should report the W's, units, study design, analytic method, and results, using the principles shown in the rows of Table 15.2, keeping in mind the format and level of detail for your intended audience.

> <u>Example</u>: For the end-of-year undergraduate research poster session at her university, Natalie must present the results of her psychology project to other students majoring in that field, to those conducting research projects in completely different fields, to faculty mentors, and to proud parents visiting to see what their children have accomplished as part of their research endeavors.
>
> > *While her professor tells Natalie to prepare her poster mostly with an **audience** of psychology researchers in mind, he also works with her to create **charts** and short **sentences** to explain her main questions and results in ways **non-experts** can understand.*

> <u>Example</u>: As a volunteer at a social service agency, you are asked to prepare and present alternative budget scenarios to staff and members of the advisory board. The scenarios differ in terms of funding source, amount, and allocation to different categories of expenditure. The agenda for that meeting is packed with other important items, so you are limited to a 5-minute presentation. Knowing that the advisory board will want to know which aspects of the budget make up the largest portion of the budget and how much that varies across the different budget scenarios, you create a couple of visualizations, accompanied by titles that convey those points.
>
> > *Having learned to think carefully about **audience** and **objective** before deciding on a **format**, you were able to communicate the key points about the data without overwhelming the advisory board with spreadsheet tables full of detailed numbers.*

TERMS AND CONCEPTS

"Garbage in, garbage out" (GIGO)   490

Practical significance   490
Practical importance   470

Practical meaning   471
Substantive significance   476

HIGHLIGHTS

- The **practical significance** of a research finding is determined by the effect size, how it compares to pertinent benchmarks or cutoffs, and whether its direction is consistent with the hypothesis and with prior literature on the subject.

- **Statistical significance** of a research finding does <u>not</u> guarantee that that finding will be of **practical importance**.

- The four facets of "importance" of a quantitative research finding—**practical meaning**, **statistical significance**, **internal validity**, and **external validity**—are distinct from one another and are affected by different aspects of study design, measurement, topic, and context.

- Only if <u>all</u> those criteria are satisfied does it make sense to design interventions or base policy on that research evidence.

- The phrase "**garbage in, garbage out**" reminds us that bad data produce faulty numeric results, where bad data can arise due to weak study design or invalid data-collection methods.

- The four main types of quantitative research tasks are **interpreting others' numeric information**, **collecting quantitative data**, **analyzing data**, and **communicating** about study objectives, methods, findings, and implications. By applying the principles from this book as you plan and conduct each of those tasks, you and your audiences will be in a good position to make sense of the resulting numbers.

RECOMMENDED READING

Amrhein, V., Greenland, S., & McShane, B. (2019). Retire statistical significance. *Nature, 567,* 305–307. https://www.nature.com/articles/d41586-019-00857-9

EXERCISES

Individual Exercises

Quantitative Reasoning in Everyday Life

1. In a local newspaper or magazine, find a solution that is being recommended to resolve a local social problem based on results of a quantitative study. Find the original research paper being summarized by the newspaper or magazine article. Evaluate whether and how the article addresses each of these aspects of "importance": (a) the practical meaning of the results, (b) whether the findings might differ by topic or context, (c) the internal validity of the study, (d) the statistical significance of the findings, and (e) the external validity of the study. (f) Given your answers to those questions, write a short description of the appropriateness of the proposed solution, based solely on the results of that study.

2. For a decision you made recently (or are in the process of making) that involves using numeric information, make a list of ways you would use the concepts and skills in each chapter of this book, working from the information in Table 15.2.

Interpreting Research

3. In a journal article in your field, find an example of an association that is statistically significant based on the $p < .05$ convention. (a) Evaluate whether the authors make it clear when they are discussing <u>statistical</u> significance. (b) Consider whether the authors also discuss the practical meaning of the association and, if so, (c) what criteria they use to assess it. (d) List any of the criteria for "importance" discussed in this chapter that the authors did <u>not</u> explicitly discuss, and (e) investigate whether the article provides information that could be used to shed light on those aspects. (f) Discuss whether you agree with the authors' presentation of the overall "importance" of their findings.

4. Do the same as in the previous exercise, but for an example of an association that does <u>not</u> meet conventional criteria for statistical significance.

Planning Research

5. Do the same as in Exercise 2, but for an assignment in a course you are currently taking or have taken recently that involves using numeric information.

Group Exercises

Quantitative Reasoning for Everyday Life

6. As a group, make a list of kinds of numeric criteria that would be of "practical importance" for each of the following issues: (a) a decision about where to live, (b) choice of a career, (c) an upcoming major purchase, and (d) choice of where to eat dinner on an upcoming trip.

Interpreting Research

7. Discuss what you wrote for Exercise 3.

8. Discuss what you wrote for Exercise 4.

9. Find a journal article in your field that reports results of an inferential statistical analysis that is being used to recommend solutions to a social or other "real-world" problem. Evaluate whether and how the article addresses each of these aspects of "importance": (a) the practical meaning of the results, (b) whether the findings differ by topic or context, (c) the internal validity of the study; (d) the statistical significance of the findings; and (e) the external validity of the study. Cite page numbers in the article where you found the information needed to answer the question.

Communicating Research

10. As a group, rewrite the conclusion to the article you used in the previous exercise, with a focus on the appropriateness of the authors' recommended solutions. Provide a comprehensive discussion about the "importance" of their numeric findings, working from the previous exercise and the guidelines in this chapter.

Appendixes

Appendix A

Why and How to Create New Variables

Learning Objectives

After reading this appendix, you will be able to do the following:

1. Explain why new variables are sometimes needed to answer a research question.

2. Know how transformations and changing scale affect the plausible values of a variable.

3. Explain how indexes and scales are created.

4. Write a formula to calculate a new continuous variable from one or more existing variables.

5. Write instructions for classifying values of existing variables into categories of a new variable.

Why New Variables Might Be Needed

Sometimes a research question can be answered using data in the form in which they were collected, referred to as the **original variables**, **existing variables**, or **raw data**. However, often the data aren't yet in the form needed to answer the research question, in which case, one or more **new variables** must be created from the existing ones. In this appendix, I explain why and how new variables are created from existing variables and how that affects level of measurement.

Once a new variable has been created, it can be used for the types of mathematical and statistical analyses described in Chapters 8, 9, 10, and 13. As with any variable, presenting the results of analyses of new variables will depend on their levels of measurement, as discussed in Chapters 6, 7, and 14.

Original (or **existing**) variables contain data in the form they were collected, without reclassifying their values or manipulating them mathematically. **New variables** are those that are created by classifying or manipulating values of one or more existing variables.

Example: To compare average heights of children who receive free school lunches and those who do not, the data can be used exactly as they were collected from school records.

> *The **original data** include a **categorical variable** indicating which children participated in the free-lunch program (the independent variable) and a **continuous measure of height** (the dependent variable). Height can be averaged separately for each of the two groups, allowing us to answer the research question using the existing variables.*

Example: If we want to see how outcomes vary for low-, moderate-, and high-income individuals, but income data were collected from tax returns to the nearest dollar, the income data are not yet in the form needed to answer the question.

> *The desired comparison requires a **new categorical income <u>group</u> variable**, which can be created by **classifying** values of the **original <u>continuous</u> income variable** into the three listed ranges.*

Example: A researcher wants to create a map of population density, updated with the latest census figures. He has data on the area of each county (in square miles) and on the population of each county (in thousands of persons).

> *The two **original variables** (population and area) from the census can be mathematically combined to calculate the **new density variable**.*

Sometimes variables are analyzed in exactly the form in which they were collected. Other times, new variables must be created from one or more existing variables.

In some situations, the new variable will be at the same level of measurement (see Chapter 4) as the variables from which it was created.

Example: Population density is at the same level of measurement as its component variables, population and area.

> *Both of the **original variables** (population and area) are at the **ratio** level of measurement. The new density variable will also be a **ratio** variable: Density in # persons per square mile = population ÷ area.*

In other situations, the new variable will have a different level of measurement than the variable(s) from which it was created. A less detailed version of a quantitative variable can be created from a more detailed version. For instance, an ordinal variable can be created from a continuous variable simply by grouping its values into ordered ranges.

> Example: Knowing someone's systolic blood pressure in millimeters of mercury (mmHg) tells us whether they fall into the normal, pre-hypertensive, or hypertensive range using standard cutoffs.
>
> *The **continuous** measure of blood pressure can be classified into **ordinal** categories.*

However, the opposite is not true: A continuous variable <u>cannot</u> be created from one with ranges (categories) of values.

> Example: Knowing that someone is hypertensive does not provide enough information to determine whether their systolic blood pressure is 131 mmHg, 137 mmHg, or some other value between 130 and 139 mmHg.
>
> *Hypertension Stage 1 encompasses systolic blood pressure values between 130 and 139 mmHg (American Heart Association, 2018). It is impossible to work backward from the **ordinal measure** of blood-pressure <u>range</u> to a **continuous** value of systolic blood pressure in single units of mmHg.*

The type of calculation or classification process used to create a new variable determines its level of measurement and its units and/or categories.

Caution: This might seem obvious, but I've seen this mistake made: New variables cannot be created if data were not collected on the concept or concepts needed to produce those new variables.

> Example: If a data set didn't collect information on age (or age group, or date of birth, or other information from which age can be calculated), nothing can be done to manufacture that information after the fact ☹.

New continuous variables can be constructed from existing variables in several ways, including by transforming the values of a variable, by combining multiple items into a scale or index, or by conducting other computations involving one or more variables.

Transformations of Numbers

A continuous variable can be **transformed** using any of a wide variety of mathematical operations, creating a new variable that will also be continuous.

Changing Scale

The **scale** of a number can be increased or decreased, either multiplying or dividing that number by a **conversion factor** that is a multiple of 10. Changing from a smaller to a larger scale (smaller to bigger "chunks") involves <u>dividing</u> by the conversion factor. Conversely, changing from a larger to a smaller scale involves <u>multiplying</u> by a conversion factor. As with other aspects of units, the scale of measurement must be reported with the numbers.

> **Changing the scale** of a number involves either multiplying or dividing the original number by a **conversion factor** that is a multiple of 10.

Example: U.S. GDP was $17,419 billion ($PPP[1] U.S.; Table A.1, Column 1), which is equivalent to $17.419 trillion (Column 2).

> *Trillions are bigger units than billions: A billion is 1/1,000th of a trillion, so when changing scale from billions to trillions, we <u>divide</u> the original value by 1,000 billions per trillion (the **conversion factor**). The scale must be specified along with the numeric value for it to be interpretable: $17 trillion is a much higher value (<u>different</u> **scale**) than $17 billion!*

Changing scale alters the level and range of plausible values to reflect the revised units (see Chapter 9).

Example: The 2015 ozone limit was specified as 70 parts per billion (ppb) instead of 0.070 parts per million (ppm)—the scale that had been used for earlier air quality standards (U.S. Environmental Protection Agency, 2018).

> *Parts per million is converted to parts per billion by multiplying ppm values by the **conversion factor**: 1,000: ppb = ppm × 1,000. With the new **scale**, users don't have to deal with all those messy decimal places, but they must recognize that the new limit has a much higher level and range than the values specified in the previous scale: 1 part per <u>million</u> vastly exceeds the ozone limit, whereas a value of 1 part per <u>billion</u> is well below the threshold.*

---

[1] $PPP: Purchasing Power Parity units; see Figure 8.7 and associated text.

Rounded Value

For many purposes, numbers are **rounded** to the nearest ten, hundred, thousand, or other **place value** (such as the "tens place" or "millions place"). A rounded number has about the same value as the original number but is less precise or exact. Numbers with decimal values can be rounded to the nearest tenth, hundredth, or other fraction of a unit, resulting in an approximate value of that number appropriate to its overall level while reducing the number of digits or decimal places. The general rule for rounding is that if the place value to which you are rounding is followed by a value of 5 or higher, round the number up. If the number in that place value is followed by a value less than 5, round it down.

Example: In 2014, China's gross domestic product (GDP) was $18.170 trillion (Table A.1, Column 2), whereas Japan's was $4.631 trillion. Rounded to the nearest whole trillion, China's GDP was $18 trillion, while Japan's was $5 trillion (Column 3).

*Numbers with the bolded blue digits in Column 2 of Table A.1 all **round up**: The digit to the right of the decimal point in Japan's GDP in trillions is a "6," so it rounds up. The digit to the right of the decimal point in China's GDP is a "1," so it **rounds down**. With GDP values that high, knowing approximate value to the nearest trillion dollars is often sufficient for international or temporal comparisons.*

Table A.1 Changing Scale, Rounding, and Truncation of a Continuous Variable

	2014 Gross Domestic Product, Purchasing Power Parity (PPP) in U.S. Dollars			
	(1) Purchasing Power Parity (billions)	**(2)** Changed scale to PPP in trillions	**(3)** Rounded to the nearest trillion	**(4)** Truncated to whole trillions
China	$18,170	$18.170	$18	$18
U.S.	$17,419	$17.419	$17	$17
India	$7,384	$7.384	$7	$7
Japan	$4,631	$4.**631**	$5	$4
Russia	$3,745	$3.**745**	$4	$3
Germany	$3,705	$3.**705**	$4	$3
Brazil	$3,264	$3.264	$3	$3
U.K.	$2,565	$2.**565**	$3	$2
Mexico	$2,145	$2.145	$2	$2
Korea, Republic of	$1,732	$1.**732**	$2	$1

Source: Data from Economics Online (2019).

Example: Mike measured 131.7 cm, which rounds to 132 cm.

> *The number to the right of the value to which we are **rounding** (<u>whole centimeters</u>) is greater than 5, so Mike's height **rounds** <u>up</u> to the next-highest (closest) centimeter.*

Truncated Value

Truncating a number involves trimming (chopping off) digits to the right of the place value to which you are truncating. Think of truncating a number as simplifying it to "completed" whole numbers (or "at least") rather than "nearest" value. Like rounding, truncating results in a less precise value of the number, with fewer digits and/or decimal places than the original value. When the digit to the right of the place value is less than 5, truncation and rounding will produce the <u>same</u> value. When the digit to the right of that place value is greater than or equal to 5, the rounded score will be greater than the corresponding truncated score; gray filled cells in Table A.1.

Rounding involves reducing the number of digits or decimal places associated with a numeric value by replacing it with a value that is the <u>nearest</u> whole unit in the place value to which you are rounding (e.g., hundreds place or tenths place). If the number in the place value to which you are rounding is followed by 5, 6, 7, 8, or 9, round <u>up</u>. If the number in that place value is followed by 0, 1, 2, 3, or 4, round <u>down</u>.

Truncating involves reducing the number of digits or decimal places associated with a numeric value by replacing it with a value that is the next-lowest <u>completed</u> unit in the scale to which you are truncating.

Example: Japan's 2014 GDP of $4.631 trillion truncates to $4 trillion (Table A.1, Column 4).

> *The **truncated** value ($4 trillion) is <u>lower</u> than the **rounded** value ($5 trillion), because Japan's GDP did not reach $5 trillion.*

Example: Mike's height (131.7 cm) **truncates** to 131 cm, so he didn't meet the minimum height requirement (132 cm) for the amusement-park ride.

> *Since Mike isn't <u>at least</u> 132 cm tall, he doesn't meet the **cutoff**.*

Rounding and truncation both decrease the precision of a number by reporting fewer digits and/or decimal places. They answer slightly different questions: Rounding produces the nearest value, whereas truncation produces the next-lowest whole ("at least") value. Truncated values are always less than or equal to the corresponding rounded values.

Logarithmic Transformations

Logarithmic transformations are commonly used to express very large or very small numbers in economics and the physical sciences. A **logarithm** is the power to which a number must be raised in order to obtain some other number; thus, taking the log of a number produces the **exponent**. In other words, a logarithm tells how many times to multiply the **base** by itself to get the number. Logarithms can only be taken of positive numbers, but the values of logarithms can be negative, zero, or positive.

Log(x) refers to the **base-10 logarithm**, so it is sometimes written as **log10**(x). **Ln**(x) refers to the **base e** logarithm, also known as **natural logarithms** (where $e = 2.718$). Consult a standard mathematics textbook for more on logarithms.[2]

Taking the **logarithm** of a number (often written "taking the log of") is a form of mathematical transformation used to express very large or very small numbers. Taking the log of a number (x) produces the **exponent** to which the **base** must be raised to produce that number. **Natural logs** (abbreviated ln(x)) use e (2.718) as their base, whereas **base-10 logarithms** (log10(x)) use 10 as the base.

If log10(x) = z, then $10^z = x$, where 10 is the base and z is the exponent (logarithm).

If ln(x) = y, then $e^y = x$; e is the base and y is the exponent (natural log).

Example: The June 2019 earthquake in Peru measuring 8.0 on the Richter scale was nearly 10 times as powerful as the one in Los Angeles that July (magnitude 7.1) and 100 times as powerful as the one in Indonesia in February of that year (magnitude 6.0; "Richter magnitude scale," 2019).

*The Richter scale is **logarithmic (base 10)**, meaning that each one-unit increase corresponds to a tenfold increase in the amount of energy released during an earthquake. Thus, the two-unit increase in Richter magnitude (from 6.0 to 8.0) is a hundredfold increase in energy: $10^8 = 1,000,000,000$, which is 100 times as large as $10^6 = 10,000,000$.*

---

[2]Logarithms and exponents "do and undo" each other, as long as the base (denoted a) is the same. Calculating a^x then **log$_a$** gets you back to x again: $\log_a\left(a^x\right) = x$

Calculating **log$_a$** then a^x gets you back to x again: $a^{\log a(x)} = x$

Example: Ella's annual income for 2018 was $38,000. The **log (base 10)** of her income is 4.58 and the ln **(natural log)** of her income is 10.55.

When a logarithm of a number is less than 1.0, that number is smaller than the base. When a logarithm is higher than 1.0, that number is greater than the base. A logarithm of 0 yields a value of 1.0, whereas negative logs yield numbers between 0 and 1.0.

Example: Decibels (dB) are a measure of sound energy, measured on a logarithmic scale.

> *The **comparison value (threshold)** for the decibel scale is the softest sound the human ear can hear without any artificial help (Ashish, 2021). Thus, a positive decibel value (value on that <u>logarithmic</u> scale) means that the sound is a few <u>times louder</u> than what humans can normally hear, while a negative dB value means that sound is a few <u>times quieter</u> than that threshold.*

Logarithms (whether base 10 or natural logs) are in completely different scales than the original variable, so plausibility checks on logarithms no longer relate to the original units.

Example: Ella's annual income is <u>not</u> $4.58!

> *The **log** of her annual income <u>cannot</u> be compared against the scale of the <u>original</u> income variable. That would imply that her <u>annual</u> income would barely be enough to buy a sandwich at today's U.S. prices!*

Mathematical transformations—such as rounding, truncating, changing scale, and taking logarithms—can only be conducted on continuous variables. They do <u>not</u> suit categorical variables, because the numeric codes for such variables do not have a mathematical interpretation.

Indexes and Scales

An **index** is a type of **composite measure** of a concept created by combining numeric measures of several aspects of that concept. The quantitative scores from the individual items are usually either summed (added together) or averaged, creating a new continuous variable. The source variables must be quantitative, since nominal categories cannot be manipulated mathematically.

Example: At a university health clinic, new students are asked to complete an intake form on which they check all symptoms they have experienced in the past 30 days, from a list of 15 specific symptoms.

Lou has been very healthy and doesn't check any of them, but his roommate Jay has been sick a lot recently and checks off 7 symptoms. An index is created to count how many symptoms each respondent had.

> For each respondent, the **index** tallies up how many symptoms they marked on the intake form. The value of the symptom index for Lou would be 0 (the minimum possible value of the index), because he didn't mark any of the symptoms, while for Jay it would be 7. The maximum possible value of the index is 15, the number of items in the entire list (for respondents who mark all the listed symptoms).

Figure A.1 Calculating an Overall Rating From a Set of Likert Items

Please rate your professor on a scale of 1 (poor) to 5 (excellent) on each of the following attributes.						
		Rating				
Mark one answer for each row.		1	2	3	4	5
a. Preparedness for class						
b. Ability to explain ideas clearly						
c. Ability to make course content interesting						
d. Fairness of grading						
e. Easiness of grading						
f. Availability to answer questions						

Calculated overall rating = average of scores on items a. through f.

Example: A teaching evaluation form asks students to rate their professor from 1 (poor) to 5 (excellent) on each of six attributes related to quality of instruction, availability, and grading (Figure A.1). A summary measure is created by averaging the scores on those six items.

> Each of the six **Likert items** on the questionnaire has a minimum value of 1 and a maximum value of 5, so the same numeric limits will apply to an **index** created by **averaging** the responses to those six items.

A **scale** is also a composite measure calculated from scores on several related items, but it combines them using different **weights** on some items.[3]

---

[3]Somewhat confusingly, the term "scale" is sometimes used as a synonym for "index," even when the items in the composite measure receive equal weighting.

Example: To create a measure that captures severity of symptoms, a scale gives more influence to life-threatening symptoms than to those that are a nuisance but not as severe.

*For the symptom-severity **scale**, chest pain might be given three times the **weight** of a mild symptom like sneezing, meaning that someone with one or two <u>severe</u> symptoms could have a higher score on the scale than someone with several <u>minor</u> symptoms.*

Example: Amazon calculates a product's star ratings by taking into account the age of a rating, whether it is from a verified purchaser, and factors that establish reviewer trustworthiness (Herrman, 2019).

*In other words, the star rating is <u>not</u> a simple average of all the individual ratings for that product. Although Amazon doesn't specify the weights used, they state that more recent ratings, those that are verified, and those that have established the trustworthiness of a reviewer are given more **weight** (emphasis) in their overall star-rating **scale** than those that are older, unverified, or from less dependable reviewers.*

Example: Researchers sought to develop a measure of family socioeconomic status (SES) based on items that could be reliably collected from adolescent respondents. They developed the Family Affluence Scale (FAS), constructed from answers to four questions: (1) number of cars the family owned; (2) number of computers they owned; (3) number of times the family traveled away from home on a holiday in the past year; and (4) whether the child had their own bedroom (Currie et al., 2008). Answers to each of those items were assigned numeric scores (Figure A.2), which were added together to arrive at the value of the new FAS variable for each respondent.

*The possible **values** of the FAS range from 0 to 9, forming a **continuous composite variable**, with higher values reflecting higher levels of SES.*

A **composite measure** is one that mathematically combines values of several different variables, often by adding or averaging values on the component items. **Indexes** and **scales** are composite measures that combine scores on several items measuring different aspects of a particular concept. **Indexes** give equal weight to each of the items in the composite measure, whereas **scales** give more weight (importance) to some items than others, based on substantive considerations for the topic.

Figure A.2 Construction of a Scale From Individual Items

The Family Affluence Scale developed for the Health Behavior in School-Aged Children Survey

Item: question	Response set	Numeric code
1) Does your family own a car, van, or truck?	No	0
	Yes, one	1
	Yes, two or more	2
2) Do you have your own bedroom for yourself?	No	0
	Yes	1
3) During the past 12 months, how many times did you travel away on holiday with your family?	Not at all	0
	Once	1
	Twice	2
	More than twice	3
4) How many computers does your family own?	None	0
	One	1
	Two	2
	More than two	3

Calculated Family Affluence Scale (FAS) = sum of scores on items 1 through 4; valid range is from 0 to 9.

Source: Reprinted from *Social Science & Medicine*, 66/6, C. Currie, et al., Researching health inequalities in adolescents: The development of the Health Behaviour in School-Aged Children (HBSC) Family Affluence Scale, 1429–1436, Copyright 2008, with permission from Elsevier.

New Continuous Variables

In addition to new continuous variables created by transforming numbers, commonly needed forms include count variables and various types of composite measures.

Count Variables

A **count variable** is created when a researcher needs to tally up (count) how many of a set of possible responses each case provided. Count variables can be created from a set of yes/no items, such as indicators from a multiple-response question or another form of list used to collect data. The symptom index mentioned earlier is an example.

Other Types of Composite Measures

A wide range of other types of composite measures are created by mathematically combining two or more continuous variables. A mathematical formula is used to calculate the new variable; thus, that variable will be continuous.

> Example: Body mass index is calculated from separate variables measuring a person's weight and height using the following formula: BMI = weight in kilograms ÷ (height in meters)^2.
>
> > *Continuous measures of weight (kilograms) and height (meters) are mathematically combined to create the new, **continuous** BMI variable. The **units** of the <u>new</u> variable (kg/m^2) are determined by the units of the <u>original</u> variables and the **formula** used to combine them.*

New Categorical Variables

New categorical variables can be created by classifying the values of one or more existing variables into a new variable with fewer values (categories). The original (source) variable can be either continuous or categorical. The categories of the new variable should be mutually exclusive and exhaustive (see Chapter 4).

Categorical Variable From a Continuous Variable

Creating a new categorical variable from a continuous variable results in an ordinal variable, because that original variable's values have an inherent order to them.

> Example: The FAS described above is often used to create a three-category variable capturing SES level: values 0 through 3 on the FAS are classified as low SES, 4 or 5 is classified as moderate SES, and 6 through 9 are classified as high SES (Boyce et al., 2006; Figure A.2).
>
> > *The **categorical** SES variable classifies values of the original **continuous** (**ratio-level**) SES scale variable into **categories** that have a logical numeric order (lowest to highest socioeconomic status), so the new variable is **ordinal** despite the use of names for each category.*

Simplified Categorical Variable From a Detailed Categorical Variable

Sometimes it can be useful to create a simplified version of a categorical variable, collapsing a large number of categories into fewer classifications. This is often done when some categories of the original variable don't have enough cases to analyze separately, or when less detail is needed. The original variable can be either nominal or ordinal, depending on the level of measurement of the original variable.

Categories that are combined with one another during the simplification process must be conceptually similar (for qualitative, nominal variables) or consecutive/adjacent (for ordinal categories).

> Example: Ages in 5-year groups can be simplified by merging them into 10-year age groups; for instance, combining the age group 0 to 4 years with the age group 5 to 9 years to create the age group 0 to 9 years.
>
> > *The <u>simplified</u> **ordinal variable** (10-year age groups) was created from a <u>detailed</u> **ordinal variable** (5-year age groups).*

> Example: The U.S. Census Bureau defines race as a person's self-identification with one or more of the following: (1) White, (2) Black or African American, (3) Asian, (4) American Indian and Alaska Native, (5) Native Hawaiian and Other Pacific Islander, (6) some other race, or (7) multiracial (U.S. Census Bureau, 2018c). In some geographic areas, the number or percentage of people in some of those groups may be so small that two or more racial groups are combined to create a less detailed racial classification for reporting and analysis—for instance, (1) White, (2) Black or African American, and (3) all other racial groups.
>
> > *A <u>simplified</u> **nominal variable** with three total categories was created from the original, <u>more detailed</u> **nominal variable** (with seven categories). Here, "conceptual similarity" is limited to the fact that each of the categories to be combined has a small sample size, even though those racial categories may be qualitatively quite distinct.*

New Categorical Variable From Two Categorical Variables

Another way to create a new categorical variable is by combining information on two characteristics, with a separate category of the new variable for each combination of the categories of those original variables, to create a set of mutually exclusive, exhaustive categories. The original variables can be either nominal or ordinal.

> Example: The 2010 U.S. Census collected information on race and Hispanic ethnicity separately (Office of Management and Budget, 1997). Information from those two variables was combined to create a single race/ethnicity variable, with categories non-Hispanic White, non-Hispanic Black, Hispanic, non-Hispanic Asian, and Other.
>
> > *Here, <u>two</u> **nominal variables**—race (classified as in the previous example) and Hispanic ethnicity (yes or no) are combined to create <u>one</u> <u>new</u> **nominal variable** that captures both characteristics simultaneously.*

Indicator Variables

Indicator variables are a specific type of categorical variable that indicates (conveys) whether a case has a particular characteristic. In other words, they classify cases into those with and without that trait. Indicator variables are at the categorical level of measurement, but they can be created from variables at any level of measurement. The criterion for assessing which category a case falls in can be either qualitative (nominal) or quantitative (ordinal, interval, or ratio).

> **Indicator** variables, also called **dichotomous** ("two-category"), **binary**, or **dummy** variables, are used to <u>indicate</u> whether each case has a characteristic of interest.

<u>Example</u>: A variable distinguishes between respondents who were married at the time of a survey and those who were not married.

> *The <u>new</u> "married"* **indicator variable** *has two categories: one for married, and the other for any of the other marital statuses (never married, separated, divorced, or widowed). Both the <u>original variables</u> and <u>the new variable</u> are* **nominal**.

<u>Example</u>: A poverty indicator differentiates between families whose income falls below the poverty threshold and those whose incomes are at or above that value.

> *The poverty indicator variable has two categories: poor and non-poor. The original income variable was* **continuous**; *the new variable is* **categorical**.

Indicator Variables From a Multiple-Response Item

As explained in Chapter 4, a multiple-response item is one for which respondents are asked to select all answers that apply to them—for some respondents, no answers may apply; for other respondents, exactly one answer may apply; and, for others, several answers may apply. Answers to multiple-response questions must be captured by a <u>set</u> of indicator variables, each indicating whether or not a respondent marked a specific one of the possible responses. Thus, if the original question had N possible responses (where N is the maximum number of distinct responses), N new indicator variables are needed to reflect the possible combinations of responses.

<u>Example</u>: A survey includes the following question to collect information on commuting patterns: "How do you commute to work? Mark all that apply."

___ Car

___ Ride-sharing

___ Bus

___ Train

___ Bike

___ Walk

___ Other

___ I work from home.

___ I am not employed.

*Respondents are asked to mark all the responses that pertain to them, so <u>no single variable</u> can easily hold all the responses. Instead, <u>nine new</u> **indicator variables** are needed—one for each of the possible ways of commuting, and—among those who didn't commute to work—to differentiate between people who work from home and those who are not employed.*

Figure A.3 shows a hypothetical data set with variables created from answers to the question about ways of commuting to work, putting the information in the form needed to analyze the data.

Figure A.3   Coding a Multiple-Response Item Into Variables

Question: "How do you commute to work? Mark all that apply."

Respondent 101:	Respondent 102:	Respondent 103:
_X_ Personal car	___ Personal car	___ Personal car
___ Ride-sharing or taxi	___ Ride-sharing or taxi	___ Ride-sharing or taxi
___ Bus	___ Bus	___ Bus
___ Train	___ Train	___ Train
___ Bike	_X_ Bike	___ Bike
___ Walk	_X_ Walk	___ Walk
___ Other	___ Other	___ Other
___ I work from home.	___ I work from home.	_X_ I work from home.
___ I am not employed.	___ I am not employed.	___ I am not employed.

Variables created from question about modes of transportation used to commute to work

Respondent ID	Personal _car	Ride-sharing	Bus	Train	Bike	Walk	Other_ trans	Work_ home	Not_ empl	N_commute_ trans	Anycommute
101	Yes	No	No	No	No	No	No	No	No	1	Yes
102	No	No	No	No	Yes	Yes	No	No	No	2	Yes
103	NA	NA	NA	NA	NA	NA	NA	Yes	No	0	No

Example: Respondent 101 marked that he commuted only by car, so for him the "Personal_car" variable is coded "Yes," while all the other commuting modality variables take on the value "No." Respondent 102 marked that she commuted by walking and biking, so, for her, each of those two variables is coded "Yes," with all other indicators coded "No." Respondent 103 works from home, so "Work_home" is coded "Yes," and all the indicators of specific commuting modalities are coded "NA" (for "not applicable").

> *Each of the response categories of the original multiple-response question yielded a <u>separate</u> **nominal indicator variable**, named after one of the modes of commuting: Personal_car, Ride-sharing, Bus, Train, Bike, Walk, and Other_trans.*

Example: The new variable N_commute_trans is created by tallying up the number of types of transportation reported by each respondent. It takes on the value 1 for Respondent 101, who indicated that he used only one mode to commute to work (personal car); the value 2 for Respondent 102, who reported commuting by both walking and biking; and the value 0 for Respondent 103, who did not commute (Figure A.3).

> *N_commute_trans is a **count (continuous) variable**, calculated as the <u>sum</u> of the number of modes of transportation each respondent marked.*

Example: The last of the new variables shown in Figure A.3, named "Anycommute," is coded "Yes" for Respondents 101 and 102 and "No" for Respondent 103.

> *"Anycommute" is a **nominal indicator variable**, differentiating between those who used <u>any</u> (1 or more) modes of commuting and those who used <u>none</u> (did not commute).*

Answers to a single-response question ("mark the best answer") can be captured with <u>one</u> variable.

Answers to a multiple-response question ("mark all that apply") must be captured by separate <u>nominal variables</u>, each indicating whether or not a respondent mentioned a specific one of the responses. If there are N possible responses to the original item (question), then N indicator variables are an efficient way to capture all possible combinations of answers.

TERMS AND CONCEPTS

Base (of logarithm)   510
Changing scale   507
Composite measure   511
   Index   511
   Scale   512
Count variable   514

Created (new) variable   504
Exponent   510
Indicator variable   517
   Dummy variable   517
Logarithm   510
Natural logarithm   510

Original (raw existing)
   variable   504
Place value   508
Rounding numbers   508
Truncating numbers   509

HIGHLIGHTS

- Sometimes variables can be analyzed in the form in which the data were **originally collected**. Other times, data aren't yet in the form needed to answer the research question, so **new** variables must be created from one or more existing variable(s).

- **Mathematical transformations**, such as rounding, truncating, changing scale, or taking logarithms, can only be conducted on continuous variables. They do <u>not</u> suit categorical variables, because the numeric codes for such variables do not have a mathematical interpretation.

- The **types of new variables** that can be created depend on the **level of measurement** of the existing variables.

- The **calculation (formula)** or **classification process** used to create a new variable will determine its **level of measurement**.

- Once a new variable has been created, it can be used for **comparisons** and **mathematical** or **statistical analyses** that suit its level of measurement.

EXERCISES

Individual Exercises

Quantitative Reasoning in Everyday Life

1. Look up the formula used to calculate a sports performance rating, such as the NFL passer rating, the basketball Performance Index Rating (PIR), or another composite measure. (a) Provide a URL where you found that information. (b) List the component items. (c) Specify the units and plausible range of values of each of those items. (d) Type the formula used to calculate the index. (e) Identify whether each component is positively or negatively associated with the value of the overall index. (f) Specify the minimum and maximum values of the composite index. (g) Indicate whether a higher or lower value is "better."

2. Go to the Heart Risk calculator at http://www.cvriskcalculator.com. (a) List the component items (risk factors); (b) for each, identify its level of measurement, (c) categories or units, (d) and plausible range of numeric values. (e) Calculate the 10-year risk of heart disease or stroke for four different combinations of risk factors. (f) Identify the direction of association between each of the component items and heart disease/stroke risk.

Interpreting Research

3. View the Short Acculturation Scale for Hispanics (SASH) at https://cansort.med. umich.edu/download/1032. List the component items, identifying (a) their level of measurement and (b) the numeric codes for each response category. (c) Write the formula used to create the scale, using abbreviations for the names of the component items. Identify (d) the cutoff used to classify scores into ranges and (e) the conceptual meaning of each of the categories.

4. Assume that your local public health department has provided you with information on number of COVID cases and number of COVID deaths in your town and asks you to calculate (a) the prevalence rate per 100,000 persons, (b) the death rate per 100,000 persons in the town, and (c) the case-fatality rate (deaths per 1,000 cases). Specify what additional information (if any) you would need in order to calculate each of those rates, and write the formulas you would use to compute each of those new measures from the raw data.

Planning Research

5. On the tab titled "Variables" for the ICPSR data set you used in Chapter 2, Exercise 3, find a nominal variable with at least three categories. (a) Write classification instructions for creating a simplified version. (b) Specify the criteria (e.g., thematic, empirical, and/or frequency of values) you used to decide how to collapse categories. (c) Show how each value of the original variable maps into the categories of the new variable. (d) Cite a published source where you identified those criteria.

6. Repeat Exercise 5 for an ordinal variable with at least three categories.

7. On the tab titled "Variables" for the ICPSR data set you used in Chapter 2, Exercise 3, find an interval or ratio variable. (a) Look up authoritative sources that discuss ways that variable is often classified, and provide citations for each. (b) Write classification instructions for creating a categorical version of that variable, showing how each value of the continuous (interval or ratio) variable maps into the categories of the new variable.

Group Exercises

Interpreting Research

8. In the scholarly literature, find three different definitions of "acculturation." Use information from Chapter 4 about reliability and validity to evaluate the Short Acculturation Scale for Hispanics (SASH) items (from Exercise 3) for each of those definitions of acculturation. Discuss why a scale was used instead of the separate individual items.

Planning Research

9. Exchange your work on Exercise 5 with a classmate. Critique each other's classification instructions for completeness and correctness, following the guidelines in this appendix. Revise your classification instructions to correct any errors found by your peer reviewer.

10. Do the same with your work on Exercise 7.

Appendix B

Sampling Weights

Learning Objectives

After reading this appendix, you will be able to do the following:

1. State the purpose of sampling weights in analysis of data from a sample.

2. Understand how to include information on use of sampling weights in tables, figures, and text.

As discussed in Chapter 11, **random sampling** is used to generate a sample that is representative of the population of interest. For random sampling, the **probability of selection** can be specified for each element in the population, which is why those methods are referred to as **probability sampling methods**. The probability of selection equals the number of elements selected for the sample (n), divided by the total number of elements in the population (N); thus, the probability of selection must fall between 0.0 and 1.0.

The Purpose of Sampling Weights

Sampling weights are used to adjust estimates based on data from a sample to reflect the corresponding pattern in the population from which it was drawn. They reflect the number of cases in the original population that are represented by each case in the sample. The **sampling weight** for a particular case is calculated as $1 \div$ probability of selection for that case, so the higher the probability of selection, the lower the sampling weight, and vice versa.

> Example: If a survey uses simple random sampling to select one out of every 1,000 people in the population, each case in the sample represents 1,000 people in the population.
>
> *The* **probability of selection** *= .001, so the* **sampling weight** *for each case = $1 \div .001 = 1,000$.*

If, instead, the survey samples one out of every 100 people in the population, each case in the sample represents 100 people in the population.

*In this hypothetical example, the **probability of selection** is <u>higher</u> than in the previous example (.01 > .001), so the **sampling weight** for each case is <u>lower</u> than in the previous example (100 < 1,000).*

Sampling weights for many large studies, such as the National Health and Nutrition Examination Survey (NHANES), also correct for variations in rates of nonresponse and attrition (CDC, 2018a).

Sampling Weights for Disproportionate Sampling

Recall from Chapter 11 that in **disproportionate random sampling**, elements from smaller **strata** of particular interest for the research question are sampled at higher rates than are elements from larger strata. We say that the groups that were sampled at higher rates were **oversampled**, meaning that their share of the sample is higher than their share in the population from which they are drawn. Thus, the probability of selection for the oversampled strata is higher than that for other strata.

When the set of elements used in an analysis was selected using disproportionate sampling, sampling weights must be used to adjust the statistics so that they correctly capture the composition of the population from which that sample was drawn. If the data are <u>not</u> adjusted for disproportionate sampling, the greater number of elements from the oversampled strata in the sample will skew population averages toward values for those groups.

<u>Example:</u> The University of Y oversampled nursing students in order to ensure that there was a sufficient number of them to analyze and compare with students from the much larger arts and sciences school (Figure 11.5). If the data were <u>not</u> adjusted (weighted) to reflect the disproportionate sampling, the sample composition would be 50% nursing, 50% arts and sciences (Table B.1, Column 3), because the sample consists of 200 students from each school. Weighted back to the population level, however, the composition was 9% nursing, 91% arts and sciences (Column 6), correctly reflecting the sizes of those two schools' overall enrollment.

*The **probability of selection** (Column 1) for the nursing students was .5, so the **sampling weight** for the nursing students was 1 ÷ .5 = 2 (Table B.1, Column 4). In other words, each nursing student in the **sample** represented <u>two</u> students from the **population** of all nursing students. The **probability of selection** for the arts and sciences students was .05, so each of them in the **sample** represented **20** students from the **population** of all arts and sciences students.*

Table B.1 Illustration of Sampling Weights

	(1) Probability of selection	(2) Unweighted *n* in sample	(3) Unweighted percentage of sample	(4) Sampling weight	(5) Weighted *N*	(6) Weighted percentage of sample
All	NA	200	100%	NA	2,200	100%
Nursing	.50	100	50%	2	200	9%
Arts and Sciences	.05	100	50%	20	2,000	91%

Notes: Sampling weight **(Column 4)** = 1 ÷ probability of selection **(Column 1)**.

Weighted *N* **(Column 5)** = Unweighted *n* **(Column 2)** × sampling weight **(Column 4)**.

Weighted percentage of sample **(Column 6)** = Weighted subgroup size **(Column 5)** ÷ Weighted total sample size **(top row of Column 5)**.

See Figure 11.5 and associated description of disproportionate sampling.

> **Sampling weights** capture the number of cases in the <u>population</u> that are represented by each case in the <u>sample</u>. For the ith case: sampling weight$_i$ = 1 ÷ probability of selection$_i$. Sampling weights also correct for differences in response rates and attrition rates across cases in the sample.

If data were collected from the full population, sampling weights are irrelevant, because the analysis includes the entire population (each case's sampling weight = 1.0). Sampling weights cannot be calculated for data selected using non-probability sampling methods, because the probability of selection for the elements in the sample is unknown.

> Sampling weights are used when analyzing data from a sample that was selected using a **probability sampling method**. They ensure that the results reflect the composition of the population from which the sample was selected. Sampling weights <u>cannot</u> be calculated for samples selected using **non-probability methods** and do <u>not</u> pertain to data for entire **populations**.

Communicating Use of Sampling Weights

When presenting results of analyses based on samples drawn using probability sampling methods to scientific audiences, the use of sampling weights should be mentioned in all tables, charts, and prose that report statistics weighted back to the population level, with a citation to documentation that describes the sampling weights for that data source. The unweighted sample size should also be reported, so that readers are aware of the actual number of cases used in the analysis; see Chapter 13 and Appendix C for more on the importance of sample size for inferential statistical results.

> <u>Example</u>: All statistics were weighted to the national level using sampling weights provided for the 2015–16 National Health and Nutrition Examination Survey (NHANES) by the Centers for Disease Control and Prevention (CDC, 2018a).
>
> *A sentence like this would be expected in the **data and methods section** of a scientific paper, explaining the use and purpose of the **sampling weights** and providing a **citation** about those weights.*

Example: In Table 13.5, the sample size column heading conveys that it is <u>unweighted</u>, while a footnote explains that the other statistics in the table are <u>weighted</u>.

> *A combination of **labeling** and **footnotes** convey which statistics are weighted and which are not. Another **footnote** cites an **authoritative source** of information about the sampling weights.*

Example: A footnote specifies that the estimates presented in Table 13.5 are **weighted** to the population level, correcting for the use of **disproportionate sampling** in the NHANES data.

TERMS AND CONCEPTS

Disproportionate sampling   523   Sampling weight   522   Weighted results   526
Probability of Selection   522   Unweighted results   526

HIGHLIGHTS

- **Sampling weights** are applied to sample statistics in order to bring them back to the population level.

- Sampling weights adjust for differences in **probability of selection** for elements with different characteristics (e.g., **disproportionate sampling**); they often also correct for differences in **response rate** and **attrition** across cases.

EXERCISES

Interpreting Statistics

1. Answer the following questions based on information in the documentation or users' guide for the data set you selected from the ICPSR Website for Chapter 2, Exercise 3. (a) Determine whether sampling weights are needed when analyzing the data from that study and (b) if so, why. (c) Identify what factors were involved in creating the sampling weights (e.g., disproportionate sampling, response rates, and attrition). (d) Cite the source from which you obtained that information.

Appendix C

Brief Technical Background on Inferential Statistics

Learning Objectives

After reading this appendix, you will be able to do the following:

1. Understand the relationship between sample size and standard error.

2. Calculate margin of error and confidence interval from a standard error.

3. Write hypotheses for inferential statistical testing.

4. Identify the numeric elements of traditional hypothesis testing.

5. Understand the logical process involved in assessing statistical significance.

6. Recognize the difference between Type I and Type II errors.

7. Assess plausibility of inferential test results.

In Chapter 13, I introduced the idea of uncertainty and its role in making sense of numbers calculated from sample data. In this appendix, I build on the concepts from that chapter, providing some additional technical details about the steps involved in traditional hypothesis testing, so that students who have had a formal statistics course can integrate that material with ideas from this book.[1] To tie the concepts introduced in this appendix to concepts from Chapter 13, I repeat several of the examples from that chapter, revising them and the associated annotations to illustrate the more advanced statistical information.

Even with the additional terms and concepts covered in this appendix, this book is <u>not</u> a substitute for a statistics textbook. For a more thorough treatment of statistical methods, and their derivation, use, and interpretation, consult a standard textbook on statistics, such as Utts and Heckard's *Mind on Statistics* (2014) or Salkind's *Statistics for People Who (Think They) Hate Statistics* (2016).

---

[1] I use the phrase "traditional" hypothesis testing to differentiate it from the compatibility interval approach to interpreting results of inferential statistics recommended by Amrhein and colleagues (2019). See "Drawbacks of Traditional Hypothesis Testing" in Chapter 13.

Standard Error and Sample Size

Recall from Chapter 13 that in studies that did <u>not</u> analyze data for the full population of interest, the true value of a **population parameter** such as a mean or a measure of difference across groups is unknown. Instead, such studies use data from a sample (smaller number of cases; $n < N$) to produce a **sample statistic** that estimates the value of the unknown population parameter. A **standard error** around a sample statistic measures the amount of variation in the sample statistic based on different samples from the same population.

In technical terms, a **standard error** of a sample statistic measures the extent of sampling variation.[2] The larger the standard error, the higher the uncertainty about the value of the population parameter. For a given amount of variation in the sample statistic, the larger the sample size, the smaller the standard error of that statistic. This is true because sample size is in the denominator of the standard error calculation for all types of sample statistics (whether means, proportions, or other statistics),[3] and, by definition, dividing by a bigger number produces a smaller result.

> <u>Example</u>: The standard error of a sample mean is the variance (s^2) divided by the square root of the sample size (n): $s^2 \div \sqrt{n}$. For the NHANES estimate of mean height among 8-year-old boys, which was based on 121 cases, variance was 8.03 cm, producing a standard error of 0.73 cm. If, instead, the estimate had been based on 250 cases, the standard error would have been smaller, because $\sqrt{250} > \sqrt{121}$. Dividing the same amount of variance by a larger number produces a smaller result.
>
> > When **sample size** (n) = 121, the **standard error of the mean** = 8.03 $\div \sqrt{121} = 8.03 \div 11 = 0.73$ cm. With the same amount of **variance** ($s^2 = 8.03$,) a hypothetical sample of <u>250</u> cases would yield a standard error of the mean = 8.03 $\div \sqrt{250} = 8.03 \div 15.8 = 0.51$ cm.

Margin of Error

The **margin of error** is calculated as standard error × a critical value, which must be a positive value. To determine the critical value, a **confidence level** is chosen by the researcher, specifying how likely it is that the true value of the population parameter falls within one margin of error on either side of the point estimate. A 95% confidence level is the most commonly used value. Once a confidence level has been selected, the **critical value** is determined using the pertinent statistical

---

[2]A standard error is the estimated standard deviation of the sampling distribution (Utts & Heckard, 2014; Chapter 9). For example, if an unlimited number of samples are drawn from the population and each of those sample means is plotted on a distribution, the standard error would equal the standard deviation of that distribution (the sampling distribution of sample means).

[3]The formula for calculating the standard error differs for different types of sample statistics. Consult a standard statistics textbook for specific formulas.

distribution,[4] the sample size, and whether the hypothesis is one-sided or two-sided (see "Writing a Hypothesis," later in this appendix). With a large sample size, the critical value for a 95% confidence level and a <u>two-sided test</u> is 1.96. Other margins of error can be calculated by substituting the appropriate critical value (e.g., 1.64 for a 90% confidence level; 2.56 for a 99% confidence level). With a large sample size, the critical value for a 95% confidence level and a <u>one-sided test</u> is 1.64.

> A **margin of error** (**MOE**) is a measure of the uncertainty of a sample estimate, calculated as MOE = **critical value** × **standard error of the estimate**. A **confidence level** specifies how likely it is that the true value of the population parameter falls within one margin of error on either side of the point estimate.

Confidence Interval

As explained in Chapter 13, a **confidence interval** (**CI**) is the range of values within which the true population parameter is expected to fall, with the degree of confidence specified by the **confidence level**. A confidence interval around a sample statistic is calculated as point estimate ± margin of error. The **lower confidence limit** (**LCL**) and **upper confidence limit** (**UCL**) are the lowest and highest values in that range, respectively.

> <u>Example</u>: The estimated prevalence of obesity among U.S. children based on the 2015–16 NHANES was 18.0%, with a margin of error of 1.0 percentage points. Thus, we can be 95% sure that the true prevalence of obesity among all U.S. children was between 17.0% and 19.0% (Figure 13.5).
>
> *The **standard error** of the estimated child obesity rate from the NHANES is 0.5%. The **critical value** for a **confidence level of 95%** and a large sample size (n = 3,115) is 1.96. The associated **margin of error** = 0.5% × 1.96 = 1.0%, yielding a **95% confidence interval** around the **point estimate** of 18.0 ± 1.0, or 17.0% to 19.0%.*

Criteria for Making Sense of Measures of Uncertainty

Table C.1 summarizes criteria for making sense of measures of uncertainty for sample estimates. The level of measurement of a variable determines the formulas for the standard error of an estimate and the test statistic. Level of measurement also determines which statistical distribution is used to ascertain the critical value used in calculating a margin of error or confidence interval.

---

[4]The critical value for proportions is based on the standard normal distribution, whereas the critical value for means is based on Student's *t*-distribution (Utts & Heckard, 2014, p. 350).

Table C.1 Criteria for Making Sense of Measures of Uncertainty

Measures of uncertainty	Definitional limits on value	Affected by		
		Units of variables?	Level of measurement of variable(s)?	Sample size?
Confidence level	Must be between 0 and 100.0.	No	No	No
Critical value	Must be positive. Maximum value: • for large sample sizes, < 3.5 • can be much higher for small sample sizes[a]	No	Affects which statistical distribution is the reference for the critical value[a]	Inversely related to sample size
Standard error of the estimate	Must be positive.	Same units as associated sample statistic[b]	Different formulas for measures related to continuous variables than for those related to categorical ones[c]	Inversely related to sample size
Margin of error = critical value × standard error			Through effect on standard error	
Confidence interval = point estimate ± margin of error	Can span negative values, positive values, or a combination of negative and positive values.			

Notes:

a. Consult a table of standard normal distribution for proportions; Student's *t*-distribution for means (Utts & Heckard, 2014, p. 350).

b. For continuous variables, measures of uncertainty will be in the units of the original variable. For categorical variables, measures of uncertainty will be in percentage points or proportion units.

c. Formulas for standard errors sample differ for continuous and for categorical variables. Consult a statistics textbook.

Critical values must be positive and are inversely related to sample size. Test statistics and critical values are not affected by the units in which the variable was measured.

Hypothesis Testing

Hypothesis testing, also known as **statistical significance testing**, uses data from a sample to assess whether a hypothesis about the value of the population parameter is supported or refuted by the data. In Chapter 12 of their textbook, Utts and Heckard (2014) outlined the following five steps for traditional hypothesis testing; see their book for a more thorough explication of each of these steps. In Chapter 13 of this book, I simplified their steps to avoid some of the more advanced statistical concepts.

Step 1: Specify Null and Alternative Hypotheses

The first step in hypothesis testing is to state the research question as a **hypothesis**, putting it into a form that can be tested using statistical methods. Two forms of the hypothesis are written: a null hypothesis and an alternative hypothesis. A **null hypothesis** (abbreviated H_0) is a statement that the population parameter is equal to the null value (often 0). For a univariate summary statistic, such as a mean or proportion, the null hypothesis usually specifies that the actual population value of that measure is 0.[5] For a bivariate statistic about the relationship between two variables, the null hypothesis implies that there is <u>no</u> relationship between those variables—in other words, that the values of the dependent variable do <u>not</u> vary according to values of the independent variable. See the following section for more on the null value for different types of numeric contrasts.

An **alternative hypothesis** (H_a) is a statement that the population parameter is <u>not</u> equal to the null value. For a univariate statistic, such as a mean, H_a suggests that that value is different from 0, taking on either a negative or a positive value. For a bivariate statistic, H_a implies that there <u>is</u> a relationship between the independent and dependent variables—in other words, that values of the dependent variable <u>do</u> vary according to values of the independent variable.

An alternative hypothesis (H_a) can be either **directional** or **nondirectional.** As its name suggests, a **directional hypothesis** conveys the predicted direction (sign) of the statistic. A directional hypothesis is also referred to as a **one-sided hypothesis**, because it specifies on which "side" of 0 (positive or negative) the statistic is expected to fall. A **nondirectional hypothesis** states only that the statistic will not equal the null value; thus, it is referred to as a **two-sided hypothesis**, because it does not predict whether the statistic will be above or below the null value (i.e., it could be to either side of that value).

---

[5]Consult a statistics textbook for examples of when a null hypothesis specifies something <u>other than </u>that the population parameter equals 0.

Example: For an evaluation of a "boot camp" to teach prospective applicants for a microloan program how to plan a 2-year budget for their proposed business, researchers conduct an experiment to test whether that training program increases the percentage of businesses that remain in operation at the end of that period. Half of the applicants are randomly assigned to receive the budget training (the treatment group); the other half receive no special training or assistance (the control group).

*The **independent variable** classifies whether each microloan applicant participated in the training, and the **dependent variable** measures the success or failure of the business. The **null hypothesis** (H_0) posits equal success rates between microloan recipients who participated in the training program and those who did not.*

There can be more than one alternative hypothesis for a research question, depending on whether a direction of association is proposed and, if so, in which direction.

Example: Two researchers on the collaborative team running the microloan boot camp each write an alternative hypothesis: Maya Singh—a first-year graduate student on the team—hypothesizes that the percentage of participants who remain in business at the end of the study period will be different in the treatment and control groups. Her mentor, Dr. Rodriguez—who designed the training to improve participants' knowledge of key business principles—specifies that the treatment group will be more likely than the control group to succeed.

*Maya's alternative hypothesis is **nondirectional**, because it states that participants in the treatment group and the control groups will have different levels of success in staying in business but doesn't indicate which group she anticipates will be more successful. Dr. Rodriguez's alternative hypothesis is **directional**, because she predicts that those who receive the specialized budget training will be more likely than those who did not receive that training to remain in business.*

A **null hypothesis** (abbreviated H_0) is a statement that the population parameter equals the **null** value (often 0). An **alternative hypothesis** (abbreviated H_a; also known as a **research hypothesis**) is a statement that the population parameter is <u>different from</u> the null value. A **directional hypothesis** (also termed a **one-sided hypothesis**) is an alternative hypothesis that expresses the predicted direction (sign) of the population parameter. There are two possibilities:

1. H_a: population parameter > null value; if the null value = 0, implies that the population parameter is <u>positive</u>

2. H_a: population parameter < null value; if the null value = 0, implies that the population parameter is <u>negative</u>

> A **nondirectional hypothesis** (also known as a **two-sided hypothesis**) simply states that the parameter does not equal the null value. It does <u>not</u> predict in which direction.
>
> H_a: population parameter ≠ null value.

Important Aside About the "Null" Value

The numeric value that reflects "no difference" varies depending on the type of mathematical comparison (see Chapter 9). When two values, x and y, are compared using <u>subtraction</u>, if $x = y$ then $x - y = 0$, so the "no difference" (null) value = 0 However, if two equal values are compared using <u>division</u>, then $x \div y = 1$. This is important to remember when the effect size is calculated using a ratio, because it means that the **null value** is 1.0, <u>not</u> 0.

> <u>Example</u>: Suppose researchers found that 75% of people who participated in the fictitious budget-planning boot camp were still in business 2 years later, versus 25% of those who did not undertake that specialized training. The associated p-value was .02. The research team specified a significance level of .05.
>
> *Comparing the success rates using <u>subtraction</u>: 75% – 25% = 50 percentage points. Because the effect size was calculated using subtraction, the null value ("no difference") = 0. Based on that measure of effect size,* **hypothesis testing** *would assess, "How likely would it be to obtain an estimate of 50 if the true value was <u>0</u>?"*
>
> *Comparing the success rates using <u>division</u>: 75% ÷ 25% = 3.0. Because the effect size was calculated using a ratio, the null value is 1.0, so instead,* **hypothesis testing** *would ask, "How likely would it be to obtain an estimate of 3.0 if the true value was <u>1.0</u>?"*
>
> *No matter which kind of math was used to make the comparison, the direction of association was the same: The treatment group had a more favorable outcome than the control group. And, regardless of in which way the effect size was calculated, the conclusion about* **statistical significance** *is the same: The* **p-value** *for the estimate is .02, which is less than the chosen* **significance level** *(.05), so the researchers reject the null hypothesis of equal success rates for the two groups with 95% confidence.*

Step 2: Calculate a Test Statistic[6]

Once the null and alternative hypotheses have been written, a **test statistic** is used to provide the numeric information needed to answer the question "If the

---

[6]In Chapter 13, this step was combined with obtaining a p-value, as the discussion about test statistics is too technical for students who have not yet had a statistics course.

null hypothesis is true about the population, what is the probability of observing sample data like that which was observed?"[7] The test statistic is computed from the **point estimate** and its **standard error**.[8] The pertinent statistical procedure depends on the levels of measurement of the variables; a t-statistic or F-statistic for continuous variables; a z-statistic or chi-square (X^2) statistic for categorical variables. Statistical software will report the calculated test statistic as part of the standard output.

Step 3: Obtain a p-Value

The third step in hypothesis testing is to obtain a **p-value** by comparing the test statistic (from Step 2) against a threshold called the **critical value**. The critical value for a test statistic depends on the pertinent statistical distribution (e.g., a t-statistic against Student's t distribution; a z-statistic against the standard normal distribution), the **degrees of freedom** (df), the level of significance chosen by the researcher, and whether the hypothesis is one-sided (directional) or two-sided (nondirectional). The degrees of freedom of an estimate is the number of independent pieces of information that went into calculating that estimate, which depends on the type of statistical procedure and the number of cases in the data set.

The **p-value** gives the probability of obtaining a result at least as large as the sample estimate if the true value in the population is the null value. The smaller the p-value, the smaller the chance of falsely rejecting the null hypothesis. Put differently, a small p-value corresponds to a very low probability of incorrectly concluding, based on the sample estimate, that the population parameter is the null value. Software will calculate and report the p-value and degrees of freedom as part of the statistical output.

A **test statistic** for a hypothesis test is a numeric data summary used to evaluate the null and alternative hypotheses. A **critical value** (denoted **critical z** or z^* in statistics books) is the value of the test statistic above which the null hypothesis is rejected. **Degrees of freedom (df)** is the number of independent pieces of information involved in calculating a statistical estimate. A **p-value** is the probability that the test statistic could take on the observed value of the sample estimate if the null hypothesis was actually true.

---

[7]Test statistics such as t, F, and X^2 statistics have known distributions when the null hypothesis is true; thus, they can be used to see whether the sample distribution is consistent with the null hypothesis (Vogt & Johnson, 2011).

[8]The general formula for a test statistic is as follows: standardized statistic = t or z = (sample statistic − null value) ÷ null standard error (Utts & Heckard, 2014, p. 458).

Step 4: Assess Statistical Significance Using the *p*-Value

The next step in traditional hypothesis testing is to compare the calculated *p*-value against the chosen **significance level** (α), which is a cutoff chosen by the researcher to determine whether a *p*-value is small enough to justify rejecting the null hypothesis. It specifies the level of risk the researcher is willing to tolerate of falsely rejecting the null hypothesis. The significance level = (100 – **confidence level**) ÷ 100 (to put it into probability terms). Thus, a 95% confidence level corresponds to $p = .05$; a 99% confidence level to a significance level of .01. The default significance level in most statistical software is .05 but can be adjusted by the researcher.

When the calculated *p*-value for a sample estimate is less than the chosen level of significance (α), the null hypothesis is rejected and we, instead, choose the alternative hypothesis; the result is then identified as **statistically significant**. A statistically significant result is one that has a high probability of supporting the alternative hypothesis (H_a). It implies a very low probability (the *p*-value) that the sample estimate could be as large as it is when the population parameter is equal to the null value, due solely to chance associated with how the sample was drawn from the population. When the *p*-value is greater than or equal to α, the null hypothesis <u>cannot</u> be rejected.

The default setting for calculating a *p*-value, in most statistical software, is a <u>two</u>-sided (**nondirectional**) hypothesis. The corresponding *p*-value for a <u>one</u>-sided (**directional**) hypothesis is calculated as α ÷ 2.

The step of comparing the *p*-value to the significance level is done by whomever is interpreting the results, whether from output based on their own statistical analysis or using a *p*-value reported by another researcher.

A **significance level** (α) is chosen by to express the risk the researcher is willing to tolerate of falsely rejecting the null hypothesis. It is mathematically related to the **confidence level**:

$$\alpha = (100 - \text{confidence level}) \div 100$$

A **statistically significant** result is one for which the calculated *p*-value for the sample estimate is less than the significance level.

As Utts and Heckard (2014, p. 465) put it,

> The logic of statistical hypothesis testing is similar to the "presumed innocent until proven guilty" principle of the U.S. judicial system. In hypothesis testing, we assume that the null hypothesis is a possible

truth until the sample data conclusively demonstrate otherwise. The "something is happening" hypothesis [H_a] is chosen only when the data show us that we can reject the "nothing is happening" hypothesis [H_0].

In a criminal trial, the standard of evidence is "beyond a reasonable doubt" (Hill & Hill, 2020), which is consistent with a 95% confidence level: high, but not 100% conclusive. The extent of certainty about the inference is expressed by the confidence level, which can never equal 100% for an estimate that is based on a sample rather than on the full population.

Step 5: Interpret the Inferential Test Result

The last step in hypothesis testing is to explain how the results of the inferential test apply to the specific topic and data used in the analysis, conveying what the results tell us about the pattern or relationship among the concepts in the hypothesis. This step is also conducted by the researcher (not the computer software!), working from their assessment of statistical significance (Step 4) in combination with principles for effective communication of statistical results (see Chapter 14).

Although many novice researchers want to be able to state conclusively that they have "proven" that their hypothesis is true (or false), as noted earlier, the uncertainty attached to statistics based on samples means that we cannot come to that definitive of a conclusion about the population. Instead, conclusions about inferential test results should be phrased in terms of the probability that the results support (or refute) the null hypothesis. In fact, if $p > .05$, researchers do not say they "accept" the null hypothesis; instead they "fail to reject" that hypothesis at the selected level of significance. Such wording conveys that because sample data were used, there is a chance that the estimates led to an incorrect conclusion about the value of that statistic in the population. See the subsequent discussion of Type I and Type II errors.

Example: In the 2015–16 U.S. NHANES sample of children aged 2 to 17 years, mean body mass index (BMI) for boys was 20.0 kg/m², versus 20.3 kg/m² for girls; $p = .29$.

Comparing the p-value for the sample estimate against the significance level, .29 > .05, we <u>fail</u> to reject the **null hypothesis** *(H_0: no difference in average BMI by gender) at the .05 significance level based on a* **two-sided (nondirectional) hypothesis**. *This result implies that the observed gender difference in mean BMI in the sample <u>could</u> be explained by sampling variation alone.*

Example: The obesity rate among children in the 2015–16 NHANES was 1.75 times as high in the lowest family income group as in the highest family income group (22.7% and 12.9%, respectively;

Table 13.4). With a X^2 statistic of 22.8, with 3 degrees of freedom, an association that large has less than a 0.1% probability ($p < .005$) of being due to random sampling alone.

> The **test statistic** (the chi-square statistic X^2) is reported in a note to the table, along with the associated number of **degrees of freedom** and **p-value** from a **one-sided** (**directional**) test, all of which would be included in the output from the software used to estimate the statistics. The use of **sampling weights** is mentioned in another footnote; see Appendix B for more on sampling weights. The second sentence conveys the probabilistic nature of the conclusion—that it is <u>not</u> 100% certain.

<u>Example</u>: In the 2015–16 NHANES child sample, as time spent watching TV or videos increased, mean BMI also increased (Table 13.6).

> A note to the table reports the F-statistic (**test statistic** for the ANOVA procedure), number of **degrees of freedom**, and **p-value** used to assess the statistical significance of differences within the table. The **asterisk** in-table reference (*) is explained in a separate **note**.

To summarize, the statistical-significance-testing process involves a combination of tasks that must be conducted by the researcher and tasks that can be done by a computer following instructions provided by the researcher. Writing the hypotheses, choosing the significance level, assessing statistical significance, and explaining the result in terms of the specific topic (Steps 1, 4, and 5 of the hypothesis-testing process) must be conducted by the researcher (human brain), using information on the test statistic and p-value provided by the statistical software (Steps 2 and 3). Researchers who are conducting their own analyses must also choose a type of statistical procedure that suits their variables, and they must correctly specify the roles of those variables, so that the software will calculate the appropriate type of test statistic and associated p-value. See Chapters 10 and 13 for how to identify the pertinent type of statistical procedure based on the level(s) of measurement of the variables.

To help tie together the concepts involved in Steps 4 and 5 of the hypothesis-testing process, Figure C.1 portrays the relationship between the significance level (α value), p-value, and conclusion about statistical significance of a sample estimate.

<u>Example</u>: Based on the 2015–16 NHANES sample, mean BMI for 2-to-17-year-old children was 2.1 kg/m²) <u>lower</u> among those watched less than 1 hour of TV per day than among those who watched 4 or more hours per day. That difference in mean BMI across TV-watching groups was statistically significantly different from 0, at $p < .001$.

> The **sample estimate** of the mean difference in BMI by amount of daily TV-watching (marked A in Figure C.1) is associated with a **p-value** of .001 (**B**), well below the **threshold for statistical significance** (p < .025 for a directional hypothesis, C). Therefore, we reject the **null hypothesis** (D: H_0 that there is no difference in children's BMI according to how

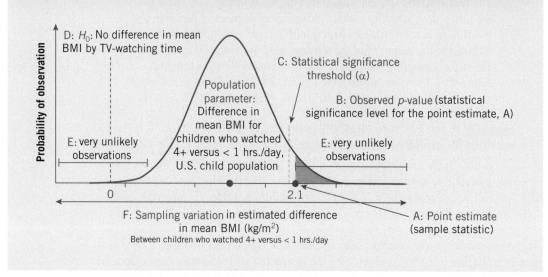

Source: Adapted from McLeod (2019).

much they watched TV) with a very high degree (99.9%) of **confidence**. The ranges marked E in both "tails" of the distribution show values of the **sample estimate** that are very unlikely based on the **sampling variation** in the data (F).

Errors in Hypothesis Testing

As you read about or conduct hypothesis testing, you may encounter a couple of additional terms related to uncertainty of numeric estimates: Type I and Type II errors. Without going into too much detail, I mention them here because they reinforce the idea that certain aspects of study design and statistical methods affect the chances of drawing an incorrect conclusion about a numeric pattern in a population based on data from a sample.

As you learned in Chapter 3, false negatives and false positives occur when we come to the wrong conclusion about how to classify an individual case based on comparison of that case's value against a numeric cutoff, such as comparing a child's screening score to a threshold for an autism diagnosis. Similarly, in traditional hypothesis testing, Type I and Type II errors involve coming to an incorrect conclusion about whether to classify a result as statistically significant. A **Type I error** is the probability of <u>rejecting</u> a null hypothesis when it is <u>true</u>—a false positive inference. The probability of a Type I error is equal to α (the significance level) chosen by the researcher.

> Example: Among children aged 2 to 17 years in the 2015–16 NHANES sample, mean BMI was 20.0 kg/m² for boys and 20.3 kg/m² for girls; p-value = .29. If we had concluded that boys' mean BMI was lower than girls', we would have made a Type I error, because the NHANES data did not support that inference.
>
> > *The **p-value** of .29 is > .05 (**α level**, the numeric cutoff for assessing statistical significance), implying that the observed gender difference in mean BMI in the sample could be explained by sampling variation. If, in the entire population, there was no difference in BMI by gender, then rejecting the null hypothesis and concluding that the difference was statistically significant would be a **false positive** inference (**Type I error**).*

A **Type II error** is the probability of accepting a null hypothesis when it is false—a **false negative** conclusion. The chances of making a Type II error decrease with increasing sample size, increasing effect size, or increasing chance of a Type I error (higher value of α); Type II error is positively associated with variability.

> Example: If we had concluded from Figure 13.3 that the levels of support for the two candidates in Poll B were not statistically significantly different from each other, we would have made a Type II error.
>
> > *The 95% **confidence intervals** around the point estimates for the two candidates based on Poll B do not overlap, so the poll data support the inference that the observed higher support for the Republican than the Democratic candidate is unlikely to be due to random error alone. Concluding that the difference in their chances of victory was not statistically significant would be a **false negative** inference (**Type II error**) if, among all voters, the Republican had higher support than the Democrat.*

A **Type I error** (denoted α) is a false positive conclusion: It occurs when the null hypothesis is incorrectly rejected. A **Type II error** (denoted β) is a false negative conclusion: It occurs when the null hypothesis is incorrectly accepted.

Recall from Chapter 3, that there is a trade-off between the chances of false negative versus false positive conclusions based on the choice of a numeric cutoff to classify cases: Changing the value of that cutoff to reduce the chances of one of those types of misclassifications increases the likelihood of the other type of misclassification. Likewise, there is a mathematically determined relationship between the chances of making Type I versus Type II errors in statistical significance testing, based on the choice of significance level (α). The lower the chance of a Type I error (α), the higher the chance of a Type II error (β), and vice versa.

As a consequence, there is always a chance of arriving at an incorrect conclusion about the pattern in a population based on data from a sample. For univariate statistics, the trade-off between Type I and Type II errors implies that there is always a risk of either (a) incorrectly concluding that the mean (or other summary statistic) is different from the null value in the population, when in fact it <u>is</u> the null value (Type I error), or (b) falsely inferring that the summary statistic for the population equals the null value, when in actuality it does <u>not</u> (Type II error). For bivariate statistics, that trade-off means there is always the possibility of either (a) incorrectly concluding that there is an association between the independent and dependent variables in the population, when in fact there is none (Type I error), or (b) falsely inferring that there is <u>not</u> an association in the population, when in fact one <u>does</u> exist (Type II error).

See "Drawbacks of Traditional Hypothesis Testing" in Chapter 13 for other issues related to interpretation of statistical significance.

> There is always some uncertainty about the values of numeric estimates based on sample data, because of the inherent tradeoff between the chances of false <u>positive</u> (Type I error) and false <u>negative</u> (Type II error) conclusions about statistical significance.

Plausibility Criteria for Inferential Test Statistics

Table C.2 summarizes criteria for making sense of numeric results of hypothesis tests. Test statistics, critical values, degrees of freedom, and p-values are <u>not</u> in the units in which the variables involved in the hypothesis test were measured. As a consequence, the criteria used to assess the plausibility of numeric values of those statistics are completely different from the criteria used to assess the plausibility of values of the variables. Instead, test statistics, critical values, degrees of freedom, and p-values are determined by the sample size, the levels of measurement of the variables, and standard statistical distributions.[9]

Therefore, the <u>same</u> numeric criteria apply to each of the aspects of hypothesis testing summarized in Table C.2 <u>regardless of</u> the topic, context, or units of the data. Significance levels (Type I error; α), p-values, and the probability of a Type II error (β) must each fall between 0 and 1. Test statistics, critical values, and p-values are inversely related to sample size, whereas the number of degrees of freedom depends on the sample size and the type of statistical test.

---

[9]The level(s) of measurement of the variable(s) in a hypothesis test determine how the test statistic is calculated; determine the statistical distribution from which the critical value is drawn; and affect how the number of degrees of freedom is calculated.

Table C.2 Criteria for Making Sense of Hypothesis Test Results

		Affected by		
	Definitional limits on value	Units of variables?	Level of measurement of variable(s)?	Sample size?
Test statistic	Can be positive, zero, or negative, depending on the sign of the point estimate	No	Determines the pertinent type of test statistic	Inversely related to sample size
Critical value	Sign will match that of the test statistic.		Determines the pertinent statistical distribution	
Degrees of freedom (df)	Must be positive.		Affects the type of test statistic, which determines how degrees of freedom are calculated	Relationship to sample size depends on the type of statistical test
p-value	Must be between 0.0 and 1.0.		No	Yes, through effect on critical value
Significance level (α) = Type I error = (100 − confidence level) ÷ 100	Depends on whether test is one-sided or two-sided.[a]			No
Type II error (β)				Inversely related to sample size

Note:

a. α for a one-sided test = (α for a two-sided test ÷ 2).

Example: When the confidence level is set at 95%, the threshold for statistical significance (α) is $p < .05$ whether the research question concerns difference in mean income by educational attainment in the United States in the year 2000, difference in poverty rates across cities in Brazil today, or any other topic, date, or setting.

Example: At a significance level (α) of .05, the critical value for a two-sided (nondirectional) t-test for difference in mean height for boys compared to girls based on a large sample is 1.96 whether height was measured in centimeters, inches, or cubits!

Example: The number of degrees of freedom for a X^2 test for a cross-tabulation of a two-category dependent variable by a three-category independent variable is 5, regardless of whether that cross-tab is assessing differences in extent of agreement with gun-control laws by political party, variation in obesity rates across ethnic groups, or any other topic.

Statistics involved in the hypothesis-testing process (including test statistics, critical values, degrees of freedom, p-values, and Type I and Type II errors) are in completely different units than the sample estimates to which they pertain. Thus, the criteria learned for assessing plausibility of hypothesis test results do not depend on topic, or context, or units; rather, they are determined by the sample size, the level(s) of measurement of the variables, and standard statistical distributions.

TERMS AND CONCEPTS

HIGHLIGHTS

- Formal **hypothesis testing** includes statement of a **null hypothesis** and an **alternative hypothesis**, which can be either **directional** or **nondirectional**.

- A calculated **test statistic** is then compared against the **critical value** from a standard statistical distribution to obtain a **p-value**—the probability that a sample statistic as large as or larger than the observed value could be found if the value of the parameter was the null value in the population from which that sample was drawn.

- **Statistical significance** is assessed by determining whether the *p*-value

is less than the **significance level** specified by the researcher—most commonly < .05.

- There is a trade-off between **Type I** and **Type II errors** in hypothesis testing: The lower the chance of incorrectly concluding that there is <u>no</u> relationship between two variables in the population, the higher the chance of incorrectly concluding that there <u>is</u> indeed a relationship. Thus, there is always a chance of coming to an incorrect conclusion about a pattern in the <u>population</u> based on data from a <u>sample</u>.

EXERCISES

Interpreting Results

1. Find a journal article in your field that reports results of inferential statistical tests as either a *p*-value or a confidence interval. Identify the authors' (a) null hypothesis, (b) alternative hypothesis, and (c) chosen significance level. (d) Interpret the statistical significance of their sample estimate for their hypothesis.

Planning Research

2. Write (a) a null hypothesis and (b) a directional research hypothesis for (i) the hypothetical study of Ritalin and student exam performance from Chapter 12 exercises, (ii) the hypothetical evaluation of a mentoring program (Chapter 12), and (iii) the study by Du Toit et al. (2015) Chapter 12.

References

Adler, N., & Stewart, J., for the Psychological Working Group, MacArthur Research Network on SES and Health. (2007). The MacArthur Scale of Subjective Social Status. The John D. and Katherine T. *MacArthur Foundation*. https://macses.ucsf.edu/research/psychosocial/subjective.php

Allcott, H., & Rogers, R. (2014). The short-run and long-run effects of behavioral interventions: Experimental evidence from energy conservation. *American Economic Review, 104*, 3003–3037. Retrieved July 2018, from https://pubs.aeaweb.org/doi/pdfplus/10.1257/aer.104.10.3003

Allemani, C. Matsuda, T., Di Carlo, V., Harewood, R., Matz, M., Nikšić, M., Bonaventure, A., Valkov, M., Johnson, C. J., Estève, J., Ogunbiyi, O. J., Azevedo e Silva, G., Chen, W.-Q., Eser, S., Engholm, G., Stiller, C. A., Monnereau, A., Woods, R. R., Visser, O., . . . Coleman, M. P. (2018). Global surveillance of trends in cancer survival 2000–14 (CONCORD-3): Analysis of individual records for 37,513,025 patients diagnosed with one of 18 cancers from 322 population-based registries in 71 countries. *Lancet, 391*(10125), 1023–1075. https://dx.doi.org/10.1016/S0140-6736(17)33326-3

Allison, P. D. (1999). *Multiple regression: A primer*. Pine Forge Press.

Amazon.com. (2018). *Merrell men's Jungle Moc slip-on shoe, taupe, 13 M US*. https://www.amazon.com/Merrell-Mens-Jungle-Slip-Boulder/dp/B0000BP54E/ref=sr_1_1_sspa?ie=UTF8&qid=1534190093&sr=8-1-spons&keywords=merrell%2Bmens%2Bjungle%2Bmoc%2Bslip-on%2Bshoe&smid=A3ETXHRYOXTLH5&th=1&psc=1

American Cancer Society. (n.d.). *Breast cancer risk factors you cannot change*. https://www.cancer.org/cancer/breast-cancer/risk-and-prevention/breast-cancer-risk-factors-you-cannot-change.html

American Heart Association. (2018). *Understanding blood pressure readings*. http://www.heart.org/HEARTORG/Conditions/HighBloodPressure/KnowYourNumbers/Understanding-Blood-Pressure-Readings_UCM_301764_Article.jsp

Amrhein, V., Greenland, S., & McShane, B. (2019). Retire statistical significance. *Nature, 567*, 305–307. https://www.nature.com/articles/d41586-019-00857-9

Arrieta, A., & Russell, L. B. (2008). Effects of leisure and non-leisure physical activity on mortality in U.S. adults over two decades. *Annals of Epidemiology, 18*(12), 889–895. https://dx.doi.org/10.1016/j.annepidem.2008.09.007

Ashish. (2021, May 5). *What is a decibel and how can negative decibels exist?* Science ABC. https://www.scienceabc.com/pure-sciences/why-negative-decibels-are-a-thing.html

Assaf, S., & Pullum, T. (2016). *Levels and trends in maternal and child health disparities by wealth and region in eleven countries with DHS surveys*. ICF International. https://www.dhsprogram.com/pubs/pdf/CR42/CR42.pdf

Benartzi, S., Beshears, J., Milkman, K. L., Sunstein, C. R., Thaler, R. H., Shankar, M., Tucker-Ray, W., Congdon, W. J., & Galing, S. (2017). Should governments invest more in nudging? *Psychological Science, 28*(8), 1041–1055. http://journals.sagepub.com/doi/10.1177/0956797617702501

Best, J. (2001). *Damned lies and statistics: Untangling numbers from the media, politicians, and activists*. University of California Press.

Bestpracticeautism.com. (2016). *Best practice review: The autism diagnostic observation schedule (ADOS)*. https://bestpracticeautism.blogspot.com/2012/01/best-practice-review-autism-diagnostic.html

Bhushan, V. (2011). What is the origin of the tall, grande, and venti nomenclature at Starbucks? *Quora*. https://www.quora.com/What-is-the-origin-of-the-Tall-Grande-and-Venti-nomenclature-at-Starbucks

Booth, W. C., Colomb, G. G., Williams, J. M., Bizup, J., & FitzGerald, W. T. (2016). *The craft of research* (4th ed.). University of Chicago Press.

Boyce, W., Torsheim, T., Currie, C., & Zambon, A. (2006). The Family Affluence Scale as a measure of national wealth: Validation of an adolescent self-report measure. *Social Indicators Research, 78*(3), 473–487.

Brynie, F. (2012, January 10). The placebo effect: How it works. *Brain Sense*. https://www.psychologytoday.com/us/blog/brain-sense/201201/the-placebo-effect-how-it-works

Card, D., & Kreuger, A. (1994). Minimum wages and employment: A case study of the fast-food industry in

New Jersey and Pennsylvania. *American Economic Review, 84*(4), 772–793.

Carrig, D. (2018, May 26). Saturday is most dangerous day of the week to drive: Afternoon rush hour worse than morning. *USA Today.* https://www.usatoday.com/story/money/nation-now/2018/05/26/driving-car-crash-deaths-speeding/640781002

Centers for Disease Control and Prevention. (n.d.-a). *Epidemiologic followup study (NHEFS).* U.S. Department of Health and Human Services. https://wwwn.cdc.gov/nchs/nhanes/nhefs/Default.aspx

Centers for Disease Control and Prevention. (n.d.-b). *NHANES 2015–2016 Overview.* U.S. Department of Health and Human Services. https://wwwn.cdc.gov/nchs/nhanes/continuousnhanes/overview.aspx?BeginYear=2015

Centers for Disease Control and Prevention. (n.d.-c). *Unweighted response rates for NHANES 2015–2016 by age and gender.* U.S. Department of Health and Human Services. https://wwwn.cdc.gov/nchs/data/nhanes3/ResponseRates/2015-2016_response_rates.pdf

Centers for Disease Control and Prevention. (2014). *Calculating BMI using the English system.* U.S. Department of Health and Human Services. Retrieved January 2019, from https://www.cdc.gov/nccdphp/dnpao/growthcharts/training/bmiage/page5_2.html

Centers for Disease Control and Prevention. (2015). *Transitioning from WHO to CDC growth charts at 2 years of age.* U.S. Department of Health and Human Services. Retrieved February 2019, from https://www.cdc.gov/nccdphp/dnpao/growthcharts/who/using/transitioning.htm

Centers for Disease Control and Prevention. (2017). *Healthy weight.* U.S. Department of Health and Human Services. Retrieved February 2019, from https://www.cdc.gov/healthyweight/assessing/bmi/adult_bmi/index.html

Centers for Disease Control and Prevention. (2018a). *National Health and Nutrition Examination Survey: Analytic guidelines, 2011–2014 and 2015–2016.* U.S. Department of Health and Human Services. https://wwwn.cdc.gov/nchs/data/nhanes/2011-2012/analyticguidelines/analytic_guidelines_11_16.pdf

Centers for Disease Control and Prevention. (2018b). *Overview of influenza surveillance in the United States.*

U.S. Department of Health and Human Services. Retrieved April 2019, from https://www.cdc.gov/flu/weekly/overview.htm

Centers for Disease Control and Prevention. (2018c). *Why I was selected.* U.S. Department of Health and Human Services. https://www.cdc.gov/nchs/nhanes/participant/participant-selected.htm

Centers for Disease Control and Prevention. (2020). *Health expenditures.* U.S. Department of Health and Human Services. Retrieved January 2021, from https://www.cdc.gov/nchs/fastats/health-expenditures.htm

Chambliss, D. F., & Schutt, R. K. (2019). *Making sense of the social world: Methods of investigation* (6th ed.). SAGE.

Chan, T. Francis. (2018, February 16). The largest annual migration on earth is happening for lunar New Year. *Business Insider.* https://www.businessinsider.com/what-is-chinese-new-year-travel-migration-2018-2

Chapman, G., Li, M., Leventhal, H., & Leventhal, E. (2016). Default clinic appointments promote influenza vaccination uptake without a displacement effect. *Behavioral Science and Policy, 2*(2). https://behavioralpolicy.org/wp-content/uploads/2017/06/chapman-web.pdf

Chou, J. (n.d.). *Fenton 2013 growth calculator for preterm infants.* PediTools. Retrieved September 2019, from https://peditools.org/fenton2013/index.php

Cleveland, W. S., & McGill, R. (1984). Graphical perception: Theory, experimentation, and application to the development of graphical methods. *Journal of the American Statistical Association, 79*(387), 531–554. https://dx.doi.org/10.1080/01621459.1984.10478080

Cleveland Clinic. (2014). *Vital signs.* https://my.clevelandclinic.org/health/articles/10881-vital-signs

Climate Change Authority. (2018). *International implementation of vehicle emissions standards.* http://www.climatechangeauthority.gov.au/reviews/light-vehicle-emissions-standards-australia/international-implementation-vehicle-emissions

Collaborative Institutional Training Initiative. (2020). *Social-behavioral-educational (SBE) comprehensive.* https://about.citiprogram.org/en/course/human-subjects-research-2

College Board. (2019). *Understanding scores.* Retrieved February 2019, from https://collegereadiness.collegeboard.org/pdf/understanding-sat-scores.pdf

Coplan, J. (2013). *DSM5: The case for double standards.* http://www.drcoplan.com/dsm5-the-case-for-double-standards

Criminal Justice Information Services (CJIS) Division Uniform Crime Reporting (UCR) Program. (2015). *Hate crime data collection guidelines and training manual, version 2.0.* Federal Bureau of Investigation, U.S. Department of Justice. https://www.fbi.gov/file-repository/ucr/ucr-hate-crime-data-collection-guidelines-training-manual-02272015.pdf/view

Cummings, H. M., & Vandewater, E. A. (2007). Relation of adolescent video game play to time spent in other activities. *Archives of Pediatrics and Adolescent Medicine, 161*(7), 684–689. https://dx.doi.org/10.1001/archpedi.161.7.684

Currie, C., Molcho, M., Boyce, W., Holstein, B., Torsheim, T., & Richter, M. (2008). Researching health inequalities in adolescents: The development of the Health Behaviour in School-Aged Children (HBSC) Family Affluence Scale. *Social Science & Medicine, 66,* 1429–1436. https://dx.doi.org/10.1016/j.socscimed.2007.11.024

DeSilver, D. (2014, December 5). For retailers, the holidays mean a hiring binge—and then a purge. *Fact Tank: News in the Numbers.* Pew Research Center. http://www.pewresearch.org/fact-tank/2014/12/05/for-retailers-the-holidays-mean-a-hiring-binge-and-then-a-purge

DeSilver, D. (2018, May 21). U.S. trails most developed countries in voter turnout. *Fact Tank: News in the Numbers.* Pew Research Center. https://www.politicalreportcards.com/wp-content/uploads/2019/08/2019-Reports-Pew-Research-U.S.-trails-most-developed-countries-in-voter-turnout-copy.pdf

Dohrenwend, B. P. (1990). Socioeconomic status (SES) and psychiatric disorders: Are the issues still compelling? *Social Psychiatry and Psychiatric Epidemiology, 25,* 41–47. http://www.med.mcgill.ca/epidemiology/hanley/c609/material/Schizophrenia/Dohrenwend1990SPPE.pdf

Duncan, O. D. (1961). A socioeconomic index for all occupations. In J. Reiss, Jr. (Ed.), *Occupations and social status* (pp. 109–138). Free Press of Glencoe.

Du Toit, G., Roberts, G., Sayre, P. H., Bahnson, H. T., Radulovic, S., Santos, A. F., Brough, H. A., Phippard, D., Basting, M., Feeney, M., Turcanu, V., Sever, M. L., Gomez Lorenzo, M., Plaut, M., & Lack, G., for the LEAP Study Team. (2015). Randomized trial of peanut consumption in infants at risk for peanut allergy. *New England Journal of Medicine, 372,* 803–813. https://dx.doi.org/10.1056/NEJMoa1414850

Economics Online. (2019). *Purchasing power parity.* Retrieved January 2019, from https://www.economicsonline.co.uk/Global_economics/Purchasing_power_parity.html

Edmunds. (2019). *Compare cars: 2018 hybrid sedans.* https://www.edmunds.com/car-comparisons/?veh1=401741147&veh2=401745711&veh3=401708205&veh4=40175225

Ehsani, J. P., Bingham, C. R., Ionides, E., & Childers, D. (2014). The impact of Michigan's text messaging restriction on motor vehicle crashes. *Journal of Adolescent Health, 54*(5S), S68–S74. https://dx.doi.org/10.1016/j.jadohealth.2014.01.003

Encyclopedia Britannica. (2016). *Cubit: Measurement.* Retrieved April 2018, from https://www.britannica.com/science/cubit

Evergreen, S. D. H. (2017). *Effective data visualization: The right chart for the right data.* SAGE.

Evergreen, S. D. H, & Emery, A. (2016). *Data visualization checklist.* http://stephanieevergreen.com/wp-content/uploads/2016/10/DataVizChecklist_May2016.pdf

Federal Bureau of Investigation. (2012). *Crimes against persons, property, and society.* U.S. Department of Justice. https://ucr.fbi.gov/nibrs/2012/resources/crimes-against-persons-property-and-society

Federal Bureau of Investigation. (2017). *UCR offense definitions.* U.S. Department of Justice. Retrieved February 2019, from https://www.ucrdatatool.gov/offenses.cfm

Federal Bureau of Investigation. (2018). *Hate crime statistics, 2017.* U.S. Department of Justice. Retrieved February 2019, from https://ucr.fbi.gov/hate-crime/2017/resource-pages/about-hate-crime

Fontenot, K., Semega, J., & Kollar, M. (2018, September). Income and poverty in the United States: 2017. U.S. Census Bureau, Current Population Reports, P60-263. U.S. Department of Commerce. https://www.census.gov/content/dam/Census/library/publications/2018/demo/p60-263.pdf

Food and Nutrition Service. (2018). *Supplemental Nutrition Assistance Program (SNAP)—Am I eligible for SNAP?* U.S. Department of Agriculture. Retrieved April 2018, from https://www.fns.usda.gov/snap/eligibility#Am%20I%20 eligible%20for%20SNAP?

Fragile Families and Child Wellbeing Study. (n.d.). *About the Fragile Families and Child Wellbeing Study*. Princeton University. https://fragilefamilies.princeton.edu/about

Fryar, C. D., Gu, Q., Ogden, C. L., & Flegal, K. M. (2016). Anthropometric reference data for children and adults: United States, 2011–2014. National Center for Health Statistics. *Vital and Health Statistics*, 3(39). https://www .cdc.gov/nchs/data/series/sr_03/sr03_039.pdf

Funk, C. (2017). Mixed messages about public trust in science. *Issues in Science and Technology*, 34(1). https:// issues.org/real-numbers-mixed-messages-about-public-trust-in-science

Geggel, L. (2016, July 28). Where do the world's tallest and shortest people live? *Live Science*. https://www.live science.com/55580-tallest-shortest-people-in-world.html

Gelman, A., Shor, B., Bafumi, J., & Park, D. (2007). Rich state, poor state, red state, blue state: What's the matter with Connecticut? *Quarterly Journal of Political Science*, (2), 345–367. http://www.stat.columbia.edu/~gelman/ research/published/rb_qjps.pdf

Gershtein, S., & Gershtein, A. (2018). *Instant capacity and volume conversion*. https://www.convert-me.com/en/convert/ volume/?u=brgallon&v=1

Ghose, T. (2013, April 2). "Just a theory": 7 misused science words. *Scientific American*. https://www.scientific american.com/article/just-a-theory-7-misused-science-words

Golnick, L., & Smith, W. (1993). *The cartoon guide to statistics*. Harper Perennial.

Golshan, T. (2018, May 3). *Most American voters prioritize the economy. Republicans are voting on national security*. Vox. https://www.vox.com/2018/5/3/17314664/2018-midterm-polls-policy-priority-voters

Gordis, L. (2009). *Epidemiology* (4th ed.). Saunders Elsevier.

Guzman, G. (2017). *Household income: 2016. American Community Survey briefs*. U.S. Census Bureau, U.S. Department of Commerce. https://www.census.gov/content/ dam/Census/library/publications/2017/acs/acsbr16-02.pdf

Hegmann, K. T., Fraser, A. M., Keaney, R. P., Moser, S. E., Nilasena, D. S., Sedlars, M., Higham-Gren, L., & Lyon, J. L.

(1993). The effect of age at smoking initiation on lung cancer risk. *Epidemiology*, 4(5), 444–448. http://www.jstor .org/stable/3703117

Herrman, J. (2019, April 19). The real stars of the internet: The rater has become the rated. *The New York Times*. https://www.nytimes.com/2019/04/19/style/star-ratings-amazon-uber-seamless.html

Hill, G., & Hill, K. (2020). Beyond a reasonable doubt. *The People's Law Dictionary*. Retrieved December 2020, from https://dictionary.law.com/Default.aspx?selected=59

Himmelfarb Health Sciences Library. (2019). *Meta-analysis: Definition*. The George Washington University. https://himmelfarb.gwu.edu/tutorials/studydesign101/ metaanalyses.cfm

HIV.gov. (2020a). *The global HIV/AIDS epidemic*. Retrieved May 2020, from https://www.hiv.gov/hiv-basics/overview/ data-and-trends/global-statistics

HIV.gov. (2020b). *U.S. statistics*. Retrieved December 2020, from https://www.hiv.gov/hiv-basics/overview/data-and-trends/statistics

Hoecker, J. (2017). *What's the best way to predict a child's adult height?* Mayo Clinic. https://www.mayoclinic.org/ healthy-lifestyle/childrens-health/expert-answers/child-growth/faq-20057990

Huang, J., Michael Strickland, S. J., & Lai, K. K. R. (2016, November 8). Election 2016: Exit polls. *The New York Times*. https://www.nytimes.com/interactive/2016/11/08/ us/politics/election-exit-polls.html

Hviid, A., Hansen, J. V., Frisch, M., & Melbye, M. (2019). Measles, mumps, rubella vaccination and autism: A nationwide cohort study. *Annals of Internal Medicine*, 170(8), 513–520. https://dx.doi.org/10.7326/M18-2101

James, N. (2018, June 20). *Recent violent crime trends in the United States*. Congressional Research Service. https://fas .org/sgp/crs/misc/R45236.pdf

Jans, M., Viana, J., Grant, D., Cochran, S. D., Lee, A. C., & Ponce, N. A. (2015). Trends in sexual orientation missing data over a decade of the California Health Interview Survey. *American Journal of Public Health*, 105(5), e43–e50. https://dx.doi.org/10.2105/ AJPH.2014.302514

Johnson, C. L., Dohrmann, S. M., Burt, V. L., & Mohadjer, L. K. (2014). National Health and Nutrition Examination

Survey: Sample design, 2011–2014. National Center for Health Statistics. *Vital and Health Statistics, 2*(162).

Keeter, S., Hatley, N., Kennedy, C., & Lau, A. (2017). *What low response rates mean for telephone surveys.* Pew Research Center. https://www.pewresearch.org/wp-content/uploads/2017/05/RDD-Non-response-Full-Report.pdf

Keith, V. M., Nguyen, A. W, Mouzon, D. M., Taylor, R. J., & Chatters, L. M. (2017). Microaggressions, discrimination, and phenotype among African Americans: A latent class analysis of the impact of skin tone and BMI. *Sociological Inquiry, 87*(2), 233–255. https://dx.doi.org/10.1111/soin.12168

Kim, J., Son, J., Kwok, P. K. Kang, J.-H., Laken, F., Daqulianea, J., Shin, H.-C., & Smith, T. W. (2012, December, 6). *Trends and correlates of income nonresponse: Forty years of the General Social Survey* (GSS Methodological Report No. 120). https://gssdataexplorer.norc.org/documents/885/download

King, B. A., Jama, A. O., Marynak, K. L., & Promoff, G. R. (2015). Attitudes toward raising the minimum age of sale for tobacco among U.S. adults. *American Journal of Preventive Medicine, 49*(4), 583–588. https://www.sciencedirect.com/science/article/pii/S0749379715002524

Klapper, L., Lusardi, A., & van Oudheusden, P. (2015). *Financial literacy around the world: Insights from the Standard and Poor's Rating Services Global Financial Literacy Survey.* World Bank Development Research Group. http://gflec.org/wp-content/uploads/2015/11/Finlit_paper_16_F2_singles.pdf

Knowles, E. (Ed.). (2016). *The Oxford dictionary of phrase and fable* (2nd ed.). Oxford University Press.

Kornegay, C. (1999). *Math dictionary with solutions: A math review* (2nd ed.). SAGE.

Kroll, M. E., Carson, C., Redshaw, M., & Quigley, M. A. (2016). Early father involvement and subsequent child behaviour at ages 3, 5 and 7 years: Prospective analysis of the UK Millennium Cohort Study. *PLoS ONE, 11*(9), e0162339. https://dx.doi.org/10.1371/journal.pone.0162339

Lewis-Beck, M. S., Bryman, A., & Liao, T. F. (2004). *The SAGE encyclopedia of social science research methods.* SAGE. http://dx.doi.org/10.4135/9781412950589

Ligon, G. D., & Clements, B. S. (2008). *Confidentiality and reliability rules for reporting educational data: A guide for establishing decision rules for disaggregating & reporting assessment results, and other indicators.* ESP Solutions Group. https://espsolutionsgroup.com/espweb/assets/files/ESP_Confidentiality_Reliability_ORG.pdf

Likert, R. (1932). A technique for the measurement of attitudes. *Archives of Psychology, 140,* 1–55.

LinkedIn Economic Graph Team. (2019, January 4). *LinkedIn Workforce Report | United States | January 2019.* https://economicgraph.linkedin.com/resources/linkedin-workforce-report-january-2019

Liptak, A. (2019, April 23). On census citizenship question, Supreme Court's conservatives appear united. *The New York Times.* https://www.nytimes.com/2019/04/23/us/politics/supreme-court-census-citizenship.html

Loftus, E. F., & Palmer, J. C. (1974). Reconstruction of automobile destruction: An example of the interaction between language and memory. *Journal of Verbal Learning and Verbal Behavior, 13,* 585–589. https://doi.org/10.1016/S0022-5371(74)80011-3

Mack, N., Woodsong, C., MacQueen, K. M., Guest, G., & Namey, E. (2005). *Qualitative research methods: A data collector's field guide.* Family Health International.

Magnani, E., & Zhu, R. (2018). Does kindness lead to happiness? Voluntary activities and subjective well-being. *Journal of Behavioral and Experimental Economics, 77,* 20–28. https://dx.doi.org/10.1016/j.socec.2018.09.009

Maker-Schoenberger, V., & Cukier, K. (2013). *Big data: A revolution that will transform how we live, work, and think.* Eamon Dolan/Mariner Books.

Marr, B. (2013). *Big Data: The mega-trend that will impact all our lives.* LinkedIn. https://www.linkedin.com/pulse/20130827231108-64875646-big-data-the-mega-trend-that-will-impact-all-our-lives

Marx, K., & Engels, F. (2002). *Manifesto of the Communist party selected works* (Vol. 1). Penguin Classics.

Mauboussin, A., & Mauboussin, M. J. (2018, July 3). If you say something is "likely," how likely do people think it is? *Harvard Business Review.* https://hbr.org/2018/07/if-you-say-something-is-likely-how-likely-do-people-think-it-is

Mayo Clinic. (2019). *Iron deficiency anemia.* Retrieved February 2019, from https://www.mayoclinic.org/diseases-conditions/iron-deficiency-anemia/diagnosis-treatment/drc-20355040

MBA Crystal Ball. (2019). *GRE score percentiles for 2019–2020*. Retrieved June 2019, from https://www.mbacrystalball.com/gre/gre-score-percentiles

McLeod, S. (2019). *What a p-value tells you about statistical significance*. Simply Psychology https://www.simplypsychology.org/p-value.html

McNeil, D. G., Jr. (2019, February 14). They've taken America's temperature—and it's running high. *The New York Times*. https://www.nytimes.com/2019/02/14/health/kinsa-flu-tracking.html

Mercer, A. (2016, September 8). 5 key things to know about the margin of error in election polls. *FactTank: Numbers in the News*. Pew Research Center. https://www.pewresearch.org/fact-tank/2016/09/08/understanding-the-margin-of-error-in-election-polls

Michael, M., Boyce, W. T., & Wilcox, A. J. (1984). *Biomedical bestiary: An epidemiologic guide to flaws and fallacies in the medical literature*. Little, Brown.

Miller, J. E. (2007). Organizing data in tables and charts: Different criteria for different tasks. *Teaching Statistics*, *29*(3), 98–101. http://dx.doi.org/10.1111/j.1467-9639.2007.00275.x

Miller, J. E. (2013). *The Chicago guide to writing about multivariate analysis* (2nd ed.). University of Chicago Press.

Miller, J. E. (2015). *The Chicago guide to writing about numbers* (2nd ed.). University of Chicago Press.

Ministry of Agriculture, Food and Rural Affairs, Ontario, Canada. (2011). *The "hand" measurement for horses*. https://web.archive.org/web/20110822161506/http://www.omafra.gov.on.ca/english/livestock/horses/facts/info_hands.htm

Mitchell, A. (2020, May 22). The U.S. is getting shorter, as mapmakers race to keep up. *The New York Times*. https://www.nytimes.com/2020/05/22/science/maps-elevation-geodetic-survey.html

The Money Converter. (2019). *Currency conversion and latest exchange rates for 90 world currencies*. Retrieved December 2019, from https://themoneyconverter.com

Muscatello, D. J., Searles, A., Macdonald, R., & Jorm, L. (2006). Communicating population health statistics through graphs: A randomised controlled trial of graph design interventions. *BMC Medicine 4*, 33. https://doi.org/10.1186/1741-7015-4-33

National Alliance on Mental Illness. (2008, June). *Schizophrenia: Public attitudes, personal needs*. https://www.nami.org/schizophreniasurvey

National Conference of State Legislatures. (2019). *State medical marijuana laws*. Retrieved March 2019, from http://www.ncsl.org/research/health/state-medical-marijuana-laws.aspx

National Environmental Research Institute of Denmark. (n.d.). Air quality standards (limit values, target values, etc.) [table]. https://www2.dmu.dk/AtmosphericEnvironment/Expost/database/docs/AQ_limit_values.pdf

National Heart, Lung, and Blood Institute. (n.d.). *High blood cholesterol*. Retrieved July 23, 2018, from https://www.nhlbi.nih.gov/health-topics/high-blood-cholesterol

National Opinion Research Center. (n.d.). *U.S. General Social Survey, 2000*. University of Chicago. https://gss.norc.org/get-the-data/spss

National Population Commission (NPC) [Nigeria] & ICF International. (2014). Nigeria Demographic and Health Survey 2013. NPC and ICF International. https://dhsprogram.com/pubs/pdf/fr293/fr293.pdf

New York City Department of Health. (2010). *Tables P2 (Population by Age) and M2 (Mortality by Age), 2010*.

Nicol, A. A. M., & Pexman, P. (2010). *Presenting your findings: A practical guide for creating tables* (6th ed.). American Psychological Association.

NJFamilyCare. (2019). *Income eligibility and cost*. Retrieved March 2019, from http://www.njfamilycare.org/income.aspx

Nordquist, R. (2020, January 17). *What is a post hoc logical fallacy?* ThoughtCo. https://www.thoughtco.com/post-hoc-fallacy-1691650

Numbeo. (2019). *Cost of living*. Retrieved December 2019, from https://www.numbeo.com/cost-of-living

Nussbaumer Knaflic, C. (2015). *Storytelling with data: A data visualization guide for business professionals*. Wiley.

OECD/Eurostat. (2012). *Eurostat-OECD methodological manual on purchasing power parities* (2012 ed.). OECD Publishing. https://dx.doi.org/10.1787/9789264189232-en

Office of Disease Prevention and Health Promotion. (2011). *Healthy people 2020: Adolescent health*. U.S. Department of Health and Human Services. https://www.healthypeople.gov/2020/topics-objectives/topic/Adolescent-Health/objectives

Office of Management and Budget. (1997, October 30). *Revisions to the standards for the classification of federal data on race and ethnicity*. Executive Office of the President. https://www.whitehouse.gov/wp-content/uploads/2017/11/Revisions-to-the-Standards-for-the-Classification-of-Federal-Data-on-Race-and-Ethnicity-October30-1997.pdf

Office of National Drug Control Policy. (2014). *2013 annual report, Arrestee Drug Abuse Monitoring Program II*. Executive Office of the President. https://www.abtassociates.com/sites/default/files/migrated_files/91485e0a-8774-442e-8ca1-5ec85ff5fb9a.pdf

Office on Smoking and Health. (2006). *The health consequences of involuntary exposure to tobacco smoke: A report of the Surgeon General*. Centers for Disease Control and Prevention, U.S. Department of Health and Human Services. https://dx.doi.org/10.1016/j.amepre.2007.02.026

Oliphant, B. (2018, June 11). Public support for the death penalty ticks up. *Fact Tank: News in the Numbers*. Pew Research Center. http://www.pewresearch.org/fact-tank/2018/06/11/us-support-for-death-penalty-ticks-up-2018

Ordway, D.-M. (2018, November 5). *The margin of error: 7 tips for journalists covering polls and surveys*. Journalist's Resource. https://journalistsresource.org/studies/politics/ads-public-opinion/margin-error-journalists-surveys-polls

Organisation for Economic Co-operation and Development. (2017). *Adult education level*. Retrieved March 2019, from https://data.oecd.org/eduatt/adult-education-level.htm#indicator-chart

Osborne, S. (2016, October, 5). Ten countries host more than half of world's refugees – and the UK urgently needs to do more, says Amnesty. *The Independent*. https://www.independent.co.uk/news/uk/home-news/refugee-crisis-amnesty-international-10-countries-host-more-half-uk-needs-to-do-more-a7344171.html

Ousey, G. C., & Kubrin, C. (2018). Immigration and crime: Assessing a contentious issue. *Annual Review of Criminology*, *1*, 63–84. https://dx.doi.org/10.1146/annurev-criminol-032317-092026

Pandey, A. V., Manivannan, A., Nov, O., Satterthwaite, M., & Bertini, E. (2014). The persuasive power of data visualization. *IEEE Transactions on Visualization and Computer Graphics*, *20*(12), 2211–2220.

Peck, J. L. (2017). *New York City drunk driving after Uber* (Working Paper No. 13). City University of New York Graduate Center, PhD Program in Economics. Retrieved July 2018, from https://ideas.repec.org/p/cgc/wpaper/013.html

Pew Research Center. (2015, July 1). *Americans, politics and science issues*. http://www.pewinternet.org/2015/07/01/americans-politics-and-science-issues

Philippine Statistical Authority. (2019). *QuickStat for 2019*. https://psa.gov.ph/statistics/quickstat/national-quickstat/all/*

Population Division. (2019). *World population prospects 2019*. Department of Economic and Social Affairs, United Nations. https://population.un.org/wpp/Download/Probabilistic/Population/July 2019

Population Reference Bureau. (2018). *2018 world population data sheet*. https://www.prb.org/wp-content/uploads/2018/08/2018_WPDS.pdf

Portman, J. (2019). *Felony classes: Charges and penalties*. Nolo. https://www.criminaldefenselawyer.com/resources/criminal-defense/felony-offense/felony-classes-charges-penalties

Pyrczak, F., & Bruce, R. R. (2016). *Writing empirical research reports: A basic guide for students of the social and behavioral sciences* (8th ed.). Routledge.

Quealy, K., Cox, A., & Katz, J. (2015, February 17). At Chipotle, how many calories do people really eat? *The New York Times*. https://www.nytimes.com/interactive/2015/02/17/upshot/what-do-people-actually-order-at-chipotle.html

Reuters. (2011, April 13). *Factbox: Facts about Mexico's education system*. https://www.reuters.com/article/us-mexico-education-factbox-idUSTRE73C4UY20110413

Reynolds, G. (2018, June 27). Walk briskly for your health: About 100 steps a minute. *The New York Times*. https://www.nytimes.com/2018/06/27/well/walk-health-exercise-steps.html

Reynolds, G. (2019, May 8). The stoner as gym rat. *The New York Times*. https://www.nytimes.com/2019/05/08/well/mind/exercise-marijuana-cannabis-pot-workout.html

Richter magnitude scale. (2019). In *Wikipedia*. Retrieved July 2019, from https://en.wikipedia.org/wiki/Richter_magnitude_scale#Richter_magnitudes

Rubin, Z. (1970). The measurement of romantic love. *Journal of Personality and Social Psychology, 16*(2), 265–273. https://dx.doi.org/10.1037/h0029841

Salkind, N. J. (2016). *Statistics for people who (think they) hate statistics* (6th ed.). SAGE.

Sanderson, M., Placek, P. J., & Keppel, K. G. (1991). The 1988 National Maternal and Infant Health Survey: Design, content, and data availability. *Birth, 18*(1), 26–32. https://dx.doi.org/10.1111/j.1523-536X.1991.tb00050.x

Sanger-Katz, M. (2018, August 15). Bleak new estimates in drug epidemic: A record 72,000 overdose deaths in 2017. *The New York Times.* https://www.nytimes.com/2018/08/15/upshot/opioids-overdose-deaths-rising-fentanyl.html

Schneider, D., & Lilienfeld, D. E. (2015). *Lilienfeld's foundations of epidemiology* (4th ed.). Oxford University Press.

Selyukh, A. (2019, March 6). *Bill raising federal minimum wage to $15 heads to U.S. House floor.* NPR. https://www.npr.org/2019/03/06/700350237/bill-raising-federal-minimum-wage-to-15-heads-to-u-s-house-floor

Semega, J. L., Fontenot, K. S., & Kollar, M. A. (2017, September). Income and poverty in the United States: 2016. *Current Population Reports*, P60-259. U.S. Census Bureau, U.S. Department of Commerce. https://www.census.gov/content/dam/Census/library/publications/2017/demo/P60-259.pdf

Shapiro, E. (2018, October 15). Homelessness in New York public schools is at a record high: 114,659 students. *The New York Times.* https://www.nytimes.com/2018/10/15/nyregion/homeless-students-nyc-schools-record.html

Sharp, T. (2017). *What is the temperature on Mars?* Space .com. Retrieved August 2018, from https://www.space.com/16907-what-is-the-temperature-of-mars.html

Shermer, M. (2014, September 1). How the survivor bias distorts reality. *Scientific American.* https://www.scientificamerican.com/article/how-the-survivor-bias-distorts-reality

Siegel Bernard, T. (2018, December 19). The Fed just raised interest rates. Here's what that means for your wallet. *The New York Times.* https://www.nytimes.com/2018/12/19/your-money/interest-rates-consumers.html

Sinclair, B., McConnell, M., & Michelson, M. R. (2013). Local canvassing: The efficacy of grassroots voter mobilization. *Political Communication, 30*(1), 42–57. https://dx.doi.org/10.1080/10584609.2012.737413

Smith, A., & Anderson, M. (2018, March 1). *Social media use in 2018.* Pew Research Center. http://www.pewinternet.org/2018/03/01/social-media-use-in-2018

Smith, R. (2018, July 13). The Google Translate World Cup. *The New York Times.* https://www.nytimes.com/2018/07/13/sports/world-cup/google-translate-app.html

State Health Access Data Assistance Center. (n.d.). *State Health Compare.* University of Minnesota. http://statehealthcompare.shadac.org/table/232/percent-of-households-with-a-broadband-internet-subscription-by-total#9,10,22,48,50/a/25/266

Statistics Canada. (2019, September 24). *Standard table symbols.* https://www.statcan.gc.ca/eng/concepts/definitions/guide-symbol

Taylor, L. E., Swerdfeger, A. L., & Eslick, G. D. (2014). Vaccines are not associated with autism: An evidence-based meta-analysis of case-control and cohort studies. *Vaccine, 32*(29), 3623–3629. https://dx.doi.org/10.1016/j.vaccine.2014.04.085

TCM Student. (2002). *Cun measurements of the body.* http://www.tcmstudent.com/study_tools/Cun%20Measurements.html

Thompson, B. (2004). The "significance" crisis in psychology and education. *Journal of Socio-Economics, 33*, 607–613. http://laits.utexas.edu/cormack/384m/homework/Journal%20of%20Socio-Economics%202004%20Thompson.pdf

Tudor-Locke, C., Han, H., Aguilar, E. J., Barriera, T. V., Schuna, J. M., Kang, M., & Rowe, D. A. (2018). How fast is fast enough? Walking cadence (steps/min) as a practical estimate of intensity in adults: A narrative review. *British Journal of Sports Medicine, 52*(12), 776–788. https://bjsm.bmj.com/content/52/12/776

UNICEF China. (2019). *Figure 1.9 sex ratio at birth, 1982–2017.* https://www.unicef.cn/en/figure-19-sex-ratio-birth-19822017

University of Chicago Press. (2017). *The Chicago manual of style: The essential guide for writers, editors, and publishers* (17th ed.). University of Chicago Press.

Urban Institute Tax Policy Center. (2017). *Briefing book.* https://www.taxpolicycenter.org/briefing-book/what-are-sources-revenue-federal-government

U.S. Bureau of Labor Statistics. (2001, October 16). *What is seasonal adjustment?* U.S. Department of Labor. https://www.bls.gov/cps/seasfaq.htm

U.S. Bureau of Labor Statistics. (2018a). Weekly and hourly earnings data from the Current Population Survey. Series LEU0252883600. *U.S. Department of Labor*. Retrieved January 2019, from https://data.bls.gov/pdq/SurveyOutputServlet

U.S. Bureau of Labor Statistics. (2018b). The Consumer Price Index. In *BLS handbook of methods*. U.S. Department of Labor. https://www.bls.gov/opub/hom/pdf/cpi-20180214.pdf

U.S. Bureau of Labor Statistics. (2019). *Usual weekly earnings of wage and salary workers, fourth quarter 2018* [News release, USDL-19-0077]. U.S. Department of Labor. https://www.bls.gov/news.release/archives/wkyeng_01172019.pdf

U.S. Bureau of Labor Statistics. (2020). *CPI inflation calculator*. U.S. Department of Labor. https://www.bls.gov/data/inflation_calculator.htm

U.S. Census Bureau. (n.d.-a). *Language spoken at home* [Table S1601]. U.S. Department of Commerce. https://data.census.gov/cedsci/table?q=S1601&tid=ACSST1Y2019.S1601

U.S. Census Bureau. (n.d.-b). *Sex by marital status for the population 15 years and over, Table B12001, 2015: ACS 1-year estimates detailed tables*. U.S. Department of Commerce. https://data.census.gov/cedsci/table?t=Marital%20Status%20and%20Marital%20History&d=ACS%201-Year%20Estimates%20Detailed%20Tables&tid=ACSDT1Y2015.B12001

U.S. Census Bureau. (n.d.-c). *Survey of income and program participation*. U.S. Department of Commerce. https://www.census.gov/sipp

U.S. Census Bureau. (2013). *Statistical quality standards*. U.S. Department of Commerce. https://www.census.gov/content/dam/Census/about/about-the-bureau/policies_and_notices/quality/statistical-quality-standards/Quality_Standards.pdf

U.S. Census Bureau. (2017). *The history of the official poverty measure*. U.S. Department of Commerce. https://www.census.gov/topics/income-poverty/poverty/about/history-of-the-poverty-measure.html

U.S. Census Bureau. (2018a). *Data protection and privacy program*. U.S. Department of Commerce. https://www.census.gov/about/policies/privacy/statistical_safeguards.html

U.S. Census Bureau. (2018c). *Race and ethnicity*. U.S. Department of Commerce. https://www2.census.gov/about/training-workshops/2020/2020-02-19-pop-presentation.pdf

U.S. Census Bureau. (2018d). *Table A-2. Annual inmigration, outmigration, net migration, and movers from abroad for regions: 1981–2018*. U.S. Department of Commerce.

U.S. Census Bureau. (2018e). *2018 poverty thresholds by size of family and number of children*. U.S. Department of Commerce. https://www2.census.gov/programs-surveys/cps/tables/time-series/historical-poverty-thresholds/thresh18.xls

U. S. Census Bureau. (2020a). *Current versus constant (or real) dollars*. U.S. Department of Commerce. https://www.census.gov/topics/income-poverty/income/guidance/current-vs-constant-dollars.html

U.S. Census Bureau. (2020b). *Population, population change, and estimated components of population change: April 1, 2010 to July 1, 2019*. U.S. Department of Commerce. https://www2.census.gov/programs-surveys/popest/datasets/2010-2019/national/totals/nst-est2019-alldata.csv

U.S. Census Bureau. (2020c). *Table A-1. Income summary measures by selected characteristics: 2017 and 2018*. U.S. Department of Commerce. https://www2.census.gov/programs-surveys/demo/tables/p60/266/tableA1.xls

U.S. Environmental Protection Agency. (2018). *Timeline of the National Ambient Air Quality Standards (NAAQS) for ozone*. https://www.epa.gov/ground-level-ozone-pollution/table-historical-ozone-national-ambient-air-quality-standards-naaqs

U.S. Inflation Calculator. (2019). *Inflation explained—Definition, examples and causes*. https://www.usinflationcalculator.com/inflation-explained-definition-examples-and-causes

U.S. National Center for Health Statistics. (2000). *CDC growth charts: United States. Stature-for-age percentiles, boys 2 to 20 years*. https://www.cdc.gov/growthcharts/data/set1clinical/cj41c021.pdf

U.S. News and World Report. (n.d.). *Best colleges*. Retrieved January 2019, from https://www.usnews.com/best-colleges

U.S. Tennis Association. (2017). *Tennis 101: Scoring*. https://www.usta.com/en/home/improve/tips-and-instruction/national/tennis-101--scoring.html

Utts, J. M. (1999). *Seeing through statistics* (2nd ed). Duxbury Press.

Utts, J., & Heckard, R. (2014). Turning data into information. *Mind on statistics* (5th ed., pp. 14–67). Cengage, Brooks Cole.

Valencia, N. (2019). These are the world's 25 tallest buildings. *ArchDaily*. https://www.archdaily.com/779178/these-are-the-worlds-25-tallest-buildings

van der Lee, J. H., Mokkink, L. B., Grootenhuis, M. A., Heymans, H. S., & Offringa, M. (2007). Definitions and measurement of chronic health conditions in childhood: A systematic review. *Journal of the American Medical Association, 297*(24), 2741–2751.

Vertex. (2009). *Body mass index (BMI) chart for adults.* https://www.vertex42.com/ExcelTemplates/bmi-chart.html

Vogt, W. P., & Johnson, R. B. (2011). *Dictionary of statistics & methodology: A nontechnical guide for the social sciences* (4th ed.). SAGE.

Wakefield, A., Murch, S. H., Anthony, A., Linnell, J., Casson, D. M., Malik, M., Berelowitz, M., Dhillon, A. P., Thomson, M. A., Harvey, P., Valentine, A., Davies, S. E., & Walker-Smith, J. A. (1998). RETRACTED: Ileal-lymphoid-nodular hyperplasia, nonspecific colitis, and pervasive developmental disorder in children. *Lancet, 351,* 637–641. https://dx.doi.org/10.1016/S0140-6736(97)11096-0

Weber, M. (2015). *Classes, stände, parties in Weber's rationalism and modern society: New translations on politics, bureaucracy and social stratification* (T. Waters & D. Waters, Ed. & Trans.). Palgrave Macmillan. (Original work published 1921)

Weisburd, D., Bushway, S., Lum, C., & Yang, S.-M. (2004). Trajectories of crime at places: A longitudinal study of street segments in the city of Seattle. *Criminology, 42*(2), 283–321.

Welsh, C. (2017). *The World Baseball Classic rules worth knowing.* Baseball Rules Academy. https://baseballrulesacademy.com/world-baseball-classic-rules-worth-knowing

Werner, S., Malaspina, D., & Rabinowitz, J. (2007). Socioeconomic status at birth is associated with risk of schizophrenia: Population-based multilevel study. *Schizophrenia Bulletin, 33*(6), 1373–1378. https://dx.doi.org/10.1093/schbul/sbm032

Williams, D. R., Yu, Y., Jackson, J. S. & Anderson, N. B. (1997). Racial differences in physical and mental health: Socio-economic status, stress and discrimination. *Journal of Health Psychology, 3*(2), 335–351. https://dx.doi.org/10.1177/135910539700200305

Wolff, T., Miller, T., & Ko, S. (2009). Aspirin for the primary prevention of cardiovascular events: An update of the evidence for the U.S. Preventive Services Task Force. *Annals of Internal Medicine, 150*(6), 405–410. https://dx.doi.org/10.7326/0003-4819-150-6-200903170-00009

WorldAtlas. (2019). *Murder rate by country.* Retrieved July 2019, from https://www.worldatlas.com/articles/murder-rates-by-country.html

World Bank Group. (2018). *Atlas of sustainable development goals 2018: From world development indicators.* https://openknowledge.worldbank.org/handle/10986/29788

World Health Organization. (1950). *Public health aspect of low birthweight.* WHO Technical Report Series, Number 27.

World Health Organization. (2006). *WHO child growth standards: Length/height-for-age, weight-for-age, weight-for-length, weight-for-height and body mass index-for-age: Methods and development.* https://www.who.int/childgrowth/standards/Technical_report.pdf

World Health Organization. (2007). *Height-for-age, boys 5-19 years.* http://www.who.int/growthref/cht_hfa_boys_perc_5_19years.pdf

World Population Review. (2019). *Countries by median age.* Retrieved June 2019, from http://worldpopulationreview.com/countries/median-age

Yahoo! Finance. (2020). *S&P 500.* Retrieved August 10, 2020, from https://finance.yahoo.com/quote/%5EGSPC/history

YorkWilliams, S. L., Gust, C. J., Mueller, R., Bidwell, L. C., Hutchison, K. E., Gillman, A. S., & Bryan, A. D. (2019). The new runner's high? Examining relationships between cannabis use and exercise behavior in states with legalized cannabis. *Frontiers in Public Health, 7,* 99. https://dx.doi.org/10.3389%2Ffpubh.2019.00099

Young, L. R., & Nestle, M. (2002). The contribution of expanding portion sizes to the US obesity epidemic. *American Journal of Public Health, 92*(2), 246–249.

Zacks, J., & Tversky, B. (1999). Bars and lines: A study of graphic communication. *Memory and Cognition, 27*(6), 1073–1079. https://dx.doi.org/10.3758/BF03201236

Ziliak, S. T., & McCloskey, D. N. (2004). Size matters: The standard error of regressions in the *American Economic Review. Journal of Socio-Economics, 33*(5), 527–546.

Ziliak, S. T., & McCloskey, D. N. (2008). *The cult of statistical significance: How the standard error costs us jobs, justice, and lives.* University of Michigan Press.

Zimmerman, K. A. (2013). Kelvin temperature scale: Facts and history. *LiveScience.* https://www.livescience.com/39994-kelvin.html

Index

difference calculation (subtraction), 242–43, 244, 533

difference in means, 293–96, 298, 299
    plausibility criteria for results of, 293, 295, 299
    units for, 293, 295

difference in percentage points, 248, 252, 446

differences, 31–32, 91–93, 219–21, 225–28, 242–45, 247–59, 265–66, 293, 298–301, 347, 375–78, 405–10, 413–19, 438–39, 445–47, 449–50, 453–55, 470–72, 525–28, 536–39
    assessing, 60, 542
    meaningful, 212, 479
    observed, 218, 370, 376–78, 468, 480
    percentage, 248, 445
    statistically significant, 5, 227–28

differential non-response rates, 326–27

digits, 143, 145–46, 153, 158, 189, 230–31, 277, 507–9

direct association. See positive association.

direction, 28–33, 137–38, 142, 147, 242, 253–55, 306–7, 351–52, 434–35, 437–40, 443, 445–47, 449–51, 455, 457–58, 461–62, 466–68, 477, 532–33

directional (2-sided) hypothesis, 403, 531–32, 537, 542

direction and magnitude, 25, 28, 30–31, 168, 170, 255, 257, 437–38, 443, 454–55, 495–96

direction and magnitude of differences, 34, 134, 195, 242, 299

direction and size of association, 32, 170, 410, 420, 438, 457, 461, 463–64, 476, 482, 486

direction of association, 28–29, 173, 455, 459, 461, 520, 532–33

disproportionate random sampling, 317, 523

disproportionate sampling, 317, 319, 494, 523, 526

distributions, 42, 83–84, 100, 143, 173, 213, 240–42, 260–62, 264–69, 271–74, 276–81, 281–83, 301, 303, 413–14, 437–38, 450–54, 481–85, 528–29
    color, 303, 346
    standard statistical, 540, 542–43

distributions of single variables.
    See univariate distributions.

diverging bar charts, 174–75

division (calculation), 237, 242–44, 253, 255–56, 258, 263, 269, 299–300, 445, 447, 450, 533

donut charts, 161–62, 167, 191

dose-response relationship, 359–60, 483, 485, 486

double-barreled questions, 329–30, 336, 343, 346

double blinding, 367, 368

double-negative questions, 329–30, 343

DV. See dependent variable.

e (base of natural logarithm), 510

ecological fallacy, 105–6, 107
    effect, 20–24, 49–50, 348–50, 352–54, 365, 367–68, 370, 380–85, 470, 472–76, 479–82, 484–85, 489, 496
    "effect" as dependent variable, 20, 348, 350, 352, 354, 365, 368, 472, 474–76, 485

effective charts, 149–50

effective data visualization, 192, 546

effective tables, 114–15

effect size, 408–10, 420, 471, 477, 479, 481–85, 501, 533

elementary schools, 9, 15, 31, 111

elements, 99, 102, 108–9, 152, 155–56, 310, 313–19, 323–24, 327–28, 389–91, 396, 399, 463–64, 522–23, 525–26
    sampled, 309, 327

eligibility criteria, 9, 96

empirical association, 350–52, 356–58, 360–61, 375, 384, 386, 482, 485–87

empirical order, 129, 131, 145, 151, 451

employed persons, 278–80

entities, 14–15, 34, 99, 102, 105, 108, 233, 314, 318

error, 11–12, 103, 105, 119–20, 145, 147, 192–94, 259, 393–400, 406, 420–23, 484–85, 527–30, 539–42, 549–50

estimates, 121, 145, 335–36, 388–96, 398–99, 401, 404–6, 408–11, 418–22, 471–72, 479, 484–85, 528–30, 533–34, 536–37

events, 27, 50, 75, 87, 124, 162, 233–34, 236, 310, 335, 354

Evergreen, 149, 152, 155–56, 161, 184, 187, 192, 546

evidentiary sentences, 434–36, 457–58, 461–62, 465, 468

example, 459, 461–3

exception, 230, 459–63, 465–66, 468, 487

exchange rate, 217, 221

exclusion criteria, 96–97, 108, 110

exercise levels, 63, 371

exhaustive categories, 78–79, 100, 329, 515–16

expected direction of association, 35, 422

experiment, 103, 365–69, 375, 381, 385–86, 403, 439, 473, 532
    versus "study", 369, 375, 381

experimental groups, 31, 377

experimental studies, 199–200, 311, 344, 347–48, 361, 365, 369–71, 375–76, 384, 386, 486–87

logistic regression, 420

lollipop charts, 131, 167–68, 170, 172

longitudinal studies, 15, 309–12, 327–28, 337, 355, 375, 486, 496. *See also* retrospective studies, prospective studies.

loss to follow-up. *See* attrition.

lower confidence limit (LCL), 396–97, 529

lung cancer, 330–31, 349, 356–59, 377–79, 383

MacArthur Scale, 61, 81–82

macro units, 105–107

magnitude, 28, 30–34, 72–73, 178–79, 235–36, 242, 252–57, 408, 434–35, 437–40, 443, 445–47, 449–51, 454–55, 461–62, 467–68, 495–96, 510, 550

maps (for presenting numeric patterns), 178, 180, 181

marginal (of table), 418, 419

margin of error, 145, 393–400, 406, 420–23, 481, 485, 527–30, 549–50

marital status, 66, 116, 121–22, 145, 328, 451, 552

mathematical comparisons, 34, 250, 254–55, 257, 263, 268, 300, 483, 533

math scores, 171–72, 477, 479

maximum values, 52–54, 57, 185, 187, 202, 230, 232, 235, 238, 248, 250–52, 265–66, 269, 274, 276, 299, 301–2, 490, 512, 520, 530

mean (average), 261–62, 263, 269, 392–93, 401, 403, 416, 418, 453, 454, 528, 531, 540

  plausibility criteria for values of, 274–75, 298, 299

measurement, 40–110, 118–19, 161, 192–93, 213–17, 229–31, 235–36, 240–42, 250–55, 260–65, 268–69, 298–301, 303–4, 399–402, 441–42, 491–96, 504–6, 520–21, 529–30, 540–42

measurement approach, 64–65, 81, 90, 215, 476

measurement bias, 306, 333–37, 339–40, 343–44, 402

measurement error, 333, 335–36, 341–43, 399, 421, 471

measurement validity, 84–85, 87, 89, 306–7, 346, 402, 421

measure of association, 119, 389, 403

measures, 9–12, 54–55, 57–63, 73–76, 81–89, 91–92, 118–20, 122–25, 224–25, 230–36, 240–42, 256–59, 263–64, 268–69, 289–90, 399–400, 440–41, 495–97, 511–13, 529–33

  common, 229–30

  new, 86–87, 521

  pertinent, 271, 303–4

  pre-intervention, 366, 373

measures of central tendency, 261, 263, 271, 274, 283, 389, 453–54

  criteria for plausibility of values, 274, 275

measures of distribution, 124, 266, 268, 301

measures of level, 229, 242, 257–58, 440, 442, 455

  criteria for plausibility of values, 235

  measures of position in a ranked list. See measures of rank.criteria for plausibility of values, 240–42

measures of rank, 229, 235, 241–42, 257, 274, 443–44.

measures of spread, 268, 274, 283, 453, 481, 484

  criteria for plausibility of values, 275–76

measures of uncertainty, 387, 392, 399–400, 421, 485, 529–30

  criteria for plausibility of values, 399–400, 529–30

measures of variation, 269, 392, 477

  units for, 74, 275–77

measuring, 4–6, 11, 16–17, 37, 40, 63–66, 81, 85, 231, 233, 271–72, 510, 513

mechanisms, 24, 350, 358–59, 374–75, 380, 383, 386, 480, 482–83, 485–86, 495

median, 173, 178, 261–63, 267, 269–71, 275, 279, 281, 283–87, 293, 296, 300–1

median income, 130–31, 133–34, 152, 170, 173, 225, 258–59, 281–82, 296

median projection, 157, 159, 398

mentoring program, 348, 359, 362–65, 377, 380, 422, 543

meta-analysis, 351, 383, 547

methods, data-collection, 328, 338, 384, 401–2, 495

methods section, 110, 457, 494–96, 525

metric system. *See* system of measurement.

micro units, 105, 106, 107

migration, 135–36, 142, 225

minimum values, 54, 68, 202, 265, 491, 512

minimum wage, 2, 61, 374, 470, 544

misclassification, 42–3, 58, 559

missing values, 8, 15–17, 79–81, 89, 193, 328, 331

missing value codes, 80

modal value, 197, 262, 269, 277, 279, 280, 281, 286, 453

  See also mode.

mode, 262–63, 271

modifiability, 475, 476

mortality rates, 120, 170–71, 183

multichotomous (multicategory) variable, 291, 293, 413–16, 418

multiple-line charts, 177, 179

multiple regression, 380, 420

multiple-response questions, 77, 79, 517–18

multistage sampling, 319, 343

mutually exclusive categories, 78–79, 100, 120, 515

named categories. *See* nominal variables.
National Health and Nutrition Examination
    Survey. *See* NHANES.
natural experiments, 373, 374
natural logarithms, 510
negative association, 29, 33, 455
negative values, 53, 68–69, 236, 244, 250, 274, 289,
    400, 479, 530
new categorical variables, 515–16
new continuous variables, 504, 506, 511, 514
new variables, xxx, 217, 274, 493–94, 499,
    504–7, 515–17, 519–21
NHANES (National Health and Nutrition Examination
    Survey), 268, 273, 281–86, 289–90, 308–9, 311,
    318–19, 325–26, 339–40, 371, 389, 392–93,
    397–98, 412–17, 523, 525, 529, 545
NHANES sample, 281, 286, 339–40, 391–93,
    405, 537, 539
nominal (current) dollars, 219–21
nominal independent variable, 147–48, 170,
    193, 294, 297, 454, 456
nominal variables, 66–67, 76, 146–47, 162, 165,
    167, 250, 254, 262, 265, 271, 279–80,
    293–95, 451–52, 516, 521
noncomparable groups, 375–76, 473
nondirectional (2-sided) hypothesis, 531–32,
    534–36, 542–43
non-probability sampling methods, 314, 320,
    323, 343, 421, 525
nonresponse, 80, 306, 326–27, 339–41, 488, 523
nonresponse bias, 307, 325, 333
non-spuriousness, 350, 356–58, 360–62, 375,
    377, 482, 485, 486
norm, 197, 200–01, 206, 223, 333
normal distribution, 269–70, 276
normal range, 42–44, 51, 72
"not applicable" response, 17, 80–81, 331–32, 519
notes to tables, use of, 121–22, 280, 283,
    413, 416, 419, 537
null hypothesis (H$_0$), 408, 531–39, 542–43
null value, 404, 531–34, 542
numerator, 138, 233–34, 236, 243–47, 251, 252, 275,
    441–42, 447–50
numeric facts, 3, 108, 161, 192, 388, 427, 435, 463
numeric measures, 6, 9, 11–12, 52, 82, 230, 235, 260,
    437, 443, 446
numeric order, 129, 147, 151, 240, 258–59
numeric values

exact, 134, 388
observed, 81, 211
particular, 5, 7, 72, 491
plausible, 57, 92
precise, 155, 192

obesity, 39, 358, 397, 413–14, 417–18,
    432–36, 455, 459–60, 462, 486, 529
obesity rates, 23, 413, 417–18, 433–35, 536, 542
observational studies, 344, 347–48, 351, 361, 364,
    370–78, 384, 386, 487
observed values, 235, 261–66, 276, 285, 299,
    376–77, 453, 458, 534, 543
  highest, 265–66, 275, 298
  lowest, 265–66
occurrence, 124, 139, 233–34, 251, 253,
    299–300, 324, 442, 451–52
OLS (Ordinary Least Squares) regression, 420
one-sided (1-sided) hypothesis. *See* directional
    hypothesis.
one-way ANOVA. *See* ANOVA.
open-ended questions, 76, 89, 91
operationalize, 59, 62–63, 65, 89, 91
optimal value, 54–56, 58–59, 90
order, 65, 68, 125–26, 130–31, 133–34, 146,
    254, 262–63, 280, 282, 293–94, 411,
    413, 446–47, 449–52
order of categories, 68, 147, 193
order of data collection (for organizing data),
    130, 135, 428–30, 459
order of magnitude, 72–73, 89, 183, 236, 246
ordinal, 65–69, 73, 75–76, 177, 179–80, 197, 253–55,
    262–63, 268–69, 289–90, 293, 295, 413–19,
    452–54, 515–17
ordinal categories, 74, 189, 281, 516
ordinal independent variables, 177, 291, 414, 455, 459
ordinal variables, 66–67, 120, 126, 165, 167, 180, 251,
    253, 271, 277, 280–82, 453, 506, 515–16, 521
Ordinary Least Squares regression. *See* OLS.
organizing data in tables and charts, 114, 125, 127, 130,
    146, 151, 549. *See also* alphabetical
    order, empirical order, order of data collection,
    thematic organization.
original variables, 212, 242, 274, 399–400, 441, 445,
    447, 505, 511, 515–17, 530
outcome. *See* dependent variable.
outlier, 150, 266–68
overgeneralization, 50, 56, 103–5, 108–9, 325

overrepresented group, 100–1
oversampling. *See* disproportionate sampling.

panel studies, 311. *See also* cohort studies.
panels, 121–26, 128, 145, 185, 187, 311,
    480, 482–85, 487
  separate, 122, 135, 480
paragraphs, 192, 427, 431–36, 463, 466, 468, 495–96
participants, 14–16, 311, 320–23, 325–27, 338–40, 351,
    361–62, 364, 365, 367–68, 370–71, 373–74, 378,
    381–82, 532
patterns
  general, 461–63, 467
  numeric, 33, 107, 156, 192, 260–61, 428,
      438–39, 538
  observed, 19–20, 22, 385
percentage, 137–42, 245, 246, 248, 263–64,
    277, 290, 442
  plausible values, 233, 235, 252
  versus proportion, 245–46, 442
percentage change, 126, 243, 247–50, 256, 449–50, 455
  plausible values, 252, 445
percentage difference, 246–49, 449–50
  plausible values, 252, 445
  versus difference in percentage points, 246, 248, 446
percentaging, direction of, in tables, 137, 302
percentage of cases. See percentage of a whole.
percentage of population, *See* percentage of a whole.
percentage of a whole, 237, 245–46, 252, 263–64,
    275, 277, 441–42
  relationship with ratio, 246
percentage points, 246, 248, 392, 396, 446
percentiles, 62, 94–95, 119, 240–41, 248–50,
    262, 265–66, 271, 274, 276, 414, 417, 443–44
perspectives, xxxiv, 33, 38, 54–58, 147, 224,
    241, 469, 471
pie charts, 150, 152, 161–62, 165–66,
    189–92, 279, 282–83
placebo effect, 367–68, 385, 544
placebos, 361, 367–68, 384
place value, 507–8, 520
plausibility, 4, 39, 51, 72, 81, 93, 487, 511.
      See also plausibility criteria, plausible values.
  of decimal values, 236, 251
  of negative values, 236, 251, 252, 274, 276, 401
  of positive values, 274, 276, 401
  of whole numbers, 236, 441
  of zero, 236, 251, 445, 541

plausibility criteria, 235, 240–41, 250, 274–75,
    297, 407, 540–42
plausible values, 51, 80–81, 233, 236, 251, 257, 301,
    491, 504, 509
point estimate, 389, 391–99, 401, 408–10, 416,
    420–23, 472, 478–79, 484, 528–29, 534, 538–39
  lower, 408–9
points in time, 87, 231, 247–48, 308–10, 355
point of view. *See* perspectives.
population, 96–103, 108, 117, 128–29, 189–90,
    236–37, 243–44, 277–78, 313–19, 321–24,
    344–46, 380–82, 387–94, 399, 421, 505,
    522–23, 525, 534–36, 538–40
  larger, 101–2, 389–90
population change, 117, 128–29, 237, 552
population composition, 373, 402
population level, 273, 281–86, 318, 397, 412,
    414–17, 419, 427, 460, 523, 525–26
population parameter, 389, 391–97, 399, 403–5, 408,
    420, 472, 528–29, 531–35, 538
population size, 238, 346
portrait layout, 142–43
position, 153, 170, 172, 176, 189–90, 235, 240–42,
    257, 271–72, 274, 301, 304, 443
position numbers, 240, 242
positive association, 28–29, 31–33, 455, 462
possible values, 30, 34, 52, 184–85, 232, 235,
    264, 276, 440, 450, 512
  lowest, 69, 236, 244, 248, 256
post-hoc fallacy, 354, 358
posttest, 365–67, 386
potential confounders, 371, 375–77, 380, 386,
    420, 482, 485–86, 495
poverty, xxxvi, 24–25, 70, 111, 114–15, 139,
    215, 232, 427, 546, 551
PPP (purchasing power parity), 117, 128–29,
    219–21, 223, 507, 546, 549
practical importance, 435, 470–71, 476,
    479–80, 484, 488–90, 500–2
practical meaning, 469, 471, 476–78,
    480–85, 488, 500–2
practical significance. *See* practical importance.
precision of numeric estimates, 65, 121, 145, 388,
    389, 395–96, 399, 510
precise values, 133, 164, 211, 428–29,
    432, 439, 448, 508
predictive validity, 86–87
presenting quantitative research, xxx, 427, 433

sampling error, 342, 389, 391–92, 399, 420

sampling fraction. *See* probability of selection.

sampling frame, 314, 316, 319–20, 339, 343, 345–46, 498

sampling methods, 313–14, 324, 337, 343, 345–46, 470, 484, 488, 494, 497–98

  random, 324, 487, 498

  use non-probability, 322, 487

sampling unit, 314, 318–19, 343, 346

sampling variation, 390–93, 399, 401, 405–6, 420–21, 528, 536, 539

sampling weights, xxxi, 16–17, 55, 82–83, 88, 119, 122, 273, 281–86, 318, 335, 340, 411–12, 414–17, 419, 427, 475, 494, 512–13, 515, 522–26, 537

scale, 72–74, 82–83, 86, 88, 121–22, 144–45, 216, 232–36, 238, 251, 268, 307, 441–42, 508–14, 520–21

  axis, 152, 184–85, 191–92

scale and range, 251, 301

scale of measurement, 59, 72–73, 89–90, 143, 231, 236, 241, 491, 509

scatter charts, 170, 172, 192

schizophrenia, 50–51, 352–54, 549, 553

scientific audiences. *See* research audiences.

scope, 38–41, 43–46, 48–51, 56–58, 60, 65, 78–79, 217, 221, 317, 324

scores, 42, 52–54, 56, 83–84, 87, 202, 240–41, 249–50, 262, 264–67, 272, 378, 380, 512–14

  scaled, 52, 54

screening scores, 42–43

screening test, 42–44, 56, 58

SD. *See* standard deviation.

seasonal adjustment, 208–09

secondary data, 65, 200, 337–38, 343

second independent variable, 176–79, 416, 418

selection, 315–20, 324, 343, 346, 399, 522–26

selection bias, 364–65, 371

selective observation, 50–51, 56, 324–25, 343–44

self-reports, 297, 339, 342

self-selection, 322, 363–65, 373–74, 376, 384, 473, 498

sentences, 226, 427, 429, 431, 433–35, 440, 442–43, 446–49, 457, 462, 466

setting. *See* context.

share of cases, 164, 264, 327

sidebars, 464, 465

SIDS (sudden infant death syndrome), 199, 360, 485

sign (of number). *See* positive values, negative values, direction of association.

significance level (α), 402, 404–7, 411, 420, 422, 533–37, 539–43

simple bar chart, 168–69, 191

simple random sampling, 315, 319, 522

single-blinding, 367, 368

single-response questions, 77, 89, 335, 519

size, 31–33, 69, 74, 186–87, 189–90, 195–96, 212, 253–54, 276, 279, 350–51, 358–60, 438–39, 445–46, 453–55, 457–58, 461–64, 476–79, 482, 484–86. *See also* magnitude.

skip pattern, 80, 81

SNAP (Supplemental Nutrition Assistance Program), 9, 96, 546

social desirability bias, 333–34, 343–44

social media platforms, 168, 174

spread. *See* variation.

spurious association, 356, 357, 378, 383, 472–73, 482, 486

stacked bar charts, 165, 167, 173–74, 191, 281–82

standard deviation, 127, 178, 267–68, 271–74, 276, 283, 301, 474–78, 481, 483, 528

standard error, 392–93, 395, 397–400, 409, 416, 420–21, 471–72, 481, 484–85, 527–30, 534

standard error calculation, 393, 528

standardized scores, 271–72, 276

standard patterns, 201, 214–15, 224

standards, 7, 9, 196–97, 199, 201, 206–7, 209–25, 429–30, 493, 548, 550

statistical analyses, 371, 397, 402, 497, 499, 502, 504, 520, 535

statistical concepts, 83, 261, 388

statistical distribution, 529–30, 540

statistically significant, 404–6, 408–9, 478–79, 484, 489, 535

statistical significance, 288–89, 350–51, 387–88, 402–3, 405–8, 410–11, 413, 419–21, 434–35, 461, 469, 471–77, 479–85, 487–90, 501–2, 536–37, 539–40, 542–44

statistical significance testing. *See* hypothesis testing.

statistical software, 396, 404, 406–7, 534–35, 537

statistical tests, 3–5, 387–88, 402, 404, 407, 410, 419, 422, 485, 540, 543

statistics, 118–19, 162, 229–32, 260–61, 275–76, 283, 286–88, 297–98, 301–2, 388–89, 391–94, 402–4, 525–28, 531, 533–34, 536–37, 540, 542, 547, 551–52

statistics textbook, 317, 388, 400, 527, 530–31

stereotype, 104

strata, 316–17, 319, 328, 378, 494, 523

stratified random sampling, 316, 319

stratum. *See* strata.

strength of association, 288–90, 350

students, xxxi–xxxiv, 6, 14–17, 27, 31–32, 83–84, 91, 104–5, 111, 232, 234, 262, 264–65, 299–300, 316–18, 346, 362–65, 448–49, 477–78, 523

Student's *t*-distribution, 529–30

study, 14–19, 21–26, 37–40, 96–103, 108–11, 197–201, 305–9, 311–17, 320–28, 330–33, 337–41, 343–49, 351–52, 358–62, 366–71, 374–76, 380–87, 409–10, 481–92, 494–97

study design, xxx, xxxiii, 305–8, 344, 347, 349, 351–52, 380, 382–84, 469–70, 480–83, 485–88, 495–96, 500–1

study nonresponse, 306, 325, 331–32, 337, 339, 344, 375–76

study participants. *See* participants.study period, 259, 310, 365, 369–70, 457, 496, 532

study respondents. *See* respondents.

study response rate. *See* response rate.

study sample, 56, 98, 102–3, 311–12, 314, 316, 331, 344, 349, 477, 487

study sites, 477–79, 489

study subjects. *See* participants.

stunting, 126–27, 178–79, 259, 310

subcharts, 185, 187, 459

subset, xxxii, 81, 99, 245–46, 252, 280, 313, 318, 340, 388–90, 433

substantive significance. *See* importance of numeric finding; practical meaning, practical importance.

subtraction (for calculating difference), 237, 242–44, 248, 253, 255–56, 258–59, 269, 272, 299–300, 441, 445–46, 450, 533

sudden infant death syndrome. *See* SIDS.

Supplemental Nutrition Assistance Program. *See* SNAP.

surveillance data, 17, 338, 340

survey data, 8, 422

Survey of Income and Program Participation (SIPP), 338, 552

survey question, 60, 75–80, 328–29, 333–35, 336. *See also* closed-ended questions; multiple-response questions; open-ended questions; single-response questions

survey samples, 97, 401, 522

survey years, 126–27

survivor bias, 312–13, 337

symptoms, 51, 134, 342–43, 511–13

system of measurement, 68, 70, 72–74, 89–90, 98, 208, 213, 216–17, 236, 241, 251, 441–42

tables, 113–31, 133–48, 245–47, 249–52, 260, 266–68, 274–78, 283–85, 289–92, 411–19, 422–23, 425–38, 443–45, 450–51, 453–55, 461–67, 480–85, 507–9, 522–26, 537, 549
  appendix, 124, 130
  design, 114, 260
  percentaging of, 137, 302
  separate, 124, 291
  well-designed, 146, 429

table shells, 147–48

table titles, 116, 118, 142, 156

take-home point, 149–51, 156, 160, 162

target population, 101–2, 108, 313–14, 324, 328, 331–32, 344–45, 483, 487, 492, 494–95, 497

target values, 7, 10, 84–85, 88, 201, 202, 206, 215, 223–24, 457–58, 549

temperature, 4–5, 53, 69, 201, 208, 244, 258, 343, 551

temporal comparisons, 200, 508. *See also* trends.

temporal design, 494–95. *See also* time structure.

t-statistic, 415, 534

t-test, 542

test-retest reliability, 83, 84

testing, 367, 369, 387–88, 402–4, 407–8, 411, 420–21, 527, 531, 533–36, 538–39, 542–43

test statistic, 481, 484, 529, 533–34, 537, 540–43

text data labels, 156, 158

text visualization, 161–62, 165, 192

The "W's". *See* "W's".

thematic organization, 116, 125, 127–29, 134, 151, 280, 451, 454, 521

theoretical criteria, 129, 202, 215, 224

theory, 18–20, 22, 33, 35, 87, 153, 348, 403, 475, 491, 545

three-way associations, 172, 179, 192, 295, 301, 377, 416, 419, 436, 468

three-way cross-tabulations, 295–97, 416–18

three-way tables, 135–36, 145, 418

thresholds, 7, 9–10, 70, 196, 200–2, 206, 208, 211, 222–26, 457, 481, 484, 510–11, 534, 537–38

TIA (transient ischemic attack), 329, 336

time intervals, 222, 445

time-lag bias, 335, 337, 343–44

time of day, 210–11

time order, 350, 352, 354–56, 358, 360–61, 372–73, 384, 386, 482, 486

time periods, 45, 62, 86, 94, 189, 232, 234, 236, 441–42, 446–47, 449

time points, 15, 126–27, 177–80, 234, 243, 248, 251–52, 308, 310–11, 450, 455

time structure, 306, 308, 337, 344, 385, 485, 488, 496–97

time trends, 200, 257, 310, 429

titles, of tables and charts, 115–16, 118–19, 121, 134, 137–38, 145–47, 149, 151, 153, 156, 158–60, 162, 177, 180, 183, 283, 296, 434, 464, 500

tools for presenting numbers, 125, 427–32, 433, 491

topic ("what"), xxix–xxxiv, 2–12, 14–16, 21–22, 24–26, 33–35, 37–110, 145–48, 200–1, 206–8, 213–16, 223–25, 235, 241, 250–51, 257–59, 275–76, 299, 301, 331–33, 431–34, 436–38, 440–41, 461–64, 470–71, 481–85, 490–93

  numeric, 9, 54

  particular, xxix, 5, 8, 21, 24, 59, 81, 89, 92, 211, 224

  unfamiliar, 11, 211

topic sentences, 433–36, 455, 457–58, 461–63, 466, 468

total number, 120, 162, 194, 205, 222, 231, 238, 240, 275, 298, 318

total number of elements, 315, 522

transient ischemic attack (TIA), 329, 336

transition sentences, 432–33, 435–36, 466, 468

treatment, 199, 345, 350, 361–62, 364–70, 373–74, 376–77, 380–81, 385–86, 388, 403

treatment group, 361–67, 372, 375, 378, 380, 381, 384, 386, 403, 473, 482, 489, 532–33

trend charts, 155, 170, 192

trend data, 5, 126

true experiments, 347, 361–62, 365–66, 369–71, 373, 375, 381, 384, 480, 489, 495

truncated value, 508–9

TV-watching levels, 414, 417–18, 433, 459, 462, 538

two-category variables. *See* dichotomous variables.

two-sided (2-sided) hypothesis.

  See nondirectional hypothesis.

two-way ANOVA. *See* ANOVA.

Type I error (α). *See* significance level.

Type II error (β) , 527, 536, 538–43

UCL. *See* upper confidence limit.

uncertainty of numeric estimates, 387–89, 391–423, 471–72, 478, 481, 484, 485, 527–30, 536, 538

under-represented group, 100–1, 326, 327, 402

United States, 49–50, 70–71, 136, 138–40, 144, 186–87, 211, 214, 219–22, 225–26, 234, 253, 291–92, 319, 341–42, 432–34, 436, 451–53, 545–48, 551–52

unit of analysis, 14, 59, 70, 73, 89–90, 241, 251, 492

units, 6–8, 67–70, 72–75, 89–90, 98–99, 118–22, 153, 158–62, 196, 211–14, 216–19, 233–36, 245–47, 250–52, 257–59, 274–77, 295–99, 399–400, 423, 440–47, 450, 468, 479–81, 483–85, 491–92, 499

  academic, 316–17

  consistent, 73, 98, 216, 224

  original, 245, 271–72, 299, 446, 511

units of measurement, 67, 70–71, 115, 118–19, 240, 242, 248, 251–52, 445, 488, 491–92

units of variables, 236, 275–76, 400, 407, 481–83, 530, 541

univariate distributions, xxx, 30, 33, 195, 261, 467

univariate statistics, 118, 260–61, 274, 277, 284, 301, 304, 403, 437, 531, 540

universe, 314–15

unweighted sample size, 273, 281–85, 397, 412, 414–17, 524

upper confidence limit, 396–97, 529

use of sampling weights. *See* sampling weights.

validity, 59, 82, 85, 87–89, 91, 340–41, 381, 401, 490, 521. *See also* external validity, internal validity, measurement validity.

  distinction versus reliability, 88

valid values, 80–82

values, 4–12, 14–17, 26–31, 51–54, 195–97, 199–202, 211–16, 218–26, 229–32, 235–69, 274–77, 297–301, 348–51, 403–10, 437–43, 445–47, 453–55, 504–13, 528–34, 536–41

  average, 118, 134, 161, 201, 211, 266

  benchmark, 224, 457, 477

  common, 262–63

  decimal, 57, 231–32, 236, 250–51, 257, 440, 507

  fractional, 212, 230–31, 236, 257, 441, 446

  lowest, 129, 187, 207, 236, 240–41

  measured, 307, 333

  median, 277, 296

  middle, 55–56, 58, 82, 262–63, 491

  midrange, 57, 89

  minimum, 68, 202, 512

  nearest, 508–9

  positive, 6, 57, 68, 274, 289, 400, 528, 530–31

  true population, 395, 401, 403

values for numerator and denominator, 441, 445
values of continuous variables, 162, 216
VAP. *See* voting-age population.
variables, 15–17, 28–35, 65–70, 118–22, 167–70,
        212–16, 250–51, 253–58, 260–66, 268–69,
        274–79, 287–91, 299–301, 303–5, 348–52,
        354–59, 450–55, 480–89, 504–6, 515–21
    existing, 504–6, 515, 520
    new, 504–7, 514–19
    original. *See* variables, existing, 517
    outcome, 147, 193
    third, 295, 356, 459, 461, 472, 485
variance, 266–69, 274, 276, 290, 293, 301,
        414, 483, 528
video-game-playing time, 473–74, 489
violent crimes, 50–51, 130, 186–87
visualizations, xxx, 113, 149–79, 182–83, 185–94,
        428–29, 431, 434, 464, 500, 550
vizzes, 149–51, 156, 170, 172, 184, 464, 491
voter participation rates, 140–41, 169
volunteers (sample of), 101, 322, 323, 340, 381, 382, 487
voters, 99, 101, 141, 239, 354, 369, 394, 406, 447, 539
voting-age population (VAP), 140–41, 169, 382

"W's", 25–26, 92, 97, 115, 118, 121, 151, 155, 156,
        159–62, 170, 197, 215, 218, 260, 283, 306,
        433–36, 446, 455, 470, 480, 491–92,
        496–97, 500
    how (as honorary W), 59, 75–76, 260, 306, 358,
        407, 470. *See also* analysis, data collection,
        measurement, study design.

how many (as an "honorary W", 25).
        See also sample size.
    "so what". *See* substantive significance,
        practical meaning.
    what. *See* topic.
    when. *See* context, setting.
    where. *See* context, setting.
    which. *See* context, setting.
    who. *See* context, setting.
Wakefield, 351, 553
weighted statistics, 273, 281–86, 397, 412,
        414–17, 419, 427, 460,
        523–24, 526
weight-for-height, 55, 274, 553
weights, sampling. *See* sampling weights.
weights, use in scales, 512–13
wording, 91, 110, 114, 328–29, 333–34, 338, 344–46,
        426–27, 437, 439–45, 447, 450, 493–95
world, 7, 110, 123, 126, 128–29, 154, 157, 159–60,
        177, 180, 188, 233–34, 237, 454–55
World Bank Group, 456, 458, 553
World Health Organization, 95, 127,
        273–74, 553
world population, 110, 157, 226, 398, 455
    projected, 154, 398
world's population, 123–24, 126,
        237, 245–46, 455

X^2 *See* Chi-squared statistic.

z-scores. *See* standardized scores.